TIMECHECK 2006

by
"Split Second"

CONTENTS

First published in 2006 by Raceform Ltd.
Compton, Newbury, Berkshire, RG20 6NL
Raceform Limited is a wholly owned subsidiary of MGN Limited

A catalogue record for this book is available from the British Library

ISBN 1-905153-06-6

Typesetting and Production: Ashley Rumney

Printed in Great Britain by William Clowes Ltd, Beccles, Suffolk

RACEFORM SPEED FIGURES

A few years ago I was in the process of setting up a computerised speed figure-based system on my home computer, and had reached the stage where I needed to work out how much to adjust the 'raw' speed figure depending on how much weight the horse carried in its previous starts, compared to how much weight it was set to carry today. At that stage, I had no preconceived ideas on the subject and had accepted like most other people that when a horse carried more weight, its raw speed figure would decrease and if it was carrying less weight, its raw speed figure would increase. I didn't believe that it was going to have the same effect on every horse so I decided to take a random sample of 1000 horses and write a program to work out how much on average their speed ratings were affected by every 1lb they carried greater or less than in their previous start.

When I ran finally the program, the results I got just did not make sense, though the results for those horses going up in weight were more or less what I had hoped for. For every 1lb extra a horse carried from its previous start, its speed figure was reduced by 0.4 of a point, which equates to one point equalling 2.5 lbs. All well and good so far, and if the results for those horses going down in weights had been anything like the complete opposite then I would have been more than happy, but they weren't. For every 1lb less a horse carried, its speed rating went down again, this time by 0.3 of a point. It was only horses that carried the same weight as in their previous start whose speed ratings actually went up. I thought there must be some sort of a bug in my program or maybe some faulty speed figures were distorting the results, but when I took a sample of 1000 different horses, the results I got were similar if not identical. Still those horses going down in weight were, on average, running slower than in their previous start.

This is the problem with conventional weight-adjusted speed ratings. Accepted wisdom states that horses will be slowed down by extra weight and my own tests did not disagree with that theory, but horses going down in weight running slower was more difficult to explain. There was no way I could program around it, as I could not treat one group of horses differently to the another by making different adjustments depending on whether the horse's weight had gone up or down. Closer inspection of particular horses' profiles showed that, more often than not, horses ran slower than in their previous start for another reason, perhaps the ground, distance or type of track, but the effect of weight was impossible to identify, certainly not in a way that could be applied in blanket-like fashion to every single horse in training. I decided to drop weight as a factor in my calculations and would leave it as something I call a 'hunch' factor, rather like a horse's fitness (something which has never been factored into any speed ratings I know of).

Having dropped weight adjustments from speed-rating calculations for my own purposes at that point, and now for Split Second, what is left is a 'pure' speed rating in the real sense of the word, with only adjustments made to take account of the ground and the class of horse running, not one which has been altered to take account of another person's opinion. What I mean is, I wanted to make sure that the highest-rated horse was the result of Split Second's calculations, not the result of an opinion by the Official Handicapper. For example, if a Flat horse runs a raw speed figure of 56 carrying 10 stone and another horse runs an 84 carrying 8 stone, adjusting to 9 stone will bring the two together if 1lb equals one point on the scale (which it does on many scales). If these two horses were then to meet at level weights, then conventional published speed figures may suggest they had an equal chance, but in real life (and from my own research) that just does not happen. The second of the two horses in my example has demonstrated an ability to run a good deal faster than the first, and I would much rather have that information available to me and make my own mind up about the effect of revised weights than have the evidence distorted before I was able to see it. The idea that the horse with the bigger weight will find the extra speed necessary to overcome his rival simply because he has a lower weight than in his previous start is fanciful to say the least, especially in view of the results of my own research shown earlier.

Another interesting point on whether or not to adjust for weight is that some other people I know (who have used and swear by making weight adjustments), have nevertheless had some doubts about whether it is desirable to artificially boost the speed ratings of horses with a very low weight. They have introduced a cut-off point, which is in effect a maximum weight adjustment they will make. In other words, if their weight adjustment is to 9 stone, they might give a horse an extra 14 points if he set to carry 8 stone today, but will also add 14 if the horse is set to carry 7st 12lb. With that doubt in mind, how many published weight-adjusted speed ratings are truly weight adjusted?

Another advantage which, in my opinion, the new system has is with the calculation of Standard Times. The new system actually uses truly average or median times rather than a theoretical Standard Time and this has the advantage that the time used to calculate the speed figures has at least been achieved by at least one horse in history, and therefore represents a truer figure. The race times used are those put up by previous winners of races run over the distance at the track going back several years, with races confined to younger horses ignored for obvious reasons.

The Split Second ratings you see are a representation of what the horse actually achieved on the day speed-wise, with one point equalling one length per mile. So if one horse has an advantage of 4 points over another and they are due to race over two miles, he has the ability to beat him by 8 lengths if conditions were identical to those under which each horse achieved their best rating and if both horses were to run to their best form.

RACEFORM MEDIAN TIMES FLAT 2005

ASCOT

5f 1m 1.92
6f 1m 16.00
6f 110y 1m 22.84
7f 1m 29.64
1m Rnd 1m 42.89
1m Str 1m 41.86
1m 2f 2m 8.73
1m 4f 2m 33.43
2m 45y 3m 34.84
2m 4f 4m 23.90
2m 6f 34y 4m 56.73

AYR

5f 1m 0.44
6f 1m 13.67
7f 50y 1m 32.72
1m 1m 43.49
1m 1f 20y 1m 55.84
1m 2f 2m 11.72
1m 2f 192y 2m 23.64
1m 5f 13y 2m 56.61
1m 7f 3m 22.47
2m 1f 105y 3m 54.77

BATH

5f 11y 1m 2.50
5f 161y 1m 11.20
1m 5y 1m 41.10
1m 2f 46y 2m 11.00
1m 3f 144y 2m 30.30
1m 5f 22y 2m 51.50
2m 1f 34y 3m 49.60

BEVERLEY

5f 1m 4.00
7f 100y 1m 34.31
1m 100y 1m 47.40
1m 1f 207y 2m 7.30
1m 4f 16y 2m 40.21
2m 35y 3m 39.50

BRIGHTON

5f 59y 1m 2.30
5f 213y 1m 10.10
6f 209y 1m 22.70
7f 214y 1m 35.04
1m 1f 209y 2m 2.60
1m 3f 196y 2m 32.20

CARLISLE

5f 1m 1.50
5f 193y 1m 13.61
6f 192y 1m 27.10
7f 200y 1m 40.09
1m 1f 61y 1m 57.56
1m 3f 206y 2m 32.40
1m 6f 32y 3m 7.30
2m 1f 52y 3m 49.90

CATTERICK

5f 1m 0.60
5f 212y 1m 14.00
7f 1m 27.36
1m 3f 214y 2m 39.00
1m 5f 175y 3m 4.50
1m 7f 177y 3m 31.40

CHEPSTOW

5f 16y 59.60
6f 16y 1m 12.40
7f 16y 1m 23.30
1m 14y 1m 36.00
1m 2f 36y 2m 9.90
1m 4f 23y 2m 38.72
2m 49y 3m 39.40
2m 2f 4m 0.62

CHESTER

5f 16y 1m 2.05
6f 18y 1m 15.65
7f 2y 1m 28.47
7f 122y 1m 34.75
1m 2f 75y 2m 13.14
1m 3f 79y 2m 25.79
1m 4f 66y 2m 40.65
1m 5f 89y 2m 55.42
1m 7f 195y 3m 33.60
2m 2f 147y 4m 5.57

DONCASTER

5f 1m 1.42
5f 140y 1m 7.94
6f 1m 14.30
6f 110y 1m 20.48
7f 1m 27.77
1m Rnd 1m 40.61
1m Str 1m 41.51
1m 2f 60y 2m 11.83
1m 4f 2m 35.53
1m 6f 132y 3m 9.74
2m 110y 3m 41.96
2m 2f 3m 57.93

EPSOM

5f 55.68
6f 1m 10.63
7f 1m 23.95
1m 114y 1m 45.74
1m 2f 18y 2m 9.04
1m 4f 10y 2m 38.73

FOLKESTONE

5f 1m 0.80
6f 1m 13.60
6f 189y 1m 25.70
7f 1m 27.90
1m 1f 149y 2m 5.21
1m 4f 2m 40.50
1m 7f 92y 3m 27.20
2m 93y 3m 40.70

GOODWOOD

5f 59.05
6f 1m 12.85
7f 1m 28.04
1m 1m 40.27
1m 1f 1m 56.86
1m 1f 192y 2m 7.75
1m 3f....................2m 27.21
1m 4f 2m 38.92
1m 6f 3m 3.97
2m 3m 30.79
2m 4f 4m 20.89

HAMILTON

5f 4y 1m 1.20
6f 5y 1m 13.10
1m 65y 1m 49.30
1m 1f 36y 1m 59.66
1m 3f 16y 2m 26.26
1m 4f 17y 2m 39.18
1m 5f 9y 2m 53.40

HAYDOCK

5f 1m 2.07
6f 1m 14.90
7f 30y 1m 32.06
1m 30y 1m 45.51
1m 2f 120y 2m 17.73
1m 3f 200y 2m 34.99
1m 6f 3m 6.29
2m 45y 3m 37.90

KEMPTON

5f 1m 1.21
6f 1m 13.07
7f Jub 1m 27.33
7f Rnd 1m 26.61
1m Jub 1m 40.55
1m Rnd 1m 39.80
1m 1f 1m 54.55
1m 2f 2m 6.36
1m 3f 30y 2m 23.27
1m 4f 2m 35.02
1m 6f 92y 3m 10.66
2m 3m 30.53

LEICESTER

5f 2y 1m 0.90
5f 218y 1m 13.20
7f 9y 1m 26.10
1m 9y 1m 42.41
1m 1f 218y 2m 8.30
1m 3f 183y 2m 34.50

LINGFIELD (TURF)

5f 58.94
6f 1m 11.67
7f 1m 24.21
7f 140y 1m 31.46
1m 1f 1m 55.29
1m 2f 2m 9.72
1m 3f 106y 2m 29.92
1m 6f 3m 6.92
2m 3m 33.26

LINGFIELD (A.W)

5f 59.78
6f 1m 12.81
7f 1m 25.89
1m 1m 39.43
1m 2f 2m 7.58
1m 4f 2m 34.08
1m 5f 2m 48.30
2m 3m 28.79

MUSSELBURGH

5f 1m 0.50
7f 30y 1m 29.94
1m 1m 42.50
1m 1f 1m 56.00
1m 4f 2m 36.90
1m 6f 3m 5.70
2m 3m 33.90

NEWBURY

5f 34y 1m 2.56
6f 8y 1m 14.32
7f 1m 27.00
7f 64y 1m 31.26
1m Str 1m 40.62
1m 7y 1m 38.73
1m 1f 1m 54.59
1m 2f 6y 2m 8.71
1m 3f 5y 2m 22.27
1m 4f 5y 2m 35.99
1m 5f 61y 2m 50.99
2m 3m 36.15

NEWCASTLE

5f 1m 1.50
6f 1m 15.09
7f 1m 28.02
1m 1m 43.48
1m 3y Str 1m 41.90
1m 1f 9y 1m 57.81
1m 2f 32y 2m 11.80
1m 4f 93y 2m 43.55
1m 6f 97y 3m 12.60
2m 19y 3m 35.20

NEWMARKET (ROWLEY)

5f 1m 0.47
6f 1m 13.10
7f 1m 26.50
1m 1m 39.37
1m 1f 1m 51.95
1m 2f 2m 5.71
1m 4f 2m 33.50
1m 6f 3m 0.13
2m 3m 26.92
2m 2f 3m 52.62

NEWMARKET (JULY)

5f 59.56
6f 1m 13.35
7f 1m 26.78
1m 1m 40.43
1m 2f 2m 6.44
1m 4f 2m 32.91

1m 6f 175y 3m 11.04
2m 24y 3m 26.99

NOTTINGHAM

5f 13y 1m 1.80
6f 15y 1m 15.00
1m 54y 1m 46.40
1m 1f 213y 2m 9.70
1m 6f 15y 3m 7.10
2m 9y 3m 33.50

PONTEFRACT

5f 1m 3.80
6f 1m 17.40
1m 4y 1m 45.70
1m 2f 6y 2m 14.08
1m 4f 8y 2m 40.30
2m 1f 22y 3m 50.50
2m 1f 216y 4m 3.00
2m 5f 122y 5m 0.80

REDCAR

5f 58.70
6f 1m 11.70
7f 1m 24.90
1m 1m 37.80
1m 1f 1m 53.40
1m 2f 2m 6.80
1m 3f 2m 21.00
1m 6f 19y 3m 5.02
2m 4y 3m 31.50

RIPON

5f 1m 0.20
6f 1m 13.00
1m 1m 41.10
1m 1f 1m 53.85
1m 2f 2m 8.00
1m 4f 60y 2m 39.90
2m 3m 33.00

SALISBURY

5f 1m 1.59
6f 1m 14.98
6f 212y 1m 29.06
1m 1m 43.09
1m 1f 198y 2m 8.46
1m 4f 2m 36.36
1m 6f 15y 3m 6.23

SANDOWN

5f 6y 1m 2.21
7f 16y 1m 31.09
1m 14y 1m 43.95
1m 1f 1m 56.11
1m 2f 7y 2m 10.24
1m 3f 91y 2m 28.07
1m 6f 3m 4.51
2m 78y 3m 38.23

SOUTHWELL (TURF)

6f 1m 16.10
7f 1m 29.20
1m 2f....................2m 14.90
1m 4f 2m 40.30
2m 3m 41.50

SOUTHWELL(A.W)

5f 1m 0.30
6f 1m 16.90
7f 1m 30.80
1m 1m 44.60
1m 3f 2m 28.90
1m 4f 2m 42.09
1m 6f 3m 9.60
2m 3m 52.30

THIRSK

5f 59.90
6f 1m 12.50
7f 1m 27.10
1m 1m 39.70
1m 4f 2m 35.20
2m 3m 31.20

WARWICK

5f 1m 0.20
5f 110y 1m 4.31
6f 21y 1m 12.10
7f 26y 1m 25.00
1m 22y 1m 39.60
1m 2f 188y 2m 19.40
1m 4f 134y 2m 43.60
1m 6f 213y 3m 15.90
2m 39y 3m 32.70

WINDSOR

5f 10y 1m 1.10
6f 1m 13.67
1m 67y 1m 45.60
1m 2f 7y 2m 8.30
1m 3f 135y 2m 30.10

WOLVERHAMPTON

5f 20y 1m 2.82
5f 216y 1m 15.81
7f 32y 1m 30.40
1m 141y 1m 51.76
1m 1f 103y 2m 2.62
1m 4f 50y 2m 42.42
1m 5f 194y 3m 7.37
2m 119y 3m 43.13

YARMOUTH

5f 43y 1m 2.80
6f 3y 1m 13.70
7f 3y 1m 26.60
1m 3y 1m 39.90
1m 2f 21y 2m 8.10
1m 3f 101y 2m 27.50
1m 6f 17y 3m 5.30
2m 3m 31.41
2m 2f 51y 4m 6.90

YORK

5f 3y 59.25
6f 3y 1m 11.50
6f 217y 1m 24.31
7f 205y 1m 38.74
1m 208y 1m 50.99
1m 2f 88y 2m 10.48
1m 3f 198y 2m 31.11
1m 5f 197y 2m 58.44
1m 7f 198y 3m 23.25

TIMECHECK REVIEW

Sprinters (5f – 6f)

There has not been a great deal between the top Group sprinters and top sprint handicappers in the last few seasons. This was emphasised in 2005 by the fact that the top time performance (119) was recorded by the handicapper **Reverence**, when taking a 0-110 handicap at Doncaster in October. Unraced as a two and three-year-old, he won four of his six races in 2005 and Eric Alston's gelding could well develop into a Pattern performer in 2006.

Benbaun was another to develop into a useful sprinter last year. He recorded his best speed figures (118 and 117) over the Curragh's five furlongs, and went on to contest the Prix de L'Abbaye and run well at Sha Tin in December. Effective over five and six furlongs, he should pay his way again in 2006.

Baron's Pit (117) earned the biggest speed figure of his career when beating **Fayr Jag** (116) in the Diadem Stakes at Newmarket. He missed much of 2004 and had struggled for form in 2005 until the first-time blinkers brought about a revival. He shares that mark with the proven Group performers Cape Of Good Hope and Whipper. **Cape Of Good Hope** came from Hong Kong to be placed twice at Royal Ascot in 2004, and a return trip brought about due reward for, after finishing fourth in the King's Stand on the opening day, he took the Golden Jubilee Stakes from **Galeota** (116). **Whipper** is a versatile performer, having won at the top level between six furlongs and a mile. He gained his figure when beating subsequent William Hill Sprint Cup winner **Goodricke** (116) in the six and a half-furlong Prix Maurice de Gheest at Deauville.

Milers (7f – 9f)

The top time performance in this category came early in the season, when **Martillo** (119) took the Prix du Muguet at Saint-Cloud from **Autumn Glory** and **Whipper** (both 117). Martillo has won six times at Group Two level, but has yet to score in the highest grade. Autumn Glory has done well in Pattern class in the last couple of years, but is not top class, having failed to score above Group Three level, unlike Whipper, who has scored at Group One level at two, three and four years of age. He has proven himself consistently capable of top-class form given cut in the ground.

Proclamation (119) shared the top figure and proved a progressive colt in 2005, moving up from Listed and Group Three company to gain his top figure when beating **Soviet Song** (118) and **Ad Valorem** (116) in the Cantor Spreadfair Sussex Stakes at Goodwood. Effective on fast and soft ground, he has joined Godolphin for the 2006 season and looks set to win more Group One races at around a mile in the coming season.

Le Vie Dei Colori had finished sixth behind Proclamation at Goodwood, but recorded his best figure (118), when running out a surprise winner of the Group Two VC Bet Challenge Stakes in October. A former Premio Parioli (Italian 2000 Guineas) winner, he was subsequently retired to stud. Another ex-Italian trained horse who will be taking up stud duties in 2006 is the 2002 Derby Italiano winner **Rakti**. He sometimes proved a handful on the track, but managed to win six European Group One races at between a mile and 12 furlongs, the last of them being the Juddmonte Lockinge Stakes at Newbury in May, where he slaughtered his rivals, lowering the track record in the process and posting a figure of 118.

Middle Distances (10f – 12f)

Not surprisingly the top speed performance in this division was posted by the best middle-distance performer in Europe. **Hurricane Run** (122) posted a fine figure when producing an exceptional performance to beat the versatile **Westerner** (120) in the Prix de L'Arc de Triomphe Lucien Barriere at Longchamp in October. He also took the Irish Derby beating the subsequent St Leger winner Scorpion. He is reported to be staying in training and is likely to carry all before him on 2006.

Westerner was better known as a stayer until the end of last season, having won six successive races over just short of two miles and further, including his second Prix Royal-Oak, his second Prix du Cadran and the Ascot Gold Cup (run at York in 2005). However, he proved top-class at shorter distances, and his second in the Arc evoked memories of Ardross, who dominated the staying ranks before filling the same position at Longchamp.

The next four home, the 2004 winner **Bago**, the subsequent Breeders' Cup Turf winner **Shirocco**, the Derby winner **Motivator** (all 119), and Irish Oaks and Prix Vermeille winner **Shawanda** (118), all recorded their best speed figures of the season, helping to further emphasise the quality of the contest.

Pride finished seventh in the Arc, but posted her best speed figure (120) in winning her trial, the Prix Foy, from subsequent Japan Cup winner **Alkaased** (119) and Shirocco. Fifth in that race was **Geordieland** (119), who had posted his best figure when beating **Fracassant** (118) in the Group Two Grand Prix de Chantilly. This was the last of three successive meetings between the pair in which there was never more than a length and a half between them, with the former edging it by two wins to one.

Pinson's figure when running away from the Prix Guillame D'Ornano in August (119) marked him down as a colt with a future, although he subsequently disappointed in the Dubai Champion Stakes at Newmarket.

Artiste Royal clocked (118) when defeating **Diamond Green** and **Autumn Glory** (both 117) in a finish of heads at Longchamp in June to complete a clean sweep of the best middle-distance speed figures for races run in France.

Stayers (13f +)

The long-distance division produced very few outstanding times but the Lady O Goodwood Cup proved the fastest, with **Distinction** (117) beating the three-year-old **Golden Quest** (116) in a close finish, with subsequent Lonsdale Cup and Doncaster Cup winner Millenary eight lengths away. In his previous race, Distinction had finished runner-up to the champion stayer Westerner in the Ascot Gold Cup, but as that was run on a new track at York while the Berkshire venue was being re-developed, no speed figures were available for that contest. **Westerner**'s best figure was recorded in the Arc (see above), but he posted 115 twice, in both the Prix Barbeville and the Prix Vicomtesse Vigier at Longchamp in the spring, when Allez Olive was his victim on each occasion.
Possibly a surprise inclusion in the list is All-Weather winner **High Action** (115), but there was no fluke about it, as his mark was recorded when winning a valuable Lingfield handicap on Polytrack in July, beating Golden Quest, whose subsequent second in the Goodwood Cup is detailed above.

Two-Year-Olds (5f – 6f)

George Washington put up one of those performances that just had to be seen to be believed when waltzing home by eight lengths in the Independent Waterford Wedgwood Phoenix Stakes at The Curragh in August. The merit of the performance was put into context when it transpired that Aidan O'Brien's colt had covered the six furlongs trip in a time half a second faster than the Group Three contest for experienced sprinters half an hour later. This spectacular effort earned the Ballydoyle inmate a superb speed figure of 116.
Balthazaar's Gift also gained his big speed figure of 115 abroad, this time in beating **Gwenseb** (114) and **Curtail** (110) by a neck and three lengths in the Criterium de Maisons-Laffitte in November. The colt loves to get his toe in, so conditions were perfect for him in France and the victory capped a memorable autumn for trainer Kevin Ryan with his juveniles.
Amongst the also-rans in the Maisons-Laffitte contest was **Manston**, but Brian Meehan's colt had already earned a place on the podium thanks to his victory in a Listed contest at Doncaster in October, a performance which earned him a figure of 112. Conditions had become very testing on Town Moor and Manston handled them that much better than the rest.
Silca's Sister (111) hit the big-time when beating the colts in the Prix Morny at Deauville in August on what turned out to be her last appearance of the season. Trained by Mick Channon then, she will be sporting the blue colours of Godolphin when she reappears at three.
Mick Channon still has **Flashy Wings** in his charge though, and the filly earned her top figure of 110 in winning the Jaguar Cars Lowther Stakes at York in August. She did not manage to win in two subsequent efforts, but neither did she enjoy the best of luck.

Alan Jarvis's **Mixed Blessing** also earned 110 for her victory in the Princess Margaret Stakes at Newbury in July. However, there was a view that she was able to take advantage of a pronounced track bias that day and her subsequent efforts give some credence to that opinion.

Two-Year-Olds (7f+)

Ballydoyle were also responsible for the top horse in this category with **Horatio Nelson** being awarded a very smart 114 for his defeat of **Opera Cape** (112) in the Prix Jean-Luc Lagardere at Longchamp on Arc day. His effort just trumped the performance of his stable-companion **George Washington**, who had previously earned 113 for his three-length victory in the Laing O'Rourke National Stakes at The Curragh the previous month. George Washington is currently favourite for the 2000 Guineas and Horatio Nelson heads the market for the Derby, but Horatio Nelson does not lack speed and it would not be a surprise to see him line up alongside his stable-companion in the Guineas.

Palace Episode (112) did his bit to make it a wonderful autumn for Kevin Ryan when ploughing through the mud to win the Racing Post Trophy at Doncaster in October. He had appeared held in Group company before this victory, but he adapted to the testing conditions that much better than anything else and his success was well deserved.

Nannina (112) proved herself out of the top drawer when edging out **Alexandrova** (111) by a short head in the relocated Meon Valley Stud Fillies' Mile at Newmarket in September. She looks a major candidate for this year's 1000 Guineas with her stamina guaranteed and her ability to handle the Rowley Mile already proven.

Quiet Royal also earned 112 for her impressive victory in the Prix Miesque at Maisons-Laffitte in November. She is in the Newmarket 1000 Guineas, but it's more likely that she will be aimed at the French version and she should be a major player for that if she trains on.

Carlotamix (111) maintained his unbeaten record with a very impressive victory in the Criterium International at Saint-Cloud in October, a race won in recent years by the likes of Dalakhani and Bago. Andre Fabre's colt will surely relish the now ten-furlong trip of the French Derby and looks a very exciting prospect.

Sir Percy is another one to look forward to and earned 111 for his victory over a possibly unlucky Horatio Nelson in the Darley Dewhurst Stakes at Newmarket in October. Unbeaten in all four of his starts at two, Marcus Tregoning's colt surely has more to offer provided he has wintered well.

Ballydoyle's success was not limited to the colts and **Rumplestiltskin** did her bit with two Group One wins including a victory over Quiet Royal in the Prix Marcel Boussac on Arc day which earned her a figure of 111.

Her stable companion **Septimus** could only finish third behind Palace Episode when odds-on for the Racing Post Trophy, but had previously earned 111 for his victory in the Beresford Stakes at The Curragh.

HOW TO READ TIMECHECK

Timecheck contains the SPLIT SECOND ratings (speed figures) for every performance of every horse that ran on the Flat between 1 January and 31 December 2005 down to a minimum rating of 99.

The data is abbreviated in the following format:

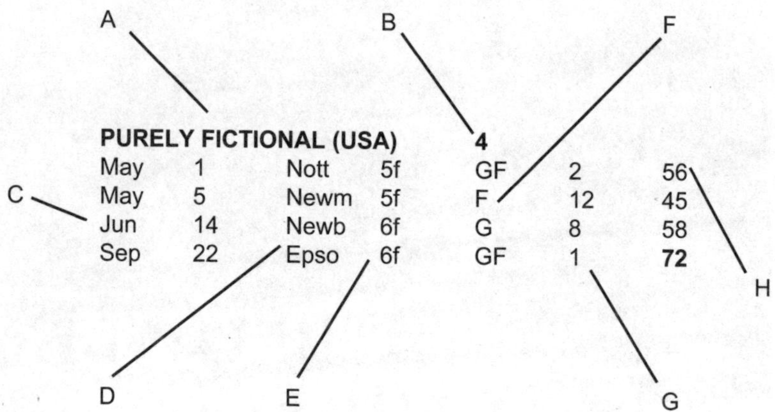

A Name of Horse
B Age as in 2004
C Date of performance
D Racecourse is always shown as the first four letters of the course name i.e. Asco, Epso, Newb, Newm, Yarm etc.
E Race distance in furlongs
F Going – signified thus: HD (hard), F (firm), GF (good to firm), G (good), GS (good to soft), S (soft), FST (fast), SF (standard to fast) ,STD (standard), SS (standard to slow), SLW (slow)
G Finishing position in race
H Speed Figure – each horse's best performance appears in **bold** type

THREE-YEAR-OLDS AND UPWARDS of 2005

A

A BIT OF FUN 4
Feb 8 Sthl 11f SD 4 **103**

A ONE 6
Jun 6 Wind 8½f G 5 **106**

A TEEN 7
Dec 29 Ling 5f G 3 **102**

A THOUSAND SMILES 3
Dec 30 Ling 10f FT 3 **100**

AAHGOWANGOWAN 6
Apr 25 Haml 6f G 5 **100**
Jun 18 Ayr 6f G 4 99

ABBEYGATE 4
Mar 8 Sthl 7f SD 1 **103**

ABERDEEN PARK 3
Jly 14 Epsm 7f G 5 **99**

ABERDOVEY 3
Jly 5 NmkJ 7f G 5 **103**
Aug 6 NmkJ 8f G 8 100
Aug 23 Yarm 8f G 2 101
Sep 3 Thsk 8f G 4 102

ADIDE 3
Jun 22 Sals 7f G 1 99
Oct 3 Wind 8½f GF 9 **102**

ABIENTOT 3
Apr 6 Ling 7f GF 2 104
Apr 22 Wolv 7f SD 1 101
May 16 Wind 5f G 1 103
Jly 10 Hayd 5f GF 3 101
Jly 29 Gdwd 5f G 1 **105**

ABLE BAKER CHARLIE 6
Jun 22 Sals 8f G 3 **103**
Jun 30 Hayd 8f GF 6 99
Jly 24 Newb 10f G 1 99
Aug 17 York 10½f G 11 101

ABLE CHARLIE 3
May 19 Donc 7f GF 5 **99**

ABLE MIND 5
Sep 19 Carl 8f G 3 **100**

ABSENT FRIENDS 8
Jan 21 Wolv 6f SD 2 **107**
Feb 11 Wolv 5f SD 8 100
Aug 12 Catt 5f GF 1 101
Aug 23 Yarm 5f G 7 99

ABSOLUTE IMAGE 3
Jun 15 Leop 7f G 1 **107**

ABSOLUTELYTHEBEST 4
May 1 Sals 14f GS 4 **107**
Jun 23 Sals 14f G 2 105

ABSTRACT FOLLY 3
Jun 23 Leic 10f GF 6 **99**
Oct 31 Wolv 8½f SD 2 **99**

ABUNDANCE 3
Aug 7 Deau 6½f G 12 109
Nov 1 MsnL 6f GF 7 **112**

ACCELERATION 5
Mar 7 Ling 16f SD 8 104

ACCENDERE 4
Feb 4 Wolv 7f SD 2 **101**

ACCOMPLISH 3
Aug 26 Bath 8f G 4 **99**
Sep 19 Folk 9½f GF 1 **99**

ACE 4
Apr 24 Lonc 10½f GS 3 111
Jun 15 York 10½f G 2 112
Jly 23 Newb 12f GF 5 109
Aug 16 York 10½f G 4 **115**
Sep 10 Leop 10f GF 4 114

ACE OF HEARTS 6
May 7 NmkR 9f GF 6 101
May 20 Hayd 8f G 8 104
May 30 Sand 8f G 3 110
Jun 11 Ripn 9f G 1 107
Jly 2 Sand 8f G 1 **116**
Jly 16 Newb 8f GF 7 101
Aug 6 Wind 8½f GF 1 110
Oct 1 NmkR 9f G 5 104

ACKNOWLEDGEMENT 3
May 5 Folk 9½f GS 5 **100**

ACOMB 5
Jan 7 Wolv 7f SW 6 103
Jan 12 Wolv 8½f SD 3 105
Feb 12 Wolv 8½f FT 1 106
Feb 18 Wolv 8½f SD 7 106
Apr 12 Muss 8f G 5 102
Jun 13 Thsk 7f G 1 105
Jun 18 Ayr 7f G 1 **110**
Jun 22 Epsm 7f G 1 106
Sep 17 Ayr 7f G 3 103

ACORAZADO 6
Feb 25 Wolv 8½f G 5 99
Apr 2 Wolv 8½f FT 2 **102**

ACROPOLIS 4
Apr 3 Curr 10f S 2 105
May 6 Ches 13½f GS 3 **107**
Sep 25 NmkR 12f G 5 101

ACTIVE ASSET 3
Jly 14 Epsm 10f G 3 102
Jly 30 Gdwd 11f G 4 99
Aug 19 Ches 10½f GF 2 100
Aug 28 Gdwd 9f G 4 **107**
Sep 24 Ripn 10f GF 3 106
Oct 10 Wind 10f G 5 99

ACTIVO 4
Nov 29 Ling 10f FT 2 **109**
Dec 17 Ling 8f FT 5 100

ACTUALITY 3
Sep 11 Gdwd 8f G 12 102
Nov 9 Wolv 7f FT 1 100
Dec 5 Ling 8f FT 2 **106**

ACUZIO 4
Apr 16 Wolv 9½f FT 2 99
Jun 27 Pont 10f G 2 **100**
Jly 5 Pont 10f G 4 99

AD VALOREM 3
Jun 14 York 8f G 2 110
Jly 3 Chan 8f G 5 113
Jly 27 Gdwd 8f GS 3 **116**

ADAALA 3
May 8 Leop 7f S 3 103
Jly 17 Curr 9f F 1 **110**
Sep 4 Curr 9f G 3 109
Sep 18 Curr 10f G 11 104
Nov 6 Leop 7f GS 7 103

ADANTINO 6
Jan 6 Wolv 6f GS 2 99
Jan 19 Ling 5f FT 4 103
Mar 21 Ling 6f FT 2 **105**
May 27 Wolv 6f SD 1 102
Jun 19 Wwck 6f G 7 **105**
Aug 6 Hayd 6f G 2 102
Aug 12 Newb 6f G 2 103
Aug 22 Wind 6f G 1 100
Sep 5 Bath 5½f GF 6 102
Sep 17 Wolv 6f FT 3 101

ADMIRAL 4
May 1 NmkR 16f G 5 101

ADMIRAL COMPTON 4
Mar 19 Ling 8f SD 4 **104**
Dec 5 Ling 8f FT 4 103
Dec 21 Ling 10f FT 3 101

ADMIRAL'S CRUISE 3
Aug 27 York 10½f G 2 105
Sep 3 NmkJ 10f G 2 106
Oct 1 NmkR 10f G 1 107
Oct 22 Newb 10f G 2 **112**

ADOBE 10
May 21 Hayd 8f GF 3 99
Jun 22 Bath 8f G 2 **101**
Jly 2 Nott 8f GF 6 99
Jly 11 Ayr 8f F 6 99
Aug 19 Ayr 8f GF 3 99
Dec 5 Wolv 8½f GF 1 100
Dec 28 Wolv 8½f GF 7 100

ADORATION 3
Apr 18 Pont 6f S 1 105
Jun 1 Bevl 7½f G 1 103
Jun 16 York 8f G 12 101
Jun 25 Newc 8f G 5 101
Jly 30 Gdwd 9f G 2 103
Aug 28 Gdwd 9f G 3 **107**
Sep 2 Hayd 8f G 2 **107**
Oct 1 Epsm 8½f GS 1 105
Oct 8 York 9f GS 7 101

ADRIATIC 5
Apr 10 Leop 7f GS 3 99
May 22 Curr 6f G 12 **100**
Aug 20 Curr 6f GF 11 99

AEGEAN DANCER 3
Jun 18 Rdcr 6f GF 2 **102**

AFRAD 4
Jly 7 NmkJ 12f G 1 103

AFRICAN BREEZE 3
Aug 3 Pont 6f G 1 **102**
Aug 24 Catt 7f G 2 99
Oct 14 Rdcr 7f GF 7 100

AFRICAN DREAM 4
Mar 19 Ling 10f SD 8 **112**
Apr 13 NmkR 9f G 8 100

AFRICAN SAHARA 6
May 2 Donc 10½f G 12 100
Jun 17 Gdwd 8f G 4 102
Jun 22 Carl 8f GF 3 103
Jun 27 Pont 8f G 3 103
Jly 2 Nott 8f GF 7 99
Jly 5 NmkJ 8f G 8 100
Jly 14 Donc 8f GF 2 103
Jly 17 Rdcr 8f G 3 99
Jly 22 Wolv 8½f FT 5 100
Oct 12 Ling 8f FT 6 101
Oct 19 Nott 8f G 1 102
Oct 31 Wolv 8½f SD 1 **105**
Nov 10 Ling 8f SD 9 99
Dec 6 Sthl 11f FT 8 103

AFRICANUS 3
Jun 23 Thsk 7f G 3 100
Aug 18 Wolv 8½f SD 2 **105**

AFTER THE SHOW 4
Oct 18 Sthl 5f SW 1 **103**
Nov 12 Wolv 5f FT 2 99
Dec 17 Ling 5f FT 1 101

AGE OF KINGS 3
Jun 25 Ches 10½f G 3 **99**

AGENDA 4
May 25 Leop 14f GF 9 101
Sep 18 Curr 10f G 10 104
Oct 9 Curr 12f GS 3 **106**

AGGI MAC 4
Nov 5 Sthl 11f FT 3 **103**

AGGRAVATION 3
Jly 8 Ling 8f SW 1 **101**

AGILETE 3
Jun 30 Epsm 7f G 5 **101**
Jly 14 Epsm 7f G 3 **101**
Aug 29 Wwck 7f GF 4 99

AHDAAF 3
Jun 1 Nott 8f G 3 103
Jly 30 Thsk 7f G 1 102
Sep 3 Thsk 8f G 2 **106**

AIDIN AND ABETTING 5
May 25 Leop 7f GF 8 101
Jun 1 Leop 7f G 14 **108**

AIGUILLE 3
Apr 1 Donc 7f G 3 **99**

AINTNECESSARILYSO 7
Jun 29 Chep 6f G 4 **100**
Jly 12 Brig 6f G 4 **100**

AIR OF ESTEEM 9
Apr 5 Sthl 8f SD 1 **100**

AIREDALE LAD 4
May 6 Haml 8½f GS 2 **101**
Jly 19 Ayr 8f G 8 **101**

AIREX 3
Jun 5 Chan 10½f G 9 **101**

AIRGUSTA 4
Nov 5 Wolv 16½f FT 3 99
Dec 12 Wolv 14f FT 8 **102**
Dec 28 Wolv 14f FT 5 100

AIRWAVE 5
May 21 Curr 8f G 1 **107**
Jun 15 York 8f G 6 105

AKAREM 4
May 21 Curr 8f G 9 **107**
Aug 14 Leop 12f F 4 103
Nov 5 Donc 12f S 2 106

AKIMBO 4
May 20 Gdwd 7f GS 2 108
Jun 1 Yarm 7f G 1 103
Jun 14 York 8f G 5 **109**
Jly 9 Ling 8f SD 10 102

AKONA MATATA 3
Jly 19 Yarm 7f G 3 **103**

AKSHAR 6
May 22 Curr 12f GS 11 103

AL EILE 5
May 25 Leop 14f GF 4 105

ALABAMA TWIST 3
Jun 29 Catt 6f G 1 99
Jly 14 Epsm 7f G 4 **100**

ALAMIYAN 3
May 2 Kemp 8f G 1 100
Jun 19 Pont 10f G 1 **108**
Jly 28 Gdwd 10f G 6 99

ALAYAN 3
Apr 10 Leop 8f S 1 104
May 8 Leop 10f S 2 **106**
Sep 10 Leop 10f GF 1 103
Oct 1 Lonc 9½f G 5 105

ALBAHJA 3
Apr 23 Leic 10f G 3 100
Jun 10 Chep 12f G 1 103
Jly 8 Chep 10f GF 2 **107**
Aug 18 York 12f G 2 103

ALBANY HALL 3
Sep 17 Lonc 10f G 7 **103**

ALBERT HALL 3
May 12 York 10½f S 5 **99**

ALBINUS 4
May 28 Gdwd 12f G 2 **107**

ALCAZAR 10
Apr 16 Newb 12f GS 6 107
Apr 27 Ling 16f S 1 113
May 13 York 14f GS 4 107
May 30 Sand 16½f G 3 101
Aug 21 Deau 15f G 1 113
Oct 23 Lonc 15½f GS 1 **114**

ALCHEMIST MASTER 6
Jun 29 Catt 7f G 2 **102**
Jly 22 York 7f G 3 101
Aug 3 Brig 8f G 9 **102**
Oct 29 Wolv 7f SD 2 101

ALDERNEY RACE 4
Apr 30 NmkR 6f G 4 **110**
Jun 18 York 6f GF 6 108
Jly 2 Hayd 6f GF 5 103

ALDORA 6
Apr 30 Gdwd 8f S 1 **109**
May 13 York 7f GS 3 101

ALERON 7
Mar 28 Wwck 11f GS 3 102

ALESSANO 3
Jan 13 Ling 10f SD 4 100
May 9 Wind 11½f GF 3 99
May 31 Leic 12f G 3 99
Oct 9 Gdwd 11f G 1 **103**

ALEXANDER GOLDRUN 4
Jun 25 Curr 10f G 1 114
Jly 5 NmkJ 8f G 2 105
Jly 30 Gdwd 10f G 1 108
Sep 10 Leop 10f GF 3 **115**
Oct 2 Lonc 10f G 3 109
Oct 15 NmkR 10f G 8 108

ALEXANDER ICEQUEEN 3
Jun 1 Leop 6f G 2 **111**
Jly 2 Leop 7f F 3 108
Aug 20 Curr 6f GF 4 107

ALEXANDER QUEEN 3
Jly 16 Curr 5f F 13 **102**

ALEXANDER SAPPHIRE 4
Jan 18 Sthl 11f F 2 **99**

ALEXIA ROSE 3
Jly 2 Hayd 6f GF 3 **102**
Dec 17 Ling 5f FT 6 99

ALFIE LEE 8
Aug 25 Muss 5f G 9 **99**

ALFIE NOAKES 3
Jly 22 Newb 10f G 1 **105**
Aug 12 Newb 13½f G 9 103
Sep 9 Donc 14½f G 7 102

ALFONSO 4
Mar 29 Pont 8f S 3 **106**
May 4 Ches 10½f GS 9 103

ALFRED THE GREAT 3
Aug 27 York 8f G 4 100
Sep 15 Pont 10f G 3 **101**

ALFRIDINI 4
Jan 19 Ling 10f FT 10 100
Feb 21 Ling 10f FT 6 101
May 20 NmkR 8f G 4 **103**

ALGHARB 3
Jun 3 Thsk 7f G 2 102
Jun 11 Ripn 6f G 1 100
Jun 25 NmkJ 6f G 5 100
Jly 16 Hayd 6f G 1 99
Aug 7 Rdcr 6f G 3 **103**
Sep 23 Ling 6f G 6 100

ALI BRUCE 5
Jan 8 Ling 8f SD 2 103
Jan 29 Ling 8f SD 4 **111**
Feb 18 Wolv 6f SD 6 103
Apr 21 Sthl 6f FT 1 100
Jun 6 Wind 8½f G 2 109
Jly 11 Wolv 7f SD 3 103
Jly 28 Epsm 7f G 2 101
Aug 6 Wind 6f GF 2 101
Aug 25 Ling 7f FT 1 104
Sep 6 Ling 7f SD 4 102

ALI D 7
Jun 24 NmkJ 8f G 1 **101**
Jly 15 NmkJ 8f G 2 99
Aug 20 Rdcr 10f G 5 99

ALI DEO 4
Jun 1 Yarm 11½f G 3 102
Jun 17 NmkJ 12f GF 7 **103**

ALKAADHEM 5
Apr 13 NmkR 9f G 6 104
Jly 18 Ayr 10f GF 3 **109**

ALKAASED 5
May 1 NmkR 12f G 1 104
Jun 3 Epsm 12f G 2 111
Jun 26 StCl 12f GF 1 118
Sep 11 Lonc 12f G 2 **119**
Oct 15 NmkR 10f G 5 109

ALL A DREAM 3
Feb 19 Wolv 8½f G 2 **104**
Dec 5 Ling 8f FT 3 101
Dec 12 Wolv 9½f FT 4 99
Dec 30 Ling 8f FT 7 101

ALL DIAMONDS 4
Nov 6 Leop 12f S 5 **99**

ALL FOR LAURA 3
Jun 24 NmkJ 6f G 2 104
Aug 14 Pont 6f G 4 **109**
Sep 18 Haml 5f F 7 101
Oct 13 NmkR 6f G 5 101

ALL IVORY 3
Apr 30 Gdwd 7f S 2 109
Jun 13 Thsk 7f G 1 105
Jly 2 Sand 7f G 5 104
Jly 16 NmkJ 7f GF 1 101
Aug 13 Newb 7f G 4 103
Aug 26 Thsk 8f GF 2 99
Sep 9 Sand 8f GS 2 102
Sep 24 NmkR 7f G 1 **115**

ALL NIGHT DANCER 3
May 22 Curr 6f G 5 **104**

ALL QUIET 4
Apr 6 Ling 7f G 1 104
May 25 NmkR 7f G 4 103
Jly 11 Wind 8½f G 1 **105**
Jly 22 Chep 7f G 4 99
Aug 15 Wind 8½f GF 1 **105**
Sep 1 Sals 7f G 5 102
Sep 27 Gdwd 8f G 3 100

ALL STAR 5
Jly 1 Sand 14f G 2 105
Aug 6 NmkJ 16f G 5 101

ALL THAT AND MORE 3
Jly 28 Epsm 8½f G 1 **101**

ALL TOO BEAUTIFUL 4
May 12 York 10½f S 1 **112**

ALLEXINA 3
Jly 17 Curr 12f F 8 106
Sep 18 Curr 10f G 6 108
Oct 9 Curr 12f GS 1 **110**

ALLEZ OLIVE 7
Apr 30 Lonc 15½f GS 2 **114**
May 22 Lonc 15½f GF 2 112
Aug 21 Deau 15f G 4 109
Oct 23 Lonc 15½f GS 9 101

ALMANSHOOD 3
May 20 NmkR 10f G 2 100
Aug 4 Hayd 10½f GF 5 100
Oct 9 Bath 10f G 3 **102**

ALMARA 5
May 11 Brig 7f G 2 **104**

ALMATY EXPRESS 3
Aug 19 Wolv 5f FT 1 **100**
Nov 28 Wolv 5f FT 1 **100**

ALMAVARA 3
Feb 18 Wolv 9½f SD 1 **99**

ALMENDRADOS 3
Apr 13 NmkR 7f G 9 **103**
May 1 NmkR 10f G 3 99

ALMIGHTY 3
Apr 10 Leop 10f S 4 **103**
May 5 Ches 12½f GS 2 102

ALMIZAN 5
May 1 NmkR 16f G 3 **106**

ALMOST INNOCENT 3
Jly 4 Wind 8½f G 1 **102**

ALMURAAD 4
Aug 29 Epsm 10f G 3 **106**
Sep 9 Donc 10½f G 5 **106**

ALONE HE STANDS 5
Mar 20 Curr 8f HY 3 **109**
Apr 3 Curr 7f S 5 105
Sep 10 Leop 7f HD 5 106
Sep 17 Curr 8f GF 7 106
Oct 23 Curr 6f S 1 **109**
Nov 6 Leop 7f GS 8 103

ALONG THE NILE 3
May 6 Haml 11f GS 2 100
May 24 Ripn 10f GS 5 99
Jun 25 Newc 8f G 3 103
Jun 27 Pont 8f G 1 **104**
Aug 14 Pont 8f G 1 102

ALOST 5
May 9 Lonc 12f G 3 **116**

ALPAGA LE JOMAGE 3
Apr 16 Thsk 5f S 3 100
May 12 York 5f GS 4 **105**
Dec 3 Wolv 6f GS 2 100

ALPINE GOLD 3
Jun 4 Hayd 12f G 9 100
Sep 17 Wwck 16f G 6 **101**

ALPINE HIDEAWAY 12
Jun 16 Bevl 8½f G 5 99

ALPINE REEL 4
May 23 Thsk 7f G 1 103
Jun 20 Wind 8½f G 1 **107**

ALPINE SPECIAL 4
Feb 14 Wolv 12f G 3 **107**
Feb 24 Sthl 14f FT 5 100

ALRAFIDAIN 3
Mar 27 Muss 12f GS 1 **106**

ALRIGHT MY SON 3
Aug 27 NmkJ 7f G 8 **100**

ALSHARQ 3
Jun 2 Brig 7f G 1 **105**

ALTA PETENS 3
Sep 13 Yarm 6f G 3 **103**
Sep 23 Ling 6f G 4 102
Oct 13 NmkR 6f G 6 100
Oct 30 Ling 6f SD 7 101

ALTIERI 7
Jly 2 Sand 10f G 3 110
Sep 4 Lonc 8f GF 6 **113**

ALUMNI 3
Apr 15 Newb 10f GS 2 99
May 4 Ches 11½f GS 1 **104**
Aug 21 Deau 10f G 6 101
Oct 13 NmkR 10f G 7 100

ALVARITA 3
Sep 13 Sals 8f G 1 99
Oct 30 Ling 8f SD 4 **101**

ALWAYS ESTEEMED 5
Mar 12 Wolv 8½f SD 3 **111**
Apr 2 Donc 8f G 9 106

ALWAYS FLYING 4
Apr 2 Wolv 8½f FT 6 **99**

AM BROSE 6
May 24 Ripn 6f G 2 100
Jun 25 Wind 6f G 8 **104**
Jly 30 Gdwd 6f G 23 100

AMANDA'S LAD 5
Jun 21 Bevl 5f G 5 99
Jun 29 Catt 5f GF 2 99
Sep 28 Newc 5f GF 4 **102**

AMAZIN 3
Jun 25 NmkJ 6f G 4 101
Jly 20 Sand 7f G 2 **107**
Aug 26 NmkJ 7f G 1 100

AMBER NECTAR TWO 5
Dec 29 Ling 5f G 5 **101**

AMEEQ 3
Sep 21 Rdcr 10f GF 2 100
Oct 5 Nott 10f G 2 100
Oct 22 Newb 10f GS 4 **103**

AMELIA 7
May 19 Newc 5f G 2 99
Sep 28 Newc 5f GF 7 **100**

AMERICAN COUSIN 10
May 23 Bevl 5f G 1 **99**

AMERIGO VESPUCCI 3
May 28 Ling 10f SW 3 **105**

AMIATA 5
Apr 3 Curr 6f S 7 **101**

AMICA 3
May 7 Ling 6f G 3 **104**
Aug 4 Chep 8f G 1 103
Aug 29 Epsm 8½f G 1 102
Sep 14 Sand 8f G 9 102

AMIE DE MIX 4
Aug 21 Deau 10f G 4 **111**

AMIR ZAMAN 7
Mar 7 Wolv 12f SD 3 **109**

AMIRA 3
May 28 Donc 5f G 5 99
Sep 5 Newc 5f F 1 **100**
Sep 13 Thsk 6f G 3 99

AMNESTY 6
May 3 Bath 10f HY 2 99

AMONG GUEST 5
Aug 7 Deau 10f GF 3 **108**

AMONGST AMIGOS 4
Apr 3 Curr 10f S 3 **109**

AMORIST 3
Aug 20 Ling 10f SD 3 99
Oct 14 Brig 8f G 2 99
Dec 10 Sthl 8f FT 1 **103**
Dec 15 Sthl 8f SD 1 100
Dec 22 Sthl 8f SD 4 101

AMOROSA BRI 3
Jun 27 Lonc 9½f G 7 **101**

AMWELL BRAVE 4
Aug 4 Chep 12f G 4 100
Oct 30 Ling 12f SD 1 **101**
Nov 12 Ling 12f FT 2 99

ANAAMIL 3
May 7 Hayd 10½f S 1 **102**

ANAK PEKAN 5
May 4 Ches 18½f GS 1 104
May 22 Lonc 15½f GF 6 **107**
Jly 2 Sand 16½f G 6 105

ANALYZE 7
Jan 8 Ling 8f SD 4 **102**

ANCHOR DATE 3
May 17 Leic 6f G 2 101
Jun 23 Thsk 7f G 2 **103**
Aug 29 Wwck 7f GF 2 102
Sep 3 Thsk 6f G 1 **103**
Sep 6 Catt 7f GF 7 99
Oct 29 Wolv 7f SD 3 100
Nov 10 Ling 8f SD 6 99

ANCIENT WORLD 5
Sep 17 Newb 9f GF 3 101
Sep 30 NmkR 8f G 2 **104**

ANDALUZA 4
Mar 24 Wolv 7f SD 1 **103**

ANDEAN 4
Aug 31 York 9f G 2 **107**

ANDRONIKOS 3
Apr 16 Newb 7f GS 5 103
Apr 27 Ling 6f GS 1 106
May 13 Newb 6f F 2 104
Jly 5 NmkJ 6f G 5 107
Aug 28 Deau 6f G 2 **111**

ANDURIL 4
Feb 25 Wolv 8½f G 1 103
Mar 7 Wolv 9½f SD 4 99
Mar 16 Wolv 9½f SD 2 **106**
Mar 24 Wolv 8½f SD 3 101
Apr 13 Bevl 10f G 6 101
May 21 Hayd 8f GF 1 103
Jun 4 Hayd 8f G 4 100
Jun 22 Carl 8f GF 9 101
Jly 13 Hayd 8f G 4 104
Jly 22 Wolv 8½f FT 2 101
Aug 3 Brig 8f G 5 104
Sep 17 Ayr 10f G 2 102
Sep 27 Gdwd 8f G 4 99
Sep 29 Ayr 10f S 4 99

ANFIELD DREAM 3
Jan 8 Ling 6f SD 2 102
Feb 22 Ling 7f SD 3 101
Mar 7 Ling 5f SD 1 **105**
Dec 20 Sthl 5f SD 2 101

ANGEL SPRINTS 3
May 28 Gdwd 6f G 7 99
Jun 11 Sand 7f G 7 102
Aug 6 Wind 6f GF 6 102
Aug 13 Gdwd 6f G 1 **105**
Aug 28 Gdwd 6f G 3 **105**
Sep 14 Sand 5f GS 1 100
Sep 29 NmkR 6f GF 5 100

ANGELO'S PRIDE 4
Feb 4 Wolv 8½f SD 5 101
Feb 14 Wolv 9½f SD 3 **102**
Feb 21 Ling 10f FT 1 101

ANGELOFTHENORTH 3
Apr 16 Nott 5f G 1 **101**
Nov 3 Muss 5f GS 3 100

ANLON 4
Apr 3 Curr 10f S 5 **106**

ANNA MONDA 3
Jun 5 Chan 8f GF 7 105
Jly 29 Gdwd 7f G 7 **107**

ANNA PALLIDA 4
Jly 8 Ling 10f G 6 103
Jly 20 Leic 12f GF 3 **105**

ANNAKITA 5
Apr 8 Sthl 14f GF 1 **103**

ANNAMBO 5
Jun 22 Epsm 12f G 2 100
Jly 16 NmkJ 15f GF 1 **102**
Nov 19 Ling 12f FT 9 100

ANNAMOE BOY 5
Jun 15 Leop 9f GF 1 **105**

ANNENKOV 3
Jly 14 Lonc 12f F 6 **108**

ANNIBALE CARO 3
Aug 1 Carl 12f G 1 **105**
Aug 6 Ayr 11f F 1 100

ANNO JUBILO 8
May 21 Curr 12f G 8 103
Jun 15 Leop 10f G 2 102
Jly 2 Leop 10f GF 1 **104**

ANNUS IUCUNDUS 4
Mar 7 Ling 16f SD 9 **104**

ANOTHER BOTTLE 4
May 15 Ripn 10f G 1 105
May 30 Rdcr 10f G 8 102
Jun 23 Newc 8f G 2 101
Jly 16 Newb 8f GF 1 **106**

ANOTHER CHOICE 4
Mar 1 Ling 10f SD 4 **107**
Apr 23 Hayd 10½f G 2 105

ANOTHER CON 4
Jan 14 Wolv 14f SW 5 **99**
Apr 18 Wolv 12f FT 1 **99**

ANOTHER FAUX PAS 4
Jun 13 Brig 8f G 2 103
Jun 20 Wind 8½f G 2 **105**
Jly 9 Nott 8f F 2 100

ANOTHER GLIMPSE 7
Jan 5 Ling 6f SD 6 **100**

ANOUSA 4
May 1 NmkR 12f G 8 **106**

ANTHEMION 8
Jly 14 Haml 8½f GF 2 105
Jly 15 Haml 9f F 1 103
Jly 19 Ayr 8f G 1 **108**
Aug 16 Haml 9f F 4 100

ANTIQUE 3						
May	15	Lonc	8f	G	5	107
Aug	2	Deau	10f	G	3	**115**
Aug	21	Deau	10f	G	4	101

ANTONIUS PIUS 4						
May	14	Newb	8f	F	8	**109**

ANUVASTEEL 4						
Jan	19	Ling	10f	FT	5	102
Jan	29	Ling	10f	SD	3	107
Feb	18	Wolv	8½f	SD	1	**108**
Feb	25	Wolv	8½f	SD	3	101

ANXIOUS MOMENTS 10						
Jun	1	Leop	14f	G	6	**106**
Jun	26	Curr	16f	F	1	104
Jly	16	Curr	16f	GF	2	105
Aug	7	Curr	16f	G	5	**106**

AONINCH 5						
May	31	Leic	10f	G	2	101
Jun	7	Sals	12f	G	3	99
Jun	23	Sals	10f	G	3	101
Jly	9	Sals	12f	G	2	**102**
Aug	11	Sals	12f	GF	1	99

APACHE POINT 8						
May	11	Newc	9f	G	1	101
Jun	17	Ayr	10f	GS	1	101
Jly	23	York	10½f	GS	3	**104**
Aug	26	Newc	9f	GF	7	103

APEX 4						
Jly	8	Ling	6f	SW	5	**106**

APPALACHIAN TRAIL 4						
Mar	12	Wolv	8½f	SD	5	107
Apr	2	Donc	8f	G	10	106
Apr	23	Sand	8f	G	6	103
May	29	NmkR	7f	GF	2	106
Jun	11	Sand	7f	G	15	102
Jly	7	NmkJ	7f	G	6	106
Jly	23	Newb	7f	GF	6	**111**
Aug	13	Newb	7f	G	1	106
Nov	11	Wolv	8½f	FT	2	**111**
Dec	9	Wolv	7f	FT	2	105

APPLEBLOSSOM PEARL 4						
Aug	7	Curr	10f	G	5	**107**

APPOLONIOUS 4						
Sep	26	Bath	8f	G	4	**99**

APSARA 4						
Aug	20	Rdcr	10f	G	4	100
Sep	17	Catt	12f	G	8	**102**

APSIS 4						
Aug	15	Deau	10f	G	2	**114**

AQUILONIA 3						
May	12	Sals	10f	G	4	**103**

ARABIAN DANCER 3						
May	31	Leic	6f	GF	2	**105**
Jun	21	Newb	6f	GF	2	100
Oct	20	Brig	6f	GS	8	99

ARABIAN MOON 9						
Jly	18	Wind	11½f	G	1	**101**

ARABIE 7						
Feb	8	Ling	10f	SD	2	99
Feb	12	Wolv	8½f	FT	5	**103**
Apr	21	Bath	10f	GS	1	**103**
May	17	Leic	10f	G	3	102
Jun	7	Ches	10½f	GF	10	99
Jly	20	Sand	10f	G	2	102

ARAGORN 3						
May	2	Donc	7f	G	1	104
May	21	NmkR	7f	G	3	102
Jun	15	York	7f	G	8	100
Jly	9	Ches	7f	GF	5	**111**

ARAKAN 5						
Apr	27	Ling	7½f	S	2	110
May	14	Newb	8f	F	5	111
Jun	25	NmkJ	7f	G	5	101
Jly	7	NmkJ	6f	G	8	105
Jly	17	Curr	7f	F	2	108
Jly	26	Gdwd	7f	G	5	111
Aug	18	York	7f	GF	1	111
Sep	8	Donc	7f	GF	4	108
Sep	27	Gdwd	7f	G	1	108
Oct	15	NmkR	7f	G	3	**114**

ARBELLA 3						
Aug	27	York	8f	G	5	**99**

ARC EL CIEL 7						
Jan	20	Sthl	7f	SD	3	**108**

ARCELIE 3						
Jly	2	Leop	10f	GF	1	**101**

ARCH FOLLY 3						
May	2	Wwck	12½f	G	7	**99**

ARCHANGE D'OR 3						
Jun	5	Chan	10½f	G	8	102
Jly	24	MsnL	10f	F	1	110
Sep	4	Lonc	8f	GF	8	**111**

ARCHIE BABE 9						
Apr	9	Newc	12½f	S	5	99

ARCHIE WRIGHT 3						
Jun	9	Brig	7f	G	4	**99**

ARCHIRONDEL 7						
Apr	13	Bevl	10f	G	1	**106**
Apr	28	Rdcr	11f	G	3	99
Aug	20	Rdcr	10f	G	6	99

ARCTIC BURST 5						
Feb	14	Ling	6f	SD	1	**100**

ARCTIC COVE 4						
Oct	10	Wolv	14f	FT	3	**99**

ARCTIC DESERT 5						
Jun	7	Sals	6f	G	5	100
Jly	23	Newb	7f	GF	2	100
Oct	31	Wolv	8½f	SD	7	**102**
Nov	10	Ling	8f	SD	4	100

ARGENT 4						
May	6	Haml	8½f	GS	1	**102**

ARGENTINA 3						
May	22	Lonc	10f	GF	2	104
Jun	12	Chan	10½f	G	2	**108**
Aug	21	Deau	10f	G	7	101

ARGENTUM 4						
Jun	23	Newc	16f	GF	1	**101**
Jly	17	Rdcr	16f	G	1	100

ARINOS 5						
Apr	16	Nott	14f	GS	5	**100**

ARISTI 4						
Jly	7	Wwck	12½f	G	3	**106**
Aug	8	Wolv	16½f	SD	1	99
Sep	12	Rdcr	14f	G	6	99

ARISTOCRATIC LADY 3						
May	1	StCl	10½f	F	7	**100**

ARMAGNAC 7						
Apr	2	Kemp	5f	GS	9	104
Aug	1	Ripn	6f	G	8	101
Aug	5	NmkJ	6f	GF	9	99
Aug	11	Sand	7f	GF	4	**107**
Aug	19	Ches	7f	GF	10	101
Sep	23	Ling	7f	G	3	99

ARMATORE 5						
Feb	25	Wolv	8½f	G	8	**99**

ARMS ACROSSTHESEA 6						
Aug	8	Thsk	8f	G	3	**100**

ARMY OF ANGELS 3						
Jly	2	Sand	7f	G	2	**107**

ARNIE DE BURGH 3						
Jun	7	Rdcr	7f	G	2	**102**

AROUS 3						
Aug	6	Rdcr	9f	G	3	**101**

ARRAN SCOUT 4						
Feb	12	Wolv	8½f	FT	8	100
Mar	16	Wolv	9½f	SD	6	99
Apr	21	Sthl	8f	FT	1	**107**
May	31	Rdcr	9f	G	2	99
Jun	16	Bevl	8½f	G	3	104
Jun	28	Haml	8½f	F	4	100

ARROW 3						
Mar	28	StCl	8f	GS	5	**102**

ARRY DASH 5						
Jan	10	Wolv	9½f	SD	6	103
Jan	29	Ling	8f	SD	8	107
Feb	16	Ling	10f	SD	4	104
Apr	4	Yarm	10f	GS	3	100
Apr	11	Ling	12f	SD	8	99
May	6	Nott	10f	G	4	100
May	13	Nott	8f	F	2	103
May	20	NmkR	8f	G	6	102
Aug	27	Wind	8½f	G	3	**111**
Sep	23	Hayd	8f	G	9	99

ART ELEGANT 3						
Jun	24	Wolv	7f	SD	4	99
Aug	19	Ayr	6f	GF	2	**101**
Oct	19	Newc	8f	GS	2	**101**

ART EYES 3						
Jun	22	Sals	12f	G	3	102
Jly	2	Leic	12f	GF	1	100
Jly	16	NmkJ	12f	GF	4	102

Jly	27	Gdwd	12f	GS	2	104
Aug	27	Gdwd	14f	G	4	108
Sep	7	Donc	14½f	GF	5	100
Sep	24	NmkR	12f	G	4	108
Sep	29	NmkR	14f	GF	1	**111**
Oct	15	NmkR	16f	G	6	100

ART MASTER 4

May	22	Lonc	7f	GF	1	**109**

ART MODERN 3

Feb	12	Ling	8f	SD	1	**103**
Aug	13	Newb	10f	G	2	102
Oct	10	Wind	10f	G	6	99

ART WORK 3

May	21	Ling	8f	SD	5	**104**
Jly	11	Wind	8½f	G	8	99

ARTIE 6

Jun	13	Thsk	6f	G	7	99
Jly	9	York	6f	G	2	105
Jly	23	York	6f	G	7	99
Jly	29	Thsk	6f	G	5	102
Aug	1	Ripn	6f	G	2	**106**
Aug	10	Bevl	5f	GF	1	105
Aug	16	York	6f	GF	5	103

ARTIST'S MUSE 3

Sep	17	Curr	8f	GF	8	**104**
Oct	9	Curr	8f	GS	3	100

ARTISTE ROYAL 4

May	9	Lonc	12f	G	4	116
Jun	16	Lonc	10f	G	1	**118**

ARTISTIC LAD 5

Jun	26	Curr	12f	F	17	**102**

ARTISTIC STYLE 5

Apr	9	Newc	7f	S	3	109
Apr	20	Epsm	10f	GS	5	107
May	4	Ches	10½f	GS	6	107
Jly	2	Sand	8f	G	9	**110**
Sep	15	Ayr	9f	G	4	105
Sep	29	Ayr	10f	S	1	107
Oct	22	Newb	10f	G	7	107

ARTURIUS 3

Jun	14	Carl	9½f	GS	1	**100**

ARTUSHOF 3

Apr	23	Wolv	9½f	SD	4	**102**

ARUM D'OR 8

Aug	7	Deau	10f	GF	9	**105**

ASAATEEL 3

Apr	26	Bath	10f	HY	1	99
Jly	31	Ches	12½f	G	3	**100**

ASAWER 3

May	12	Sals	10f	G	1	**109**
Jun	16	York	12f	G	3	102
Jly	16	NmkJ	12f	GF	2	105
Aug	18	York	12f	G	4	100
Sep	14	Yarm	10f	G	1	106
Sep	24	NmkR	12f	G	3	108
Oct	13	NmkR	10f	G	3	106

ASHARON 3

Jan	15	Ling	7f	SD	1	100
Feb	5	Ling	10f	SD	1	104
May	18	Gdwd	9f	G	3	**109**

ASHDOWN EXPRESS 6

Apr	14	NmkR	6f	G	2	107
Apr	30	NmkR	5f	G	2	112
May	23	Wind	6f	F	6	104
May	31	Sand	5f	G	6	110
Jly	7	NmkJ	6f	G	6	107
Jly	16	Newb	6f	GF	2	**115**
Jly	26	Gdwd	7f	G	7	109
Aug	27	NmkJ	6f	G	4	103
Sep	3	Hayd	6f	F	3	105
Sep	10	Gdwd	6f	GF	1	113
Sep	25	NmkR	6f	G	7	110

ASHES 3

Jun	26	Wind	5f	G	1	**99**

ASHKAL WAY 3

May	28	Muss	8f	G	2	108
Jun	21	Bevl	8½f	G	1	102
Jly	7	NmkJ	8f	G	3	106
Jly	28	Gdwd	10f	G	2	106
Aug	20	Bevl	10f	GF	1	109
Sep	17	Newb	10f	GF	7	**111**

ASK CAROL 4

Jly	2	Leop	10f	GF	4	**101**

ASK THE CLERK 4

Apr	2	Kemp	7f	GS	6	101
Aug	3	Yarm	6f	G	5	103
Sep	2	NmkJ	8f	G	4	**107**

ASTROCHARM 6

Jun	19	Pont	12f	G	3	**110**
Jun	25	Newc	16f	G	4	**110**
Jly	28	Gdwd	14f	G	3	101
Aug	16	York	16f	G	5	102
Aug	27	Gdwd	14f	G	5	107
Sep	24	NmkR	16f	G	8	104

ASTRONOMICAL 3

May	13	Nott	8f	F	1	**106**
May	27	Pont	8f	GF	4	99
Aug	27	York	10½f	G	6	101

ASWAN 7

Jan	12	Wolv	8½f	SD	6	102
Feb	25	Wolv	8½f	SD	5	100
Nov	26	Wolv	8½f	FT	1	**103**

ATACAMA STAR 3

Jly	3	Brig	10f	G	1	99
Aug	9	Bath	11½f	GF	3	**101**

ATHANOR 3

Jun	27	Lonc	9f	G	5	**108**

ATHENS 3

Jun	27	Wolv	12f	SD	4	**99**

ATHLUMNEY LAD 6

May	8	Leop	12f	S	7	104
May	22	Curr	12f	GS	7	**108**
Jun	26	Curr	12f	F	4	**108**
Sep	18	Curr	16f	G	2	**108**
Oct	9	Curr	16f	GS	13	99

ATLANTIC ACE 8

Feb	25	Wolv	8½f	GS	4	**100**
Mar	16	Wolv	9½f	SD	4	99

ATLANTIC AIR 3

Aug	2	Deau	10f	G	7	**103**

ATLANTIC QUEST 6

Jan	7	Wolv	7f	SW	1	**104**
Dec	26	Wolv	7f	SD	1	103

ATLANTIC VIKING 10

Jun	4	Epsm	5f	G	10	100
Jun	24	Newc	5f	G	12	**101**

ATTACCA 4

May	12	Carl	6f	G	3	99
Aug	19	Ayr	7f	GF	6	99
Sep	1	Carl	7f	G	1	**103**

ATTORNEY 7

Jan	12	Ling	5f	SD	1	99
Jan	18	Sthl	6f	SD	1	103
Mar	21	Ling	6f	SD	7	102
Apr	8	Ling	6f	SD	1	**104**
Apr	19	Folk	6f	GS	1	99
May	20	Gdwd	5f	G	2	99
Jun	23	Haml	6f	G	2	100
Sep	17	Wolv	6f	FT	2	101
Sep	21	Gdwd	5f	GF	1	99

ATTRACTION 4

Aug	13	Newb	7f	G	4	103
Sep	10	Leop	8f	GF	1	**117**

ATTUNE 4

May	7	Ling	7f	G	6	105
Aug	13	Newb	7f	G	5	103
Sep	8	Donc	7f	G	3	108
Sep	25	NmkR	7f	G	2	**113**
Oct	30	Ling	8f	SD	3	102

AUBONNE 5

Apr	10	Lonc	10f	S	9	**105**

AUDIENCE 5

Mar	31	Donc	8f	G	5	104
May	28	Gdwd	8f	G	3	104
Jun	22	Sals	8f	G	1	106
Jly	2	Sand	8f	G	12	106
Jly	29	Gdwd	8f	G	10	**110**
Aug	18	York	8f	G	16	101
Sep	30	NmkR	8f	G	7	101
Oct	9	Gdwd	10f	G	8	103
Oct	29	NmkR	8f	S	4	107

AUDITORIUM 4

May	20	Gdwd	7f	GS	3	105
Jly	30	NmkJ	8f	GF	5	**111**
Aug	17	York	10½f	G	10	101

AUGUSTINE 4

Feb	22	Ling	10f	SD	9	99
Mar	2	Sthl	8f	SD	1	**101**
Dec	22	Sthl	8f	SD	3	**101**
Dec	27	Sthl	8f	SD	2	100

AUNT JULIA 3

Jly	31	Newb	12f	G	3	**108**
Aug	17	York	12f	G	7	105

AUNTY EURO 3

May	22	Curr	8f	G	2	**109**

AUSTRALIE 4
- Sep 30 NmkR 12f G 3 **106**

AUTHENTICATE 3
- Aug 29 Wwck 7f GF 3 100
- Oct 14 Rdcr 7f GF 4 **101**

AUTHORITY 5
- Apr 4 Yarm 10f GS 1 **102**

AUTUMN GLORY 5
- Mar 31 Donc 8f G 1 **117**
- May 1 StCl 8f HD 2 **117**
- Jun 16 Lonc 10f G 3 **117**
- Jly 9 Ling 8f SD 1 114
- Jly 26 Gdwd 7f G 13 99
- Sep 3 Hayd 8f GF 5 101

AUTUMN WEALTH 4
- Jly 31 Newb 12f G 4 **108**
- Sep 24 NmkR 12f G 5 107
- Oct 1 Lonc 12½f G 7 105
- Oct 25 Yarm 14f S 2 100

AUVERGNE 3
- May 24 Ling 7f G 4 100
- Jly 2 Nott 8f GF 2 104
- Aug 7 Curr 7f G 3 **108**

AUWITESWEETHEART 3
- Mar 30 Folk 6f S 2 100
- May 16 Wind 5f G 2 **102**
- Jun 20 Wind 6f G 2 **102**
- Jun 27 Wind 6f G 2 99
- Jly 29 Gdwd 5f G 5 101

AVALON 3
- Aug 16 York 12f G 3 104
- Sep 29 NmkR 14f GF 4 **105**

AVANTI AVANTI 3
- Jan 15 Ling 8f SD 1 **103**

AVENTURA 5
- Jan 6 Wolv 8½f SD 1 **103**
- Jan 12 Wolv 8½f SD 5 101
- Feb 3 Sthl 8f SD 3 102

AVERSHAM 5
- Apr 30 NmkR 6f G 25 99
- Jly 5 Pont 6f G 6 103
- Jly 29 NmkJ 6f G 4 **105**

AVICIA 3
- Aug 20 Ling 12f SD 3 99
- Sep 30 Ling 13f FT 3 **100**

AVIEMORE 3
- Apr 23 Leic 10f G 4 **100**

AVONBRIDGE 5
- Apr 30 NmkR 5f G 1 113
- Jun 5 Chan 5f G 3 110
- Jly 7 NmkJ 6f G 2 112
- Aug 18 York 5f GF 7 110
- Sep 25 NmkR 6f G 3 **115**
- Oct 2 Lonc 5f G 1 **115**

AVONTUUR 3
- Jun 17 Ayr 7f GS 2 **99**

AWAKE 8
- Jan 3 Sthl 6f SD 2 **104**
- Feb 17 Sthl 5f SD 5 99
- Mar 1 Ling 6f SD 9 100

AWAKEN 4
- Aug 7 Rdcr 11f G 4 **100**

AWARDING 5
- Dec 30 Ling 7f FT 2 **101**

AYAM ZAMAN 3
- May 7 Ling 11½f G 3 **102**

AYLMER ROAD 3
- Jun 11 Bath 11½f G 1 **105**
- Jly 21 Sand 14f GF 4 101
- Sep 27 Nott 16f GF 5 102

AZAMOUR 4
- Jun 15 York 10½f G 1 114
- Jly 23 Newb 12f GF 1 **115**
- Sep 10 Leop 10f GF 5 114

AZAROLE 4
- Mar 28 Wwck 7f GS 1 104
- Apr 23 Leic 7f G 7 102
- May 23 Leic 7f G 1 100
- Jun 15 York 8f G 3 **111**
- Jly 26 Gdwd 7f G 10 107
- Dec 17 Ling 8f FT 2 104

AZREME 5
- Apr 2 Kemp 7f GS 9 **101**
- Jun 17 Ayr 8f G 3 100

AZUREE 3
- Jun 13 Wwck 6f GF 1 100
- Sep 5 Newc 6f F 1 **101**

B

BABBLE ON 6
- Jun 15 Leop 10f G 5 101
- Jun 26 Curr 12f F 8 **108**

BABE MACCOOL 3
- Jun 10 Sand 8f GF 3 **100**
- Jly 2 Leic 8f GF 1 99
- Jly 15 NmkJ 10f G 1 **100**
- Sep 7 Donc 10½f GF 13 99

BABODANA 5
- Mar 28 StCl 8f GS 7 108
- Apr 23 Sand 8f G 3 104
- Jly 9 Ling 8f SD 4 111
- Jly 29 Gdwd 8f G 5 **113**
- Aug 18 York 7f GF 3 109
- Aug 28 Gdwd 8f G 4 108
- Sep 30 NmkR 8f G 4 103
- Oct 15 NmkR 7f G 11 99
- Oct 29 NmkR 8f S 5 101

BABY BARRY 8
- Jun 14 Carl 8f GS 3 99
- Jly 1 Wolv 8½f GS 2 99
- Sep 20 Bevl 10f GF 7 **100**
- Oct 19 Newc 8f GS 2 99

BACHELOR AFFAIR 3
- May 17 Bevl 7½f GF 2 **100**

BACK TO PARIS 3
- Jun 15 Leop 10f G 4 **101**

BACKGAMMON 4
- May 1 Haml 13f S 1 **110**
- May 12 York 14f S 9 99
- Jun 8 Haml 12f G 6 100

BADDAM 3
- May 6 Nott 14f G 1 **105**
- May 31 Sand 14f G 2 102
- Jly 21 Sand 14f GF 1 **105**
- Aug 26 NmkJ 15f G 1 101

BAGGIO 4
- May 22 Curr 6f G 1 108
- Jun 1 Leop 7f G 3 108
- Jly 16 Curr 7f F 3 100
- Sep 17 Curr 5f G 1 **112**
- Oct 23 Curr 6f S 11 101

BAGO 4
- Apr 24 Lonc 10½f GS 1 113
- Jun 26 StCl 12f GF 3 115
- Jly 23 Newb 12f GF 3 114
- Oct 2 Lonc 12f G 3 **119**

BAHAMIAN BALLET 3
- Oct 3 Wind 6f GF 1 **100**
- Dec 2 Wolv 6f SD 8 99

BAHAMIAN PIRATE 10
- Jun 25 Newc 6f G 6 101
- Jly 2 Sand 5f G 5 103
- Jly 7 NmkJ 6f G 7 106
- Aug 18 York 5f GF 8 **110**
- Sep 20 Bevl 5f GF 4 102
- Sep 25 NmkR 6f G 11 105

BAHAR SHUMAAL 3
- Jun 26 Curr 12f F 5 **104**

BAHARA 3
- May 1 Haml 5f G 2 **103**

BAHIA BREEZE 3
- Apr 13 NmkR 7f G 7 104
- May 1 NmkR 8f G 8 106
- Jun 5 Chan 8f GF 4 **110**

BAHIANO 4
- Mar 19 Ling 7f SD 5 105
- Apr 9 Ling 7f FT 4 106
- May 7 Ling 7f G 6 108
- May 29 NmkR 7f GF 3 105
- Jun 4 Epsm 6f G 2 107
- Jun 16 York 7f GF 4 105
- Jly 9 Ling 8f SD 8 108
- Aug 6 NmkJ 7f G 3 **112**
- Aug 13 Newb 7f G 8 101
- Aug 27 Gdwd 6f G 9 100
- Nov 11 Wolv 8½f FT 7 106
- Nov 26 Ling 8f FT 3 107

BAIE DES FLAMANDS 3
- Jly 15 Pont 10f GF 2 100
- Oct 1 Rdcr 10f GF 6 99
- Oct 10 Wind 10f G 2 **101**
- Oct 17 Wind 10f G 8 100

BAILEY GATE 3
- Jun 27 Wind 6f G 1 **102**

Aug 14 Pont 6f G 14 99
Sep 11 Gdwd 6f G 9 101

BAILEYS BEST 3
Jly 16 Curr 10f GF 4 **102**

BAILIEBOROUGH 6
Jun 27 Muss 9f GF 1 103
Aug 15 Brig 7f G 4 102
Sep 6 Catt 7f GF 1 **108**
Sep 15 Pont 8f G 1 **108**

BAKERMAN 3
Apr 3 Lonc 10f S 3 **106**

BALAKIREF 6
Jun 25 Donc 6f GF 5 104
Jly 9 York 6f G 5 102
Aug 12 Newc 6f GS 2 105
Sep 29 Ayr 6f G 1 **106**
Oct 29 Ayr 6f S 2 104
Nov 25 Wolv 6f FT 7 102
Dec 16 Wolv 6f FT 4 103

BALANCE OF POWER 3
Jly 22 NmkJ 12f G 2 **100**

BALAVISTA 4
Apr 19 Sthl 7f GF 2 101
Jun 4 Hayd 8f G 1 **102**
Jly 13 Ling 8f SW 8 99
Sep 17 Ayr 8f G 2 101
Oct 7 York 8f G 11 **102**

BALEARIC STAR 4
May 13 Nott 8f F 3 **101**
Jun 20 Wind 8½f G 5 99
Sep 13 Sals 7f G 7 99
Dec 15 Sthl 8f SD 3 100

BALERNO 6
Feb 23 Ling 7f SD 10 99
Apr 1 Ling 8f SD 6 **101**
Sep 17 Wolv 7f FT 1 100

BALI ROYAL 7
Jun 26 Curr 5f GF 12 104
Jly 16 Curr 5f F 1 **115**
Aug 20 Curr 6f GF 9 103

BALKAN KNIGHT 5
Apr 20 Epsm 12f GS 2 110
May 1 Sals 14f GS 1 **111**
Jun 4 Epsm 12f G 2 108
Jun 25 Newc 16f G 6 110
Jly 26 Gdwd 14f G 2 107
Aug 17 York 14f G 4 107
Sep 3 Hayd 14f GF 1 107

BALL BOY 3
Feb 16 Ling 12f SD 1 **101**

BALLAST 4
Apr 30 Thsk 8f S 1 100
Jun 15 York 8f G 2 **113**
Jly 7 NmkJ 7f G 15 101
Aug 18 York 8f G 15 103

BALLET BALLON 3
Sep 3 NmkJ 10f G 8 **101**
Oct 1 Rdcr 10f GF 4 100
Oct 27 Ling 12f SD 4 **101**

BALLETOMAINE 3
Oct 1 Rdcr 14f GF 3 **101**

BALLINTRY GUEST 9
Jly 2 Leop 12f GF 7 **101**

BALLYBUNION 6
Jan 6 Wolv 6f GF 3 101
Jan 10 Wolv 6f SD 2 99
Jun 5 Bath 5f G 4 99
Jly 14 Leic 6f GF 4 **104**
Aug 24 Catt 5f GF 1 102

BALLYCROY GIRL 3
Aug 19 Ayr 7f GF 1 **104**

BALLYGALLY BAY 3
Jun 30 Yarm 11½f G 3 **101**

BALLYGRIFFIN KID 5
Jan 8 Ling 7f SD 3 100
Feb 4 Wolv 8½f SD 4 102
Feb 16 Ling 8f SD 1 **106**
Feb 18 Wolv 7f SD 3 100
Feb 24 Sthl 8f FT 2 105
Apr 2 Wolv 8½f FT 4 100
Jun 4 Ling 12f SD 3 99
Jun 11 Ling 10f SW 5 100

BALLYHURRY 8
Jan 6 Wolv 8½f SW 5 101
Apr 6 Catt 7f G 1 100
Apr 29 Muss 8f G 4 99
May 16 Muss 7f G 2 102
May 28 Muss 8f G 1 **104**
Jun 27 Muss 7f GF 5 101
Jly 13 Hayd 8f G 7 101
Jly 28 Muss 7f G 4 100
Aug 19 Ayr 7f GF 3 103
Aug 25 Muss 8f G 5 **104**
Sep 12 Muss 9f GF 1 **104**

BALLYRUSH 5
Nov 5 Sthl 8f FT 1 **101**

BALMACARA 6
Jun 13 Brig 10f G 4 99
Jly 12 Brig 10f G 5 **100**

BALMONT 4
Apr 14 NmkR 6f G 8 101
May 31 Sand 5f G 3 **114**
Jun 18 York 6f GF 3 **114**
Jly 7 NmkJ 6f G 5 107
Aug 7 Curr 6f G 2 111
Aug 18 York 5f GF 15 103

BALTIC DIP 3
Mar 26 Kemp 8f GS 5 **102**
Apr 30 Gdwd 8f S 4 101
May 31 Leic 7f GF 6 100

BALTIC KING 5
Apr 15 Newb 5f GS 4 103
Apr 30 NmkR 6f G 2 **115**
May 23 Wind 6f F 1 109
Jly 16 Newb 6f GF 6 112
Aug 20 Bevl 5f G 2 109
Sep 7 Donc 5½f GF 9 106
Sep 17 Newb 5f GF 5 107
Sep 25 NmkR 6f G 4 113
Oct 14 NmkR 6f G 2 112

BALWEARIE 4
Jly 19 Ayr 10f G 1 **103**
Sep 5 Newc 10f G 4 102
Sep 13 Thsk 12f G 1 102

BALYAN 4
May 4 Ches 18½f GS 8 **101**

BAMZOOKI 3
Jly 19 Yarm 8f G 3 100
Dec 20 Ling 10f G 8 **101**

BANASAN 7
Aug 7 Curr 16f G 2 **108**

BANBA 3
May 24 Ripn 10f GS 4 100
Jly 16 NmkJ 8f GF 4 100
Sep 7 Donc 10½f GF 8 **104**

BAND 5
May 4 Chep 8f S 5 100
Jly 25 Sthl 8f S 1 **101**
Aug 22 Wolv 8½f S 1 **101**
Dec 22 Sthl 8f SD 5 99

BANDARI 6
Apr 16 Newb 12f GS 9 100
May 1 NmkR 12f G 3 102
Jun 3 Epsm 12f G 5 108
Jun 18 York 12f G 1 **115**
Sep 3 NmkJ 12f G 4 102

BANDOS 5
Sep 10 Muss 8f G 3 **101**

BANJO BAY 7
Apr 29 Muss 7f G 2 99
May 6 Nott 6f G 1 **101**
May 7 Thsk 7f GS 2 100
May 16 Muss 7f G 7 99
Sep 12 Rdcr 6f G 7 100

BANJO PATTERSON 3
Jun 25 Wind 6f G 1 103
Jly 13 Hayd 6f G 1 100
Jly 19 Yarm 7f G 1 **111**

BANJUL 4
Aug 20 Curr 6f GF 9 **100**

BANK ON HIM 10
Jan 15 Ling 10f SD 1 **100**

BANKNOTE 3
Apr 18 Wind 8½f G 1 104
Jun 30 Hayd 8f GF 1 103
Aug 27 Wind 8½f G 1 **112**

BARATHEA DREAMS 4
Jan 5 Ling 7f SD 11 99
Apr 1 Donc 8f G 1 106
May 2 Kemp 8f G 7 99
May 21 Curr 8f G 10 **107**
Jun 15 Nott 8f GF 7 101
Aug 19 Sand 8f GS 1 106
Aug 27 Wind 8½f G 9 106

BARBIROLLI 3
Jun 7 Ches 10½f GF 3 99
Jly 31 Ches 10½f G 1 **101**
Aug 18 Wolv 8½f SD 3 100

Aug 19 Ches 10½f GF 4 99

BARCARDERO 3
Apr 12 Muss 9f G 1 **106**
Jun 9 Ripn 12f GF 1 100

BARGAIN HUNT 4
Jly 28 Muss 8f G 3 **101**

BARKING MAD 7
Mar 7 Wolv 9½f SD 1 99
Mar 16 Wolv 9½f SD 3 103
Mar 28 Wwck 11f GS 2 102
Apr 11 Sthl 12f G 1 99
May 11 York 12f S 2 108
Jun 21 Bevl 12f G 1 **109**
Jly 15 Carl 12f G 3 100

BARNBROOK EMPIRE 3
Jly 23 Ling 10f SW 3 **100**
Aug 11 Chep 12f G 3 99

BAROLO 6
May 28 Gdwd 12f G 3 **107**

BARON DE FEYPO 7
Jun 1 Leop 16f G 2 105

BARON RHODES 4
Apr 28 Rdcr 5f GF 3 103
May 7 Bevl 5f GF 9 100
May 15 Ripn 6f G 6 99
May 19 Donc 6f GF 1 103
Jly 30 Haml 5f F 5 101
Aug 10 Bevl 5f GF 2 **104**
Sep 25 Muss 7f G 7 102

BARON'S PIT 5
Jly 16 Newb 6f GF 3 115
Aug 7 Curr 6f G 7 104
Sep 10 Gdwd 6f GF 5 108
Sep 25 NmkR 6f G 1 **117**
Oct 15 NmkR 7f G 10 100

BARONS SPY 4
Dec 3 Wolv 8½f G 1 **101**
Dec 20 Ling 10f G 10 99

BARTON SANDS 8
Feb 5 Ling 10f G 5 101
Feb 8 Ling 10f SD 1 100
Feb 12 Ling 10f SD 2 103
Feb 23 Ling 10f SD 1 99
Mar 1 Ling 10f SD 4 101
Mar 23 Ling 12f SD 3 101
Apr 8 Ling 10f SD 1 100
May 20 NmkR 8f G 1 **108**
Jun 13 Wind 8½f G 2 99
Jun 27 Wind 8½f G 4 100
Dec 30 Ling 10f FT 2 101

BARTRA ROCK 6
Jun 15 Haml 13f GS 2 102
Aug 2 Catt 14f G 3 **107**
Sep 1 Rdcr 14f G 1 100
Sep 17 Catt 12f G 4 104
Oct 1 Rdcr 14f GF 5 100

BARYSSHAW 3
Jun 27 Lonc 9½f G 4 **106**

BARZAK 5
Jan 10 Wolv 7f SD 1 **103**
Feb 25 Wolv 8½f SD 1 99
Mar 4 Wolv 8½f SD 5 100
Apr 16 Wolv 8½f FT 5 101

BASILEA GOLD 3
Aug 2 Deau 10f G 7 **111**

BASINET 7
Sep 20 Bevl 10f GF 10 **99**

BASSERAH 3
Jly 29 Thsk 8f G 1 102
Aug 31 York 8f G 2 **109**
Sep 19 Leic 8½f G 10 99

BASTET 3
Sep 4 Lonc 10f GF 3 **104**

BATIK 4
May 12 Sals 12f G 1 99
Jly 8 York 12f GS 5 **102**
Sep 24 Hayd 14f GF 13 99

BATTLEDRESS 3
Apr 4 Wolv 12f FT 2 **105**
Jun 22 Bath 11½f G 1 100

BATTLING MAC 7
Nov 29 Ling 8f FT 12 **100**

BAVARICA 3
Sep 16 Nott 8f GF 5 **100**
Nov 16 Sthl 8f FT 3 99

BAWAADER 3
Sep 10 Leop 9f GF 6 **106**

BAY BOY 3
Sep 18 Curr 7f GF 2 **99**

BAY STORY 3
Jun 22 Sals 12f G 2 103
Jly 8 York 12f GS 6 101
Jly 23 Newb 12f GF 1 **110**
Jly 27 Gdwd 12f GS 5 99
Sep 3 Hayd 14f GF 3 106
Sep 9 Donc 14½f G 6 102

BAYEUX 4
Jly 21 Sand 10f GF 6 **100**

BAYEUX DE MOI 3
Jly 15 NmkJ 10f G 2 99
Jly 27 Gdwd 12f GS 4 102
Aug 20 Sand 10f G 5 101
Sep 2 NmkJ 12f G 3 **106**
Oct 1 NmkR 10f G 4 103

BAYLAW STAR 4
Feb 24 Sthl 8f FT 6 99
Apr 21 Bevl 7½f S 1 **108**
Jun 21 Bevl 7½f G 1 102
Jly 18 Bevl 7½f G 3 101
Jly 26 Bevl 8½f G 1 106
Aug 20 Bevl 7½f GF 1 104
Sep 4 Curr 8f G 13 103

BAYTOWN FLYER 5
May 16 Wolv 6f FT 1 **100**

BAZELLE 3
Jun 11 Ripn 10f G 2 100
Jly 11 Wind 11½f G 5 **102**
Dec 10 Wolv 9½f FT 4 101
Dec 26 Wolv 12f SD 5 **102**

BE LUCKY LADY 3
Jun 25 Ling 10f SW 9 **99**

BE WISE GIRL 4
Mar 3 Ling 10f SW 4 **100**

BEAMISH PRINCE 6
Sep 20 Bevl 10f GF 9 **100**

BEAMSLEY BEACON 4
Apr 5 Sthl 5f FT 3 **99**
Dec 28 Wolv 6f FT 3 **99**

BEAU CHAPEAU 3
Aug 2 Deau 10f G 8 **103**

BEAUCHAMP TIGER 3
Sep 30 Ling 13f FT 2 **100**

BEAUCHAMP TRUMP 3
Aug 6 Rdcr 9f G 4 100
Sep 27 Gdwd 16f G 1 **101**
Oct 27 Ling 12f SD 7 100

BEAUCHAMP TURBO 3
May 28 Ling 10f SW 2 **103**

BEAUCHAMP TWIST 3
May 2 Wwck 12½f G 4 **101**
Jly 18 Wind 11½f G 2 100

BEAUMONT GIRL 3
Sep 17 Catt 14f G 1 **101**

BEAUTIFIX 3
May 15 Lonc 5f G 8 103
Jun 5 Chan 5f G 7 **107**
Sep 4 Lonc 5f GF 7 103

BEAUTIFUL AFFAIR 4
May 21 Curr 12f G 5 **106**

BEAUTY OF DREAMS 4
Feb 5 Ling 7f G 4 100
Feb 8 Ling 8f SD 6 100
May 12 Carl 9½f G 2 101
Jly 2 Nott 8f GF 5 101
Aug 17 Carl 8f GF 2 **105**

BEAUTYANDTHEBEAST 3
Jun 15 York 8f G 1 107
Jly 2 Leop 7f F 4 **108**
Sep 18 Curr 10f G 8 104

BEAVER PATROL 3
Mar 26 Kemp 8f GS 4 103
May 21 Hayd 8f GF 5 106
Jun 16 York 8f G 7 105
Jly 6 NmkJ 10f G 8 99
Aug 13 Gdwd 10f G 5 102
Aug 27 NmkJ 7f G 6 103
Sep 3 NmkJ 6f G 4 **108**
Sep 21 Gdwd 6f GF 1 **108**
Oct 8 York 6f GS 6 102
Oct 21 Newb 6f G 3 103

BECKERMET 3
Apr 27 Ling 6f GS 4 101
May 5 Ches 5f GS 4 101
May 21 Hayd 5f F 3 101
May 28 Muss 5f G 12 100
Jun 11 Ripn 6f G 2 107
Jun 18 York 6f GF 2 113
Jly 2 Hayd 6f GF 4 108
Jly 16 Newb 6f GF 1 **116**
Sep 10 Gdwd 6f GF 3 111
Sep 17 Newb 5f GF 11 100

BECTIVE RANGER 3
May 25 Leop 10f GF 1 **107**
Jun 25 Curr 10f G 3 106

BEEF OR SALMON 9
Oct 9 Curr 16f GS 9 105

BEHASNI 7
Aug 21 Deau 15f G 9 **102**

BEHKIYRA 3
Sep 10 Leop 12f GF 11 **102**

BELENUS 3
May 18 Gdwd 11f G 3 104
Jun 16 York 10½f G 2 105
Jly 16 Newb 10f GF 2 **111**

BELISCO 4
Jan 7 Wolv 8½f SW 3 **108**

BELLA MIRANDA 3
Sep 20 Brig 12f G 1 **103**

BELLA PAVLINA 7
Jan 14 Wolv 12f SW 6 100
Mar 4 Wolv 8½f SD 1 **102**
May 3 Leic 10f S 1 99

BELLALOU 3
May 27 Wolv 12f SD 1 **100**

BELLAMY CAY 3
Jly 14 Lonc 12f F 5 **109**
Sep 17 Lonc 10f G 6 105

BELLE ARTISTE 3
May 8 Leop 7f S 1 **105**

BELLEINGA 4
Jly 16 Curr 5f F 8 **106**
Sep 17 Curr 5f G 8 104

BELLY DANCER 3
Apr 2 Donc 7f G 2 103
Apr 13 NmkR 7f G 2 101
May 6 Ches 7f GS 1 **104**
Jun 25 Ches 7f G 5 101

BEN HUR 6
May 27 Brig 10f GF 1 **99**
Jly 16 Ling 10f SW 2 **99**
Aug 25 Muss 9f G 3 **99**

BENBAUN 4
Jun 5 Chan 5f G 2 111
Jun 26 Curr 5f GF 1 **118**
Aug 18 York 5f GF 5 111
Sep 4 Curr 5f G 1 117
Sep 17 Curr 6f G 2 114
Oct 2 Lonc 5f G 10 107

BENDARSHAAN 5
Apr 20 Epsm 12f GS 4 **106**
May 1 NmkR 12f G 10 105
May 14 Newb 12f G 5 **106**
May 23 Thsk 12f G 3 103
Jun 8 Haml 12f G 7 99
Jun 30 Hayd 14f GF 5 103
Jly 12 Bevl 16f GF 2 102
Jly 16 NmkJ 15f GF 6 99

BENEDICT 3
Jun 4 Hayd 8f G 1 100
Jly 24 NmkJ 8f G 2 106
Aug 13 NmkJ 8f G 1 **109**
Oct 7 York 8f G 2 108
Oct 22 Newb 10f G 4 **109**

BENEKING 5
Dec 29 Ling 8f G 2 **101**
Dec 30 Ling 7f FT 2 **101**

BENNY THE BUS 3
Jly 1 Wolv 6f FT 2 **100**
Aug 19 Wolv 7f FT 3 **100**

BENS GEORGIE 3
Jun 25 Wind 6f G 2 **102**
Jly 22 Wolv 6f FT 1 101

BENTLEY BROOK 3
May 30 Chep 8f G 1 102
Jun 9 Ripn 8f G 3 **103**
Jun 16 York 8f G 10 102
Aug 19 Ayr 8f GF 3 102
Dec 6 Sthl 11f FT 10 99

BENWILT BREEZE 3
Jly 6 Naas 6f GF 1 106
Jly 20 Naas 6f GF 1 **107**
Sep 17 Curr 6f G 8 101

BESSEMER 4
Jun 27 Muss 9f GF 2 102
Jly 30 Haml 8½f F 1 **105**
Aug 19 Wolv 7f FT 4 99
Sep 8 Epsm 7f G 3 **105**
Nov 15 Sthl 8f FT 3 102
Dec 10 Wolv 6f FT 1 102

BEST BE GOING 5
Jun 30 Epsm 10f G 3 99
Jly 21 Sand 10f GF 2 **102**

BEST BEFORE 5
Mar 18 Ling 8f SD 2 **104**

BEST FLIGHT 5
Apr 13 Bevl 10f G 7 **100**

BEST GAME 3
Mar 3 Ling 8f SW 4 **102**
May 16 Muss 8f G 1 100
Aug 1 Carl 7f G 1 99

BEST LEAD 6
Feb 28 Wolv 5f SD 4 99
Aug 16 Haml 5f F 1 **100**

BEST OF THE BLUES 5
Jun 13 Wwck 7f GF 7 **100**

BEST PORT 9
Apr 2 Wolv 12f FT 6 99
May 7 Bevl 16f G 8 99
May 30 Rdcr 14f G 3 100
Jun 10 Catt 16f GF 1 **108**

BEST PROSPECT 3
May 19 Newc 10f G 1 99
Jun 6 Pont 10f GF 2 102
Jly 8 Ches 10½f F 2 103
Jly 28 Gdwd 10f G 3 104
Aug 20 Bevl 10f GF 4 103
Sep 15 Ayr 9f G 3 **106**
Oct 3 Pont 8f G 5 102

BEST SIDE 3
May 22 Curr 8f G 1 **110**
Jun 26 Curr 8f F 2 102
Jly 17 Curr 9f F 5 107

BETHANYS BOY 4
Sep 23 Hayd 12f G 4 99
Oct 1 Wolv 12f FT 1 **106**
Oct 10 Wolv 14f FT 2 101
Nov 16 Sthl 12f FT 1 105
Dec 26 Wolv 12f SD 3 104

BETSEN 3
Aug 20 Curr 6f GF 10 **99**

BEVELLER 6
Jan 27 Sthl 6f SD 5 **102**
Feb 11 Wolv 7f SD 4 100

BEVERLEY BEAU 3
Jly 17 Rdcr 5f G 7 **100**

BEYOND THE CLOUDS 9
May 7 Bevl 5f GF 5 **102**

BID FOR FAME 8
Jun 3 Wolv 14f FT 1 **109**
Jun 24 Wolv 12f SD 3 99

BIENHEUREUX 4
Jan 5 Ling 13f SD 3 99
Jan 21 Wolv 12f SD 4 103
Feb 14 Wolv 12f SD 2 **108**
Jun 23 Leic 12f GF 3 101
Sep 17 Wolv 12f FT 3 100
Nov 12 Ling 12f FT 3 99
Dec 10 Wolv 12f FT 3 102

BIENS NANTI 3
Apr 3 Lonc 10f S 1 **109**

BIG BAD BOB 5
Jun 4 Donc 10½f GF 2 104
Aug 29 Epsm 10f G 2 **108**

BIG BAND MUSIC 3
Feb 26 Ling 7f SD 2 **105**

BIG BERTHA 7
Jan 14 Wolv 12f SW 1 **106**
Jan 22 Ling 16f FT 2 **106**

BIG BRADFORD 4
Jly 14 Leic 6f GF 3 104
Jly 22 Chep 7f G 3 99
Sep 8 Epsm 7f G 2 **106**
Nov 15 Ling 7f FT 5 104

BIG MOMENT 7
May 4 Ches 18½f GS 9 101
Jly 2 Sand 16½f G 4 107
Jly 26 Gdwd 14f G 9 101
Sep 3 Hayd 14f GF 9 103

BIGALOS BANDIT 3
May 14 Thsk 5f G 2 **102**
Jun 11 Sand 5f G 2 101

BIJOU DAN 4
Jan 12 Wolv 8½f SD 3 102
Feb 19 Wolv 7f SD 3 **104**
Apr 2 Wolv 7f FT 2 100
May 3 Catt 7f GS 4 100
May 16 Muss 7f G 3 101
Nov 12 Wolv 8½f FT 1 103

BILL BENNETT 4
Mar 17 Sthl 12f FT 4 **101**

BILLY ALLEN 4
Mar 19 Ling 10f SD 11 **110**

BILLY THE KID 7
Apr 30 Lonc 15½f GS 8 **108**

BINAA 4
Jan 21 Wolv 8½f SD 4 **100**

BINANTI 5
Feb 1 Ling 8f SD 3 109
May 30 Sand 8f G 4 109
Jun 11 Sand 7f G 5 **111**
Jly 13 Ling 8f SW 6 102
Aug 27 Gdwd 7f G 4 106
Sep 27 Gdwd 7f G 5 103
Nov 15 Ling 7f FT 2 106
Nov 29 Ling 8f FT 3 106

BINNION BAY 4
Jan 13 Ling 8f SD 5 99
Feb 16 Ling 8f SD 5 101
Feb 23 Ling 7f SD 3 **102**

BINT IL SULTAN 3
Jly 15 Carl 9½f G 4 **100**

BINT ROYAL 7
Apr 12 Muss 5f G 3 **102**
May 19 Donc 6f GF 4 100

BINTY 3
Aug 10 Yarm 6f GF 1 **100**

BIRD OF PARADISE 3
Jun 27 Lonc 10½f G 1 **109**

BIRD OVER 3
Apr 25 Wolv 7f FT 1 102
May 5 Folk 6f G 1 99
Jun 22 Epsm 6f G 1 **106**
Jly 5 NmkJ 7f G 8 100
Aug 28 Gdwd 6f G 7 102
Sep 30 Ling 7f FT 8 99

BIRTHDAY STAR 3
Mar 3 Ling 8f SW 3 **102**

BISHOPS COURT 11
Apr 1 Donc 5f G 7 100
Apr 20 Epsm 5f GS 1 **109**
Jun 21 Bevl 5f G 5 99
Jly 11 Ayr 5f GF 4 101
Jly 29 Nott 5f G 7 100

BISHOPS FINGER 5
Mar 3 Ling 10f SW 10 **103**
Mar 23 Ling 10f SD 1 100
Jly 16 Ling 10f SW 1 100
Dec 20 Ling 10f SW 6 102

BLACK FALCON 5
Jan 22 Ling 12f FT 7 102
Jun 25 Newc 10f G 4 99
Aug 11 Hayd 10½f GF 2 **104**

BLACK OUZEL 5
Jun 1 Leop 14f G 15 **106**

BLACK OVAL 4
Jly 14 Leic 6f GF 2 **105**

BLACK VELVET 3
Jun 11 Sand 7f G 9 **110**
Jly 2 Sand 7f G 7 102

BLACK WISH 6
Jun 15 Leop 14f G 5 **103**

BLACKHEATH 9
May 27 Catt 6f GF 5 100
Jun 13 Thsk 6f G 6 100
Jun 24 Newc 6f G 7 99
Aug 10 Haml 6f GF 3 **101**
Aug 16 Haml 6f F 1 99
Sep 11 Carl 6f GF 5 **101**

BLACKMAIL 7
Jan 15 Ling 10f SD 2 100
Jan 29 Ling 10f SD 5 **107**
Feb 12 Ling 10f SD 7 100
Apr 11 Ling 8f SD 1 99
May 11 Brig 8f G 3 100
Jun 2 Brig 12f G 1 104
Jun 21 Brig 12f G 2 101
Jun 30 Epsm 12f G 2 100
Jly 14 Epsm 12f G 2 99
Aug 3 Epsm 10f G 7 104
Aug 17 Epsm 12f G 1 99

BLADES BOY 3
Apr 25 Haml 5f G 1 **101**

BLAEBERRY 4
May 17 Rdcr 10f G 3 101

BLAISE HOLLOW 3
Mar 28 Kemp 9f G 4 99
Apr 14 NmkR 10f G 1 100
Jun 26 Wind 10f G 3 **103**

BLAKESHALL QUEST 5
May 9 Sthl 6f FT 1 **100**

BLATANT 6
May 9 Wind 8½f GF 4 108
Sep 24 NmkR 8f G 3 **112**
Oct 29 NmkR 8f S 4 103

BLAZE OF COLOUR 4
Jan 13 Ling 12f SD 2 **111**
Jan 22 Ling 12f FT 2 105
Feb 5 Ling 12f FT 2 102
Jly 16 NmkJ 12f GF 3 103

BLAZING BAILEY 3
Jly 23 Sals 14f G 2 **103**

BLAZING THE TRAIL 5
Aug 5 Ling 11½f GS 4 **99**

BLESSED PLACE 5
Mar 31 Ling 5f SD 3 99
Apr 19 Brig 5½f G 2 99
Jun 5 Bath 5½f G 1 99
Sep 1 Sals 5f G 4 99
Sep 15 Yarm 6f GS 1 **101**

BLESSYOURPINKSOX 4
Jun 26 Curr 12f F 18 100
Jly 17 Curr 9f F 8 104
Sep 10 Leop 12f GF 4 **110**

BLING BLING 3
Aug 21 Folk 9½f G 4 **100**

BLONDE STREAK 5
May 25 Ripn 8f G 2 **110**
Jun 22 Carl 8f GF 8 101
Jly 11 Wind 8½f G 4 102
Sep 2 Hayd 8f G 8 100
Sep 16 Ayr 8f G 1 105

BLOW THE LOT 3
Aug 2 Deau 10f G 9 **99**

BLUE AWAY 7
Jun 1 Leop 16f G 8 **104**
Jun 26 Curr 16f F 4 103

BLUE BAJAN 3
Jun 7 Ches 10½f GF 2 99
Jun 23 Leic 12f GF 1 103
Jly 17 Rdcr 11f G 3 102
Oct 27 Ling 12f SD 1 **104**

BLUE CANARI 4
Apr 24 Lonc 10½f GS 7 109
Jun 5 Chan 12f G 6 **116**

BLUE CORRIG 5
May 22 Curr 12f GS 3 **114**
Sep 18 Curr 8f GF 12 99

BLUE CREST 3
Mar 28 StCl 8f GS 6 **104**

BLUE EMPIRE 4
Jan 17 Wolv 8½f SD 5 **106**
Mar 16 Wolv 7f SD 3 102
Mar 24 Wolv 7f SD 6 99
Apr 4 Wolv 8½f FT 1 102
Jun 9 Wolv 8½f SD 5 99
Jun 21 Bevl 7½f G 2 99
Jly 9 Ches 7½f GF 1 99

BLUE HEDGES 3
Jun 27 Wind 10f G 5 **99**
Aug 28 Yarm 14f G 7 **99**

BLUE HILLS 4
Jan 7 Wolv 12f SW 3 103
Jan 12 Wolv 14f SD 3 104
Feb 25 Wolv 12f SD 2 101
Mar 4 Wolv 12f SD 5 100

Mar 17 Sthl 12f SD 3 103
Apr 8 Sthl 12f SD 1 99
Jly 7 Wwck 12½f G 10 99
Dec 28 Wolv 14f G 1 **105**

BLUE JAVA 4
May 20 NmkR 8f G 3 **105**
Jun 10 Gdwd 7f G 1 103
Jly 2 Leic 7f GF 4 101
Sep 9 Sand 7f GS 4 99

BLUE KNIGHT 6
Jan 19 Ling 5f FT 3 103
May 5 Chep 6f GS 8 100
May 17 Rdcr 6f G 5 99
Sep 28 Newc 5f GF 1 **110**

BLUE LULLABY 3
Aug 2 Brig 7f G 1 **105**
Aug 14 Bath 8f G 2 100

BLUE MAEVE 5
Dec 21 Ling 6f G 2 **100**

BLUE MONDAY 4
May 4 Ches 10½f GS 3 107
May 30 Rdcr 10f G 1 106
Jun 18 York 12f G 4 106
Sep 17 Newb 10f GF 2 **112**
Oct 1 NmkR 9f G 1 111

BLUE MOON HITMAN 4
Jun 5 Bath 5f G 2 **100**

BLUE OPAL 3
Dec 22 Sthl 12f SD 4 **100**

BLUE PATRICK 5
Jan 11 Sthl 11f SW 3 103
Feb 3 Sthl 8f SD 2 104
Apr 4 Wolv 9½f FT 1 102
May 7 Bevl 10f GS 1 101
May 12 Carl 9½f G 5 99
Jun 7 Ches 10½f GF 6 100
Aug 19 Wolv 7f FT 5 99
Dec 16 Wolv 9½f FT 1 103
Dec 27 Sthl 8f SD 2 **106**

BLUE POWER 4
Apr 11 Sthl 5f FT 3 **100**

BLUE QUIVER 5
Dec 3 Wolv 8½f FT 3 **100**
Dec 20 Ling 10f FT 9 **100**

BLUE SPINNAKER 6
Apr 2 Donc 8f G 11 105
May 12 York 7f GS 2 **110**
May 30 Rdcr 10f G 9 102
Jun 17 York 10½f G 12 102
Aug 18 York 8f G 13 106
Aug 27 York 9f G 6 101
Sep 10 Donc 10½f GS 3 101
Oct 7 York 8f G 14 99

BLUE TOMATO 4
Jan 15 Ling 6f SD 6 102
Feb 19 Wolv 5f SD 6 **104**
Jly 21 Donc 6f GF 3 100
Jly 29 Gdwd 6f G 9 99

BLUE TORPEDO 3
May 21 Ling 10f GS 1 105
Aug 29 Epsm 10f G 2 **108**
Sep 8 Epsm 10f G 3 104
Sep 21 Gdwd 11f G 1 105
Oct 4 Leic 12f G 5 104
Oct 14 NmkR 12f G 4 103

BLUE TRAIN 3
Apr 23 Wolv 9½f SD 1 **106**

BLUE TROJAN 5
Mar 19 Ling 8f SD 3 **105**
Sep 10 Gdwd 9f G 11 103
Oct 7 York 8f G 9 103
Oct 29 Wolv 9½f SD 8 103
Nov 12 Ling 8f FT 7 100
Nov 26 Wolv 9½f FT 4 101

BLUEBERRY TART 3
Apr 18 Wind 8½f G 4 **102**
Jun 30 Newb 10f G 7 99
Dec 10 Sthl 8f FT 2 101

BLUEBOK 4
Jun 2 Hayd 6f G 4 99
Jun 12 Sals 5f G 2 **109**
Jun 17 Rdcr 5f G 4 99
Jun 22 Bath 5½f GF 1 99
Jly 2 Hayd 5f GF 1 106
Jly 15 Wwck 5½f G 3 104
Jly 22 York 5f G 2 108
Jly 29 Nott 5f G 2 106
Jly 31 Newb 5f G 6 101

BLUFF 3
Jun 6 Folk 7f G 1 100
Jly 20 Sand 7f G 7 **104**
Aug 15 Yarm 7f G 2 102
Oct 14 Rdcr 7f GF 6 100

BLUSHING RUSSIAN 3
Dec 28 Wolv 7f GF 3 **99**

BLYTHE KNIGHT 5
Mar 19 Ling 10f SD 2 **115**
Mar 28 Kemp 10f GS 2 104
Apr 2 Donc 8f G 6 108
Apr 30 NmkR 10f G 3 99
May 7 NmkR 9f GF 4 102
Jun 3 Epsm 10f G 12 103
Jun 15 York 8f G 8 108
Jly 23 Newb 10f GF 4 100
Aug 6 Hayd 10½f GF 7 106
Sep 9 Donc 10½f G 3 109
Oct 1 NmkR 9f G 7 103
Oct 14 NmkR 8f G 8 105

BLYTHE SPIRIT 6
Jan 20 Sthl 5f FT 4 99
Feb 8 Ling 6f SD 8 **101**
Feb 11 Wolv 5f SD 6 **101**
Feb 26 Ling 5f SD 5 **101**
Dec 16 Wolv 6f FT 2 **101**

BO MCGINTY 4
Apr 13 Bevl 5f G 6 100
Jun 11 Sand 7f G 8 **110**
Jun 25 Newc 7f G 4 102
Jly 15 Haml 6f F 3 102
Aug 5 Hayd 6f F 5 103
Aug 16 York 6f GF 2 104

Aug 27 York 6f G 9 99
Sep 11 Carl 6f GF 1 107
Oct 16 Muss 5f GF 9 99

BOANERGES 8
Oct 3 Brig 5½f G 2 **99**

BOBBY CHARLES 4
Jan 5 Ling 10f SD 1 100
Feb 5 Ling 10f SD 6 100
Mar 3 Ling 10f SW 2 **107**
Apr 5 Folk 9½f S 1 103
Oct 25 Yarm 10f S 1 105

BOBERING 5
Dec 21 Wolv 9½f FT 3 **100**

BOBS PRIDE 3
Apr 10 Leop 10f S 1 **108**
May 8 Leop 10f S 4 101

BOBSKI 3
May 19 Donc 7f GF 1 **105**
Aug 22 Haml 8½f F 6 101

BOBSLEIGH 6
Jly 1 Sand 14f G 8 99
Jly 13 Ling 16f G 5 99
Aug 11 Sals 14f GF 1 102

BOCACCIO 7
Sep 17 Curr 8f GF 14 **100**

BODDEN BAY 3
Dec 30 Ling 7f FT 4 **99**

BODHI TREE 3
Oct 19 Bath 10f GS 5 **104**

BOGAZ 3
May 14 Nott 8f F 3 **103**
Jun 20 Nott 8f F 3 100

BOISDALE 7
Jun 16 Wolv 6f F 2 99
Aug 12 Newc 6f GS 2 **102**

BOJANGLES 6
Jan 3 Sthl 12f SD 4 100
Feb 8 Sthl 11f SD 5 101
Mar 29 Wwck 11f S 4 102
May 3 Bath 10f HY 1 101
Jun 15 Chep 10f GS 2 **104**
Jun 30 Newb 11f G 6 102
Aug 1 Wind 11½f GS 2 103

BOLD ACT 3
Sep 27 Nott 8f GF 2 102
Oct 17 Wind 8½f G 3 **103**

BOLD CHEVERAK 3
Mar 7 Ling 5f SD 6 **101**
Aug 3 Brig 6f G 1 99

BOLD DIKTATOR 3
May 28 Ling 10f SW 5 100
Jun 17 NmkJ 8f GF 3 102
Aug 20 Ling 7f G 1 101
Aug 31 York 8f G 7 100
Sep 13 Sals 8f G 5 102
Sep 17 Newb 7f GF 4 **104**
Sep 26 Bath 8f G 2 100

BOLD EAGLE 3
Oct 4 Leic 12f G 6 **103**

BOLD HAZE 3
May 25 Ripn 6f GS 2 99
Jly 21 Donc 6f GF 3 **102**
Aug 29 Ripn 6f G 4 99

BOLD MAGGIE 3
Jun 23 Leic 5f GF 2 **99**

BOLD MARC 3
Apr 16 Thsk 5f S 2 101
May 5 Ches 5f GS 2 101
May 14 Thsk 5f G 4 100
Jun 11 Ripn 6f G 10 99
Jly 2 Hayd 6f GF 2 **104**
Jly 8 Ches 5f F 2 101
Oct 30 Ling 6f SD 12 100

BOLD MINSTREL 3
May 31 Rdcr 5f G 1 **103**

BOLD TRUMP 4
Jun 29 Chep 12f G 9 99
Jly 7 Wwck 12½f G 7 **102**
Dec 19 Wolv 8½f FT 3 100

BOLERO AGAIN 3
May 28 Ling 10f SW 2 **105**
Aug 28 Bevl 10f GS 1 104

BOLLIN BILLY 3
Jun 17 Rdcr 5f G 5 99
Jly 16 Ripn 6f G 3 99
Oct 24 Ling 6f SW 1 **102**

BOLLIN EDWARD 6
May 7 Thsk 7f GS 3 99
Jun 8 Bevl 7½f G 1 **105**
Jly 18 Bevl 7½f G 4 99

BOLLIN MICHAEL 3
Apr 9 Newc 9f S 4 **106**

BOLLIN THOMAS 7
May 3 Catt 12f GS 2 101
Jly 30 Thsk 16f G 4 101
Sep 17 Ayr 13f G 5 100

BOLODENKA 3
May 7 NmkR 8f GF 1 **102**
Jly 16 NmkJ 8f GF 5 99
Jly 29 NmkJ 8f G 1 99
Oct 8 York 9f GS 6 **102**

BOLTON HALL 3
May 2 Wwck 7f G 3 99
May 17 Leic 7f G 1 99
Jun 10 Sand 8f GF 5 100
Jun 20 Nott 8f F 2 **104**
Aug 10 Haml 9f F 4 99
Sep 12 Muss 9f GF 2 103
Sep 16 Ayr 8f G 3 103

BON NUIT 3
Apr 13 NmkR 7f G 8 104
May 31 Leic 7f GF 2 104
Jun 15 York 8f G 3 104
Jly 2 Sand 8f G 1 **107**
Aug 10 Sals 10f G 2 **107**
Sep 18 Curr 10f G 7 106

BONANZA 3
May 25 Leop 8f GF 4 **105**
Jly 20 Naas 6f GF 4 101

BOND BOY 8
May 28 Muss 5f G 1 **109**
Jun 17 Rdcr 6f G 3 107
Jun 21 Bevl 5f G 4 99
Jun 24 Newc 5f G 6 106
Jly 29 Nott 5f G 1 108
Sep 4 York 6f G 6 100
Sep 24 Hayd 5f GF 10 102

BOND CITY 3
May 5 Ches 5f GS 3 101
Jun 4 Epsm 5f G 14 99
Jun 11 Leic 5f G 4 101
Jun 18 NmkJ 5f G 1 101
Jly 15 Haml 6f F 4 99
Aug 15 Nott 5f GF 5 101
Aug 20 Bevl 5f G 6 103
Aug 29 Epsm 5f G 3 **108**
Sep 3 Hayd 5f F 10 102

BOND DIAMOND 8
Sep 4 York 8f G 8 **103**
Sep 20 Bevl 7½f GF 4 102

BOND FINESSE 3
May 30 Rdcr 7f G 1 **100**
Aug 17 Carl 8f GF 6 **100**

BOND MILLENNIUM 7
Jan 12 Wolv 8½f SD 9 99
Mar 24 Wolv 8½f SD 6 99
Apr 13 Bevl 10f G 8 **100**

DONNABEE 3
Sep 13 Yarm 11½f G 5 **104**
Sep 28 Ling 12f SD 8 100

BONNE DE FLEUR 4
Feb 18 Wolv 6f SD 9 101
Apr 4 Wolv 5f FT 1 101
Apr 28 Rdcr 5f GF 4 102
May 7 Bevl 5f GF 2 **105**
Jly 9 Nott 5f F 2 104
Aug 25 Muss 5f G 6 100

BONUS 5
May 7 NmkR 6f GF 3 104
Jun 25 Wind 6f G 12 99
Jly 8 Ling 6f SW 6 105
Aug 8 Wind 6f GF 4 102
Aug 15 Wind 6f GF 1 99
Dec 2 Wolv 6f SD 1 **112**

BOO 3
Jun 1 Wolv 8½f FT 1 105
Jun 20 Nott 8f F 4 99
Jly 11 Ayr 8f F 1 105
Jly 15 Carl 9½f G 1 104
Jly 21 Folk 9½f G 3 102
Aug 4 Hayd 8f GF 2 **109**
Dec 10 Wolv 9½f FT 1 105
Dec 31 Wolv 9½f SD 1 107

BOOGIE STREET 4
May 28 Gdwd 5f G 1 107
Jun 14 York 5f G 2 108
Aug 18 York 5f GF 4 111
Sep 4 Curr 5f G 4 **113**
Sep 10 Gdwd 6f GF 6 107
Sep 17 Newb 5f GF 3 108
Sep 29 NmkR 5f GF 1 108

BOOK MATCHED 4
Jan 3 Sthl 8f SD 1 **102**
Jan 11 Sthl 8f SW 7 101

BOOT 'N TOOT 4
Mar 3 Ling 7f SW 2 101
Jly 13 Ling 8f SW 7 99
Aug 2 Brig 12f G 1 107
Nov 19 Ling 8f FT 3 103
Nov 29 Ling 10f FT 4 **108**

BOPPYS PRINCESS 4
Apr 13 Bevl 10f G 3 **105**
Apr 21 Bevl 10f S 1 104
May 17 Leic 10f G 1 103

BORDER ARTIST 6
Sep 8 Epsm 7f G 5 **102**

BORDER CASTLE 4
Jun 25 Wind 11½f G 3 105
Jly 8 York 10½f GS 7 101

BORDER EDGE 7
Jan 13 Ling 6f SD 7 101
May 28 Ling 7f GF 1 102
Jun 27 Wind 8½f G 4 101
Jun 30 Epsm 7f G 6 99
Aug 21 Folk 7f G 1 99
Aug 24 Brig 7f S 1 101
Aug 27 Wind 8½f G 10 **106**

BORDER MUSIC 4
Apr 27 Ling 8f FT 4 103
May 20 Hayd 8f G 6 106
Jun 10 Gdwd 7f G 3 101
Jun 22 Epsm 7f G 6 100
Jly 9 York 8f G 4 107
Aug 8 Wolv 7f SD 1 **112**
Sep 3 NmkJ 6f G 3 108
Sep 27 Gdwd 7f G 4 104
Oct 27 Ling 7f SD 1 111
Oct 30 Ling 6f SD 1 110

BORDERLESCOTT 3
Jun 30 Hayd 6f GF 1 103
Aug 7 Rdcr 6f G 1 105
Aug 29 Ripn 6f G 1 105
Sep 11 Gdwd 6f G 2 106
Sep 23 Ling 6f G 3 104
Oct 8 York 6f GS 1 **109**

BORN FOR DANCING 3
Aug 20 Bevl 5f G 1 **103**
Aug 29 Ripn 6f G 3 99

BORN TO BE BOLD 3
Oct 17 Wind 6f G 4 **101**

BORODINSKY 4
Aug 2 Catt 7f G 1 **103**
Aug 12 Catt 7f G 3 99

BOROUJ 3
Sep 26 Haml 9f G 1 **102**

BORTHWICK GIRL 3
Mar 26 Kemp 8f GS 3 **107**

Apr 9 Ling 8f FT 3 102
Jun 15 York 8f G 2 106
Oct 29 NmkR 8f S 3 105

BOULE D'OR 4
Jun 3 Epsm 10f G 9 **109**
Jun 17 York 10½f G 7 104
Aug 11 Sals 8f GF 8 107
Nov 19 Ling 10f FT 2 102

BOUNDLESS PROSPECT 6
Jly 15 NmkJ 8f G 1 101
Aug 3 Brig 8f G 3 104
Aug 19 Sand 8f GS 2 103
Aug 27 NmkJ 10f G 2 99
Sep 2 NmkJ 8f G 6 **105**
Sep 14 Yarm 8f GF 1 103
Sep 30 NmkR 8f G 3 **105**
Nov 10 Ling 8f SD 2 104
Nov 19 Ling 8f FT 7 99

BOURGAINVILLE 7
Feb 5 Ling 12f FT 10 99
Feb 12 Ling 10f SD 4 **108**
Mar 1 Ling 10f SD 5 107
Jly 21 Sand 10f GF 3 102
Aug 11 Sand 9f GF 1 105

BOWERMAN 3
Jly 2 Leop 10f GF 4 **99**

BOWLED OUT 3
Jly 15 NmkJ 10f G 3 99
Aug 22 Wolv 12f G 2 99
Sep 13 Yarm 11½f G 1 **106**
Sep 28 Ling 12f SD 3 102
Oct 27 Ling 12f SD 5 101

BOWNESS 3
Jly 26 Bevl 5f G 1 103
Jly 30 Donc 5f G 3 **104**
Sep 14 Sand 5f GS 2 99

BOWSTRING 4
Jly 8 Chep 10f GF 5 **99**

BOX BUILDER 8
Feb 24 Sthl 14f FT 4 100
Mar 7 Ling 16f SD 4 **105**

BRACE OF DOVES 3
Mar 27 Muss 7f GS 2 99
Apr 6 Nott 8f GS 3 **104**
Apr 28 Rdcr 8f GF 1 99
May 14 Thsk 8f G 6 100
May 28 Muss 8f G 5 100

BRACKLINN 3
Jly 1 Hayd 8f G 5 **99**

BRADS HOUSE 3
Apr 25 Haml 11f G 1 101
May 14 Newb 11f G 5 101
Jun 4 Hayd 12f G 3 **105**
Jun 17 Gdwd 12f G 1 **105**
Aug 3 Pont 12f G 4 104
Sep 24 Hayd 14f GF 4 104

BRAHMINY KITE 3
Jun 17 York 12f G 2 **106**
Jun 26 Curr 12f F 4 105
Jly 26 Gdwd 12f G 3 103

Sep 9 Donc 12f G 2 103

BRAMANTINO 5
May 2 Newc 12½f G 1 102
Jun 8 Haml 12f G 8 99

BRAVE BEAR 3
Jun 2 Haml 5f G 1 101
Jun 23 Haml 5f G 2 **106**
Sep 11 Carl 5f GF 1 100
Sep 13 Thsk 6f G 2 100
Sep 26 Haml 5f F 1 102

BRAVE CHIEF 4
May 9 Sthl 7f FT 1 **100**
Oct 1 Sthl 6f SD 1 99
Oct 18 Sthl 8f SD 2 **100**

BRAVEMORE 3
Apr 4 Wolv 12f FT 1 **110**
May 21 Ling 10f GS 4 101
Jun 7 Ches 10½f GF 3 102

BRAVO MAESTRO 4
Mar 19 Ling 7f SD 9 101
May 25 NmkR 7f G 9 100
Jly 13 Ling 8f SW 5 **103**
Sep 23 Ling 10f SW 10 101

BREAKING SHADOW 3
Apr 21 Bevl 7½f S 3 100
Jly 23 York 7f G 1 101
Sep 25 Muss 7f G 5 **103**
Oct 3 Pont 8f G 4 **103**

BREATHING FIRE 3
May 5 Chep 8f GS 2 101
Oct 3 Wind 11½f GF 2 101
Oct 10 Wind 10f G 1 **104**

BRECON BEACON 3
Apr 9 Ling 8f FT 2 103
May 2 Donc 8f G 2 103
Jun 16 York 8f G 2 **112**
Jly 30 Gdwd 8f G 8 99

BRENNIE 4
Jly 19 Yarm 11½f G 2 **102**
Aug 8 Thsk 16f G 2 100
Sep 20 Brig 12f G 3 99

BRETTON 4
Mar 31 Ling 10f SD 8 **99**

BRIANNIE 3
May 28 Ling 10f SW 6 **99**

BRIANNSTA 3
May 5 Ches 6f GS 1 103
May 21 NmkR 6f G 7 101
Jun 11 Ripn 6f G 7 **104**
Jly 5 NmkJ 6f G 9 **104**
Jly 29 Gdwd 6f G 4 103
Aug 6 Wind 6f GF 8 100
Sep 11 Gdwd 6f G 4 **104**
Oct 30 Ling 6f SD 8 101

BRICKS AND PORTER 5
Oct 9 Curr 8f GS 1 103
Oct 23 Curr 6f S 5 **105**

BRIDEGROOM 3
Oct 9 Gdwd 8f G 8 **99**

BRIDGE LOAN 3
Feb 23 Ling 10f G 1 100
Jly 30 NmkJ 10f GF 1 **102**
Aug 31 York 12f G 8 101
Sep 25 NmkR 12f G 6 101

BRIDGEWATER BOYS 4
May 17 Bevl 8½f GF 6 100
Oct 19 Nott 8f G 2 100
Dec 22 Sthl 8f SD 2 **102**

BRIEF GOODBYE 5
Apr 12 Muss 8f G 10 99
May 17 Rdcr 8f G 6 100
May 30 Sand 10f G 1 101
Jun 19 Pont 10f G 3 **106**
Jly 30 NmkJ 10f GF 3 101

BRIGADORE 6
Jly 23 Newc 5f GF 4 99
Aug 10 Bevl 5f GF 5 100
Aug 19 Ayr 6f GF 2 101
Sep 27 Nott 6f G 1 **103**

BRIGHT SUN 4
May 17 Rdcr 10f G 5 100
May 31 Rdcr 9f G 3 99
Jly 11 Ayr 11f F 2 **106**
Jly 17 Rdcr 9f G 1 104
Jly 23 York 12f GS 5 103
Sep 4 York 8f G 6 104
Oct 9 Newc 10f G 3 105

BRINDISI 4
Aug 14 Bath 8f G 4 108
Sep 4 Curr 9f G 6 106
Sep 24 NmkR 8f G 4 **110**
Oct 1 NmkR 9f G 12 99
Oct 30 Ling 8f SD 2 103
Nov 11 Wolv 8½f FT 4 **110**

BRIOLETTE 3
Sep 4 Curr 9f G 5 106
Sep 10 Leop 12f GF 1 **112**
Sep 24 NmkR 12f G 2 109
Oct 10 Wind 11½f G 6 100

BROGELLA 5
Oct 9 Curr 16f GS 12 100
Nov 6 Leop 16f S 9 101

BRONWEN 3
Apr 12 Muss 9f G 2 102
Apr 29 Muss 9f G 1 103
Jun 9 Yarm 14f G 3 102
Jly 1 Bevl 12f G 1 **106**
Jly 7 Folk 12f G 2 101
Jly 24 NmkJ 15f GS 1 105

BRONX BOMBER 7
Nov 4 Yarm 6f S 6 **101**

BRONZE DANCER 3
May 24 Ripn 10f GS 2 101
Jly 5 Pont 10f G 4 99
Sep 17 Catt 12f G 5 **104**

BROOKLYN'S GOLD 10
Oct 5 Nott 10f G 10 100

BROOMFIELD LAD 4
Jly 2 Leop 10f GF 5 **101**

BROUGHTON BUZZER 4
May 4 Chep 10f S 1 **106**

BROUGHTON KNOWS 8
Jan 14 Wolv 14f SW 2 103
Feb 11 Wolv 12f SD 1 **105**
Feb 24 Sthl 14f FT 3 102

BROWN DRAGON 4
Jan 27 Sthl 6f SD 3 **103**

BRUNEL 4
Apr 23 Sand 8f G 2 104
Jun 4 Epsm 8½f G 2 105
Jun 27 Lonc 7f G 1 **114**
Jly 17 Curr 7f F 4 104

BRUT 3
Jly 6 Catt 7f GS 4 99
Jly 29 Thsk 6f G 1 **100**
Aug 2 Catt 6f G 5 **100**
Sep 12 Rdcr 6f G 8 99
Sep 18 Haml 6f F 2 99
Sep 26 Haml 5f F 2 **100**

BUBBLING FUN 4
Jan 14 Wolv 12f SW 7 99
Feb 14 Wolv 12f SW 1 **109**
Feb 28 Wolv 12f SD 4 99
Mar 7 Wolv 12f SD 8 107
May 17 Leic 12f G 6 101

BUCHRA INCHALLA 6
Apr 3 Curr 6f S 3 **103**
May 22 Curr 6f G 10 100

BUCK WHALEY 5
Nov 5 Sthl 11f FT 1 **105**

BUCKS 8
Aug 2 Brig 12f G 3 **105**
Aug 14 Pont 12f G 5 102

BULBERRY HILL 4
Jly 19 Yarm 11½f G 5 **101**

BULWARK 3
May 2 Wwck 12½f G 1 105
May 31 Leic 12f G 2 100
Jun 9 Yarm 14f G 1 104
Jly 21 Sand 14f GF 3 103
Sep 3 NmkJ 15f G 1 103
Sep 17 Wwck 16f G 2 105
Sep 27 Nott 16f GF 1 **108**

BUNDABERG 5
Feb 1 Ling 10f SD 6 99
Feb 3 Sthl 8f SD 1 101
Feb 8 Sthl 11f SD 6 101
Mar 3 Ling 10f SW 12 **102**
Aug 4 Brig 8f G 2 99
Sep 21 Gdwd 8f G 2 99

BUNDY 9
Apr 25 Haml 6f G 2 **103**

BUREAUCRAT 3
Jun 22 Sals 10f G 1 **103**
Jly 2 Nott 10f GF 1 100
Sep 23 Ling 10f GF 8 102

BURGUNDY 8
Jan 15 Ling 10f SD 1 101
Jan 29 Ling 10f SD 13 102
Feb 12 Ling 10f SD 3 103
Feb 16 Ling 10f SD 3 105
Mar 1 Ling 10f SD 6 100
Jun 30 Epsm 10f G 2 99
Aug 3 Epsm 10f G 1 **110**
Aug 29 Epsm 10f G 3 108
Sep 8 Epsm 10f G 4 103
Oct 27 Ling 12f SD 2 102
Nov 19 Ling 8f FT 5 99
Dec 21 Ling 10f FT 6 101

BURHAAN 3
Oct 31 Wolv 8½f SD 1 **103**

BURLEY FLAME 4
Apr 12 Muss 8f G 7 101
May 23 Thsk 7f G 4 101
Jun 13 Thsk 6f G 9 99
Jly 18 Bevl 7½f G 2 102
Aug 6 Rdcr 7f G 2 **103**
Sep 9 Sand 7f GS 3 100
Sep 25 Muss 7f G 10 100
Oct 10 Wolv 7f FT 2 102
Oct 29 NmkR 7f S 9 99

BURNLEY AL 3
Jun 15 Nott 8f GF 4 **102**
Aug 19 Ayr 8f GF 2 **102**
Sep 25 Muss 8f G 2 101

BURREN ROSE 3
Sep 10 Leop 12f GF 2 **111**

BURTON ASH 3
May 14 Nott 8f F 4 100
Jun 15 Nott 8f GF 5 102
Jly 1 Hayd 8f G 2 **106**
Aug 17 Carl 8f GF 5 102
Aug 31 York 8f G 6 103

BUSACO 3
Apr 6 Nott 8f GS 6 99
May 28 Gdwd 11f G 5 100
Jun 9 Brig 12f G 2 101
Jly 7 Folk 12f G 1 **102**

BUSCADOR 6
Feb 25 Wolv 8½f G 2 102
Mar 4 Wolv 8½f SD 2 103
Mar 16 Wolv 9½f SD 1 **104**
Apr 4 Wolv 8½f FT 2 101

BUSH MAIDEN 5
Sep 10 Leop 9f GF 2 **108**

BUSTER HYVONEN 3
Jly 13 Ling 8f SW 1 **104**

BUY ON THE RED 4
Apr 30 NmkR 6f G 19 104
Jun 4 Epsm 6f G 9 102
Jun 22 Epsm 7f G 5 100
Jly 23 Newb 7f GF 7 **111**
Aug 6 NmkJ 7f G 12 109
Aug 11 Sand 7f GF 6 106
Aug 27 NmkJ 6f G 11 100

BYGONE DAYS 4
May 12 York 5f GS 10 99
Jun 2 Hayd 6f G 1 107
Jun 26 Curr 6½f GF 8 99
Sep 17 Ayr 6f G 6 **111**
Sep 24 Hayd 6f GF 1 106

BYO 7
Jan 12 Wolv 5f SD 3 99
Feb 28 Wolv 5f SD 6 99
Mar 8 Sthl 5f SD 1 101
Apr 19 Folk 5f GS 5 101
Jly 7 Folk 5f G 5 **104**
Jly 20 Sand 5f GF 5 99
Aug 15 Brig 5½f G 4 100

BYRON 4
May 22 Lonc 7f GF 2 **108**
Jun 18 York 6f GF 6 **108**

BYRON BAY 3
Jun 17 Ayr 8f G 2 100
Jly 11 Ayr 8f F 5 100
Sep 29 Ayr 10f S 2 101
Oct 29 Ayr 8f HY 2 104
Dec 27 Sthl 8f SD 1 **107**

BYWAYOFTHESTARS 4
Sep 4 Curr 9f G 8 **99**

C

CACIQUE 4
May 1 StCl 8f HD 5 **115**
May 22 Lonc 9f GF 3 106
Jun 12 Chan 8f GF 1 105
Sep 4 Lonc 8f GF 7 112

CADOGEN SQUARE 3
Sep 17 Catt 7f G 1 **100**

CAESAR BEWARE 3
Sep 8 Epsm 7f G 3 **104**

CAHEERLOCH 3
Sep 18 Curr 8f GF 11 100
Nov 6 Leop 8f S 4 **104**

CAIRDEAS 4
Apr 3 Curr 10f S 3 105
Jun 5 Chan 12f G 7 115
Aug 7 Curr 10f G 2 **116**

CAIRLINN 3
Jly 16 Curr 5f F 10 **106**
Sep 17 Curr 5f G 11 103

CALAMINTHA 5
Apr 16 Nott 14f GS 1 **107**

CALATAGAN 6
Mar 7 Wolv 12f SD 4 **108**
Oct 4 Catt 12f GF 2 101

CALCULAITE 4
Jun 9 Wolv 8½f SD 1 **103**
Jly 2 Hayd 8f GF 1 **103**
Sep 19 Carl 8f G 5 99
Sep 22 Pont 10f G 1 100

CALCUTTA 9
Mar 31 Donc 8f G 4 105
May 30 Sand 8f G 8 103
Jly 2 Sand 8f G 10 109
Jly 16 Newb 8f GF 5 102
Aug 6 Rdcr 8f G 2 108
Aug 18 York 8f G 3 **110**

CALEDONIAN 4
Jan 15 Ling 10f SD 7 104
Feb 12 Ling 10f SD 3 **109**
Feb 26 Ling 10f SD 5 104

CALIFORNIA LAWS 3
Jun 4 Donc 5f G 5 **99**

CALL ME MAX 3
Apr 9 Newc 9f S 2 **106**
Apr 25 Wolv 8½f FT 2 99
Jun 8 Bevl 7½f G 1 105
Aug 15 Yarm 7f G 1 103
Aug 27 NmkJ 7f G 4 103

CALLOW LAKE 5
Apr 10 Leop 12f GS 4 106
May 22 Curr 12f GS 2 **114**
Jun 26 Curr 12f F 13 107

CALORANDO 6
May 21 Curr 8f G 6 **108**
Sep 17 Curr 8f GF 15 100

CALUKI 8
Mar 19 Ling 10f SD 13 **109**

CALY DANCER 3
Jun 26 Wind 8½f G 6 **100**

CAMACHO 3
May 21 Hayd 6f F 1 **108**
Jun 15 York 7f G 2 106
Jly 7 NmkJ 6f G 10 104
Oct 14 NmkR 6f G 7 100

CAMARGUE 7
May 21 Curr 8f G 7 **108**

CAMBO 4
Mar 7 Ling 16f SD 6 **105**

CAMERON ORCHID 3
Jun 25 Ling 10f SW 3 **102**
Jly 6 Ling 12f SW 4 **102**

CAMILLE PISSARRO 5
May 18 Sthl 7f FT 1 **100**
May 24 Nott 6f G 1 99

CAMPBELLS LAD 4
Aug 8 Thsk 8f G 4 **100**

CAMPEON 3
May 11 Brig 5½f G 2 **104**
Nov 3 Muss 5f GS 1 102

CAMROSE 4
May 1 NmkR 12f G 6 107
Jun 4 Epsm 12f G 4 107
Jly 2 Hayd 12f GF 8 105
Jly 26 Gdwd 14f G 4 105
Sep 9 Donc 14½f G 8 99
Sep 25 NmkR 12f G 2 **108**
Oct 13 NmkR 12f G 3 **108**

CANADIAN DANEHILL 3
May 11 Brig 5½f G 1 **106**
May 25 NmkR 6f G 1 100

CANARY DANCER 3
Jly 12 Brig 6f G 5 **101**

CANTARNA 4
Apr 23 Hayd 8f G 3 **103**
May 23 Leic 7f G 4 99
Jly 2 Leic 7f GF 3 102
Oct 19 Nott 8f G 3 100
Nov 5 Wolv 8½f FT 2 99

CANTRIP 5
May 16 Bath 13f G 1 100
Jun 21 Newb 13½f G 2 101
Aug 21 Folk 12f G 2 100
Oct 20 Brig 12f GS 1 **103**

CAPABLE GUEST 3
Mar 26 Kemp 8f GS 2 104
Apr 30 NmkR 8f G 14 99
Jly 28 Gdwd 7f G 7 100
Aug 6 NmkJ 7f G 2 **112**
Aug 13 Newb 7f G 12 100

CAPE COLUMBINE 3
Apr 13 NmkR 7f G 2 107
May 1 NmkR 8f G 5 **108**
Jun 17 York 8f G 4 **108**

CAPE ENTERPRISE 3
Apr 20 Ling 10f FT 5 100
May 28 Gdwd 11f G 3 **101**

CAPE FEAR 4
Apr 9 Ling 7f FT 3 108
Apr 23 Leic 7f G 2 107
Jun 1 Nott 8f G 5 108
Jun 16 York 7f GF 5 104
Jly 29 Gdwd 8f G 9 **111**

CAPE GREKO 3
Jun 25 Wind 8½f G 5 **103**

CAPE OF GOOD HOPE 7
Jun 14 York 5f G 4 107
Jun 18 York 6f GF 1 **117**

CAPE ROYAL 5
Mar 27 Muss 5f G 4 99
Apr 1 Donc 5f G 1 108
Apr 20 Epsm 5f GS 3 108
May 12 York 5f GS 5 105
May 28 Muss 5f G 10 102
Jun 4 Epsm 5f G 13 99
Jun 24 Newc 5f G 11 101
Jly 24 Newb 5f G 11 105
Jly 27 Gdwd 5f G 8 99
Aug 20 Sand 5f GS 1 **109**
Aug 29 Epsm 5f G 2 108
Sep 3 Hayd 5f F 6 106
Sep 7 Donc 5½f GF 5 107
Sep 19 Leic 5f F 2 100
Sep 24 Hayd 5f GF 2 108
Oct 1 Epsm 5f G 2 107
Oct 13 NmkR 5f G 4 108
Oct 22 Donc 5f S 9 106

CAPE ST VINCENT 5
Jan 5 Ling 7f SD 6 104
Jan 29 Ling 8f SD 9 **105**
Feb 9 Ling 7f SD 2 101
Apr 5 Folk 6f G 4 99
May 20 Bath 5½f G 1 101
Jun 11 Bath 5½f G 4 100

CAPITANA 4
May 12 Sals 10f G 5 **103**
Jly 4 Wind 10f G 4 100

CAPO ROSSO 6
May 9 Lonc 12f G 8 **103**

CAPRAROLA 3
Nov 6 Leop 7f GS 10 **102**

CAPRICHO 8
Mar 31 Donc 6f G 4 102
Apr 30 NmkR 6f G 10 **108**
Sep 17 Ayr 6f G 16 103
Oct 14 NmkR 7f G 20 99

CAPTAIN CLIPPER 5
Jun 24 NmkJ 10f G 5 **102**
Jly 7 NmkJ 12f G 8 100

CAPTAIN CLOUDY 5
Aug 4 Folk 9½f GF 1 **101**

CAPTAIN DARLING 5
Jan 8 Ling 7f SD 1 **104**
Mar 21 Ling 6f SD 4 **104**
Apr 6 Ling 7f SD 5 99
May 25 Ling 6f SD 3 99
Nov 22 Sthl 8f SW 2 102
Dec 18 Sthl 7f SW 1 99
Dec 30 Ling 7f FT 1 102

CAPTAIN JOHNNO 3
Feb 9 Ling 6f FT 2 99
Mar 7 Ling 5f SD 4 103
May 7 Ling 6f G 4 **104**
May 31 Leic 6f GF 3 102

CAPTAIN MARGARET 3
Nov 12 Ling 12f FT 1 100
Dec 21 Ling 12f FT 1 **102**

CARADAK 4
Jun 1 Leop 8f G 9 102
Jun 26 Curr 8f F 1 112
Jly 17 Curr 7f F 1 112
Aug 14 Leop 8f F 1 112
Oct 1 Lonc 7f G 2 **114**

CARAGH MIA 3
Aug 18 Wolv 8½f SD 2 100
Sep 3 Thsk 8f G 3 **105**
Oct 12 Ling 8f G 4 102
Nov 10 Ling 8f SD 5 101
Nov 19 Ling 8f FT 4 101

CARAMAN 7
Mar 4 Wolv 12f SD 3 **101**

CARDINAL VENTURE 7
Jan 20 Sthl 7f SD 4 **108**
Jan 28 Wolv 8½f SD 4 103
Feb 10 Sthl 7f SD 1 105
Apr 2 Donc 8f G 14 102

May	28	Donc	7f	G	3	105
Jun	16	York	7f	GF	6	102
Aug	29	Ripn	8f	G	11	99
Sep	17	Ayr	7f	G	5	100
Nov	5	Donc	7f	GS	1	105
Nov	11	Wolv	8½f	FT	9	102

CARGO 6

Jan	5	Ling	6f	SD	3	**104**
Feb	14	Wolv	5f	SD	2	100

CARIBBEAN CORAL 6

Jun	4	Epsm	5f	G	11	100
Jun	18	York	6f	GF	7	**108**
Jun	24	Newc	5f	G	10	103
Jly	30	Gdwd	6f	G	22	100
Aug	6	Hayd	5f	G	17	100

CARIBBEAN DANCER 3

Jly	13	Hayd	10½f	G	3	100
Jly	18	Bevl	10f	G	1	**105**
Jly	25	Yarm	10f	GS	1	102
Jly	29	Nott	10f	G	3	99

CARIBBEAN PEARL 3

Oct	9	Newc	10f	G	1	99
Oct	28	NmkR	12f	GS	1	**106**

CAROUBIER 5

Jan	11	Sthl	11f	SW	5	**100**

CARPET RIDE 3

May	28	Gdwd	11f	G	6	**100**

CARRY ON DOC 4

May	31	Sand	8f	G	8	**100**

CARTE DIAMOND 4

Aug	17	York	14f	G	2	**108**

CASEMATE 3

Apr	6	Ling	8f	G	1	101
Jun	15	Nott	8f	GF	2	**103**
Jun	24	Wolv	7f	SD	1	**103**
Jly	9	Ling	8f	SD	4	101
Aug	8	Wolv	7f	SD	3	100
Aug	31	Ling	7f	SD	6	100
Oct	12	Ling	8f	SD	5	101

CASH ON 3

Jun	25	Ling	10f	SW	6	**101**

CASHBAR 4

May	31	Sand	8f	G	9	**100**

CASHEL HOUSE 3

Aug	7	Curr	7f	G	13	**100**

CASHEL MEAD 5

Jan	12	Wolv	5f	SD	1	**101**
Apr	26	Wwck	5f	G	4	100

CASHIER 3

Apr	12	NmkR	7f	GF	2	101
May	7	Thsk	8f	GS	1	100
Sep	17	Ayr	8f	G	1	**102**

CASSYDORA 3

May	7	Ling	11½f	G	1	**107**
Jly	30	Gdwd	10f	G	2	**107**
Aug	21	Deau	10f	G	3	102

CASTANZA 3

Jly	30	Ling	7f	GS	1	**100**

CASTELLETTO 3

Jly	28	Gdwd	5f	G	4	**109**
Aug	15	Nott	5f	GF	6	100
Sep	4	Lonc	5f	GF	9	99
Sep	24	Hayd	5f	GF	11	101

CASTEROSSA 3

Oct	9	Bath	5½f	G	2	**99**

CASUAL GLANCE 3

May	28	Gdwd	11f	G	7	100
Sep	28	Ling	12f	SD	9	100
Oct	14	Brig	12f	G	1	**101**

CATCH THE CAT 6

Apr	30	Thsk	5f	S	3	101
May	14	Nott	5f	HD	1	**103**

CATCH THE WIND 4

May	14	Thsk	5f	G	5	103
Jun	2	Sand	5f	G	5	102
Jun	28	Brig	5½f	F	3	**104**
Aug	23	Yarm	5f	G	5	102

CAUSTIC WIT 7

Jly	21	Donc	6f	GF	4	99
Aug	6	Ling	6f	G	2	102
Sep	5	Bath	5½f	GF	4	**103**

CAUTIOUSLY 4

Jan	7	Wolv	8½f	SW	9	**105**

CAVA BIEN 3

May	6	Nott	14f	G	2	103

CAVALLINI 3

Jun	11	Sand	10f	G	1	**99**

CAVAN GAEL 3

Apr	18	Wind	8½f	G	3	**102**

CAVERAL 4

Jly	11	Wind	8½f	G	2	103
Jly	22	Newb	8f	G	3	101
Jly	29	Gdwd	7f	G	10	99
Sep	8	Donc	7f	G	4	102
Sep	24	NmkR	8f	G	9	**105**

CAYMAN BREEZE 5

Jun	9	Brig	7f	G	1	101
Jly	18	Brig	6f	G	1	99
Aug	15	Brig	7f	G	1	**105**
Dec	21	Ling	6f	G	3	100
Dec	30	Ling	7f	FT	3	101

CAYMAN CALYPSO 4

Mar	17	Sthl	12f	FT	5	100
Apr	5	Sthl	14f	SD	1	**101**

CD EUROPE 7

Apr	1	Donc	5f	G	3	**104**

CD FLYER 8

Apr	9	Newc	7f	S	5	**105**
Apr	23	Leic	6f	G	5	104
Jun	4	Donc	7f	G	4	100
Sep	29	Ayr	6f	G	3	102

CEIRIOG VALLEY 3

Aug	13	Ripn	12f	GS	1	**105**
Oct	28	NmkR	12f	GS	2	**105**

CELLARMASTER 4

Apr	3	Curr	10f	S	12	**101**

CELLO 4

Jly	29	Gdwd	8f	G	15	**104**

CELTIC BLAZE 6

Apr	18	Pont	21½f	S	4	**101**

CELTIC MILL 7

Apr	30	NmkR	5f	G	4	109
May	23	Wind	6f	F	3	107
May	31	Sand	5f	G	1	**115**
Sep	8	Donc	5f	F	3	110
Sep	17	Newb	5f	GF	8	105
Oct	30	Ling	6f	SD	3	105
Nov	16	Sthl	5f	FT	1	109

CELTIC PROMISE 3

May	6	Nott	14f	G	4	**100**

CELTIC SPA 3

Jly	9	Sals	8f	G	2	100
Jly	23	Sals	8f	G	1	99
Aug	10	Sals	8f	G	9	100
Sep	14	Sand	8f	G	5	**104**

CELTIC THUNDER 4

May	7	Bevl	5f	GF	8	**100**
Jly	1	Wolv	6f	GF	3	99
Aug	6	Hayd	6f	G	6	**100**

CELTICELLO 3

May	24	Ripn	8f	GS	1	99
Jun	25	Newc	8f	G	1	**100**
Jly	18	Ayr	8f	GF	0	101

CELTIQUE 3

Jun	1	Nott	8f	G	5	101
Jly	16	Ling	10f	SW	2	102
Aug	21	Folk	9½f	G	2	101
Oct	14	Brig	12f	G	2	**103**
Oct	29	Wolv	9½f	SD	1	102
Dec	19	Wolv	9½f	FT	4	100

CENTAURUS 3

May	2	Donc	8f	G	5	101
Aug	12	NmkJ	12f	G	1	**115**
Aug	27	Gdwd	14f	G	3	108
Sep	29	NmkR	14f	GF	2	108

CENTIFOLIA 3

May	15	Lonc	5f	G	6	104
Jun	5	Chan	5f	G	9	**105**
Sep	4	Lonc	5f	GF	10	99

CEREBUS 3

Jan	14	Wolv	7f	SW	2	101
Jan	27	Sthl	6f	SD	1	100
Feb	22	Ling	7f	SD	6	99
Sep	9	Donc	5f	G	7	**106**
Sep	15	Pont	6f	G	2	**106**
Sep	22	Pont	5f	G	3	103
Nov	3	Muss	5f	GS	5	99

CERTAIN JUSTICE 7

Feb	7	Sthl	7f	SD	1	**104**
Jun	20	Wind	8½f	G	3	102

Jly 2 Leic 7f GF 2 102
Jly 25 Sthl 6f GF 1 101
Aug 1 Wind 6f G 4 99
Oct 5 Nott 8f GF 6 99

CERULEAN ROSE 6
May 26 Bath 5½f G 2 101
Jun 3 Thsk 5f G 3 99
Jun 11 Bath 5½f G 2 101
Jly 11 Wind 5f G 3 99
Jly 22 Chep 5f G 2 **103**
Jly 27 Gdwd 5f G 5 102
Aug 9 Bath 5f GF 5 101
Aug 13 Gdwd 6f G 4 100
Sep 5 Bath 5½f GF 10 99
Sep 16 Nott 6f GF 3 99

CESARE 4
May 25 Ripn 8f G 1 111
Jly 13 Ling 8f SW 1 111
Jly 29 Gdwd 8f G 3 **114**

CHAINED EMOTION 4
Apr 3 Curr 6f S 6 101
May 25 Leop 7f GF 2 **108**
Jun 8 Leop 8f F 4 104
Jun 26 Curr 6½f GF 3 102
Jly 17 Curr 8f F 1 99
Sep 10 Leop 7f HD 3 107
Oct 23 Curr 6f S 4 107

CHAKA ZULU 8
Jly 13 Catt 12f GF 2 99
Jly 28 Carl 14f GS 2 100
Aug 12 Catt 12f G 1 **104**

CHALET 3
Jun 22 Bath 11½f G 2 **99**

CHALISON 3
Oct 17 Wind 8½f G 6 **101**

CHAMPAGNE CRACKER 4
Jun 28 Haml 5f F 3 100
Jly 4 Muss 5f GF 2 **104**
Jly 28 Muss 5f F 1 101
Jly 30 Haml 5f F 3 102

CHAMPAGNE SHADOW 4
Jun 11 Ling 12f SW 1 **101**

CHAMPAIN SANDS 6
Apr 22 Wolv 8½f SD 5 100
Jly 28 Carl 9½f G 2 **104**
Aug 26 Newc 9f GF 9 101
Sep 19 Carl 8f G 4 99

CHAMPION LION 6
Nov 25 Wolv 12f FT 2 **101**

CHANCELLOR 7
Apr 23 Sand 10f G 6 100
May 5 Ches 10½f G 6 106
Jun 3 Epsm 10f G 3 **111**
Jly 2 Hayd 12f GF 14 100
Aug 15 Deau 10f G 5 107
Sep 10 Donc 12f S 5 104

CHANTACO 3
Feb 22 Ling 7f SD 1 102
Feb 26 Ling 7f SD 3 101
Aug 22 Wind 8½f G 3 **103**

Sep 9 Sand 10f GS 4 99
Oct 9 Gdwd 11f G 3 101
Oct 21 Donc 10½f GS 1 99

CHANTELLE'S DREAM 3
Dec 14 Ling 5f FT 2 **100**

CHANTILLY BEAUTY 3
Jun 15 York 8f G 4 102
Oct 1 Lonc 8f G 7 **108**

CHAPTER 3
Sep 7 Epsm 8½f G 5 **102**

CHARADE 3
Mar 4 Wolv 12f SD 4 **100**

CHARLESTON LOVER 4
Aug 4 Folk 9½f GF 3 **100**

CHARLIE BEAR 4
Sep 11 Gdwd 8f G 6 **105**

CHARLIE GEORGE 4
May 10 Muss 9f G 4 **99**

CHARLIE KENNET 7
Feb 25 Wolv 12f G 1 102
Mar 17 Sthl 12f G 4 101
Apr 2 Wolv 12f FT 5 100
Jun 18 Ling 10f SW 1 **104**
Jly 18 Wind 10f G 1 **104**
Jly 27 Leic 10f G 1 **104**
Sep 10 Ches 10½f GS 1 101
Sep 23 Hayd 10½f G 6 100
Oct 21 Newb 10f GS 3 99

CHARLIE TANGO 4
May 31 Rdcr 9f G 1 **100**
Jly 28 Carl 9½f G 6 99

CHARLIES FIRST 5
Aug 7 Curr 16f G 6 105

CHARLOTTE VALE 4
May 1 Haml 13f S 3 **105**
Jun 8 Haml 12f G 2 103
Jun 30 Hayd 14f GF 7 101
Jly 23 York 12f GS 7 101
Sep 17 Catt 12f G 3 **105**

CHARMATIC 4
Apr 26 Wwck 12½f GS 2 **105**
Jly 9 Nott 8f F 3 100
Aug 11 Hayd 10½f GF 4 102
Oct 9 Newc 10f G 10 102

CHARMED FOREST 4
May 21 Curr 8f G 5 **109**
Jun 8 Leop 8f F 10 100
Sep 4 Curr 8f G 7 108
Sep 17 Curr 8f GF 6 106

CHARMO 4
May 22 Lonc 9f GF 5 104
Jun 16 Lonc 10f G 4 **116**
Jly 24 MsnL 8f F 5 113

CHATEAU NICOL 6
Jan 15 Ling 6f SD 3 **107**
Apr 2 Kemp 7f GS 4 103
Apr 18 Pont 6f S 3 101

May 6 Ches 7½f GS 2 **107**
Jun 11 Sand 7f G 13 103
Aug 13 Newb 7f G 13 99
Aug 27 NmkJ 6f G 3 103
Oct 27 Ling 7f SD 10 102
Nov 25 Wolv 6f FT 1 106
Dec 9 Wolv 7f FT 5 103
Dec 17 Ling 6f FT 7 103

CHATER KNIGHT 4
Dec 10 Sthl 11f FT 1 **103**

CHATSHOW 4
Feb 14 Wolv 5f FT 1 101
Feb 28 Wolv 5f SD 5 102
Mar 8 Sthl 5f SD 2 102
Apr 8 Ling 6f SD 4 102
Apr 11 Sthl 5f FT 1 105
Apr 24 Brig 5½f GF 1 104
Apr 28 Sthl 5f GF 4 100
May 6 Ling 5f G 4 105
May 27 Brig 5½f GF 5 100
Jun 12 Sals 5f G 3 106
Jun 19 Wwck 6f G 5 106
Jun 25 Wind 6f G 1 102
Jly 5 Pont 6f G 2 **108**
Jly 15 Wwck 5½f G 9 100
Jly 24 Pont 6f G 5 102
Jly 31 Newb 5f G 3 103

CHEERLEADER 3
Jun 13 Wind 10f G 2 **100**
Jly 6 Carl 9½f G 1 **100**

CHEESE 'N BISCUITS 5
Jan 22 Ling 7f FT 1 100
Feb 9 Ling 7f FT 1 103
Mar 3 Ling 7f SW 3 100
Nov 15 Ling 7f FT 6 **104**

CHELOUMOFF 3
Mar 20 Curr 6f HY 4 **99**

CHELSEA ROSE 3
Jun 8 Leop 10f F 1 109
Jun 25 Curr 10f G 9 109
Jly 17 Curr 12f F 9 105
Aug 14 Leop 12f F 1 108
Sep 4 Curr 9f G 1 **113**
Sep 18 Curr 10f G 4 109

CHERISHED NUMBER 6
Jan 12 Wolv 8½f SD 1 **106**
Feb 25 Wolv 8½f SD 1 102
Mar 24 Wolv 8½f SD 2 104
Aug 10 Haml 8½f F 1 101

CHEROKEE 3
Jun 1 Leop 6f G 5 **109**

CHEROKEE NATION 4
Jan 29 Ling 7f SD 6 **108**
Feb 12 Ling 8f SD 5 99
Mar 4 Wolv 6f SD 5 103

CHERRY MIX 4
Oct 2 Lonc 12f G 12 **108**

CHIC 5
Jly 9 Ling 8f SD 6 109
Jly 27 Gdwd 8f GS 12 104
Aug 28 Gdwd 8f G 1 **115**

Sep 10 Leop 8f GF 2 **116**
Oct 1 NmkR 8f G 5 103
Oct 15 NmkR 10f G 7 109

CHICKEN SOUP 3
Aug 31 York 8f G 5 **104**

CHIEF DIPPER 3
Feb 28 Wolv 8½f SD 1 100
Mar 3 Ling 8f SW 1 **104**
Apr 20 Ling 10f FT 3 101

CHIEF EXEC 3
Feb 26 Ling 7f SD 4 99
Jly 8 Ling 6f SW 4 **106**
Aug 25 Ling 7f FT 5 99
Aug 31 Ling 7f FT 4 101
Dec 20 Ling 8f FT 8 100

CHIEF SCOUT 3
May 5 Ches 7½f GS 4 **104**
Oct 14 NmkR 7f G 14 103
Oct 29 NmkR 7f S 4 **104**

CHIGORIN 4
Apr 23 Leic 10f G 3 **99**
Sep 23 Hayd 10½f G 1 **99**

CHILLY CRACKER 3
May 3 Bath 5½f HY 2 101
Jly 2 Leic 6f GF 2 100
Jly 14 Leic 6f GF 9 100
Jly 30 Donc 5f G 2 **104**

CHIMALI 4
Mar 1 Ling 6f SD 8 **102**

CHINALEA 3
May 16 Wind 5f G 4 99
May 25 NmkR 6f G 2 99
Jun 10 Gdwd 6f GF 2 100
Aug 20 Sand 5f GS 1 **102**
Oct 7 York 5f G 3 100
Oct 17 Wind 6f G 8 99

CHINEUR 4
May 15 Lonc 5f G 1 111
Jun 14 York 5f G 1 111
Aug 18 York 5f GF 9 109
Oct 2 Lonc 5f G 4 112
Nov 1 MsnL 6f GF 5 **113**

CHOCOLATE BOY 6
Feb 12 Ling 12f SD 2 100
Mar 23 Ling 12f SD 1 **103**
Sep 28 Ling 12f SD 7 101

CHOCOLATE CARAMEL 3
Apr 22 Sand 10f G 5 99
May 23 Leic 10f G 1 101
Sep 7 Epsm 12f G 5 102
Oct 1 NmkR 14f G 2 **106**

CHOOKIE HEITON 7
Apr 30 NmkR 6f G 24 100
Jun 24 Newc 5f G 2 108
Aug 7 Curr 6f G 3 109
Aug 20 Bevl 5f G 1 **111**
Sep 7 Donc 5½f GF 7 106
Sep 17 Ayr 6f G 12 108

CHOREOGRAPHIC 3
May 6 Haml 5f GS 3 **100**
Jun 7 Rdcr 7f G 8 99

CHORISTAR 4
Jan 19 Ling 6f FT 2 101
Feb 21 Ling 7f SD 4 99
Mar 21 Ling 6f SD 8 **102**
May 22 Brig 7f G 5 99
Jun 13 Brig 10f G 3 99

CHORUS 8
Jan 3 Sthl 7f SD 3 102
Jan 5 Sthl 7f SD 2 **103**

CHRYSANDER 3
Apr 16 Newb 8f GS 1 106
May 2 Donc 8f G 3 103
May 20 NmkR 8f G 2 **111**
Jun 12 Chan 8f GF 4 108
Jly 24 MsnL 10f F 4 109
Aug 20 Deau 10f GS 6 105
Nov 2 Nott 8f GS 1 105

CIARAS DIAMOND 3
May 22 Curr 8f G 9 **102**

CIMYLA 4
Mar 29 Pont 8f S 2 106
Apr 23 Sand 8f G 7 103
Sep 10 Donc 8f GS 4 108
Nov 11 Wolv 8½f FT 1 **114**
Nov 29 Ling 10f FT 1 110

CIRCASSIAN 4
Aug 10 Bevl 16f GF 1 **110**

CIRCUIT DANCER 6
Aug 5 Hayd 6f F 9 **99**

CIRRIOUS 4
Jun 5 Bath 11½f G 1 **102**

CLARA ALLEN 7
Aug 7 Curr 16f G 1 109
Oct 9 Curr 16f GS 1 **111**
Nov 6 Leop 16f S 3 109

CLARA BOW 3
Apr 29 Nott 8f G 2 102
Jly 16 NmkJ 7f GF 1 100
Jly 27 Sand 7f GS 2 **104**
Aug 27 NmkJ 7f G 5 103
Sep 14 Sand 8f G 7 103
Oct 1 Epsm 7f GS 4 101
Nov 15 Ling 7f FT 8 100

CLARET AND AMBER 3
Oct 3 Pont 8f G 8 99
Nov 19 Ling 7f FT 9 105
Dec 9 Wolv 8½f FT 2 **108**
Dec 31 Wolv 7f SD 3 101

CLASH OF THE ASH 3
Mar 20 Curr 7f HY 4 100
Apr 10 Leop 10f S 3 **104**
Apr 30 NmkR 10f G 4 101

CLASSIC EVENT 4
Jun 17 Rdcr 16f G 2 **102**

CLASSIC ROLE 6
Jan 13 Ling 12f SD 7 105

CLEAR THINKING 5
Apr 27 Ling 16f S 5 **107**

CLEARING SKY 4
Jun 24 Wolv 6f SD 2 100
Sep 8 Bath 5f GF 1 **101**

CLEARWATERDREAMER 4
Jun 15 Leop 14f G 3 **105**

CLEAVER 4
Oct 19 Newc 10f GS 1 **100**

CLETY 9
Aug 21 Deau 15f G 6 **108**

CLIMATE CHANGE 3
Aug 28 Gdwd 9f G 1 **109**
Sep 15 Ayr 9f G 2 106
Oct 4 Leic 12f G 7 103

CLINET 3
May 9 Wolv 8½f FT 1 102
May 21 Ling 8f SD 6 102
Jun 25 NmkJ 8f G 2 106
Jly 5 NmkJ 7f G 1 107
Jly 14 Donc 7f GF 3 101
Jly 29 Gdwd 7f G 8 105
Aug 14 Bath 8f G 3 108
Sep 1 Sals 7f G 2 109
Sep 24 NmkR 8f G 3 110
Sep 25 NmkR 7f G 3 **112**

CLIPPER HOY 3
Nov 29 Sthl 5f SD 2 102
Dec 31 Wolv 5f SD 1 **103**

CLIPPERDOWN 4
Jun 11 Ripn 8f G 1 106
Jun 26 Wind 8½f G 4 105
Jly 16 Ripn 10f G 1 103
Jly 30 NmkJ 10f GF 6 99
Aug 29 Epsm 10f G 7 101
Sep 14 Yarm 10f G 2 **108**
Sep 23 Ling 10f G 1 107

CLOANN 3
May 11 Brig 5½f G 4 101
Jly 21 Folk 6f GF 2 **102**

CLONARD 3
Aug 20 Curr 10f GF 5 **102**

CLONEDEN 5
May 21 Curr 12f G 2 **108**

CLOONE RIVER 9
Jun 26 Curr 12f F 1 **110**

CLOUD DANCER 6
Jan 1 Sthl 8f SD 7 101
Jan 17 Wolv 8½f SD 2 **110**
Jun 17 Rdcr 6f G 5 105

CLOVE 3
Jun 11 Leic 5f G 5 **99**

CLUELESS 3
May 23 Leic 12f G 2 100

Jly 22 NmkJ 12f G 1 101
Aug 31 York 12f G 5 102
Sep 14 Yarm 10f G 1 **109**
Oct 1 NmkR 10f G 2 104

COCONUT BEACH 4
Apr 3 Curr 16f HY 5 **106**
May 4 Ches 18½f GS 5 102

COCONUT MOON 3
Nov 5 Wolv 5f FT 1 **102**

COCONUT SQUEAK 3
Apr 25 Wolv 7f FT 2 99
Jun 22 Sals 6f G 1 100
Jly 27 Leic 6f G 2 102
Jly 28 Epsm 6f G 2 102
Aug 10 Yarm 6f GF 3 102
Aug 20 Ling 6f G 2 102
Aug 28 Gdwd 6f G 2 105
Sep 21 Gdwd 6f GF 3 105
Sep 25 NmkR 7f G 4 **111**
Oct 13 NmkR 6f G 1 108
Nov 1 MsnL 6f GF 10 107

CODE ORANGE 3
Jun 2 Hayd 6f G 2 **104**

COEUR COURAGEUX 3
Mar 1 Ling 7f SD 2 **108**
Mar 18 Ling 7f SD 1 104
May 28 Gdwd 8f G 3 104

COIS NA TINE EILE 3
Aug 4 Brig 12f G 3 99
Aug 29 Chep 16f G 2 **100**

COLD TURKEY 5
Jan 13 Ling 12f SD 1 **112**
Jan 22 Ling 12f FT 3 105
Feb 5 Ling 12f FT 1 103
Mar 4 Wolv 12f SD 2 99
Mar 26 Kemp 16f S 1 107
May 4 Ches 18½f GS 12 99
May 21 Ling 16f SD 2 105
Jun 25 Newc 16f G 10 108
Jly 9 Ling 16f SD 8 110
Oct 30 Ling 16f SD 3 106
Dec 16 Wolv 12f FT 1 103

COLEMANSTOWN 5
Jan 11 Sthl 8f SW 3 **104**
Apr 21 Sthl 8f FT 3 **104**

COLEORTON DANCER 3
May 5 Ches 7½f GS 5 102
May 21 NmkR 6f G 2 **106**
Sep 17 Ayr 6f G 20 99

COLEORTON DANE 3
Apr 21 Bevl 7½f S 2 101
May 14 Thsk 8f G 4 **102**

COLINCA'S LAD 3
Oct 28 NmkR 10f GS 5 **101**

COLISAY 6
Apr 30 NmkR 10f G 2 100
Jun 3 Epsm 10f G 5 **110**
Jun 17 York 10½f G 17 100
Aug 29 Epsm 10f G 5 105
Sep 17 Newb 9f GF 5 99

Oct 1 NmkR 9f G 9 100
Oct 14 NmkR 8f G 2 **110**
Oct 28 NmkR 10f GS 4 102
Nov 19 Ling 10f FT 9 99

COLLECT 3
Aug 28 Bevl 10f GS 4 **100**

COLLETON RIVER 4
Jan 7 Wolv 12f SW 1 **107**
Apr 19 Sthl 16f GF 2 103
May 7 Bevl 16f G 3 101
Jun 4 Chep 18f GS 7 100

COLLIER HILL 7
Sep 17 Curr 14f G 1 **105**

COLLOQUIAL 4
Sep 17 Wwck 16f G 10 99
Sep 28 Sals 14f G 1 102
Oct 21 Newb 16f GS 1 **104**

COLONEL BILKO 3
Mar 21 Ling 6f GS 8 100
Apr 26 Wwck 7f GS 7 **104**
Jly 14 Epsm 7f G 2 101

COLONEL COTTON 6
Jun 4 Epsm 5f G 5 103
Jun 26 Curr 5f GF 13 103
Jly 30 Gdwd 6f G 18 102
Aug 29 Epsm 5f G 8 **104**

COLOURFUL ERA 11
Feb 4 Wolv 7f SD 3 101
Feb 23 Ling 7f SD 7 100
Apr 23 Wolv 6f SD 1 99
May 5 Chep 6f GS 2 **107**

COME AWAY WITH ME 5
May 28 Ling 5f GF 1 **102**
Jun 19 Wwck 5f GF 3 101

COME ON 6
Jly 4 Muss 8f GF 2 **103**

COME ON JONNY 3
Mar 31 Donc 10½f G 1 99
Apr 22 Sand 10f G 3 102
May 4 Ches 12½f GS 2 101
Jun 4 Hayd 12f G 1 107
Jly 8 York 12f GS 4 103
Sep 10 Donc 10½f GS 2 108
Nov 5 Donc 12f S 1 **111**

COME WHAT JULY 4
Jan 6 Wolv 12f S 6 104
Jan 14 Wolv 14f SW 1 105
Jan 20 Sthl 12f SD 1 106
Feb 8 Sthl 11f SD 3 **110**
Feb 12 Wolv 12f FT 3 109
Feb 19 Wolv 12f FT 8 102
Feb 26 Sthl 12f FT 2 106
Jun 1 Wolv 14f FT 1 104
Jun 17 NmkJ 12f GF 8 103
Jly 26 Bevl 12f G 6 99

COMEINTOTHESPACE 3
Apr 20 Ling 10f FT 4 101
May 12 Carl 8f G 2 **102**
Aug 19 Ayr 8f GF 4 101
Sep 2 Hayd 8f G 7 101

COMFORT ZONE 4
Mar 20 Curr 8f HY 5 **108**

COMIC STRIP 3
Jly 28 Gdwd 10f G 4 **102**

COMMANDO SCOTT 4
Oct 14 NmkR 7f G 3 **107**
Oct 29 NmkR 7f S 6 102

COMMITMENT LECTURE 5
Apr 25 Haml 9f G 2 101
May 11 Newc 9f G 2 100
Jly 11 Ayr 8f F 4 101
Jly 19 Ayr 8f G 3 **107**
Jly 29 Nott 8f G 1 99
Oct 9 Newc 8f G 2 100

COMMON VENTURE 7
Jun 15 Leop 9f GF 1 **101**

COMMON WORLD 6
Mar 20 Curr 8f HY 15 99
Apr 2 Donc 8f G 3 **111**
Apr 16 Newb 8f GS 2 99
May 21 Curr 8f G 12 106
Jun 15 York 8f G 5 109
Aug 27 Wind 10f G 7 106
Sep 18 Curr 8f GF 5 106
Oct 30 StCl 8f G 7 110
Nov 6 Leop 7f GS 9 103

COMMUNICATION 3
May 31 Rdcr 10f G 4 **99**

COMPETITOR 4
Jan 29 Ling 10f SD 7 **105**
Oct 24 Ling 12f SW 10 100
Dec 30 Ling 10f FT 1 103

COMPTON BOLTER 8
Jan 15 Ling 10f SD 2 107
Jan 28 Wolv 8½f SD 2 107
Feb 5 Ling 12f SD 3 101
Feb 26 Ling 10f SD 4 107
Mar 19 Ling 10f SD 4 **113**
Apr 2 Donc 12f G 2 110
Apr 16 Newb 12f GS 8 101
May 7 NmkR 12f GF 1 106
May 14 Newb 13½f G 5 99
May 28 Gdwd 12f G 4 106
Sep 16 Newb 11f G 1 107
Sep 25 NmkR 12f G 3 102
Nov 19 Ling 10f FT 3 101
Dec 16 Wolv 12f FT 2 102

COMPTON CLASSIC 3
May 6 Haml 5f GS 2 **101**
Jly 18 Ayr 5f GF 4 **101**

COMPTON COURT 3
Oct 9 Gdwd 8f G 2 **106**

COMPTON DRAGON 6
Jan 7 Wolv 8½f SW 8 **105**
Jan 17 Wolv 8½f SD 8 101
Jun 1 Newc 8f G 5 101
Aug 26 Newc 9f GF 6 103
Oct 9 Newc 10f G 12 101

COMPTON DRAKE 6
Jan 19 Ling 10f FT 4 102

Mar 28 Wwck 11f GS 1 **104**
Apr 30 NmkR 10f G 7 101
May 15 Ripn 10f G 11 99

COMPTON ECLAIRE 5
Aug 8 Thsk 16f G 1 **103**

COMPTON ECLIPSE 5
Aug 19 Ayr 8f GF 1 **100**
Sep 1 Carl 8f G 4 **100**

COMPTON PLUME 5
Jly 20 Catt 6f G 2 **106**
Aug 2 Catt 6f G 1 105
Aug 10 Bevl 5f GF 6 99
Sep 1 Rdcr 6f G 5 99
Sep 14 Bevl 5f G 3 101

COMPTON'S ELEVEN 4
Apr 15 Newb 5f GS 3 106
Apr 30 NmkR 6f G 13 106
May 28 Donc 7f G 2 105
Jun 16 York 7f GF 8 102
Jun 25 Newc 7f G 5 101
Jly 7 NmkJ 7f G 12 102
Jly 28 Gdwd 7f G 2 103
Aug 19 Ches 7f GF 5 104
Aug 27 Gdwd 7f G 5 103
Sep 10 Gdwd 7f G 6 **109**
Sep 30 NmkR 7f G 2 **109**
Oct 14 NmkR 7f G 2 108
Oct 27 Ling 7f SD 6 107

CONJECTURE 3
Feb 5 Ling 5f SD 1 99
Apr 29 Muss 5f G 1 99
Jly 10 Hayd 5f GF 2 **103**
Jly 17 Rdcr 5f G 3 **103**

CONJUROR 4
May 7 NmkR 6f GF 8 99
May 23 Wind 6f F 3 102
Jun 13 Wind 6f GF 5 99
Sep 1 Rdcr 7f G 2 99
Sep 8 Donc 7f G 3 101
Sep 23 Ling 7f G 1 **104**

CONNECT 8
May 28 Gdwd 6f G 5 101
Jun 17 Rdcr 6f G 2 107
Jly 2 Bevl 5f G 7 99
Jly 22 York 5f G 1 **109**
Jly 23 York 6f G 2 106
Jly 30 Gdwd 6f G 21 100
Aug 16 York 6f GF 8 101
Sep 4 York 6f G 4 104
Sep 7 Donc 5½f GF 10 105
Sep 17 Ayr 6f G 11 108
Oct 8 York 6f GS 5 104
Oct 13 NmkR 5f G 7 104

CONNOTATION 3
Jan 5 Ling 8f SD 5 **101**
Dec 26 Wolv 9½f SD 1 99

CONSCRIPT 3
Aug 15 Yarm 11½f G 2 100
Aug 29 Newc 10f GF 1 102
Sep 14 Yarm 10f G 6 **106**

CONSENSUS 6
Feb 11 Wolv 5f SD 7 **101**

CONSIDINE 4
Feb 14 Wolv 12f SD 4 **107**
May 21 Catt 14f GF 4 103
Jun 10 Catt 16f GF 2 **107**
Jun 17 Rdcr 16f G 3 101

CONSONANT 8
Mar 1 Ling 10f SD 2 **108**
Aug 6 Wind 8½f GF 5 105
Sep 3 NmkJ 10f G 9 101
Dec 12 Wolv 9½f FT 2 100
Dec 19 Wolv 9½f FT 1 104

CONSTABLE BURTON 4
Jun 21 Bevl 7½f G 3 99
Aug 25 Muss 8f G 7 **104**

CONSTRUCTOR 4
Feb 21 Ling 7f SD 2 **102**
Jly 13 Ling 8f SW 4 101
Oct 27 Ling 7f SD 3 100

CONSULAR 3
Jun 3 Hayd 12f G 1 100
Jun 17 York 12f G 3 **106**
Aug 31 York 12f G 6 101

CONTACT DANCER 6
May 4 Ches 18½f GS 3 103
Jun 4 Hayd 16f G 3 **104**
Jun 25 Newc 16f G 18 103

CONTENTED 3
Jan 29 Ling 8f SD 4 **101**

CONTINENT 8
Sep 7 Donc 5½f GF 3 **107**

CONVINCE 4
Jun 2 Hayd 6f G 4 102
Jun 18 Ling 5f G 5 **104**
Sep 9 Sand 5f G 5 101

COOL HUNTER 4
Aug 26 Sals 10f G 1 **106**
Sep 14 Sand 10f G 4 99

COOL PANIC 3
Apr 2 Donc 7f G 1 **108**
Apr 14 NmkR 7f G 6 102
May 11 York 7f GS 2 103

COOL SANDS 3
Nov 21 Sthl 5f GS 2 **100**

COOL TEMPER 9
Jly 8 Chep 8f GF 5 **101**

COOLFORE JADE 5
Feb 14 Wolv 9½f GF 6 **100**

COPELAND 10
May 4 Ches 18½f GS 13 99

COPPERMALT 7
Dec 12 Wolv 14f FT 5 **102**

COPPICE 4
Aug 17 Nott 8f F 2 102
Sep 13 Sals 8f G 1 106
Sep 19 Leic 8½f G 1 **107**
Oct 8 Sals 8f GF 4 100

COQUETERIA 4
May 7 Ling 7f G 5 **105**
Sep 14 Yarm 10f G 2 **105**

COQUETTE ROUGE 4
May 8 Leop 12f S 4 **108**
Jun 26 Curr 12f F 12 107

COQUIN D'ALEZAN 4
Feb 19 Wolv 8½f F 7 99
Mar 1 Ling 7f SD 3 **102**

CORAL DAWN 5
Aug 7 Curr 10f G 11 **105**

CORANGLAIS 5
Jly 2 Hayd 5f GF 5 102
Jly 14 Leic 6f GF 1 **106**
Aug 2 Brig 5½f G 3 99
Aug 6 Hayd 6f G 3 102
Sep 17 Wwck 5½f G 3 99

CORCORAN 3
May 18 Gdwd 10f G 3 99
Jly 14 Lonc 12f F 5 **106**

CORDAGE 3
Mar 29 Pont 10f S 3 **102**
Jly 19 Ayr 8f G 6 101
Aug 1 Ripn 10f G 4 99

CORDIAL 5
Jan 10 Wolv 9½f SD 3 **108**
Jan 19 Ling 10f FT 1 104
Feb 8 Ling 12f SD 1 103
Feb 12 Wolv 12f FT 10 100
Sep 24 Hayd 14f GF 5 103

CORKY 4
Jun 3 Gdwd 7f GS 1 **108**
Jun 26 Wind 8½f G 8 99
Aug 27 Wind 8½f G 12 105
Oct 31 Wolv 8½f SD 10 99
Dec 5 Ling 7f FT 4 99
Dec 19 Wolv 8½f FT 3 103

CORMORANT WHARF 5
Mar 1 Ling 10f SD 2 **103**

CORNUS 3
Apr 13 NmkR 7f G 6 101
May 13 Newb 6f F 3 103
Jly 9 Ling 5f SD 4 100
Sep 6 Leic 5f GF 5 101
Sep 20 Bevl 5f GF 1 105
Nov 25 Wolv 6f FT 5 104
Dec 3 Wolv 5f FT 3 102
Dec 17 Ling 6f FT 3 **106**

CORONADO FOREST 6
Sep 17 Ling 8f SD 1 **99**

CORRE CAMINOS 3
Aug 2 Deau 10f G 2 108
Sep 17 Lonc 10f G 1 **110**
Oct 1 Lonc 9½f G 7 104

CORRIB ECLIPSE 6
Apr 27 Ling 16f S 7 99
Jly 9 Ling 16f SD 5 **112**
Sep 15 Pont 18f G 2 102

CORRIDOR CREEPER 8
Apr 30 Gdwd 5f G 1 106
May 21 Hayd 5f F 1 102
May 28 Gdwd 5f G 4 102
Jun 4 Epsm 5f G 3 106
Jun 25 Newc 6f G 5 103
Jly 9 Ches 5f GF 4 108
Jly 24 Newb 5f G 1 **114**
Aug 20 Bevl 5f G 4 106
Sep 20 Bevl 5f GF 5 101
Sep 29 NmkR 5f GF 2 106
Oct 13 NmkR 5f G 3 108

CORRIOLANUS 5
Mar 19 Ling 10f SD 5 **112**
Apr 2 Donc 12f G 6 103

COSMIC DESTINY 3
Aug 7 Ling 5f G 3 **99**
Sep 10 Gdwd 5f GF 1 **99**

COST ANALYSIS 3
Aug 15 Yarm 7f G 3 **101**

COTTINGHAM 4
Sep 20 Bevl 10f GF 5 **101**

COTTON EYED JOE 4
Dec 12 Sthl 11f FT 2 **99**

COUGAR CAT 3
Jly 6 Naas 6f GF 2 **105**

COUNCELLOR 3
Aug 3 Epsm 6f G 2 103
Aug 11 Sals 7f GF 2 100
Aug 17 Epsm 7f G 1 100
Aug 28 Gdwd 6f G 4 103
Sep 8 Epsm 7f G 1 **107**
Oct 1 Epsm 8½f GS 3 101
Dec 31 Wolv 7f SD 2 102

COUNCIL MEMBER 3
May 21 NmkR 7f G 1 108
Jun 15 York 7f G 7 100
Jly 30 Gdwd 8f G 5 102
Oct 1 Rdcr 7f GF 1 **111**
Oct 15 NmkR 7f G 12 99

COUNSEL'S OPINION 8
Feb 12 Ling 10f SD 1 **111**
Mar 19 Ling 10f SD 12 110
Apr 2 Donc 12f G 1 **111**
Apr 20 Epsm 10f GS 3 109
May 5 Ches 10½f G 3 **111**
Jly 16 Newb 10f GF 5 109
Aug 27 Wind 11½f G 2 106
Sep 16 Newb 11f G 4 101

COUNT BORIS 4
Mar 29 Wwck 11f S 1 **105**

COUNT COUGAR 5
Jan 27 Sthl 6f SD 4 100
Jun 24 Wolv 6f SD 1 102
Jun 27 Wolv 6f SD 1 **104**
Aug 2 Catt 5f GF 3 100

COUNT KRISTO 3
May 20 Hayd 10½f G 3 **99**

COUNTBACK 6
Dec 12 Wolv 14f FT 4 **103**

COUNTDOWN 3
Nov 25 Wolv 6f FT 3 **104**
Dec 16 Wolv 6f FT 3 **104**

COUNTERCLAIM 5
Aug 7 Deau 10f GF 7 **107**

COUNTRY PURSUIT 3
Jly 5 NmkJ 10f G 6 99
Jly 24 Newb 12f G 3 99
Aug 13 Newb 10f G 3 101
Aug 31 Ling 12f G 1 103
Sep 21 Gdwd 12f G 2 **109**
Sep 29 NmkR 14f GF 6 102

COUNTRY REEL 5
May 23 Wind 6f F 8 **101**

COUNTRYWIDE LUCK 4
Jly 23 Newb 12f GF 7 **105**
Sep 16 Newb 11f G 6 **105**
Dec 21 Ling 12f G 3 101
Dec 26 Wolv 12f SD 4 102

COUP D'ETAT 3
Mar 28 Kemp 7f GS 1 107
Jun 11 Sand 7f G 1 **110**
Jly 7 NmkJ 8f G 2 106

COUPE DE CHAMPE 4
May 22 Lonc 7f GF 4 107
Jun 27 Lonc 7f G 1 **114**
Jly 31 Deau 8f G 7 111
Oct 1 Lonc 7f G 5 112

COURAGEOUS DUKE 6
May 25 NmkR 10f G 4 101
Jun 17 York 10½f G 6 105
Jly 23 Newb 10f GF 2 102
Aug 6 Hayd 10½f GF 1 **109**
Aug 17 York 10½f G 13 99

COURS DE LA REINE 3
Sep 4 Lonc 10f GF 4 **102**

COURT MASTERPIECE 5
May 7 Ling 7f G 4 112
May 23 Leic 7f G 2 99
Jun 3 Gdwd 8f GS 1 115
Jun 25 NmkJ 7f G 2 108
Jly 9 Ling 8f SD 2 113
Jly 26 Gdwd 7f G 1 **117**
Aug 28 Gdwd 8f G 3 109
Sep 8 Donc 7f GF 3 108
Oct 1 Lonc 7f G 1 115

COURT OF APPEAL 8
Apr 26 Sthl 12f FT 1 101
May 3 Catt 12f GS 3 101
Jly 13 Catt 12f GF 1 **103**
Aug 6 Rdcr 14f G 3 **103**

COUSTOU 5
Apr 5 Folk 12f S 1 99

COVE MOUNTAIN 3
Mar 20 Curr 6f HY 2 **104**

COVENTINA 4
Mar 26 Kemp 16f S 2 106
Apr 6 Nott 14f GS 3 **110**

COVER UP 8
Jly 2 Sand 16½f G 3 **112**
Aug 16 York 16f G 4 102
Oct 15 NmkR 16f G 1 **112**

COZZENE'S HONOR 5
May 21 Curr 12f G 6 **105**

CRAFTY FANCY 4
Jan 29 Ling 8f SD 10 **104**

CRAIC SA CEILI 5
Jan 31 Wolv 7f SD 6 101
Feb 24 Sthl 7f FT 2 **103**
Mar 24 Wolv 8½f SD 5 99

CRAIL 5
Jan 12 Wolv 8½f SD 1 **107**
Oct 5 Nott 8f GF 8 99
Nov 26 Wolv 9½f FT 2 104
Dec 10 Wolv 9½f FT 3 103

CRATHORNE 5
Apr 6 Catt 16f G 3 100
Apr 20 Catt 12f S 2 102
Jun 10 Catt 12f GF 1 99
Aug 2 Catt 14f G 5 100

CRAZY RHYTHM 3
Jun 27 Lonc 7f G 5 **102**

CREAM OF ESTEEM 3
Aug 7 Rdcr 11f G 5 **99**

CREE 3
Jun 22 Epsm 6f G 3 **104**
Jly 4 Bath 5½f G 2 99
Jly 28 Epsm 6f G 1 103

CRESKELD 6
Jan 1 Sthl 8f SD 1 **116**

CRESTED POCHARD 4
Apr 10 Leop 12f GS 5 105
May 22 Curr 12f GS 4 **114**
Jun 26 Curr 16f F 10 99
Sep 4 Curr 10f G 3 106
Sep 18 Curr 16f G 7 104

CRETE 3
May 31 Leic 12f G 1 102
Jun 9 Ripn 12f GF 3 99
Aug 18 York 14f G 6 **103**

CRIMSON SUN 3
Sep 16 Newb 7f GF 3 105
Oct 1 Rdcr 7f GF 5 **106**

CRIPSEY BROOK 7
Jun 18 Rdcr 10f G 2 **107**
Jun 25 Newc 10f G 2 103
Jly 16 Ripn 12f G 6 103
Jly 23 Newc 10f GF 3 100
Oct 1 Rdcr 10f GF 1 102
Oct 9 Newc 10f G 11 101

CRISTOFORO 8
Jly 1 Sand 14f G 1 **107**

Sep 9 Donc 14½f G 2 105
Sep 25 NmkR 12f G 4 **107**

CRITICAL STAGE 6
May 17 Leic 12f G 7 **99**

CROOKED THROW 6
Jun 1 Leop 14f G 8 **106**

CROSS MY MIND 3
Jly 8 Wolv 6f FT 2 101
Jly 16 NmkJ 7f GF 2 99
Aug 11 Sals 7f GF 1 101
Aug 27 NmkJ 7f G 2 **104**

CROSS MY SHADOW 3
Jun 13 Brig 7f G 3 **99**

CROSS THE LINE 3
Aug 31 York 8f G 1 **110**
Oct 24 Ling 8f SW 2 101

CROSS TIME 3
Mar 28 Yarm 8f GS 2 103
Apr 12 Muss 9f G 3 101
May 1 Sals 10f GS 5 99
May 27 Pont 8f GF 1 106
Jun 16 York 8f G 14 100
Jun 25 Donc 8f GF 2 **107**
Aug 10 Sals 8f G 7 101
Aug 27 York 10½f G 4 104
Sep 7 Epsm 12f G 2 105
Sep 21 Gdwd 12f G 3 106
Oct 9 Gdwd 11f G 6 100

CROSSOVER 3
Sep 4 Lonc 5f GF 5 **108**

CROSSPEACE 3
Apr 12 NmkR 6f GF 2 102
Apr 22 Sand 8f G 8 101
May 1 NmkR 7f G 1 110
Jly 23 Newb 7f GF 12 108
Jly 29 Gdwd 8f G 2 **114**
Sep 17 Newb 10f GF 3 112
Oct 1 NmkR 9f G 4 105
Nov 5 Donc 12f HY 1 111

CROW WOOD 6
Mar 26 Kemp 10f GS 12 99
Apr 20 Epsm 10f GS 6 107
May 11 York 10½f S 5 102
May 30 Rdcr 10f G 3 105
Jun 4 Epsm 12f G 1 **110**
Jun 18 York 12f G 2 108
Jly 9 York 10½f G 2 106
Aug 17 York 14f G 10 104
Sep 3 Hayd 14f GF 11 102

CROWN OF MEDINA 3
Sep 28 Ling 6f SD 3 **101**

CROWNFIELD 6
Jun 17 Rdcr 16f G 5 **100**

CRUISE DIRECTOR 5
Jan 22 Ling 12f FT 4 105
Feb 12 Wolv 12f FT 2 110
Feb 19 Wolv 12f FT 5 105
May 11 York 12f S 1 **111**

CRUSOE 8
Jan 2 Sthl 7f SD 1 100
Jan 27 Sthl 6f SD 1 **104**
Mar 4 Wolv 8½f SD 4 100

CRUZSPIEL 5
Apr 27 Ling 16f S 8 99
May 7 NmkR 12f GF 4 103

CRYFIELD 8
Sep 14 Bevl 8½f G 3 99
Sep 20 Bevl 10f GF 4 **101**

CRYSTAL 4
Apr 11 Ling 12f SD 4 **101**

CRYSTAL MYSTIC 3
Jun 10 Chep 6f G 1 **102**
Jly 6 Catt 6f GS 2 101

CRYSTAL VIEW 3
Apr 10 Leop 7f GS 3 99
Jun 26 Curr 8f F 8 99
Sep 4 Curr 8f G 14 101
Sep 18 Curr 8f GF 8 **104**

CULTURED 4
May 2 Wwck 8f G 5 **99**

CUMBRIAN KNIGHT 7
Jun 17 Rdcr 11f G 4 99
Aug 12 Catt 12f G 4 **101**
Nov 28 Wolv 14f FT 1 99

CUMBRIAN PRINCESS 8
Feb 11 Wolv 9½f SD 1 **100**

CUP OF LOVE 3
Sep 3 Folk 9½f GF 1 **101**
Dec 22 Sthl 8f SD 7 99

CUPID'S BOW 5
Nov 6 Leop 8f S 8 **100**

CUPID'S GLORY 3
Jly 30 Gdwd 8f G 7 100
Aug 18 Ches 7½f F 1 104
Aug 28 Deau 8f G 2 103
Sep 8 Epsm 7f G 2 **108**

CUPIDS RAY 4
Mar 20 Curr 5f HY 2 100
Apr 3 Curr 6f S 2 **104**
Aug 20 Curr 6f GF 8 103
Oct 9 Curr 5f GS 1 103

CURRENCY 8
Jan 5 Ling 7f SD 3 105
Feb 8 Ling 6f SD 10 99
Jun 7 Sals 6f G 4 100
Jun 11 Bath 5½f G 5 99
Jun 19 Wwck 6f G 1 **110**
Jly 9 York 6f G 1 106
Jly 29 Thsk 6f G 7 102
Aug 11 Hayd 6f GF 1 102
Aug 27 Gdwd 6f G 3 105
Sep 3 NmkJ 6f G 6 104
Sep 21 Gdwd 6f GF 13 101

CURSUM PERFICIO 3
Jun 20 Nott 8f F 1 **101**

CURTAIN BLUFF 3
Apr 30 Gdwd 7f S 5 100
May 17 Bevl 7½f GF 1 107
Jun 25 Newc 8f G 2 **108**
Jly 9 Ling 8f SD 3 101
Jly 20 Sand 7f G 8 103
Sep 2 Hayd 8f G 3 106

CUSOON 3
Jun 11 Sand 7f G 8 101
Jly 4 Wind 8½f G 1 100
Jly 14 Epsm 7f G 6 99
Aug 27 Wind 8½f G 11 **105**
Oct 12 Ling 10f G 2 101

CUT AND DRIED 4
Jan 4 Ling 5f FT 7 **100**

CYCLICAL 3
Sep 24 Hayd 6f GF 6 **100**

CYCLONIC 3
Sep 5 Bath 5½f GF 2 **100**

CYFRWYS 4
May 21 Catt 7f GF 5 99
May 26 Bath 5½f G 3 99
Jun 29 Chep 6f G 1 **106**
Jly 15 Pont 6f GF 2 100
Jly 23 Newc 6f GF 4 101
Oct 4 Leic 6f G 2 101

D

DA BOOKIE 5
Aug 7 Curr 7f G 10 **103**
Aug 14 Leop 9f F 2 100

DABBERS RIDGE 3
Apr 1 Donc 7f G 2 101
May 2 Donc 7f G 2 99
May 11 York 7f GS 1 102
Jun 25 Ches 7f G 2 102
Jly 31 Ches 7½f G 4 101
Sep 16 Newb 7f GF 4 99
Oct 29 NmkR 7f S 2 **108**

DAFARABAD 3
Jly 6 Naas 10f GF 1 **104**

DAFORE 4
Aug 1 Wind 8½f GS 5 99
Oct 3 Wind 8½f GF 6 **102**

DAGOLA 4
Apr 8 Ling 10f SD 4 **99**

DAHLIYEV 3
May 14 Thsk 8f G 8 **100**

DAHMAN 3
Jly 14 Epsm 10f G 2 **103**
Jly 30 Gdwd 11f G 3 100

DAHTEER 3
May 1 Sals 6f G 3 99
May 14 Nott 6f F 3 **103**
Jun 3 Epsm 7f G 5 100
Jun 25 Newc 6f G 8 100
Jly 5 NmkJ 6f G 10 **103**

DAKOTA RAIN 3						
Aug	3	Pont	8f	G	2	99
Aug	27	York	8f	G	2	102
Sep	16	Nott	8f	GF	1	**107**
Oct	8	Sals	8f	GF	6	99

DALDINI 3						
May	19	Donc	7f	GF	6	99
Aug	28	Gdwd	9f	G	12	**100**

DALVENTO 7						
Jun	26	Curr	16f	F	8	**101**

DAME DE NOCHE 5						
Apr	26	Bath	5f	HY	4	102
Jun	2	Sand	5f	G	3	104
Jun	21	Bevl	5f	G	2	102
Jun	24	Newc	5f	G	5	**106**
Jly	18	Ayr	5f	GF	9	101
Jly	24	Newb	5f	G	9	**106**
Aug	14	Pont	6f	G	12	101

DAME NOIR 4						
May	8	Leop	8f	S	6	**109**

DAMSON 3						
May	22	Curr	8f	G	9	**110**
Jun	17	York	8f	G	7	101
Aug	7	Curr	6f	G	9	102

DAN DI CANIO 4						
Jan	13	Ling	8f	SD	2	101
Jan	21	Wolv	8½f	SD	2	**104**

DANAKIM 8						
Mar	31	Ling	5f	SD	3	**99**

DANCE IN STYLE 4						
Jly	25	Sthl	8f	SD	2	**100**

DANCE ON THE TOP 7						
Feb	1	Ling	8f	SD	4	108
Mar	19	Ling	8f	SD	6	100
Apr	1	Ling	7f	SD	3	101
Apr	24	Brig	8f	GF	2	102
Jun	6	Wind	8½f	G	3	**109**
Jun	20	Wind	8½f	G	4	101
Jly	9	Nott	8f	F	1	101
Sep	2	NmkJ	8f	G	9	104
Oct	5	Nott	8f	GF	7	99

DANCE PARTNER 3						
Jun	11	Ling	12f	SW	2	100
Jun	25	Ling	10f	SW	1	104
Jly	31	Newb	10f	G	1	101
Aug	12	Folk	9½f	G	1	106
Oct	9	Gdwd	12f	G	1	**110**

DANCE TO MY TUNE 4						
Mar	31	Donc	12f	G	2	99
Apr	21	Bevl	10f	S	4	99
May	2	Newc	12½f	G	2	101
Jun	8	Haml	12f	G	1	**105**
Jly	8	York	10½f	GS	5	104
Jly	30	Donc	10½f	G	7	100

DANCE TO THE BLUES 4						
Jan	31	Wolv	6f	SD	2	100
Apr	24	Brig	5½f	GF	3	101
Aug	15	Brig	5½f	G	1	**102**
Sep	1	Sals	5f	G	2	**102**
Oct	4	Leic	6f	G	1	**102**

DANCE WORLD 5						
Mar	26	Kemp	16f	S	6	102

DANCEINTHEVALLEY 3						
Apr	11	Sthl	10f	G	2	**106**
May	21	Carl	9½f	G	4	99
Jun	15	Haml	8½f	GS	1	105

DANCER'S SERENADE 3						
May	24	Ripn	10f	GS	1	**109**
Jun	4	Hayd	12f	G	7	102
Jun	25	Newc	10f	G	1	108
Sep	24	Ripn	10f	GF	6	101

DANCES WITH ANGELS 5						
Jan	24	Wolv	14f	SD	4	99
Feb	21	Wolv	14f	FT	2	**101**

DANCING BAY 8						
Jly	28	Gdwd	16f	G	5	110
Oct	15	NmkR	16f	G	4	**111**

DANCING DEANO 3						
Jun	7	Rdcr	7f	G	3	**102**
Jun	19	Pont	6f	G	2	**102**
Sep	15	Ayr	7f	G	4	100

DANCING LYRA 4						
May	15	Ripn	10f	G	6	102
Jun	12	Sals	12f	G	3	104
Jun	22	Epsm	12f	G	4	99
Aug	2	Brig	12f	G	6	104
Aug	12	Newb	13½f	G	4	106
Sep	16	Newb	11f	G	8	105
Oct	24	Ling	12f	SW	3	**107**

DANCING MYSTERY 11						
Jan	1	Sthl	5f	FT	1	**107**
Mar	19	Ling	5f	SD	1	106
May	6	Ling	5f	G	5	105
May	27	Brig	5½f	GF	4	100
Jun	12	Sals	5f	G	7	100
Jly	24	Newb	5f	G	10	106
Aug	23	Yarm	5f	G	3	105
Oct	17	Wind	6f	G	6	100
Oct	30	Ling	6f	SD	9	99
Nov	16	Sthl	5f	FT	8	102
Dec	6	Sthl	5f	FT	8	100

DANCING ROSE 3						
Aug	27	NmkJ	7f	G	3	**104**
Sep	16	Newb	7f	GF	5	99

DANCING WATER 6						
Nov	6	Leop	12f	S	2	100

DANCINGINTHECLOUDS 3						
Jly	1	Hayd	12f	G	5	**100**

DANDOUN 7						
Jan	7	Wolv	8½f	SW	4	**112**

DANDYGREY RUSSETT 4						
Jan	15	Ling	10f	SD	5	99
Jan	29	Ling	10f	SD	4	**107**
May	25	Ling	10f	G	2	105

DANE RHAPSODY 4						
Aug	4	Brig	6f	G	7	**99**

DANE'S ROCK 3						
Sep	5	Bath	8f	GF	1	**99**

DANEHILL DAZZLER 3						
Jun	1	Nott	8f	G	4	101
Jun	11	Sand	7f	G	4	**107**
Aug	28	Gdwd	7f	G	1	102
Sep	16	Ayr	8f	G	5	100

DANEHILL STROLLER 5						
Aug	29	Wwck	6f	GF	3	100
Sep	5	Bath	5½f	GF	5	**102**

DANEHILL WILLY 3						
May	16	Wind	11½f	G	6	101
Jun	19	Pont	10f	G	2	107
Jly	6	NmkJ	10f	G	1	**109**
Jly	14	Epsm	10f	G	1	104
Sep	17	Newb	10f	GF	13	107

DANELOR 7						
Jan	10	Wolv	9½f	SD	5	106
Jan	28	Wolv	9½f	SD	4	105
Feb	8	Sthl	11f	SD	1	**111**
Feb	21	Ling	10f	FT	5	102
Mar	26	Kemp	10f	GS	6	103
Mar	29	Pont	10f	S	1	110
May	2	Donc	10½f	G	8	103
Jun	3	Epsm	10f	G	14	102
Jly	23	York	10½f	GS	5	102
Sep	29	Ayr	10f	S	3	99
Nov	26	Wolv	9½f	FT	5	99
Dec	6	Sthl	11f	FT	2	105
Dec	20	Sthl	11f	SW	2	108

DANETIME LADY 5						
Jly	6	Naas	6f	GF	4	**101**
Jly	20	Naas	6f	GF	2	100

DANETTIE 4						
Aug	6	Rdcr	9f	G	2	101
Dec	7	Ling	8f	FT	1	100
Dec	28	Wolv	8½f	FT	2	**103**

DANGER BIRD 5						
Jan	14	Wolv	9½f	SW	3	**102**

DANGER ZONE 3						
Dec	17	Ling	10f	FT	2	**100**

DANIEL O'DONNELL 3						
Apr	6	Ling	7f	FT	5	**99**

DANIELLA 3						
Jun	4	Ling	7f	G	3	102
Jun	30	Yarm	7f	G	2	103
Aug	10	Yarm	6f	GF	1	**105**
Aug	28	Gdwd	6f	G	5	103

DANIELLE'S LAD 9						
Jun	16	Wolv	8½f	G	5	101
Jly	8	Chep	8f	GF	1	**105**
Oct	3	Wind	8½f	GF	10	99
Dec	19	Wolv	8½f	FT	5	100

DANIFAH 4						
May	5	Chep	6f	GS	1	**108**

DANSE SPECTRE 3						
Dec	30	Ling	10f	FT	1	**102**

DANSILI DANCER 3						
May	30	Leic	8f	G	2	99
Jun	10	Gdwd	8f	G	1	101
Jly	7	NmkJ	8f	G	5	103

Jly 28 Gdwd 10f G 5 102
Sep 7 Epsm 10f G 2 **105**

DANTE'S DIAMOND 3
Jun 7 Rdcr 7f G 5 100
Jun 23 Thsk 7f G 2 **104**

DANZIG RIVER 4
May 6 Ches 5f GS 4 **106**
May 12 York 5f GS 6 105
Jly 9 York 6f G 8 100
Jly 29 Gdwd 6f G 3 103
Aug 12 Newc 6f GS 3 105

DANZILI BAY 3
May 31 Leic 6f GF 1 **106**
Jly 2 Hayd 6f GF 1 **106**
Jly 23 York 6f G 4 103

DANZOLIN 4
Sep 11 Gdwd 8f G 10 **103**
Sep 26 Bath 8f G 2 101

DARA MAC 6
Jun 23 Thsk 8f G 4 100
Jly 29 Thsk 7f G 5 **104**
Aug 8 Thsk 8f G 6 99

DARGHAN 5
Jun 27 Wind 8½f G 8 **100**

DARING AFFAIR 4
Nov 29 Sthl 12f SD 3 101
Dec 20 Sthl 11f SW 3 **103**

DARING RANSOM 3
Apr 30 NmkR 10f G 2 **103**
Jun 17 York 16f G 4 100

DARK CHAMPION 5
May 17 Rdcr 7f G 2 99
Jly 29 Thsk 6f G 2 99
Sep 12 Rdcr 6f G 6 101
Oct 14 Rdcr 6f GF 2 **103**

DARK CHARM 6
Jun 8 Haml 8½f G 1 **109**
Jun 11 Ripn 8f G 4 103

DARK CHEETAH 3
Jun 3 Epsm 7f G 6 103
Jun 26 Curr 6½f GF 4 101
Jly 16 Curr 5f F 11 105
Aug 20 Curr 6f GF 2 **110**

DARK PARADE 4
Jan 12 Ling 16f SD 1 100
Feb 7 Sthl 14f SD 1 103
Mar 7 Ling 16f SD 3 **106**

DARK SOCIETY 7
Feb 1 Ling 10f SD 1 103

DARLING DEANIE 3
Aug 1 Wind 11½f GS 1 **105**
Sep 1 Sals 14f G 6 99
Oct 1 NmkR 14f G 9 99

DARN GOOD 4
May 26 Bath 17½f G 4 101
Jun 4 Chep 18f GS 6 100
Jun 23 Sals 14f G 5 100

Jly 16 Hayd 16f GF 2 **104**
Aug 14 Pont 17f G 6 101

DART ALONG 3
May 27 Pont 6f GF 1 100
Jun 11 Sand 7f G 5 **105**
Jun 22 Epsm 6f G 4 100

DASAR 5
Jan 5 Sthl 7f SD 4 **101**

DASH TO THE TOP 3
Jun 23 Newc 10f GF 1 **109**
Jly 17 Curr 12f F 5 108
Aug 17 York 12f G 2 **109**
Sep 11 Lonc 12f G 4 108

DASHING HOME 6
Jun 17 York 10½f G 9 **103**

DAVENPORT 3
Feb 19 Wolv 8½f G 4 103
Apr 6 Nott 8f GS 1 **106**
Apr 25 Wind 8½f GS 1 104
Aug 29 Epsm 8½f G 4 99
Oct 5 Nott 8f GF 3 101
Oct 28 NmkR 8f GS 1 101
Nov 12 Ling 8f FT 4 102

DAVID JUNIOR 3
Apr 30 NmkR 8f G 11 106
Jly 1 Sand 10f G 1 112
Jly 27 Gdwd 8f GS 7 **113**
Oct 15 NmkR 10f G 1 **113**

DAVORIN 4
Jun 26 Curr 8f F 4 100
Sep 10 Leop 9f GF 10 **105**

DAWN AT SEA 3
Jly 26 Bevl 12f G 4 **100**

DAY FLIGHT 4
Mar 28 Kemp 10f GS 1 107
Apr 16 Newb 12f GS 1 **113**
May 6 Ches 13½f GS 1 108
Jly 6 NmkJ 12f G 2 102
Oct 22 Newb 12f G 1 109
Nov 5 Donc 12f HY 2 101

DAY ONE 4
Jan 7 Wolv 12f SW 4 **102**

DAY TO REMEMBER 4
Sep 3 Hayd 14f GF 15 **100**

DAYBREAK DANCER 3
Jly 16 Ripn 6f G 1 **107**
Jly 23 Ling 7f GF 1 103

DAYDREAM DANCER 4
May 30 Leic 12f G 2 **104**
Jun 29 Chep 12f G 6 101
Aug 4 Chep 12f G 2 102

DAYOFF 4
Apr 3 Curr 10f S 15 **99**

DAZZLING BAY 5
Apr 30 NmkR 6f G 22 101
May 28 Muss 5f G 6 **106**
Jun 17 Rdcr 6f G 7 102

Jun 24 Newc 5f G 9 104

DEBBIE 6
Feb 27 Wolv 12f G 1 100

DECISIVE 6
May 21 Ling 16f SD 9 102
Jun 18 NmkJ 15f G 6 100

DEEPER IN DEBT 7
Sep 11 Gdwd 8f G 1 **111**
Oct 3 Wind 8½f GF 3 105
Nov 10 Ling 8f SD 10 99
Dec 10 Wolv 7f FT 2 99
Dec 19 Wolv 8½f FT 1 106

DEERPARK 3
Jun 26 Curr 8f F 1 **105**

DEFI 3
Apr 30 NmkR 8f G 2 **103**
Jun 9 Ripn 8f G 6 100
Aug 4 Hayd 8f GF 5 **103**
Aug 22 Haml 8½f F 3 **103**
Oct 29 Wolv 9½f SD 9 101

DEFINING 6
May 13 York 14f GS 3 108
May 30 Sand 16½f G 5 100
Jly 15 NmkJ 12f G 1 **115**
Aug 17 York 14f G 14 100
Sep 30 NmkR 12f G 2 108

DEL MAR SUNSET 6
Apr 5 Folk 9½f S 2 100
Jly 13 Hayd 8f G 1 103
Aug 3 Brig 10f G 1 104
Sep 7 Epsm 8½f G 4 102
Sep 8 Epsm 10f G 2 104
Oct 1 Rdcr 10f GF 2 101
Oct 9 Newc 10f G 2 105
Oct 29 Wolv 9½f SD 5 105
Nov 11 Wolv 8½f FT 6 **107**

DELFOS 4
Apr 3 Lonc 10f S 1 **116**
Oct 1 Lonc 9½f G 9 99

DELLA SALUTE 3
Jun 2 Brig 7f G 3 101
Jun 13 Brig 8f G 1 **104**
Jly 8 Chep 8f GF 2 99
Jly 21 Bath 10f GF 3 99
Aug 14 Bath 8f G 1 102
Sep 27 Gdwd 8f G 5 99

DELLAGIO 4
Apr 8 Ling 6f SD 8 99
Nov 5 Sthl 5f FT 1 101
Dec 27 Sthl 5f SD 2 **104**

DELPHIE QUEEN 4
Apr 2 Donc 6f G 6 103
Aug 6 NmkJ 7f G 11 **109**
Aug 14 Pont 6f G 5 107
Sep 8 Donc 7f G 5 100
Sep 24 NmkR 8f G 14 100

DEMI TASSE 3
Jun 6 Folk 9½f G 4 **99**

DEMOCRATIC DEFICIT 3
Apr 14 NmkR 8f G 1 101
Apr 30 NmkR 8f G 6 108
May 21 Curr 8f G 3 99
Jun 8 Leop 7f G 1 **109**
Jly 16 Curr 8f GF 3 106
Aug 14 Leop 8f F 6 104
Aug 31 York 9f G 4 101
Oct 15 NmkR 9f G 5 103

DENNICK 3
Jun 7 Rdcr 7f G 6 99

DEPRESSED 3
Jun 20 Wind 6f G 3 100
Jun 22 Epsm 6f G 2 **105**

DESERT ARC 7
May 30 Leic 6f G 5 **100**

DESERT CHIEF 3
Jun 2 Sand 8f G 1 **103**

DESERT CRISTAL 4
May 28 Gdwd 8f G 8 100
Jun 25 NmkJ 8f G 6 101
Aug 27 NmkJ 10f G 1 100
Oct 9 Gdwd 10f G 7 103
Nov 29 Ling 10f FT 7 **107**

DESERT DESTINY 5
Jly 7 NmkJ 7f G 9 105
Aug 6 NmkJ 7f G 13 **108**
Aug 27 York 9f G 7 101
Oct 1 NmkR 9f G 6 104

DESERT DREAMER 4
Mar 18 Ling 7f SD 2 **105**
Apr 27 Ling 8f FT 5 102
May 7 NmkR 6f GF 4 103
May 18 Gdwd 7f G 6 102
Jun 13 Wind 6f GF 4 100
Jly 8 Ling 6f SW 9 99
Aug 3 Brig 8f G 7 102
Aug 12 NmkJ 6f G 1 100
Sep 6 Ling 7f SD 1 104
Sep 28 Sals 6f G 3 100
Oct 1 Epsm 7f GS 2 102

DESERT FANTASY 6
May 21 Curr 8f G 17 101
Jun 2 Hayd 7f G 3 **112**

DESERT GOLD 4
Aug 14 Leop 7f F 3 103
Sep 10 Leop 7f HD 6 **105**

DESERT HAWK 4
Jun 27 Wind 10f G 3 **99**
Aug 11 Chep 8f G 6 **99**
Dec 28 Wolv 14f G 7 **99**

DESERT HILL 8
Jun 8 Leop 8f F 6 **104**

DESERT IMAGE 4
Sep 28 Ling 12f SD 2 **103**

DESERT IMP 3
May 14 Newb 7f F 1 **102**
Jly 5 NmkJ 7f G 9 100
Jly 24 NmkJ 8f G 6 99
Aug 10 Sand 7f GF 2 **102**
Nov 12 Ling 8f FT 10 99

DESERT ISLAND DISC 8
Jun 12 Sals 12f G 6 103
Jly 20 Sand 10f G 6 99
Aug 2 Brig 12f G 10 101
Aug 13 Gdwd 11f G 2 99
Aug 23 Brig 12f G 2 99
Sep 5 Wwck 16f G 1 101
Sep 17 Wwck 16f G 4 104
Sep 27 Gdwd 16f G 3 99
Oct 19 Bath 11½f GS 7 99
Oct 28 NmkR 16f GS 3 **105**

DESERT LEADER 4
Oct 29 Wolv 9½f SD 3 99
Nov 12 Wolv 9½f FT 1 103
Dec 3 Wolv 9½f FT 1 **104**
Dec 10 Wolv 9½f FT 2 103

DESERT LIGHTNING 3
Aug 13 NmkJ 8f G 3 **99**

DESERT LORD 5
Jun 7 Ches 7f GF 6 99
Jun 17 Rdcr 6f G 9 100
Jly 5 Pont 6f G 5 103
Jly 15 Pont 5f GF 1 **108**
Aug 6 Hayd 5f G 6 106
Sep 24 Hayd 5f GF 6 105

DESERT LOVER 3
Nov 19 Sthl 7f SW 1 99
Dec 28 Wolv 8½f SW 6 **100**

DESERT MOVE 3
May 1 NmkR 10f G 4 99
Aug 18 York 12f G 3 **101**

DESERT OF GOLD 4
May 21 Curr 12f G 11 **101**

DESERT OPAL 5
Aug 27 York 6f G 10 99
Sep 3 Wolv 6f FT 1 100
Sep 17 Wolv 6f FT 1 **102**

DESERT PLUS 6
Aug 7 Deau 10f GF 4 **107**

DESERT QUEST 5
May 25 NmkR 10f G 3 101
Jun 17 York 10½f G 4 107

DESERT REIGN 4
May 15 Ripn 10f G 3 **103**

DESERT SECRETS 3
Jun 26 Wind 11½f G 2 **99**

DESERT STATION 4
Jun 1 Leop 14f G 14 **106**

DESERT STREAM 4
Jun 7 Rdcr 11f G 2 **100**

DESIDERATUM 3
Apr 10 Lonc 10½f S 4 107
Jly 14 Lonc 12f F 2 **112**

DESPERATE DAN 4
Jly 1 Sand 5f G 6 101
Jly 22 Newb 6f G 4 102
Aug 5 Hayd 6f F 3 104
Sep 24 Hayd 6f GF 2 102
Nov 16 Sthl 5f FT 4 **106**
Dec 2 Wolv 6f SD 6 105

DESPERATION 3
Jan 13 Ling 10f SD 1 101
Mar 23 Ling 12f SD 4 **104**
Jly 17 Rdcr 11f G 6 100
Sep 6 Ling 10f SD 2 99
Dec 10 Sthl 11f FT 2 102

DETONATE 3
Jly 30 Donc 5f G 5 **100**
Aug 23 Yarm 5f G 8 99

DETONATEUR 7
Jly 7 Wwck 12½f G 8 100

DETROIT CITY 3
Mar 23 Ling 12f SD 1 **106**
May 31 Sand 14f G 6 99

DEVINE COMMAND 4
Jan 13 Ling 8f SD 1 **102**
Apr 11 Ling 8f SD 3 99
Jly 19 Yarm 11½f G 3 **102**

DEVIOUS DIVA 3
Apr 10 Leop 7f GS 2 101
Sep 10 Leop 9f GF 4 107
Sep 17 Curr 8f GF 2 **110**
Oct 9 Curr 8f GS 5 99

DEVON FLAME 6
May 16 Wind 6f G 1 100
Jly 9 Sals 6f G 1 99
Jly 23 York 6f G 3 **104**
Aug 20 Sand 5f GS 3 102

DHAULAR DHAR 3
Jun 16 York 8f G 8 104
Jly 20 Sand 7f G 6 104
Aug 11 Sand 9f GF 4 102
Aug 28 Gdwd 9f G 5 **107**
Sep 7 Epsm 8½f G 2 104
Oct 1 Epsm 8½f GS 5 101
Oct 9 Gdwd 8f G 1 **107**

DHEHDAAH 4
Mar 28 Yarm 11½f S 1 101
Apr 9 Newc 12½f S 4 100
Apr 26 Wwck 12½f GS 9 100
May 17 Leic 12f G 5 102

DIACONATE 4
Jun 26 Curr 16f F 9 **99**

DIAL SQUARE 4
Feb 2 Ling 10f F 1 99
Feb 21 Ling 10f FT 4 100
Mar 31 Ling 10f SD 7 **103**

DIAMOND CIRCLE 3
Jun 11 Ripn 10f G 1 101
Sep 3 NmkJ 15f G 2 102
Oct 1 NmkR 14f G 1 **107**

DIAMOND DAN 3
Dec 29 Ling 8f G 6 **99**

DIAMOND DIGGINS 3
Aug 12 NmkJ 12f G 3 **99**

DIAMOND GREEN 4
Jun 16 Lonc 10f G 2 **117**

DIAMOND JOSH 3
Oct 22 Wolv 6f SD 1 **99**

DIAMOND KATIE 3
Jun 25 Wind 6f G 3 100
Jly 30 Haml 5f F 4 **102**

DIAMOND MAX 7
Jan 5 Ling 7f SD 10 99
Feb 8 Ling 6f SD 6 102
Apr 1 Ling 8f SD 4 101
Apr 16 Thsk 8f HY 4 **108**

DIAMOND TANGO 4
Apr 10 Lonc 10f S 6 **107**

DIAMONDS AND DUST 3
Apr 9 Ling 8f FT 4 100
Apr 22 Sand 8f G 9 99
Jly 7 NmkJ 8f G 1 **107**

DIAMONDS FOR LUCK 3
Jly 6 Naas 6f GF 3 104
Jly 20 Naas 6f GF 3 103
Aug 20 Curr 6f GF 1 **105**

DICTATION 3
Sep 4 Curr 10f G 9 **103**

DIDNT TELL MY WIFE 6
Jan 12 Wolv 8½f SD 10 **99**

DIEGO CAO 4
Oct 9 Gdwd 10f G 3 105

DIG DEEP 3
Jan 19 Ling 6f FT 4 99
Sep 17 Newb 7f GF 1 **107**
Sep 30 Ling 7f FT 4 100

DIGITAL 8
Apr 2 Kemp 7f GS 7 101
Apr 9 Newc 7f S 4 **107**
Jun 13 Wwck 7f GF 2 105
Jly 2 Leic 7f GF 5 101
Jly 15 Carl 7f G 1 99
Aug 6 Wind 6f GF 1 102
Aug 10 Haml 6f GF 2 102

DILALA 3
Jly 15 Wwck 11f G 3 **102**
Aug 28 Bevl 10f GS 2 99

DIMASHQ 3
Sep 17 Catt 14f G 3 **99**

DIMPLE CHAD 6
Jun 8 Haml 12f G 9 **99**

DINNER DATE 3
May 14 Nott 8f F 5 **100**
Aug 10 Yarm 10f G 1 99

DISCOMANIA 3
May 6 Nott 14f G 3 **103**

DISCUSS 3
May 26 Bath 8f G 1 99
Jun 17 York 8f G 8 101
Jly 8 Chep 10f GF 4 103
Aug 14 Bath 8f G 2 **109**
Sep 24 NmkR 8f G 8 107
Oct 30 Ling 8f SD 5 100

DISPOL FOXTROT 7
Apr 23 Hayd 8f G 1 104
May 1 Haml 8½f S 3 101
Jly 9 Haml 9f F 3 **105**
Sep 2 Hayd 8f G 6 102
Sep 26 Haml 9f G 1 104
Oct 11 Leic 10f G 2 100
Dec 22 Sthl 8f SD 1 103

DISPOL KATIE 4
May 14 Thsk 5f G 8 102
May 27 Catt 7f GF 1 104
Jun 27 Muss 7f GF 2 103
Jun 29 Catt 7f G 4 99
Jly 8 York 7f G 1 102
Jly 14 Donc 7f GF 5 100
Aug 19 Ches 7f GF 4 **105**
Sep 3 Thsk 8f G 5 99

DISPOL PETO 5
Jan 3 Sthl 7f SD 4 101
Jan 5 Sthl 7f SD 1 **104**

DISPOL VELETA 4
Apr 23 Hayd 8f G 4 102
May 1 Haml 8½f S 1 **104**
May 6 Haml 8½f GS 1 102
May 25 Ripn 8f G 7 99
Jly 30 Donc 10½f G 5 100
Aug 13 Ripn 10f GS 4 99

DISTANT COUNTRY 6
Mar 18 Ling 8f SD 1 **105**
Jun 6 Wind 8½f G 6 101
Aug 11 Chep 8f G 5 99
Aug 18 Chep 8f GF 6 101

DISTANT COUSIN 8
Jun 3 Wolv 14f FT 5 99
Jun 25 Ling 12f SW 1 **101**
Aug 8 Wolv 12f SD 2 100

DISTANT PROSPECT 8
May 4 Ches 18½f GS 11 100
Oct 15 NmkR 18f G 10 101

DISTANT TIMES 4
Jun 2 Hayd 6f G 1 **105**

DISTINCTION 6
Jly 28 Gdwd 16f G 1 **117**
Aug 16 York 16f G 2 103
Sep 8 Donc 18f G 6 106

DISTINCTLY GAME 3
Jun 5 Chan 5f G 6 **109**
Jun 14 York 5f G 9 101
Jun 26 Curr 5f GF 11 104
Jly 9 Ches 5f GF 8 104

DIUM MAC 4
May 17 Rdcr 6f G 4 **100**
Aug 6 Rdcr 9f G 5 99

DIVINE GIFT 4
Apr 2 Donc 8f G 8 107
May 4 Ches 10½f GS 2 **108**
May 30 Rdcr 10f G 2 105
Jun 18 Rdcr 10f G 3 107

DIVINE PROPORTIONS 3
May 15 Lonc 8f G 1 **117**
Jun 12 Chan 10½f G 1 111
Jly 31 Deau 8f G 1 **117**
Aug 14 Deau 8f GF 4 112

DIVINE SPIRIT 4
May 7 Bevl 5f GF 11 99
Jun 1 Newc 6f G 5 100
Jun 24 Newc 6f G 2 **105**
Jun 30 Hayd 6f GF 2 102
Jly 11 Ayr 5f GF 3 103
Aug 5 Hayd 6f F 6 102
Aug 10 Bevl 5f GF 3 101
Sep 16 Ayr 5f GF 4 100
Oct 29 Wolv 6f SD 3 100
Nov 3 Muss 5f GS 7 99

DIVINELY DECADENT 3
Apr 13 NmkR 7f G 5 **105**
Aug 10 Sals 10f G 8 100
Sep 25 NmkR 7f G 12 103

DIXIEANNA 3
Jun 25 NmkJ 6f G 3 **101**

DIZZY IN THE HEAD 6
Jun 15 Haml 5f G 2 103
Jun 28 Haml 5f F 1 104
Jly 2 Carl 6f GF 2 **106**
Aug 12 Newc 6f GS 7 101
Nov 1 Catt 5f G 1 103

DOCTOR DENNIS 8
Dec 30 Ling 7f FT 3 **99**

DOCTOR DINO 3
Jun 5 Chan 10½f G 7 102
Jun 27 Lonc 9f G 6 **108**

DOCTOR'S CAVE 3
Mar 7 Ling 5f SD 7 99
May 31 Leic 6f GF 5 **100**
Dec 30 Ling 6f FT 9 99

DOCTORED 4
Jun 21 Newb 10f G 2 102
Jun 30 Newb 11f G 4 **105**
Jly 13 Hayd 10½f G 2 101

DOITFORREEL 3
Jun 25 Ling 7f G 1 99
Aug 4 Yarm 7f GF 2 **102**

DOITNOW 4
Mar 12 Wolv 6f SD 7 **103**
May 28 Donc 7f G 7 100
Aug 27 NmkJ 6f G 8 101

DOLCE PICCATA 4
Aug 9 Bath 5f GF 2 **102**

DOLLARS ROCK 5
Jun 1 Leop 7f G 4 **108**
Aug 7 Curr 7f G 12 101

DOLMA 4
Nov 1 MsnL 6f GF 8 **110**

DOLPHIN BAY 5
Aug 7 Curr 10f G 4 **108**

DOMIRATI 5
May 7 Bevl 5f GF 7 **100**
Jun 7 Ches 5f GF 5 **100**
Jun 24 Newc 6f G 6 99

DON PASQUALE 3
Feb 19 Wolv 8½f G 2 **105**
Mar 28 Yarm 8f GS 4 102

DON PELE 3
Jun 12 Sals 6f G 4 99
Jly 5 NmkJ 6f G 14 **100**
Jly 22 Newb 6f G 7 99

DON'T BE BITIN 4
Nov 6 Leop 16f S 5 107

DON'T TELL MUM 3
May 2 Kemp 6f G 1 **101**

DONALDSON 3
Jly 24 MsnL 10f F 6 **107**

DONASTRELA 4
May 1 Sals 14f GS 5 **105**
May 16 Bath 13f G 3 99
Jly 20 Sand 10f G 5 99
Oct 31 Wolv 14f SD 3 99

DONEGAL SHORE 6
Jan 13 Sthl 7f SD 1 99
Jan 27 Sthl 6f SD 2 **107**

DONNA'S DOUBLE 10
Jun 17 Ayr 10f GS 2 99
Jly 19 Ayr 10f G 5 101
Aug 12 Newc 10f GS 1 101
Aug 20 Rdcr 10f G 3 101
Sep 5 Newc 10f G 2 102
Sep 15 Pont 10f G 3 100

DONT CALL ME DEREK 4
Nov 5 Donc 16½f S 1 109

DOOHULLA 4
Apr 26 Bath 5f HY 6 99
Jun 27 Pont 6f G 1 **109**
Aug 20 Ches 5f G 4 103

DOONAREE 9
May 8 Leop 12f S 8 **104**

DORCHESTER 8
Jun 25 Wind 6f G 2 **101**

DORIC 4
Jly 28 Gdwd 7f G 7 100
Aug 16 York 6f GF 3 103
Aug 18 York 8f G 7 **108**
Sep 4 York 6f G 2 105

DORINGO 4
Aug 4 Brig 8f G 1 **100**

DORIS SOUTER 5
Mar 3 Ling 10f SW 13 99

DORN DANCER 3
Jly 30 Donc 5f G 4 **102**

DORN HILL 3
Aug 18 Chep 6f GF 2 **100**

DOUBLE DEPUTY 4
Aug 14 Pont 12f G 3 **104**

DOUBLE GREEN 4
Apr 10 Lonc 10f S 2 **110**

DOUBLE KUDOS 3
Mar 23 Ling 12f SD 3 **105**

DOUBLE M 8
Jan 4 Ling 5f FT 5 102
Jan 13 Ling 6f SD 1 **105**
Jan 26 Ling 7f FT 1 101

DOUBLE RANSOM 6
Feb 5 Ling 10f FT 7 **99**

DOUBLE VODKA 4
Apr 9 Newc 8f S 2 102
May 17 Bevl 8½f GF 4 102
May 26 Ayr 10f G 1 **105**
Jun 19 Pont 10f G 5 99
Jly 5 NmkJ 8f G 10 100

DOVE COTTAGE 3
Aug 28 Gdwd 10f G 1 **99**
Sep 10 Ches 10½f GS 3 **99**

DOVEDALE 5
Jun 17 NmkJ 12f GF 5 **107**

DOVEDON HERO 5
Jan 13 Ling 12f SD 3 **110**
Feb 5 Ling 12f SD 4 101
Feb 19 Wolv 12f SD 6 104
Apr 11 Ling 12f SD 6 100
May 1 NmkR 16f G 1 107
May 20 NmkR 12f G 6 99
Jly 16 Hayd 16f GF 3 102
Nov 16 Sthl 12f FT 7 99
Dec 6 Sthl 14f FT 5 100
Dec 21 Ling 12f FT 9 99
Dec 27 Sthl 12f SD 3 100

DOVER STREET 3
Jun 15 Nott 8f GF 6 **102**

DOWER HOUSE 10
Jan 10 Wolv 9½f SD 1 **111**
Jan 28 Wolv 9½f SD 5 104
Feb 12 Wolv 12f FT 1 **111**
Feb 21 Ling 10f FT 4 102
Mar 8 Sthl 12f SD 1 101
Oct 17 Wind 10f G 9 100
Dec 21 Ling 10f G 1 102

DOWN MEXICO WAY 3
Jly 6 Naas 10f GF 4 **101**

DOWNLAND 9
May 16 Muss 7f G 6 99
Jun 23 Thsk 8f G 3 100
Jun 30 Yarm 7f G 1 **105**
Jly 7 Donc 7f GF 2 99
Jly 29 Thsk 7f G 9 100

DOYEN 5
Jun 18 York 12f G 5 105
Jly 23 Newb 12f GF 6 **108**
Aug 16 York 10½f G 6 105

DR KNOCK 7
Apr 10 Leop 12f GS 6 **105**

DR SHARP 5
May 4 Ches 18½f GS 10 101
Jun 4 Hayd 16f G 2 104
Sep 3 Hayd 14f GF 13 102
Sep 24 Hayd 14f GF 6 101
Oct 8 York 20f HY 2 **105**

DR SYNN 4
Aug 27 Gdwd 7f G 1 99
Oct 25 Yarm 7f S 6 **100**

DR THONG 4
Jly 18 Ayr 8f GF 3 104
Aug 3 Brig 8f G 6 104
Aug 11 Sand 7f GF 12 99
Aug 22 Wind 8½f G 5 100
Nov 10 Ling 8f SD 1 103
Nov 29 Ling 8f FT 5 **105**
Dec 9 Wolv 8½f FT 6 104

DRAGON FLYER 6
Feb 19 Wolv 5f FT 5 104
Mar 19 Ling 5f SD 6 100
May 28 Muss 5f G 8 **105**
Sep 29 NmkR 5f GF 7 99

DRAGON INN DANCER 4
May 25 Leop 7f GF 10 **101**

DRAGON SLAYER 3
Mar 2 Sthl 6f SD 1 100
Aug 3 Epsm 8½f G 1 100
Dec 12 Wolv 9½f FT 2 101
Dec 19 Wolv 9½f FT 2 **102**

DREADNOUGHT 3
Jun 27 Wolv 12f SD 6 **99**

DREAM CATCH 5
Nov 6 Leop 8f S 2 **105**

DREAM MAGIC 7
Jan 31 Wolv 9½f SD 3 **100**
Feb 17 Sthl 12f SD 3 **100**

DREAM MERCHANT 5
May 23 Wind 11½f GF 2 **101**
Jun 3 Hayd 14f G 4 99
Jly 23 Sals 14f G 5 **101**

DREAM OF DUBAI 4
Dec 29 Ling 8f G 5 **99**

DREAM TO DRESS 3
Jun 25 Curr 10f G 7 **111**
Sep 4 Curr 9f G 7 100
Oct 9 Curr 12f GS 6 99

DREAM TONIC 3
Jly 23 Sals 8f G 1 101
Aug 8 Thsk 8f G 1 100
Aug 19 Ayr 8f GF 1 **103**

DRURY LANE 5
Jly 18 Ayr 6f GF 1 **102**

DUBAI DREAMS 5
Jan 4 Wolv 9½f SD 2 99
Jan 13 Sthl 8f SD 1 **105**
Jan 18 Sthl 11f SD 1 101

DUBAI SUCCESS 5
Apr 16 Newb 12f GS 3 **112**
Apr 27 Ling 16f S 3 110
Jly 6 NmkJ 12f G 3 100
Jly 29 Gdwd 12f G 2 103
Aug 17 York 14f G 17 99
Sep 10 Donc 12f S 1 109
Sep 24 NmkR 16f G 5 110
Oct 22 Newb 12f G 7 101

DUBAI SURPRISE 3
Oct 11 Leic 8½f G 1 **107**

DUBAI VENTURE 3
May 20 NmkR 10f G 1 101
Jun 2 Sand 10f G 2 101
Aug 11 Bevl 10f GF 2 104
Sep 2 NmkJ 12f G 2 **108**

DUBAWI 3
Apr 30 NmkR 8f G 5 109
May 21 Curr 8f G 1 107
Jun 4 Epsm 12f G 3 108
Aug 14 Deau 8f GF 1 **117**
Sep 24 NmkR 8f G 2 114

DUC'S DREAM 7
Feb 8 Sthl 11f SD 7 99
May 18 Sthl 12f FT 1 **106**

DUCK ROW 10
Oct 1 NmkR 9f G 10 100
Oct 14 NmkR 8f G 9 **105**
Oct 29 NmkR 8f S 6 **105**

DUDLEY DOCKER 3
May 21 Carl 8f G 5 **102**
Jun 2 Brig 7f G 2 **102**
Jun 17 NmkJ 8f GF 1 100
Oct 24 Ling 8f SW 4 99

DUE RESPECT 5
Mar 20 Curr 8f HY 2 **114**
May 21 Curr 8f G 13 106

DUELLING BANJOS 6
Apr 19 Folk 9½f S 1 **102**
Dec 17 Ling 10f FT 4 100

DUKE OF VENICE 4
Sep 30 NmkR 12f G 6 **102**

DUKESTREET 4
May 8 Leop 8f S 12 **100**

DUMARAN 7
Mar 1 Ling 10f SD 8 **105**
Mar 26 Kemp 10f GS 4 **105**
Apr 20 Epsm 10f GS 9 101
May 4 Chep 10f S 4 99

DUMNONI 4
Mar 26 Kemp 8f GS 2 103
May 13 York 7f GS 2 106
Jun 6 Pont 8f GF 4 99
Sep 25 NmkR 7f G 7 **109**
Oct 30 Ling 8f SD 6 100

DUNASKIN 5
Mar 26 Kemp 10f GS 3 **106**
Aug 6 Hayd 10½f GF 12 101

DUNDONALD 6
Jan 7 Wolv 8½f SW 5 **104**
Feb 27 Wolv 7f SW 1 99

DUNDRY 4
Mar 28 Wwck 11f GS 5 99
May 1 Sals 14f GS 2 110
May 12 York 14f S 1 **111**
Jun 30 Hayd 14f GF 8 99
Sep 24 Hayd 14f GF 11 100

DUNE RAIDER 4
Jly 27 Leic 10f G 7 101
Aug 3 Pont 12f G 5 104
Aug 22 Haml 11f F 2 **105**
Sep 3 Thsk 12f G 2 101

DUNN DEAL 5
Apr 14 Ripn 5f S 3 99
May 6 Nott 6f G 3 100
Jun 8 Haml 5f G 3 100
Jun 23 Thsk 5f GF 5 99
Jun 29 Chep 6f G 2 105
Jly 18 Ayr 6f GF 3 100
Jly 23 Nowc 6f GF 1 106
Jly 29 Thsk 6f G 1 **107**
Aug 3 Yarm 6f G 8 101

DUROOB 3
Jun 25 Ches 12½f G 3 **101**
Aug 15 Nott 14f GF 5 100
Sep 3 NmkJ 15f G 4 100

DUSTY DAZZLER 5
Feb 5 Ling 5f G 9 **101**

DUSTY DIAMOND 5
Jun 1 Leop 16f G 6 **104**

DUTCH KEY CARD 4
Jan 4 Ling 5f FT 3 104
Jan 19 Ling 5f FT 1 100
Feb 12 Ling 6f SD 7 **105**

DVINSKY 4
Feb 19 Wolv 7f SD 2 105
Mar 16 Wolv 7f SD 4 100
Mar 21 Ling 6f SD 2 **106**
Apr 6 Ling 7f SD 2 102
May 23 Wind 6f F 4 101
May 27 Brig 7f GF 2 99
Jun 25 Donc 6f GF 8 99
Jly 22 Chep 7f G 2 101
Aug 11 Chep 8f G 3 100
Aug 19 Wolv 7f FT 6 99
Aug 24 Brig 7f S 2 100

DYNAH MO HUM 3
May 25 Leop 10f GF 4 **103**

E

EAGLE THYME 6
Jly 2 Leop 10f GF 2 **103**

EAMON AN CHNOIC 4
May 21 Curr 12f G 12 **101**

EARLSFIELD RAIDER 5
Apr 18 Pont 21½f S 3 101

EARLY MARCH 3
May 15 Lonc 8f G 5 **110**
Jun 12 Chan 8f GF 3 **110**

EASIBET DOT NET 5
Jly 11 Ayr 11f F 1 **107**
Aug 22 Haml 11f F 4 102

EAST CAPE 8
Jly 8 Wolv 14f FT 3 99
Jly 11 Wolv 14f SD 7 **100**

EASTBOROUGH 6
Jan 15 Ling 10f SD 4 99
Jan 31 Wolv 12f SD 1 99
Feb 12 Wolv 12f FT 6 106
Feb 21 Ling 10f FT 7 101
Apr 26 Wwck 12½f GS 1 **108**
Jun 19 Wwck 12½f G 2 101
Dec 9 Wolv 8½f FT 8 103
Dec 21 Ling 10f FT 10 99
Dec 26 Wolv 12f SD 7 101

EASTER OGIL 10
Feb 16 Ling 8f SD 3 103
Feb 22 Ling 10f SD 1 **106**
Nov 10 Ling 12f FT 11 99

EASTERN HOPE 6
Jan 6 Wolv 8½f FT 8 **99**

EASTERN MANDARIN 3
Jun 27 Muss 7f GF 3 **100**

EASY FEELING 3
Aug 4 Yarm 7f GF 3 **101**
Dec 30 Ling 6f FT 6 **101**

EASY LAUGHTER 4
Nov 12 Wolv 9½f FT 3 **101**

EASY MOVER 3
Jly 18 Bevl 10f G 3 100
Aug 6 NmkJ 8f G 3 **103**

EBAZIYAN 4
May 22 Curr 12f GS 8 **107**

EBONY SHADES 4
Jun 1 Leop 14f G 4 106
Jun 15 Leop 14f G 1 **107**

EBTIKAAR 3
Apr 27 Pont 10f GS 2 99
May 20 Hayd 12f G 1 99
Aug 31 York 12f G 2 106
Sep 30 NmkR 12f G 3 105
Oct 13 NmkR 12f G 1 **109**

ECCENTRIC 4
Jan 29 Ling 10f SD 1 99

Feb 1 Ling 8f SD 1 **116**
Feb 12 Ling 10f SD 2 109
Feb 26 Ling 10f SD 1 111
Mar 19 Ling 10f SD 1 **116**
Jun 3 Epsm 10f G 1 112
Jly 9 Ling 8f SD 9 108
Jly 26 Gdwd 10f G 6 104
Aug 6 Hayd 10½f GF 2 108
Aug 27 Wind 10f G 1 112
Sep 17 Newb 10f GF 8 110
Oct 15 NmkR 9f G 8 101

ECHELON 3
Apr 16 Newb 7f GS 3 101
May 1 NmkR 8f G 9 104
Jun 4 Hayd 6f G 3 100
Jly 2 Sand 8f G 2 106
Jly 22 Newb 8f G 1 106
Sep 25 NmkR 7f G 1 **114**

ECHO OF LIGHT 3
May 7 NmkR 8f GF 2 100
Aug 15 Yarm 11½f G 1 106
Sep 9 Donc 10½f G 1 **117**

ECLAIR D'IRLANDE 5
Nov 6 Leop 8f S 9 **100**

ECOMIUM 4
Mar 19 Ling 10f SD 6 **112**
Sep 9 Donc 10½f G 4 107
Sep 30 NmkR 8f G 7 101
Oct 28 NmkR 10f GS 2 109

EDAS 3
May 5 Folk 9½f GS 4 104
Jun 6 Folk 9½f G 1 **109**
Jly 21 Folk 9½f G 4 101
Aug 2 Brig 12f G 11 101
Aug 28 Gdwd 9f G 10 101

EDEN ROCK 4
May 18 Gdwd 8f G 1 105
Jun 15 York 8f G 12 100
Jly 2 Sand 8f G 8 **111**
Aug 18 York 8f G 4 109
Sep 10 Gdwd 9f G 13 102

EDGE FUND 3
Sep 13 Sals 7f G 5 **100**

EDGED IN GOLD 3
Jly 1 Wolv 5f G 1 **99**

EDGEHILL 4
Feb 16 Ling 10f SD 5 104
Mar 3 Ling 10f SW 6 105
Jly 25 Wind 11½f GS 4 99

EDIN BURGHER 4
Feb 16 Ling 8f SD 7 99
Dec 21 Ling 6f SD 1 **101**

EFFECTIVE 5
Apr 1 Ling 7f SD 5 99
Apr 15 Thsk 7f S 3 100
May 21 Ling 7f G 5 99
May 28 Ling 7f GF 3 101
Jun 17 Gdwd 6f G 1 99
Jun 23 Leic 5f GF 1 102
Jly 2 Carl 6f GF 1 107
Aug 12 Newc 6f GS 1 **110**

Aug 27 Gdwd 6f G 7 101

EFIDIUM 7
May 31 Rdcr 7f G 3 99
Jun 18 Rdcr 7f GF 2 **105**
Jly 2 Carl 7f GF 4 103
Jly 29 Thsk 7f G 7 101
Aug 7 Rdcr 8f G 3 99
Sep 13 Thsk 8f G 1 100

EFISTORM 4
Dec 20 Sthl 5f SD 3 **99**

EFORETTA 3
May 18 Sthl 7f FT 1 **99**

EFRHINA 5
Jan 3 Sthl 12f SD 1 104
Jan 5 Sthl 11f SD 1 100
Jan 14 Wolv 12f SW 2 **105**
Mar 17 Sthl 12f SW 5 101
May 9 Wolv 14f FT 1 104
Nov 15 Sthl 11f FT 1 **105**
Dec 15 Sthl 12f SD 7 101

EGERIA 3
Jly 5 Pont 12f G 5 **102**

EGO TRIP 4
Apr 20 Catt 12f S 5 **100**
Oct 8 York 14f S 2 99

EHSAN 3
May 22 Curr 10f GS 5 **100**

EIJAAZ 4
Jan 26 Ling 10f FT 1 103
Feb 5 Ling 10f FT 3 102
Mar 3 Ling 10f SW 4 **106**
Jly 20 Sand 10f G 4 99

EISTEDDFOD 4
Mar 28 Kemp 6f G 3 108
Apr 12 NmkR 7f GF 4 100
May 13 York 6f GS 5 105
May 28 Gdwd 6f G 1 105
Jun 25 Wind 6f G 1 110
Jly 31 Ches 6f G 2 109
Aug 28 Deau 6f G 1 **113**
Oct 2 Lonc 5f G 7 111

EKLIM 5
Sep 18 Curr 8f GF 6 105
Nov 6 Leop 7f GS 4 **107**

EL CHAPARRAL 5
Jan 29 Ling 10f SD 9 105
Mar 16 Wolv 9½f SD 1 **107**
May 23 Wind 11½f GF 3 101
Jun 16 Wolv 12f GF 1 100
Oct 1 Wolv 12f FT 2 105
Dec 3 Wolv 9½f FT 2 102

EL COTO 5
May 12 York 7f GS 6 **106**
May 28 Donc 7f G 1 **106**

EL PALMAR 4
Jan 3 Sthl 7f SD 2 102
Jan 11 Sthl 8f SW 4 **103**
Apr 26 Sthl 8f FT 1 **103**

EL POTRO 3
Nov 29 Sthl 5f SD 1 **103**
Dec 31 Wolv 5f SD 1 99

EL REY DEL MAMBO 3
Jly 2 Sand 7f G 4 **104**
Jly 27 Sand 7f GS 4 102
Aug 10 Sals 8f G 8 101

EL REY ROYALE 3
Jly 18 Bevl 10f G 2 **101**

ELA PAPAROUNA 4
Jun 25 NmkJ 8f G 4 101
Aug 25 Ling 7f FT 2 **102**

ELDORADO 4
Apr 3 Curr 10f S 6 **106**

ELECTROCUTIONIST 4
Aug 16 York 10½f G 1 **116**

ELEMENT OF TRUTH 3
May 7 NmkR 8f GF 1 102
Jun 18 Wwck 7f G 3 **108**
Sep 24 NmkR 8f G 12 104

ELGIN MARBLES 3
May 31 Leic 6f GF 4 **101**

ELIDORE 5
Jun 29 Chep 8f G 3 99
Jly 8 Chep 8f GF 6 100
Aug 11 Chep 8f G 1 **105**
Aug 18 Chep 8f GF 1 **105**
Sep 19 Leic 8½f G 8 100

ELISHA 3
Aug 21 Folk 5f G 5 **101**

ELIZABETHAN AGE 3
Sep 12 Folk 9½f GF 3 99
Oct 3 Pont 8f G 2 99
Oct 17 Wind 8½f G 2 **104**

ELKHORN 3
Oct 17 Wind 6f G 7 **100**

ELLE DONNE 3
Jun 27 Lonc 10½f G 7 **105**

ELLEN MOONEY 6
Feb 4 Wolv 8½f SD 6 **101**

ELLENS ACADEMY 10
Apr 30 NmkR 6f G 5 **110**
May 14 Thsk 5f G 2 105
Jun 1 Newc 6f G 3 102
Jun 25 Newc 6f G 2 109
Jly 16 Curr 5f F 5 109
Aug 16 York 6f GF 7 101
Sep 11 Carl 6f GF 9 99

ELLINA 4
Mar 30 Folk 12f HY 3 **104**
Apr 20 Ling 12f FT 5 99
Jly 11 Wolv 14f SD 1 103
Oct 10 Wolv 14f FT 1 102

ELLIOTS WORLD 3
Apr 20 Epsm 10f GS 2 102
May 21 Hayd 8f GF 9 103

Jun 3 Gdwd 8f GS 2 106
Jun 16 York 10½f G 3 101
Jly 6 NmkJ 10f G 3 106
Jly 29 Gdwd 8f G 4 **114**
Aug 18 York 8f G 2 111
Sep 9 Donc 8f G 1 108

ELLWAY HEIGHTS 8
Aug 11 Bevl 16f GF 1 **101**

ELMS SCHOOLBOY 3
Oct 11 Sthl 8f GF 1 **100**

ELOPA 4
Jun 25 Curr 10f G 3 **112**

ELOQUENT KNIGHT 3
Dec 6 Sthl 11f FT 5 **104**

ELRAAWY 3
Jly 5 NmkJ 10f G 2 **101**
Aug 22 Leic 12f G 1 **101**

ELRAFA MUJAHID 3
Feb 22 Ling 7f SD 4 100
May 10 Yarm 7f GF 1 100
Nov 15 Sthl 8f FT 1 **105**

ELSIE HART 3
May 13 York 7f GS 5 **101**

ELUSIVE DOUBLE 3
Sep 4 Curr 8f G 10 **105**

ELUSIVE DREAM 4
Sep 3 Hayd 14f GF 4 **106**
Oct 15 NmkR 18f G 5 103
Nov 5 Donc 16½f S 3 101

ELVINA 4
Jly 2 Hayd 5f GF 6 99
Aug 26 Thsk 5f GF 1 100
Sep 1 Sals 5f G 3 **101**
Nov 21 Sthl 5f G 3 99

ELVINA HILLS 3
Jun 2 Brig 7f G 4 **100**

ELVSTROEM 5
May 14 Newb 8f F 4 111
May 22 Lonc 9f GF 2 107
Jun 15 York 10½f G 3 108
Jun 26 StCl 12f GF 4 **115**

EMERALD BAY 3
Jun 3 Hayd 8f G 1 100
Jun 20 Nott 8f F 1 **106**
Jly 14 Donc 8f GF 3 99
Jly 24 Pont 10f G 3 103

EMERALD CAT 3
Sep 18 Curr 8f GF 9 **104**

EMERALD LODGE 3
Jun 10 Gdwd 6f GF 1 **101**

EMERALD STORM 3
Jun 27 Pont 10f G 1 **101**

EMILE ZOLA 3
May 16 Wind 11½f G 5 **101**

EMPANGENI 3
Jun 21 Newb 13½f G 1 **102**
Sep 28 Newc 16f GF 3 99

EMPEROR'S WELL 6
Aug 25 Muss 8f G 4 **104**
Sep 4 York 8f G 5 **104**
Sep 15 Pont 8f G 2 102

ENCHANTMENT 4
Jly 18 Ayr 5f GF 10 **99**

ENDLESS PEACE 4
Feb 28 Wolv 8½f SD 2 **99**

ENDLESS SUMMER 8
May 12 York 5f GS 11 99
Jun 2 Hayd 6f G 4 **103**
Sep 11 Gdwd 6f G 11 99
Oct 16 Muss 5f GF 8 101

ENFIELD CHASE 4
Jun 1 Leop 7f G 1 **111**
Jly 2 Leop 7f F 1 106
Sep 17 Curr 5f G 10 104

ENFORCER 3
Apr 2 Donc 7f G 4 100
Apr 15 Newb 8f GS 2 103
Apr 22 Sand 8f G 3 106
May 18 Gdwd 9f G 1 **110**
May 21 Hayd 8f GF 3 106
Jun 4 Epsm 10f G 1 106
Jun 16 York 8f G 13 101
Jly 6 NmkJ 10f G 9 99
Jly 28 Gdwd 10f G 1 107
Aug 20 Bevl 10f GF 3 104
Sep 21 Gdwd 10f G 2 108
Oct 15 NmkR 9f G 1 105

ENFORD PRINCESS 4
May 25 NmkR 7f G 7 101
Jly 14 Donc 7f GF 2 103
Aug 6 NmkJ 8f G 6 101
Aug 22 Wind 8½f G 2 **105**
Oct 1 Epsm 7f GS 3 102

ENGLISH VICTORY 3
Aug 31 Ling 12f GS 4 **99**

ENJOY THE BUZZ 6
Jly 7 Folk 5f G 4 **106**

ENNISTOWN LADY 6
May 21 Curr 12f G 7 105

ENTAILMENT 3
Jun 27 Wind 8½f G 2 **106**
Dec 9 Wolv 14f FT 7 99

EQDAAM 3
May 21 Ling 10f GS 5 99
Aug 10 Sals 8f G 5 **102**

EQUILIBRIA 3
Oct 20 Brig 12f GS 2 **102**

ERASER 3
Jun 5 Chan 10½f G 13 100
Jly 2 Hayd 12f GF 2 101
Sep 11 Lonc 12f G 4 **109**

ERMINE GREY 4
Jan 28 Wolv 9½f SD 6 104
Feb 18 Wolv 8½f SD 2 **106**
Apr 1 Donc 8f G 4 103
Jly 8 Chep 8f GF 10 99
Jly 25 Wind 10f GS 4 101
Jly 27 Leic 10f G 3 103

ESCAYOLA 5
Sep 15 Yarm 16f GS 5 **104**
Oct 15 NmkR 18f G 8 102
Oct 30 Ling 16f SD 5 101

ESCOBAR 4
Mar 21 Ling 10f SD 6 100
Mar 31 Ling 10f SD 6 **104**

ESPERANCE 5
Mar 31 Ling 10f SD 1 **108**

ESPRIT DE CORPS 3
Dec 30 Ling 10f FT 6 **99**

ESSEX STAR 4
May 6 Nott 6f G 2 **100**

ESTABLISHMENT 8
Aug 6 NmkJ 16f G 4 102
Sep 10 Gdwd 16f G 3 100
Oct 28 NmkR 16f GS 4 **104**

ESTEPONA 4
Apr 13 Bevl 10f G 4 104
Jun 8 Bevl 10f G 2 100
Jly 2 Bevl 10f G 2 99
Jly 10 Hayd 10½f GF 2 99
Aug 4 Hayd 12f GF 1 99
Nov 5 Donc 12f S 3 **105**

ESTOILLE 4
Jly 9 Nott 5f F 5 **99**

ESTRELLE 3
Jun 30 Yarm 11½f G 2 101
Oct 3 Wind 11½f GF 4 99
Oct 28 NmkR 12f GS 5 **102**

ESWARAH 3
Apr 15 Newb 10f GS 1 101
Jun 3 Epsm 12f G 1 **107**
Jly 23 Newb 12f GF 8 102
Aug 17 York 12f G 4 **107**

ETCHING 5
Oct 9 Newc 12½f G 2 **99**

ETESAAL 5
Apr 30 NmkR 10f G 1 101
Jun 17 York 10½f G 11 102
Jly 2 Hayd 12f GF 10 103
Aug 29 Epsm 10f G 1 **109**
Sep 21 Gdwd 10f G 1 **109**

ETLAALA 3
May 31 Sand 5f G 7 107
Jun 18 York 6f GF 7 106
Jly 7 NmkJ 6f G 3 **110**
Sep 3 Hayd 6f F 6 104
Sep 25 NmkR 6f G 10 105
Oct 15 NmkR 7f G 8 106

ETOILE RUSSE 3
Sep 20 Bevl 8½f GF 3 **99**

ETON 9
Jly 5 Pont 10f G 1 **102**

ETTRICK WATER 6
May 28 Gdwd 8f G 6 102
Aug 6 NmkJ 7f G 5 **111**
Aug 20 Ches 7½f G 7 99

EUROLINK ROOSTER 7
Apr 10 Leop 7f GS 1 **105**

EUROPAEA 6
Jun 1 Leop 7f G 15 **108**

EVALUATOR 4
Apr 1 Donc 8f G 6 101
Apr 23 Sand 8f G 11 100
Jun 24 NmkJ 10f G 2 106
Jly 26 Gdwd 10f G 1 **108**
Sep 17 Newb 10f GF 12 **108**
Oct 1 NmkR 9f G 2 **108**

EVER CHEERFUL 4
Jan 6 Wolv 7f G 1 99
Jly 7 Folk 5f G 7 100
Sep 17 Wolv 7f FT 3 99
Dec 5 Ling 7f FT 1 **102**
Dec 17 Ling 5f FT 2 100
Dec 20 Ling 6f FT 4 100

EVEREST 8
Jun 11 Ripn 8f G 6 100
Jly 5 NmkJ 8f G 6 102
Jly 24 Newb 8f G 4 101
Aug 12 NmkJ 8f G 1 105
Sep 2 NmkJ 8f G 1 **108**
Sep 16 Ayr 8f G 7 100
Sep 30 NmkR 8f G 9 101

EVOLUTION EX 3
May 7 Hayd 10½f S 2 100
May 23 Wind 10f GF 1 99
Jun 4 Epsm 10f G 4 **103**
Jly 8 Ches 10½f F 3 102
Sep 18 Haml 8½f F 6 99

EXCUSEZ MOI 3
Apr 4 Yarm 7f G 1 105
Jun 3 Epsm 7f G 3 108
Jun 11 Ripn 6f G 8 102
Jly 5 NmkJ 6f G 13 102
Jly 23 Newb 7f GF 9 **110**
Aug 13 NmkJ 6f G 2 103
Aug 27 York 6f G 4 106

EXHIBIT ONE 3
Jly 15 Wwck 11f G 2 **105**
Aug 12 Catt 12f G 1 99

EXMOOR 3
Jun 1 Nott 6f G 2 **102**
Aug 5 Hayd 6f F 7 **102**

EXPLOSIVE FOX 4
Mar 7 Ling 16f SD 7 **104**
Jun 18 Rdcr 14f G 3 99

EXTEMPORISE 5
Nov 4 Yarm 6f S 7 **100**

EXTREME BEAUTY 3
Jly 19 Yarm 7f G 1 100
Aug 14 Bath 8f G 10 **102**

EXTREMELY RARE 4
Jly 25 Wind 6f G 2 99
Aug 1 Wind 6f G 1 103
Aug 26 Bath 5f G 1 **105**
Aug 29 Wwck 6f GF 2 102
Sep 9 Sand 5f G 3 102
Oct 17 Wind 6f G 1 103

EZZ ELKHEIL 6
Feb 28 Wolv 12f SD 2 **99**

F

FABRIAN 7
Jun 29 Chep 8f G 1 101
Jly 8 Chep 8f GF 3 104
Jly 15 NmkJ 8f G 3 99
Aug 1 Wind 8½f GS 1 105
Aug 13 Gdwd 10f G 4 103
Aug 27 Wind 8½f G 6 **110**
Sep 9 Sand 7f GS 2 100
Sep 19 Leic 8½f G 2 106

FACTUAL LAD 7
Jun 15 Chep 10f GS 3 **103**
Aug 29 Epsm 10f G 8 101

FAIR ALONG 3
Feb 10 Sthl 11f SD 1 102

FAIR COMPTON 4
Apr 8 Ling 6f SD 5 **102**
May 27 Brig 6f GF 1 99
Jly 12 Brig 6f G 5 99

FAIR SHAKE 5
Apr 15 Thsk 7f S 1 104
May 23 Thsk 8f G 2 99
Jun 8 Haml 8½f G 2 **108**
Jly 30 Thsk 8f G 3 107

FAIR SPIN 5
Apr 9 Newc 12½f S 3 100

FAIRGAME MAN 7
Aug 6 Ling 6f G 3 **99**
Aug 26 Newc 6f GF 1 **99**

FAIRLIE 4
Jun 27 Pont 8f G 1 **107**
Aug 17 Carl 8f GF 8 99
Sep 5 Newc 10f G 1 103
Oct 9 Newc 10f G 5 104

FAIRMILE 3
Sep 9 Sand 10f GS 1 **102**
Oct 3 Wind 11½f GF 1 **102**

FAIRY MONARCH 6
May 23 Bevl 10f G 3 99
May 24 Nott 8f G 2 **101**
Jun 29 Catt 12f G 6 **101**
Aug 26 Newc 9f GF 12 100

FAIRY OF THE NIGHT 3
Sep 18 Curr 8f GF 4 **106**

FAIRY PASS 4
May 22 Curr 6f G 4 104
Jun 26 Curr 6½f GF 7 99
Jly 16 Curr 5f F 9 **106**
Aug 14 Leop 6f G 4 99
Oct 23 Curr 6f S 8 103

FALEH 3
Aug 28 Gdwd 7f G 3 **100**

FALSTAFF 3
May 12 York 10½f S 3 **106**

FANTAISISTE 3
May 29 NmkR 6f GF 2 101
Jun 18 NmkJ 7f G 3 100
Aug 31 Ling 7f G 2 103
Sep 17 Newb 7f GF 2 **106**
Sep 30 Ling 7f FT 7 99

FANTASY BELIEVER 7
May 28 Donc 7f G 5 103
Jun 25 Newc 6f G 5 104
Jun 30 Epsm 6f G 1 107
Jly 5 Pont 6f G 3 107
Jly 15 Haml 6f F 2 102
Jly 23 York 6f G 6 102
Jly 30 Gdwd 6f G 3 109
Sep 7 Donc 5½f GF 13 104
Sep 17 Ayr 6f G 5 **111**

FANTASY CRUSADER 6
Jun 13 Brig 10f G 2 **100**

FANTASY DEFENDER 3
Jun 27 Muss 7f GF 1 **101**
Dec 5 Wolv 8½f GF 2 99

FANTORINI 3
May 7 Ling 10f G 4 101
Aug 10 Sand 10f GF 1 100
Oct 10 Wind 10f G 1 **102**

FAR NOTE 7
Dec 6 Sthl 6f FT 1 **100**

FAR PAVILIONS 6
Apr 6 Catt 14f G 1 100
May 14 Nott 14f F 1 101
May 28 Muss 14f G 1 104
Jun 25 Newc 16f G 3 **110**

FAREWELL GIFT 4
Aug 11 Sand 7f GF 7 **105**
Aug 29 Epsm 8½f G 2 101

FARNBOROUGH 4
Jun 1 Wolv 8½f FT 1 99
Jun 9 Wolv 12f SD 2 **101**
Jun 16 Wolv 8½f SD 3 **101**
Jly 25 Wind 11½f GS 3 **101**
Aug 1 Wind 11½f GS 3 **101**

FARRIERS CHARM 4
Jun 27 Wind 8½f G 3 **103**

FASHION HOUSE 3
Jly 1 Hayd 8f G 4 **103**

FASHIONABLE 3
Apr 13 NmkR 8f G 1 100
May 1 NmkR 10f G 1 101

Aug 10 Sals 10f G 7 **102**

FAST HEART 4
Mar 19 Ling 5f SD 2 105
Apr 20 Epsm 5f GS 6 106
Apr 30 NmkR 5f G 6 **108**
May 21 Hayd 5f F 2 101
Jun 4 Epsm 5f G 9 100
Jun 24 Newc 5f G 8 105
Jly 2 Sand 5f G 6 101
Jly 9 Ling 5f SD 5 99
Aug 6 Hayd 5f G 10 105
Sep 7 Donc 5½f GF 12 104

FASYLITATOR 3
Jly 8 Wolv 8½f FT 1 102
Sep 1 Sals 8f G 2 100
Oct 12 Ling 10f G 1 105
Dec 5 Ling 8f FT 1 **107**

FAVOURABLE TERMS 5
Sep 8 Donc 7f G 1 **114**

FAVOURITA 3
Apr 13 NmkR 7f G 3 **106**
May 1 NmkR 8f G 12 101
Jun 8 Newb 10f GF 3 99
Sep 14 Yarm 10f G 4 104
Sep 24 NmkR 8f G 15 100

FAYR JAG 6
Jun 14 York 5f G 8 101
Jly 16 Newb 6f GF 4 114
Jly 31 Ches 6f G 3 107
Aug 18 York 5f GF 6 110
Sep 3 Hayd 6f F 5 104
Sep 13 Yarm 6f G 2 105
Sep 25 NmkR 6f G 2 **116**
Oct 1 Rdcr 7f GF 7 106

FEARLESS SPIRIT 3
Jly 5 NmkJ 10f G 5 99
Aug 11 Chep 12f G 1 **105**

FEAST OF ROMANCE 8
Feb 26 Sthl 7f FT 1 100
Mar 28 Yarm 6f GS 2 **101**

FEED THE METER 5
May 11 Newc 12½f G 1 101
May 17 Leic 12f G 4 102
May 19 Donc 12f F 1 103
May 23 Wind 11½f GF 1 102
May 27 Pont 12f GF 1 101
Jun 4 Donc 12f GF 3 105
Jun 17 NmkJ 12f GF 3 **108**
Jun 24 NmkJ 12f G 2 101

FEN GAME 3
Jly 30 NmkJ 12f GF 1 **99**

FEN SHUI 3
May 1 NmkR 8f G 10 **103**

FERRARA FLAME 3
Feb 10 Sthl 11f SD 4 **100**

FEU INDIEN 4
Mar 28 StCl 8f GS 5 **109**

FICTIONAL 4
May 7 Bevl 5f GF 3 100
May 12 York 5f GS 9 100
Jun 24 Newc 5f G 3 **108**
Jly 8 York 5f G 3 101
Jly 16 NmkJ 5f GF 1 99
Aug 6 Hayd 5f G 14 103
Aug 16 York 6f GF 1 105

FIDDLERS CREEK 6
Jan 17 Wolv 8½f SD 1 **111**
Feb 5 Ling 12f SD 9 100
Feb 12 Wolv 12f FT 9 102
May 1 Haml 8½f S 2 102

FIEFDOM 3
May 21 Hayd 8f GF 4 **106**

FIELD SPARK 5
Jan 10 Wolv 12f SD 2 102
May 17 Leic 12f G 3 102
May 30 Leic 12f G 3 **104**
Jly 11 Wolv 14f SD 4 101

FIELDS OF JOY 4
Sep 4 Curr 8f G 4 110
Sep 10 Leop 9f GF 1 110
Sep 17 Curr 8f GF 1 **111**

FIGARO'S QUEST 3
Sep 20 Brig 12f G 2 **99**

FIGHT YOUR CORNER 6
May 30 Sand 16½f G 1 **102**

FILEY BUOY 3
Nov 28 Sthl 7f SD 1 **102**

FILLAMEENA 5
Jun 20 Chep 12f G 3 103
Jly 7 Wwck 12½f G 4 **106**
Jly 11 Wolv 14f SD 2 102
Aug 31 Ling 16f SD 4 100

FINAL OPINION 5
May 8 Leop 12f S 3 **108**

FINAL PROMISE 3
Apr 26 Wwck 7f GS 3 **107**
Jly 7 Wwck 8f G 1 103
Aug 28 Gdwd 9f G 11 100

FINALMENTE 3
Aug 28 Yarm 14f G 1 **105**

FINE SILVER 4
Apr 16 Newb 8f GS 1 100
Apr 23 Sand 8f G 12 100
May 12 York 7f GS 7 **103**
Jun 3 Epsm 8½f G 11 99
Jun 17 York 10½f G 13 102
Aug 6 Wind 8½f GF 8 102

FINISHED ARTICLE 8
May 2 Donc 10½f G 9 **102**

FIRE FINCH 4
Sep 4 Curr 10f G 10 **100**

FIRE UP THE BAND 6
May 6 Ches 5f GS 1 109
May 12 York 5f GS 8 101
Jun 4 Epsm 5f G 1 109
Jun 18 York 6f GF 10 100
Jun 26 Curr 5f GF 4 109
Jly 9 Ches 5f GF 3 109
Jly 28 Gdwd 5f G 1 **113**
Aug 18 York 5f GF 13 106
Oct 2 Lonc 5f G 3 112

FIRENZE 4
Jun 2 Hayd 6f G 3 **103**
Jun 11 Leic 6f G 1 101
Aug 16 York 6f GF 6 102
Sep 29 NmkR 6f GF 3 101

FIRESONG 3
Aug 17 Nott 10f G 2 **104**
Oct 8 Sals 8f GF 7 99

FIREWORK 7
Jly 16 Ling 6f G 1 **103**

FIRST BALLOT 9
May 7 NmkR 12f GF 3 **104**
May 30 Sand 16½f G 7 99

FIRST DYNASTY 5
Apr 13 Bevl 10f G 5 101
Apr 26 Wwck 12½f GS 3 **105**

FIRST FOUGHT 3
May 20 Hayd 8f G 2 99

FIRST OF MAY 4
Dec 29 Ling 8f G 8 **99**

FIRST RHAPSODY 3
Jun 27 Pont 6f G 3 **105**

FIRST ROW 3
Apr 7 Leic 12f S 1 100
May 5 Ches 12½f GS 3 **102**
Sep 1 Sals 14f G 5 **102**

FIRST SHOW 3
Aug 31 York 8f G 4 **108**
Oct 17 Wind 8½f G 1 106
Oct 28 NmkR 8f GS 2 100

FISBERRY 3
Jun 2 Hayd 6f G 1 **105**
Jun 20 Wind 6f G 1 103

FISBY 4
Jan 12 Wolv 8½f SD 4 101
Feb 12 Ling 10f SD 1 104
Feb 25 Wolv 9½f SD 2 99
Mar 3 Ling 10f SW 1 **108**
Oct 1 Wolv 8½f FT 3 100
Oct 14 Brig 12f G 2 100

FIT THE COVE 5
Jun 1 Leop 8f G 7 **104**
Sep 10 Leop 7f HD 13 99

FIVE FIELDS 3
Oct 13 NmkR 10f G 8 **99**

FIVEOCLOCK EXPRESS 5
Jan 6 Wolv 12f G 9 100
Jan 14 Wolv 9½f SW 1 **107**
Jan 31 Wolv 9½f SD 2 101
Mar 1 Ling 10f SD 5 101
Jun 13 Brig 10f G 1 102
Aug 3 Brig 10f G 4 100

FIZA	**6**					
Apr	3	Curr	16f	HY	7	**101**

FIZZLEPHUT	**3**					
Jun	3	Hayd	5f	G	1	**101**

FLAG LIEUTENANT	**3**					
Apr	25	Haml	11f	G	2	**100**

FLAG OF TRUCE	**3**					
Aug	27	NmkJ	8f	G	3	**100**

FLAG POINT	**3**					
Jun	11	Bath	11½f	G	3	**99**

FLAMBOYANT LAD	**4**					
May	14	Newb	12f	G	1	**111**
Jly	2	Hayd	12f	GF	11	101
Aug	6	Hayd	10½f	GF	4	107

FLAMING EYES	**4**					
Jan	14	Wolv	12f	SW	3	**102**

FLAMJICA	**4**					
Aug	6	NmkJ	8f	G	10	**99**

FLARAN	**5**					
Sep	5	Bath	5½f	GF	9	**100**

FLASH RAM	**4**					
Jun	1	Newc	8f	G	1	**106**
Jun	14	Carl	8f	GS	1	104
Jly	1	Bevl	8½f	G	3	105

FLEECE	**3**					
Aug	22	Leic	12f	G	2	**100**

FLIGHT OF ESTEEM	**5**					
Aug	3	Pont	12f	G	3	**105**
Aug	13	NmkJ	12f	G	5	100
Sep	23	Ling	12f	G	3	103

FLIGHTY FELLOW	**5**					
May	28	Donc	7f	G	6	**102**
Jun	7	Rdcr	8f	G	5	99
Aug	6	Hayd	8f	GF	6	100

FLINT RIVER	**7**					
Jan	29	Ling	8f	SD	7	**108**
Feb	10	Sthl	7f	SD	3	102
Apr	2	Kemp	7f	GS	1	107
May	18	Gdwd	7f	G	3	103
Jun	22	Epsm	7f	G	4	101
Jly	8	Chep	7f	GF	3	105
Aug	3	Brig	8f	G	10	101
Aug	11	Sand	7f	GF	11	100
Aug	27	NmkJ	6f	G	5	103
Sep	3	NmkJ	6f	G	9	103
Oct	7	Newb	7f	GF	5	101

FLIPANDO	**4**					
Apr	1	Donc	8f	G	2	104
Aug	6	Rdcr	8f	G	5	107
Aug	18	York	8f	G	5	**109**
Aug	29	Ripn	8f	G	6	105
Oct	1	Rdcr	8f	GF	2	100
Oct	7	York	8f	G	3	107

FLITE OF ARABY	**8**					
Feb	14	Wolv	9½f	G	7	99
Mar	4	Wolv	8½f	SD	2	**101**

FLORIDA HEART	**4**					
May	21	Ling	8f	SD	4	**104**

FLOTTA	**6**					
Apr	11	Ling	12f	SD	2	102
Jun	4	Donc	12f	GF	1	106
Jun	12	Sals	12f	G	7	103
Jly	1	Sand	14f	G	3	104
Sep	16	Newb	11f	G	4	**107**

FLUR NA H ALBA	**6**					
Jly	15	Pont	5f	GF	3	101
Jly	24	Pont	6f	G	4	105
Aug	17	Nott	5f	GF	1	**107**

FLUSHING MEADOWS	**4**					
May	25	NmkR	7f	G	8	**100**

FLY MORE	**8**					
Jun	15	Chep	6f	GS	1	**106**

FLY TO DUBAI	**3**					
May	7	Bevl	8½f	GS	2	99
May	12	Carl	8f	G	1	103
Jun	1	Wolv	8½f	FT	3	101
Jun	9	Ripn	8f	G	1	**106**
Jun	20	Nott	8f	F	3	103

FLYING BANTAM	**4**					
Apr	18	Pont	6f	S	1	103
Apr	23	Ripn	6f	S	5	99
May	21	Catt	7f	GF	7	102
Jun	7	Ches	7f	GF	4	102
Aug	1	Ripn	6f	G	5	103
Aug	12	Newc	6f	GS	6	102
Sep	6	Catt	7f	GF	5	100
Sep	25	Muss	7f	G	3	**105**
Oct	10	Wolv	7f	FT	5	99
Oct	20	Brig	6f	GS	5	102
Oct	29	NmkR	7f	S	5	103

FLYING DANCER	**3**					
Jly	4	Bath	5f	G	2	**99**

FLYING EDGE	**5**					
May	17	Rdcr	6f	G	3	101
Jun	23	Haml	6f	G	1	101
Jly	20	Catt	6f	G	3	**104**
Aug	17	Carl	7f	GF	2	99
Sep	24	Ripn	6f	GF	1	100

FLYING SPIRIT	**6**					
Aug	2	Brig	12f	G	5	104

FLYING TACKLE	**7**					
Jun	21	Bevl	5f	G	2	101
Jly	12	Bevl	5f	GF	1	**102**
Aug	26	Newc	5f	GF	4	100

FOCUS GROUP	**4**					
Sep	30	NmkR	8f	G	1	**108**

FOLEY MILLENNIUM	**7**					
Feb	11	Wolv	5f	SD	1	107
Feb	26	Ling	5f	SD	1	107
Apr	2	Kemp	5f	GS	2	109
Jun	7	Ches	5f	GF	4	104
Jly	6	NmkJ	5f	GF	3	102
Jly	15	Wwck	5½f	G	1	105
Jly	29	Nott	5f	G	3	104
Aug	20	Ches	5f	G	1	**110**
Aug	23	Yarm	5f	G	1	108
Sep	6	Leic	5f	GF	1	106

FOLGA	**3**					
Apr	12	Muss	5f	G	5	101
May	13	Nott	6f	F	2	100
May	20	Bath	5f	G	1	99
Jun	11	Sand	5f	G	2	99
Jun	22	Carl	5f	GF	2	**103**
Jun	24	NmkJ	5f	G	2	99
Jly	21	Donc	6f	GF	2	**103**
Jly	29	Gdwd	5f	G	6	100
Aug	17	York	5f	F	1	**103**
Aug	27	York	6f	G	9	100

FOLIO	**5**					
Jan	8	Ling	8f	SD	6	102
Jan	29	Ling	8f	SD	6	**109**
Feb	22	Ling	7f	SD	6	104
Mar	12	Wolv	7f	SD	7	102
Sep	2	NmkJ	8f	G	2	107
Oct	5	Nott	10f	G	2	108
Oct	17	Wind	10f	G	11	99

FOLLOW MY LEAD	**3**					
Aug	15	Wind	8½f	GF	1	100
Aug	27	Wind	8½f	G	3	**101**

FOLLOWING FLOW	**3**					
Jan	5	Ling	8f	SD	8	99
Jan	21	Wolv	8½f	SD	2	103
May	27	Pont	8f	GF	2	101
Oct	29	Wolv	9½f	SD	10	100
Dec	9	Wolv	8½f	FT	5	**106**

FONTHILL ROAD	**5**					
Apr	13	Bevl	5f	G	1	106
May	6	Ches	5f	GS	2	108
May	13	York	6f	GS	2	109
May	28	Muss	5f	G	7	106
Jun	26	Curr	6½f	GF	5	101
Jly	30	Gdwd	6f	G	2	**112**
Aug	20	Bevl	5f	G	7	101
Sep	17	Ayr	6f	G	2	**112**

FOODBROKER FOUNDER	**5**					
Oct	17	Wind	10f	G	3	102

FOOLISH GROOM	**4**					
May	4	Chep	8f	S	3	**103**
May	21	Hayd	8f	GF	2	99
Aug	5	Hayd	8f	F	1	100
Sep	4	York	8f	G	9	100

FOOTBALL CRAZY	**6**					
Aug	2	Catt	14f	G	2	107

FOOTSTEPSINTHESAND	**3**					
Apr	30	NmkR	8f	G	1	**112**

FOR SCARLETT	**3**					
Jun	4	Donc	5f	G	4	**101**

FOREIGN AFFAIRS	**7**					
Aug	12	NmkJ	12f	G	2	105
Oct	9	Curr	12f	GS	2	**106**

FOREIGN EDITION	**3**					
Apr	2	Donc	6f	G	1	**107**
Apr	14	NmkR	7f	G	7	102

FOREST DANE	**5**					
Feb	23	Ling	7f	G	8	**100**

Oct 3 Brig 5½f G 1 **100**

FOREST OF LOVE 3
Jly 5 Wolv 8½f FT 2 **101**
Jly 13 Ling 8f SW 5 100
Sep 3 Wolv 7f FT 1 99

FOREST VIKING 3
May 23 Bevl 10f G 2 **99**

FORESTIER 5
Apr 30 Lonc 15½f GS 9 107
May 22 Lonc 15½f GF 4 **111**
Aug 21 Deau 15f G 5 109
Oct 23 Lonc 15½f GS 7 108

FOREVER MY LORD 7
Aug 3 Brig 12f G 1 **99**

FOREVER PHOENIX 5
Jan 1 Sthl 5f FT 4 104
May 14 Nott 6f F 2 105
May 28 Muss 5f G 11 102
Jun 24 NmkJ 6f G 4 102
Jly 9 Ling 5f SD 3 101
Jly 18 Ayr 5f GF 4 104
Jly 24 Newb 5f G 6 **109**
Jly 31 Ches 6f G 7 101
Aug 6 Hayd 5f G 3 107

FORFEITER 3
Jun 11 Sand 7f G 10 **99**

FORGERY 3
Apr 22 Sand 10f G 2 **102**
May 14 Newb 11f G 6 101

FORMAL APPROVAL 3
Jun 8 Bevl 7½f G 3 **100**
Oct 4 Catt 12f GF 5 99
Nov 3 Muss 12f GS 3 99

FORMIDABLE WILL 3
Oct 13 Sthl 8f SD 1 101
Oct 18 Sthl 8f SD 1 **105**

FORREST GUMP 5
Jun 27 Muss 12f G 6 **99**

FORT DIGNITY 4
Apr 13 NmkR 9f G 4 108
May 9 Wind 8½f GF 1 **111**
May 22 Lonc 9f GF 7 101

FORTUNE ISLAND 6
Mar 26 Kemp 16f S 5 103
Jly 6 NmkJ 16f G 1 102
Jly 12 Bevl 16f GF 3 101
Oct 28 NmkR 16f GS 2 **107**

FORTUNES FAVOURITE 5
Jan 14 Wolv 12f SW 5 **100**
Aug 5 Ling 10f GS 3 **100**

FORWARD MOVE 3
Apr 14 NmkR 8f G 6 99
May 6 Ches 10½f GS 4 106
Jly 1 Sand 10f G 2 **108**
Jly 30 Gdwd 8f G 1 107
Sep 30 NmkR 8f G 8 99

FOSSGATE 4
Oct 11 Leic 10f G 1 **101**

FOUR AMIGOS 4
Apr 15 Thsk 5f S 2 **100**
Jun 18 Ayr 5f G 4 99

FOURSQUARE FLYER 3
Jun 25 Donc 10½f GF 3 **101**

FOX 3
Aug 29 Wwck 7f GF 2 **107**
Oct 1 Rdcr 7f GF 8 100
Oct 27 Ling 7f SD 13 101

FOXHAVEN 3
May 21 Hayd 8f GF 10 102
Jun 2 Sand 10f G 4 100
Jun 26 Wind 10f G 2 104
Jly 6 NmkJ 10f G 5 101
Jly 27 Gdwd 12f GS 1 **106**

FOXY GWYNNE 3
Jun 15 Chep 8f GS 2 103
Jun 30 Newb 10f G 3 **104**

FRACAS 3
Apr 10 Leop 10f S 1 100
Apr 22 Sand 10f G 1 102
May 8 Leop 10f S 1 107
Jun 4 Epsm 12f G 4 **108**

FRACASSANT 4
May 9 Lonc 12f G 1 117
Jun 5 Chan 12f G 2 **118**

FRALOGA 3
Jly 14 Lonc 12f F 2 112
Oct 1 Lonc 15f G 2 **113**

FRANCIS CADELL 3
Jan 26 Ling 6f FT 2 **105**
Mar 19 Ling 7f SD 2 103

FRANCIS FLUTE 7
Apr 6 Catt 7f G 2 **101**

FRANK SONATA 4
Apr 6 Nott 14f GS 2 111
Apr 16 Newb 12f GS 2 **112**
May 13 York 14f GS 7 104
Aug 27 Wind 11½f G 3 105
Sep 30 NmkR 12f G 4 105
Oct 22 Newb 12f G 5 103

FRANK'S QUEST 5
Aug 22 Wolv 8½f G 2 **100**

FRANKLINS GARDENS 5
Apr 27 Ling 16f S 2 **112**
May 13 York 14f GS 1 110

FRANKSALOT 5
Apr 20 Ling 6f FT 2 100
May 22 Brig 7f G 4 99
Jun 30 Epsm 7f G 2 103
Aug 17 Epsm 7f G 3 103
Sep 8 Epsm 7f G 4 104
Sep 13 Sals 7f G 6 100
Dec 30 Ling 6f FT 1 **105**

FRASCATI 5
Apr 15 Thsk 5f S 4 99
May 28 Muss 5f G 6 100
Jly 4 Muss 5f GF 4 102
Jly 9 Nott 5f F 3 103
Jly 30 Haml 5f F 2 104
Aug 20 Ches 5f G 2 103
Aug 25 Muss 5f G 3 102
Sep 9 Donc 5f G 8 104
Sep 18 Haml 5f F 2 **106**
Oct 16 Muss 5f GF 5 102
Nov 16 Sthl 5f FT 6 103
Dec 6 Sthl 5f FT 5 103

FRATERNITY 8
Feb 6 Wolv 8½f SD 1 100
Feb 15 Sthl 8f FT 1 101
Feb 21 Wolv 8½f FT 1 101
Feb 27 Wolv 6f FT 1 102
Mar 2 Sthl 8f SD 2 100
Mar 24 Wolv 8½f SD 1 **105**

FREAK OCCURENCE 4
May 26 Bath 10f G 1 99
May 31 Leic 10f G 3 100
Oct 19 Bath 8f GS 4 **101**
Oct 25 Yarm 10f S 8 99

FREE ANGEL 3
Oct 24 Wolv 7f SD 1 **101**

FREE LIFT 3
Jun 11 Sand 7f G 9 99
Jly 5 NmkJ 7f G 7 **101**
Jly 18 Wind 6f G 1 100

FREE STYLE 5
Jan 6 Wolv 12f G 5 **105**
Apr 28 Ling 13f FT 1 99
Jly 6 Ling 12f SW 1 104
Nov 12 Ling 12f FT 4 99

FREE WHEELIN 5
May 5 Folk 6f G 6 **101**
Aug 6 Ling 6f G 4 99

FREEFALL 4
Feb 25 Wolv 12f G 5 **99**

FREELOADER 5
May 31 Sand 8f G 1 **110**
Jun 22 Sals 8f G 2 104
Aug 6 Wind 8½f GF 3 106
Aug 19 Sand 8f GS 3 101
Sep 10 Gdwd 9f G 6 106
Sep 23 Ling 10f G 9 102
Oct 8 Sals 8f GF 5 100

FRENCH MANNEQUIN 6
Feb 18 Wolv 12f SD 1 **102**
Mar 16 Wolv 16½f SD 1 100
Mar 30 Folk 12f HY 5 100
Apr 19 Sthl 16f GF 6 100
May 16 Bath 13f G 2 99
Aug 6 Rdcr 14f G 5 100

FRENCHMANS LODGE 5
Apr 19 Brig 5½f G 3 99
Jun 10 Chep 6f G 2 **100**

FRIEDHELMO 9
May 3 Catt 12f GS 4 99

Jly 28 Carl 14f GS 1 **103**
Aug 11 Bevl 16f GF 5 99

FRIENDS HOPE 4
Feb 28 Wolv 8½f SD 1 100
Mar 8 Sthl 7f SD 4 100
May 20 Bath 10f G 2 101
Dec 20 Ling 10f G 7 **102**

FROMSONG 7
Apr 2 Kemp 5f GS 7 104
May 6 Ling 5f G 3 106
Jun 12 Sals 5f G 1 110
Jun 23 Sals 5f G 2 102
Jly 29 Nott 5f G 4 104
Aug 6 Hayd 5f G 4 107
Aug 20 Sand 5f GS 7 99
Oct 30 Ling 6f SD 1 **112**
Nov 12 Ling 5f FT 1 105
Dec 2 Wolv 6f SD 7 104
Dec 17 Ling 6f FT 2 108

FRONT STAGE 3
Jun 26 Wind 10f G 1 **105**
Aug 31 York 12f G 7 101

FRONTIER 8
Jun 15 Chep 10f GS 4 103
Jly 9 Ches 10½f GF 1 99

FRONTLINEFINANCIER 5
Mar 13 Wolv 14f FT 1 100
Mar 26 Wolv 14f FT 2 **102**
Jly 7 Folk 16½f G 1 100

FRUHLINGSSTURM 5
May 5 Ches 10½f G 5 106
Jun 3 Epsm 10f G 13 102
Aug 27 Wind 10f G 3 110
Sep 17 Ayr 10f G 1 **111**

FRUIT OF GLORY 6
May 15 Ripn 6f G 1 103
Jun 4 Epsm 5f G 4 104
Jun 24 NmkJ 6f G 3 103
Jly 18 Ayr 5f GF 2 107
Jly 30 Gdwd 6f G 12 105
Aug 14 Pont 6f G 1 **113**
Aug 29 Epsm 5f G 11 101
Sep 17 Newb 5f GF 10 100

FU MANCHU 3
Apr 30 NmkR 10f G 3 **103**

FUEL CELL 4
Mar 1 Ling 10f SD 3 102
May 6 Ling 8f SD 4 100
Jun 27 Wind 8½f G 6 100
Aug 20 Ling 10f SD 1 **103**

FUERTA VENTURA 3
Oct 10 Wind 11½f G 4 **100**

FULL OF ZEST 3
Aug 18 Wolv 8½f SD 4 **103**
Oct 29 Wolv 9½f SD 4 99

FULL SPATE 10
May 5 Chep 6f GS 6 **103**
Jun 2 Hayd 6f G 6 99
Jun 9 Ripn 6f G 1 100
Jun 25 Wind 6f G 3 99

Aug 5 Hayd 6f F 1 99

FULLANDBY 3
Apr 23 Wolv 9½f SD 2 105
Jly 29 NmkJ 6f G 2 105
Aug 19 Ayr 6f GF 1 103
Sep 11 Gdwd 6f G 8 102
Oct 16 Muss 5f GF 2 **106**
Oct 28 NmkR 6f GS 1 **106**

FULVIO 5
Jan 12 Ling 8f SD 2 99
May 11 Brig 7f G 4 **103**

FUN TO RIDE 4
Jly 22 York 5f G 6 **101**
Sep 15 Pont 6f G 3 99

FUNFAIR WANE 6
May 7 Bevl 5f GF 2 **102**
Sep 7 Donc 5½f GF 18 100

FURTHER OUTLOOK 11
Apr 2 Kemp 5f GS 5 **106**
Apr 20 Epsm 5f GS 10 103
May 6 Ling 5f G 6 105
May 16 Wind 6f G 2 99
Jun 6 Wind 5f G 4 102
Jly 31 Newb 5f G 2 103
Aug 27 NmkJ 6f G 6 102
Sep 14 Sand 5f GS 1 **106**

FUSS 4
Jly 25 Yarm 16f GS 1 **101**
Aug 8 Thsk 16f G 3 99

FUTOO 4
Jun 2 Haml 9f GS 1 103
Jun 8 Haml 8½f G 5 103
Jun 20 Ripn 10f G 3 **104**

FUTURE DEAL 4
Jly 11 Wolv 7f SD 5 **101**

FYODOR 4
Sep 14 Bevl 5f G 2 101
Oct 1 Rdcr 5f GF 1 104
Oct 29 Wolv 6f SD 1 103
Nov 12 Ling 5f FT 2 103
Dec 6 Sthl 5f FT 1 **108**

G

GABOR 6
Jly 22 Chep 16f G 3 102
Aug 11 Bevl 16f GF 2 100

GAELIC PRINCESS 5
Jan 8 Ling 8f SD 3 102
Jan 29 Ling 8f SD 3 **111**
Feb 18 Wolv 8½f SD 8 105
Jun 12 Sals 7f G 1 102
Jly 5 NmkJ 8f G 9 100
Jly 23 Sals 7f G 1 101
Aug 12 NmkJ 7f G 4 101
Sep 1 Sals 7f G 6 99
Oct 1 Wolv 8½f FT 5 99
Oct 31 Wolv 8½f SD 5 103
Dec 5 Ling 8f FT 6 100

GAFF 3
Jun 8 Leop 7f G 4 **106**

GALA EVENING 3
May 20 Hayd 10½f G 2 **99**

GALA SUNDAY 5
Jun 29 Catt 12f G 3 **103**

GALEOTA 3
Apr 16 Newb 7f GS 3 106
Jun 3 Epsm 7f G 1 110
Jun 18 York 6f GF 2 **116**

GALLANT BOY 6
Jly 14 Epsm 12f G 1 100
Jly 15 Wwck 12½f G 1 **101**

GALLANTRY 3
Jun 18 Wwck 7f G 1 101
Jly 20 Sand 7f G 4 **106**

GALLEGO 3
Apr 18 Wolv 8½f FT 2 99
Jly 2 Hayd 8f GF 2 **102**
Jly 7 Wwck 8f G 2 **102**
Jly 13 Hayd 8f G 2 **102**

GALLERY BREEZE 6
Jan 31 Wolv 9½f SD 1 **103**
Jun 5 Bath 8f G 2 102
Jun 15 Haml 9f GS 1 100
Jun 22 Carl 9½f GF 3 102
Aug 13 Ripn 10f GS 1 **103**

GALLEY LAW 5
Apr 25 Sthl 8f FT 1 **99**
Nov 9 Wolv 12f FT 5 **99**

GAMBLING SPIRIT 3
Sep 30 Ling 13f FT 1 **101**

GAME GURU 6
Mar 17 Sthl 12f FT 1 **105**
Mar 29 Wwck 11f S 3 102

GAME LAD 3
Jun 25 NmkJ 6f G 2 103
Jly 12 Bevl 7½f GF 3 100
Aug 27 NmkJ 7f G 11 99
Sep 24 Ripn 10f GF 4 104
Oct 3 Pont 8f G 3 104
Oct 16 Muss 7f G 1 104
Oct 29 NmkR 7f S 1 **111**

GAMUT 6
May 1 NmkR 12f G 2 103
Jun 18 York 12f G 3 **111**
Jly 6 NmkJ 12f G 1 108
Jly 23 Newb 12f GF 9 102
Aug 13 Newb 13½f G 5 101
Sep 17 Curr 14f G 5 102

GANDALF 3
Jly 1 Wolv 12f G 1 **104**
Sep 2 Hayd 12f G 6 99

GANYMEDE 4
May 28 Donc 12f GF 2 **102**

GARDEN SOCIETY 8
Mar 12 Wolv 16½f SD 2 99

Aug 12 Newb 13½f G 1 107
Aug 20 Ches 13½f G 8 102
Sep 15 Yarm 16f GS 1 107
Oct 30 Ling 16f SD 1 **108**

GARIBALDI 3
Feb 12 Ling 8f SD 2 101
Nov 10 Ling 12f SD 1 **102**

GARNETT 4
Mar 7 Ling 16f SD 1 **107**

GARPLE BURN 3
May 28 Ling 12f SW 3 **99**

GARRIGON 4
Jan 1 Sthl 11f SD 2 **100**
Jan 15 Ling 10f SD 6 **100**

GAUDALPIN 3
Dec 21 Ling 6f SD 2 **100**

GAVEMERS 4
Jun 1 Leop 7f G 6 **108**

GAVROCHE 4
Jun 7 Ches 10½f GF 2 102
Jly 23 York 10½f GS 1 105
Aug 13 Gdwd 10f G 3 104
Aug 29 Epsm 10f G 1 **110**
Sep 8 Epsm 10f G 1 105
Oct 22 Newb 10f G 11 103
Dec 31 Wolv 9½f SD 4 104

GEM BIEN 7
Apr 4 Sthl 8f SD 1 100
Jly 11 Wolv 8½f SD 1 **102**
Jly 28 Carl 9½f G 7 99

GEMS OF ARABY 3
May 7 Ling 10f G 2 **102**

GENERAL FEELING 4
May 31 Sand 8f G 7 101
Oct 17 Wind 6f G 5 100
Oct 29 Wolv 7f SD 4 99
Nov 26 Ling 6f FT 1 99
Dec 10 Wolv 7f FT 1 100
Dec 30 Ling 6f FT 2 **104**

GENERAL FLUMPA 4
Apr 26 Wwck 12½f GS 7 103
May 21 Catt 14f GF 6 100
Jly 7 Wwck 12½f G 1 **108**

GENERATOR 3
Nov 16 Sthl 6f FT 2 **99**

GENEROUS OPTION 3
Jun 25 Newc 7f G 7 99
Aug 17 Epsm 7f G 5 **102**

GENTLE PEACE 4
Nov 9 Wolv 12f FT 1 **102**
Dec 12 Wolv 9½f FT 5 99

GEORDIELAND 4
May 9 Lonc 12f G 2 116
Jun 5 Chan 12f G 1 **119**
Jun 26 StCl 12f GF 8 105
Sep 11 Lonc 12f G 5 113

GEORGINA 3
May 22 Curr 8f G 3 **106**

GERMANICUS 3
Jly 13 Catt 12f GF 1 **100**

GESTURE 3
Jun 27 Lonc 7f G 6 **101**

GHARIR 3
May 15 Lonc 8f G 3 **112**
Jun 5 Chan 10½f G 4 103

GHURRA 3
May 1 NmkR 7f G 7 102
May 19 Donc 7f GF 2 103
Jun 3 Epsm 7f G 6 99
Jun 25 NmkJ 8f G 5 101
Jly 14 Donc 7f GF 4 100
Jly 27 Gdwd 9f GS 2 103
Aug 12 Folk 9½f G 5 **104**

GIBRALTAR BAY 3
Jan 6 Wolv 9½f G 1 100
Jan 17 Wolv 9½f SD 1 99
Mar 23 Ling 12f SD 5 104
Apr 25 Wind 11½f GS 1 101
May 16 Wind 11½f G 2 **105**
May 31 Sand 14f G 3 101

GIFT HORSE 5
May 2 Donc 6f G 1 102
May 13 York 6f GS 3 108
Jun 4 Epsm 6f G 1 108
Jly 30 Gdwd 6f G 1 **113**

GIFT RANGE 3
Oct 9 Curr 12f GS 5 **102**

GIFTED FLAME 6
Jly 2 Carl 7f GF 2 **105**
Jly 6 Carl 7f G 1 101
Jly 26 Bevl 8½f G 3 100

GIFTED GAMBLE 3
Apr 7 Leic 6f S 2 **112**
May 11 York 7f GS 3 99
Jun 3 Epsm 7f G 5 106
Aug 27 York 6f G 7 101

GIG HARBOR 6
Jan 22 Ling 12f FT 1 106
Feb 5 Ling 12f FT 5 101
Feb 26 Ling 10f SD 2 108
Mar 4 Wolv 12f SD 1 100
Mar 19 Ling 10f SD 10 **111**
Jly 9 Ling 16f SD 11 107

GILBERTO 4
May 8 Leop 8f S 10 **105**
Nov 6 Leop 12f S 3 100

GILDED COVE 5
Feb 12 Ling 6f SD 5 **106**
Apr 2 Wolv 6f FT 1 101
Apr 28 Sthl 5f FT 1 104
Aug 19 Wolv 6f FT 2 101
Oct 18 Sthl 5f SW 3 99
Nov 12 Wolv 5f FT 1 100
Nov 25 Wolv 5f FT 2 100
Dec 2 Wolv 6f SD 2 100

GIMASHA 3
Jly 2 Bevl 5f G 1 107
Jly 15 Wwck 6f GF 1 99
Aug 6 Wind 6f GF 1 **108**
Aug 27 York 6f G 11 99
Sep 23 Ling 6f G 1 107

GINGER SPICE 3
Jly 24 Newb 8f G 1 **99**

GINGKO 8
Feb 16 Ling 10f SD 1 **107**
Dec 21 Ling 10f SD 5 101

GIOCOSO 5
Jun 17 Gdwd 8f G 1 **111**
Jly 8 Chep 7f GF 6 102

GIRLSWEEKEND 3
Apr 19 Folk 5f GS 4 **103**

GITCHE MANITO 3
Jly 15 Wwck 11f G 4 **101**
Jly 31 Ches 10½f G 3 99

GIUNCHIGLIO 6
Mar 7 Wolv 12f SD 6 **108**
Jly 11 Ayr 11f F 6 103
Dec 29 Ling 10f F 10 100

GIVE ME FIVE 4
Aug 21 Deau 10f G 9 **104**

GIVEN A CHANCE 4
May 30 Leic 12f G 5 99

GIVEN A CHOICE 3
Apr 29 Muss 9f G 4 101
May 30 Rdcr 11f G 1 103
Jly 17 Rdcr 11f G 1 **104**
Sep 7 Donc 10½f GF 7 **104**

GJOVIC 4
May 13 Newb 10f GF 2 100
Jun 6 Wind 10f G 3 100
Jun 30 Hayd 8f GF 5 99
Aug 3 Epsm 10f G 2 **109**
Aug 11 Hayd 10½f GF 3 103

GLARAMARA 4
Jan 20 Sthl 7f SD 2 **109**
Feb 1 Ling 8f SD 6 106
Feb 3 Sthl 6f SD 1 105
Feb 10 Sthl 7f SD 4 100
Mar 31 Donc 6f G 6 100
Apr 30 NmkR 6f G 20 102
May 6 Ches 7½f GS 6 102
Jun 25 Donc 6f GF 2 106
Jly 5 Pont 6f G 8 100
Aug 5 Hayd 6f F 4 104

GLAZED FROST 3
Mar 28 StCl 8f GS 5 **105**

GLEN IDA 3
Mar 28 Kemp 9f G 1 **106**
Apr 22 Sand 10f G 5 99
Aug 27 York 9f G 4 105

GLEN INNES 4
Jan 7 Wolv 8½f SW 2 **115**

GLENCAIRN STAR 4
Jan 6 Wolv 6f SW 2 102
Feb 19 Wolv 7f SW 5 101
Jun 2 Hayd 6f G 2 **104**
Jun 13 Thsk 6f G 3 101

GLENCALVIE 4
Aug 6 Ling 6f G 3 100
Sep 13 Sals 7f G 4 100
Oct 3 Wind 8½f GF 1 106
Nov 10 Ling 8f SD 3 100
Dec 5 Ling 8f FT 3 106
Dec 30 Ling 8f FT 1 **107**

GLENDALE 4
Jan 22 Ling 10f FT 2 101
Feb 1 Ling 10f SD 5 100
Feb 12 Ling 12f SD 3 99
Mar 21 Ling 10f SD 1 102
Mar 31 Ling 10f SD 3 **106**

GLENREE 4
Dec 3 Wolv 8½f SD 2 **100**

GLISTENING 3
Jun 25 Wind 11½f G 5 104
Aug 18 York 14f G 2 **108**
Sep 3 Hayd 14f GF 6 106
Sep 29 NmkR 14f GF 5 104

GLOBAL ACHIEVER 4
Jan 13 Ling 6f SD 5 **101**
Feb 18 Wolv 6f SD 11 99
Feb 26 Ling 5f SD 7 100
Dec 21 Ling 6f SD 4 99

GLOBALIZED 3
Jly 2 Leop 10f GF 2 **100**

GLOIREZ 4
Apr 30 Lonc 15½f GS 3 **114**
May 22 Lonc 15½f GF 5 109

GLOVED HAND 3
Jly 4 Ripn 6f G 1 101
Aug 14 Pont 6f G 7 **106**
Sep 10 Muss 8f G 4 105
Oct 30 Ling 8f SD 8 99

GO FREE 4
May 17 Ling 13f SD 1 99
Jun 29 Chep 12f G 2 **103**
Aug 4 Chep 12f G 5 100

GO GARUDA 4
Feb 9 Ling 8f G 3 **100**
May 25 Ling 8f SD 2 99

GO GREEN 4
May 5 Chep 12f S 1 **101**

GO MO 3
Jun 6 Folk 6f G 1 104
Jly 20 Sand 7f G 1 **108**
Jly 27 Sand 7f GS 6 99
Aug 6 Wind 6f GF 10 99
Oct 20 Brig 6f GS 4 102
Oct 30 Ling 6f SD 6 107

GO PADERO 4
Jun 18 Ayr 7f G 3 **105**
Jly 9 York 8f G 7 100
Jly 23 Newb 7f GF 15 **105**

GO SOLO 4
May 21 Carl 8f G 6 101
Jun 17 Rdcr 8f G 1 103
Jun 28 Haml 8½f F 2 101
Jly 17 Rdcr 8f G 1 103
Jly 30 Haml 9f F 1 **107**
Aug 10 Haml 9f F 3 104
Aug 30 Ripn 10f F 3 103
Sep 17 Ayr 10f G 4 100

GO TECH 5
May 20 Hayd 8f G 7 104
May 30 Rdcr 10f G 11 101
Jun 11 Ripn 9f G 8 101
Jun 18 Rdcr 10f G 1 108
Aug 6 Hayd 10½f GF 8 106
Aug 11 Bevl 10f GF 6 100
Aug 17 York 10½f G 5 107
Sep 22 Pont 10f G 1 **113**
Nov 19 Ling 12f FT 4 102
Nov 29 Ling 10f FT 8 106

GO THE DISTANCE 3
May 25 Leop 8f GF 6 **102**

GOLANO 5
Feb 19 Wolv 12f GF 1 **107**
Oct 17 Wind 10f G 7 101

GOLBAND 3
Jly 17 Rdcr 5f G 8 99
Aug 10 Yarm 6f GF 2 **104**
Sep 28 Ling 6f SD 1 **104**

GOLD GUEST 6
Jan 14 Wolv 9½f SW 1 99
Mar 3 Ling 10f SW 11 102
Apr 4 Wolv 9½f FT 2 101
May 3 Catt 12f GS 1 102
Jun 1 Yarm 11½f G 6 99
Jly 8 Chep 8f GF 7 100
Jly 21 Bath 10f GF 1 100

GOLD GUN 3
Oct 4 Leic 12f G 3 **104**

GOLD HERITAGE 3
Aug 4 Hayd 10½f GF 6 99
Oct 5 Nott 10f G 3 **100**

GOLD QUEEN 3
Apr 2 Kemp 9f S 3 **100**

GOLD RING 5
May 11 York 12f S 4 105
Jun 4 Epsm 12f G 11 101
Jun 25 Newc 16f G 9 108

GOLD SOUND 3
Apr 10 Lonc 10½f S 2 107
Jun 5 Chan 10½f G 10 101
Aug 20 Deau 10f GS 5 **113**
Sep 17 Lonc 10f G 9 101

GOLDEN ANTHEM 3
Apr 13 NmkR 7f G 12 100
Jun 18 Wwck 7f G 9 **104**

GOLDEN APPLAUSE 3
Aug 8 Wind 8½f GF 2 102
Aug 20 Sand 8f G 1 **104**

GOLDEN ASHA 3
Jun 1 Nott 5f G 2 100
Jly 12 Brig 6f G 1 **109**
Aug 20 Rdcr 6f G 2 101
Aug 28 Yarm 5f G 2 103
Sep 14 Bevl 5f G 1 103
Sep 22 Pont 5f G 1 104
Oct 17 Pont 5f G 2 101
Nov 3 Muss 5f GS 8 99

GOLDEN CHALICE 6
Aug 6 Wind 8½f GF 7 103

GOLDEN CHANCE 8
Aug 12 Catt 12f G 5 **100**

GOLDEN CROSS 6
Nov 6 Leop 16f S 1 111

GOLDEN DIXIE 6
Jan 21 Wolv 6f SD 1 108
Feb 18 Wolv 6f SD 7 102
May 20 Gdwd 5f G 1 103
Jun 2 Sand 5f G 1 106
Jun 7 Sals 6f G 3 101
Jun 18 NmkJ 6f G 6 99
Jun 30 Epsm 6f G 5 103
Jly 15 Wwck 5½f G 4 104
Jly 22 Newb 6f G 8 99
Aug 10 Sand 5f GF 2 104
Sep 9 Donc 5f G 2 **114**
Sep 16 Ayr 6f GF 3 101
Sep 21 Gdwd 6f GF 5 104

GOLDEN FURY 3
Jly 28 Epsm 8½f G 2 99
Aug 8 Wind 8½f GF 4 102
Sep 7 Epsm 8½f G 1 **105**

GOLDEN GATE 3
Jun 9 Brig 12f G 3 **99**

GOLDEN GRIMSHAW 3
Jun 25 Ches 10½f G 1 102
Aug 7 Curr 10f G 1 **110**

GOLDEN ISLAND 4
Jun 6 Pont 8f GF 3 101
Jun 23 Haml 8½f G 2 **106**
Aug 20 Sand 8f G 2 100

GOLDEN LEGACY 3
Apr 13 NmkR 7f G 6 **104**
May 1 NmkR 8f G 11 101

GOLDEN MEASURE 5
May 21 Catt 14f GF 2 **104**

GOLDEN QUEST 4
Jun 4 Hayd 16f G 1 106
Jly 9 Ling 16f SD 2 114
Jly 26 Gdwd 14f G 1 108
Jly 28 Gdwd 16f G 2 **116**

GOLDEN SPECTRUM 6
Feb 4 Wolv 8½f SD 9 99
Apr 6 Catt 7f G 3 100
Apr 13 Bevl 8½f G 1 **102**
Apr 21 Bevl 7½f S 3 99
Jly 3 Brig 8f G 1 99

Oct 24 Wolv 7f SD 2 99
Nov 28 Sthl 7f SD 2 100

GOLDEN SQUARE 3
May 11 Brig 8f G 2 100
Jly 7 Wwck 8f G 3 99
Oct 6 Sthl 8f G 2 **101**

GOLDEVA 6
May 11 York 6f S 5 108
Jun 1 Leop 6f G 7 108
Aug 14 Pont 6f G 3 **111**
Sep 25 NmkR 6f G 13 105

GOLDHILL PRINCE 3
Mar 7 Ling 5f SD 3 **104**

GOLDSTAR DANCER 3
Jly 4 Muss 9f GF 7 **100**

GOLO GAL 3
Dec 30 Ling 10f FT 7 **99**

GOLOVIN 8
Aug 7 Curr 16f G 11 **102**

GONE FISHING 3
Aug 27 Wind 8½f G 1 **103**

GONE TOO FAR 7
Jun 27 Muss 16f G 1 102

GONE'N'DUNNETT 6
Jan 1 Sthl 6f SD 1 99
Jan 13 Ling 6f SD 3 103
Feb 11 Wolv 5f SD 10 99
Feb 12 Ling 6f SD 10 100
Mar 4 Wolv 6f SD 7 99
Mar 21 Ling 6f SD 7 100
Apr 4 Yarm 5f G 1 **105**
Apr 20 Ling 6f FT 3 99
May 6 Ling 5f G 9 99
Jly 23 Newc 6f GF 6 99
Aug 3 Yarm 6f G 6 103
Dec 2 Wolv 6f SD 2 100
Dec 17 Ling 5f FT 5 99

GONFILIA 5
Oct 30 Ling 8f SD 7 **100**

GOOD MORNING ALL 3
Jun 15 Leop 8f GF 4 **99**

GOOD SURPRISE 4
Sep 10 Leop 10f GF 2 **102**

GOODBYE MR BOND 5
May 2 Kemp 8f G 5 100
May 19 Donc 8f GF 4 99
May 25 Ripn 8f G 3 **108**
Jun 22 Carl 8f GF 2 104
Jun 30 Hayd 8f GF 3 101
Jly 13 Hayd 8f G 2 106
Jly 30 Donc 10½f G 2 104
Aug 17 York 10½f G 8 103
Sep 7 Donc 10½f GF 10 103
Sep 18 Haml 8½f F 3 102
Sep 23 Hayd 8f G 6 101
Oct 8 York 9f GS 2 104
Oct 29 NmkR 8f S 3 107

GOODENOUGH MOVER 9
May 7 NmkR 6f GF 6 101
Jun 11 Bath 5½f G 1 102
Jun 25 Wind 6f G 10 103
Aug 27 Gdwd 6f G 10 99
Sep 11 Carl 6f GF 8 100
Sep 28 Sals 6f G 2 100
Oct 30 Ling 6f SD 3 **109**
Nov 15 Ling 7f FT 1 108

GOODRICKE 3
May 1 Sals 6f G 1 106
Jun 3 Epsm 7f G 2 108
Jun 30 Newb 6f G 1 106
Jly 23 Newb 7f GF 2 114
Aug 7 Deau 6½f G 2 **116**
Sep 3 Hayd 6f F 1 108

GOODWOOD SPIRIT 3
May 5 Chep 8f GS 3 100
Jun 16 Newb 8f G 1 **104**
Jly 26 Gdwd 8f G 5 102
Aug 17 Epsm 7f G 4 102
Oct 8 Sals 8f GF 3 101

GOOSE CHASE 3
Apr 16 Nott 8f GS 1 **103**

GORELLA 3
Jun 5 Chan 8f GF 1 113
Jly 31 Deau 8f G 3 114
Sep 4 Lonc 8f GF 2 **117**

GORTUMBLO 3
May 7 Ling 6f G 5 **103**

GRACEFUL AIR 4
Apr 29 Muss 9f G 3 101
Jun 22 Carl 9½f GF 1 **105**

GRAHAM ISLAND 4
Aug 2 Catt 14f G 1 **108**
Aug 26 Thsk 16f GF 5 103

GRAMADA 3
Dec 12 Wolv 9½f FT 3 **101**

GRAMPIAN 6
Apr 2 Donc 12f G 4 107
Apr 27 Ling 16f S 6 103
May 23 Thsk 12f G 1 106
Jun 18 York 12f G 6 102
Jly 2 Hayd 12f GF 4 107
Aug 17 York 14f G 3 **108**
Sep 3 Hayd 14f GF 5 106

GRANARY GIRL 3
Oct 5 Nott 10f G 1 99
Oct 15 Ling 10f SD 1 **100**

GRAND BAHAMA 3
Apr 10 Lonc 10½f S 5 **101**

GRAND CENTRAL 3
Apr 10 Leop 8f S 2 100
May 8 Leop 10f S 3 **106**
Jun 4 Epsm 12f G 9 102
Jun 26 Curr 8f F 7 99

GRAND DISPLAY 4
Jly 2 Leop 12f GF 4 **105**

GRAND EMPORIUM 5
May 14 Newb 8f F 7 **110**
Jun 4 Epsm 8½f G 3 105

GRAND IDEAS 6
Jan 13 Ling 8f SD 2 101
Mar 18 Ling 8f SD 3 **103**

GRAND OPENING 3
Aug 2 Deau 10f G 10 **108**

GRAND PASSION 5
Mar 19 Ling 10f SD 9 **111**
May 5 Ches 10½f G 7 102
May 31 Sand 10f G 4 110
Jly 1 Sand 10f G 4 106
Jly 16 Newb 10f GF 4 109

GRAND SEIGNEUR 3
Jan 22 Ling 10f FT 1 **101**

GRAND VIEW 9
Apr 15 Wolv 6f SD 1 **99**

GRANDE ROCHE 3
Oct 9 Bath 10f G 2 **106**
Dec 19 Wolv 8½f FT 2 101

GRANDE TERRE 4
Jly 1 Bevl 7½f G 1 **101**
Jly 4 Ripn 8f G 1 100
Jly 11 Ayr 8f F 7 99
Sep 10 Muss 8f G 8 99
Sep 19 Carl 8f G 7 99

GRANDMA LILY 7
Jan 11 Sthl 8f SW 6 **102**
Mar 4 Wolv 6f SD 8 100

GRANGEHILL DANCER 4
May 8 Leop 8f S 8 **107**

GRANSTON 4
Apr 1 Donc 8f G 5 102
May 2 Kemp 8f G 2 103
May 17 Bevl 8½f GF 2 104
Jun 7 Rdcr 8f G 3 103
Jly 9 York 8f G 6 104
Aug 29 Ripn 8f G 1 **110**
Oct 1 Rdcr 8f GF 3 99
Oct 29 NmkR 8f S 9 99

GRASP 3
Aug 15 Nott 14f GF 7 **99**
Sep 27 Gdwd 16f G 4 **99**
Oct 19 Bath 17f GS 1 **99**

GRAVARDLAX 4
Jan 22 Ling 10f FT 4 **101**

GRAZE ON 3
Sep 11 Carl 6f GF 7 **101**
Oct 9 Bath 5½f G 1 100

GREAT BRITAIN 3
Aug 26 Newc 7f GF 1 102
Sep 16 Newb 7f GF 4 **105**

GREAT FOX 4
Sep 13 Yarm 5f G 1 101
Sep 21 Gdwd 6f GF 9 **102**

GREAT ORATOR 3
- Oct 10 Wind 10f G 2 103
- Oct 22 Newb 10f GS 3 **104**

GREAT PLAINS 3
- Apr 30 Gdwd 7f S 1 **112**
- May 21 NmkR 8f G 3 102
- Sep 14 Yarm 10f G 7 101

GREAT VIEW 6
- May 27 Pont 12f GF 2 100
- Jun 30 Newb 11f G 7 **102**
- Jly 26 Bevl 12f G 5 100

GREEN FALCON 4
- Jun 21 Bevl 12f G 2 **101**

GREEN GIRL 3
- Mar 28 StCl 8f GS 1 **110**
- May 1 StCl 10½f F 3 103
- May 22 Lonc 10f GF 5 102
- Jun 12 Chan 10½f G 8 103

GREEN MANALISHI 4
- Jly 29 Nott 5f G 5 103
- Aug 10 Sand 5f GF 1 105
- Aug 13 Newb 5f G 1 101
- Aug 20 Sand 5f GS 4 102
- Sep 3 Hayd 5f F 2 109
- Sep 7 Donc 5½f GF 8 106
- Sep 24 Hayd 5f GF 1 **110**
- Oct 13 NmkR 5f G 8 100
- Dec 2 Wolv 6f SD 4 106
- Dec 17 Ling 6f FT 4 105

GREEN NOON 4
- Jly 1 Sand 10f G 3 **107**
- Jly 31 Newb 12f G 6 102
- Sep 24 NmkR 8f G 13 102

GREEN PIRATE 3
- Jan 14 Wolv 7f SW 1 **103**

GREENBELT 4
- Dec 22 Sthl 8f SD 2 99
- Dec 27 Sthl 8f SD 1 **101**

GREENHALL RAMBLER 6
- Jun 1 Leop 14f G 1 **110**

GREENSLADES 6
- May 7 Ling 7f G 8 101
- Jun 2 Hayd 6f G 2 105
- Jun 25 Wind 6f G 4 **107**
- Jly 29 NmkJ 6f G 1 **107**
- Aug 27 Gdwd 6f G 2 106
- Sep 24 Hayd 6f GF 4 102
- Oct 27 Ling 7f SD 7 105

GREENWICH MEANTIME 5
- Mar 31 Donc 12f G 1 101
- Apr 6 Catt 14f G 2 99
- Jun 6 Pont 17f GF 4 100
- Jly 10 Hayd 14f GF 2 102
- Jly 22 York 14f G 5 **107**

GREENWOOD 7
- Jan 26 Ling 7f FT 3 100
- Feb 12 Ling 6f SD 4 **106**
- May 18 Gdwd 7f G 2 105
- Jun 3 Gdwd 7f GS 7 102
- Jun 13 Wwck 7f GF 4 102
- Oct 10 Wind 6f G 1 100
- Oct 17 Wind 6f G 3 102

GREY BOY 4
- Jly 2 Nott 8f GF 1 **106**
- Sep 13 Sals 8f G 3 104

GREY CLOUDS 5
- Jun 21 Bevl 10f G 4 **101**

GREY COSSACK 8
- May 30 Leic 6f G 3 **101**
- Jun 25 Donc 6f GF 7 99

GREY PLOVER 3
- Oct 19 Newc 12½f GS 1 **103**
- Nov 1 Catt 14f GS 2 99

GREY SWALLOW 4
- Jly 23 Newb 12f GF 7 106
- Sep 10 Leop 10f GF 6 **110**

GREZIE 3
- Mar 3 Ling 8f SW 5 **102**

GRIGOROVITCH 3
- May 16 Wind 5f G 3 100
- Aug 25 Muss 5f G 1 104
- Sep 9 Donc 5f G 6 **106**
- Sep 16 Ayr 5f GF 1 104
- Oct 1 Epsm 5f G 3 **106**
- Oct 16 Muss 5f GF 4 103

GRINGO 3
- Jun 20 Nott 8f F 1 **104**
- Aug 10 Sand 10f GF 2 99
- Oct 25 Yarm 10f S 6 101

GRISCHA 3
- Jun 27 Lonc 10½f G 8 **104**

GRIZEDALE 6
- May 18 Gdwd 7f G 4 **102**
- Aug 11 Sand 7f GF 10 101
- Oct 8 Sals 7f GF 2 **102**

GROSVENOR SQUARE 3
- Sep 10 Gdwd 9f G 12 **102**
- Oct 1 NmkR 10f G 7 100

GROUP CAPTAIN 3
- Mar 19 Ling 10f SD 1 100
- Jly 2 Sand 10f G 1 99
- Jly 11 Wind 11½f G 4 102
- Jly 30 Gdwd 11f G 1 104
- Aug 20 Bevl 10f GF 8 100
- Oct 22 Donc 12f S 1 **107**
- Nov 5 Donc 12f S 5 100

GROWLER 4
- May 21 Carl 8f G 1 **104**

GRUMPYINTMORNING 6
- Mar 23 Ling 7f SD 2 **99**

GUADALAJARA 4
- Oct 1 Lonc 12½f G 3 **111**

GUADALOUP 3
- May 23 Thsk 7f G 2 **102**
- Jly 30 Thsk 7f G 2 100

GUEST ARTIST 5
- Apr 3 Curr 10f S 7 **105**
- Aug 7 Curr 10f G 14 100

GUILDENSTERN 3
- May 7 Ling 6f G 1 **106**
- May 21 NmkR 6f G 3 103
- Jun 3 Epsm 7f G 2 103
- Jly 5 NmkJ 6f G 16 99

GULF 6
- May 14 Newb 13½f G 2 **100**

GUNS BLAZING 6
- Aug 13 NmkJ 5f GS 3 **100**

GURRUN 3
- Mar 23 Ling 12f SD 2 105
- Jun 9 Brig 12f G 1 102
- Jun 17 NmkJ 12f GF 1 **109**

GUSTAVO 4
- Apr 23 Leic 10f G 1 101

GYPSY FAIR 3
- Mar 2 Sthl 6f SD 3 **99**

GYPSY KING 3
- May 6 Ches 10½f GS 1 **108**
- Jun 4 Epsm 12f G 5 107

H

H HARRISON 5
- May 21 Catt 7f GF 9 100
- Jly 27 Muss 7f GF 1 102
- Jly 28 Muss 7f G 1 105
- Aug 4 Brig 7f G 3 102
- Aug 17 Epsm 6f G 2 103
- Aug 19 Ches 7f GF 2 **108**
- Aug 20 Ches 7½f G 2 100

HABANERO 4
- Apr 27 Ling 8f FT 3 103
- Jun 6 Wind 10f G 1 103
- Jun 13 Wind 8½f G 1 101
- Jly 12 Brig 8f G 2 103
- Jly 24 Newb 8f G 2 103
- Aug 8 Wind 8½f GF 2 108
- Aug 22 Wind 8½f G 1 106
- Aug 27 Wind 8½f G 2 **111**

HABSHAN 5
- Jly 14 Donc 8f GF 1 104
- Aug 27 Wind 8½f G 5 **110**

HACHITA 3
- Apr 30 NmkR 8f G 3 102
- May 31 Leic 7f GF 1 **105**
- Aug 14 Bath 8f G 7 103

HADATH 8
- Feb 22 Ling 6f SD 1 101
- Mar 7 Ling 6f SD 2 99
- Apr 1 Ling 7f SD 2 101
- Apr 6 Ling 6f SD 1 99
- Apr 20 Ling 7f FT 1 99
- May 25 Ling 6f SD 1 102
- Dec 30 Ling 6f FT 3 **104**

HADRIAN 3
Apr 14 NmkR 7f G 4 105
May 13 Nott 8f F 4 101
May 19 Donc 7f GF 7 99
Jun 3 Epsm 7f G 7 99
Jun 22 Epsm 8½f G 1 105
Jly 13 Hayd 8f G 1 **107**
Jly 30 NmkJ 10f GF 2 101

HAIL THE CHIEF 8
Nov 11 Wolv 8½f FT 8 105
Nov 29 Ling 8f FT 2 107
Dec 9 Wolv 8½f FT 1 **109**
Dec 17 Ling 8f FT 3 103
Dec 31 Wolv 9½f SD 3 104

HAITI 3
Jun 1 Leop 7f G 5 **100**

HALCYON MAGIC 7
Feb 27 Wolv 12f G 3 99
Mar 13 Wolv 12f FT 5 99
May 4 Chep 8f S 2 **103**
May 17 Ling 10f S 1 101
Jun 17 NmkJ 8f GF 4 99
Dec 21 Wolv 9½f FT 2 100

HALKIN 3
Aug 27 NmkJ 8f G 2 **102**

HALLA SAN 3
Jly 16 Ripn 10f G 4 **99**

HALLE BOP 3
Aug 28 Gdwd 7f G 2 **100**

HALLHOO 3
Apr 2 Donc 8f G 3 102
Apr 20 Epsm 10f GS 1 **103**
Jun 4 Epsm 10f G 3 **103**

HALLOWED DREAM 3
May 1 NmkR 10f G 2 **100**

HALLUCINATE 3
Jun 7 Rdcr 11f G 3 **99**

HALMAHERA 10
Jun 18 York 6f GF 8 103
Jly 30 Gdwd 6f G 19 101
Sep 7 Donc 5½f GF 11 **105**

HAMAASY 4
Mar 27 Muss 7f GS 1 **102**
Aug 2 Catt 6f G 6 99

HAMBLEDEN 8
Jly 15 NmkJ 12f G 2 **109**
Jly 23 Newb 12f GF 9 102
Sep 2 NmkJ 12f G 5 102

HAMMER OF THE GODS 5
Jan 4 Ling 5f FT 2 104
Mar 21 Ling 6f FT 1 **108**

HANA DEE 4
Feb 7 Wolv 8½f FT 6 99
Jly 25 Yarm 16f GS 3 **100**
Aug 31 Ling 16f GS 5 99

HAND CHIME 8
Sep 3 Wolv 7f FT 1 **100**
Nov 19 Ling 8f FT 4 99

HANDSOME CROSS 4
May 14 Thsk 5f G 4 104
May 28 Muss 5f G 2 104
Jun 7 Ches 5f GF 2 **106**
Jun 25 Ches 5f G 1 103

HANORLA 6
Aug 7 Curr 16f G 9 **102**

HANSEATIC LEAGUE 3
May 7 Ling 6f G 8 99
May 27 Pont 8f GF 3 **100**

HANSOMELLE 3
May 14 Thsk 8f G 7 **100**
Aug 19 Ayr 8f GF 7 99

HAPPY TO CHAT 3
Aug 20 Curr 8f GF 1 **103**

HARBOUR HOUSE 6
Mar 22 Ling 5f SD 6 **99**

HARCOURT 5
May 17 Leic 10f G 2 **102**

HARD ROCK CITY 5
Aug 14 Leop 7f F 1 107
Sep 10 Leop 7f HD 1 108
Oct 9 Curr 6f GS 3 103
Nov 6 Leop 7f GS 2 **109**

HARD TO CATCH 7
Aug 6 Ling 7f SD 2 102
Aug 26 Bath 5f G 2 **103**
Dec 20 Ling 6f G 2 102

HARD TOP 3
Jly 20 Ling 11½f G 1 **109**
Aug 16 York 12f G 1 105
Sep 10 Donc 14½f S 5 99

HARLEM DANCER 3
Jly 14 Lonc 12f F 3 **110**

HARLESTONE LINN 3
Sep 27 Gdwd 16f G 5 **99**

HARRISON'S FLYER 4
May 28 Muss 5f G 1 **105**
Jun 18 Ayr 5f G 3 103
Jly 25 Sthl 6f G 1 100
Aug 20 Ches 5f G 5 102
Oct 7 York 5f G 1 103

HARRY UP 4
Aug 17 Carl 5f GF 2 100
Dec 19 Wolv 6f FT 1 **103**

HARRYS HOUSE 3
Oct 10 Ayr 5f G 1 **100**

HARTSHEAD 6
May 23 Thsk 7f G 3 101
Jun 22 Carl 8f GF 1 105
Jly 23 Newc 7f GF 2 100
Aug 6 Rdcr 8f G 3 108
Aug 16 York 6f GF 9 101
Aug 29 Ripn 8f G 4 107
Oct 7 York 8f G 1 **109**

HARVEST WARRIOR 3
Aug 27 York 6f G 8 101
Sep 24 NmkR 7f G 10 **110**
Oct 3 Pont 8f G 2 100
Oct 29 NmkR 8f S 7 102

HASAINM 4
Jly 6 Naas 7f GF 3 100
Aug 20 Curr 6f GF 7 **101**

HATHLEN 4
Aug 11 Sals 14f GF 3 101

HATTAN 3
Apr 22 Sand 10f G 3 100
May 5 Ches 12½f GS 1 103
Jun 4 Epsm 12f G 6 105
Aug 27 Wind 10f G 2 **111**

HAUNT THE ZOO 10
Mar 17 Sthl 8f G 1 **100**

HAUNTING MEMORIES 3
Aug 7 Leic 7f G 4 **102**

HAWK ARROW 3
May 9 Wind 11½f GF 1 **100**

HAWKES BAY 3
Mar 30 Folk 7f S 1 101
Apr 14 NmkR 7f G 3 106
Jun 16 York 8f G 3 **111**

HAWKES RUN 7
Jan 7 Wolv 12f SW 2 **104**
Jan 22 Ling 16f FT 6 **104**

HAWKIT 4
Mar 16 Wolv 7f SD 2 102
Apr 16 Wolv 8½f FT 4 102
May 4 Chep 10f S 2 **105**

HAWRIDGE KING 3
Apr 25 Wind 8½f GS 3 100
Oct 10 Wind 11½f G 2 101

HAWRIDGE PRINCE 5
Apr 23 Sand 10f G 5 **101**

HAWRIDGE STAR 3
Aug 26 Sals 10f G 2 **103**

HAYYANI 3
Sep 30 Ling 7f FT 2 102
Nov 29 Ling 8f FT 4 **105**

HAZARISTA 4
Jun 25 Curr 10f G 5 **111**
Jly 30 Gdwd 10f G 9 99

HAZEWIND 4
Jun 5 Bath 8f G 4 101
Jun 7 Ches 10½f GF 7 100
Jun 11 Ripn 8f G 3 **104**
Jly 2 Leic 7f GF 1 103
Jly 23 Newb 7f GF 3 99
Sep 8 Epsm 7f G 7 102

HAZYVIEW 4
Apr 13 NmkR 9f G 5 105
Apr 23 Sand 10f G 2 106
May 7 NmkR 9f GF 3 104

Jun 4 Epsm 8½f G 1 108
Jun 25 Wind 8½f G 1 **109**
Jly 2 Sand 10f G 4 **109**
Aug 14 Leop 8f F 5 **109**
Sep 21 Gdwd 10f G 4 105
Oct 15 NmkR 9f G 6 102

HE'S A DIAMOND 3
Mar 3 Ling 8f SW 8 **99**

HE'S A ROCKET 4
Feb 21 Wolv 5f FT 1 99
Mar 22 Ling 5f SD 1 **106**
Apr 5 Sthl 5f FT 2 100
Jun 3 Thsk 5f G 2 100
Jly 2 Hayd 5f GF 4 103
Jly 11 Wolv 5f SD 1 99
Nov 9 Wolv 5f FT 1 99
Nov 21 Sthl 5f FT 1 101

HE'S A STAR 3
Mar 29 Wwck 7f GS 1 102
Nov 21 Sthl 14f SW 2 **105**
Dec 10 Sthl 14f FT 3 99

HEAD TO KERRY 5
Jun 18 Ling 10f SW 4 **101**
Jly 11 Wolv 14f SD 5 **101**

HEADLAND 7
Jan 10 Wolv 6f SD 1 **100**
Feb 24 Sthl 6f FT 4 **100**
Jly 5 Wolv 6f FT 3 99

HEART SPRINGS 5
May 26 Bath 17½f G 1 104
Jun 4 Chep 18f GS 2 **106**
Jly 7 Wwck 16f G 3 102

HEARTCRUSHER 3
Dec 19 Wolv 8½f FT 1 **105**

HEARTHSTEAD WINGS 3
Apr 22 Sand 10f G 4 99
Jun 4 Epsm 10f G 8 99
Jly 2 Hayd 12f GF 3 100
Jly 28 Gdwd 16f G 6 **109**
Sep 3 Hayd 14f GF 14 101
Sep 10 Donc 12f S 3 106
Sep 26 Haml 13f G 1 107
Nov 3 Muss 16f GS 2 103

HEAT OF THE NIGHT 3
Mar 26 Kemp 8f GS 6 99
Jun 18 Wwck 7f G 7 **105**
Jly 2 Sand 8f G 5 99
Jly 22 Newb 8f G 4 99

HEATHWOOD 3
Apr 6 Ling 7f G 1 **106**
Apr 18 Wind 8½f G 6 99
Sep 26 Bath 8f G 4 99

HEATHYARDS PRIDE 5
Jly 5 Wolv 12f FT 3 100
Jly 20 Leic 12f GF 2 **106**
Jly 26 Bevl 12f G 2 101
Oct 1 Wolv 12f FT 3 104
Nov 16 Sthl 12f FT 3 103
Dec 6 Sthl 14f FT 1 105
Dec 26 Wolv 12f SD 1 **106**

HEAVENLY DREAMER 3
May 25 Leop 8f GF 5 **104**

HEAVENS WALK 4
Aug 12 Folk 5f GF 5 **100**

HEGRID 4
Apr 3 Curr 10f S 14 **99**

HEIDENHEIM 3
Jun 1 Leop 7f G 4 102
Jun 15 Leop 7f G 4 **104**

HEIDI'S DASH 3
Jly 21 Bath 5f G 1 **99**
Aug 9 Bath 5f GF 7 **99**

HEISSE 5
Feb 12 Wolv 12f FT 7 **105**

HELIOS QUERCUS 3
Mar 28 StCl 8f GS 1 113
Apr 24 Lonc 10f GS 2 99
May 15 Lonc 8f G 6 108
Jly 3 Chan 8f G 7 112
Oct 30 StCl 8f G 2 **114**

HELLBENT 6
Mar 22 Ling 5f SD 2 **103**

HELLO IT'S ME 4
Jan 22 Ling 12f FT 6 **104**
Mar 18 Ling 13f SD 2 99
Mar 26 Kemp 16f S 4 103
May 23 Thsk 12f G 6 99
Aug 3 Pont 12f G 6 103

HELM BANK 5
Jan 7 Wolv 8½f SW 5 110
May 29 NmkR 7f GF 6 102
Jun 17 York 10½f G 16 100
Jun 23 Newc 8f G 1 102
Jly 2 Sand 8f G 4 **115**
Jly 29 Gdwd 8f G 7 112
Aug 11 Sals 8f GF 4 110
Oct 15 NmkR 9f G 7 102
Nov 19 Ling 10f FT 7 100

HELVETIO 3
May 22 Curr 10f GS 1 **103**
Jun 17 York 16f G 3 101
Jun 26 Curr 12f F 6 102

HEMARIS 3
Jly 20 Naas 6f GF 1 101
Aug 20 Curr 6f GF 2 **103**

HENRY HALL 9
May 14 Thsk 5f G 10 100
Jun 9 Ripn 5f G 2 **105**
Jly 2 Bevl 5f G 3 102
Jly 8 York 5f G 4 99
Jly 22 York 5f G 4 101

HENRY TUN 7
Jan 28 Wolv 5f SD 1 100
Apr 11 Sthl 5f FT 4 100
Apr 28 Sthl 5f FT 2 **103**

HERMITAGE COURT 4
Oct 29 Wolv 7f SD 5 **99**

HERNANDO'S BOY 4
May 21 Catt 14f GF 3 104
Nov 1 Catt 14f GS 1 102

HERON'S WING 4
Jan 15 Ling 10f SD 2 **103**

HEWARAAT 3
Aug 3 Epsm 6f G 1 **104**
Aug 28 Gdwd 6f G 9 99

HEY PRESTO 5
Apr 6 Ling 7f G 3 102
Sep 13 Sals 7f G 1 **104**

HEYBROOK BOY 3
Jan 28 Wolv 9½f SD 1 **99**

HIAMOVI 3
Mar 12 Wolv 5f SD 2 **101**

HIAWATHA 6
Jly 15 Wwck 12½f G 3 **99**

HICCUPS 5
Apr 23 Ripn 6f S 4 100
Jun 1 Newc 6f G 4 100
Jun 29 Catt 7f G 1 **104**
Jly 22 NmkJ 6f G 6 101
Aug 11 Hayd 6f GF 5 99

HIDDEN CHANCE 3
May 27 Brig 10f GF 2 99
Oct 14 NmkR 12f G 3 **104**

HIDDEN DRAGON 6
Jan 27 Sthl 5f FT 1 107
Feb 3 Sthl 6f SD 2 104
Feb 5 Ling 5f SD 3 105
Feb 19 Wolv 5f SD 2 107
Mar 12 Wolv 6f SD 4 105
Apr 20 Epsm 5f GS 2 **108**
May 6 Ches 5f GS 8 100
Jun 16 York 7f GF 12 99
Jly 30 Gdwd 6f G 13 105
Aug 1 Ripn 6f G 3 105
Sep 13 Yarm 6f G 5 99

HIDDEN HOPE 4
Jly 2 Hayd 12f GF 2 **102**

HIDDEN STAR 3
Jun 10 Chep 6f G 3 99
Jly 2 Nott 8f GF 3 **103**
Jly 27 Leic 8½f G 2 99

HIDDENSEE 3
Apr 1 Donc 10½f GS 3 103
Apr 23 Leic 12f G 1 105
Jun 17 York 12f G 6 102
Aug 12 Newb 13½f G 2 **106**
Aug 18 York 14f G 8 102
Sep 24 Hayd 14f GF 2 105

HIGH ACCOLADE 5
May 14 Newb 13½f G 3 **100**

HIGH ACTION 5
May 1 NmkR 12f G 1 113
May 13 Haml 12f F 2 102
Jun 25 Newc 16f G 13 107
Jly 9 Ling 16f SD 1 **115**

Aug 17 York 14f G 11 103
Aug 20 Ches 13½f G 4 105
Sep 8 Donc 18f G 4 109
Sep 24 NmkR 16f G 7 105

HIGH BRAY 4
Apr 24 Brig 8f GF 1 105
May 13 Newb 10f GF 1 102
Aug 29 Epsm 8½f G 3 100
Sep 27 Gdwd 7f G 1 **107**
Oct 8 Sals 7f GF 1 104
Oct 29 NmkR 7f S 3 104

HIGH CARD 3
Oct 9 Gdwd 8f G 7 **99**

HIGH CHART 3
Jun 2 Brig 7f G 5 **99**

HIGH CHARTER 4
Apr 29 Nott 14f G 1 **99**

HIGH DYKE 3
Jan 21 Wolv 8½f SD 4 99
Mar 24 Wolv 9½f SD 1 102
Jun 10 Sand 8f GF 1 **103**
Aug 20 Bevl 10f GF 5 **103**

HIGH FREQUENCY 4
Aug 20 Ling 10f SD 4 **99**

HIGH KICK 4
Apr 30 Thsk 12f S 2 **100**

HIGH POINT 7
May 21 Ling 16f SD 5 103
Jun 4 Hayd 16f G 7 99
Jly 9 Ling 16f SD 10 **109**
Sep 15 Yarm 16f GS 6 103
Oct 15 NmkR 18f G 12 100
Oct 28 NmkR 10f GS 5 100

HIGH PRIESTESS 6
May 25 Leop 14f GF 5 **104**

HIGH REACH 5
Mar 28 Kemp 6f G 2 **110**
Apr 6 Nott 5f S 1 105
Apr 15 Newb 5f GS 5 102
Apr 30 NmkR 6f G 15 106
May 28 Gdwd 6f G 3 101
Jun 25 Wind 6f G 5 107
Jly 7 NmkJ 7f G 11 104
Aug 8 Wind 6f GF 8 99

HIGH REEF 7
Jun 1 Leop 7f G 8 108
Sep 10 Leop 12f GF 6 **109**

HIGH RESERVE 4
Apr 21 Bevl 10f S 2 102
Jly 8 Ling 10f G 5 104
Jly 29 Nott 10f G 1 **105**
Oct 13 NmkR 10f G 6 102

HIGH RHYTHM 3
Dec 30 Ling 7f FT 6 **99**

HIGH RIDGE 6
Apr 26 Wwck 5f G 3 100
May 5 Chep 6f GS 5 104
May 23 Wind 6f F 1 104

Jun 13 Wind 6f GF 6 99
Jly 9 York 6f G 3 103
Jly 22 Newb 6f G 5 101
Jly 29 Thsk 6f G 4 103
Aug 5 Hayd 6f F 8 101
Aug 11 Hayd 6f GF 3 100
Aug 27 Gdwd 6f G 4 **105**
Sep 11 Carl 6f GF 3 103
Sep 16 Ayr 6f GF 5 99

HIGH TREASON 3
Jun 4 Ling 12f SD 2 **100**

HIGH VOLTAGE 4
Apr 2 Donc 6f G 7 **102**

HIGHER LOVE 3
Apr 5 Folk 9½f S 1 **104**
May 4 Ches 11½f GS 2 103

HIGHER STATE 4
Aug 28 Bevl 12f GS 1 **101**
Oct 7 York 12f G 5 **101**

HIGHEST LOVER 3
Oct 1 Lonc 15f G 7 **101**

HIGHEST REGARD 3
Aug 18 Wolv 8½f SD 1 **101**

HIGHLAND GAMES 5
May 14 Newb 12f G 6 104
Aug 26 Thsk 16f GF 2 **105**
Sep 15 Yarm 16f GS 2 **105**

HIGHLAND WARRIOR 6
Apr 23 Ripn 5f GS 1 104
Apr 30 Thsk 5f S 7 99
May 14 Thsk 6f G 2 100
May 28 Muss 5f G 2 **107**
Aug 25 Muss 5f G 8 99
Sep 3 Hayd 5f F 4 **107**
Oct 16 Muss 5f GF 10 99

HIGHLINER 3
Dec 30 Ling 10f FT 8 **99**

HILLS OF GOLD 6
Apr 1 Donc 8f G 10 99
Jun 17 Ayr 8f G 2 101
Jun 22 Carl 8f GF 4 **103**

HILLS SPITFIRE 4
Jly 1 Wolv 12f GF 6 **99**

HILLTIME 5
Jun 29 Catt 12f G 1 105
Jly 5 Pont 10f G 2 101

HILLTOP RHAPSODY 4
May 20 NmkR 8f G 7 **100**

HINTERLAND 3
Aug 27 NmkJ 8f G 1 103
Sep 23 Hayd 8f G 1 **107**
Oct 3 Pont 8f G 9 99

HIPPODROME 3
Jun 25 Curr 10f G 2 **106**

HISTORIC PLACE 5
Jun 4 Hayd 16f G 6 100

Jly 7 Wwck 16f G 2 **103**
Oct 21 Newb 16f GS 2 102

HISTORIX 3
Jun 27 Lonc 10½f G 5 **107**

HIT'S ONLY MONEY 5
Dec 19 Wolv 8½f FT 6 **99**

HITS ONLY CASH 3
Aug 27 NmkJ 6f G 7 **102**

HITS ONLY HEAVEN 3
Sep 13 Yarm 6f G 2 102
Nov 10 Ling 8f SD 1 **106**
Dec 20 Ling 8f SD 1 **106**

HOCKNEY 3
Oct 1 Lonc 15f G 5 **111**

HOH BLEU DEE 4
Sep 21 Gdwd 8f G 3 **99**

HOH HOH HOH 3
Sep 6 Leic 5f GF 2 **105**

HOH MY DARLING 3
May 27 Brig 10f GF 1 **100**
Jly 21 Bath 10f GF 2 **100**

HOLBECK GHYLL 3
Aug 14 Bath 5½f G 2 102
Sep 1 Sals 5f G 1 103
Sep 5 Bath 5½f GF 1 **108**
Sep 9 Sand 5f G 1 103

HOLIDAY CAMP 3
Jly 24 Pont 8f G 1 104
Aug 10 Sals 8f G 4 102
Sep 9 Sand 8f GS 1 **105**
Sep 24 Ripn 10f GF 7 100
Oct 7 York 8f G 6 **105**

HOLIDAY COCKTAIL 3
Aug 13 Ripn 5f G 3 **100**
Oct 25 Yarm 7f S 7 99
Dec 20 Ling 7f S 1 99

HOLLOW JO 5
Nov 28 Sthl 7f SD 3 99
Dec 21 Ling 6f SD 1 **102**

HOLLY SPRINGS 3
May 28 Donc 5f G 2 **101**

HOLY ORDERS 8
Sep 18 Curr 16f G 1 **109**
Oct 9 Curr 16f GS 6 107
Nov 6 Leop 16f S 7 105

HOME AFFAIRS 3
May 21 Hayd 8f GF 1 110
Jun 15 York 7f G 3 105
Jly 3 Chan 8f G 4 **115**
Aug 11 Sals 8f GF 7 108
Sep 30 NmkR 8f G 6 102

HOMEGROWN 4
Sep 18 Curr 8f GF 10 **104**

HONEY RYDER 3
May 7 NmkR 6f GF 1 100

May 14 Nott 6f F 7 99
Jun 18 Wwck 7f G 5 **107**

HOPE AN GLORY 3
May 16 Bath 10f G 1 99
Jun 11 Bath 11½f G 2 **101**
Aug 1 Carl 12f G 3 **101**

HOPE SOUND 5
Apr 20 Catt 12f S 4 **102**

HOREION DIRECTA 6
Apr 27 Ling 7½f S 1 **112**
Aug 7 Deau 6½f G 8 110

HORNPIPE 3
Jun 24 NmkJ 5f G 1 100
Aug 17 York 5f F 4 101
Sep 3 Hayd 5f F 9 **105**

HORS LA LOI 9
Jan 12 Wolv 14f SD 5 **102**

HOUSE MARTIN 3
Jly 8 Ling 10f G 4 **105**
Jly 31 Newb 10f G 2 99

HOUSE OF KAISER 3
Aug 26 Newc 9f GF 3 **104**

HOWARDS PRINCESS 3
Jun 17 Rdcr 5f G 1 **101**
Jun 23 Haml 5f G 4 99
Sep 18 Haml 6f F 1 100
Sep 26 Haml 5f F 3 99
Nov 3 Muss 5f GS 2 **101**

HOWLE HILL 5
Jan 15 Ling 10f SD 1 108
Mar 19 Ling 10f SD 14 104
May 14 Newb 13½f G 6 99
May 28 Gdwd 12f G 5 106
Jly 9 Ling 16f SD 9 110
Aug 17 York 14f G 12 102

HUE 4
Apr 9 Newc 9f S 5 **105**

HUGS DESTINY 4
Mar 4 Wolv 12f SD 6 100
Jly 6 Carl 9½f G 2 99
Jly 23 York 12f GS 6 101

HULA BALLEW 5
Jun 1 Newc 8f G 6 100
Jun 14 Carl 8f GS 2 100
Jun 27 Pont 8f G 2 106
Jly 9 Haml 9f F 2 **109**
Jly 14 Haml 8½f GF 3 103
Aug 17 Carl 8f GF 1 107
Sep 1 Carl 8f G 2 102
Sep 15 Pont 8f G 5 99

HUMBLE OPINION 3
May 21 NmkR 8f G 2 102
Jun 16 Newb 8f G 2 103
Jly 12 Bevl 7½f GF 2 100
Jly 16 NmkJ 8f GF 3 102
Sep 10 Gdwd 9f G 7 **106**

HUMOUROUS 3
Jun 25 Wind 11½f G 7 **99**

HUNTING LODGE 4
Jly 16 Ling 8f SW 1 **105**
Aug 6 Wind 8½f GF 9 100

HURRICANE ALAN 5
Mar 19 Ling 10f SD 3 114
Mar 31 Donc 8f G 2 **115**
Apr 13 NmkR 9f G 2 109
Apr 23 Sand 8f G 1 105
May 14 Newb 8f F 3 112
Jly 2 Sand 10f G 5 105

HURRICANE COAST 6
Jan 29 Ling 7f SD 10 102
Feb 8 Ling 6f SD 3 **106**
Feb 9 Ling 7f SD 9 99
Feb 18 Wolv 6f SD 2 **106**
Mar 4 Wolv 6f SD 7 102
Mar 12 Wolv 6f SD 10 100
Mar 18 Ling 6f SD 4 102
Apr 25 Wolv 7f FT 1 101
Jly 8 Ling 6f SW 10 99
Oct 17 Wind 6f G 2 102
Oct 25 Yarm 7f S 1 103
Oct 30 Ling 6f SD 9 101
Nov 15 Ling 7f FT 8 102
Nov 29 Ling 8f FT 11 101
Dec 19 Wolv 8½f FT 2 104
Dec 30 Ling 8f FT 3 104

HURRICANE JAMES 3
Oct 1 Lonc 8f G 5 **110**

HURRICANE RUN 3
May 9 Lonc 11f G 1 108
Jun 5 Chan 10½f G 2 104
Jun 26 Curr 12f F 1 111
Sep 11 Lonc 12f G 1 116
Oct 2 Lonc 12f G 1 **122**

HUXLEY 6
Jun 29 Chep 8f G 1 **100**

HYPNOTIC 3
Aug 23 Yarm 8f G 1 **102**

I

I HAVE DREAMED 3
Aug 21 Folk 9½f G 1 **102**

I WISH 7
Jan 13 Ling 8f SD 4 99
May 5 Chep 6f GS 3 **105**
Jun 3 Wolv 6f FT 1 101
Aug 4 Brig 6f G 1 104

I'LL DO IT TODAY 4
Dec 31 Wolv 14f SD 1 **100**

I'M SO LUCKY 3
Apr 23 Leic 12f G 3 103
May 14 Newb 11f G 1 **105**
Jun 4 Hayd 12f G 6 102
Jun 17 York 12f G 4 104
Jly 1 Sand 10f G 1 102
Jly 9 York 10½f G 6 102
Jly 23 Newb 10f GF 5 99

IAMBACK 5
Aug 11 Bevl 16f GF 3 **100**
Oct 15 Ling 13f SD 2 **100**

IBERUS 7
Dec 15 Sthl 8f SD 4 99

ICANNSHIFT 5
Mar 29 Wwck 11f S 2 **104**
Jun 30 Newb 11f G 8 99
Jly 12 Brig 10f G 2 101
Sep 3 Folk 9½f GF 3 99

ICE AND FIRE 6
Dec 12 Wolv 14f FT 6 **102**
Dec 28 Wolv 14f FT 6 100

ICE DRAGON 4
Jly 1 Wolv 8½f FT 3 **99**

ICE PLANET 4
Jun 3 Thsk 5f G 1 102
Jun 8 Haml 5f G 2 105
Jun 9 Ripn 5f G 4 105
Jun 25 Donc 6f GF 1 **109**
Jly 22 NmkJ 6f G 2 105
Jly 29 NmkJ 6f G 5 105
Aug 13 Ripn 6f G 1 108

ICECAP 5
Jly 12 Brig 10f G 3 **100**

ICED DIAMOND 6
Feb 9 Ling 7f G 1 99
Feb 18 Wolv 7f SD 1 **103**
Feb 23 Ling 7f SD 6 101

ICEMAN 3
Apr 14 NmkR 8f G 4 **100**
Apr 30 NmkR 8f G 13 **100**

ICKLINGHAM 5
Apr 3 Curr 16f HY 1 109
Apr 10 Leop 12f GS 1 **111**

IDEALISTIC 4
Jun 12 Sals 12f G 5 104
Jly 16 Ripn 12f G 4 **107**
Aug 14 Bath 11½f G 1 102
Oct 10 Wind 11½f G 5 100

IDLE POWER 7
Apr 2 Kemp 7f GS 8 101
Apr 30 Gdwd 6f G 1 105
Jun 11 Sand 7f G 12 107
Jun 22 Epsm 7f G 3 103
Jly 19 Yarm 7f G 2 **110**
Jly 29 Gdwd 6f G 1 107
Aug 27 Gdwd 6f G 5 103
Sep 10 Gdwd 7f G 8 106
Sep 11 Gdwd 6f G 10 100
Oct 21 Newb 6f G 4 102
Oct 30 Ling 6f SD 5 105
Nov 15 Ling 7f FT 7 103
Nov 25 Wolv 6f FT 10 100

IF PARADISE 4
Mar 19 Ling 5f SD 7 99
Mar 28 Kemp 6f G 2 101
Apr 15 Newb 5f GS 1 **110**
May 28 Gdwd 5f G 5 102
Jly 2 Hayd 6f GF 6 99
Jly 9 Ches 5f GF 6 105
Jly 16 Newb 6f GF 8 100

Jly	24	Newb	5f	G	7	109
Aug	15	Nott	5f	GF	4	102
Sep	3	Hayd	5f	F	8	105
Sep	29	NmkR	5f	GF	4	105
Oct	13	NmkR	5f	G	5	107

IFFRAAJ 4						
Mar	28	Kemp	6f	G	1	112
May	7	Ling	7f	G	1	**116**
Jun	18	York	6f	GF	1	**116**
Jly	7	NmkJ	6f	G	14	100
Sep	8	Donc	7f	GF	1	112
Oct	1	Lonc	7f	G	7	111

IFFY 4						
Jun	23	Sals	10f	G	2	102
Jun	30	Epsm	10f	G	1	102
Jly	20	Sand	10f	G	1	103
Aug	3	Epsm	10f	G	6	**105**

IFTIKHAR 6						
Jan	10	Wolv	12f	SD	4	101
Feb	4	Wolv	8½f	SD	3	**103**
Feb	14	Wolv	9½f	SD	1	**103**
Feb	28	Wolv	9½f	SD	6	**103**

IGNITION 3						
Jun	20	Muss	8f	GF	1	99
Jly	15	Carl	9½f	G	2	**100**
Sep	15	Ayr	8f	G	1	99

IL PRANZO 3						
Jan	4	Ling	6f	FT	1	101
Feb	22	Ling	7f	SD	2	101
Mar	1	Ling	6f	SD	10	100
Mar	4	Wolv	6f	SD	5	102
Mar	7	Ling	5f	SD	2	**104**

ILE MICHEL 8						
Apr	24	Brig	8f	GF	4	99
May	12	Carl	9½f	G	3	**100**

IM SPARTACUS 3						
Apr	22	Sand	10f	G	4	101
May	6	Ches	10½f	GS	2	**107**
May	13	York	10½f	GS	1	101
May	22	Curr	10f	GS	1	102

IMAGO MUNDI 5						
Apr	24	Lonc	10½f	GS	8	108
Jun	26	StCl	12f	GF	7	**112**

IMCO SASIHILL 5						
Feb	28	Wolv	5f	SD	2	**104**

IMPARTIAL 4						
Oct	9	Curr	16f	GS	4	**108**
Nov	6	Leop	16f	S	6	106

IMPELLER 6						
May	28	Gdwd	8f	G	4	104
Jun	3	Epsm	10f	G	7	110
Jun	22	Sals	8f	G	7	101
Jly	9	York	10½f	G	9	101
Jly	26	Gdwd	10f	G	10	101
Jly	29	Gdwd	8f	G	8	**112**
Aug	3	Epsm	8½f	G	1	104
Aug	6	Hayd	10½f	GF	5	106
Aug	27	York	9f	G	2	106
Sep	10	Gdwd	9f	G	2	107
Sep	17	Newb	10f	GF	5	111
Sep	21	Gdwd	10f	G	6	100

Oct	1	NmkR	9f	G	8	101
Oct	14	NmkR	8f	G	7	106
Oct	22	Newb	10f	G	10	104

IMPERIAL ECHO 4						
Jun	25	Donc	6f	GF	6	**103**
Jly	10	Hayd	6f	GF	2	101
Jly	22	NmkJ	6f	G	5	102
Aug	17	Epsm	6f	G	3	102
Aug	27	York	6f	G	8	99
Sep	6	Catt	7f	GF	6	100
Sep	16	Ayr	6f	GF	6	99
Oct	29	NmkR	7f	S	8	100

IMPERIAL ROSE 3						
May	8	Leop	12f	S	1	110
May	22	Curr	12f	GS	5	**113**
Jun	26	Curr	12f	F	3	108
Sep	10	Leop	12f	GF	13	100

IMPERIAL RULE 3						
Oct	3	Wind	6f	GF	2	99
Oct	9	Gdwd	6f	G	1	**103**

IMPERIAL STRIDE 4						
May	12	York	7f	GS	10	100
Jun	17	York	10½f	G	1	**115**
Jun	25	NmkJ	12f	G	1	109
Jly	18	Ayr	10f	GF	1	114
Sep	3	NmkJ	12f	G	1	114

IMPERIAL TREASURE 3						
Aug	20	Ling	10f	SD	4	**99**

IMPERIALISTIC 4						
Apr	16	Thsk	8f	HY	3	**109**
Jun	8	Haml	8½f	G	6	100
Sep	2	Hayd	8f	G	5	105
Oct	16	Muss	7f	G	3	102
Nov	1	Catt	7f	GS	3	101

IMPERIUM 4						
Jun	6	Wind	5f	G	8	100
Jly	12	Brig	6f	G	3	**101**

IMPROVISE 3						
Mar	29	Pont	6f	S	1	103
May	7	Ling	7f	G	7	102
Jun	18	Wwck	7f	G	2	**108**

IMPULSIVO 5						
Mar	31	Ling	10f	SD	5	**105**

IMSHY 4						
Sep	4	Lonc	5f	GF	11	**99**

IMTALKINGGIBBERISH 4						
Feb	28	Wolv	5f	SD	2	100
Jun	6	Wind	5f	G	5	**102**

IN CLOVER 3						
Sep	4	Lonc	10f	GF	2	**104**

IN GOOD FAITH 4						
Jly	16	Ling	10f	SW	5	**99**

IN THE DARK 5						
Jun	5	Chan	12f	G	9	**100**

IN THE FAN 3						
Sep	30	NmkR	7f	G	10	**100**

IN THE LEAD 3						
May	12	Sals	10f	G	3	99
Jun	10	Chep	12f	G	2	100
Jly	5	Pont	12f	G	4	103
Aug	5	Ling	11½f	GS	2	102
Oct	19	Bath	10f	GS	2	**106**

IN THE PINK 5						
May	9	Rdcr	7f	GS	5	**104**
May	17	Rdcr	8f	G	1	99
Aug	6	NmkJ	8f	G	7	101
Aug	15	Wind	8½f	GF	2	103

IN THE RIBBONS 3						
May	25	Leop	14f	GF	11	**99**

IN TIME'S EYE 6						
Sep	10	Leop	10f	GF	3	**100**

INCENSE 3						
Aug	28	Gdwd	7f	G	4	**99**

INCH BY INCH 6						
Jun	18	Ling	5f	G	3	**105**
Jly	12	Brig	6f	G	1	104
Aug	21	Folk	5f	G	4	103
Sep	9	Sand	5f	G	6	101
Sep	21	Gdwd	6f	GF	6	104

INCH ISLAND 5						
Apr	10	Leop	7f	GS	2	99
May	21	Curr	8f	G	16	**103**

INCHDURA 7						
Nov	5	Sthl	8f	FT	5	**99**

INCHLOCH 3						
Oct	5	Nott	10f	G	4	**106**
Oct	25	Yarm	10f	S	5	102

INCHLOSS 4						
Jun	15	Nott	8f	GF	3	**103**

INCHNADAMPH 5						
Jun	3	Hayd	14f	G	1	102
Jun	30	Hayd	14f	GF	1	**106**
Aug	6	NmkJ	16f	G	1	104
Sep	24	Hayd	14f	GF	12	100
Oct	15	NmkR	18f	G	3	105

INCHPAST 4						
Jun	23	Sals	14f	G	1	106
Jly	9	Ling	16f	SD	6	**110**
Jly	22	York	14f	G	2	109
Aug	20	Ches	16f	G	3	108
Sep	15	Yarm	16f	GS	7	102

INCROYABLE 4						
Aug	20	Ches	16f	G	5	**108**
Sep	10	Muss	14f	G	2	99

INCURSION 4						
Jly	31	Ches	12½f	G	6	99

INDALO GREY 9						
Feb	11	Wolv	12f	SD	2	**99**

INDANEHILL 3						
Jun	27	Lonc	9½f	G	2	**106**

INDEBTED 3						
Mar	12	Wolv	8½f	SD	1	99

Oct 1 Wolv 8½f FT 2 **101**
Dec 12 Wolv 9½f FT 3 99

INDESATCHEL 3
Apr 3 Curr 7f S 1 111
Apr 16 Newb 7f GS 1 108
May 15 Lonc 8f G 2 **112**

INDIAN BAZAAR 9
Jly 12 Bevl 5f GF 3 **100**
Jly 22 Chep 5f G 4 **100**

INDIAN BLAZE 11
Feb 22 Ling 10f SD 4 **103**

INDIAN CHASE 8
Jly 8 Wolv 14f FT 4 **99**
Jly 11 Wolv 14f SD 8 **99**

INDIAN MAIDEN 5
Jan 6 Wolv 6f SD 4 99
Feb 12 Ling 6f SD 1 110
Mar 18 Ling 6f SD 1 107
Apr 26 Bath 5f HY 1 111
May 14 Nott 6f F 4 103
May 28 Gdwd 5f G 3 104
Jun 4 Hayd 6f G 1 106
Jly 8 York 6f G 3 108
Jly 28 Gdwd 5f G 8 102
Jly 31 Ches 6f G 1 110
Aug 7 Curr 6f G 6 104
Aug 14 Pont 6f G 2 **112**
Sep 3 Hayd 6f F 10 102
Sep 10 Ches 6f GS 1 109
Sep 29 NmkR 5f GF 3 105

INDIAN PACE 4
Jun 1 Leop 7f G 10 **108**

INDIAN PEARL 3
Apr 19 Folk 5f GS 2 **99**

INDIAN PIPE DREAM 3
Apr 1 Donc 10½f GS 1 105
Apr 23 Leic 12f G 4 103
May 31 Sand 14f G 1 103
Sep 24 Hayd 14f GF 1 106
Oct 28 NmkR 16f GS 1 **108**

INDIAN SPARK 11
Jly 18 Ayr 6f GF 5 99
Aug 12 Newc 6f GS 5 **103**
Sep 1 Rdcr 6f G 3 100
Sep 28 Newc 5f GF 3 **103**

INDIAN STEPPES 6
Jan 7 Wolv 7f SW 2 103
Jan 27 Sthl 5f FT 3 102
Feb 9 Ling 7f FT 5 100
Feb 22 Ling 7f SD 5 105
Mar 18 Ling 7f SD 1 **110**
Apr 12 NmkR 7f GF 6 100
Apr 27 Ling 7½f S 5 107

INDIAN TRAIL 5
Apr 30 NmkR 6f G 1 **116**
Sep 7 Donc 5½f GF 6 106
Sep 24 Hayd 6f GF 8 99

INDIAN'S FEATHER 4
Nov 6 Leop 7f GS 6 **104**

INDIGO CAT 3
May 7 Ling 10f G 1 103
May 18 Gdwd 11f G 2 105
Jun 16 York 10½f G 1 **107**

INDONESIA 3
Mar 23 Ling 12f SD 6 **104**

INDUSTRIAL SPIRIT 3
May 20 NmkR 8f G 4 **107**

INFATUATE 3
May 30 Leic 8f G 1 **100**

INGLETON 3
Jly 1 Sand 5f G 5 102
Aug 28 Gdwd 6f G 8 100
Nov 3 Muss 5f GS 5 **103**

INHERIT 3
Sep 3 Thsk 6f G 3 **99**

INISHMOT LADY 7
Jun 15 Leop 9f GF 3 **103**

INK IN GOLD 4
Aug 4 Chep 12f G 6 **99**

INNCLASSIC 4
Dec 29 Ling 5f G 6 **100**

INNOCENT REBEL 4
Jly 7 Wwck 16f G 6 99

INNOCENT SPLENDOUR 3
Jun 7 Sals 10f G 5 99
Sep 19 Leic 8½f G 9 **100**
Oct 10 Wolv 9½f FT 1 **100**

INSIGNIA 3
Dec 28 Wolv 8½f FT 3 **102**

INSPECTORS CHOICE 4
Jun 1 Leop 7f G 2 **109**

INSTANT HIT 6
Jan 6 Wolv 8½f G 4 **102**
Feb 25 Wolv 8½f G 6 99

INSTRUCTOR 4
Feb 18 Wolv 8½f SD 3 106
Feb 26 Sthl 8f FT 1 **113**
Mar 8 Sthl 8f SD 7 104
Jun 8 Bevl 10f G 4 99
Jly 10 Hayd 10½f GF 1 100
Jly 28 Carl 9½f G 1 105
Aug 6 Ayr 10f F 3 100
Sep 22 Pont 10f G 6 105
Oct 7 York 10½f G 2 105

INTAVAC BOY 4
Aug 26 Newc 9f GF 5 **103**
Sep 5 Newc 10f G 3 102
Sep 20 Bevl 10f GF 2 **103**
Oct 9 Newc 12½f G 1 100
Nov 9 Wolv 12f FT 2 100
Dec 10 Wolv 12f FT 4 101

INTEND TO LEAVE 3
Oct 22 Newb 10f GS 2 **104**

INTER VISION 5
Jan 7 Wolv 7f SW 5 103
Feb 18 Wolv 6f SD 8 101
Apr 30 Thsk 5f S 4 101
May 14 Thsk 5f G 7 103
Jun 1 Newc 6f G 6 99
Jun 9 Ripn 5f G 3 105
Jun 10 Catt 6f GF 1 102
Jun 24 Newc 6f G 1 **109**
Jly 23 Newc 6f GF 3 102
Aug 1 Ripn 6f G 1 107

INTERIM PAYMENT 3
Jly 4 Bath 10f G 1 **103**
Aug 19 Ches 10½f GF 3 100
Sep 21 Gdwd 11f G 5 102

INTERNATIONALGUEST 6
Apr 26 Wwck 12½f GS 11 **99**

INTO THE BREEZE 5
Aug 18 Ches 7f F 1 **101**

INTO THE DARK 4
Sep 16 Newb 11f G 2 **106**
Sep 30 NmkR 12f G 5 103
Oct 15 NmkR 9f G 4 103
Oct 28 NmkR 10f GS 3 105

INTO THE SHADOWS 5
Apr 29 Muss 14f G 2 102
May 6 Ches 12½f GS 1 101
Sep 23 Hayd 10½f G 3 104
Oct 9 Gdwd 12f G 5 **105**
Oct 28 NmkR 12f GS 6 101

INTOXICATING 3
Apr 12 NmkR 6f GF 4 99
May 1 NmkR 7f G 2 **109**
May 14 Nott 6f F 1 106
May 21 NmkR 6f G 5 102
Jly 5 NmkJ 6f G 11 103
Aug 7 Leic 7f G 6 101
Sep 4 York 6f G 1 106

INTREPID JACK 3
May 13 Newb 6f F 1 106
Aug 6 Wind 6f GF 4 104
Aug 27 York 6f G 2 **110**

INTRICATE WEB 9
Apr 23 Hayd 10½f G 4 **103**
May 17 Rdcr 10f G 2 102
Jun 20 Ripn 10f G 4 **103**
Jly 27 Leic 10f G 6 101
Oct 9 Newc 10f G 9 102

INTRIGUING GLIMPSE 4
Apr 2 Kemp 5f GS 8 104
May 6 Ling 5f G 7 102
Jun 12 Donc 5f F 3 101
Jun 18 Ling 5f G 1 **107**
Jly 1 Sand 5f G 3 **107**
Jly 27 Gdwd 5f G 3 104
Aug 2 Brig 5½f G 1 106
Aug 10 Sand 5f GF 3 102
Aug 29 Epsm 5f G 5 **107**
Oct 1 Epsm 5f G 4 105
Oct 20 Brig 6f GS 6 101

INVASIAN 4
Jly 30 NmkJ 8f GF 8 **101**

IONIAN SPRING 10
Mar 1 Ling 10f SD 3 **107**
Mar 12 Wolv 8½f SD 6 **107**
Mar 29 Pont 10f S 3 102
May 4 Ches 10½f GS 4 **107**
Jun 25 Ches 10½f G 1 101
Jly 30 Donc 10½f G 4 102
Sep 7 Donc 10½f GF 6 104
Sep 15 Ayr 9f G 2 103
Oct 10 Ayr 10f S 2 100
Oct 29 Wolv 9½f SD 7 103

IOTA 3
Aug 17 York 12f G 5 **106**

IPLEDGEALLEGIANCE 9
Aug 6 Rdcr 14f G 4 101

IRISH BALLAD 3
Aug 26 Bath 13f G 6 **99**

IRISH QUESTION 3
Sep 10 Leop 9f GF 8 **106**

IRISH RISE 3
May 25 Leop 8f GF 7 **100**

IRONY 6
Jun 11 Sand 7f G 4 **112**
Jly 2 Carl 7f GF 1 107
Jly 8 Ling 7f G 2 105
Aug 6 NmkJ 7f G 17 103
Aug 11 Sand 7f GF 9 102
Aug 29 Ripn 8f G 10 102
Sep 10 Gdwd 7f G 10 105
Oct 7 Newb 7f GF 9 99

IRUNARRI 3
Jun 27 Lonc 10½f G 10 **103**

ISA'AF 6
Mar 7 Wolv 12f SD 2 **109**
Dec 21 Ling 12f SD 5 100

ISIDORE BONHEUR 4
Jun 18 Rdcr 10f G 5 106
Jly 28 Muss 7f G 2 103
Aug 6 Rdcr 7f G 4 101
Sep 7 Donc 10½f GF 3 106
Sep 15 Ayr 9f G 1 **107**
Oct 7 York 10½f G 5 103

ISKANDER 4
May 13 Nott 8f F 1 **104**
May 21 Carl 8f G 2 103
Jun 1 Newc 8f G 3 **104**
Jun 11 Leic 10f G 2 102
Aug 26 Newc 9f GF 11 100

ISLAND RAPTURE 5
Jan 17 Wolv 8½f SD 4 **107**
Feb 8 Ling 8f SD 4 101
Mar 3 Ling 8f SW 2 104
Jun 27 Pont 8f G 4 103
Jly 11 Wind 8½f G 5 101
Dec 5 Ling 8f FT 2 106
Dec 20 Ling 8f FT 2 104
Dec 30 Ling 8f FT 11 99

ISLAND SOUND 8
Apr 20 Epsm 10f GS 8 **107**

ISLANDS FAREWELL 5
Jan 2 Sthl 11f SD 3 **103**

ISLE DE MAURICE 3
Mar 4 Wolv 12f SD 1 **104**
Apr 23 Leic 12f G 5 99

ISTAN 3
Jly 9 Deau 6f GF 7 **105**

IT MUST BE SPEECH 4
Dec 29 Ling 10f GF 9 **100**

IT'S THE LIMIT 6
May 14 Newb 12f G 3 108

ITALIAN MIST 6
Jan 13 Ling 6f SD 4 **102**

ITQAAN 3
Aug 3 Pont 8f G 1 **100**

ITSONLYWOODY 3
May 22 Curr 6f G 13 99
Jun 15 Leop 7f G 3 **104**
Aug 7 Curr 7f G 11 101
Nov 6 Leop 12f S 1 102

ITZMO 3
Jun 27 Lonc 7f G 4 **103**

IVORY LACE 4
Feb 26 Ling 6f SD 3 99
Mar 21 Ling 6f SD 6 103
Jun 18 Ling 5f G 2 **106**
Sep 5 Bath 5½f GF 7 101
Oct 4 Leic 6f G 4 99
Oct 27 Ling 7f SD 2 100
Dec 20 Ling 6f SD 5 100

IWUNDER 3
Aug 20 Sand 8f G 3 **102**

IZENAH 3
Jun 27 Lonc 9½f G 8 **101**

J

J R STEVENSON 9
Feb 28 Wolv 9½f SD 3 **107**
Oct 30 Ling 12f SD 2 100

JAAFI 3
Jun 7 Rdcr 11f G 1 **101**
Jly 4 Ripn 12f G 2 100

JAAMID 3
Sep 20 Bevl 8½f GF 5 **99**

JACARANDA 5
Mar 3 Ling 10f SW 7 **105**
Apr 1 Ling 12f SD 3 102

JACK DAWSON 8
Feb 12 Wolv 12f FT 5 107
May 7 Thsk 16f GS 5 101
May 21 Ling 16f SD 4 103

JACK OF TRUMPS 5
Apr 11 Ling 12f SD 1 103
Jun 4 Donc 12f GF 2 105
Jly 23 Newb 12f GF 2 **108**
Oct 22 Newb 10f G 6 107

JACK SULLIVAN 4
Jly 9 Ling 8f SD 7 109
Jly 26 Gdwd 7f G 2 **116**
Aug 11 Sals 8f GF 2 114
Sep 8 Donc 7f GF 8 100

JACK THE GIANT 3
Sep 1 Rdcr 9f G 2 101
Sep 8 Epsm 8½f G 1 **105**
Sep 20 Bevl 8½f GF 4 99

JACKIE KIELY 4
May 5 Ches 10½f G 9 99
Jun 11 Leic 10f G 3 **102**
Jly 12 Brig 10f G 4 100
Aug 23 Brig 10f G 1 99
Aug 29 Chep 10f G 1 99
Nov 8 Sthl 12f G 1 99

JACKS ESTATE 10
Sep 17 Curr 5f G 15 **101**

JADAN 4
Apr 30 Thsk 5f S 6 99
Jly 23 Newc 5f GF 1 **105**
Aug 10 Bevl 5f GF 4 100
Aug 20 Ches 5f G 7 99
Sep 10 Ches 5f GS 7 100

JADEERON 6
Jan 12 Wolv 14f SD 2 **106**
Jan 22 Ling 16f FT 9 100

JAGGED 5
Aug 12 Folk 5f GF 4 **100**

JAGGER 5
Jly 29 Gdwd 12f G 3 101
Aug 17 York 14f G 6 106
Aug 20 Ches 13½f G 1 107
Sep 8 Donc 18f G 5 108
Sep 24 NmkR 16f G 6 **109**

JAGUAR ON THE RUN 3
Jly 6 Naas 6f GF 6 **100**

JAHIA 6
Mar 31 Ling 8f SD 2 **100**

JAIR OHMSFORD 6
Apr 9 Newc 12½f S 2 101
May 12 York 14f S 3 107
Jun 3 Hayd 14f G 3 99

JAKARMI 4
Mar 7 Wolv 12f SD 9 **101**
Apr 21 Bath 10f GS 2 99
Jly 22 Wolv 8½f FT 3 100

JAKE BLACK 5
Mar 7 Wolv 12f SD 11 100

JALAMID 3
Apr 15 Newb 8f GS 1 107
Aug 6 Rdcr 8f G 1 **109**
Oct 1 Rdcr 8f GF 4 99

JALISSA 3
May 1 Sals 6f G 1 99

Aug 12 NmkJ 7f G 3 102
Sep 14 Sand 8f G 4 **104**

JALLDEE 3
Sep 1 Rdcr 9f G 1 103
Sep 14 Sand 10f G 1 101
Oct 4 Leic 12f G 4 **104**

JALMIRA 4
Sep 4 Curr 8f G 2 **112**

JALOUHAR 5
Dec 28 Wolv 6f G 1 **102**

JAMAICAN 3
May 28 Ling 12f SW 1 **104**
Jun 21 Brig 12f G 5 99

JAMES CAIRD 5
May 20 Hayd 8f G 5 **106**
May 30 Rdcr 10f G 4 104
Jun 7 Rdcr 8f G 2 104
Jly 9 York 10½f G 4 104
Jly 30 Gdwd 9f G 1 105
Aug 17 York 10½f G 7 104
Aug 27 York 9f G 3 105
Sep 15 Ayr 9f G 6 99
Oct 7 York 8f G 12 101

JARDINES LOOKOUT 8
May 13 York 14f GS 6 **104**

JARVO 4
Jun 22 Bath 10f G 2 **99**

JASMINE PEARL 4
Jun 15 Chep 6f GS 3 **102**
Aug 4 Brig 6f G 4 101
Aug 15 Brig 6f G 1 **102**

JATH 4
Apr 14 Ripn 10f S 1 **104**
May 13 York 7f GS 4 101
Sep 14 Yarm 10f G 6 103
Nov 5 Donc 10½f S 5 99

JAYANJAY 6
Jun 25 Wind 6f G 9 104
Jun 30 Epsm 6f G 3 105
Jly 8 Ling 6f SW 8 103
Aug 29 Epsm 5f G 6 106
Oct 1 Epsm 5f G 1 **109**
Oct 20 Brig 6f GS 1 105
Oct 30 Ling 6f SD 11 100
Nov 15 Ling 7f FT 4 105

JAYER GILLES 5
May 1 Sals 14f GS 10 99
May 26 Bath 17½f G 2 **103**
Jun 4 Chep 18f GS 5 102
Jly 7 Wwck 16f G 4 101
Sep 17 Wwck 16f G 5 **103**

JAYMITO 3
Jun 27 Lonc 7f G 7 **101**

JAZZ D'ALLIER 8
Apr 30 Lonc 15½f GS 5 **111**
May 22 Lonc 15½f GF 7 99

JAZZ PRINCESS 3
May 8 Leop 7f S 4 100

May 22 Curr 8f G 9 **110**
Jly 17 Curr 9f F 2 109

JAZZ SCENE 4
Mar 26 Kemp 10f GS 8 101
Apr 2 Donc 8f G 13 103
Jun 3 Epsm 8½f G 8 102
Jun 11 Ripn 9f G 3 106
Jun 18 Rdcr 10f G 4 **107**
Jly 23 York 10½f GS 2 104
Aug 11 Hayd 10½f GF 1 105
Aug 30 Ripn 10f F 7 99
Sep 4 York 9f G 2 99

JE SUIS BELLE 3
Oct 12 Ling 10f G 8 99
Nov 15 Sthl 11f FT 3 **100**

JEDBURGH 4
Apr 12 NmkR 7f GF 1 103
May 7 Ling 7f G 10 99
May 29 NmkR 7f GF 5 102
Jun 16 York 7f GF 1 109
Jly 16 Newb 6f GF 5 **113**
Aug 18 York 7f GF 4 108
Sep 8 Epsm 7f G 5 102
Oct 1 Rdcr 7f GF 6 106

JEEPSTAR 5
Apr 20 Epsm 12f GS 9 99
May 23 Thsk 12f G 2 104
Jun 4 Donc 12f GF 4 104
Jun 30 Hayd 14f GF 3 105
Jly 12 Bevl 16f GF 1 103
Sep 3 Hayd 14f GF 2 **106**
Sep 24 Hayd 14f GF 7 101

JEMMY JOHN 5
May 25 Leop 7f GF 5 **104**

JEMMY'S BROTHER 4
Mar 20 Curr 8f HY 12 **102**

JENKINS LANE 3
Aug 14 Leop 7f F 5 **102**

JENNVERSE 3
Mar 21 Ling 7f F 1 **99**

JEROME 4
Jly 29 Thsk 7f G 8 **101**

JEWEL IN THE SAND 3
Jun 11 Sand 5f G 3 **100**

JIDIYA 6
Jan 29 Ling 10f SD 10 **104**
Feb 21 Ling 10f FT 8 99
Mar 7 Wolv 14f SD 1 102

JILLY WHY 4
Feb 11 Wolv 5f SD 9 100
Sep 16 Nott 6f GF 1 101
Sep 21 Rdcr 5f GF 4 **102**

JIMMY RYAN 4
May 28 Gdwd 5f G 2 **106**

JOHN FORBES 3
May 6 Haml 11f GS 1 **102**
May 13 York 12f GS 4 100

JOHN ROBIE 3
May 17 Leic 6f G 3 101
Jun 4 Donc 5f G 3 **102**

JOHNNY ALLJAYS 4
Mar 26 Wolv 14f FT 1 **104**
Apr 5 Sthl 14f SD 3 99

JOHNNY JUMPUP 3
Apr 16 Newb 7f GS 2 106
Jun 12 Chan 8f GF 5 **108**

JOHNNY PARKES 4
Sep 9 Donc 5f G 9 **103**
Sep 21 Gdwd 6f GF 11 101
Oct 7 York 5f G 2 102

JOHNSTON'S DIAMOND 7
Jan 11 Sthl 6f SW 4 100
Feb 17 Sthl 5f SD 4 **102**
Mar 31 Donc 6f G 3 **102**
May 6 Ches 5f GS 7 100
Jun 7 Ches 7f GF 5 99
Aug 19 Wolv 6f FT 3 101
Sep 2 Hayd 6f GF 1 **102**
Sep 16 Ayr 6f GF 7 99
Sep 26 Haml 6f F 3 100

JOINT AGREEMENT 8
Apr 3 Curr 16f HY 3 107

JOINT ASPIRATION 3
Mar 26 Kemp 8f GS 2 107
May 1 NmkR 8f G 13 101
May 22 Curr 8f G 7 **111**
Jly 17 Curr 9f F 9 100
Jly 30 Gdwd 10f G 8 103
Sep 9 Donc 8f G 4 103
Sep 24 NmkR 8f G 2 **111**

JOLIE 3
May 2 Wwck 8f G 3 **101**
May 30 Chep 6f G 1 99

JOMUS 4
Mar 3 Ling 10f SW 9 104
Apr 1 Ling 8f SD 5 101
Apr 8 Ling 10f SD 2 99
Aug 5 Ling 10f GS 4 99
Dec 20 Ling 10f GS 2 **105**

JONANAUD 6
May 1 Sals 14f GS 6 **104**

JONATHAN JOSH 4
May 11 York 12f S 5 **100**

JONNY EBENEEZER 6
May 28 Gdwd 5f G 6 **102**

JONQUIL 3
May 18 Gdwd 9f G 4 **106**

JOOLS 7
Mar 16 Wolv 7f SD 3 100
Mar 24 Wolv 8½f SD 3 101
May 22 Brig 7f G 3 99
Jun 6 Wind 8½f G 1 **111**
Jun 26 Wind 8½f G 1 107

JORDANS ELECT 5
Jun 28 Haml 9f F 2 99

Jly 18 Ayr 8f GF 4 103
Jly 30 Haml 9f F 3 **104**
Sep 18 Haml 8½f F 4 101
Sep 26 Haml 9f G 2 99
Oct 9 Newc 10f G 14 100

JORDANS SPARK 4
Oct 19 Newc 8f GS 1 **100**

JOSEAR 3
Apr 11 Sthl 10f G 4 101
May 27 Wolv 12f SD 2 99
May 28 Ling 12f SW 2 **103**

JOSEPH HENRY 3
May 1 NmkR 7f G 3 **107**
Jun 3 Epsm 7f G 4 **107**
Jly 5 NmkJ 6f G 12 102
Jly 28 Gdwd 7f G 4 102

JOSEPHUS 4
Aug 6 NmkJ 7f G 10 **109**

JOSH 3
Apr 13 NmkR 7f G 5 **105**
May 13 Newb 6f F 4 99
May 21 Hayd 6f F 3 100
Aug 18 Ches 7½f F 2 100
Aug 29 Wwck 7f GF 5 **105**
Sep 17 Ayr 8f G 4 100
Sep 30 NmkR 7f G 12 99

JOSHUA'S GOLD 4
Apr 22 Wolv 8½f SD 2 101
May 21 Catt 7f GF 3 100
Jly 6 Catt 7f GS 1 100
Jly 29 Thsk 7f G 3 105
Sep 4 York 8f G 3 **109**
Sep 10 Muss 8f G 2 102
Sep 12 Muss 8f GF 2 100
Oct 9 Newc 8f G 4 99

JOSTLE 3
Mar 3 Ling 8f SW 6 **102**

JOY AND PAIN 4
Jan 26 Ling 7f FT 4 100
Feb 5 Ling 7f FT 2 103
Feb 12 Ling 6f SD 2 **109**
Mar 21 Ling 6f SD 1 106

JOYEAUX 3
Apr 6 Nott 5f S 1 100
Jun 23 Haml 5f G 3 **105**
Dec 2 Wolv 6f SD 4 102
Dec 17 Ling 5f FT 2 104

JUBILANT NOTE 3
May 25 Leop 8f GF 2 **109**
Aug 20 Curr 10f GF 4 104

JUBILEE STREET 6
May 21 Catt 7f GF 1 101
May 28 Donc 7f G 1 100
Jun 1 Newc 8f G 2 105
Jun 8 Bevl 7½f G 2 104
Jun 17 Rdcr 8f G 2 102
Jun 29 Catt 7f G 5 99
Sep 6 Catt 7f GF 2 **106**
Sep 20 Bevl 7½f GF 1 105
Oct 1 Rdcr 8f GF 1 101

JUDD STREET 3
Jly 8 Ches 5f F 3 99
Aug 5 Ling 6f SD 1 100
Sep 9 Sand 5f G 2 **102**
Sep 16 Ayr 5f GF 2 **102**

JUMEIRAH SCARER 4
May 28 Muss 8f G 3 **103**

JUNGLE LION 7
Feb 1 Sthl 12f FT 2 **99**

JUST A GLIMMER 5
Jan 29 Ling 7f SD 11 **100**

JUST A TRY 3
Mar 3 Ling 8f SW 3 103
Apr 26 Wwck 7f GS 5 **104**
May 2 Kemp 9f G 6 99
Jun 17 NmkJ 8f GF 5 99

JUST BOND 3
Jly 6 Catt 7f GS 3 **99**

JUST FLY 5
Jan 29 Ling 7f SD 7 **108**
Aug 3 Brig 8f G 12 99
Sep 19 Leic 8½f G 7 101
Oct 8 Sals 7f GF 4 100
Dec 5 Ling 8f FT 4 101
Dec 21 Ling 10f FT 4 101

JUST JAMES 6
Jly 7 NmkJ 7f G 10 **104**
Jly 23 Newb 7f GF 18 102

JUST WAZ 3
Jly 4 Ripn 12f G 3 99
Aug 1 Ripn 10f G 3 **100**

JUST WIZ 9
Jan 7 Wolv 8½f SW 7 **101**
Jan 14 Wolv 9½f SW 4 99

JUSTALORD 7
Jan 1 Sthl 5f FT 6 99
Feb 5 Ling 5f FT 10 100
Feb 19 Wolv 5f FT 8 102
Feb 26 Ling 5f SD 2 **103**

JUSTAQUESTION 3
Aug 12 NmkJ 7f G 6 **99**
Sep 14 Sand 8f G 11 **99**

JUSTE POUR L'AMOUR 5
Jun 3 Gdwd 7f GS 6 103
Jun 10 Gdwd 7f G 3 101
Jun 17 Gdwd 8f G 2 **110**

K

KABEER 7
Jan 15 Ling 10f SD 2 103
Jan 22 Ling 10f FT 2 104
Feb 9 Ling 8f FT 1 103
Feb 26 Ling 10f SD 7 103
Mar 19 Ling 8f SD 1 **107**
Jun 13 Wwck 7f GF 6 101

KABIS AMIGOS 3
Aug 30 Ripn 8f F 1 **101**

KALAMKAR 3
May 5 Ches 12½f GS 4 **101**

KALANI STAR 5
Jan 11 Sthl 8f SW 5 **103**
Feb 25 Wolv 8½f SW 4 100
Mar 4 Wolv 8½f SD 5 102
Mar 16 Wolv 9½f SD 3 100
May 30 Rdcr 7f G 2 99
Jun 9 Brig 7f G 2 100
Aug 2 Catt 7f G 2 101
Aug 12 Catt 7f G 2 99
Aug 24 Brig 7f S 3 99
Sep 1 Carl 7f G 3 102
Sep 10 Muss 8f G 7 99
Sep 12 Muss 8f GF 3 99

KALISHKA 4
Apr 25 Haml 9f G 3 **101**

KALLISTA'S PRIDE 5
Jan 4 Ling 6f FT 3 100
Jun 18 Ling 5f G 8 102
Jly 30 Thsk 6f G 1 100
Aug 21 Folk 5f G 1 **108**
Sep 5 Bath 5½f GF 2 106
Sep 17 Wwck 5½f G 2 100

KALUANA COURT 9
May 26 Bath 17½f G 5 100
Jun 18 NmkJ 15f G 4 **106**

KAMAKIRI 3
Apr 13 NmkR 7f G 1 **109**
May 15 Lonc 8f G 10 105
Jun 25 Wind 8½f G 3 105
Jly 26 Gdwd 7f G 12 101

KAMANDA LAUGH 4
Apr 1 Donc 8f G 9 99
May 6 Ches 7½f GS 3 106
Jly 5 NmkJ 6f G 1 **109**
Jly 7 NmkJ 7f G 7 105
Jly 29 Gdwd 8f G 11 108
Sep 10 Donc 8f GS 6 102

KAMES PARK 3
May 13 York 10½f GS 2 99
Aug 4 Hayd 8f GF 3 **107**

KANAD 3
May 13 Nott 8f F 5 100
May 24 Ripn 10f GS 3 101
Jly 17 Rdcr 11f G 4 **102**
Aug 3 Epsm 10f G 8 **102**

KANDIDATE 3
Jan 28 Wolv 8½f SD 1 **111**
Apr 14 NmkR 8f G 3 100
Apr 30 NmkR 8f G 3 110
May 12 York 10½f S 4 104
Jun 14 York 8f G 5 104
Jly 27 Gdwd 8f GS 9 **111**
Aug 11 Sals 8f GF 5 110
Nov 19 Ling 10f FT 5 101

KANGARILLA ROAD 6
Feb 28 Wolv 5f SD 1 **103**
May 27 Catt 5f GF 3 101
Jun 10 Catt 6f GF 3 99
Jun 23 Thsk 5f GF 4 101

KANPAI 3
Aug 11 Chep 12f G 2 **100**

KARAOKE 5
Jan 10 Wolv 9½f SD 7 **103**
Feb 8 Ling 12f SD 4 99
Feb 21 Ling 10f FT 2 **103**
Apr 8 Ling 10f SD 2 100
May 6 Nott 10f G 2 100
Dec 21 Ling 10f G 2 99

KARATHAENA 5
Aug 28 Bevl 10f GS 5 99

KAREEB 8
Jan 31 Wolv 7f SD 1 104
Feb 12 Ling 8f SD 3 99
Jly 8 Ling 7f G 3 99
Sep 4 York 7f GF 3 99
Sep 11 Gdwd 8f G 4 **107**

KAREN'S CAPER 3
Apr 13 NmkR 7f G 1 108
May 1 NmkR 8f G 4 108
Jun 17 York 8f G 2 111
Jly 5 NmkJ 8f G 4 104
Sep 10 Leop 8f GF 6 **114**

KARLIYNA 3
Jun 8 Newb 10f GF 2 **99**

KARLU 3
Jun 25 Ches 12½f G 2 102
Sep 2 Hayd 12f G 1 **104**

KARMINSKEY PARK 6
Apr 8 Ling 6f SD 2 **103**
Apr 29 Nott 6f GS 1 101

KARRAMALU 4
Aug 7 Curr 10f G 3 **108**
Sep 4 Curr 10f G 4 106

KASALI 4
Oct 30 StCl 8f G 9 **106**

KASTHARI 6
Sep 8 Donc 18f G 3 109

KASTORIA 4
Aug 18 York 12f G 1 104
Sep 7 Donc 14½f GF 2 102
Oct 1 Lonc 12½f G 2 **112**

KATHOLOGY 8
Jan 19 Ling 5f FT 1 **107**

KATHRYN JANEWAY 3
May 2 Wwck 8f G 2 102
May 25 Ling 10f G 4 **103**

KATIYPOUR 8
Feb 22 Ling 7f SD 2 106
Mar 1 Ling 6f SD 1 **110**
Mar 12 Wolv 6f SD 1 107
Mar 19 Ling 7f SD 4 105
Jun 22 Epsm 7f G 2 103
Jly 8 Ling 7f G 1 107
Aug 3 Epsm 8½f G 6 100
Aug 11 Sand 7f GF 3 108
Sep 10 Gdwd 7f G 4 **110**
Sep 21 Gdwd 6f GF 10 102
Sep 27 Gdwd 7f G 3 105
Dec 17 Ling 6f FT 6 103

KAURI FOREST 4
Mar 20 Curr 6f HY 3 **102**

KAVI 5
Feb 12 Ling 12f SD 1 **102**
Feb 28 Wolv 12f SD 1 100
Apr 1 Ling 12f SD 2 **102**
Jly 15 Wwck 12½f G 5 99

KAY TWO 3
Jun 26 Curr 5f GF 6 108
Jly 9 Ches 5f GF 5 106
Jly 16 Curr 5f F 6 107
Aug 20 Curr 6f GF 3 108
Sep 17 Curr 6f G 5 **110**
Oct 9 Curr 6f GS 4 101

KAYMICH PERFECTO 5
May 4 Chep 8f S 4 102
May 21 Catt 7f GF 3 100
May 31 Rdcr 9f G 1 100
Jly 17 Rdcr 9f G 3 103
Jly 28 Carl 9½f G 5 100
Aug 7 Rdcr 8f G 1 100
Aug 11 Chep 8f G 2 **104**
Sep 13 Thsk 8f G 2 99
Sep 18 Haml 8½f F 5 99

KAZATZKA 3
Jun 25 Ling 10f SW 8 **100**

KEEN LOOK 6
Jly 6 Naas 6f GF 5 101
Aug 7 Curr 7f G 8 104
Aug 14 Leop 7f F 6 100
Sep 4 Curr 8f G 5 **109**
Sep 10 Leop 9f GF 3 108
Sep 17 Curr 8f GF 10 102

KEENELAND SWAN 6
Jun 18 York 6f GF 10 **102**
Jly 7 NmkJ 6f G 12 101

KEEP ON MOVIN' 4
Mar 30 Folk 12f HY 4 **103**

KEEPER'S LODGE 4
Jun 11 Ripn 8f G 7 99
Jly 8 York 10½f GS 8 **100**
Sep 2 Hayd 8f G 9 99

KEEPERS KNIGHT 4
Jan 6 Wolv 12f G 10 99
Mar 17 Sthl 12f G 2 **103**
May 16 Muss 16f G 2 99
Jun 17 Rdcr 16f G 4 100

KELATAKAN 4
Aug 7 Curr 10f G 9 **105**

KELLY NICOLE 3
May 9 Rdcr 10f G 1 **99**
Jun 25 Curr 10f G 12 **99**

KELTIC RAINBOW 4
Feb 8 Sthl 11f SD 8 99
May 5 Chep 12f S 3 99
Jun 29 Chep 12f G 4 **101**

KELTOS 7
May 1 StCl 8f HD 8 **113**

KELUCIA 4
Jly 14 Donc 7f GF 7 99
Jly 24 Newb 8f G 5 **100**
Aug 20 Rdcr 8f G 1 99

KEMPSEY 3
Jan 8 Ling 5f SD 3 99
Aug 7 Ling 5f G 1 **104**
Oct 28 NmkR 6f GS 4 100

KENACKY 5
Aug 7 Deau 10f GF 1 **109**

KENDOR DINE 3
Apr 3 Lonc 10f S 2 108
Apr 24 Lonc 10f GS 1 100
Jun 27 Lonc 9f G 3 111
Jly 24 MsnL 10f F 7 107
Aug 20 Deau 10f GS 3 **113**
Sep 17 Lonc 10f G 3 107

KENMORE 3
Apr 29 Nott 6f GS 1 99
Jly 28 Gdwd 7f G 4 102
Aug 27 Gdwd 7f G 6 100
Sep 24 NmkR 7f G 14 104
Oct 14 NmkR 7f G 1 **110**

KENNINGTON 5
Mar 28 Yarm 6f GS 1 102
Aug 3 Yarm 6f G 3 105
Aug 22 Leic 5f G 4 99
Sep 21 Rdcr 6f GF 1 101
Sep 27 Nott 6f G 4 100
Dec 3 Wolv 6f G 3 99
Dec 17 Ling 5f FT 1 **106**

KENSINGTON 4
Aug 15 Brig 6f G 3 99
Aug 23 Brig 7f G 3 101
Sep 15 Ayr 5f GF 1 **102**
Oct 30 Ling 7f SD 1 **102**
Dec 19 Wolv 6f FT 2 101

KENTUCKY BULLET 9
Jan 2 Sthl 11f SD 4 **101**
Apr 4 Sthl 11f SD 3 **101**
Jly 25 Sthl 12f SD 1 100

KENTUCKY CHARM 4
Apr 3 Curr 16f HY 4 **107**

KERASHAN 3
May 2 Kemp 9f G 1 104
Jun 4 Epsm 10f G 2 104
Jly 6 NmkJ 10f G 2 107
Sep 23 Ling 10f G 3 105
Oct 4 Leic 12f G 1 107
Oct 13 NmkR 12f G 4 **108**

KERESFORTH 3
Jan 8 Ling 5f SD 1 **102**

KERNEL DOWERY 5
May 30 Leic 12f G 4 **102**
Jun 19 Wwck 12½f G 3 100
Jly 15 Wwck 12½f G 2 100

KESHYA 4
Apr 23 Hayd 8f G 2 103
Jun 16 Wolv 8½f G 1 **104**
Aug 27 Wind 8½f G 2 102

KESTREL CROSS 3
Jun 25 Curr 10f G 7 102
Aug 20 Curr 10f GF 3 106
Sep 4 Curr 8f G 1 **113**
Sep 10 Leop 7f HD 7 104

KEW GREEN 7
Jan 19 Ling 10f FT 2 103
Jan 28 Wolv 9½f SD 3 105
Feb 21 Ling 10f FT 1 104
Mar 26 Kemp 10f GS 1 107
May 7 NmkR 9f GF 1 **108**
Nov 19 Ling 10f FT 1 103

KEW THE MUSIC 5
Jan 31 Wolv 7f SD 1 100
Feb 5 Ling 7f SD 3 101
Feb 9 Ling 8f SD 4 100
Feb 19 Wolv 7f SD 4 **103**
Apr 11 Sthl 7f G 3 99
Apr 24 Brig 8f GF 3 101
Apr 29 Muss 8f G 2 102
Jun 13 Thsk 7f G 3 101
Jun 21 Brig 7f G 4 100
Oct 25 Yarm 7f S 4 101
Dec 2 Wolv 6f SD 6 100

KEY TIME 3
Aug 24 Brig 12f GS 2 **100**
Aug 27 Gdwd 16f G 1 99

KEY TO THE KINGDOM 5
Jly 2 Leop 12f GF 5 **104**

KEYAKI 4
Aug 6 NmkJ 8f G 9 **100**
Sep 27 Gdwd 7f G 7 **100**

KEYS OF CYPRUS 3
Aug 24 Catt 6f G 1 **100**

KHABFAIR 4
Jun 16 York 7f GF 9 101
Aug 8 Wind 6f GF 6 100
Sep 10 Gdwd 6f GF 4 **110**
Sep 17 Ayr 6f G 7 **110**
Oct 1 Rdcr 7f GF 4 108
Oct 21 Newb 6f G 5 102

KHALIDIA 4
Feb 22 Ling 7f SD 11 **99**

KHANJAR 5
Aug 6 Hayd 8f GF 2 103
Aug 22 Haml 8½f F 5 102
Sep 12 Muss 9f GF 4 100
Oct 31 Wolv 8½f SD 3 104
Nov 12 Wolv 9½f FT 2 101
Dec 3 Wolv 9½f FT 3 100
Dec 15 Sthl 12f SD 3 **114**
Dec 22 Sthl 12f SD 1 106

KHARISH 3
May 14 Newb 11f G 2 104
Jun 17 York 12f G 8 101
Jly 15 NmkJ 10f G 3 99
Aug 17 York 10½f G 6 **105**

KHE SANH 3
Feb 23 Ling 8f G 1 100
Jun 27 Pont 8f G 5 **102**
Nov 19 Ling 8f FT 6 101

KHYBER KIM 3
Aug 4 Hayd 10½f GF 1 105
Sep 9 Donc 10½f G 2 111
Oct 22 Newb 10f G 1 **113**

KIAMA 3
Jly 6 Ling 12f SW 2 **103**

KID CREOLE 7
Jly 2 Leop 7f F 6 101
Jly 16 Curr 7f F 2 100
Aug 7 Curr 7f G 6 **105**
Sep 17 Curr 5f G 6 **105**

KID'Z'PLAY 9
May 1 Haml 13f S 5 99

KILL CAT 4
Mar 19 Ling 7f SD 8 **101**

KILLENA BOY 3
Apr 29 Nott 8f G 1 100
Jun 16 Newb 8f G 3 101
Jly 7 NmkJ 8f G 6 **103**
Sep 14 Yarm 8f GF 2 102
Oct 1 Epsm 8½f GS 4 101

KILMANNIN 5
May 8 Leop 8f S 1 **114**
Sep 18 Curr 7f GF 4 99

KILMORE PRINCESS 4
May 25 Leop 7f GF 6 103
Jun 1 Leop 7f G 9 **108**

KIND 4
Apr 26 Bath 5f HY 3 105
May 14 Nott 6f F 1 106
Jun 1 Leop 6f G 3 **111**
Jly 8 York 6f G 5 106
Aug 7 Curr 6f G 5 105

KIND EMPEROR 8
Jun 1 Yarm 11½f G 1 **105**
Jun 30 Yarm 10f G 1 99

KINDLELIGHT DEBUT 5
Jun 1 Yarm 8f G 1 101
Jun 17 NmkJ 8f GF 2 99
Jun 30 Yarm 7f G 3 100
Jly 5 Wolv 7f FT 1 99
Jly 11 Wolv 7f SD 1 105
Aug 6 NmkJ 8f G 5 102
Sep 2 NmkJ 8f G 5 **106**
Oct 3 Wind 8½f GF 4 104
Nov 19 Ling 8f FT 6 99

KINDLING 3
May 15 Ripn 12f G 4 99
Jly 31 Ches 12½f G 5 99
Sep 2 Hayd 12f G 4 101
Sep 23 Hayd 12f G 1 103
Nov 3 Muss 16f GS 1 **104**

KINDNESS 5
May 2 Wwck 8f G 4 100
Jun 2 Brig 8f G 1 100
Aug 3 Epsm 8½f G 2 99
Sep 11 Gdwd 8f G 13 **102**

KING AFTER 3
Sep 12 Muss 8f GF 1 **102**

KING AT LAST 6
Apr 22 Wolv 8½f SD 3 **101**

KING CAREW 7
Jun 26 Curr 12f F 15 **105**

KING EIDER 6
Feb 12 Wolv 12f FT 4 **107**
May 21 NmkR 14f GS 3 102

KING FLYER 9
Jan 1 Sthl 16f SD 1 **103**
Aug 6 Rdcr 14f G 2 **103**

KING HARSON 6
Apr 9 Newc 7f S 6 104
Apr 30 Thsk 7f S 1 107
Aug 19 Ches 7f GF 7 103
Sep 8 Donc 7f G 4 100
Sep 24 NmkR 7f G 8 **111**

KING JOCK 4
Apr 3 Curr 7f S 4 **107**
Jun 16 York 7f GF 2 **107**
Sep 10 Leop 7f HD 12 101

KING MARJU 3
Apr 12 NmkR 7f GF 3 99
Jun 15 York 7f G 10 99
Jly 5 NmkJ 6f G 6 106
Jly 28 Gdwd 7f G 5 102
Aug 13 Newb 7f G 2 105
Aug 27 Gdwd 7f G 3 107
Sep 24 NmkR 7f G 9 **110**

KING NICHOLAS 6
Jan 6 Wolv 8½f G 3 102
Feb 12 Wolv 8½f FT 2 **105**
Apr 2 Wolv 8½f FT 5 100

KING OF DIAMONDS 4
Jan 8 Ling 8f SD 5 102
Jan 13 Ling 12f SD 11 100
Aug 3 Epsm 10f G 5 **105**

KING OF KNIGHT 4
Jan 22 Ling 10f FT 1 **106**
Feb 12 Ling 10f SD 5 102
Jun 11 Ling 10f SW 2 102

KING OF MEZE 4
Nov 4 Yarm 6f S 8 **99**

KING OF MUSIC 4
Feb 5 Ling 10f S 4 101
Feb 16 Ling 10f SD 7 **103**

KING OF PEACE 12
Jun 26 Curr 12f F 14 **105**

KING OF TORY 3
May 25 Leop 7f GF 9 101
Sep 10 Leop 9f GF 13 104
Sep 17 Curr 8f GF 5 **107**

KING REVO 5
May 4 Ches 18½f GS 7 102
Sep 24 Hayd 14f GF 10 100
Oct 15 NmkR 18f G 2 106

KING ZAFEEN 3
Jly 4 Muss 9f GF 2 **106**

KING'S CAPRICE 4
Sep 11 Gdwd 6f G 3 104
Sep 16 Newb 7f GF 2 102
Sep 30 NmkR 7f G 8 102
Oct 14 NmkR 7f G 12 104
Oct 27 Ling 7f SD 4 107
Nov 19 Ling 7f FT 2 **112**
Nov 26 Ling 8f FT 8 103

KING'S GAIT 3
Aug 13 NmkJ 6f G 1 105
Sep 24 Hayd 5f GF 4 106
Oct 16 Muss 5f GF 1 107
Oct 22 Donc 5f S 2 **113**

KING'S KAMA 3
Apr 16 Wolv 8½f FT 1 **102**
May 15 Ripn 10f G 8 101

KING'S MAJESTY 3
Aug 27 NmkJ 7f G 1 **105**

KING'S MINSTREL 4
Feb 22 Ling 10f SD 7 **102**

KING'S THOUGHT 6
Mar 12 Wolv 8½f SD 8 106
Mar 26 Kemp 10f GS 5 104
Apr 14 Ripn 10f S 3 101
Apr 20 Epsm 10f GS 1 **111**
May 4 Ches 10½f GS 5 107

KINGDOM OF DREAMS 3
Jun 22 Sals 12f G 4 101
Sep 21 Gdwd 11f G 7 99
Oct 5 Nott 10f G 3 **107**
Oct 10 Wind 10f G 3 100

KINGS COLLEGE BOY 5
Jun 8 Haml 5f G 4 99
Jun 25 Ches 5f G 3 100
Jun 28 Haml 5f F 4 100
Jly 20 Sand 5f GF 1 103
Jly 23 Newc 6f GF 5 101
Aug 17 Nott 5f GF 2 105
Aug 27 York 6f G 5 102
Sep 9 Sand 5f G 4 101
Sep 10 Ches 5f GS 2 **109**
Sep 16 Ayr 5f GF 3 102
Oct 7 York 5f G 6 99

KINGS POINT 4
May 12 York 7f GS 3 110
Jun 26 Curr 8f F 2 110
Jly 29 Gdwd 8f G 14 105
Aug 18 York 7f GF 5 108
Sep 18 Curr 8f GF 1 **111**
Sep 27 Gdwd 7f G 6 99

KINGS QUAY 3
Mar 26 Kemp 8f GS 5 100
Apr 14 NmkR 9f G 2 101
Apr 22 Sand 10f G 6 99
Jun 27 Lonc 9f G 7 106
Jly 16 Newb 10f GF 3 **110**
Aug 29 Epsm 10f G 4 105
Oct 9 Gdwd 10f G 5 104

KINGS TOPIC 5
May 27 Wolv 9½f SD 1 **100**

KINGSCROSS 7
Apr 5 Folk 6f G 3 100
Apr 30 Gdwd 6f G 4 99
Jun 18 NmkJ 6f G 5 100
Aug 5 Hayd 6f F 1 106
Aug 17 Epsm 6f G 6 100
Aug 27 NmkJ 6f G 4 103
Sep 3 NmkJ 6f G 2 **108**
Sep 11 Gdwd 6f G 7 102
Sep 28 Sals 6f G 4 99
Oct 21 Newb 6f G 7 100

KINGSDALE GIRL 7
Jun 1 Leop 14f G 16 **106**

KINGSDON 8
Jun 18 Ling 10f SW 3 **101**

KINGSHOLM 3
Aug 13 Gdwd 8f G 2 100
Aug 28 Gdwd 9f G 6 **106**
Oct 17 Wind 10f G 1 104

KINGSMAITE 4
Mar 4 Wolv 6f SD 1 **110**
Mar 12 Wolv 6f SD 5 105
Dec 16 Wolv 6f FT 6 101

KINGSTON HARBOUR 4
Jan 11 Sthl 11f SW 1 **104**
Apr 4 Yarm 10f GS 4 99

KINNAIRD 4
May 21 Curr 8f G 3 105
Sep 18 Curr 10f G 3 **110**
Oct 2 Lonc 10f G 1 **110**

KINRANDE 3
Jun 18 Wwck 11f G 1 100
Jun 25 Ches 12½f G 1 **103**
Oct 9 Bath 11½f G 2 101

KINSMAN 8
Jan 8 Ling 7f SD 2 **102**
Dec 14 Ling 8f FT 1 100
Dec 29 Ling 10f FT 8 **102**

KINTBURY CROSS 3
Apr 16 Newb 8f GS 3 99
Jun 17 Gdwd 9f G 2 101
Jly 11 Wind 11½f G 3 **103**

KIRIN 3
Sep 12 Rdcr 7f G 3 **100**

KIRKBY'S TREASURE 7
Mar 27 Muss 7f GS 1 103
May 21 Catt 7f GF 8 102
Jly 2 Carl 7f GF 3 104
Jly 27 Muss 7f GF 3 100
Aug 13 NmkJ 6f G 3 101
Aug 18 Ches 7f F 3 99
Sep 6 Catt 7f GF 3 **105**
Sep 11 Carl 6f GF 4 103
Sep 25 Muss 7f G 4 103

KISS THE RAIN 5
Feb 14 Wolv 5f G 1 101
Mar 22 Ling 5f SD 3 **103**
Jun 5 Bath 5f G 3 100
Aug 9 Bath 5f GF 4 101

KISSING LIGHTS 3
Jun 18 Wwck 7f G 8 **105**
Jly 18 Ayr 5f GF 7 103
Sep 4 York 6f G 3 **105**

KISWAHILI 3
Nov 3 Muss 16f GS 3 **101**

KITTY O'SHEA 3
Mar 20 Curr 8f HY 1 **105**

KNICKYKNACKIENOO 4
Feb 4 Wolv 8½f SD 8 **99**

KNOCK ABBEY CASTLE 5
Sep 10 Leop 12f GF 9 **108**

KNOCK BRIDGE 3
Apr 6 Nott 8f GS 2 **105**
Jly 18 Wind 8½f G 2 99
Oct 9 Gdwd 8f G 4 104

KNOCKTOPHER ABBEY 8
Aug 18 Chep 8f GF 7 **100**

KNOT IN WOOD 3
Jun 7 Rdcr 7f G 4 102
Jly 14 Haml 6f GF 1 **105**
Jly 21 Donc 6f GF 1 104
Aug 29 Ripn 6f G 2 100

KOCAB 3
Jly 24 MsnL 10f F 3 109
Aug 20 Deau 10f GS 4 **113**
Oct 16 Lonc 12f G 2 111

KODIAC 4
May 18 Gdwd 7f G 5 102
Jun 18 NmkJ 6f G 1 104
Jly 22 Newb 6f G 1 **108**
Aug 7 Curr 6f G 4 107
Sep 10 Gdwd 6f GF 8 103

KOMREYEV STAR 3
Jly 4 Muss 9f GF 6 **101**
Oct 29 Ayr 9f HY 1 **101**

KONG 3
Aug 16 York 12f G 4 **101**
Sep 10 Donc 14½f S 4 100
Sep 25 NmkR 12f G 4 **101**

KOOL OVATION 3
Jun 23 Newc 6f G 1 **101**

KOSTAR 4
Jun 13 Wind 6f GF 1 105
Jun 23 Sals 5f G 4 99
Jly 10 Hayd 6f GF 1 103
Dec 2 Wolv 6f SD 2 **111**

KOUKALOVA 4
May 22 Curr 6f G 7 **102**
Jun 15 Leop 9f GF 2 100
Sep 18 Curr 7f GF 1 **102**

KOVA HALL 3
- May 25 Leop 10f GF 3 **105**
- Jun 25 Curr 10f G 8 101

KRAMER 9
- May 21 Curr 12f G 9 **102**

KRATAIOS 5
- May 22 Lonc 9f GF 8 **101**
- Jun 12 Chan 8f GF 5 **101**

KRISTENSEN 6
- Apr 25 Haml 12f G 3 102
- May 7 Thsk 16f GS 6 101
- Aug 10 Bevl 16f GF 4 **104**

KRUGERRAND 6
- Apr 1 Donc 8f G 7 101
- Apr 23 Sand 8f G 8 102
- May 20 Hayd 8f G 2 **108**
- May 30 Sand 8f G 7 106
- Jun 11 Ripn 9f G 2 106
- Sep 10 Gdwd 9f G 8 105
- Sep 23 Hayd 8f G 7 101
- Oct 8 York 9f GS 1 105

KRYSSA 4
- May 18 Gdwd 8f G 5 100
- Jly 8 Ling 10f G 3 **105**
- Jly 27 Gdwd 9f GS 3 102
- Aug 12 Folk 9½f G 4 104
- Oct 19 Bath 8f GS 3 102

KUMAKAWA 7
- Feb 22 Sthl 7f SW 1 **100**
- Nov 5 Sthl 8f FT 4 99
- Nov 19 Sthl 8f SW 3 99
- Nov 28 Sthl 8f SD 1 99

KYATIKYO 4
- Jun 1 Leop 14f G 17 **106**

KYDD GLOVES 3
- Aug 10 Sand 8f GF 1 101
- Aug 27 York 10½f G 1 106
- Oct 9 Gdwd 12f G 4 **107**

KYLE OF LOCHALSH 5
- Jly 14 Haml 11f GF 4 99

KYLEBEG DANCER 4
- Jun 26 Curr 16f F 6 **102**

KYLES PRINCE 3
- Oct 22 Newb 10f GS 5 **101**
- Dec 3 Wolv 12f GS 1 100

KYLKENNY 10
- Feb 17 Sthl 12f GS 1 107
- Feb 26 Sthl 12f FT 3 104
- Mar 8 Sthl 12f SD 2 100
- Jly 5 Pont 10f G 3 99
- Jly 26 Bevl 10f G 1 101
- Sep 26 Haml 11f G 1 103
- Dec 6 Sthl 11f FT 4 104
- Dec 20 Sthl 11f SW 1 **109**
- Dec 27 Sthl 12f SD 1 102

L

LA BELLA GRANDE 3
- Jun 15 Nott 8f GF 1 **104**
- Jun 30 Newb 10f G 4 103
- Jly 22 NmkJ 8f G 1 102
- Aug 13 Newb 10f G 1 103

LA COMMARA 3
- May 22 Curr 8f G 4 **104**

LA CUCARACHA 4
- Apr 2 Donc 6f G 1 109
- May 11 York 6f S 9 105
- Jun 1 Leop 6f G 1 112
- Jly 8 York 6f G 2 110
- Jly 23 York 6f G 1 107
- Aug 18 York 5f GF 1 **114**
- Sep 3 Hayd 6f F 2 106

LA GESSA 3
- Sep 14 Yarm 10f G 1 **101**

LA MANDRAGOLA 8
- Aug 7 Curr 16f G 10 102

LA PERSIANA 4
- May 1 NmkR 9f G 3 **111**
- May 12 York 10½f S 2 **111**
- Jun 23 Newc 10f GF 2 107
- Aug 10 Sals 10f G 1 108
- Aug 23 Yarm 10f G 1 107
- Sep 18 Curr 10f G 5 108
- Oct 13 NmkR 10f G 4 106

LA VIE EST BELLE 4
- Apr 12 Muss 5f G 2 **103**
- Apr 14 Ripn 5f S 2 100
- May 23 Thsk 5f G 2 **103**
- Aug 10 Bevl 5f GF 7 99
- Sep 15 Ayr 5f GF 2 101

LABELLED WITH LOVE 5
- Jan 19 Ling 6f FT 2 99
- Jly 30 Ling 6f GS 2 101
- Aug 6 Ling 6f G 1 **102**

LACONICOS 3
- Apr 20 Ling 10f FT 6 **100**
- Aug 3 Newc 9f G 2 99
- Oct 12 Ling 10f G 4 **100**

LADEENA 3
- Sep 12 Rdcr 7f G 1 **103**

LADIES KNIGHT 5
- Feb 14 Wolv 5f G 2 **100**

LADY ALGARHOUD 3
- Nov 21 Sthl 6f SW 3 **99**

LADY DIKTAT 3
- Jun 6 Pont 10f GF 4 **100**

LADY FILLY 3
- May 16 Wind 5f G 5 99
- May 31 Rdcr 5f G 2 **101**

LADY GEORGINA 4
- Aug 11 Sand 9f GF 2 **104**
- Sep 24 NmkR 8f G 17 99

LADY HEN 3
- Feb 28 Wolv 8½f SD 2 **99**

LADY HOPEFUL 3
- Nov 30 Wolv 5f SD 1 100
- Dec 29 Ling 5f SD 4 **101**

LADY IN GREY 3
- May 1 StCl 10½f F 4 **103**
- Sep 4 Lonc 10f GF 5 102

LADY KARR 4
- Jun 10 Catt 16f GF 4 **106**
- Jly 23 York 12f GS 3 103
- Jly 29 NmkJ 12f G 2 102
- Sep 12 Rdcr 14f G 3 102

LADY MCNAIR 5
- Jan 29 Ling 8f SD 11 **99**

LADY MISHA 3
- Dec 9 Wolv 14f FT 4 **100**

LADY PEKAN 6
- Jan 12 Ling 5f SD 2 **100**
- Feb 7 Sthl 5f SD 1 99
- Apr 6 Ling 5f FT 2 **100**

LADY PILOT 3
- Dec 30 Ling 10f FT 2 **100**

LADY PORTIA 4
- Oct 9 Curr 5f GS 3 **101**

LADY SINGSPIEL 4
- Jun 1 Leop 14f G 12 **106**

LADY TAVERNER 4
- May 17 Ling 10f G 3 100
- Aug 5 Ling 10f GS 1 **104**
- Dec 10 Wolv 12f FT 1 103
- Dec 20 Ling 10f FT 3 **104**
- Dec 31 Wolv 14f SD 3 99

LADY WEASLEY 3
- Jun 5 Chan 8f GF 9 **99**

LAFI 6
- Apr 1 Donc 5f G 6 101
- Jly 2 Sand 5f G 2 107
- Jly 24 Newb 5f G 2 **112**
- Jly 30 Gdwd 6f G 8 107
- Aug 27 NmkJ 6f G 2 107

LAGO D'ORTA 5
- Jun 3 Epsm 8½f G 9 **101**

LAHIBA 4
- Mar 20 Curr 6f HY 1 **105**
- Oct 23 Curr 6f S 10 103

LAKE ANDRE 4
- Nov 16 Sthl 5f FT 5 **105**

LAKE CHINI 3
- Nov 26 Ling 6f FT 1 **99**

LAKE DIVA 4
- Jan 5 Sthl 11f SD 1 **100**

LAKE VERDI 6
- Jan 7 Wolv 8½f SW 8 **100**

LAKE WAKATIPU 3
- Dec 19 Wolv 8½f FT 4 **104**

LAKESIDE GUY 4
Feb 27 Wolv 6f FT 3 **99**

LAKOTA BRAVE 11
Jan 12 Wolv 8½f SD 5 **104**
Feb 9 Ling 8f SD 2 101

LAMH EILE 3
May 13 York 7f GS 3 **105**
Jun 25 NmkJ 8f G 3 102

LAND 'N STARS 5
Mar 18 Ling 13f SD 1 100
May 4 Ches 18½f GS 6 102
May 21 Ling 16f SD 3 105
Aug 6 NmkJ 16f G 6 101
Aug 26 NmkJ 15f G 2 100
Sep 1 Sals 14f G 2 107
Sep 24 NmkR 16f G 1 **114**
Oct 15 NmkR 18f G 6 103

LANDUCCI 4
May 22 Brig 7f G 1 103
Jun 21 Brig 7f G 1 104
Jun 30 Epsm 7f G 3 102
Jly 12 Brig 8f G 1 **105**
Aug 3 Epsm 8½f G 3 102
Aug 6 Hayd 8f GF 4 101
Aug 20 Ches 7½f G 6 99
Sep 10 Gdwd 7f G 9 **105**

LANGFORD 5
May 17 Rdcr 8f G 7 99
May 31 Sand 8f G 2 **109**
Jun 12 Donc 8f F 1 99
Jun 22 Epsm 8½f G 2 104
Jun 25 Donc 8f GF 1 108
Jly 13 Ling 8f SW 2 **109**
Jly 24 Pont 8f G 2 108
Aug 18 York 8f G 6 108
Aug 29 Ripn 8f G 2 **109**

LANGSTON BOY 3
Jan 5 Ling 8f SD 2 **104**
Apr 26 Wwck 7f GS 6 **104**
Aug 31 Ling 7f GS 7 99

LAOCH NA MARA 6
Apr 3 Curr 10f S 10 **103**

LAPWING 7
Jun 25 Wind 6f G 6 106
Aug 27 Wind 8½f G 7 **108**

LARA FALANA 7
Feb 8 Ling 8f SD 2 101
Feb 16 Ling 10f SD 8 **103**

LARAD 4
Feb 12 Ling 12f SD 4 **99**

LARGS 5
Aug 16 Haml 5f F 2 **99**

LARKWING 4
May 4 Ches 18½f GS 4 102
Jly 26 Gdwd 14f G 5 104
Aug 6 NmkJ 16f G 3 102
Aug 26 NmkJ 15f G 3 100
Sep 24 NmkR 16f G 2 **113**

LARKY'S LOB 6
Oct 10 Wolv 5f FT 4 **100**

LAST PIONEER 3
May 6 Haml 11f GS 3 **99**

LATE ARRIVAL 8
Jun 7 Rdcr 16f G 1 **99**

LATEEN SAILS 5
Jun 1 Nott 8f G 2 111
Jun 25 Wind 8½f G 4 103
Jly 30 NmkJ 8f GF 3 112
Aug 15 Deau 10f G 4 **113**
Sep 25 NmkR 12f G 7 99

LATIF 4
Jun 16 Bevl 8½f G 2 **104**
Jun 27 Pont 8f G 4 102

LATIN QUEEN 5
Jun 29 Chep 12f G 8 99

LATINO MAGIC 5
Jun 1 Leop 8f G 3 108
Jun 8 Leop 10f F 5 99
Jun 26 Curr 8f F 5 105
Aug 7 Curr 10f G 3 **114**

LAUGH 'N CRY 4
May 6 Ling 10f G 2 99
May 21 Ling 8f SD 3 **104**

LAUREN LOUISE 3
Aug 10 Yarm 6f GF 3 **99**

LAURO 5
May 20 Hayd 10½f G 6 **102**

LAVEROCK 3
Mar 28 StCl 8f GS 3 **109**
May 15 Lonc 8f G 7 108
Jun 5 Chan 10½f G 6 104
Jly 14 Lonc 12f F 7 106
Jly 24 MsnL 10f F 2 **109**
Oct 1 Lonc 9½f G 6 104

LAW BREAKER 7
Apr 18 Pont 6f S 6 99
Apr 30 Gdwd 6f G 3 100
May 21 Ling 7f G 2 101
Jun 10 Gdwd 7f G 2 102
Oct 31 Wolv 8½f SD 2 **104**
Nov 10 Ling 8f SD 8 101

LAW MAKER 5
Mar 31 Ling 5f SD 2 99
Jun 9 Brig 5½f G 2 100
Jun 29 Catt 5f GF 1 100
Jly 2 Hayd 5f GF 2 **104**
Jly 5 Wolv 6f FT 1 102
Aug 19 Wolv 6f FT 1 **104**
Sep 17 Wolv 6f FT 4 99
Nov 25 Wolv 5f FT 1 101

LAWAAHEB 4
Feb 21 Ling 10f FT 3 100
Mar 3 Ling 10f SW 1 102
Dec 29 Ling 10f SW 6 103

LAXLOVA 3
Mar 28 StCl 8f GS 2 **107**
May 1 StCl 10½f F 6 102

LAY A WHISPER 3
Jun 30 Hayd 8f GF 3 **101**
Sep 13 Sals 7f G 8 99

LAYED BACK ROCKY 3
Jun 15 Haml 8½f GS 3 **100**
Dec 19 Wolv 8½f FT 4 99

LAYMAN 3
Aug 11 Sals 8f GF 1 **116**
Aug 28 Gdwd 8f G 6 101
Oct 15 NmkR 10f G 9 108

LAZIO 4
May 22 Lonc 7f GF 5 107
Jun 27 Lonc 7f G 4 **112**

LAZZAZ 7
Apr 2 Wolv 12f FT 1 **104**
Jun 1 Wolv 14f FT 5 99

LE CARRE 7
Apr 30 Lonc 15½f GS 4 **113**
Aug 21 Deau 15f G 8 104

LE CHIFFRE 3
Oct 3 Pont 8f G 1 **101**

LE CORVEE 3
Apr 22 Sand 8f G 5 103
May 14 Newb 11f G 4 102
Jun 4 Hayd 12f G 8 100
Sep 23 Ling 10f G 5 **104**
Oct 9 Gdwd 10f G 12 99

LE LEOPARD 5
Aug 7 Curr 16f G 3 **108**

LE PRINCE CHARMANT 4
Jun 16 Lonc 10f G 7 **114**

LE SOLEIL 4
Sep 26 Wolv 12f FT 1 **100**

LE TISS 4
May 1 NmkR 12f G 5 **110**
May 14 Newb 12f G 7 101
May 21 NmkR 14f GS 4 99
Aug 12 Newb 13½f G 5 105
Sep 10 Gdwd 16f G 5 100

LE VIE DEI COLORI 5
Apr 23 Leic 7f G 1 108
May 14 Newb 8f F 6 110
Jun 25 NmkJ 7f G 6 101
Jly 27 Gdwd 8f GS 6 113
Aug 28 Gdwd 8f G 5 103
Oct 15 NmkR 7f G 1 **118**

LEAGUE OF NATIONS 3
Aug 2 Brig 12f G 12 99
Aug 4 Brig 12f G 1 **103**

LEAH'S PRIDE 4
Dec 14 Ling 5f FT 1 **101**

LEAPING BRAVE 4
May 5 Chep 8f GS 3 **99**

Horse / Date		Course	Dist	Going	Pos	Rating
LEG SPINNER 4						
Jun	1	Leop	16f	G	7	**104**
LEGAL DRAM 4						
Dec	19	Wolv	8½f	FT	5	**103**
LEGAL LOVER 3						
Nov	8	Sthl	8f	FT	1	99
Nov	19	Sthl	8f	SW	1	**103**
LEGAL SET 9						
Jan	19	Ling	6f	FT	1	100
Feb	28	Wolv	5f	SD	4	103
Mar	4	Wolv	6f	SD	6	102
Apr	20	Catt	6f	S	1	99
Apr	26	Sthl	6f	FT	3	99
May	30	Leic	6f	G	7	99
Jun	19	Wwck	6f	G	9	103
Dec	29	Ling	5f	G	2	**104**
LEGS LAWLOR 3						
Jun	1	Leop	7f	G	3	104
Jun	15	Leop	8f	GF	1	**105**
LEIGHTON BUZZARD 3						
Oct	14	Rdcr	7f	GF	5	**101**
LEITRIM HOUSE 4						
Jun	12	Sals	6f	G	1	**108**
Sep	16	Newb	7f	GF	7	101
LENNEL 7						
Jan	21	Wolv	12f	SD	2	**104**
Feb	4	Wolv	12f	SD	3	101
Feb	8	Ling	12f	SD	5	99
Feb	14	Wolv	12f	SD	6	103
May	20	Hayd	10½f	G	7	100
Jun	29	Catt	12f	G	2	**104**
LENWADE 4						
Oct	20	Brig	12f	GS	3	**100**
LEO'S LUCKY STAR 3						
Mar	26	Kemp	8f	GS	6	100
Apr	2	Donc	8f	G	2	**103**
Aug	29	Ripn	8f	G	12	99
LEO'S LUCKYMAN 6						
Sep	10	Donc	10½f	GS	1	**109**
LEOBALLERO 5						
Nov	19	Ling	7f	FT	8	**106**
Nov	26	Ling	8f	FT	10	100
LEONARDO DE VINCI 5						
Apr	3	Curr	16f	HY	6	**106**
LEPORELLO 5						
Jly	1	Sand	10f	G	5	106
Jly	16	Newb	10f	GF	7	**108**
LES ARCS 5						
Jan	7	Wolv	7f	SW	3	107
Jan	29	Ling	8f	SD	2	**113**
Feb	22	Ling	7f	SD	2	106
Mar	27	Muss	7f	GS	2	102
Apr	1	Donc	8f	G	8	100
May	28	Muss	7f	G	1	104
Jun	7	Ches	7f	GF	1	108
Sep	17	Ayr	7f	G	2	104
Sep	24	NmkR	7f	G	11	109
Oct	8	York	6f	GS	4	106
Oct	27	Ling	7f	SD	8	105
Dec	17	Ling	6f	FT	1	109
LESLINGTAYLOR 3						
Jun	15	Nott	8f	GF	8	100
Sep	15	Pont	10f	G	1	103
Oct	4	Catt	12f	GF	1	**105**
LET IT BE 4						
Jun	18	Rdcr	14f	G	1	102
Jly	1	Hayd	12f	G	3	**105**
Jly	10	Hayd	14f	GF	1	103
Sep	12	Rdcr	14f	G	7	99
Oct	1	Rdcr	14f	GF	2	101
LET SLIP 3						
Sep	16	Nott	8f	GF	4	**100**
LETS GET IT ON 4						
May	12	Carl	6f	G	2	**100**
LETS ROLL 4						
May	11	York	12f	S	3	106
May	20	NmkR	12f	G	4	101
Jly	7	NmkJ	12f	G	9	100
Jly	16	NmkJ	15f	GF	3	101
Sep	17	Ayr	13f	G	1	**111**
Oct	15	NmkR	18f	G	14	99
LEVITSKI 4						
Apr	3	Lonc	10f	S	6	113
May	9	Lonc	12f	G	5	**116**
LIAKOURA 3						
Sep	30	NmkR	8f	G	6	102
Oct	14	NmkR	8f	G	12	**103**
LIBERTY SEEKER 6						
Apr	29	Muss	14f	G	4	99
Aug	6	Ayr	10f	F	1	102
LIBRAS CHILD 6						
Jun	26	Curr	6½f	GF	9	99
Jly	16	Curr	5f	F	4	**109**
Aug	20	Curr	6f	GF	10	100
Sep	17	Curr	5f	G	3	108
Oct	9	Curr	5f	GS	4	100
LIBRE 5						
Jan	10	Wolv	9½f	SD	4	**107**
Feb	18	Wolv	8½f	SD	10	100
Apr	6	Nott	10f	GS	2	102
Apr	13	Bevl	10f	G	2	105
May	6	Nott	10f	G	3	100
May	18	Gdwd	8f	G	3	102
Jun	4	Hayd	8f	G	2	100
Jly	13	Hayd	8f	G	6	101
Dec	21	Ling	10f	G	1	100
LICENCE 5						
Oct	9	Curr	16f	GS	7	**106**
LIFFEY 5						
Mar	20	Curr	8f	HY	6	**107**
LIFTED WAY 6						
May	31	Sand	8f	G	6	**108**
Jun	26	Wind	8½f	G	7	99
LIGHT OF MORN 4						
Jly	16	NmkJ	12f	GF	5	101
Aug	20	Ches	13½f	G	3	**105**
Sep	7	Donc	14½f	GF	6	99
LIGHTNING FLASH 3						
May	21	Ling	7f	SD	1	**100**
LIGNE D'EAU 4						
Apr	8	Ling	6f	SD	3	**103**
LILAC MIST 3						
Aug	4	Hayd	10½f	GF	2	**104**
Sep	12	Folk	9½f	GF	2	99
LILLEBROR 7						
Mar	28	Yarm	11½f	S	2	**99**
LILLY GEE 4						
Jan	27	Sthl	6f	SD	6	**101**
LIMIT 3						
Apr	6	Nott	8f	GS	4	**101**
LINCOLN DANCER 8						
Apr	13	Bevl	5f	G	5	**100**
LINCOLNEUROCRUISER 3						
Sep	27	Nott	6f	G	3	**101**
LINDA GREEN 4						
Jan	19	Ling	5f	FT	5	100
Apr	12	Muss	5f	G	7	99
Apr	24	Brig	5½f	GF	6	99
May	3	Bath	5½f	HY	2	102
May	26	Bath	5½f	G	1	102
Jun	5	Bath	5f	G	1	101
Jun	18	Ayr	6f	G	3	100
Jly	14	Leic	6f	GF	5	**103**
Jly	20	Sand	5f	GF	4	100
Jly	25	Wind	6f	G	1	101
Aug	13	Gdwd	6f	G	3	**103**
Oct	25	Yarm	7f	S	3	101
LINDA REGINA 4						
Aug	21	Deau	10f	G	8	**107**
LINDA'S COLIN 3						
Mar	18	Ling	7f	SD	7	**99**
LINDBERGH 3						
Jun	21	Newb	5f	GF	1	**103**
Jly	8	Ches	5f	F	4	99
Jly	29	Gdwd	5f	G	3	**103**
Dec	17	Ling	6f	FT	10	99
LINDEN LIME 3						
Oct	12	Ling	10f	FT	6	**100**
LINDEN'S LADY 5						
May	21	Catt	7f	GF	6	99
Jly	2	Carl	6f	GF	3	101
Jly	27	Muss	8f	GF	3	100
Aug	8	Thsk	8f	G	1	102
Aug	12	Catt	7f	G	1	100
Aug	17	Carl	8f	GF	3	**104**
LINENS FLAME 6						
Apr	2	Kemp	14½f	S	1	**100**
May	1	Sals	14f	GS	9	**100**
LINNET 3						
May	2	Wwck	8f	G	1	**103**
Jun	30	Newb	10f	G	6	101
Oct	3	Wind	11½f	GF	3	100

Oct 9 Gdwd 11f G 4 101

LINNGARI 3
Sep 3 Hayd 8f GF 1 **107**

LINNING WINE 9
Jan 15 Ling 10f SD 3 **106**
Jan 22 Ling 12f FT 5 104
Mar 7 Wolv 9½f SD 3 100
Mar 16 Wolv 9½f SD 2 102

LION HUNTER 6
Jan 15 Ling 10f SD 9 **100**

LISCARA 5
Jly 2 Leop 12f GF 6 **102**

LISCARRA LAD 3
Jun 25 Curr 10f G 6 **103**

LISCOA 4
Apr 3 Curr 10f S 13 **100**

LISCUNE 3
Aug 7 Curr 10f G 8 **106**

LISS ARD 4
May 22 Curr 12f GS 9 **106**
May 25 Leop 14f GF 6 103

LISTEN TO REASON 4
Jan 21 Wolv 12f SD 6 **102**
Mar 24 Wolv 8½f SD 5 99

LITERATIM 5
Aug 6 Hayd 8f GF 5 101
Aug 29 Ripn 8f G 7 **104**

LITTLE BOB 4
Jun 20 Ripn 10f G 2 **105**
Sep 27 Nott 10f GF 2 99
Oct 29 Ayr 9f HY 1 **105**
Nov 2 Nott 10f S 4 101

LITTLE EDWARD 7
Jun 28 Brig 5½f F 6 **103**

LITTLE EYE 4
Jun 6 Wind 10f G 5 99
Jly 18 Wind 10f G 2 **103**
Jly 25 Wind 10f GS 5 100
Aug 13 Gdwd 11f G 1 100
Aug 28 Gdwd 12f G 2 99
Sep 27 Nott 10f GF 1 101

LITTLE GOOD BAY 5
May 6 Ches 7½f GS 4 106
May 28 Gdwd 8f G 7 101
Jun 7 Ches 7f GF 2 106
Jun 15 York 8f G 7 109
Jly 2 Sand 8f G 13 105
Aug 6 Wind 8½f GF 6 104
Aug 20 Ches 7½f G 5 99
Sep 10 Gdwd 9f G 4 107
Sep 22 Pont 10f G 2 **111**
Oct 22 Newb 10f G 5 108

LITTLE JIMBOB 4
Apr 12 Muss 8f G 1 108
May 17 Rdcr 8f G 2 102
Jun 3 Epsm 8½f G 7 103
Jun 19 Pont 10f G 4 105
Jly 1 Bevl 8½f G 2 **109**
Jly 13 Hayd 8f G 3 105
Jly 31 Ches 7½f G 3 101
Aug 18 York 8f G 8 108
Sep 15 Ayr 9f G 5 104

LITTLE MISS GRACIE 3
Mar 26 Kemp 8f GS 4 106
Jun 23 Haml 8½f G 1 **107**
Sep 10 Muss 8f G 2 **107**
Oct 11 Leic 8½f G 2 106

LITTLE RICHARD 6
Feb 21 Wolv 14f FT 3 101
Feb 27 Wolv 12f FT 2 99
Mar 13 Wolv 12f FT 1 101
Dec 28 Wolv 14f FT 2 **104**

LITTLE RIDGE 4
Jan 20 Sthl 5f FT 1 **105**
Feb 17 Sthl 5f SD 3 103
Apr 2 Kemp 5f GS 10 99

LITTLE VENICE 5
Apr 30 Thsk 7f S 3 102
Aug 12 NmkJ 7f G 1 **104**

LITTLE WHISPER 4
Mar 20 Curr 8f HY 14 **100**

LITTLETON TELCHAR 5
Oct 3 Wind 8½f GF 8 **102**

LITTLETON ZEPHIR 6
Apr 9 Ling 8f FT 1 101
Apr 11 Ling 8f SD 4 99
May 6 Ling 8f SD 1 **105**
Jun 27 Wind 8½f G 7 100

LIVE IN FEAR 3
Sep 17 Curr 5f G 16 **99**

LIZARAZU 6
Jly 14 Epsm 7f G 1 105
Aug 3 Epsm 8½f G 3 99
Aug 4 Brig 7f G 5 102
Sep 11 Gdwd 8f G 2 **110**
Sep 20 Bevl 7½f GF 5 100
Oct 9 Bath 8f G 1 101
Oct 31 Wolv 8½f SD 6 102
Nov 10 Ling 8f SD 5 99
Dec 5 Ling 8f FT 7 99

LLAMADAS 3
Feb 11 Wolv 7f SD 2 100
Mar 2 Sthl 7f SD 1 **109**
Mar 28 Kemp 9f G 5 99
Dec 5 Ling 8f FT 1 107

LOADED GUN 5
Feb 7 Wolv 8½f FT 1 **103**

LOADERFUN 3
May 28 Gdwd 6f G 6 99
Aug 20 Sand 5f GS 6 **101**

LOBLOLLY BAY 3
May 25 Leop 10f GF 2 **106**
Jun 15 Leop 8f GF 5 99
Sep 4 Curr 8f G 15 101

LOCAL POET 4
Apr 30 NmkR 6f G 14 106
Jun 24 Newc 6f G 5 100
Aug 5 Hayd 6f F 10 99
Sep 29 Ayr 6f G 8 99
Dec 20 Sthl 7f SW 1 **108**

LOCH QUEST 3
May 16 Wind 11½f G 1 **106**
May 30 Rdcr 11f G 3 101
Sep 3 NmkJ 10f G 6 103
Sep 21 Gdwd 12f G 4 104
Oct 3 Wind 11½f GF 7 99

LOCHBUIE 4
Apr 2 Donc 12f G 3 110
May 6 Ches 13½f GS 4 106
May 30 Sand 16½f G 2 101
Jun 25 Newc 16f G 12 108
Jly 28 Gdwd 16f G 4 **112**
Aug 13 Newb 13½f G 1 104
Aug 21 Deau 15f G 7 107
Oct 15 NmkR 16f G 5 111

LOCK AND KEY 3
Jly 2 Leop 7f F 2 108
Jly 16 Curr 8f GF 2 106
Sep 17 Curr 6f G 4 **110**
Oct 9 Curr 6f GS 6 100

LOCKSTOCK 7
Feb 12 Wolv 8½f FT 4 **104**
Mar 16 Wolv 7f SD 2 102
Mar 24 Wolv 7f SD 3 100
Apr 2 Wolv 8½f FT 3 102
Apr 21 Sthl 8f FT 4 102
May 3 Bath 8f HY 1 **104**
May 21 Ling 7f G 4 99
Jun 9 Wolv 8½f SD 4 99

LOCOMBE HILL 9
May 26 Ayr 7f G 2 **104**
Jun 9 Wolv 7f SD 1 99

LOGISTICAL 5
Mar 31 Ling 8f SD 1 **101**

LOGSDAIL 5
Sep 9 Sand 7f GS 1 **105**
Sep 13 Sals 8f G 2 **105**
Oct 7 Newb 7f GF 3 102
Oct 29 Wolv 9½f SD 6 104
Nov 10 Ling 8f SD 3 103

LOLA SAPOLA 3
Jun 21 Brig 12f G 1 **104**
Aug 2 Brig 12f G 9 102

LONDONER 7
Feb 16 Ling 10f SD 9 **101**
Feb 25 Wolv 8½f SD 7 99
Apr 1 Ling 8f SD 8 99
Dec 3 Wolv 8½f SD 6 99

LONE PLAINSMAN 4
Sep 17 Curr 5f G 2 **109**

LONG WEEKEND 7
Feb 16 Ling 8f SD 6 **100**

LOOK AGAIN 4
May 15 Ripn 10f G 4 103

Jun 10 Sand 10f GF 2 102
Jly 1 Sand 10f G 2 101
Jly 23 Newb 12f GF 3 **106**
Sep 17 Newb 10f GF 17 104

LOOK BETWEEN US 8
Jun 1 Leop 14f G 10 **106**

LOOK HERE'S CAROL 5
Apr 2 Donc 6f G 3 107
Apr 12 NmkR 7f GF 8 99
Jly 8 York 6f G 4 107
Aug 6 NmkJ 7f G 6 **111**

LOOK OF EAGLES 3
Nov 21 Sthl 6f SW 2 100
Nov 29 Sthl 7f SD 1 **101**
Dec 20 Sthl 7f SW 5 100

LOOKS COULD KILL 3
Apr 14 NmkR 7f G 5 104
May 1 NmkR 7f G 5 103
May 5 Ches 7½f GS 3 105
May 21 Hayd 8f GF 6 104
Jun 4 Epsm 10f G 6 100
Aug 7 Rdcr 6f G 4 103
Aug 20 Sand 5f GS 3 101
Aug 31 Ling 7f GS 3 102
Nov 25 Wolv 6f FT 2 105
Dec 2 Wolv 6f SD 3 **106**
Dec 9 Wolv 7f FT 4 103

LOOKS THE BUSINESS 4
Jly 1 Wolv 12f FT 1 100
Aug 4 Brig 12f G 2 100
Aug 20 Ling 10f SD 5 99

LOOP THE LOUP 9
Jly 22 Chep 16f G 1 104
Aug 6 Rdcr 14f G 1 **105**
Sep 12 Rdcr 14f G 6 100

LORD ADMIRAL 4
Jun 1 Leop 8f G 1 **113**
Jun 26 Curr 8f F 4 107
Aug 14 Leop 8f F 4 109

LORD BASKERVILLE 4
May 9 Rdcr 6f GS 5 **99**

LORD CHAMBERLAIN 12
Apr 2 Wolv 7f FT 1 **103**
Jly 11 Wolv 7f SD 4 102
Sep 21 Gdwd 8f G 1 101

LORD DU SUD 4
Apr 3 Lonc 10f S 5 **115**
May 9 Lonc 12f G 6 113

LORD LINKS 4
Apr 2 Kemp 7f GS 2 104
May 30 Sand 8f G 5 106
Jun 17 Gdwd 8f G 3 **109**
Jun 22 Sals 8f G 4 103
Aug 6 Wind 8½f GF 4 105

LORD MAYOR 4
Apr 13 NmkR 9f G 7 102
Oct 22 Newb 10f G 3 **111**
Nov 19 Ling 10f FT 8 100

LORD NELLSSON 9
Jly 7 Folk 16½f G 2 99
Jly 23 Sals 14f G 4 **101**

LORD OF DREAMS 3
Jly 9 Ling 8f SD 7 99
Nov 12 Wolv 8½f FT 2 99
Dec 19 Wolv 8½f FT 3 **104**

LORD OF THE EAST 6
May 9 Rdcr 6f GS 2 101
May 31 Rdcr 7f G 2 102
Jun 6 Pont 6f GF 1 102
Jun 16 Wolv 6f GF 3 99
Jun 30 Epsm 6f G 6 101
Jly 28 Epsm 7f G 1 103
Aug 19 Ches 7f GF 3 **107**
Sep 6 Catt 7f GF 4 105
Sep 8 Donc 7f G 1 105
Sep 17 Ayr 7f G 1 105
Sep 21 Gdwd 6f GF 8 102
Sep 30 NmkR 7f G 4 104
Oct 14 NmkR 7f G 8 106

LORES JOY 6
Sep 4 Lonc 5f GF 8 **100**

LORIKEET 6
Jly 16 Curr 16f GF 3 **102**

LOS ORGANOS 3
Aug 6 Rdcr 9f G 1 **105**

LOST SOLDIER THREE 4
May 30 Sand 16½f G 6 100
Jly 28 Gdwd 16f G 8 **107**
Aug 16 York 16f G 6 100
Sep 0 Donc 14½f G 3 104

LOUGHLORIEN 6
Jun 21 Bevl 5f G 3 100
Aug 26 Newc 5f GF 3 **104**

LOUISE D'ARZENS 3
Aug 21 Folk 9½f G 3 **101**
Sep 8 Bath 11½f GF 2 100

LOUISIADE 4
Apr 4 Wolv 7f FT 1 99
Apr 22 Wolv 7f SD 1 **104**
May 17 Rdcr 6f G 1 103
May 27 Wolv 6f SD 3 99
Jun 13 Thsk 6f G 4 101
Jly 29 Thsk 6f G 10 100

LOUISVILLE 6
Jun 8 Leop 8f F 9 **101**

LOUISVILLE PRINCE 4
Aug 4 Brig 6f G 8 **99**

LOUPHOLE 3
Sep 30 Ling 7f FT 6 100
Nov 15 Ling 7f FT 5 **105**
Nov 29 Ling 8f FT 7 104
Dec 16 Wolv 6f FT 7 99
Dec 30 Ling 6f FT 4 103

LOUVE HEUREUSE 4
Oct 19 Bath 10f GS 6 **100**

LOVE AFFAIR 3
Jun 1 Nott 8f G 1 **104**
Sep 19 Leic 8½f G 6 103

LOVE ALWAYS 3
May 12 Sals 10f G 2 **107**

LOVE ANGEL 3
Jun 25 Ches 10½f G 2 100
Aug 25 Muss 8f G 10 100
Sep 4 York 10½f G 1 103
Sep 8 Bath 10f GF 1 102
Sep 13 Yarm 11½f G 4 **104**
Sep 26 Haml 11f G 2 101

LOVE ATTACK 3
Oct 15 Ling 10f SD 1 **99**

LOVE CITY 3
Aug 20 Curr 8f GF 2 **102**

LOVE GREEN 4
May 22 Lonc 7f GF 10 **103**

LOVE IN SEATTLE 5
Jun 16 Bevl 8½f G 1 **105**

LOVE PALACE 3
Jun 16 York 8f G 11 101
Aug 13 Newb 7f G 10 101
Aug 24 Catt 7f G 1 **102**

LOVE THIRTY 3
Apr 16 Newb 7f GS 4 100
May 31 Leic 7f GF 3 **102**
Sep 25 NmkR 7f G 13 **102**

LOVES TRAVELLING 5
Jly 23 York 12f GS 4 **103**

LOW CLOUD 5
Jun 7 Ches 10½f GF 5 101
Jun 16 Bevl 8½f G 4 **102**
Jun 27 Pont 8f G 6 101

LOWLANDER 6
Jun 1 Leop 16f G 3 **105**

LOYAL FOCUS 4
Sep 18 Curr 16f G 8 103

LOYAL TYCOON 7
May 7 NmkR 6f GF 7 101
Jun 4 Epsm 5f G 12 99
Jun 13 Thsk 6f G 2 101
Jun 30 Epsm 6f G 7 100
Aug 8 Wind 6f GF 5 101
Aug 16 York 6f GF 3 **103**
Sep 4 York 6f G 7 100
Oct 7 Newb 7f GF 8 100
Oct 30 Ling 6f SD 8 102

LUAS LINE 3
May 22 Curr 8f G 3 **112**
Jun 15 York 7f G 5 102

LUCAYAN DANCER 5
May 17 Rdcr 10f G 1 **105**
Jun 7 Ches 10½f GF 1 103
Jly 23 Newc 10f GF 2 101
Jly 30 Gdwd 9f G 3 103

LUCAYAN LEGEND 4
Apr 2 Donc 8f G 12 **105**
Apr 23 Sand 8f G 9 101
Jun 15 Nott 8f GF 1 **105**
Jun 26 Wind 8½f G 5 101
Jly 5 NmkJ 8f G 7 101

LUCE 4
Jan 7 Wolv 12f SW 5 **99**

LUCID DREAMS 6
Apr 11 Ling 8f SD 1 **100**
May 6 Ling 8f SD 5 **100**

LUCIUS VERRUS 5
Feb 27 Wolv 6f SD 2 **100**

LUCKY LEO 5
Apr 23 Leic 10f G 2 100
May 17 Leic 12f G 1 **104**
Jun 4 Donc 12f GF 10 99
Jly 30 NmkJ 12f GF 9 99

LUCKY RED PEPPER 3
Jun 18 NmkJ 7f G 2 **101**

LUCKY SPIN 4
May 7 Ling 7f G 1 110
Jly 8 York 6f G 1 **114**
Jly 29 Gdwd 7f G 3 110
Aug 7 Deau 6½f G 4 112
Sep 3 Hayd 6f F 8 103
Sep 25 NmkR 6f G 6 110
Oct 13 NmkR 6f G 3 107

LUJAIN ROSE 3
May 28 Ling 10f SW 7 **99**

LUKE AFTER ME 5
Apr 6 Catt 7f G 4 **99**

LUNA TACUMANA 5
Jly 2 Leop 10f GF 6 **99**

LUNAR PROMISE 3
Sep 11 Gdwd 10f G 1 **100**

LUNAR SKY 3
Jun 3 Wolv 12f FT 1 99
Jun 27 Wolv 12f SD 2 **101**

LUNE D'OR 4
Aug 17 York 12f G 3 **108**
Sep 11 Lonc 12f G 5 **108**

LUXI RIVER 5
Nov 6 Leop 12f S 6 **99**

LYGETON LAD 7
Jan 7 Wolv 8½f SW 7 106
Jan 15 Ling 10f SD 4 105
Mar 12 Wolv 8½f SD 10 103
Mar 19 Ling 7f SD 2 108
Apr 9 Ling 7f FT 5 105
Jun 24 NmkJ 8f G 2 100
Jly 9 Ling 8f SD 11 100
Nov 19 Ling 7f FT 3 **109**

LYONELS GLORY 4
Apr 3 Lonc 10f S 7 **106**

LYRICAL WAY 6
May 22 Brig 10f G 1 **100**

LYSANDER'S QUEST 7
Jun 24 Folk 12f GF 2 99
Aug 31 Ling 16f GF 1 **101**

LYSANDRA 3
Jun 7 Sals 10f G 3 102
Jun 30 Newb 10f G 1 **106**
Jly 30 Donc 10½f G 9 99

LYTHAM 4
Apr 9 Newc 8f S 5 **99**
May 12 Carl 9½f G 4 **99**

M

MA'AM 3
Apr 16 Newb 8f GS 2 101
Oct 9 Gdwd 12f G 7 101
Oct 19 Bath 10f GS 3 **106**

MAC 5
Aug 7 Curr 16f G 7 **104**

MAC LOVE 4
Apr 27 Ling 7½f S 4 108
May 14 Newb 8f F 2 **113**
Jun 4 Epsm 8½f G 5 101
Jun 14 York 8f G 4 110
Jly 9 Ling 8f SD 5 110
Jly 27 Gdwd 8f GS 11 109
Aug 11 Sals 8f GF 9 107
Sep 8 Donc 7f GF 5 105
Sep 16 Newb 7f GF 6 103

MAC'S ELAN 5
May 4 Chep 8f S 6 100

MACARONI GOLD 5
Jan 1 Sthl 16f SD 2 **102**
Mar 21 Sthl 16f SD 2 101
Jun 21 Newb 13½f G 4 101

MACAULAY 3
Jun 7 Sals 7f G 1 102
Jly 16 NmkJ 8f GF 7 99
Aug 4 Hayd 8f GF 6 **103**

MACHINIST 5
May 14 Thsk 6f G 4 99
Jun 4 Epsm 6f G 7 103
Aug 27 NmkJ 6f G 9 101
Sep 3 NmkJ 6f G 5 107
Sep 16 Ayr 6f GF 1 104
Oct 8 York 6f GS 2 **108**

MACPURSIE 4
Jun 15 Leop 9f GF 2 **104**

MAD 4
Jan 13 Ling 8f SD 3 101
Feb 1 Ling 10f SD 4 100
Feb 8 Ling 8f SD 5 101
Feb 16 Ling 8f SD 2 **104**
Feb 23 Ling 7f SD 4 102
Dec 14 Ling 8f FT 1 99

MAD CAREW 6
Jan 19 Ling 10f FT 3 102
Apr 11 Ling 12f SD 3 101
May 30 Sand 10f G 3 99
Jun 6 Wind 11½f G 1 100
Jly 15 Carl 12f G 1 104
Nov 16 Sthl 12f FT 4 103
Dec 6 Sthl 11f FT 3 **105**
Dec 21 Ling 10f FT 8 100
Dec 27 Sthl 12f SD 2 101

MADAM CAVERSFIELD 3
Jun 27 Pont 8f G 3 **105**

MADDIE'S A JEM 5
Jun 4 Donc 6f G 2 100
Jun 27 Pont 6f G 4 **101**

MADEMOISELLE 3
Sep 29 Ayr 8f S 2 99
Oct 14 Brig 8f G 1 **100**

MADHAVI 3
May 7 NmkR 6f GF 2 99
May 30 Sand 7f G 4 99
Jly 11 Wind 8½f G 3 **102**

MADIBA 6
Feb 12 Wolv 12f FT 8 **105**
Feb 24 Sthl 14f FT 2 103
Jly 9 Ches 16f GF 7 99

MADRAGO 3
Jun 27 Lonc 7f G 2 **104**

MADRASEE 7
Jan 4 Ling 5f FT 1 **105**
Jan 19 Ling 5f FT 2 **105**
Jly 21 Bath 5f G 1 100
Oct 10 Wolv 5f FT 3 103
Dec 16 Wolv 6f FT 4 100

MADRID BEAUTY 3
Jun 27 Lonc 10½f G 3 **108**

MAFAHEEM 3
Apr 14 Ripn 6f S 2 99
May 1 Haml 5f G 3 **103**
Jun 3 Epsm 7f G 3 102

MAGGIE TULLIVER 3
Jun 27 Wolv 12f SD 3 101
Jly 21 Sand 14f GF 2 **104**
Aug 15 Nott 14f GF 1 103
Sep 27 Nott 16f GF 6 101

MAGHAZI 3
Jun 7 Sals 7f G 2 102
Jun 23 Thsk 7f G 1 **104**

MAGIC AMIGO 4
Mar 28 Wwck 11f GS 4 99
Nov 4 Yarm 10f HY 1 **101**

MAGIC AMOUR 7
May 17 Leic 7f G 1 **99**
May 22 Brig 7f G 1 **99**

MAGIC FLO 3
May 20 NmkR 8f G 2 **105**
Sep 20 Bevl 8½f GF 2 100

MAGIC GLADE 6
Jan 1 Sthl 5f FT 3 105

Jan 27 Sthl 5f FT 2 106
Feb 19 Wolv 5f FT 3 106
Apr 30 NmkR 6f G 12 107
May 12 York 5f GS 2 108
May 21 Hayd 5f F 4 100
Jly 24 Newb 5f G 4 **110**
Aug 6 Hayd 5f G 13 103
Nov 16 Sthl 5f FT 11 101

MAGIC INSTINCT 3
May 16 Bath 10f G 1 **106**
Jun 22 Sals 12f G 1 104
Aug 18 York 14f G 7 102

MAGIC MERLIN 4
Sep 27 Gdwd 7f G 6 **102**
Dec 30 Ling 8f FT 9 100

MAGIC RED 5
Dec 28 Wolv 14f FT 3 **102**

MAGIC STING 4
Apr 28 Rdcr 11f G 1 **103**
May 5 Folk 9½f GS 1 99
May 30 Rdcr 10f G 14 99
Jun 25 Newc 10f G 5 99
Aug 22 Wind 10f G 1 100

MAGIC VERSE 4
Jun 29 Catt 12f G 7 **100**

MAGIC WARRIOR 5
Sep 10 Wolv 8½f FT 1 **99**

MAGICAL ROMANCE 3
May 15 Lonc 8f G 6 **105**
Jun 3 Epsm 12f G 6 99
Sep 8 Epsm 7f G 6 101

MAGICAL WIT 5
May 6 Ling 10f G 3 **99**

MAGNESIUM 5
Apr 20 Epsm 12f GS 8 99

MAGNOLIA LANE 3
May 8 Leop 10f S 2 **108**

MAHMJRA 3
Apr 11 Sthl 10f G 3 **105**
Apr 19 Sthl 10f GF 1 100
May 2 Wwck 12½f G 2 104
May 15 Ripn 12f G 2 102
May 28 Gdwd 11f G 2 101
Jun 9 Yarm 14f G 2 103
Jun 25 Ches 12½f G 4 100

MAIDS CAUSEWAY 3
May 1 NmkR 8f G 2 109
May 22 Curr 8f G 5 111
Jun 17 York 8f G 1 **112**

MAINLY MINE 6
Apr 3 Curr 6f S 8 **99**

MAJEHAR 3
Dec 28 Wolv 8½f S 4 **101**

MAJESTIC DESERT 4
Apr 30 Gdwd 8f S 3 106
Jun 15 York 8f G 4 106
Jly 29 Gdwd 7f G 1 **112**
Aug 14 Leop 8f F 3 111
Sep 10 Leop 8f GF 9 110

MAJESTIC MISSILE 4
May 15 Lonc 5f G 4 106
Jun 26 Curr 5f GF 3 114
Jly 9 Ches 5f GF 2 109
Aug 18 York 5f GF 3 112
Sep 8 Donc 5f F 1 **115**
Sep 17 Newb 5f GF 2 110
Oct 2 Lonc 5f G 9 107

MAJESTIC TIMES 5
Apr 3 Curr 6f S 1 106
Jun 26 Curr 6½f GF 2 103
Jly 16 Curr 5f F 2 **114**
Aug 20 Curr 6f GF 5 107
Sep 17 Ayr 6f G 3 112
Oct 9 Curr 6f GS 2 107

MAJESTIC VISION 4
Jun 21 Brig 12f G 3 **100**

MAJESTICAL 3
May 11 Brig 5½f G 3 **102**
Jun 23 Newc 6f G 2 100
Nov 28 Wolv 5f FT 2 99

MAJIK 6
Jan 3 Sthl 6f SD 1 105
Jan 11 Sthl 6f SW 1 104
Jan 20 Sthl 5f FT 2 103
Nov 4 Yarm 6f S 2 **106**

MAJOR FAUX PAS 3
Jan 5 Ling 8f SD 3 104
Aug 3 Epsm 10f G 4 **105**

MAJOR MAGPIE 3
May 23 Thsk 7f G 3 **102**
Jun 20 Nott 8f F 2 100

MAJOR TITLE 6
Jun 8 Leop 8f F 5 104
Sep 4 Curr 8f G 3 **111**
Sep 17 Curr 8f GF 9 104
Nov 6 Leop 8f S 6 103

MAJORS CAST 4
Jly 26 Gdwd 7f G 3 113
Aug 13 Newb 7f G 2 109
Aug 28 Gdwd 8f G 2 114
Sep 4 Lonc 8f GF 3 **117**

MAKARIM 9
Aug 31 Ling 16f GF 2 **100**

MAKE MY HAY 6
Jan 24 Wolv 14f SD 1 102

MAKTAVISH 6
Nov 3 Muss 5f GS 1 **107**

MAKUTI 3
May 22 Curr 8f G 6 104
Aug 7 Curr 7f G 5 **106**

MALAHEM 3
Aug 11 Hayd 8f GF 1 100
Sep 7 Epsm 8½f G 3 **102**

MALAPROPISM 5
May 20 Gdwd 5f G 4 100
May 28 Muss 5f G 3 107
Jly 11 Ayr 5f GF 5 100
Aug 20 Sand 5f GS 5 102
Aug 25 Muss 5f G 3 102
Sep 9 Donc 5f G 5 107
Oct 1 Epsm 5f G 5 103
Oct 15 Catt 5f G 2 99
Oct 16 Muss 5f GF 3 105
Oct 22 Donc 5f S 5 **110**

MALARKEY 8
May 7 Thsk 16f GS 1 **107**
Jun 4 Hayd 16f G 5 102
Jly 30 Thsk 16f G 6 101
Sep 15 Yarm 16f GS 4 105

MALCHEEK 3
Jun 3 Thsk 7f G 1 104
Jun 23 Thsk 7f G 1 **106**

MALIBU 4
Jan 19 Ling 10f FT 8 101
Mar 3 Ling 10f SW 8 **105**
Apr 6 Ling 12f SW 1 99

MALINSA BLUE 3
May 14 Thsk 8f G 2 **105**
Sep 8 Donc 7f G 2 103
Sep 17 Newb 7f GF 6 102

MALTESE FALCON 5
Jly 22 NmkJ 5f G 1 100
Jly 28 Gdwd 5f G 9 100
Aug 6 Hayd 5f G 12 104
Aug 15 Nott 5f GF 2 105
Sep 4 Lonc 5f GF 2 **110**
Sep 17 Newb 5f GF 4 107
Sep 29 NmkR 5f GF 5 103

MALVERN LIGHT 4
May 14 Nott 6f F 6 102
Jly 13 Ling 8f SW 4 103
Aug 18 York 8f G 10 107
Sep 1 Sals 7f G 3 107
Sep 10 Gdwd 7f G 11 101
Sep 25 NmkR 7f G 9 **108**

MAMBAZO 3
Aug 19 Wolv 5f FT 2 **99**

MAMBO PRINCESS 3
Sep 12 Folk 9½f GF 1 **100**

MAMCAZMA 7
May 1 NmkR 12f G 9 **105**

MAMOOL 6
Jly 29 Gdwd 12f G 1 104
Aug 13 Newb 13½f G 4 102
Sep 3 NmkJ 12f G 2 **113**

MAN CRAZY 4
Feb 27 Wolv 6f G 4 **99**
Mar 7 Ling 6f SD 3 **99**

MAN OF ARAN 5
Jly 2 Leop 10f GF 3 **103**

MANDA ISLAND 3
Jun 30 Newb 10f G 8 **99**

MANDARIN SPIRIT 5
Jan 6 Wolv 8½f G 6 100
Feb 12 Wolv 7f FT 1 100
Mar 1 Ling 6f SD 3 105
May 3 Catt 7f GS 3 102
May 5 Folk 6f G 1 **107**
May 23 Wind 6f F 6 100
May 27 Catt 6f GF 2 103
Jly 15 Wwck 5½f G 7 101
Jly 21 Donc 6f GF 5 99

MANDATUM 4
Jun 7 Sals 12f G 1 101
Jly 16 NmkJ 15f GF 2 101
Aug 12 Newb 13½f G 8 **104**
Aug 31 York 14f G 3 99
Sep 17 Wwck 16f G 8 100

MANDINKA 5
Jan 2 Sthl 11f SD 1 **109**
Jan 11 Sthl 11f SW 2 103

MANEKI NEKO 3
Jly 12 Brig 8f G 4 **101**
Sep 7 Epsm 8½f G 6 **101**

MANGO MISCHIEF 4
May 1 NmkR 9f G 6 104
Jly 8 Chep 10f GF 1 108
Aug 21 Deau 10f G 5 **111**
Sep 24 NmkR 12f G 7 103
Nov 5 Donc 10½f S 4 99

MANIATIS 8
Mar 23 Ling 12f SD 2 102
Apr 22 Wolv 12f SD 1 99
Apr 26 Sthl 12f FT 2 100
Jun 3 Wolv 14f FT 3 **103**

MANIC 3
Jun 1 Nott 6f G 3 **100**
Jly 28 Epsm 6f G 3 99
Dec 30 Ling 6f FT 8 **100**

MANYANA 4
Sep 1 Sals 14f G 4 **106**

MARAAHEL 4
Apr 16 Newb 12f GS 5 107
May 5 Ches 10½f G 1 113
Jun 18 York 12f G 2 114
Aug 16 York 10½f G 3 **115**
Aug 31 York 9f G 3 104
Oct 15 NmkR 10f G 3 111

MARAAKEB 4
Mar 29 Pont 10f S 4 101
Apr 16 Newb 10f GS 1 101
May 2 Donc 10½f G 7 104
May 25 NmkR 10f G 5 100
Jly 2 Hayd 12f GF 7 105
Jly 23 Newb 12f GF 4 **106**
Aug 6 Hayd 10½f GF 9 104
Sep 7 Donc 10½f GF 11 102

MARCHETTA 3
May 31 Sand 9f G 1 100
Jly 16 Ling 10f SW 1 **103**

MARCHING SONG 3
Jly 20 Sand 7f G 3 106
Aug 6 Wind 6f GF 2 107
Aug 27 York 6f G 5 103
Sep 10 Gdwd 7f G 7 **109**
Oct 14 NmkR 7f G 16 103

MARCUS EILE 4
Aug 7 Rdcr 11f G 2 **101**
Sep 20 Bevl 10f GF 11 99

MAREDSOUS 5
May 9 Lonc 12f G 6 **113**

MAREN 4
May 23 Thsk 8f G 3 **99**

MARGARET'S DREAM 4
Dec 29 Ling 8f G 4 **101**

MARGERY DAW 5
Jan 22 Ling 10f FT 3 100
Jan 26 Ling 10f FT 3 101
Feb 1 Ling 10f SD 7 99
Feb 22 Ling 10f SD 2 **105**

MARHABA MILLION 3
Aug 24 Brig 12f GS 3 **99**

MARIA DELFINA 3
Aug 26 Bath 13f G 4 **100**

MARIA VETSERA 4
Jly 29 Thsk 8f G 2 101
Aug 7 Ling 10f G 2 **102**

MARIAS MAGIC 4
Apr 25 Haml 12f G 2 103
May 1 Haml 13f S 2 **108**
Jly 30 NmkJ 12f GF 6 101
Aug 3 Pont 12f G 8 99
Aug 29 Newc 14½f GF 1 101

MARINAITE 4
Mar 8 Sthl 5f GF 3 101
Mar 21 Sthl 8f SD 1 **109**
Apr 13 Bevl 10f G 9 100

MARKER 5
Apr 2 Kemp 5f GS 4 **106**

MARKET TREND 3
Apr 2 Kemp 9f S 1 **108**
Aug 13 Ripn 12f GS 3 101
Aug 31 York 12f G 9 101
Sep 17 Catt 12f G 6 104

MARKET WATCHER 4
Sep 17 Curr 8f GF 13 **101**

MARKO JADEO 7
Jan 8 Ling 8f SD 7 101
Jan 29 Ling 7f SD 8 **107**
Feb 9 Ling 7f SD 6 100
Mar 4 Wolv 6f SD 1 106
Sep 6 Ling 7f SD 5 101
Dec 5 Ling 7f FT 2 100
Dec 20 Ling 8f FT 7 101

MARSAD 11
Mar 28 Kemp 6f G 7 100
Jly 14 Leic 6f GF 7 **102**

MARSH ORCHID 4
Mar 4 Wolv 12f SD 7 **99**

MARSHALLSPARK 6
Apr 2 Wolv 7f FT 3 **99**

MARSHMAN 6
Apr 18 Pont 6f S 4 100
May 7 Ling 7f G 11 99
Jun 25 Newc 7f G 1 105
Jly 7 NmkJ 7f G 14 101
Aug 6 NmkJ 7f G 9 **109**
Aug 27 Gdwd 7f G 7 100
Sep 17 Ayr 7f G 4 101
Sep 30 NmkR 7f G 6 102
Oct 14 NmkR 7f G 9 105
Oct 27 Ling 7f SD 3 107
Nov 19 Ling 7f FT 6 108
Nov 26 Ling 8f FT 7 103

MARTILLO 5
May 1 StCl 8f HD 1 **119**
Jun 14 York 8f G 6 106

MARY CARLETON 4
Feb 22 Sthl 8f SW 1 **99**

MARY GRAY 3
Jly 1 Hayd 14f G 1 **99**

MARYS ISLE 6
Jun 1 Leop 14f G 9 **106**

MASAFI 4
Jly 26 Gdwd 10f G 7 104
Aug 14 Pont 12f G 2 **107**
Aug 20 Ches 13½f G 2 106

MASKED 4
May 1 NmkR 16f G 2 **106**

MASQUERADER 3
Jun 20 Nott 8f F 2 103
Aug 31 Ling 12f F 1 103
Sep 23 Ling 12f F 2 104
Oct 29 Wolv 9½f SD 2 **110**

MASSEY 9
Jan 3 Sthl 6f SD 3 **103**
Jan 20 Sthl 7f SD 2 102
Jan 29 Ling 7f SD 12 100
Apr 8 Sthl 6f SD 2 102

MASSIF CENTRALE 4
May 13 York 14f GS 8 99
May 28 Gdwd 12f G 7 **104**

MASTER COBBLER 3
Jun 16 Newb 12f G 3 **102**
Jly 21 Sand 10f GF 8 99
Sep 3 NmkJ 15f G 3 101
Sep 28 Sals 14f G 2 99

MASTER JOSEPH 3
Aug 15 Yarm 7f G 4 99
Oct 14 Rdcr 7f GF 3 **102**

MASTER MAHOGANY 4
May 3 Bath 8f HY 2 103
May 16 Bath 8f G 1 103
Jun 5 Bath 8f G 3 101
Jun 26 Wind 8½f G 2 106
Jly 9 York 8f G 2 109
Jly 24 Pont 8f G 4 104
Aug 27 Wind 8½f G 4 **110**

MASTER ROBBIE 6
Mar 19 Ling 7f SD 1 **109**
Apr 30 NmkR 6f G 16 105
Jly 14 Leic 7f GF 1 105
Jly 19 Yarm 7f G 4 108
Aug 11 Sand 7f GF 8 102
Aug 19 Ches 7f GF 9 101
Oct 7 Newb 7f GF 7 100

MASTER THEO 4
Jan 10 Wolv 9½f SD 2 109
Jan 28 Wolv 9½f SD 1 106
Feb 18 Wolv 8½f SD 6 106
Mar 26 Kemp 10f GS 10 100
Nov 11 Wolv 8½f FT 3 **110**
Dec 9 Wolv 8½f FT 3 107

MASTER WELLS 4
May 7 Thsk 16f GS 4 **103**

MASTER'N COMMANDER 3
Aug 31 Ling 12f GS 3 **99**

MASTERMAN READY 4
Sep 17 Wwck 16f G 3 **105**

MATERIAL WITNESS 8
Apr 23 Leic 7f G 6 102
Jly 7 NmkJ 7f G 17 100
Jly 28 Gdwd 7f G 3 102
Aug 13 Newb 7f G 9 101
Sep 6 Ling 7f SD 2 **103**
Sep 24 NmkR 7f G 15 **103**

MATHEMATICIAN 3
Jun 12 Chan 8f GF 2 112
Jly 3 Chan 8f G 6 **113**
Oct 1 Lonc 8f G 3 **113**

MATLOOB 4
Aug 27 Wind 11½f G 6 **103**

MATRIX 4
Nov 1 MsnL 6f GF 6 **112**

MATSUNOSUKE 3
Jun 24 NmkJ 5f G 3 **99**

MATTY TUN 6
Jly 29 Nott 5f G 6 101
Aug 26 NmkJ 5f G 1 99
Sep 3 Hayd 5f F 5 **106**
Sep 9 Donc 5f G 11 100
Oct 22 Donc 5f S 10 105

MAXAMILLION 3
Oct 25 Yarm 10f S 3 **103**
Nov 4 Yarm 10f HY 2 100

MAY MORNING 3
Jun 13 Thsk 7f G 4 99
Jly 19 Yarm 7f G 1 **104**

MAYADEEN 3
May 28 Donc 10½f GF 2 **100**

MAYSTOCK 5
Jly 29 NmkJ 12f G 1 **104**
Sep 28 Sals 14f G 3 99
Nov 10 Ling 13f SD 1 99

MAZINDAR 3
Mar 3 Ling 8f SW 2 **103**

MAZUNA 4
May 14 Newb 13½f G 4 **99**
Sep 7 Donc 14½f GF 7 **99**

MCBAIN 6
Jun 7 Ches 10½f GF 8 100

MCELDOWNEY 3
Jly 14 Haml 8½f GF 1 **107**
Aug 22 Haml 11f F 1 106
Aug 24 Brig 12f GS 1 101

MEADOW 4
Jly 6 Naas 6f GF 8 **99**

MEAN MACHINE 3
Jly 6 Naas 10f GF 5 **99**

MEAS 4
Jun 1 Leop 14f G 2 **108**

MEASURED RESPONSE 3
Sep 15 Pont 8f G 3 **100**

MECCA'S MATE 4
Apr 12 Muss 5f G 1 105
Apr 28 Rdcr 5f GF 2 103
May 7 Thsk 6f GS 1 103
Jun 4 Donc 6f G 3 100
Jun 18 Ayr 5f G 1 **109**
Jun 25 Newc 6f G 4 105
Jly 8 York 5f G 1 105
Jly 18 Ayr 5f GF 1 **109**
Jly 28 Gdwd 5f G 5 108
Jly 30 Gdwd 6f G 14 104
Aug 20 Bevl 5f G 3 106
Sep 18 Haml 5f F 6 103
Oct 13 NmkR 5f G 2 **109**

MEDIA HORA 5
Feb 5 Ling 5f G 7 **103**

MEDICINAL 4
Jun 16 Lonc 10f G 6 **115**

MEDITATION 3
Aug 20 Ling 7f G 2 **99**

MEDJUGORJE MESSAGE 3
Nov 5 Sthl 11f FT 2 **104**

MEELUP 5
Jun 6 Wind 8½f G 4 **106**
Jly 24 Newb 8f G 3 102

MEGGIDO 3
Mar 28 Kemp 7f GS 4 **100**
Jun 21 Bevl 8½f G 3 **100**

MEHMAAS 9
Jly 4 Muss 8f GF 3 **102**
Jly 28 Muss 8f G 5 99

MEIJIN 5
Aug 15 Brig 7f G 5 **100**

MEIKLE BARFIL 3
Sep 14 Sand 5f GS 3 99
Oct 7 York 5f G 4 **100**

MEJHAR 5
Jun 18 Rdcr 10f G 8 **103**

MELALCHRIST 3
Jun 20 Ripn 6f G 2 **106**
Jly 2 Bevl 5f G 4 101
Aug 18 Ches 6f F 1 99
Sep 24 Hayd 5f GF 9 104

MELANDRE 3
Jun 23 Thsk 5f GF 3 **101**
Jly 17 Rdcr 5f G 6 100

MELANOSPORUM 3
Jun 27 Lonc 9f G 2 **111**

MELODY ISLAND 3
May 8 Leop 8f S 4 **110**
Oct 23 Curr 6f S 3 107
Nov 6 Leop 8f S 5 103

MELROSE AVENUE 3
Apr 20 Catt 12f S 1 **104**
Jun 17 York 16f G 1 103

MELVINO 3
Feb 9 Ling 8f G 3 **102**
Mar 3 Ling 8f SW 7 100
Sep 15 Pont 10f G 5 99
Oct 4 Catt 12f GF 3 100
Oct 10 Wind 11½f G 1 **102**

MEMBERSHIP 5
Apr 12 NmkR 7f GF 3 **101**

MENESTROL 3
Aug 2 Deau 10f G 5 **106**
Sep 17 Lonc 10f G 5 105

MENWAAL 3
May 8 Leop 10f S 3 **100**

MERAYAAT 3
Aug 28 Yarm 14f G 2 **101**

MERCARI 3
Jly 4 Muss 9f GF 3 **105**

MERDIFF 6
Jan 6 Wolv 6f GF 1 100
Mar 16 Wolv 7f SD 5 99
Mar 24 Wolv 7f SD 2 **102**

MERGER 3
Apr 3 Curr 7f S 2 107
Apr 22 Sand 10f G 2 100
Jun 8 Leop 10f F 2 **108**
Jun 26 Curr 8f F 3 107

MERLIN'S DANCER 5
Mar 31 Donc 6f G 1 106
Jly 24 Newb 5f G 5 **110**
Jly 30 Gdwd 6f G 4 108
Sep 7 Donc 5½f GF 16 101

MERLINS PROFIT 5
Jun 27 Muss 9f GF 3 102
Jly 27 Muss 8f GF 1 103
Aug 2 Catt 7f G 3 100
Aug 25 Muss 8f G 1 **107**

MERMAID ISLAND 3
May 22 Curr 8f G 5 104
Jly 17 Curr 9f F 7 **106**
Sep 18 Curr 8f GF 7 104

MERRYMADCAP 3
Mar 24 Wolv 9½f SD 3 99
Jly 5 Wolv 8½f FT 3 101
Sep 26 Bath 8f G 1 **102**

MERRYMAKER 5
Apr 26 Wwck 12½f GS 8 102
Jun 4 Donc 12f GF 5 102
Jun 24 NmkJ 12f G 3 101
Jly 31 Ches 12½f G 2 100
Sep 17 Catt 12f G 1 **108**
Oct 24 Ling 12f SW 8 103

MERSEY SOUND 7
Jun 18 NmkJ 15f G 1 **109**
Jly 9 Sals 12f G 3 99
Jly 13 Ling 16f G 2 100
Jly 23 Sals 14f G 1 104
Aug 11 Sals 14f GF 4 99

MESHAHEER 6
Apr 23 Leic 7f G 5 103
May 7 Hayd 7f GS 3 **108**
Jun 3 Gdwd 8f GS 3 103

MESMERIC 7
May 1 Sals 14f GS 7 101
May 12 York 14f S 6 **105**

MEXICAN 6
Feb 1 Sthl 8f FT 2 **106**

MEXICAN PETE 5
Jun 8 Haml 12f G 4 102
Jly 20 Leic 12f GF 4 103

MEZUZAH 5
Apr 18 Pont 8f S 2 102
Apr 25 Haml 9f G 4 99
Jun 2 Haml 9f GS 1 **106**
Jun 8 Haml 8½f G 7 99
Jly 30 NmkJ 10f GF 5 100
Oct 8 York 9f GS 4 102

MI ODDS 9
Jan 1 Sthl 8f SD 6 106
Jan 7 Wolv 8½f SW 6 **110**
Jan 20 Sthl 7f SD 7 103
Jan 28 Wolv 8½f SD 6 101
Jun 16 Wolv 12f SD 2 99
Nov 15 Sthl 11f FT 2 104
Nov 29 Sthl 12f SD 2 102
Dec 6 Sthl 11f FT 1 106
Dec 20 Sthl 11f SW 5 102

MICHABO 4
May 21 NmkR 14f GS 2 **104**

MICHAELS DREAM 6
Jly 7 Wwck 12½f G 9 99

MICHAELS PRIDE 3
Jun 23 Sals 10f G 1 **103**
Jly 2 Bevl 10f G 1 100
Jly 14 Haml 11f GF 2 101
Jly 21 Bath 10f GF 1 101
Oct 19 Bath 11½f GS 4 100
Oct 29 Ayr 9f HY 3 101

MICKEHAHA 3
Apr 25 Wind 8½f GS 4 99
May 28 Ling 10f SW 1 **104**
Aug 25 Ling 10f GS 3 100

MICKLEDOR 5
Aug 2 Catt 7f G 5 **99**

MICKLEY 8
Jan 6 Wolv 12f G 7 **103**

MICKMACMAGOOLE 3
Dec 12 Sthl 11f FT 1 **100**

MIDAS WAY 5
Apr 20 Epsm 12f GS 3 108
May 7 NmkR 12f GF 2 105
Jly 2 Sand 16½f G 2 **112**
Jly 29 Gdwd 12f G 5 99

MIDCAP 3
Aug 18 Chep 7f GF 1 **99**

MIDDLE EARTH 3
Jan 15 Ling 7f SD 2 **99**

MIDDLE EASTERN 3
Nov 16 Sthl 6f FT 1 **100**

MIDDLEMARCH 5
Jly 2 Sand 8f G 7 **111**
Jly 18 Ayr 8f GF 5 103
Aug 6 Hayd 10½f GF 13 100
Aug 17 York 10½f G 9 102

MIDDLETON GREY 7
Jan 20 Sthl 7f SD 5 108
Jun 3 Gdwd 7f GS 8 102
Jun 19 Wwck 6f G 2 **109**
Aug 13 NmkJ 6f G 1 106
Dec 2 Wolv 6f SD 8 102

MIDNIGHT GRACE 3
Sep 17 Curr 5f G 13 **102**

MIDNIGHT LACE 3
Jly 23 Ling 7f GF 1 99
Sep 20 Bevl 7½f GF 6 99
Nov 5 Wolv 8½f FT 1 **100**

MIDSHIPMAN 7
Feb 25 Wolv 9½f FT 1 **100**
May 7 Hayd 8f S 1 **100**

MIGHTY BEAU 6
Jun 14 York 5f G 5 **105**
Jun 18 York 6f GF 11 100

MIKAO 4
Apr 25 Wind 10f GS 3 99
May 26 Ayr 10f G 2 103
Aug 3 Pont 12f G 2 **106**
Aug 26 NmkJ 15f G 4 100
Sep 17 Wwck 16f G 1 **106**

MILADY'S PRIDE 4
Feb 25 Wolv 8½f G 2 101
Mar 4 Wolv 8½f SD 1 **102**

MILESIUS 3
Jly 16 Curr 8f GF 5 **103**

MILK IT MICK 4
Jly 9 Ches 7f GF 6 **102**

MILLAGROS 5
Apr 25 Haml 12f G 5 99
Jly 14 Haml 11f GF 1 102
Sep 17 Ayr 13f G 3 **103**
Nov 3 Muss 12f GS 2 100

MILLENARY 8
Jly 6 NmkJ 12f G 4 99
Jly 28 Gdwd 16f G 3 **112**
Aug 16 York 16f G 1 105
Sep 8 Donc 18f G 1 111
Oct 15 NmkR 16f G 3 111

MILLENIO 5
Feb 16 Ling 10f SD 10 **101**

MILLENNIUM FORCE 7
Mar 28 Wwck 7f GS 3 100
Apr 27 Ling 7½f S 3 **108**
Jly 7 NmkJ 7f G 5 106
Aug 6 NmkJ 7f G 16 104

MILLENNIUM HALL 6
Apr 25 Haml 12f G 4 101
May 2 Newc 12½f G 3 101
Jun 2 Haml 13f GS 1 99
Jun 8 Haml 12f G 3 **102**

MILLINSKY 4
May 28 Ling 5f GF 2 99
Jly 7 Folk 5f G 1 **109**
Jly 31 Newb 5f G 7 99
Aug 21 Folk 5f G 3 104
Sep 21 Rdcr 5f GF 1 104
Oct 1 Rdcr 5f GF 2 101

MILLION PERCENT 6
Feb 8 Ling 6f SD 9 100
Mar 18 Ling 6f SD 2 105
Jun 1 Newc 6f G 7 99
Jun 13 Thsk 6f G 5 100
Jun 17 Rdcr 6f G 8 101
Jly 8 Ling 6f SW 3 **106**
Aug 3 Yarm 6f G 4 104
Aug 17 Nott 5f GF 4 102
Dec 3 Wolv 6f GF 4 99
Dec 30 Ling 6f FT 5 102

MILLION WISHES 3
Nov 1 MsnL 6f GF 11 **107**

MILLKOM ELEGANCE 6
Jan 21 Wolv 12f SD 7 100
Feb 21 Wolv 14f FT 1 **102**

MILLVILLE 5
Apr 20 Epsm 12f GS 5 104
Jun 4 Epsm 12f G 5 106
Jun 30 Hayd 14f GF 2 105
Jly 16 Ripn 12f G 2 **108**
Aug 3 Pont 12f G 1 **108**
Aug 17 York 14f G 13 102
Sep 3 Hayd 14f GF 8 104
Nov 19 Ling 12f FT 3 103

MILLY WATERS 4
Aug 12 NmkJ 7f G 5 **100**

MIMI MOUSE 3
May 14 Thsk 5f G 1 105
Jly 22 York 5f G 3 **107**
Sep 18 Haml 5f F 4 104

MIMIC 5
May 5 Folk 6f G 8 99
Aug 3 Yarm 6f G 2 **106**
Sep 12 Rdcr 6f G 5 102

MINA 3
Sep 3 Thsk 6f G 2 **101**
Oct 9 Gdwd 6f G 2 **101**

MINA A SALEM 3
Jly 20 Ling 11½f G 3 99
Sep 2 NmkJ 8f G 8 **104**
Oct 24 Ling 8f SW 1 103
Nov 19 Ling 8f FT 2 103

MIND HOW YOU GO 7
May 27 Catt 12f GF 2 99

MINE 7
Apr 2 Donc 8f G 7 108
Apr 16 Thsk 8f HY 2 **111**
May 12 York 7f GS 5 108
Jun 15 York 8f G 11 106
Jly 7 NmkJ 7f G 1 108
Jly 23 Newb 7f GF 10 110
Aug 11 Sals 8f GF 10 105
Oct 1 Rdcr 7f GF 9 100

MINE BEHIND 5
Jun 25 Wind 6f G 11 102
Jly 23 Newb 7f GF 1 101
Aug 5 NmkJ 6f GF 1 **104**
Aug 13 Ripn 6f G 6 99

MINEKO 3
Jly 5 Pont 12f G 2 **104**

MINERAL STAR 3
Mar 28 Yarm 8f GS 1 105
May 13 York 7f GS 1 **107**
Aug 10 Sand 7f GF 1 104
Sep 23 Hayd 8f G 8 100

MINIMUM BID 4
Jan 19 Ling 6f FT 1 103
Feb 26 Ling 6f SD 1 105
Mar 3 Ling 7f SW 4 99
Mar 21 Ling 6f SW 3 **106**
Aug 6 Ling 7f SD 3 101
Aug 12 Newb 6f G 1 104

MINNESINGER 3
Apr 23 Leic 10f G 1 **103**
Sep 8 Epsm 10f G 5 100
Oct 5 Nott 10f G 8 102

MINORITY REPORT 5
May 19 Donc 8f GF 2 100
Sep 18 Haml 8½f F 2 **104**
Sep 27 Gdwd 8f G 2 101
Oct 7 Newb 7f GF 1 **104**

MINTLAW 3
Jun 23 Haml 8½f G 3 **101**

MIRABILIS 3
Jun 5 Chan 8f GF 5 108
Jly 31 Deau 8f G 5 112
Oct 1 Lonc 7f G 3 **114**

MIRASOL PRINCESS 4
Jun 18 Ling 5f G 4 **104**
Jly 20 Sand 5f GF 6 99

MIRJAN 9
May 11 York 12f S 7 99
Jun 25 Newc 16f G 8 **109**
Sep 3 Hayd 14f GF 12 102
Oct 15 NmkR 18f G 7 103

MIRPOUR 6
May 22 Curr 12f GS 13 100
Jun 26 Curr 16f F 3 103

MISARO 4
Oct 10 Wolv 5f FT 1 **107**
Oct 18 Sthl 6f SD 2 100

MISS ADELAIDE 4
Jan 13 Ling 6f SD 2 **103**

MISS AILBHE 3
Jun 25 Curr 10f G 11 **99**

MISS ALABAMA 4
Apr 10 Lonc 10f S 7 **107**

MISS AMOUR 3
May 28 Ling 10f SW 3 **102**

MISS CARUSO 3
Mar 20 Curr 7f HY 3 **102**
Apr 10 Leop 7f GS 4 99
Aug 7 Curr 7f G 17 99
Nov 6 Leop 8f S 10 99

MISS CHAUSSINI 3
Jun 1 Leop 7f G 2 **106**

MISS ELOISE 4
Jan 14 Wolv 12f SW 8 **99**

MISS EMMA 5
May 15 Lonc 5f G 2 108
Jun 5 Chan 5f G 8 105
Jly 9 Deau 6f GF 4 108
Sep 4 Lonc 5f GF 3 110
Oct 2 Lonc 5f G 13 105
Nov 1 MsnL 6f GF 1 **115**

MISS GLORY BE 7
Apr 4 Wolv 9½f FT 3 100
Jly 12 Brig 10f G 1 **102**
Nov 5 Sthl 8f FT 3 100
Dec 29 Ling 8f FT 7 99

MISS ISABELA 3
May 22 Curr 6f G 8 101
Jly 6 Naas 6f GF 7 99
Aug 14 Leop 6f G 3 100
Aug 20 Curr 6f GF 3 **103**

MISS MADAME 4
Apr 24 Brig 8f GF 5 **99**

MISS MALONE 3
Mar 1 Ling 7f SD 4 **101**

MISS MAMBO 4
Sep 10 Leop 8f GF 4 **115**

MISS MEGGY 3
Sep 30 Ling 7f FT 5 **100**

MISS PARTICULAR 3
Apr 16 Newb 8f GS 2 100
Jun 30 Newb 10f G 2 **105**
Jly 24 Newb 12f G 1 100

MISS PATRICIA 3
Mar 23 Ling 7f SD 2 99
Apr 18 Wind 8½f G 2 **103**
May 14 Newb 7f F 2 99
Jun 1 Nott 8f G 2 **103**
Aug 8 Wind 8½f GF 6 99

MISS PEBBLES 5
Jly 16 Ling 10f SW 4 100
Jly 25 Wind 10f GS 3 101
Jly 28 Epsm 8½f G 1 100
Aug 3 Epsm 8½f G 2 102
Aug 6 NmkJ 8f G 4 103

MISS POLARIS 4
Feb 12 Ling 8f SD 2 99
Apr 27 Ling 8f FT 1 **105**
May 15 Ripn 10f G 2 104

MISS PORCIA 4
Aug 4 Brig 6f G 6 **100**

MISS PROVVIDENCE 3
Aug 7 Ling 10f G 1 103
Sep 7 Donc 10½f GF 1 107
Oct 24 Ling 12f SW 1 **108**

MISS SALLY 3
Jun 28 Curr 6½f GF 1 104
Jly 2 Leop 7f F 1 109
Sep 17 Curr 6f G 3 **112**
Oct 9 Curr 6f GS 1 109

MISS THE BOAT 3
May 5 Folk 9½f GS 2 **106**
Jun 6 Folk 9½f G 3 105
Jun 26 Wind 11½f G 1 100

MISS TOULON 7
Jun 1 Leop 14f G 5 106

MISS TRISH 5
Mar 20 Curr 8f HY 13 100
Apr 3 Curr 10f S 6 103
May 21 Curr 8f G 2 **106**

MISS UNA 3
Oct 23 Curr 7f S 1 **102**

MISS WIND 4
Apr 10 Lonc 10f S 1 **112**
Aug 21 Deau 10f G 11 104

MISS WIZZ 5
Jly 28 Muss 8f G 2 **101**
Aug 17 Carl 8f GF 7 99

MISSATACAMA 3
Jan 21 Wolv 8½f SD 3 **103**
May 21 NmkR 8f G 1 **103**
Jun 10 Sand 8f GF 4 100

Horse / Date	Course	Dist	Going	Pos	Rating
Dec 10	Wolv	9½f	FT	7	99
Dec 30	Ling	8f	FT	4	**103**
MISSED A BEAT 3					
May 24	Ling	7f	G	3	101
Jly 9	Sals	7f	G	2	99
Aug 10	Sals	8f	G	6	102
Sep 14	Sand	8f	G	10	101
Nov 10	Ling	8f	SD	4	**103**
MISSIE BAILEYS 3					
May 28	Ling	10f	SW	4	101
Jly 23	Ling	10f	SW	2	**102**
Aug 20	Ling	10f	SD	2	101
MISSION AFFIRMED 4					
Apr 21	Sthl	7f	FT	1	103
Jly 29	Thsk	7f	G	6	**104**
MISSPERON 3					
Sep 15	Ayr	5f	GF	3	**99**
MISSUS LINKS 4					
Apr 1	Ling	7f	SD	4	**100**
MISSY CINOFAZ 3					
Jan 8	Ling	6f	SD	3	**100**
MISTER ARJAY 5					
May 28	Muss	8f	G	4	103
Jun 11	Leic	10f	G	5	99
MISTER AZIZ 3					
Jun 7	Rdcr	7f	G	7	**99**
MISTER BENJI 6					
Jan 5	Sthl	7f	SD	1	101
Jan 11	Sthl	8f	SW	2	**106**
MISTER CHARM 5					
Aug 28	Deau	8f	G	5	**99**
MISTER CLINTON 8					
Aug 4	Brig	7f	G	4	**102**
Dec 21	Wolv	9½f	FT	1	**102**
MISTER COMPLETELY 4					
Nov 5	Sthl	11f	FT	4	**100**
MISTER GENEPI 3					
Apr 14	NmkR	8f	G	5	99
Apr 30	NmkR	8f	G	7	**107**
May 22	Curr	10f	GS	3	101
Jun 5	Chan	10½f	G	14	99
Jly 30	Gdwd	8f	G	4	103
MISTER HIGHT 3					
Apr 10	Leop	10f	S	2	106
May 22	Curr	10f	GS	4	100
Jun 26	Curr	12f	F	7	**108**
MISTER MAL 9					
Apr 14	Ripn	5f	S	3	99
May 5	Chep	6f	GS	4	**104**
MISTER MARMADUKE 4					
Jan 12	Wolv	5f	SD	2	100
Feb 11	Wolv	5f	SD	3	**103**
MISTER RIGHT 4					
May 20	Bath	10f	G	1	102
Jun 6	Wind	10f	G	4	100
Jun 21	Newb	10f	G	1	**103**
Aug 2	Brig	12f	G	7	**103**
MISTER SWEETS 6					
Aug 16	York	6f	GF	11	100
Aug 27	York	6f	G	6	**101**
MISTRAL SKY 6					
Jan 7	Wolv	7f	SW	4	**107**
Feb 18	Wolv	6f	SD	4	104
Mar 4	Wolv	6f	SD	4	104
Mar 12	Wolv	7f	SD	1	101
Apr 23	Leic	6f	G	7	99
May 30	Leic	6f	G	2	101
Jun 19	Wwck	6f	G	6	105
Jly 14	Leic	6f	GF	8	102
Dec 16	Wolv	6f	FT	8	99
MISTRESS TWISTER 4					
May 17	Rdcr	8f	G	5	101
Jun 25	Newc	10f	G	3	103
Jly 23	York	10½f	GS	2	**105**
Aug 13	Ripn	10f	GS	3	102
Oct 1	Rdcr	10f	GF	3	101
Oct 9	Newc	10f	G	6	103
MISTY DANCER 6					
Jun 10	Sand	10f	GF	4	101
Jun 22	Epsm	12f	G	1	101
MISTY HEIGHTS 4					
May 21	Curr	8f	G	5	100
Jun 1	Leop	8f	G	5	**107**
Jly 2	Leop	7f	F	6	103
MISTY MAN 7					
Jan 21	Wolv	12f	SD	5	**102**
MITH HILL 4					
Apr 11	Ling	12f	SD	7	100
Apr 25	Haml	12f	G	1	**104**
May 23	Thsk	12f	G	4	101
MIXING 3					
Jly 1	Sand	14f	G	9	**99**
MIZZ TEE 3					
Jun 9	Ripn	8f	G	4	101
Jun 25	Ches	7f	G	4	101
Aug 7	Rdcr	6f	G	5	101
Nov 26	Wolv	9½f	FT	3	**104**
Dec 31	Wolv	9½f	SD	2	**104**
MKUZI 6					
May 25	Leop	14f	GF	3	**105**
Sep 17	Curr	14f	G	6	101
MOAYED 6					
Jan 7	Wolv	8½f	SW	1	**116**
Jan 15	Ling	6f	SD	2	108
Jan 28	Wolv	8½f	SD	5	101
Mar 12	Wolv	7f	SD	2	100
Mar 19	Ling	10f	SD	7	112
Apr 30	NmkR	6f	G	8	109
May 7	Ling	7f	G	2	113
Jun 16	York	7f	GF	7	102
Jly 7	NmkJ	7f	G	13	102
Jly 23	Newb	7f	GF	20	100
Jly 30	Gdwd	6f	G	9	107
Aug 6	NmkJ	7f	G	14	107
Sep 24	NmkR	7f	G	2	114
Nov 19	Ling	10f	FT	10	99
Dec 2	Wolv	6f	SD	5	105
Dec 9	Wolv	7f	FT	3	104
Dec 31	Wolv	9½f	SD	5	102
MOBANE FLYER 5					
May 21	Carl	8f	G	4	**102**
Jun 2	Haml	9f	GS	2	**102**
MOBO-BACO 8					
Jan 21	Wolv	12f	SD	3	**102**
Feb 25	Wolv	8½f	SD	3	100
Mar 4	Wolv	8½f	SD	7	99
MOBS JAGGER 5					
Jun 1	Leop	14f	G	19	**106**
MOCCA 4					
May 1	NmkR	12f	G	2	**112**
Jun 4	Epsm	12f	G	6	106
Jun 23	Newc	10f	GF	4	101
Sep 19	Carl	12f	G	6	100
MODAFFAA 5					
Jan 13	Ling	12f	SD	10	**102**
MOGAAMER 3					
Feb 16	Ling	7f	SD	2	103
Mar 1	Ling	7f	SD	1	**109**
Mar 19	Ling	7f	SD	4	103
May 28	Gdwd	8f	G	6	102
MOHAFAZAAT 3					
Oct 19	Bath	10f	GS	4	**104**
Nov 15	Ling	10f	FT	1	99
MOHANDAS 4					
Jun 16	Lonc	10f	G	5	**116**
MOKARABA 3					
Apr 30	Thsk	12f	S	1	101
Jun 4	Hayd	12f	G	4	**104**
Jly 1	Sand	14f	G	5	102
MOKTABES 3					
Jly 19	Yarm	7f	G	2	103
Sep 28	Ling	8f	SD	1	**107**
Oct 12	Ling	8f	SD	1	106
MOLDAVIA 4					
Jan 1	Sthl	11f	SD	1	101
Feb 14	Wolv	12f	SD	5	**103**
MOLEM 3					
Oct 9	Bath	8f	G	2	**99**
MOLINIA 4					
Feb 17	Sthl	7f	G	2	102
Feb 24	Sthl	7f	FT	4	102
Mar 21	Sthl	8f	SD	2	**104**
MOLLY MARIE 3					
Jun 4	Donc	5f	G	2	102
Jun 18	Rdcr	6f	GF	1	**106**
Jly 2	Hayd	6f	GF	5	100
MOLLY'S SECRET 7					
Jun 3	Wolv	14f	FT	2	**104**
MOLLYPUTTHEKETELON 4					
Jun 13	Wind	8½f	G	3	99
Jly 2	Nott	8f	GF	4	**102**
Sep 7	Epsm	8½f	G	7	101

Sep 28 Ling 12f SD 12 99
Dec 16 Wolv 9½f FT 2 100

MOLLZAM 3
Jun 1 Wolv 8½f FT 4 **100**

MOLOTOV 5
Jun 21 Bevl 5f G 4 **99**

MOMENT OF CLARITY 3
May 28 Ling 10f SW 8 **100**

MOMTIC 4
Apr 23 Sand 8f G 1 107
May 7 NmkR 9f GF 5 101
May 30 Sand 8f G 2 110
Jun 3 Epsm 8½f G 1 113
Jly 2 Sand 8f G 2 **115**
Aug 18 York 8f G 1 112

MON SECRET 7
Apr 26 Sthl 7f FT 2 **102**

MONA LISA 3
May 22 Curr 8f G 11 109
Jun 17 York 8f G 3 108
Jun 25 Curr 10f G 6 **111**
Jly 17 Curr 12f F 3 110
Sep 10 Leop 10f GF 7 108
Oct 2 Lonc 10f G 2 109

MONASH LAD 3
Aug 28 Gdwd 9f G 8 **105**
Oct 11 Leic 10f G 3 100

MONASHEE PRINCE 3
Jan 8 Ling 5f SD 2 **101**
Dec 19 Wolv 0f FT 3 100

MONKEY MADGE 3
Dec 28 Wolv 7f FT 4 **99**

MONKSTOWN ROAD 3
Apr 2 Donc 6f G 3 **99**

MONSUSU 3
Aug 7 Curr 7f G 16 **99**

MONT SAINT MICHEL 3
May 4 Ches 12½f GS 3 101
Jly 15 Wwck 11f G 1 **106**
Sep 14 Yarm 10f G 9 100

MONTANA 5
Aug 3 Epsm 6f G 3 101
Aug 12 Folk 5f GF 3 101
Nov 4 Yarm 6f S 3 **104**

MONTARA 6
May 10 Muss 9f G 1 **101**
Sep 14 Bevl 8½f G 2 100

MONTARE 3
May 1 StCl 10½f F 2 104
Oct 16 Lonc 12f G 1 **112**

MONTE CRISTO 7
Oct 12 Ling 16f G 1 101

MONTE MAYOR BOY 3
Nov 16 Sthl 8f FT 1 **102**

MONTECARMELO 3
Jun 27 Lonc 7f G 3 **103**

MONTECITO 3
Jly 1 Hayd 12f G 1 **107**
Aug 20 Sand 10f G 2 102
Oct 19 Bath 11½f GS 2 102
Oct 28 NmkR 12f GS 4 103

MONTERIGGIONI 3
Aug 7 Curr 7f G 1 **110**
Sep 18 Curr 7f GF 3 99

MONTGOMERY'S ARCH 3
May 15 Lonc 8f G 12 102
Jly 26 Gdwd 7f G 11 **106**
Aug 28 Deau 6f G 6 105

MONTJEU BABY 3
Sep 8 Bath 10f GF 3 **100**

MONTOLIVO 3
Aug 7 Deau 6½f SD 2 **99**

MONTOSARI 6
Jan 22 Ling 16f FT 3 **105**
Mar 7 Ling 16f SD 5 **105**
Apr 20 Ling 12f FT 1 101
Oct 12 Ling 16f FT 2 99

MOON AT MIDNIGHT 5
May 25 Leop 7f GF 7 103
Jun 1 Leop 7f G 11 **108**
Jly 2 Leop 7f F 2 105
Aug 7 Curr 7f G 4 107
Aug 14 Leop 7f F 2 106

MOON BIRD 3
Jun 24 Wolv 7f SD 2 **100**

MOON EMPEROR 8
Mar 7 Ling 16f SD 2 **106**
Apr 19 Sthl 16f GF 3 102
Jun 18 NmkJ 15f G 2 **106**
Jly 1 Sand 14f G 6 102

MOON SHOT 9
Feb 17 Sthl 12f G 2 **105**
Nov 25 Wolv 12f FT 4 99

MOON SPINNER 8
Jan 22 Ling 10f FT 5 **100**
Feb 23 Ling 16f FT 3 99
Mar 26 Wolv 14f FT 4 99

MOON UNIT 4
Mar 20 Curr 5f HY 3 100
Jun 1 Leop 6f G 4 109
Jun 26 Curr 5f GF 7 108
Aug 7 Curr 6f G 11 99
Aug 20 Curr 6f GF 1 **111**
Sep 4 Curr 5f G 5 109
Sep 17 Curr 6f G 7 103

MOONDANCER 6
Dec 14 Ling 8f FT 2 **99**

MOONFLEET 3
May 21 Carl 9½f G 2 100
Jly 7 Folk 9½f G 1 **101**

MOONLIGHT DANCE 3
Jun 15 Leop 8f GF 3 101
Jly 16 Curr 8f GF 1 **107**

MOONLIGHT MAN 4
Mar 28 Kemp 6f G 3 100
May 7 Ling 7f G 7 104
May 23 Wind 6f F 9 101
May 29 NmkR 7f GF 7 101
Jly 2 Sand 8f G 3 **115**
Jly 8 Chep 7f GF 1 107
Jly 16 Newb 8f GF 2 104
Jly 23 Newb 7f GF 14 105
Aug 20 Ches 7½f G 4 100

MOONMAIDEN 3
Mar 28 Kemp 7f GS 2 101
Jly 4 Bath 5½f G 1 **103**

MOONSHINE BEACH 7
Jun 4 Chep 18f GS 4 103
Jly 7 Wwck 16f G 1 **104**
Aug 26 Thsk 16f GF 4 103
Sep 5 Wwck 16f G 2 100
Sep 17 Wwck 16f G 7 100

MOONSHINE BILL 6
Mar 21 Ling 10f G 7 99
Apr 2 Wolv 12f FT 4 **101**
Jun 27 Pont 10f G 4 99

MOORS MYTH 4
May 20 NmkR 8f G 5 **103**

MOR MORTAS 3
Jly 6 Naas 7f GF 2 **101**

MORDOR 3
May 0 Ches 10½f GS 5 **104**

MORE RAINBOWS 5
May 22 Curr 12f GS 6 **110**
Jun 26 Curr 12f F 5 108
Oct 9 Curr 16f GS 3 108

MORGAN LEWIS 4
Apr 23 Leic 6f G 6 100
Jly 9 York 6f G 6 **102**
Oct 25 Yarm 7f S 2 101

MORNING GLOW 3
Jly 2 Leop 10f GF 3 **100**

MORSE 4
Apr 5 Folk 6f G 2 100
Apr 23 Leic 6f G 4 104
Apr 30 Gdwd 6f G 1 **105**
Jun 3 Gdwd 7f GS 5 103
Aug 17 Nott 8f F 5 99
Nov 1 Catt 7f GS 6 99

MOSS VALE 4
Apr 30 NmkR 5f G 7 107
Jun 14 York 5f G 3 107
Jly 7 NmkJ 6f G 11 104
Jly 28 Gdwd 5f G 3 110
Aug 18 York 5f GF 12 108
Aug 27 NmkJ 6f G 5 101
Sep 10 Gdwd 6f GF 1 **113**
Sep 17 Newb 5f GF 9 103
Sep 25 NmkR 6f G 5 **113**
Oct 14 NmkR 6f G 3 112

MOSSMANN GORGE 3
May 24 Ling 7f G 2 **102**
Dec 15 Sthl 12f SD 6 **102**

MOST DEFINITELY 5
Apr 29 Muss 14f G 1 103
May 7 Thsk 16f GS 3 106
May 28 Muss 14f G 7 99
Jly 8 York 12f GS 7 101
Jly 16 Ripn 12f G 1 **110**
Aug 20 Ches 13½f G 5 104
Sep 3 Hayd 14f GF 7 105
Sep 9 Donc 14½f G 4 104
Sep 19 Carl 12f G 3 103

MOSTARSIL 7
Dec 7 Ling 12f FT 1 **99**

MOSTASHAAR 3
Apr 19 Folk 7f GS 1 100
May 5 Ches 7½f GS 2 106
Jun 16 York 8f G 1 **115**

MOTHECOMBE DREAM 3
Jan 4 Ling 6f FT 3 **99**

MOTIVATOR 3
May 12 York 10½f S 1 111
Jun 4 Epsm 12f G 1 114
Jly 2 Sand 10f G 2 112
Sep 10 Leop 10f GF 2 115
Oct 2 Lonc 12f G 5 **119**

MOTIVE 4
Jly 2 Hayd 12f GF 6 106
Jly 26 Gdwd 10f G 9 102
Aug 17 York 10½f G 3 **109**

MOTTSEY 6
Jun 1 Leop 7f G 7 **108**

MOTU 4
Apr 11 Ling 8f SD 2 **99**
May 11 Brig 8f G 4 **99**

MOUFTARI 4
Jun 1 Leop 14f G 20 106

MOUNT HILLABY 5
Mar 24 Wolv 8½f SD 2 **105**
May 9 Rdcr 7f GS 4 104
Jun 28 Haml 8½f F 3 100
Jly 11 Ayr 8f F 2 104

MOUNT ROYALE 7
Feb 24 Sthl 7f FT 5 **102**
Apr 26 Sthl 7f FT 3 **102**
Dec 28 Wolv 7f FT 2 99

MOUNT VETTORE 4
Jun 17 Rdcr 8f G 3 **99**

MOUNTAIN HIGH 3
Jun 17 York 12f G 4 **105**

MOUNTAIN SNOW 5
Jly 16 Curr 10f GF 5 **101**

MOVEOVERROVER 3
May 22 Curr 8f G 8 **102**

MOYENNE 3
Aug 7 Curr 6f G 8 103
Sep 17 Curr 6f G 6 **107**
Oct 9 Curr 6f GS 5 100
Nov 6 Leop 7f GS 11 101

MPENZI 3
Aug 23 Brig 12f G 1 **103**
Aug 26 Bath 13f G 1 **103**
Sep 7 Epsm 12f G 3 **103**
Oct 19 Bath 11½f GS 3 102

MR AITCH 3
Jly 9 Ling 8f SD 6 100
Aug 26 Newc 9f GF 8 **102**
Sep 26 Bath 8f G 1 101

MR BELVEDERE 4
Dec 29 Ling 8f G 3 **101**

MR DINOS 6
Jly 2 Sand 16½f G 5 **106**

MR DIP 5
Feb 7 Wolv 14f FT 1 **100**
Feb 21 Wolv 14f FT 5 99
Mar 13 Wolv 12f FT 4 99

MR JACK DANIELLS 4
May 21 Curr 10f G 1 99
Jun 15 Leop 10f G 1 104
Jun 26 Curr 12f F 10 **107**

MR KALANDI 3
Apr 16 Nott 8f GS 2 **100**

MR LAMBROS 4
Jan 29 Ling 7f SD 1 110
Mar 19 Ling 7f SD 7 102
Apr 30 NmkR 6f G 3 **111**
Jun 2 Hayd 6f G 6 99
Jly 22 NmkJ 6f G 4 102

MR MALARKEY 5
May 14 Thsk 6f G 1 101
May 27 Catt 6f GF 4 101
Jun 13 Thsk 6f G 8 99
Jun 25 Newc 6f G 7 101
Jly 22 NmkJ 6f G 3 103
Aug 8 Wind 6f GF 7 99
Aug 23 Yarm 5f G 4 **104**
Sep 3 NmkJ 6f G 7 103
Sep 6 Leic 5f GF 3 **104**

MR MAXIM 3
Jun 7 Rdcr 11f G 4 **99**
Sep 6 Catt 14f GF 3 **99**

MR MIDASMAN 4
May 20 Hayd 10½f G 2 **105**
Jun 11 Leic 10f G 4 101
Jly 27 Leic 10f G 8 101
Aug 4 Hayd 10½f GF 1 99
Aug 11 Hayd 10½f GF 5 100

MR MISCHIEF 5
May 30 Rdcr 14f G 2 100
Jun 3 Hayd 14f G 2 101
Jun 6 Pont 17f GF 2 102

MR STROWGER 4
Feb 22 Ling 10f SD 10 **99**

MR TAMBOURINE MAN 4
Apr 11 Ling 12f SD 5 **100**

MR TWINS 4
Feb 22 Ling 10f SD 8 100

MR VEGAS 3
May 10 Yarm 11½f GS 2 99
May 23 Leic 12f G 1 **103**
Jun 17 York 16f G 2 102
Aug 21 Deau 15f G 11 101

MR VELOCITY 5
Jun 15 Nott 8f GF 4 **102**

MR WOLF 4
Jun 28 Haml 5f F 5 99
Jly 11 Ayr 6f GF 1 101
Jly 15 Pont 6f GF 1 104
Jly 24 Pont 6f G 1 **107**
Jly 29 Thsk 6f G 3 104
Aug 3 Pont 5f G 1 106
Sep 3 Hayd 5f F 11 100
Sep 7 Donc 5½f GF 17 100
Sep 20 Bevl 5f GF 2 104
Oct 1 Epsm 5f G 8 101

MRS GILLOW 4
Jun 26 Curr 16f F 5 103
Jly 16 Curr 16f GF 1 106
Sep 18 Curr 16f G 4 106
Oct 9 Curr 16f GS 2 **110**

MRS MOH 4
Jun 25 Newc 7f G 8 99
Oct 15 Catt 7f GS 1 **101**

MRS SPENCE 4
Apr 12 Muss 5f G 4 **102**

MT DESERT 3
Sep 2 Hayd 12f G 5 100
Sep 17 Ayr 13f G 2 **104**

MUBTAKER 8
May 31 Sand 10f G 3 110
Jly 23 Newb 12f GF 11 101
Aug 13 Newb 13½f G 2 103
Aug 27 Gdwd 14f G 1 111
Sep 9 Donc 12f G 1 106
Sep 25 NmkR 12f G 1 105
Oct 2 Lonc 12f G 9 **114**
Oct 22 Newb 12f G 4 105

MUCH REALITY 3
Jly 6 Naas 10f GF 3 **100**

MUFREH 7
Jan 1 Sthl 8f SD 4 **109**
Feb 26 Sthl 8f FT 3 **109**
Mar 8 Sthl 8f SD 4 105

MUGEBA 4
Jan 5 Sthl 7f SD 3 99
Jly 4 Wind 6f G 4 99
Aug 3 Yarm 7f G 1 99
Nov 4 Yarm 6f S 1 **107**

MUJAZAF 3
May 6 Nott 14f G 5 **99**

MUKAFEH 4

Jun 1	Nott	8f	G	3	109
Jly 16	Newb	8f	GF	3	103
Jly 30	NmkJ	8f	GF	6	**111**
Aug 18	York	8f	G	14	105

MUKTASB 4

Feb 28	Wolv	5f	SD	5	**99**

MULAN PRINCESS 5

Mar 4	Wolv	8½f	SD	6	**99**

MULBERRY LAD 3

Jly 12	Brig	6f	G	6	**100**

MULLINS BAY 4

Mar 20	Curr	8f	HY	8	105
May 21	Curr	8f	G	3	111
Jun 17	York	10½f	G	2	**113**
Jly 9	York	10½f	G	1	109
Aug 31	York	9f	G	1	108
Sep 24	NmkR	8f	G	6	109
Oct 15	NmkR	9f	G	2	104

MULTAHAB 6

Jly 3	Brig	5½f	G	1	**100**
Dec 28	Wolv	6f	G	4	99

MUMBLING 7

Aug 14	Pont	17f	G	2	**104**

MUNAAWASHAT 4

May 30	Leic	8f	G	1	99
Aug 22	Wind	8½f	G	4	**102**

MUNADDAM 3

Oct 14	NmkR	7f	G	19	**100**

MUNGO JERRY 4

Apr 9	Newc	12½f	S	1	**102**
Apr 23	Hayd	10½f	G	5	101

MUNSEF 3

Jun 17	York	12f	G	1	108
Sep 30	NmkR	12f	G	1	**109**
Oct 22	Newb	12f	G	3	105

MUNTAMI 4

Nov 2	Nott	10f	S	2	**102**

MURAABET 3

Mar 28	Yarm	8f	GS	5	**102**

MUSEEB 3

Apr 1	Donc	7f	G	1	**107**
Apr 12	NmkR	7f	GF	2	100
May 21	NmkR	7f	G	2	**107**
Jun 15	York	7f	G	4	102
Jly 30	Gdwd	8f	G	3	104
Aug 18	York	7f	GF	9	103

MUSIC TEACHER 3

Dec 30	Ling	6f	FT	7	**101**

MUSICAL FAIR 5

May 7	Bevl	5f	GF	4	103
May 14	Thsk	5f	G	3	**105**
May 19	Donc	6f	GF	3	101
Jun 6	Wind	5f	G	10	99
Sep 21	Rdcr	5f	GF	6	101

MUSICAL GIFT 5

Feb 7	Sthl	7f	SD	2	103
Feb 28	Wolv	9½f	SD	4	**107**

MUSICANNA 4

Jun 25	NmkJ	8f	G	1	**107**
Jly 24	Newb	8f	G	1	105
Aug 20	Sand	8f	G	1	102
Oct 1	NmkR	8f	G	3	**107**

MUSIOTAL 4

Apr 25	Haml	6f	G	3	**102**

MUSKETIER 3

Jun 5	Chan	10½f	G	11	101
Jun 27	Lonc	9f	G	4	**110**
Jly 14	Lonc	12f	F	8	106
Sep 17	Lonc	10f	G	4	106

MUSTAJED 4

Jun 11	Sand	7f	G	14	103
Jun 22	Sals	8f	G	6	102
Jly 4	Wind	10f	G	2	101
Jly 21	Sand	10f	GF	1	103
Jly 30	Donc	10½f	G	3	103
Aug 13	Gdwd	10f	G	2	**106**
Sep 2	Hayd	12f	G	3	102
Sep 16	Newb	11f	G	11	104
Oct 9	Bath	11½f	G	1	102

MUSTAMEET 4

Apr 3	Curr	7f	S	1	**112**
Jun 1	Leop	8f	G	2	111
Jly 17	Curr	7f	F	5	103
Aug 14	Leop	8f	F	2	111

MUSTANG ALI 4

Jan 6	Wolv	12f	F	4	**106**
Sep 1	Carl	12f	G	1	99

MUTADAREK 4

May 25	Leop	7f	GF	4	105
Sep 4	Curr	10f	G	2	**106**
Sep 10	Leop	9f	GF	9	105

MUTAJAMMEL 3

Sep 14	Yarm	10f	G	8	**100**

MUTAKARRIM 8

May 25	Leop	14f	GF	2	106
Jun 26	Curr	12f	F	6	**108**

MUTAMARED 5

Jun 3	Gdwd	7f	GS	4	105
Sep 3	NmkJ	6f	G	1	**109**
Sep 28	Sals	6f	G	1	102

MUTARED 7

Oct 29	Sthl	8f	SD	1	**101**

MUTASSEM 4

Mar 28	Yarm	7f	GS	2	100
Apr 5	Sthl	7f	SD	1	**103**

MUTAWAFFER 4

May 13	York	6f	GS	4	**106**
Jly 7	NmkJ	7f	G	8	105
Jly 23	York	6f	G	5	103
Jly 30	Gdwd	6f	G	17	103
Sep 10	Donc	8f	GS	8	99
Oct 7	York	8f	G	10	103

MUTAWAQED 7

Apr 30	NmkR	6f	G	9	**108**
Aug 6	NmkJ	7f	G	15	106

MUTAYAM 5

Jly 4	Muss	5f	GF	5	**101**

MUZDAHER 3

Jun 21	Bevl	8½f	G	2	101
Jun 30	Hayd	8f	GF	2	**103**
Jly 27	Muss	7f	GF	2	100
Aug 6	Rdcr	7f	G	5	100
Aug 26	Thsk	8f	GF	1	100

MUZDAHERHA 3

Aug 28	Gdwd	12f	G	1	**100**

MY GACHO 3

Feb 9	Ling	6f	G	1	**100**
May 7	Ling	6f	G	7	**100**
May 13	Newb	6f	F	2	99
Nov 29	Sthl	6f	SD	2	**100**

MY GALLIANO 9

Jly 28	Epsm	10f	G	1	101

MY GIRL PEARL 5

Aug 10	Sals	6f	G	1	**100**

MY IMMORTAL 3

Jly 1	Wolv	12f	G	2	103
Aug 5	Ling	14f	GS	1	102
Aug 20	Ches	16f	G	1	109

MY LEGAL EAGLE 11

Apr 16	Nott	14f	GS	2	**104**
May 7	Bevl	16f	G	6	100
Jun 21	Newb	13½f	G	5	99

MY LILLI 5

Mar 31	Ling	10f	SD	2	**106**
Jun 18	Ling	10f	SW	5	100

MY MAN 3

Jun 27	Lonc	7f	G	3	**112**
Nov 1	MsnL	6f	GF	12	107

MY MICHELLE 4

May 23	Leic	7f	G	1	**102**

MY ONLY SUNSHINE 6

Apr 4	Yarm	5f	G	4	99
Apr 25	Haml	6f	G	6	99
May 5	Folk	6f	G	2	**106**
Aug 1	Wind	6f	G	2	102
Aug 27	NmkJ	6f	G	12	99

MY PARIS 4

Apr 12	NmkR	7f	GF	5	100
Apr 30	Thsk	8f	S	2	99
May 11	York	10½f	S	4	103
Jun 15	York	8f	G	6	109
Jly 7	NmkJ	7f	G	16	100
Aug 6	NmkJ	7f	G	1	**113**
Aug 18	York	8f	G	12	106
Sep 10	Donc	8f	GS	1	109
Oct 1	NmkR	9f	G	3	106

MY PENSION 4

Jan 17	Wolv	8½f	SD	7	102
Mar 1	Ling	10f	SD	1	**104**
Oct 1	Wolv	8½f	FT	4	100

MY PRINCESS 3

Jly	9	Sals	8f	G	1	101
Jly	16	NmkJ	8f	GF	6	99
Jly	24	NmkJ	8f	G	3	**105**
Aug	6	NmkJ	8f	G	1	104
Aug	27	NmkJ	7f	G	9	100

MY RASCAL 3

Sep	13	Thsk	6f	G	1	**102**

MY SPECIAL 4

Aug	21	Deau	10f	G	12	**104**

MYND 5

Apr	14	Ripn	5f	S	1	**103**

MYSTERY LOT 3

Apr	26	Bath	10f	HY	1	100
May	1	Sals	10f	GS	4	100
Jun	7	Sals	10f	G	2	**103**

MYSTERY PIPS 5

Aug	12	Catt	5f	GF	2	**100**
Aug	24	Catt	5f	GF	2	99

MYSTIC LAD 4

Feb	21	Ling	7f	SD	3	101
Apr	1	Ling	8f	SD	3	**102**
Apr	11	Ling	8f	SD	1	99
Oct	12	Ling	8f	SD	3	**102**

MYSTIC MAN 7

Apr	9	Newc	7f	S	8	102
Apr	30	Thsk	7f	S	4	101
Jun	22	Carl	8f	GF	10	100
Jly	22	York	7f	G	1	**103**
Oct	10	Wolv	7f	FT	3	100
Dec	3	Wolv	6f	FT	1	102
Dec	26	Wolv	7f	SD	2	102

MYSTICAL AYR 3

Sep	29	Ayr	8f	S	1	102
Oct	10	Ayr	8f	S	1	**103**

MYSTICAL LAND 3

Aug	15	Nott	5f	GF	1	106
Sep	4	Lonc	5f	GF	6	**107**

MYTHICAL CHARM 6

Aug	13	Gdwd	8f	G	1	**101**

MYTHICAL KING 8

Jun	4	Chep	18f	GS	3	105

MYTTON'S BELL 3

Apr	25	Haml	5f	G	2	**99**

N

NABIR 5

Dec	6	Sthl	11f	FT	6	**104**
Dec	15	Sthl	12f	SD	5	103

NAHEEF 6

Aug	27	Wind	11½f	G	5	**104**

NAISSANCE ROYALE 3

Mar	28	StCl	8f	GS	7	102
May	22	Lonc	10f	GF	4	**103**

NAJAABA 5

Jan	28	Wolv	9½f	SD	8	102
Feb	26	Sthl	8f	FT	7	101
Mar	3	Ling	7f	SW	1	102
May	9	Rdcr	7f	GS	2	**105**

NAJEEBON 6

Apr	5	Folk	6f	G	1	101
May	7	NmkR	6f	GF	5	102
Jun	11	Bath	5½f	G	3	101
Jun	17	Rdcr	6f	G	4	**105**
Jly	29	NmkJ	6f	G	7	102
Aug	11	Hayd	6f	GF	2	101
Aug	17	Epsm	6f	G	4	102
Aug	27	NmkJ	6f	G	2	104

NAMAT 4

Jun	20	Ripn	10f	G	1	**106**
Jun	24	NmkJ	12f	G	1	102
Jly	30	NmkJ	12f	GF	4	103

NAMATHEJ 3

May	30	Rdcr	11f	G	2	102
Jun	18	NmkJ	10f	G	2	99
Jly	8	Ling	10f	G	2	**105**
Aug	22	Leic	10f	G	5	101

NAMIR 3

Apr	2	Donc	6f	G	2	100
Apr	16	Thsk	5f	S	1	**104**
May	1	Haml	5f	G	1	**104**
May	14	Thsk	5f	G	3	101

NAMROC 4

May	20	Hayd	8f	G	4	**106**
May	30	Sand	8f	G	6	**106**
Jly	30	NmkJ	10f	GF	4	100

NAMROUD 6

May	26	Ayr	7f	G	1	105
Jun	18	Ayr	7f	G	2	109
Jun	25	Newc	7f	G	6	100
Jly	9	York	8f	G	1	**110**
Jly	30	Thsk	8f	G	6	103
Oct	7	York	8f	G	13	100
Oct	29	Ayr	8f	HY	1	107
Nov	12	Ling	8f	FT	9	100

NAN JAN 3

Feb	11	Wolv	7f	SD	1	105
Sep	17	Wolv	7f	FT	2	99
Nov	21	Sthl	6f	SW	1	101
Dec	2	Wolv	6f	SD	1	**106**

NAN SCURRY 3

Aug	10	Yarm	6f	GF	2	**99**
Sep	5	Bath	5½f	GF	3	**99**

NANTON 3

Jun	22	Sals	10f	G	3	99
Jly	16	Hayd	8f	GF	1	101
Jly	23	Nott	8f	F	1	101
Aug	1	Wind	8½f	GS	3	101
Aug	28	Gdwd	9f	G	9	**102**

NANTUCKET SOUND 4

Feb	19	Wolv	12f	G	7	**103**
Feb	28	Wolv	12f	SD	3	99
Mar	17	Sthl	12f	SD	6	100
Jly	19	Yarm	11½f	G	8	99

NAPPER TANDY 5

Apr	3	Curr	10f	S	5	104
Jun	1	Leop	8f	G	4	**107**
Jun	8	Leop	10f	F	3	105

NARNIA 3

Aug	2	Deau	10f	G	6	**113**

NASHAAB 8

May	28	Donc	7f	G	3	**105**
Jun	7	Ches	7f	GF	3	104
Jun	11	Ripn	9f	G	4	103
Jun	16	York	7f	GF	11	101
Jly	13	Hayd	8f	G	8	99
Jly	16	Newb	8f	GF	4	103

NATALIE JANE 3

Jun	7	Sals	10f	G	1	107
Jly	2	Hayd	12f	GF	3	102
Jly	31	Newb	12f	G	2	**109**

NATHAN JONES 6

Jly	6	Naas	6f	GF	4	**102**

NATIONAL SWAGGER 3

Jun	1	Leop	6f	G	8	105
Jly	6	Naas	7f	GF	1	**106**

NATIONAL TRUST 3

Jun	17	York	12f	G	5	**104**

NATIVE TITLE 7

Apr	1	Donc	5f	G	2	106
Apr	13	Bevl	5f	G	4	100
May	6	Ches	5f	GS	6	105
Jun	4	Epsm	6f	G	4	**107**
Jun	24	Newc	5f	G	4	**107**
Jly	15	Pont	5f	GF	5	100

NAUGHTY GIRL 5

May	24	Nott	8f	G	1	**103**

NAUTICAL 7

Jun	13	Wind	6f	GF	2	103
Jun	18	NmkJ	6f	G	2	102
Jly	4	Wind	6f	G	1	103
Jly	21	Donc	6f	GF	2	101
Jly	23	Newb	7f	GF	4	99
Sep	9	Sand	5f	G	8	99
Sep	21	Gdwd	6f	GF	7	**104**
Dec	12	Wolv	9½f	FT	6	100

NAVIGATION 3

Jly	9	Haml	5f	F	2	99
Jly	17	Rdcr	5f	G	5	**101**
Sep	5	Bath	5½f	GF	1	**101**
Sep	14	Bevl	5f	G	6	99
Nov	3	Muss	5f	GS	4	99

NAWAMEES 7

Jan	15	Ling	10f	SD	8	102
Sep	16	Newb	11f	G	9	105
Sep	30	NmkR	12f	G	2	106
Oct	30	Ling	16f	SD	2	**107**

NAWOW 5

Jan	5	Ling	13f	SD	1	101
Jan	13	Ling	12f	SD	8	**104**
Feb	26	Sthl	12f	FT	4	103

NAYYIR 7

Jun	25	NmkJ	7f	G	3	108

Jly 27 Gdwd 8f GS 4 **115**
Aug 13 Newb 7f G 6 102
Sep 27 Gdwd 7f G 4 105

NDOLA 6
Feb 15 Sthl 11f FT 1 **100**

NEARLY A FOOL 7
Jan 12 Wolv 8½f SD 7 **100**
Feb 5 Ling 7f SD 6 99
Mar 3 Ling 8f SW 6 99

NEBDI 4
May 22 Curr 6f G 11 **100**

NEBRASKA CITY 4
Aug 4 Brig 6f G 9 **99**

NECKAR VALLEY 6
May 17 Rdcr 10f G 6 **99**

NEEDLE ROCK 4
Jun 5 Chan 12f G 8 **102**

NEEDLECRAFT 3
Jly 31 Deau 8f G 8 **106**

NEEZE 5
Jly 16 Curr 5f F 14 **102**

NEON BLUE 4
Sep 1 Rdcr 6f G 1 **104**
Sep 4 York 7f GF 1 101
Sep 15 Ayr 7f G 3 101

NEPHETRITI WAY 4
May 7 NmkR 6f GF 3 99
Nov 11 Wolv 7f FT 1 **100**

NEPHIN 3
Jun 1 Leop 7f G 8 **100**
Aug 7 Curr 7f G 14 **100**

NEPTUNE 9
Mar 13 Wolv 12f FT 3 **99**

NERO'S RETURN 4
Mar 29 Pont 8f S 1 107
Apr 9 Newc 7f S 7 102
Apr 23 Sand 8f G 4 104
May 28 Gdwd 8f G 2 105
Jun 3 Epsm 8½f G 3 105
Jun 11 Ripn 9f G 5 103
Jun 18 Rdcr 10f G 7 105
Jly 5 NmkJ 8f G 4 104
Jly 9 York 10½f G 7 102
Jly 26 Gdwd 10f G 3 106
Jly 29 Gdwd 8f G 12 108
Aug 6 Hayd 10½f GF 10 104
Sep 10 Gdwd 9f G 1 108
Sep 17 Newb 10f GF 10 **109**
Oct 9 Gdwd 10f G 10 102
Oct 29 Ayr 8f HY 3 99

NESSEN DORMA 4
May 12 York 14f S 8 101
Jun 4 Hayd 16f G 4 103
Jun 30 Hayd 14f GF 4 103
Jly 30 NmkJ 12f GF 2 **104**
Sep 2 Hayd 12f G 2 103
Sep 30 NmkR 12f G 5 101

NEUTRINO 3
Aug 7 Leic 12f GF 2 **100**

NEVADA DESERT 5
Jan 19 Ling 10f FT 9 100
Apr 15 Thsk 8f S 1 100
May 15 Ripn 10f G 5 103
Jun 8 Haml 8½f G 4 106
Jun 11 Ripn 8f G 2 105
Jun 22 Carl 8f GF 5 102
Jly 1 Bevl 8½f G 6 103
Jly 30 Thsk 8f G 5 105
Aug 11 Bevl 10f GF 3 103
Aug 30 Ripn 10f F 4 102
Oct 8 York 9f GS 3 104
Oct 29 Wolv 9½f SD 1 **111**
Nov 11 Wolv 8½f FT 5 108

NEVER WITHOUT ME 5
Aug 22 Leic 5f G 1 **103**
Sep 1 Rdcr 6f G 3 100
Sep 14 Bevl 5f G 4 101

NEVERLETME GO 3
Jun 4 Donc 5f G 1 104
Jun 12 Donc 5f F 2 101
Jly 9 Nott 5f F 1 **105**

NEVINSTOWN 5
Aug 6 Rdcr 6f G 2 **101**

NEW ENGLAND 3
Dec 28 Wolv 8½f G 1 **104**

NEW LARGUE 3
Jun 5 Chan 8f GF 6 **108**

NEW MORNING 4
May 31 Sand 10f G 1 **112**
Jun 25 Curr 10f G 4 **112**
Aug 16 York 10½f G 7 100

NEW OPTIONS 8
Jly 18 Ayr 5f GF 5 **100**
Aug 26 Newc 5f GF 5 99

NEW REALM 3
May 28 Ling 10f SW 6 **102**

NEW SAGA 3
Jun 12 Chan 10½f G 5 **106**

NEW SEEKER 5
Apr 2 Donc 8f G 2 112
May 7 Ling 7f G 9 99
Jun 15 York 8f G 1 114
Jly 23 Newb 7f GF 1 **115**
Aug 11 Sals 8f GF 3 112
Sep 16 Newb 7f GF 1 111
Sep 27 Gdwd 7f G 3 106
Oct 15 NmkR 7f G 9 104

NEW SOUTH WALES 5
May 28 Gdwd 12f G 1 **108**

NEW WAVE 3
Jan 31 Wolv 7f SD 2 99
Sep 12 Rdcr 7f G 4 **100**

NEW WISH 5
Apr 26 Sthl 7f FT 4 **102**
Jly 11 Wolv 8½f SD 3 100

NEWCORP LAD 5
Sep 14 Bevl 8½f G 1 **101**

NEWLANDS NORTH 4
Jun 26 Curr 12f F 16 **103**

NEWNHAM 4
Sep 23 Ling 12f F 4 **102**
Oct 19 Bath 11½f GS 6 99
Nov 10 Ling 12f SD 2 101

NEWTONIAN 6
Jan 11 Sthl 12f SW 2 **103**
Mar 8 Sthl 12f SD 4 99
Nov 16 Sthl 12f FT 5 99

NEXT FLIGHT 6
Jun 15 Haml 13f GS 1 **103**

NEXT TIME 3
Mar 22 Ling 5f SD 5 **100**

NICE TUNE 3
Sep 3 Thsk 8f G 6 99
Oct 12 Ling 8f G 2 **103**
Nov 19 Ling 8f FT 2 **103**

NID D'ABEILLES 3
Jly 24 MsnL 8f F 6 **109**

NIGHT AIR 4
Jan 7 Wolv 7f SW 1 109
Jan 29 Ling 8f SD 1 **115**
Mar 12 Wolv 8½f SD 1 112
Jly 23 Newb 7f GF 8 111
Aug 13 Newb 7f G 11 100

NIGHT BRIDGE 3
Jun 25 Curr 10f G 10 **100**

NIGHT FAIRY 4
Sep 10 Leop 9f GF 17 **100**

NIGHT PROSPECTOR 5
May 20 Gdwd 5f G 3 102
Jly 28 Gdwd 5f G 6 **107**
Aug 6 Hayd 5f G 11 104
Aug 29 Epsm 5f G 9 104
Oct 20 Brig 6f GS 3 102

NIGHT SIGHT 8
May 6 Nott 10f G 5 99
Jun 21 Bevl 10f G 2 102
Jly 1 Bevl 12f G 4 100
Aug 10 Bevl 16f GF 2 **107**
Aug 26 Thsk 16f GF 6 102
Nov 21 Sthl 14f SW 5 105
Dec 6 Sthl 14f FT 4 100

NIGHT SPOT 4
May 2 Donc 10½f G 4 107
Jun 3 Epsm 10f G 4 **110**
Jun 25 Wind 11½f G 2 105
Jly 23 Newb 12f GF 6 106
Aug 29 Epsm 10f G 5 106

NIGHT STORM 4
Mar 7 Ling 6f SD 1 101
Aug 23 Brig 7f G 1 **102**
Sep 8 Bath 8f GF 1 100
Dec 17 Ling 10f FT 1 101

Horse / Date		Course	Dist	Going	Pos	Rating
NIGHT WARRIOR 5						
Jly	7	Wwck	12½f	G	6	**104**
Dec	18	Sthl	12f	SW	1	99
NIGHT WOLF 5						
Mar	18	Ling	8f	SD	4	102
May	11	Brig	8f	G	1	**103**
Aug	4	Brig	7f	G	2	**103**
Sep	20	Brig	8f	G	1	101
NIGHTDANCE FOREST 4						
Jly	31	Deau	8f	G	6	**112**
NIMELLO 9						
Jan	28	Wolv	9½f	SD	7	**103**
Feb	26	Sthl	8f	FT	6	101
Mar	7	Wolv	9½f	SD	1	**103**
May	4	Chep	10f	S	3	99
Oct	31	Wolv	8½f	SD	11	99
Nov	15	Sthl	8f	FT	2	**103**
NINA FONTENAIL 4						
May	17	Ling	10f	FT	2	100
Jun	24	Folk	12f	GF	1	100
Jly	7	Wwck	12½f	G	2	**107**
NINTH HOUSE 3						
Dec	19	Wolv	8½f	FT	1	**104**
NIPPING 3						
May	15	Lonc	5f	G	5	106
Jun	5	Chan	5f	G	5	110
Jly	9	Deau	6f	GF	2	112
Aug	18	York	5f	GF	10	109
Sep	4	Lonc	5f	GF	1	**113**
Oct	2	Lonc	5f	G	15	101
NISR 8						
Mar	28	Yarm	6f	GS	3	100
Dec	29	Ling	10f	GS	4	**104**
NISTAKI 4						
Jly	14	Leic	6f	GF	6	103
Aug	20	Rdcr	6f	G	1	103
Aug	27	York	6f	G	2	**104**
NITEOWL LAD 3						
Jun	17	Rdcr	5f	G	3	99
Jly	17	Rdcr	5f	G	1	**107**
Jly	30	Donc	5f	G	6	100
Aug	8	Thsk	5f	GF	1	103
Aug	15	Wind	5f	GF	1	101
NIVERNAIS 6						
Apr	5	Folk	6f	G	5	**99**
Aug	6	Ling	6f	G	5	**99**
NIZAMAR 4						
Sep	4	Curr	10f	G	5	**105**
NO COMMISSION 3						
Apr	16	Wolv	8½f	FT	3	**102**
NO FRONTIER 7						
Aug	7	Curr	7f	G	2	**109**
NO GROUSE 5						
Apr	11	Sthl	7f	G	1	101
Jun	13	Thsk	6f	G	1	**102**
Dec	2	Wolv	6f	SD	9	99
NO SOUND 4						
Apr	3	Curr	10f	S	9	**104**
NO TIME 5						
Feb	5	Ling	5f	S	2	**105**
Feb	19	Wolv	5f	S	7	102
Mar	1	Ling	6f	SD	4	104
Mar	18	Ling	6f	SD	5	101
May	14	Thsk	5f	G	9	101
NOAHS ARK 4						
Jun	25	Curr	10f	G	10	**105**
NOBBLER 3						
Jly	7	Wwck	16f	G	5	**101**
NOBELIX 3						
Aug	5	Ling	11½f	GS	1	**103**
Aug	28	Bevl	12f	GS	3	99
NOBLE FUTURE 3						
Jun	25	Ling	10f	SW	2	**103**
Jly	29	Nott	8f	G	2	101
Sep	20	Bevl	8½f	GF	1	101
Oct	5	Nott	10f	G	6	102
NOBLE MIND 4						
Feb	25	Wolv	12f	G	3	**100**
Mar	24	Wolv	12f	SD	2	99
NOBLE MOUNT 4						
Jan	4	Ling	6f	FT	4	99
Jun	21	Bevl	5f	G	1	**102**
Jly	4	Bath	5f	G	3	99
NOELANI 3						
Sep	17	Curr	6f	G	1	**115**
NOEND 3						
May	21	Curr	12f	G	3	**107**
Sep	18	Curr	16f	G	5	106
NOORA 4						
Sep	1	Sals	8f	G	1	101
Sep	19	Leic	8½f	G	4	**104**
Oct	7	Newb	10f	GF	1	99
NORBORNE BANDIT 4						
Jly	16	Curr	10f	GF	6	**100**
NORCROFT 3						
Jan	5	Ling	8f	SD	7	100
Apr	21	Sthl	6f	FT	2	99
May	7	Ling	6f	G	2	**105**
Jun	19	Pont	6f	G	1	103
Jly	8	Ling	8f	SW	2	100
Sep	28	Ling	6f	SD	2	101
NORDWIND 4						
May	14	Newb	12f	G	4	**107**
May	28	Muss	14f	G	6	102
NORSE DANCER 5						
Apr	13	NmkR	9f	G	1	110
Apr	23	Sand	8f	G	5	103
Jly	23	Newb	12f	GF	2	**114**
Aug	16	York	10½f	G	5	112
Sep	10	Leop	10f	GF	8	108
Oct	2	Lonc	12f	G	11	109
NORTH LIGHT 4						
May	31	Sand	10f	G	2	**111**
NORTH QUEEN 3						
Aug	2	Deau	10f	G	5	**113**
NORTH SHORE 3						
May	2	Kemp	9f	G	4	100
May	18	Gdwd	9f	G	8	**103**
May	30	Sand	7f	G	3	99
Aug	29	Wwck	7f	GF	5	99
NORTHERN DESERT 6						
Jan	5	Ling	7f	SD	4	104
Jan	8	Ling	8f	SD	1	104
Jan	29	Ling	8f	SD	5	**109**
Mar	12	Wolv	7f	SD	3	104
Mar	18	Ling	7f	SD	5	101
Jun	3	Gdwd	7f	GS	9	102
Dec	20	Ling	8f	GS	3	104
Dec	30	Ling	8f	FT	2	105
NORTHERN NYMPH 6						
Apr	16	Nott	14f	GS	3	**102**
NORTHSIDE LODGE 7						
Jan	13	Ling	12f	SD	6	**106**
Aug	3	Brig	10f	G	2	103
Dec	21	Ling	12f	G	7	99
NORTON 8						
Mar	29	Pont	8f	S	5	102
May	30	Sand	8f	G	1	**111**
Jly	2	Sand	8f	G	11	108
Jly	16	Newb	8f	GF	6	102
Aug	6	Wind	8½f	GF	2	108
Sep	10	Gdwd	9f	G	5	106
NORWEGIAN 4						
Jun	27	Wind	8½f	G	5	**101**
NOSE ONE'S WAY 3						
Aug	7	Curr	7f	G	15	**99**
NOT AMUSED 5						
Feb	19	Wolv	12f	G	10	100
Mar	7	Wolv	12f	SD	5	**108**
NOT SO DUSTY 5						
Feb	11	Wolv	5f	SD	2	**105**
Feb	26	Ling	5f	SD	6	100
NOTA BENE 3						
Apr	12	NmkR	6f	GF	1	104
May	13	Newb	6f	F	1	**108**
NOTABILITY 3						
Apr	22	Sand	8f	G	2	107
May	5	Ches	7½f	GS	1	108
May	21	Hayd	8f	GF	2	**109**
Jun	16	York	8f	G	9	104
NOTABLE GUEST 4						
Apr	30	NmkR	10f	G	1	108
Jun	18	York	12f	G	1	**109**
Sep	16	Newb	11f	G	3	103
NOTJUSTAPRETTYFACE 3						
Jun	30	Newb	6f	G	3	100
Jly	18	Ayr	5f	GF	3	**106**
Aug	14	Pont	6f	G	8	105
Sep	8	Donc	5f	F	5	105
Sep	18	Haml	5f	F	3	**106**

NOTNOWCATO 3

Apr 12 NmkR 7f GF 3 99
Apr 30 NmkR 8f G 1 105
May 18 Gdwd 9f G 7 103
Sep 24 NmkR 7f G 13 107
Sep 30 NmkR 8f G 2 107
Oct 14 NmkR 8f G 1 **111**

NOTTE ITALIANA 3

Sep 17 Catt 14f G 2 **100**

NOUBIAN 3

May 2 Kemp 9f G 3 **100**

NOUL 6

Jan 20 Sthl 7f SD 1 **104**

NOUVELLE NOBLESSE 3

Aug 2 Deau 10f G 7 **111**

NOVA TOR 3

Mar 12 Wolv 5f SD 1 **102**
Apr 16 Wolv 5f FT 1 99

NOW LOOK AWAY 4

Jan 21 Wolv 8½f SD 3 **102**

NOWADAY 3

Jly 2 Bevl 16f G 1 **99**

NUFOOS 3

Apr 7 Leic 6f S 4 107
May 7 Ling 7f G 2 109
May 21 Hayd 6f F 2 104
Jun 18 Wwck 7f G 1 **111**
Sep 8 Donc 7f G 2 **111**
Sep 24 NmkR 8f G 5 109

NUMERO DUE 3

Jly 13 Catt 12f GF 2 99
Aug 1 Carl 12f G 2 104
Aug 26 Thsk 16f GF 1 **106**
Sep 27 Nott 16f GF 2 **106**

NUMMENOR 8

Aug 7 Deau 10f GF 8 **106**

NURENBERG 3

Sep 10 Leop 9f GF 14 **104**

NUTLEY KING 6

Apr 3 Curr 10f S 4 **108**
May 8 Leop 12f S 6 106

NUWARA ELIYA 3

Jly 5 NmkJ 10f G 1 **102**
Aug 14 Pont 12f G 6 101

NYASA 4

Aug 7 Curr 7f G 18 99
Sep 10 Leop 9f GF 16 **102**

O

OAKBRIDGE 3

Jly 23 Sals 6f G 1 **102**

OAKLEY ABSOLUTE 3

May 28 Gdwd 11f G 4 100
Jun 23 Leic 10f GF 3 **102**

OATCAKE 3

Sep 25 Muss 8f G 3 **101**

OBE BOLD 4

May 12 Carl 6f G 4 99
Jly 20 Catt 6f G 5 **100**

OBE GOLD 3

Mar 28 Kemp 6f G 1 103
Apr 13 NmkR 7f G 2 **108**
Jun 25 Newc 6f G 4 105
Jly 16 Curr 5f F 15 102
Aug 7 Curr 6f G 10 102
Aug 18 York 7f GF 7 106
Sep 10 Gdwd 6f GF 7 104
Sep 23 Ling 6f G 2 105

OBEZYANA 3

Oct 3 Pont 8f G 1 101
Nov 19 Ling 8f FT 1 **104**

OBLIQUE 3

Aug 3 Newc 9f G 1 102
Sep 7 Epsm 12f G 1 **107**

OBRIGADO 5

Jun 25 Donc 8f GF 3 **107**
Aug 5 NmkJ 6f GF 7 99
Sep 14 Yarm 8f GF 3 101
Nov 12 Ling 8f FT 1 103
Dec 9 Wolv 8½f FT 4 **107**

OCEAN AVENUE 6

Jly 23 Newb 12f GF 11 **101**
Sep 21 Gdwd 12f G 5 99

OCEAN GIFT 3

May 29 NmkR 7f GF 2 102
Jun 7 Sals 7f G 1 103
Aug 28 Gdwd 6f G 1 **108**
Sep 11 Gdwd 6f G 5 104

OCEAN KING 4

Dec 12 Wolv 14f FT 2 **104**

OCEAN OF STORMS 10

Jun 27 Wind 8½f G 5 **100**

OCEAN ROCK 4

Jly 8 Wolv 14f FT 1 **100**
Jly 11 Wolv 14f SD 6 **100**
Aug 31 Ling 16f SD 3 **100**
Sep 10 Wolv 12f FT 1 99

OCEANCOOKIE 3

May 2 Wwck 7f G 1 **100**

OCEANICO DOT COM 3

Sep 10 Ches 5f GS 3 **107**
Dec 17 Ling 5f FT 4 99

ODABELLA 5

Jan 21 Wolv 8½f SD 5 **99**

ODDSHOES 3

Apr 10 Leop 7f GS 1 102
May 8 Leop 8f S 3 **110**

ODDSMAKER 4

May 31 Sand 8f G 4 **108**

ODIENNE JEM 3

Jun 27 Lonc 10½f G 9 **103**

ODIHAM 4

May 1 NmkR 12f G 4 110
May 21 Ling 16f SD 1 108
Jun 25 Newc 16f G 5 110
Jly 9 Ling 16f SD 4 **113**
Aug 17 York 14f G 8 104
Sep 9 Donc 14½f G 5 103

OFARABY 5

Apr 30 NmkR 10f G 8 99
Jly 8 York 10½f GS 1 106
Jly 26 Gdwd 10f G 2 **107**
Aug 17 York 10½f G 4 **107**
Sep 23 Ling 10f G 2 106
Oct 9 Gdwd 10f G 1 **107**
Oct 22 Newb 10f G 8 106

OFF COLOUR 3

Jly 2 Nott 10f GF 2 99
Jly 25 Wind 11½f GS 2 **102**

OH DANNY BOY 4

Nov 12 Wolv 8½f FT 1 **100**

OH SO ROSIE 5

Jan 13 Ling 8f SD 1 **102**

OISEAU RARE 3

Oct 1 Lonc 12½f G 1 **113**
Oct 23 Lonc 15½f GS 5 110

OK PAL 5

Apr 1 Donc 5f G 5 102
May 6 Ling 5f G 8 101
Jun 2 Sand 5f G 4 102
Oct 22 Donc 5f S 12 104
Dec 3 Wolv 5f S 1 **106**
Dec 20 Sthl 5f SD 1 105

OLD BAILEY 5

Jan 1 Sthl 6f SD 1 **104**
Feb 10 Sthl 6f SD 2 101
Feb 26 Sthl 7f FT 2 100
Apr 8 Sthl 6f FT 1 103

OLDENWAY 6

May 15 Ripn 10f G 10 99
Jun 7 Ches 10½f GF 4 102
Jun 21 Bevl 10f G 1 104
Aug 11 Bevl 10f GF 5 101
Oct 29 Ayr 9f HY 2 101
Nov 12 Wolv 9½f FT 4 100
Dec 15 Sthl 12f SD 2 **114**
Dec 22 Sthl 12f SD 3 105

OLIGARCH 3

Apr 14 NmkR 7f G 2 **106**
Apr 22 Sand 8f G 4 105
Jun 24 NmkJ 10f G 3 104
Jun 26 Wind 10f G 5 99
Aug 13 Gdwd 10f G 6 100
Sep 14 Yarm 10f G 5 **106**

OLIVIA ROSE 6

Jun 18 NmkJ 10f G 1 **101**

OLIVINO 4

Dec 20 Ling 10f G 4 **103**

OMAHA CITY 11
Jun 27 Wind 8½f G 6 99
Jly 8 Chep 8f GF 8 **100**

OMAN GULF 4
Apr 28 Rdcr 11f G 2 **102**

OMETSZ 4
Aug 21 Deau 10f G 9 **104**

ON THE WATERLINE 3
May 7 Ling 6f G 10 **99**

ON THE WING 4
May 18 Gdwd 8f G 4 **101**

ONE GREAT IDEA 3
Jly 9 Haml 5f F 1 **100**

ONE MORE ROUND 7
Sep 10 Leop 7f HD 10 **103**
Dec 9 Wolv 7f FT 7 102

ONE PUTRA 3
Apr 7 Leic 6f S 3 **108**
May 28 Gdwd 5f G 7 102
Jun 11 Leic 5f G 1 105
Jly 5 NmkJ 6f G 8 104
Jly 30 Gdwd 6f G 6 107
Aug 6 Wind 6f GF 3 106
Aug 29 Epsm 5f G 12 100
Sep 26 Haml 6f F 2 104
Nov 5 Donc 6f HY 3 99

ONE TO WIN 3
Jun 13 Wind 10f G 1 101
Jly 4 Wind 10f G 1 **103**
Aug 23 Yarm 10f G 4 **103**

ONE UPMANSHIP 4
May 5 Chep 12f S 2 100
Jly 7 Wwck 12½f G 5 **105**
Jly 18 Wind 11½f G 5 99

ONE WAY TICKET 5
Apr 24 Brig 5½f GF 4 101
May 14 Nott 5f HD 2 101
Jun 9 Ripn 5f G 1 **106**
Jun 19 Wwck 5f GF 1 103
Jly 15 Wwck 5½f G 2 104
Jly 20 Catt 5f GF 1 103
Sep 13 Yarm 5f G 2 99

ONE WON ONE 11
Apr 3 Curr 6f S 9 99
Jun 8 Leop 8f F 3 **105**

ONLY IF I LAUGH 4
Jan 21 Wolv 6f SD 6 **102**
Feb 7 Sthl 7f SD 5 99

ONLY MAKE BELIEVE 3
Apr 3 Curr 7f S 5 100
May 21 Curr 8f G 2 **112**

ONLYTIME WILL TELL 7
Aug 29 Epsm 6f G 1 **99**

ONYERGO 3
Jun 27 Muss 7f GF 3 **103**

OODACHEE 6
Apr 3 Curr 16f HY 2 108
Jun 1 Leop 16f G 1 106
Sep 18 Curr 16f G 6 105
Oct 9 Curr 16f GS 10 103

OONAGH MACCOOL 3
Sep 14 Sand 8f G 1 **107**

OOPS 6
Jly 25 Yarm 16f GS 2 **100**

OPEN OFFER 5
Apr 10 Lonc 10f S 3 **110**

OPENING CEREMONY 6
Jun 11 Ripn 9f G 6 102
Jun 22 Carl 9½f GF 2 104
Jly 16 Ripn 10f G 3 102
Jly 23 York 10½f GS 3 102
Jly 30 Donc 10½f G 8 99
Aug 11 Bevl 10f GF 1 **105**

OPERA BELLE 3
Oct 12 Ling 10f GF 5 **100**

OPTIMISE 3
May 25 Leop 10f GF 5 **103**

OPTIMUM 3
Feb 10 Sthl 11f SD 2 **101**

ORANGINO 7
Jly 28 Muss 8f G 4 **99**

ORANMORE CASTLE 3
Apr 14 NmkR 6f G 1 100
May 14 Nott 6f F 5 99
Jly 22 Newb 6f G 6 **101**
Jly 29 Gdwd 5f G 7 99

ORATORIO 3
Apr 30 NmkR 8f G 4 109
May 21 Curr 8f G 2 105
Jun 14 York 8f G 3 108
Jly 2 Sand 10f G 1 113
Sep 10 Leop 10f GF 1 **116**
Oct 15 NmkR 10f G 4 110

ORCADIAN 4
Jly 15 NmkJ 12f G 3 **109**
Aug 27 Wind 11½f G 1 108
Oct 23 Lonc 15½f GS 8 105
Nov 5 Donc 12f HY 3 99

ORCHESTRATION 4
Jan 27 Sthl 6f SD 3 **102**
Dec 21 Ling 6f SD 5 99

ORIENTAL BEN 7
Aug 14 Leop 9f F 3 99
Sep 4 Curr 8f G 11 **105**

ORIENTOR 7
Apr 15 Newb 5f GS 2 108
May 11 York 6f S 8 106
May 31 Sand 5f G 2 **114**
Jly 2 Sand 5f G 4 103
Jly 30 Donc 6f G 3 103
Aug 18 York 5f GF 16 100
Sep 3 Hayd 6f F 12 99
Oct 2 Lonc 5f G 12 105
Oct 13 NmkR 5f G 6 107

ORINOCOVSKY 6
May 9 Wolv 14f FT 3 101
Jun 1 Wolv 14f FT 3 101
Jly 5 Wolv 12f FT 5 99

ORION STAR 3
May 9 Lonc 11f G 3 103
Jly 14 Lonc 12f F 3 **111**

ORLAR 3
Aug 18 Wolv 8½f SD 3 **103**

ORPAILLEUR 4
Aug 7 Curr 10f G 12 102
Sep 10 Leop 9f GF 11 **105**

ORPEN QUEST 3
Nov 22 Sthl 8f SW 3 **101**

ORPEN WIDE 3
Apr 18 Wind 8½f G 7 99
Jly 2 Bevl 5f G 5 100
Sep 12 Rdcr 6f G 9 99
Oct 9 Newc 8f G 1 **101**

ORPHAN 3
May 2 Newc 6f G 1 101
Jun 11 Ripn 6f G 1 **108**
Jly 2 Hayd 6f GF 6 99

OSSIANA 3
May 25 Leop 10f GF 7 **100**
Jly 16 Curr 16f GF 6 99

OSTANKINO 4
Aug 21 Deau 15f G 3 **111**
Oct 23 Lonc 15½f GS 6 110

OSTERHASE 6
Jun 26 Curr 5f GF 2 **115**
Aug 7 Curr 6f G 1 112
Aug 20 Curr 6f GF 6 106
Oct 2 Lonc 5f G 14 105

OTAGO 4
Jan 5 Ling 13f SD 2 100
Jan 12 Wolv 14f SD 4 **103**
Jly 15 NmkJ 10f G 1 101
Sep 28 Ling 12f SD 11 100

OUDE 3
Jly 30 Gdwd 8f G 2 **106**

OUIJA BOARD 4
Sep 24 NmkR 12f G 1 **111**

OULAN BATOR 5
Jly 30 Haml 9f F 5 102
Aug 16 Haml 9f F 1 **104**
Aug 22 Haml 11f F 3 102

OUNINPOHJA 4
Jun 8 Bevl 10f G 3 100
Jly 23 Newc 10f GF 1 103
Aug 14 Pont 12f G 1 108
Sep 2 NmkJ 12f G 1 109
Sep 25 NmkR 12f G 1 **110**

OUR CHOICE 3
Mar 24 Wolv 9½f SD 2 **101**

Horse	Month	Day	Course	Dist	Going	Pos	Rating
	Aug	26	Bath	13f	G	2	**101**
	Sep	6	Catt	12f	GF	1	99
	Sep	28	Newc	16f	GF	2	99
	Nov	7	Wolv	14f	FT	1	99
OUR DESTINY 7							
	Jan	26	Ling	10f	FT	4	**100**
OUR FUGITIVE 3							
	May	5	Ches	5f	GS	5	**100**
	Oct	1	Epsm	5f	G	9	**100**
OUR JAFFA 4							
	Sep	10	Leop	12f	GF	5	**110**
	Nov	6	Leop	8f	S	3	105
OUR KES 3							
	Jan	8	Ling	7f	SD	1	**100**
OUR LITTLE SECRET 3							
	Aug	1	Ripn	5f	G	1	99
	Aug	26	Thsk	5f	GF	2	99
	Sep	28	Newc	5f	GF	5	**101**
OUR MONOGRAM 9							
	Jun	4	Chep	18f	GS	1	107
	Jly	13	Ling	16f	G	3	100
	Aug	14	Pont	17f	G	1	**108**
OUR TEDDY 5							
	Jan	8	Ling	8f	SD	9	99
	May	2	Donc	10½f	G	6	105
	May	19	Donc	8f	GF	3	99
	May	31	Sand	8f	G	5	**108**
	Jun	4	Donc	12f	GF	8	100
	Jun	27	Pont	8f	G	2	103
	Jly	21	Sand	10f	GF	4	101
	Aug	11	Bevl	10f	GF	8	99
	Aug	22	Haml	8½f	F	4	103
	Sep	19	Leic	8½f	G	5	104
OUT AFTER DARK 4							
	Apr	23	Leic	6f	G	2	106
	May	7	Bevl	5f	GF	1	107
	May	28	Gdwd	6f	G	4	101
	Jun	21	Bevl	5f	G	1	103
	Jun	24	Newc	5f	G	1	**109**
	Jly	30	Gdwd	6f	G	5	107
	Aug	20	Sand	5f	GS	2	108
	Sep	7	Donc	5½f	GF	1	**109**
	Sep	17	Ayr	6f	G	14	107
OUT FOR A STROLL 6							
	Jan	13	Ling	6f	SD	8	99
	Aug	17	Nott	8f	F	1	104
	Aug	23	Brig	8f	G	1	105
	Sep	3	NmkJ	6f	G	8	103
	Sep	4	York	8f	G	4	**107**
	Dec	30	Ling	8f	FT	10	99
OUT OF INDIA 3							
	Apr	22	Wolv	7f	SD	2	100
	Oct	14	Rdcr	7f	GF	1	**107**
OUTER HEBRIDES 4							
	Jan	5	Ling	7f	SD	7	102
	Jan	29	Ling	7f	SD	5	**108**
	Feb	22	Ling	7f	SD	4	106
	May	2	Donc	6f	G	1	100
	Jun	25	Donc	6f	GF	4	105
	Jly	10	Hayd	6f	GF	3	100
	Jly	24	Pont	6f	G	6	101
	Jly	29	NmkJ	6f	G	6	103
	Aug	19	Sals	7f	GS	1	105
	Sep	8	Donc	7f	G	5	100
	Sep	16	Newb	7f	GF	3	101
	Oct	7	Newb	7f	GF	4	101
OUTRAGEOUS FLIRT 3							
	Jun	27	Muss	7f	GF	4	**99**
OVERDRAWN 4							
	Jun	8	Bevl	7½f	G	5	99
	Jun	20	Ripn	10f	G	5	**103**
	Aug	19	Ayr	7f	GF	5	101
OVERLORD WAY 3							
	Jly	13	Ling	8f	SW	2	103
	Aug	6	Ling	10f	SD	2	99
	Aug	18	Wolv	8½f	SD	1	**108**
OVERSIGHTED 4							
	Apr	3	Curr	6f	S	4	**102**
	Jly	6	Naas	6f	GF	3	101
OWED 3							
	Dec	6	Sthl	6f	FT	2	99
	Dec	15	Sthl	7f	SD	1	**103**
OZONE BERE 3							
	Mar	28	StCl	8f	GS	4	**105**
P							
PACE SHOT 3							
	Jly	1	Wolv	12f	GS	4	103
	Aug	20	Ling	12f	SD	2	99
PACHA DE RETZ 3							
	Jun	27	Lonc	9½f	G	5	**107**
PADRE NOSTRO 6							
	Dec	20	Sthl	11f	SW	4	**102**
PAGAN DANCE 6							
	May	11	York	12f	S	8	99
	Jun	4	Epsm	12f	G	8	103
	Jun	25	Newc	16f	G	15	104
	Jly	26	Gdwd	14f	G	8	101
	Aug	12	Newb	13½f	G	3	**106**
	Oct	9	Bath	11½f	G	3	101
PAGAN MAGIC 4							
	Jly	30	NmkJ	12f	GF	5	101
	Aug	13	NmkJ	12f	G	2	103
	Aug	28	Yarm	14f	G	6	99
	Sep	13	Yarm	11½f	G	3	**105**
PAGAN QUEST 3							
	Jly	12	Brig	6f	G	3	**105**
PAGAN SKY 6							
	May	11	York	10½f	S	2	106
	Jly	2	Hayd	12f	GF	12	101
	Jly	26	Gdwd	10f	G	12	100
	Aug	20	Sand	10f	G	1	103
	Sep	14	Yarm	10f	G	3	108
	Sep	22	Pont	10f	G	3	**111**
	Oct	7	York	10½f	G	4	103
	Oct	24	Ling	12f	SW	2	107
	Nov	19	Ling	12f	FT	6	101
PAGAN SWORD 3							
	Apr	6	Ling	7f	FT	3	102
	Apr	20	Ling	10f	FT	1	102
	May	1	Sals	10f	GS	1	101
	May	28	Donc	10½f	GF	1	101
	Jun	6	Pont	10f	GF	3	101
	Aug	9	Bath	11½f	GF	2	102
	Sep	3	NmkJ	10f	G	1	**107**
PAITA 3							
	Jun	12	Chan	10½f	G	3	108
	Sep	11	Lonc	12f	G	3	109
	Oct	16	Lonc	12f	G	3	**111**
PALACE STAR 4							
	May	21	Curr	8f	G	4	102
	Jun	1	Leop	8f	G	6	**105**
	Sep	10	Leop	7f	HD	8	104
	Sep	17	Curr	8f	GF	12	102
PALACE THEATRE 4							
	Mar	4	Wolv	6f	SD	4	**104**
PALOMAR 3							
	Oct	1	Lonc	15f	G	6	**109**
PAMIR 3							
	May	7	Ling	6f	G	6	**102**
	Sep	6	Ling	7f	SD	3	**102**
	Sep	30	Ling	7f	FT	3	100
PANGO 6							
	May	25	NmkR	7f	G	3	104
	Jun	17	Gdwd	8f	G	5	101
	Jly	26	Gdwd	8f	G	2	107
	Aug	17	Epsm	7f	G	1	108
	Sep	10	Gdwd	7f	G	3	110
	Sep	24	NmkR	7f	G	3	**113**
	Sep	30	NmkR	7f	G	1	110
	Oct	14	NmkR	7f	G	18	101
	Oct	21	Newb	6f	G	6	101
PANSHIR 4							
	Jly	5	Pont	6f	G	9	**99**
PANZER 4							
	May	23	Wind	11½f	GF	4	100
	Jun	7	Sals	12f	G	2	100
	Jly	30	NmkJ	12f	GF	1	**105**
PAPALITY 3							
	Jly	5	NmkJ	10f	G	3	100
	Sep	6	Leic	10f	GF	2	99
	Oct	9	Bath	10f	G	1	**107**
PAPARAAZI 3							
	Jan	5	Ling	8f	SD	4	102
	Aug	20	Rdcr	10f	G	1	**104**
PAPEETE 4							
	May	11	Brig	12f	G	1	99
	May	16	Bath	13f	G	4	99
	Jly	13	Ling	16f	G	1	**101**
PAPER TALK 3							
	Apr	12	NmkR	7f	GF	1	102
	May	1	NmkR	7f	G	4	105
	Jly	16	NmkJ	8f	GF	1	103
	Aug	20	Ches	7½f	G	3	100
	Sep	24	NmkR	7f	G	4	**112**

PAPINEAU 5
May 13 York 14f GS 5 **107**

PARADISE FLIGHT 4
Jan 22 Ling 16f FT 1 **107**
Apr 6 Catt 16f G 2 101
Jun 6 Pont 17f GF 1 103
Jly 9 Ches 16f GF 3 105

PARADISE ISLE 4
Jun 24 NmkJ 6f G 1 **107**
Jly 18 Ayr 5f GF 8 101
Aug 14 Pont 6f G 10 102
Sep 7 Donc 5½f GF 15 101
Sep 29 NmkR 6f GF 1 103
Oct 13 NmkR 6f G 4 101

PARADISE MILL 3
Aug 10 Sand 8f GF 2 **99**

PARC AUX BOULES 4
Jan 27 Sthl 7f SD 2 99
Mar 8 Sthl 7f SD 2 **101**
Sep 17 Ling 6f SD 1 99

PARIS BELL 3
May 25 Ripn 6f GS 1 100
Jun 11 Ripn 6f G 5 **105**
Jun 20 Ripn 6f G 5 101
Aug 13 NmkJ 6f G 4 100
Sep 11 Carl 6f GF 6 101
Oct 29 Ayr 6f S 3 99

PARIS DREAMER 4
Feb 7 Wolv 14f FT 2 **99**

PARIS HEIGHTS 3
Jly 6 Catt 7f GS 2 **100**

PARIS SUE 5
Aug 20 Curr 6f GF 6 **102**

PARISETTE 3
Apr 18 Wind 8½f G 1 **100**

PARISIAN PLAYBOY 5
Jly 19 Ayr 8f G 7 **101**

PARISIEN STAR 9
Jly 15 NmkJ 10f G 4 **99**

PARK LAW 3
Jly 29 Gdwd 7f G 9 **101**

PARK ROMANCE 3
Sep 24 NmkR 8f G 16 **99**

PARKSIDE PURSUIT 7
Jly 11 Wind 5f G 2 101
Jly 22 Chep 5f G 1 **106**
Aug 15 Brig 5½f G 2 101
Aug 28 Yarm 5f G 3 99
Sep 5 Bath 5½f GF 3 104

PARKVIEW LOVE 4
Aug 8 Wolv 7f SD 4 **100**
Aug 31 Ling 8f SD 1 **100**
Nov 16 Sthl 8f FT 2 **100**
Dec 6 Sthl 7f FT 1 99

PARMELIE 5
Aug 7 Deau 10f GF 2 **108**

PARNASSIAN 5
Apr 2 Kemp 7f GS 3 103
Jly 29 Nott 10f G 2 102
Aug 27 Wind 8½f G 8 **107**
Oct 3 Wind 8½f GF 2 105
Oct 17 Wind 10f G 5 101
Nov 2 Nott 10f S 1 103

PARSLEY'S RETURN 3
Jly 4 Muss 9f GF 5 **105**
Sep 3 Folk 12f GF 1 99

PARTNERS IN JAZZ 4
May 13 York 6f GS 7 100
May 24 Ripn 6f G 1 101
Jun 4 Epsm 6f G 6 103
Jun 25 Newc 7f G 2 104
Jly 7 NmkJ 7f G 4 107
Jly 23 Newb 7f GF 3 **114**
Jly 30 Gdwd 6f G 11 106
Sep 17 Ayr 6f G 15 105
Sep 24 NmkR 7f G 12 108

PARTY BOSS 3
Jan 21 Wolv 8½f SD 1 104
Feb 19 Wolv 8½f SD 1 **110**
Feb 26 Ling 7f SD 1 106
Mar 19 Ling 7f SD 1 105
Apr 9 Ling 8f FT 1 106
Apr 30 NmkR 8f G 12 105
Oct 7 York 8f G 7 105
Nov 19 Ling 7f FT 5 108

PARTY PRINCESS 4
Aug 17 Nott 6f GF 1 **99**

PASO DOBLE 7
Dec 20 Sthl 7f SW 1 **99**

PASS THE PORT 4
Jan 7 Wolv 7f SW 6 99
Feb 12 Wolv 8½f FT 7 101
Mar 17 Sthl 12f FT 1 **106**
May 12 York 14f S 5 **106**
Nov 16 Sthl 12f FT 2 104
Dec 26 Wolv 12f SD 2 105

PASSION FRUIT 4
Jly 29 Thsk 7f G 1 **107**

PASSIONATELY ROYAL 3
May 12 Carl 8f G 3 **100**

PASTORAL PURSUITS 4
Jun 14 York 8f G 7 100
Jly 7 NmkJ 6f G 1 **114**

PATAVELLIAN 7
Apr 14 NmkR 6f G 6 103
May 11 York 6f S 7 107
May 23 Wind 6f F 2 108
Aug 7 Deau 6½f G 3 **113**
Sep 3 Hayd 6f F 7 104
Sep 13 Yarm 6f G 1 109
Oct 2 Lonc 5f G 5 111
Oct 14 NmkR 6f G 4 111

PATRICIA PHILOMENA 7
Jun 27 Muss 12f G 3 **102**

PATRONAGE 3
Jun 17 Rdcr 11f G 1 **105**
Oct 1 Rdcr 10f GF 5 100

PATXARAN 3
Jun 16 Bevl 10f G 2 99
Aug 13 Ripn 12f GS 5 **101**

PAULINE'S PRINCE 3
Apr 7 Leic 6f S 5 **104**

PAWAN 5
Jan 11 Sthl 6f SW 3 102
Jan 27 Sthl 5f FT 5 100
Feb 7 Sthl 7f SD 3 103
Feb 17 Sthl 5f SD 2 104
Feb 24 Sthl 6f FT 2 102
Feb 26 Sthl 7f FT 1 101
Mar 8 Sthl 8f SD 9 99
Apr 16 Thsk 8f HY 5 106
May 3 Catt 7f GS 2 **107**
Sep 20 Bevl 5f GF 3 102
Nov 3 Muss 5f GS 2 104
Dec 6 Sthl 5f FT 4 104

PAWN BROKER 8
Jly 2 Sand 8f G 14 **103**

PAWN IN LIFE 7
Jan 3 Sthl 8f SD 2 101
Jan 11 Sthl 8f SW 1 **110**
Feb 7 Sthl 8f SD 1 100
Feb 26 Sthl 7f FT 3 100

PAX 8
Apr 15 Thsk 5f S 3 100
Apr 23 Ripn 6f S 3 **104**
Sep 15 Ayr 7f G 2 102

PAX ROMANA 3
May 7 Ling 11½f G 4 **101**
May 14 Newb 11f G 8 99

PEACE EMBLEM 4
Mar 4 Wolv 8½f SD 3 **103**

PEACE LILY 3
Jly 15 Pont 6f GF 3 **100**

PEACE OFFERING 5
Apr 3 Curr 6f S 5 101
May 28 Muss 5f G 4 107
Jun 4 Epsm 5f G 2 106
Jun 26 Curr 5f GF 5 **108**
Jly 30 Donc 6f G 2 104
Aug 15 Nott 5f GF 3 103
Sep 17 Ayr 6f G 13 **108**

PEACEFUL LOVE 3
Aug 2 Deau 10f G 4 **115**

PEAK OF PERFECTION 4
May 1 NmkR 12f G 12 101
May 11 York 12f S 6 100
May 28 Muss 14f G 2 **103**
Jly 9 Ling 16f SD 12 100

PEAK PARK 5
Jan 22 Ling 16f FT 5 104
Feb 10 Sthl 16f SD 1 101
Feb 24 Sthl 14f FT 1 104
Mar 21 Sthl 16f SD 1 103
May 21 Ling 16f SD 8 102
Nov 21 Sthl 14f SW 4 **105**

Dec 6 Sthl 14f FT 3 101

PEARL KING 3
Jly 16 NmkJ 8f GF 2 102
Jly 24 NmkJ 8f G 4 102
Aug 14 Pont 8f G 2 101
Sep 24 Ripn 10f GF 2 **108**
Oct 7 York 10½f G 3 104

PEARL OF LOVE 4
Jun 1 Nott 8f G 4 **108**

PEARL'S A SINGER 3
Jun 23 Leic 12f GF 2 **102**
Jly 18 Brig 12f G 1 99
Aug 26 Bath 13f G 3 100

PEARLY JACK 7
Nov 6 Leop 16f S 10 101

PEARSON GLEN 6
Feb 14 Wolv 9½f S 2 **102**
Feb 21 Ling 10f FT 6 99

PEDRILLO 4
Jly 29 Gdwd 8f G 13 107
Aug 18 York 8f G 9 107
Aug 27 York 9f G 1 **108**

PEE JAY'S DREAM 3
Oct 10 Ayr 15f S 2 **99**

PEERESS 4
May 13 York 7f GS 1 109
Jun 15 York 8f G 1 **115**
Jly 5 NmkJ 8f G 3 105
Oct 1 NmkR 8f G 1 111
Oct 15 NmkR 7f G 4 110

PEINEVE 5
Oct 9 Curr 8f GS 2 **101**
Nov 6 Leop 8f S 11 99

PEKING BEAUTY 3
Jun 27 Lonc 10½f G 2 **108**

PELAGIAS STAR 4
May 8 Leop 12f S 2 109
Sep 10 Leop 12f GF 3 **110**

PELLA 4
Aug 27 Wind 8½f G 8 99
Sep 11 Gdwd 8f G 9 **103**
Sep 23 Hayd 12f G 3 100

PENDING 4
Jun 23 Thsk 8f G 2 101
Aug 4 Chep 8f G 1 **102**
Sep 1 Carl 8f G 5 99
Dec 15 Sthl 8f SD 2 **102**

PENEL 4
Sep 20 Bevl 10f GF 6 **100**

PENKENNA PRINCESS 3
Apr 16 Newb 7f GS 1 102
May 22 Curr 8f G 2 **112**
Jly 5 NmkJ 8f G 5 102
Jly 30 Gdwd 10f G 7 103

PENNY RICH 11
May 21 Curr 12f G 10 102

PENNY WEDDING 3
May 5 Folk 9½f GS 1 **107**

PENTECOST 6
Apr 16 Thsk 8f HY 1 **112**
Apr 23 Sand 8f G 6 101
May 9 Wind 8½f GF 3 108
Jun 4 Epsm 8½f G 6 99
Jly 2 Sand 8f G 5 **112**

PENWAY 4
Jan 22 Ling 10f FT 3 **102**
Feb 21 Ling 7f SD 5 99

PENWELL HILL 6
Feb 8 Sthl 11f SD 5 100
Feb 26 Sthl 8f FT 4 107
Mar 8 Sthl 8f SD 1 **114**
Jly 25 Sthl 6f SD 2 99

PEOPLETON BROOK 3
Jun 11 Sand 5f G 1 100
Jly 6 Carl 5f G 2 103
Jly 10 Hayd 5f GF 1 **104**
Jly 29 Gdwd 5f G 2 103
Aug 8 Thsk 5f GF 2 101
Aug 15 Wind 5f GF 2 100
Aug 17 York 5f F 3 101
Oct 16 Muss 5f GF 7 101
Nov 3 Muss 5f GS 3 103

PEPPER ROAD 6
Sep 1 Carl 7f G 5 **100**
Sep 20 Brig 8f G 4 99

PEPPERMINT TEA 3
May 6 Haml 8½f GS 3 **101**

PERCUSSIONIST 4
May 13 York 14f GS 2 **109**

PERCY'S PEARL 3
Jly 25 Wind 8½f GS 1 99
Aug 10 Sals 8f G 3 **104**
Sep 7 Donc 10½f GF 12 100

PEREGRINE HAWK 4
Feb 15 Sthl 8f FT 2 **99**

PERFECT BALANCE 4
Jan 3 Sthl 12f SD 2 **102**

PERFECT BLEND 3
Aug 8 Wind 8½f GF 1 **103**
Oct 5 Nott 8f GF 4 100

PERFECT HEDGE 3
May 22 Lonc 10f GF 3 103
Jun 12 Chan 10½f G 6 106
Aug 21 Deau 10f G 5 101
Sep 11 Lonc 12f G 3 **111**
Oct 1 Lonc 12½f G 5 110

PERFECT MURDER 3
Jly 24 MsnL 10f F 5 **109**
Sep 17 Lonc 10f G 8 103

PERFECT STORY 3
Jan 15 Ling 8f SD 2 100
Jan 29 Ling 8f SD 2 106
Aug 4 Folk 6f F 1 100
Sep 17 Newb 7f GF 3 105

Oct 28 NmkR 6f GS 3 102
Nov 15 Ling 7f FT 1 **107**
Dec 5 Ling 7f FT 1 99
Dec 17 Ling 6f FT 5 103

PERFECT TONE 3
May 12 Sals 10f G 3 103
May 28 Ling 10f SW 1 **106**

PERFIDIOUS 7
Jan 10 Wolv 9½f SD 9 102
Feb 16 Ling 10f SD 11 100
Mar 3 Ling 10f SW 3 **107**
Apr 20 Ling 12f FT 2 99
Jun 17 Gdwd 12f G 5 101
Aug 5 Ling 11½f GS 3 100
Aug 21 Folk 12f G 1 101
Sep 28 Ling 12f SD 4 102

PERLE D'OR 4
Apr 25 Wind 10f GS 1 101
Jly 30 Donc 10½f G 1 **105**
Aug 23 Yarm 10f G 5 102
Oct 22 Donc 12f S 3 101

PERSEA 4
Feb 19 Wolv 6f S 2 100
Feb 28 Wolv 6f SD 1 99
Mar 21 Ling 6f SD 6 **101**

PERSIAN GENIE 4
May 26 Bath 17½f G 6 **100**

PERSIAN KNIGHT 6
Sep 4 Curr 10f G 1 **107**

PERSIAN LIGHTNING 6
May 21 Ling 11½f GS 1 **106**
Jun 17 York 10½f G 14 101

PERSIAN MAJESTY 5
May 21 Ling 11½f GS 4 100
Jun 4 Donc 10½f GF 3 100
Jun 19 Pont 12f G 4 **108**

PERSIAN ROCK 3
Aug 19 Sals 7f GS 2 **104**

PERSONA 3
Jly 17 Rdcr 9f G 4 **99**

PERTEMPS MAGUS 5
Jun 18 Ayr 6f G 1 **103**

PERUVIAN STYLE 4
Jan 5 Ling 7f SD 9 100
Jan 7 Wolv 7f SW 5 99
Feb 8 Ling 7f SD 2 102
Feb 22 Ling 7f SD 9 **103**
Sep 5 Bath 5½f GF 8 100

PESPITA 4
Jun 17 NmkJ 12f GF 9 **102**

PETANA 5
Aug 4 Brig 6f G 5 **101**

PETARDIAS MAGIC 4
Feb 8 Ling 6f SD 4 **103**
Apr 20 Ling 6f FT 1 101
Sep 3 NmkJ 6f G 10 102

PETER PAUL RUBENS 4
May 23 Wind 6f F 5 106
Jun 18 York 6f GF 3 110
Jly 23 Newb 7f GF 4 **113**
Aug 29 Wwck 7f GF 4 105

PETER'S IMP 10
Jun 27 Pont 10f G 3 100

PETERS DELITE 3
Apr 20 Catt 7f S 2 99
Jun 13 Thsk 7f G 2 **102**
Jun 23 Thsk 7f G 4 99

PETITE BOIS 3
Aug 14 Leop 6f G 1 **102**
Aug 20 Curr 6f GF 8 100

PETITE COLLEEN 4
Jan 6 Wolv 12f GF 8 **101**

PETITE MAC 5
Aug 6 Rdcr 6f G 1 102
Sep 12 Rdcr 6f G 4 **104**

PETITE PARAMOUR 4
Dec 9 Wolv 14f FT 3 **101**

PETITE SPECIALE 6
Apr 10 Lonc 10f S 10 **103**

PEVENSEY 3
May 13 Nott 8f F 2 **104**
May 21 Hayd 8f GF 7 **104**
Jun 16 Newb 12f G 4 102
Jly 6 NmkJ 10f G 4 **104**
Jly 22 York 10½f G 1 99
Aug 20 Bevl 10f GF 7 100
Aug 27 York 10½f G 5 103
Oct 4 Leic 12f G 8 102

PHARAOH PRINCE 4
Oct 15 Ling 13f SD 3 **99**
Nov 9 Wolv 12f FT 3 **99**

PHAROAH'S GOLD 7
Feb 7 Sthl 8f SD 2 **99**

PHECKLESS 6
Feb 14 Ling 8f SD 1 99
Mar 23 Ling 7f SD 1 **101**
Apr 8 Ling 6f SD 7 100

PHILHARMONIC 4
Apr 13 Bevl 5f G 2 105
May 7 Bevl 5f GF 1 **107**
Jun 26 Curr 5f GF 10 106
Jly 30 Gdwd 6f G 16 103
Sep 17 Ayr 6f G 17 102

PHLUKE 4
May 6 Ling 8f G 2 104
May 22 Brig 7f G 2 100
Jun 5 Bath 8f G 5 99
Jun 13 Wwck 7f GF 1 **106**
Jun 30 Epsm 7f G 3 102
Aug 4 Brig 7f G 1 105
Aug 18 Ches 7f F 2 99
Sep 6 Catt 7f GF 8 99

PHOEBE WOODSTOCK 3
Jun 27 Pont 10f G 2 **99**

PHOENIX EYE 4
Mar 26 Wolv 14f FT 3 100
Jun 29 Catt 12f G 5 101
Jly 9 Ches 16f GF 6 **102**

PHOENIX REACH 5
Jly 23 Newb 12f GF 10 **102**

PIANOFORTE 3
Jan 5 Ling 8f SD 6 100
Jan 31 Wolv 7f SD 1 100
Mar 2 Sthl 7f SD 2 **102**

PIC UP STICKS 6
Mar 28 Kemp 6f G 4 106
Apr 30 NmkR 6f G 18 105
Jun 4 Epsm 6f G 10 99
Jly 31 Newb 5f G 5 101
Sep 11 Gdwd 6f G 1 **107**
Sep 21 Gdwd 6f GF 4 104

PICCLED 7
Jun 7 Ches 5f GF 6 99
Sep 9 Donc 5f G 12 99
Nov 16 Sthl 5f FT 7 103
Dec 3 Wolv 5f FT 2 **104**

PICCLEYES 4
Jun 16 Wolv 6f FT 1 **100**
Jun 27 Wolv 6f SD 5 99

PICCOLO PRINCE 4
Apr 25 Haml 6f G 7 **99**

PICKAPEPPA 3
May 7 Ling 6f G 9 **99**

PICTAVIA 3
May 1 NmkR 8f G 7 107
Jun 3 Epsm 12f G 3 104
Sep 4 Curr 9f G 2 **111**
Sep 18 Curr 10f G 2 110

PIETER BRUEGHEL 6
Apr 18 Pont 6f S 4 100
Jun 1 Newc 6f G 2 102
Jly 5 Pont 6f G 1 **109**
Jly 30 Gdwd 6f G 7 107
Aug 13 Ripn 6f G 2 104
Sep 7 Donc 5½f GF 2 108

PIKE BISHOP 3
Jly 5 NmkJ 6f G 7 **105**
Aug 6 Wind 6f GF 7 100
Aug 13 NmkJ 6f G 3 102
Sep 24 Hayd 6f GF 9 99

PILLARS OF WISDOM 3
Aug 4 Brig 8f G 1 101
Sep 23 Ling 7f G 2 **103**

PINCHBECK 6
Jly 8 Ling 6f SW 1 **107**
Nov 15 Ling 7f FT 3 106
Dec 22 Sthl 6f SD 1 101

PINE BAY 4
Aug 13 Gdwd 6f G 2 **104**
Aug 20 Ling 6f G 3 99
Aug 22 Wind 6f G 2 99
Sep 8 Epsm 7f G 9 99

PINE CONE 3
Jly 4 Wind 8½f G 4 100
Jly 18 Wind 10f G 1 100
Aug 22 Leic 10f G 2 **102**
Sep 14 Sand 10f G 3 99
Oct 10 Wind 10f G 4 100

PINE VALLEY 4
Aug 7 Curr 10f G 10 **105**

PINK BAY 3
Aug 18 Chep 6f GF 1 101
Sep 13 Sals 7f G 3 **103**
Sep 26 Bath 8f G 3 100

PINK PALACE 4
Apr 10 Lonc 10f S 5 **109**

PINPOINT 3
Jly 7 Donc 8f GF 1 **107**
Sep 9 Sand 8f GS 2 102
Sep 30 NmkR 8f G 5 102
Oct 8 Sals 8f GF 1 106

PINSON 3
Jun 27 Lonc 9f G 1 113
Aug 20 Deau 10f GS 1 **119**
Oct 15 NmkR 10f G 10 103

PINTLE 5
Aug 28 Yarm 7f G 1 102
Sep 25 NmkR 7f G 8 **108**

PIPER GENERAL 3
Nov 21 Sthl 12f SW 1 110
Dec 9 Wolv 14f FT 1 104
Dec 15 Sthl 12f SD 1 **115**

PIPPA'S DANCER 3
May 16 Bath 5f GF 1 **99**

PIPS PEARL 3
Jun 22 Bath 8f G 3 **100**

PIQUET 7
Jan 26 Ling 10f FT 2 101
Feb 1 Ling 10f SD 2 101
Jun 18 Ling 10f SW 2 102
Jly 6 Ling 12f SW 3 **103**
Dec 29 Ling 10f SW 7 102

PITCH UP 3
Jun 6 Folk 6f G 3 **99**

PITTSBURGH 3
Feb 19 Wolv 8½f G 5 **102**

PIVOTAL FLAME 3
Apr 16 Newb 7f GS 4 105
May 21 Hayd 8f GF 13 99
Jun 15 York 7f G 6 101
Jly 7 NmkJ 7f G 3 107
Jly 23 Newb 7f GF 11 108
Aug 13 Newb 7f G 3 109
Oct 1 Rdcr 7f GF 3 **110**
Oct 15 NmkR 7f G 7 107

PIVOTAL ROLE 3
Aug 18 Wolv 8½f SD 5 **102**

PIVOTAL'S PRINCESS 3
May 28 Donc 5f G 1 103

Jun 12 Donc 5f F 1 102
Jun 23 Haml 5f G 1 **109**
Jly 8 Ches 5f F 1 104
Jly 18 Ayr 5f GF 5 104
Sep 10 Ches 6f GS 3 105
Sep 24 Hayd 5f GF 3 107
Sep 29 NmkR 5f GF 6 103

PLANET 3
May 28 Gdwd 11f G 1 **104**

PLANTERS PUNCH 4
Oct 9 Newc 10f G 13 101

PLATEAU 6
Apr 20 Epsm 5f GS 4 106
Jun 4 Epsm 5f G 7 102
Jun 7 Ches 5f GF 1 **107**
Jly 6 NmkJ 5f GF 4 100
Jly 27 Gdwd 5f G 7 100
Aug 20 Ches 5f G 2 103
Sep 9 Donc 5f G 10 101

PLATINUM CHARMER 5
Jun 22 Bath 10f G 1 101
Jun 27 Muss 12f G 1 **104**
Nov 3 Muss 12f GS 1 102

PLATONIC AFFAIR 4
May 22 Curr 6f G 9 **101**

PLAUSABELLE 4
Jan 4 Wolv 9½f SD 1 102
Jan 14 Wolv 9½f SW 1 99
Feb 8 Ling 8f SD 1 103
Feb 28 Wolv 9½f SD 2 **108**
Apr 1 Ling 8f SD 1 103

PLAY ME 3
Oct 5 Nott 10f G 1 **101**

PLAYFUL ACT 3
Jly 2 Hayd 12f GF 1 103
Jly 17 Curr 12f F 2 **111**
Oct 2 Lonc 10f G 8 107

PLAYFUL DANE 8
Jly 11 Ayr 5f GF 2 103
Aug 17 Carl 5f GF 1 103
Aug 25 Muss 5f G 2 102
Sep 9 Donc 5f G 3 **112**
Sep 24 Hayd 5f GF 5 106
Oct 15 Catt 5f G 1 101
Oct 22 Donc 5f S 11 105

PLAYTIME BLUE 5
Jun 18 Ling 5f G 6 **103**

PLEA BARGAIN 3
Apr 22 Sand 8f G 1 100
Jun 17 York 12f G 1 107
Jly 14 Lonc 12f F 4 **110**

PLEASANT 4
Jly 9 Sals 12f G 4 99
Jly 25 Wind 11½f GS 1 **103**

PLECTRUM 4
Mar 28 Kemp 7f GS 3 101
Jun 8 Bevl 7½f G 2 103
Jun 17 Gdwd 9f G 3 100
Jly 26 Gdwd 8f G 1 **112**

PLEIN D'ESTIME 3
Aug 2 Deau 10f G 3 **107**

POCKETWOOD 3
Apr 23 Leic 12f G 2 **104**

POETICAL 4
Jly 2 Leop 7f F 7 **100**

POINT CALIMERE 4
Sep 17 Curr 5f G 7 **105**

POINT OF DISPUTE 10
Jan 5 Ling 6f SD 2 **104**
Feb 8 Ling 7f SD 3 100
Mar 1 Ling 6f SD 6 103
Mar 4 Wolv 8½f SD 2 101
Mar 21 Ling 6f SD 4 102

POKER PLAYER 3
Jly 7 Donc 8f GF 2 **102**
Jly 22 NmkJ 8f G 2 101
Oct 3 Wind 6f GF 1 101

POLAR BEAR 5
Apr 23 Leic 7f G 3 106
May 12 York 7f GS 8 101
Sep 17 Newb 9f GF 1 103
Oct 1 Lonc 8f G 2 **115**

POLAR BEN 6
May 7 Hayd 7f GS 4 103
Jly 9 Ches 7f GF 4 112
Jly 30 NmkJ 8f GF 2 **113**
Sep 3 Hayd 8f GF 4 104
Sep 30 NmkR 8f G 3 103
Oct 22 Donc 7f S 1 102

POLAR DAWN 3
Jly 8 Chep 8f GF 1 100
Aug 27 Wind 8½f G 5 **101**

POLAR FORCE 5
May 10 Yarm 6f GF 1 99
Jun 3 Thsk 5f G 4 99
Jun 7 Sals 6f G 2 102
Aug 28 Yarm 5f G 1 104
Sep 12 Rdcr 6f G 1 **108**

POLAR HAZE 8
Aug 4 Brig 6f G 2 **102**

POLAR JEM 5
Jly 16 NmkJ 12f GF 1 106
Aug 10 Sals 10f G 4 106
Aug 27 Wind 10f G 4 **110**
Sep 3 NmkJ 12f G 5 100
Sep 24 NmkR 12f G 6 104
Oct 10 Wind 11½f G 1 103

POLAR KINGDOM 7
Mar 4 Wolv 6f SD 6 **101**

POLAR MAGIC 4
Apr 19 Sthl 7f GF 1 102
May 25 NmkR 7f G 2 107
Jun 11 Sand 7f G 3 **112**
Jly 7 NmkJ 7f G 2 107
Jly 23 Newb 7f GF 13 105
Sep 10 Donc 8f GS 5 106

POLAR SUN 4
Jun 9 Wolv 8½f SD 2 **102**
Jun 16 Wolv 8½f SD 6 99

POLAR WAY 6
Jly 23 Newb 7f GF 17 **102**

POLICY MAKER 5
Jun 5 Chan 12f G 5 **117**
Jun 26 StCl 12f GF 2 116
Jly 23 Newb 12f GF 12 99

POLISH CORRIDOR 6
May 2 Donc 10½f G 2 **108**

POLISH EMPEROR 5
Feb 5 Ling 5f G 5 105
Feb 19 Wolv 5f G 1 **108**
Apr 1 Donc 5f G 4 104
Apr 20 Epsm 5f GS 5 106
Jun 23 Sals 5f G 1 104
Aug 6 Hayd 5f G 5 107
Oct 1 Epsm 5f G 7 101
Nov 16 Sthl 5f FT 3 107
Dec 6 Sthl 5f FT 7 100
Dec 17 Ling 6f FT 8 102

POLISH FLAME 7
Jly 12 Bevl 16f GF 5 **99**

POLISH SPIRIT 10
Apr 26 Bath 10f HY 1 **100**
May 3 Bath 10f HY 3 99
Jun 27 Wind 10f G 4 99

POLITICAL INTRIGUE 3
Jun 25 Donc 10½f GF 2 101
Jly 5 Pont 12f G 1 **107**
Jly 20 Leic 12f GF 1 **107**

POLY DANCE 4
May 22 Lonc 7f GF 6 **107**

POLYGONAL 5
Apr 30 NmkR 10f G 3 **105**
May 14 Newb 12f G 8 100
May 25 NmkR 10f G 8 99
May 30 Rdcr 10f G 13 100
Jun 18 Rdcr 10f G 6 **105**

POMFRET LAD 7
Jun 10 Catt 6f GF 2 101
Jun 30 Hayd 6f GF 3 99
Jly 27 Gdwd 5f G 2 **105**
Aug 5 Hayd 6f F 2 **105**
Aug 27 York 6f G 3 103

PONT D'OR 6
Apr 3 Lonc 10f S 4 **115**

PONT NEUF 5
Mar 30 Folk 12f HY 1 **106**
Jun 15 Chep 10f GS 5 101
Jly 18 Wind 11½f G 4 99

POP UP AGAIN 5
Aug 19 Ayr 7f GF 4 **102**
Sep 1 Carl 7f G 2 **102**
Sep 10 Muss 8f G 5 100

POPPYS FOOTPRINT 4
May 20 Hayd 8f G 3 **107**

Jun 4 Hayd 8f G 5 99
Jly 14 Donc 7f GF 6 100
Dec 19 Wolv 9½f FT 3 100

PORT 'N STARBOARD 4
Aug 4 Brig 12f G 4 99
Aug 20 Ling 10f SD 2 **101**
Sep 6 Ling 10f SD 3 99

PORTHCAWL 4
May 2 Kemp 8f G 3 **103**
May 19 Donc 8f GF 1 **103**

PORTMEIRION 4
Jly 30 Ling 6f GS 1 **103**
Aug 6 Ling 6f G 4 99
Aug 20 Ling 6f G 1 **103**
Sep 16 Nott 6f GF 2 100

PORTRAYAL 3
Oct 13 NmkR 10f G 1 **109**

PORTSMOUTH 3
Aug 7 Curr 10f G 5 **103**

POSTGRADUATE 3
May 26 Ayr 7f G 1 101
Aug 27 NmkJ 7f G 7 102
Sep 23 Hayd 8f G 5 101
Oct 3 Pont 8f G 2 **106**

POUSSIN 7
Apr 30 Lonc 15½f GS 6 **111**

POWERSCOURT 5
Jun 18 York 12f G 4 108
Jly 18 Ayr 10f GF 2 **113**

PRAGMATICA 4
Jly 19 Yarm 8f G 2 **100**
Aug 10 Yarm 7f GF 2 99

PRAIRIE LAW 5
Jly 15 Wwck 12½f G 4 99
Jly 18 Wind 11½f G 3 100
Aug 7 Rdcr 11f G 1 **103**

PRAIRIE OYSTER 4
Jun 27 Wind 8½f G 2 **101**
Jly 11 Wind 8½f G 6 **101**
Aug 27 Wind 8½f G 7 99

PRAIRIE SUN 4
May 16 Muss 16f G 1 101
May 21 Catt 14f GF 1 106
May 25 Ripn 16f G 1 **108**
May 30 Rdcr 14f G 1 101
Jun 6 Pont 17f GF 3 102
Jly 17 Rdcr 16f G 2 99
Jly 22 York 14f G 4 **108**
Jly 30 Thsk 16f G 7 100

PRE EMINANCE 4
Jun 30 Newb 11f G 2 **107**
Aug 2 Brig 12f G 8 102

PRECIOUS MYSTERY 5
Mar 7 Wolv 14f SD 3 100
Mar 29 Wwck 15f S 1 99
May 1 Sals 14f GS 3 **107**
Sep 17 Wwck 16f G 9 100
Oct 31 Wolv 14f SD 2 99

PRECIPITOUS 4
Jly 2 Leop 7f F 3 **104**
Jly 16 Curr 7f F 1 102

PRELUDE 4
Apr 21 Bevl 10f S 3 102
Aug 13 Ripn 10f GS 2 102
Aug 28 Bevl 10f GS 2 **103**
Sep 10 Ches 10½f GS 2 100
Sep 26 Haml 11f G 3 99

PREMIER DANE 3
Apr 10 Leop 10f S 5 100
May 25 Leop 10f GF 6 102
Jun 15 Leop 10f G 6 101
Jly 6 Naas 10f GF 1 **104**

PREMIER FANTASY 3
Dec 3 Wolv 5f GF 6 **99**

PREMIER GRAND 5
Jly 25 Sthl 6f GF 2 **99**

PREMIER PROSPECT 4
Jly 11 Ayr 6f GF 2 99
Jly 16 Ripn 6f G 2 100
Aug 19 Ayr 6f GF 1 **102**

PREMIER ROUGE 4
Apr 6 Ling 7f GF 4 101
Jun 1 Yarm 8f G 2 99
Jun 11 Ling 10f SW 4 101
Jun 23 Leic 12f GF 4 99
Jun 27 Wind 10f G 1 **104**

PRESS EXPRESS 3
Aug 20 Rdcr 10f G 2 103
Aug 26 Newc 9f GF 1 **106**
Oct 9 Newc 10f G 1 **106**

PRESTO SHINKO 4
Mar 18 Ling 6f SD 1 103
Mar 28 Kemp 6f G 6 101
Apr 23 Leic 6f G 1 108
Jun 25 Wind 6f G 2 109
Jun 30 Epsm 6f G 2 106
Jly 22 Newb 6f G 3 103
Jly 30 Gdwd 6f G 15 103
Aug 6 NmkJ 7f G 7 111
Aug 8 Wind 6f GF 1 104
Aug 27 Gdwd 6f G 1 107
Sep 17 Ayr 6f G 1 **113**
Nov 5 Donc 6f HY 1 111

PRESUMPTIVE 5
Jun 11 Sand 7f G 1 **115**

PRETTY KOOL 5
Jly 11 Wind 5f G 1 103
Aug 13 NmkJ 5f GS 2 102
Aug 21 Folk 5f G 2 **106**

PRIDE 5
Apr 24 Lonc 10½f GS 6 112
Jun 3 Epsm 12f G 6 107
Aug 21 Deau 10f G 1 116
Sep 11 Lonc 12f G 1 **121**
Oct 2 Lonc 12f G 7 117
Oct 15 NmkR 10f G 2 112

PRIDE OF KINLOCH 5
Jun 17 Ayr 7f GS 1 **103**

PRIDE OF NATION 3
Sep 16 Nott 8f GF 2 104
Sep 27 Nott 8f GF 1 **105**

PRIMARILY 3
Apr 18 Pont 6f S 2 **102**
Jun 2 Hayd 6f G 3 100
Aug 3 Pont 6f G 3 100

PRIME CONTENDER 3
Sep 16 Nott 8f GF 3 102

PRIME NUMBER 3
Apr 30 Gdwd 7f S 3 107
May 29 NmkR 7f GF 3 101
Jun 17 Gdwd 9f G 1 103
Aug 8 Wind 8½f GF 1 **110**
Sep 18 Haml 8½f F 1 105
Oct 9 Gdwd 10f G 11 101

PRIME OFFER 9
Sep 11 Gdwd 8f G 3 **107**

PRIME POWERED 4
Mar 26 Kemp 10f GS 11 **99**

PRIME RECREATION 8
Apr 19 Folk 5f GS 3 **103**

PRIMESHADE PROMISE 4
May 4 Chep 8f S 1 **105**
Jun 16 Wolv 8½f S 2 102
Aug 4 Chep 8f G 2 102

PRIMO WAY 4
May 21 Ling 7f G 1 105
Jly 31 Ches 7½f G 2 102
Aug 13 Newb 7f G 3 104
Sep 4 Curr 8f G 9 **106**
Oct 14 NmkR 7f G 15 103

PRIMUS INTER PARES 4
Sep 17 Ayr 6f G 8 **110**

PRINCE AARON 5
Apr 14 NmkR 6f G 4 104
Apr 30 NmkR 5f G 5 109
May 23 Wind 6f F 7 101
May 31 Sand 5f G 4 **113**

PRINCE CHARMING 3
Jly 31 Ches 6f G 6 **102**

PRINCE CYRANO 6
May 30 Leic 6f G 1 **104**
Jly 29 Gdwd 6f G 8 100
Aug 5 NmkJ 6f GF 8 99
Aug 29 Wwck 6f GF 1 103

PRINCE DAYJUR 6
Jan 3 Sthl 7f SD 1 **105**
Jan 15 Ling 6f SD 4 **105**
Sep 3 Wolv 7f FT 2 99
Sep 25 Muss 7f G 2 **105**

PRINCE DOLOIS 7
Aug 7 Deau 10f GF 5 **107**

PRINCE NAMID 3
Jun 21 Bevl 5f G 3 100
Jly 29 Thsk 6f G 2 **106**
Aug 8 Thsk 5f GF 3 99

Sep 11 Carl 6f GF 2 103
Sep 29 Ayr 6f G 7 101
Oct 17 Pont 5f G 3 100
Nov 3 Muss 5f GS 6 101

PRINCE NUREYEV 5
Jly 1 Sand 10f G 4 101
Aug 20 Sand 10f G 6 99
Oct 9 Gdwd 10f G 4 **105**
Oct 22 Newb 10f G 13 99

PRINCE OF GOLD 5
Jan 31 Wolv 7f SD 5 **102**
Feb 12 Wolv 7f FT 3 99
Feb 28 Wolv 5f SD 3 99
May 30 Leic 6f G 4 101
Aug 6 Hayd 6f G 5 100
Aug 19 Wolv 6f FT 5 99
Dec 28 Wolv 7f FT 1 100

PRINCE OF THEBES 4
Apr 12 NmkR 7f GF 2 101
Jly 8 Chep 7f GF 4 104
Aug 13 Newb 7f G 7 101
Aug 29 Wwck 7f GF 1 **109**
Sep 8 Epsm 7f G 4 103
Sep 30 NmkR 7f G 7 102

PRINCE SAMOS 3
Apr 8 Ling 8f SD 1 100
Apr 22 Sand 8f G 1 **110**
Aug 4 Hayd 8f GF 7 100
Sep 17 Ayr 8f G 5 99
Sep 24 Ripn 10f GF 5 104
Oct 9 Gdwd 10f G 6 104
Oct 14 NmkR 8f G 10 104

PRINCE SOLOR 3
Jun 27 Lonc 9½f G 6 **104**

PRINCE TUM TUM 5
Jan 7 Wolv 6f SW 1 **113**
Jan 15 Ling 6f SD 5 105
Mar 12 Wolv 8½f SD 9 104
Mar 28 Wwck 7f GS 2 103
Apr 9 Ling 7f FT 6 104
Apr 14 NmkR 6f G 5 104
Apr 30 NmkR 6f G 17 105
Jun 3 Epsm 8½f G 10 100
Jly 28 Gdwd 7f G 6 100
Aug 25 Muss 9f G 1 103
Oct 30 Ling 6f SD 7 104
Nov 25 Wolv 6f FT 6 104
Dec 16 Wolv 6f FT 2 106

PRINCE VECTOR 3
Jun 6 Wind 10f G 2 102
Jly 11 Wind 11½f G 2 **104**
Sep 6 Leic 10f GF 1 100
Sep 21 Gdwd 11f G 4 103
Oct 17 Wind 10f G 2 103

PRINCE VETTORI 3
Jly 8 Wolv 8½f FT 2 100
Oct 6 Sthl 8f FT 1 **102**

PRINCELET 3
Oct 5 Nott 10f G 1 **103**

PRINCELYWALLYWOGAN 3
Apr 6 Ling 7f G 4 101
Oct 12 Ling 10f G 3 101

Oct 17 Pont 10f G 1 **103**

PRINCESS JONES 5
Jun 27 Lonc 7f G 7 **104**

PRINCESS KIOTTO 4
May 7 Bevl 16f G 4 **100**
May 19 Newc 16f G 1 **100**
Jun 23 Newc 16f GF 2 **100**

PRINCESS NALA 3
May 22 Curr 10f GS 2 **101**

PRIORINA 3
Jun 22 Bath 8f G 2 **100**

PRIVY SEAL 4
May 5 Ches 10½f G 8 **99**

PRIZE FIGHTER 3
Oct 29 NmkR 8f S 8 100

PRO TEMPORE 3
Aug 12 Folk 5f GF 2 **101**

PROCLAMATION 3
May 28 Gdwd 8f G 1 110
Jun 15 York 7f G 1 109
Jly 27 Gdwd 8f GS 1 **119**
Sep 3 Hayd 6f F 11 100

PROFIT'S REALITY 3
May 2 Wwck 7f G 2 101
May 5 Chep 8f GS 1 **103**
May 21 Hayd 8f GF 8 **103**
Jun 2 Sand 10f G 1 102
Jun 16 York 10½f G 4 99
Jly 6 NmkJ 10f G 0 101

PROMOTION 5
Apr 30 NmkR 10f G 4 104
Jun 17 York 10½f G 5 105
Jly 2 Hayd 12f GF 5 **107**
Jly 26 Gdwd 10f G 11 101

PROPINQUITY 3
May 21 Hayd 8f GF 11 **102**

PROSPECT PARK 4
Oct 15 NmkR 10f G 11 **102**

PROUD TO BE IRISH 6
Jun 1 Leop 14f G 3 **106**
Jly 16 Curr 16f GF 4 101

PROUD WESTERN 7
Aug 8 Thsk 8f G 5 **99**

PROUDANCE 3
Oct 1 Lonc 8f G 4 **111**

PSEUDONYM 3
May 28 Ling 10f SW 7 **102**
Aug 20 Ling 10f SD 3 101

PSYCHIATRIST 4
Apr 9 Ling 7f FT 2 109
May 20 Gdwd 7f GS 4 104
Aug 13 Newb 7f G 5 103
Sep 24 NmkR 7f G 6 **111**
Oct 14 NmkR 7f G 7 106
Oct 27 Ling 7f SD 12 101
Nov 19 Ling 7f FT 4 109
Nov 26 Ling 8f FT 2 108
Dec 17 Ling 8f FT 1 105

PTARMIGAN RIDGE 9
Apr 20 Epsm 5f GS 7 **105**
May 28 Muss 5f G 14 99
Aug 13 Ripn 6f G 4 102
Aug 25 Muss 5f G 5 101
Aug 29 Epsm 5f G 10 103

PUBLIC EYE 4
Jun 30 Newb 11f G 3 **105**

PUGILIST 3
Jly 4 Bath 10f G 2 102
Sep 7 Donc 10½f GF 4 **106**

PUKKA 4
Jun 17 York 10½f G 15 101
Aug 20 Ches 13½f G 6 103
Sep 10 Donc 12f S 4 **105**
Oct 13 NmkR 12f G 6 **105**

PULSE 7
Mar 31 Ling 5f SD 1 100
Apr 24 Brig 5½f GF 2 101
Apr 26 Wwck 5f G 1 **103**
May 27 Catt 5f GF 4 101
Jun 9 Ripn 5f G 5 101
Jun 16 Bevl 5f G 1 101
Jun 19 Wwck 5f GF 2 101
Jun 28 Brig 5½f F 7 102

PUNCTILIOUS 4
May 31 Sand 10f G 5 110
Jly 2 Hayd 12f GF 7 101
Jly 31 Newb 12f G 1 **111**
Aug 17 York 12f G 1 110
Sep 7 Donc 14½f GF 4 101

PURE IMAGINATION 4
May 5 Folk 6f G 4 104
Jun 2 Hayd 6f G 5 101
Jun 10 Chep 7f G 1 102
Jly 8 Chep 7f GF 7 102
Aug 27 NmkJ 6f G 1 **105**
Sep 25 Muss 7f G 8 102
Oct 5 Nott 8f GF 1 103
Oct 16 Muss 7f G 2 103

PURE MISCHIEF 6
Jan 29 Ling 10f SD 6 **105**
Feb 9 Ling 8f SD 6 99

PURPLE DANCER 3
Aug 19 Ayr 8f GF 6 99
Sep 15 Pont 10f G 2 **100**

PUSSIGNY 7
Aug 7 Deau 10f GF 6 **107**

PUTRA KUANTAN 5
Apr 23 Sand 8f G 13 99
Jun 22 Sals 8f G 8 100
Aug 3 Epsm 8½f G 5 101
Aug 30 Ripn 10f F 2 **105**
Sep 7 Epsm 10f G 4 99

PUTRA PEKAN 7
Mar 31 Donc 8f G 3 **114**

PYRANA 3
May 1 StCl 10½f F 5 102
Jly 14 Lonc 12f F 4 **110**

Q

QAADMAH 3
Jun 30 Yarm 11½f G 5 **101**

QAASI 3
Aug 4 Hayd 10½f GF 4 **101**
Aug 27 York 8f G 3 **101**

QADAR 3
Aug 7 Leic 7f G 3 **102**
Sep 10 Gdwd 7f G 12 100

QOBTAAN 6
Apr 22 Wolv 8½f SD 1 **102**

QUALITAIR WINGS 6
May 3 Catt 7f GS 5 100
Jly 14 Haml 8½f GF 4 102
Jly 26 Bevl 8½f G 4 99
Sep 4 York 8f G 2 **110**
Oct 9 Newc 8f G 3 99
Oct 17 Pont 10f G 2 99

QUALITY STREET 3
Aug 21 Folk 5f G 8 **99**

QUANTICA 6
May 17 Rdcr 6f G 2 **101**
Jly 30 Ling 6f GS 3 100
Aug 10 Yarm 7f GF 1 100
Sep 29 Ayr 7f S 2 100

QUANTUM LEAP 8
Jan 26 Ling 7f FT 2 100
Feb 5 Ling 7f FT 1 **105**
Feb 9 Ling 7f FT 3 101
Feb 22 Ling 7f SD 8 104
Jun 3 Gdwd 7f GS 10 101
Jun 30 Epsm 7f G 1 104
Aug 3 Epsm 8½f G 7 99
Nov 10 Ling 8f SD 7 99
Dec 5 Ling 8f FT 5 100

QUDRAAT 4
Aug 7 Curr 10f G 13 **102**

QUEDEX 9
Oct 15 NmkR 18f G 11 **101**

QUEEN ASTRID 5
Oct 9 Curr 16f GS 5 **108**
Nov 6 Leop 16f S 4 **108**

QUEEN OF ICENI 3
Apr 2 Kemp 9f S 2 **106**
Jly 8 Ling 10f G 8 100
Jly 24 NmkJ 15f GS 2 103
Oct 1 NmkR 14f G 5 104

QUEEN OF NIGHT 5
Jan 3 Sthl 6f SD 4 100
Mar 8 Sthl 5f SD 4 **101**
Jun 3 Wolv 6f FT 2 100
Jly 26 Bevl 5f G 3 99

QUEEN TITI 3
May 22 Curr 8f G 15 104
Jly 6 Naas 10f GF 2 103
Jly 17 Curr 9f F 3 **109**
Sep 18 Curr 10f G 9 104

QUEEN TOMYRA 3
Apr 20 Ling 10f FT 2 **101**
Aug 22 Wolv 12f FT 1 **101**

QUEEN'S DANCER 3
Oct 10 Wind 11½f G 3 100
Nov 4 Yarm 10f HY 3 99
Nov 21 Sthl 14f SW 6 **105**

QUEEN'S ECHO 4
May 23 Leic 7f G 2 **101**
May 26 Ayr 8f G 1 **101**

QUEEN'S LODGE 5
Jun 4 Donc 6f G 1 101
Jun 17 Rdcr 6f G 10 99
Jly 8 York 6f G 6 **105**
Aug 14 Pont 6f G 9 103

QUEENS RHAPSODY 5
Jun 18 Ayr 7f G 4 **103**
Nov 15 Ling 7f FT 6 **103**
Nov 25 Wolv 6f FT 9 100
Nov 29 Sthl 6f SD 3 99

QUEENSTOWN 4
Feb 24 Sthl 8f FT 1 **106**
Jly 16 Ling 8f SW 4 100

QUEL FONTENAILLES 7
Mar 21 Ling 13f SW 1 **99**

QUERIDO 3
Sep 10 Gdwd 16f G 4 **100**

QUEST ON AIR 6
Mar 13 Wolv 12f FT 2 **100**
Mar 31 Ling 12f SD 1 99

QUICKFIRE 3
Jun 15 York 8f G 5 101
Jly 29 Gdwd 7f G 2 **110**
Aug 14 Pont 6f G 11 101
Sep 25 NmkR 7f G 5 **110**
Oct 11 Leic 8½f G 3 106

QUIET READING 8
Feb 3 Sthl 8f SD 5 99
Feb 7 Sthl 7f SD 4 **100**
Dec 22 Sthl 8f SD 1 **100**

QUIET TIMES 6
Jan 7 Wolv 6f SW 3 **110**
Jan 15 Ling 6f SD 1 109
Mar 12 Wolv 6f SD 9 102
Oct 30 Ling 6f SD 4 105
Nov 16 Sthl 5f FT 9 102
Dec 22 Sthl 6f SD 2 99

QUIFF 4
Apr 23 Sand 10f G 4 **101**

QUINCANNON 4
Jan 5 Sthl 7f SD 3 **103**
Aug 8 Wolv 7f SD 2 101

QUITO 8
Jan 20 Sthl 7f SD 8 102
Apr 2 Donc 6f G 5 105
Apr 14 NmkR 6f G 1 108
May 7 Hayd 7f GS 2 109
May 12 York 7f GS 1 111
May 23 Wind 6f F 4 107
Jun 2 Hayd 7f G 5 110
Jun 18 York 6f GF 9 105
Jun 25 Newc 6f G 2 107
Jly 2 Hayd 6f GF 2 110
Jly 7 NmkJ 6f G 9 104
Jly 27 Gdwd 8f GS 8 **112**
Aug 18 York 7f GF 2 110
Aug 27 NmkJ 6f G 1 109
Sep 3 Hayd 8f GF 3 105
Sep 8 Donc 7f GF 7 104
Sep 25 NmkR 6f G 9 107

QUIZZENE 3
Apr 22 Sand 10f G 1 **103**
May 4 Ches 12½f GS 1 102

QUIZZICAL QUESTION 3
Aug 6 Ling 10f SD 1 **100**

R

RACCOON 5
Sep 1 Rdcr 6f G 2 **100**
Sep 14 Bevl 5f G 5 99

RACE THE ACE 4
Jly 6 NmkJ 16f G 2 **101**

RADLETT LADY 4
Jly 30 Ling 6f GS 4 99
Aug 6 Ling 6f G 2 **100**

RAFFERTY 6
Jan 1 Sthl 8f SD 2 **115**
Jan 7 Wolv 7f SW 3 102
Jan 20 Sthl 7f SD 6 103
Feb 1 Ling 8f SD 5 107
Feb 26 Sthl 8f FT 5 106
Mar 27 Muss 7f GS 3 102
Apr 19 Sthl 7f GF 3 99
Sep 25 Muss 7f G 6 102
Oct 10 Wolv 7f FT 1 103
Nov 1 Catt 7f GS 5 99

RAFFISH 3
Jly 13 Ling 10f G 1 **99**

RAGASAH 7
Feb 7 Wolv 8½f FT 5 **99**
Nov 28 Sthl 7f SD 4 **99**

RAGEMAN 5
Oct 30 StCl 8f G 1 **115**

RAGGTIME TOON 5
Apr 10 Leop 12f GS 3 109
May 22 Curr 12f GS 1 **115**
Jun 26 Curr 12f F 9 108
Sep 10 Leop 12f GF 7 109

RAIN STOPS PLAY 3
Mar 28 Kemp 9f G 2 103
Apr 30 NmkR 8f G 5 100
May 13 York 7f GS 4 **104**

May 19 Donc 7f GF 4 102
Sep 7 Epsm 7f G 1 99

RAINBOW RISING 3
May 7 Thsk 6f GS 1 101
Jun 20 Ripn 6f G 3 105
Aug 1 Ripn 6f G 7 101
Aug 27 York 6f G 6 103
Oct 22 Donc 5f S 7 **109**

RAINBOW SKY 3
Jly 23 York 10½f GS 5 **99**

RAJAYOGA 4
Jly 25 Yarm 16f GS 4 99

RAKTI 6
May 14 Newb 8f F 1 **118**
Jun 14 York 8f G 2 114
Sep 24 NmkR 8f G 4 111
Oct 15 NmkR 10f G 6 109

RAMPAGE 4
Oct 10 Wind 6f G 2 99
Oct 18 Sthl 6f SD 1 101
Oct 29 Wolv 7f SD 1 **102**

RAMSGILL 3
Sep 6 Ling 10f SD 1 **102**
Sep 22 Pont 10f G 2 99
Nov 12 Ling 10f FT 1 100
Dec 12 Wolv 9½f FT 4 101

RANCHO CUCAMONGA 3
Feb 9 Ling 6f FT 3 99
Mar 17 Sthl 6f FT 1 **104**
Jun 10 Wolv 6f SD 1 101
Jly 14 Haml 6f GF 3 100
Jly 10 Ayr 6f G 1 102

RANDOM QUEST 7
Aug 20 Ches 16f G 7 **107**

RANGOON 4
Jly 2 Leop 7f F 5 **101**

RAPID RIVER 3
Aug 20 Bevl 5f G 3 99
Sep 14 Sand 5f GS 2 **103**

RARE COINCIDENCE 4
Mar 7 Wolv 9½f SD 2 101
Mar 29 Wwck 11f S 6 100
Apr 16 Wolv 9½f FT 1 102
Apr 22 Wolv 8½f SD 7 99
Jun 24 Wolv 12f SD 1 102
Jly 11 Ayr 11f F 3 106
Aug 12 Catt 12f G 2 102

RARE CROSS 3
Jun 11 Leic 5f G 3 **102**

RASID 7
Jan 6 Wolv 12f G 3 **107**
Jan 21 Wolv 12f SD 8 101
Mar 16 Wolv 9½f SD 4 103
Apr 1 Ling 12f SD 4 102
Apr 20 Ling 12f FT 3 99
May 20 Hayd 10½f G 5 102
Jun 11 Ling 10f SW 3 101

RATHGOWNEY LAD 5
Mar 20 Curr 8f HY 4 109
May 21 Curr 8f G 1 **113**

RATHOR 3
Apr 23 Leic 10f G 2 101
Jly 5 Pont 10f G 1 107
Jly 23 Nott 8f F 1 104
Aug 11 Sals 8f GF 6 **108**
Oct 7 York 8f G 5 106

RATIO 7
May 22 Lonc 7f GF 9 104
Aug 7 Deau 6½f G 5 **111**
Aug 28 Deau 6f G 3 109

RAUL SAHARA 3
Aug 26 Bath 8f G 2 **103**

RAVE REVIEWS 4
Apr 16 Newb 12f GS 4 **108**
Jly 28 Gdwd 14f G 4 99

RAWAABET 3
Apr 18 Wind 8½f G 5 100
Apr 25 Wind 8½f GS 2 **101**

RAWDON 4
Apr 16 Wolv 8½f FT 2 101
May 20 Hayd 10½f G 1 101
Jun 24 NmkJ 10f G 1 107
Aug 13 NmkJ 12f G 3 102
Sep 3 NmkJ 10f G 5 103
Sep 23 Hayd 10½f G 1 **108**

RAYMOND'S PRIDE 5
Jan 1 Sthl 6f SD 2 101
Jan 31 Wolv 7f SD 3 103
Apr 23 Ripn 6f S 1 **108**
Aug 1 Ripn 6f G 9 99
Oct 17 Pont 5f G 4 100
Oct 29 Ayr 6f S 1 105

RAZE 3
May 12 Sals 10f G 1 **103**

RAZKALLA 7
May 21 Ling 11½f GS 3 **102**

REACHING OUT 3
May 21 Ling 10f GS 2 **102**
Aug 25 Ling 10f GS 2 **102**
Oct 5 Nott 10f G 9 101

READ FEDERICA 3
Apr 13 NmkR 7f G 11 **101**

REAL COOL CAT 3
Jun 16 Bevl 10f G 1 101
Jun 23 Leic 10f GF 1 **104**

REAL QUALITY 3
May 2 Donc 8f G 1 106
Jun 16 York 8f G 6 105
Aug 20 Bevl 10f GF 6 102
Sep 17 Ayr 10f G 2 **108**

REALISM 5
May 30 Rdcr 10f G 5 103
Jun 3 Epsm 10f G 2 **111**
Jly 9 York 10½f G 3 106
Jly 26 Gdwd 10f G 13 100

Aug 17 York 10½f G 1 **111**
Oct 7 York 10½f G 1 106

REAP 7
Mar 24 Wolv 8½f SD 4 **100**

REBEL RAIDER 6
Feb 4 Wolv 8½f SD 7 100

REBEL REBEL 3
Mar 26 Kemp 8f GS 1 105
Apr 30 NmkR 8f G 2 **110**

REBUTTAL 3
May 28 Gdwd 8f G 5 **103**

RED ADMIRAL 3
Aug 19 Sals 12f G 1 **102**

RED BIRR 4
Dec 20 Ling 10f G 1 **107**

RED BLOOM 4
May 1 NmkR 9f G 5 106
Jun 6 Pont 8f GF 1 105
Jun 25 Curr 10f G 2 112
Jly 30 Gdwd 10f G 3 106
Aug 21 Deau 10f G 2 **115**
Sep 18 Curr 10f G 1 112
Oct 2 Lonc 10f G 6 108

RED CHAIRMAN 3
Jan 13 Ling 10f SD 2 **100**

RED CONTACT 4
Feb 10 Sthl 7f SD 2 102
Mar 8 Sthl 8f SD 2 **112**

RED DAMSON 4
Jly 26 Gdwd 14f G 8 **103**
Aug 6 NmkJ 16f G 2 102

RED FINESSE 3
Oct 4 Leic 6f G 3 **100**

RED FOREST 6
Jly 30 Thsk 16f G 2 **104**
Aug 10 Bevl 16f GF 5 102
Nov 21 Sthl 14f SW 7 99

RED HAPPY 3
Jly 6 Naas 10f GF 2 **103**
Jly 16 Curr 10f GF 2 **103**

RED LANCER 4
Feb 5 Ling 12f GF 7 100
Mar 12 Wolv 8½f SD 7 106
Mar 28 Kemp 10f GS 3 103
Apr 16 Newb 12f GS 7 102
May 6 Ches 13½f GS 5 103
May 21 Ling 11½f GS 2 103
Jun 3 Epsm 10f G 6 **110**
Jun 17 York 10½f G 10 103
Jly 2 Hayd 12f GF 2 107
Jly 9 York 10½f G 8 101
Jly 18 Ayr 10f GF 4 105
Aug 6 Hayd 10½f GF 6 106
Aug 20 Ches 13½f G 7 103
Aug 27 Wind 11½f G 7 102

RED MO 4
Jun 27 Lonc 7f G 5 **111**

RED MONARCH 4						
Apr	26	Sthl	6f	FT	2	**99**
May	5	Folk	6f	G	7	**99**

RED OPERA 3						
Sep	6	Catt	14f	GF	1	**105**
Sep	12	Rdcr	14f	G	4	100

RED PEONY 3						
Aug	10	Sals	10f	G	6	102
Aug	23	Yarm	10f	G	2	106
Aug	31	York	12f	G	1	**108**
Oct	10	Wind	11½f	G	2	102

RED RACKETEER 3						
Aug	1	Ripn	10f	G	1	103
Aug	13	Ripn	12f	GS	2	102
Sep	7	Epsm	10f	G	3	105
Sep	24	Ripn	10f	GF	1	**109**
Oct	1	NmkR	10f	G	6	101

RED RIVER REBEL 7						
May	30	Leic	12f	G	1	**105**
Jly	1	Bevl	12f	G	3	101
Jly	26	Bevl	12f	G	1	102

RED ROMEO 4						
Apr	30	NmkR	6f	G	21	102
Jly	24	Pont	8f	G	5	101
Sep	25	Muss	7f	G	1	**107**
Nov	12	Ling	8f	FT	2	102
Nov	19	Ling	7f	FT	10	101

RED RUDY 3						
Aug	26	Newc	9f	GF	4	**104**

RED SAIL 4						
Jun	1	Yarm	11½f	G	5	102
Jun	17	NmkJ	12f	GF	6	**105**
Nov	9	Wolv	12f	FT	4	99

RED SANS 3						
Dec	30	Ling	10f	FT	4	**100**

RED SCORPION 6						
Jun	18	NmkJ	15f	G	3	**106**

RED SOVEREIGN 4						
Jan	5	Ling	6f	SD	7	99
May	27	Brig	5½f	GF	1	**105**
Jun	28	Brig	5½f	F	8	101
Aug	6	Ling	6f	G	1	103

RED SPELL 4						
Apr	23	Sand	8f	G	3	105
May	7	NmkR	9f	GF	7	101
May	28	Gdwd	8f	G	1	106
Jun	11	Sand	7f	G	7	110
Jun	22	Sals	8f	G	5	103
Jly	5	NmkJ	8f	G	12	99
Sep	10	Gdwd	9f	G	3	107
Sep	23	Ling	10f	G	6	103
Oct	27	Ling	7f	SD	2	108
Nov	19	Ling	7f	FT	1	**114**
Nov	26	Ling	8f	FT	1	109
Dec	9	Wolv	7f	FT	6	103

RED SQUARE LADY 7						
Jun	1	Leop	14f	G	7	106
Jly	2	Leop	12f	GF	3	**107**

RED SUN 8						
Jly	9	Ches	16f	GF	4	**104**

REDSPIN 5						
May	7	Bevl	16f	G	7	100

REDWOOD ROCKS 4						
Jun	18	Rdcr	7f	GF	1	**107**
Sep	1	Carl	8f	G	1	104

REDWOOD STAR 5						
Apr	24	Brig	5½f	GF	5	99
Jun	9	Brig	5½f	G	1	101
Jun	28	Brig	5½f	F	1	**106**
Jly	22	Chep	5f	G	3	102
Aug	2	Brig	5½f	G	2	99
Aug	9	Bath	5f	GF	1	103
Aug	15	Brig	5½f	G	3	100
Aug	26	Bath	5f	G	3	100

REEFSCAPE 4						
Apr	24	Lonc	10½f	GS	2	111
Jun	3	Epsm	12f	G	3	109
Jun	26	StCl	12f	GF	5	**114**
Aug	21	Deau	15f	G	2	111
Oct	23	Lonc	15½f	GS	2	113

REGAL ATTIRE 3						
May	30	Chep	12f	G	4	**101**

REGAL DREAM 3						
May	16	Wind	5f	G	6	99
May	27	Brig	6f	GF	1	99
Jly	14	Epsm	7f	G	1	**102**
Jly	23	York	7f	G	2	99
Aug	19	Wolv	7f	FT	1	101

REGENCY RED 7						
Jan	2	Sthl	11f	SD	5	100
Jan	21	Wolv	12f	SD	2	105
Jan	24	Wolv	14f	SD	2	101
Feb	8	Sthl	11f	SD	2	**107**
Mar	16	Wolv	9½f	SD	5	101
Apr	2	Wolv	12f	FT	3	101
Jun	27	Muss	12f	G	4	101
Jly	19	Yarm	11½f	G	7	100
Aug	8	Wolv	12f	SD	3	99

REGENT'S SECRET 5						
May	11	Newc	9f	G	4	99
May	17	Rdcr	10f	G	4	100
Jun	28	Haml	9f	F	1	100
Jly	9	Haml	9f	F	1	**111**
Jly	15	Haml	9f	F	2	102
Jly	21	Sand	10f	GF	7	99
Jly	30	Haml	9f	F	2	105
Aug	10	Haml	9f	F	1	106
Aug	16	Haml	9f	F	2	103
Aug	22	Haml	8½f	F	2	103

REGGAE RHYTHM 11						
Mar	16	Wolv	16½f	SD	2	99
Apr	19	Sthl	16f	GF	5	100
Sep	26	Wolv	16½f	FT	1	**101**
Nov	5	Wolv	16½f	FT	2	100

REGINA 3						
Jun	11	Leic	5f	G	2	**103**

REGISTRAR 3						
May	30	Sand	7f	G	2	100
Sep	6	Ling	7f	G	1	100
Sep	17	Newb	7f	GF	7	**101**

REHEARSAL 4						
Jun	18	York	12f	G	3	107
Aug	6	Hayd	10½f	GF	3	107
Sep	17	Newb	10f	GF	15	106
Dec	16	Wolv	12f	FT	3	102

REINE ANNICKA 3						
Jun	27	Lonc	10½f	G	4	**107**

REISK SUPERMAN 7						
Jun	15	Leop	14f	G	2	**106**

RELUCTANT SUITOR 3						
Jun	19	Pont	12f	G	2	**102**

REM TIME 5						
Aug	10	Yarm	10f	G	2	**99**

REMAAL 3						
Jun	19	Pont	12f	G	1	**103**
Aug	15	Nott	14f	GF	4	101

REQUESTED PLEASURE 3						
May	25	Leop	8f	GF	1	**110**
Jun	25	Curr	10f	G	1	108
Jly	17	Curr	9f	F	10	100

RESONATE 7						
Jan	15	Ling	10f	SD	3	99
Feb	12	Wolv	8½f	FT	6	103
Mar	3	Ling	10f	SW	5	106
Jun	3	Epsm	10f	G	8	**109**
Jly	2	Hayd	12f	GF	3	107
Aug	2	Brig	12f	G	13	99
Aug	14	Bath	11½f	G	3	100
Sep	14	Yarm	10f	G	4	108
Dec	17	Ling	10f	FT	3	100

RESPLENDENT GLORY 3						
Jan	8	Ling	6f	SD	1	104
Jan	26	Ling	6f	FT	1	106
Apr	12	NmkR	6f	GF	3	100
May	1	Sals	6f	G	1	106
May	21	NmkR	6f	G	1	107
Jun	11	Sand	5f	G	1	105
Jly	2	Sand	5f	G	1	**108**

RESPLENDENT NOVA 3						
Feb	23	Ling	8f	G	2	99
Mar	7	Ling	7f	SD	1	99
Apr	26	Wwck	7f	GS	4	**107**
Jun	1	Wolv	8½f	FT	2	104
Jly	9	Ling	8f	SD	5	100
Aug	31	Ling	7f	SD	1	105

RESPLENDENT ONE 4						
Apr	2	Donc	8f	G	4	**110**
Sep	30	NmkR	8f	G	8	101

RESPLENDENT PRINCE 3						
Dec	20	Sthl	7f	SW	4	**103**

RESTART 4						
Apr	8	Sthl	14f	SW	3	100
Apr	16	Nott	14f	GS	4	101

RESTORATION 3						
Apr	16	Newb	8f	GS	1	102
Jly	22	NmkJ	8f	G	3	101
Sep	2	Hayd	8f	G	4	**105**

RESULT 5
Jun 1 Leop 14f G 21 **106**

RETIREMENT 6
Jun 27 Wind 8½f G 3 **100**

REVERENCE 4
Aug 13 Ripn 5f G 1 107
Aug 27 NmkJ 6f G 10 100
Sep 9 Donc 5f G 1 115
Oct 17 Pont 5f G 1 103
Oct 22 Donc 5f S 1 **119**

REVERIE SOLITAIRE 4
Apr 10 Lonc 10f S 4 **110**

REVERSIONARY 4
Jan 13 Sthl 8f SD 3 99
Apr 26 Sthl 8f FT 2 **100**

REVIEN 3
Feb 12 Ling 5f SD 1 99
Aug 7 Ling 5f G 2 **101**

REVOLVE 5
Oct 15 Ling 13f SD 4 **99**

REZZAGO 5
May 28 Donc 7f G 2 99
Jun 13 Thsk 7f G 4 101
Jly 1 Wolv 6f G 1 102
Jly 9 Ling 6f SD 1 99
Jly 21 Donc 6f GF 1 102
Aug 5 NmkJ 6f GF 3 **103**

RHODESIAN WINNER 6
Oct 15 NmkR 16f G 7 **99**

RICHTEE 4
Jun 20 Ripn 12f G 1 **99**

RIDGE BOY 4
May 2 Kemp 8f G 4 101
May 18 Gdwd 8f G 2 104
Jun 3 Epsm 8½f G 2 **108**
Jly 26 Gdwd 8f G 3 106
Aug 3 Epsm 8½f G 4 101

RIGHT ANSWER 3
Jun 24 Newc 5f G 7 **106**
Jly 18 Ayr 5f GF 6 103
Aug 6 Hayd 5f G 9 105

RIGHT KEY 3
Jly 17 Curr 12f F 4 **109**

RIGHTFUL RULER 3
Apr 23 Wolv 9½f SD 3 102
May 16 Bath 10f G 3 **105**

RILEY BOYS 4
Mar 29 Pont 8f S 4 105
May 17 Bevl 8½f GF 3 102
May 25 Ripn 8f G 6 104
Jun 22 Carl 8f GF 7 101
Jly 1 Bevl 8½f G 1 **110**

RING OF DESTINY 6
May 20 NmkR 12f G 5 **101**
Jun 4 Donc 12f GF 9 99
Jly 20 Sand 10f G 3 100
Aug 13 NmkJ 12f G 4 **101**

RINGMOOR DOWN 6
Apr 30 NmkR 5f G 3 **109**
May 14 Nott 6f F 3 104
May 31 Sand 5f G 9 103
Jun 26 Curr 5f GF 8 107

RINGSEND LADY 4
Jun 1 Leop 7f G 9 **100**

RINGSIDER 4
Mar 18 Ling 13f SD 3 99
May 1 NmkR 12f G 3 **112**
Sep 23 Ling 10f G 7 102

RIO RIVA 3
Apr 2 Donc 6f G 3 99
Apr 30 Thsk 7f S 2 102
Jly 12 Bevl 7½f GF 1 102
Oct 3 Pont 8f G 1 **108**
Oct 29 Wolv 9½f SD 4 106

RIQUEWIHR 5
Feb 18 Wolv 7f SD 2 101
Feb 23 Ling 7f SD 1 **104**
Mar 21 Ling 6f SD 11 99
Apr 8 Ling 6f SD 6 101
Apr 19 Folk 5f GS 2 **104**
May 3 Bath 5½f HY 1 103

RISE 4
Feb 12 Ling 6f SD 8 **105**
Feb 26 Ling 6f SD 3 99

RISING SHADOW 4
Apr 18 Pont 6f S 2 102
May 7 Bevl 5f GF 6 101
May 13 York 6f GS 6 101
Jun 1 Newc 6f G 1 103
Jun 4 Epsm 6f G 3 107
Jun 25 Newc 6f G 3 **108**
Jly 23 Newc 6f GF 2 104
Jly 30 Gdwd 6f G 10 106
Sep 24 Hayd 6f GF 5 100
Oct 8 York 6f GS 3 107
Oct 14 NmkR 7f G 5 107

RISK FREE 8
Jan 7 Wolv 8½f SW 2 **108**
Feb 4 Wolv 8½f SD 2 103
Feb 16 Ling 8f SD 4 102
Feb 24 Sthl 8f FT 3 103

RIVER ALHAARTH 3
May 2 Kemp 9f G 2 **103**

RIVER FALCON 5
Apr 15 Thsk 5f S 1 107
May 12 York 5f GS 1 **112**
May 28 Muss 5f G 5 107
Jun 18 York 6f GF 5 109
Jly 24 Newb 5f G 8 107
Aug 13 Ripn 6f G 3 103
Sep 17 Ayr 6f G 10 108
Oct 22 Donc 5f S 8 109

RIVER OF BABYLON 4
Apr 19 Sthl 7f GF 6 99
May 6 Haml 8½f GS 2 101
May 9 Rdcr 7f GS 1 **106**
Jun 25 Donc 8f GF 4 **106**
Jly 15 Wwck 7f GF 1 99
Aug 12 NmkJ 7f G 2 103
Aug 19 Sals 7f GS 3 102
Oct 7 Newb 7f GF 6 100

RIVER OF DIAMONDS 4
Aug 23 Brig 10f G 1 **99**

RIVER ROYALE 3
Mar 28 Wwck 7f GS 1 101
Apr 14 NmkR 7f G 1 **107**

RIVIERA RED 5
Dec 29 Ling 8f G 1 **103**

ROB ROY 3
Apr 14 NmkR 8f G 2 100
Sep 9 Donc 8f G 3 **105**
Sep 30 NmkR 8f G 1 **105**
Oct 15 NmkR 10f G 14 99

ROBBIE CAN CAN 6
Mar 24 Wolv 8½f SD 4 **101**

ROBESON 3
May 14 Thsk 8f G 5 **102**

ROBINZAL 3
Oct 19 Newc 8f GS 1 **103**

ROBWILLCALL 5
Aug 8 Thsk 8f G 2 **100**

ROCAMADOUR 3
Apr 14 NmkR 9f G 1 102
Apr 30 NmkR 10f G 1 105
Jun 5 Chan 10½f G 3 103
Jun 14 York 8f G 4 107
Jly 3 Chan 8f G 3 **115**

ROCK CHICK 3
May 28 Ling 10f SW 4 **105**
Oct 29 Wolv 9½f SD 2 100

ROCK CONCERT 7
Jan 5 Sthl 11f SD 3 99
Feb 14 Wolv 9½f SD 5 **100**

ROCK FEVER 3
Dec 29 Ling 5f SD 1 **105**

ROCK HAVEN 3
Jun 15 Nott 8f GF 3 **103**

ROCK LOBSTER 4
May 13 Nott 8f F 4 **101**
May 31 Rdcr 9f G 2 99

ROCK MUSIC 3
Jan 26 Ling 8f FT 1 102
Oct 14 NmkR 7f G 11 **104**

ROCKAZAR 4
Jun 8 Leop 8f F 11 **100**

ROCKET FORCE 5
Jly 22 York 14f G 6 **106**
Aug 2 Catt 14f G 4 104
Sep 23 Hayd 10½f G 4 104

ROCKY REPPIN 5
Mar 8 Sthl 7f SD 3 **101**
Apr 5 Sthl 7f SD 2 100

ROHAANI 3						
Apr	27	Pont	10f	GS	1	100
Jly	30	Thsk	8f	G	1	108
Sep	17	Newb	10f	GF	4	**112**

ROKOCOKO 3						
Jun	1	Leop	7f	G	10	**100**

ROLEX FREE 7						
Feb	17	Sthl	12f	G	4	100
Mar	4	Wolv	8½f	SD	1	**104**

ROMAN ARMY 3						
May	2	Wwck	12½f	G	5	**101**
Jun	21	Newb	13½f	G	3	**101**

ROMAN MAZE 5						
Jan	7	Wolv	7f	SW	4	101
Jan	29	Ling	7f	SD	3	108
Feb	8	Ling	6f	SD	2	**109**
Feb	18	Wolv	6f	SD	1	107
Mar	4	Wolv	6f	SD	3	104
Mar	12	Wolv	6f	SD	8	103
Aug	6	Rdcr	7f	G	1	106
Aug	12	NmkJ	6f	G	2	99
Aug	19	Ches	7f	GF	6	103
Aug	20	Ches	7½f	G	1	102
Sep	16	Ayr	6f	GF	2	102
Sep	30	NmkR	7f	G	5	104
Oct	8	York	6f	GS	7	100
Oct	27	Ling	7f	SD	9	104

ROMAN QUINTET 5						
Jan	29	Ling	10f	SD	11	102
Feb	12	Ling	6f	SD	3	**108**
Mar	3	Ling	8f	SW	1	105
Apr	11	Sthl	7f	G	2	99
May	23	Wind	6f	F	2	102
Jun	13	Wind	6f	GF	3	101
Jly	27	Leic	6f	G	1	103

ROMAN THE PARK 4						
May	10	Muss	9f	G	3	**99**

ROMANY NIGHTS 5						
May	23	Wind	6f	F	5	101
Jun	18	NmkJ	6f	G	3	100
Jly	22	NmkJ	6f	G	1	**106**
Aug	17	Epsm	6f	G	1	105
Sep	3	NmkJ	6f	G	11	102
Sep	21	Gdwd	6f	GF	14	99
Oct	29	NmkR	7f	S	7	100
Dec	20	Ling	6f	S	6	100

ROMIL STAR 8						
Jan	11	Sthl	12f	SW	1	104
Feb	3	Sthl	12f	SD	1	101
Feb	8	Sthl	11f	SD	2	**110**
Feb	17	Sthl	12f	SD	5	99
Feb	26	Sthl	12f	FT	5	102
Nov	29	Sthl	12f	SD	1	103
Dec	10	Sthl	14f	FT	2	102

RONSARD 3						
Jun	25	Newc	8f	G	4	102
Oct	9	Gdwd	8f	G	3	**105**

ROOD BOY 4						
Dec	4	Sthl	11f	FT	1	100

ROODEYE 3						
May	21	NmkR	6f	G	6	101
Jun	6	Folk	6f	G	2	100
Jun	11	Sand	7f	G	3	109
Jly	5	NmkJ	7f	G	4	103
Jly	14	Donc	7f	GF	1	104
Jly	29	Gdwd	7f	G	4	**110**
Aug	14	Bath	8f	G	8	103
Sep	8	Donc	7f	G	6	100
Sep	25	NmkR	7f	G	6	109

ROOFTOP PROTEST 8						
Jun	1	Leop	16f	G	4	105
Jun	26	Curr	16f	F	7	101
Aug	7	Curr	16f	G	8	103
Sep	18	Curr	16f	G	3	106
Oct	9	Curr	16f	GS	11	102
Nov	3	Muss	16f	GS	1	102

ROSAPENNA 3						
Apr	26	Wwck	7f	GS	2	**107**
Jly	21	Folk	6f	GF	1	103
Aug	12	Newb	6f	G	2	100

ROSAWA 3						
Sep	4	Lonc	10f	GF	1	**106**
Oct	2	Lonc	10f	G	9	103

ROSE BIEN 3						
Nov	10	Ling	12f	SD	5	**99**

ROSECLIFF 3						
Feb	12	Ling	8f	SD	4	99
Mar	28	Kemp	9f	G	3	**102**
May	1	Sals	10f	GS	2	100
Jun	3	Thsk	12f	G	1	99
Oct	19	Bath	11½f	GS	8	99

ROSEIN 3						
Sep	10	Ches	5f	GS	4	**105**

ROSIE'S RESULT 5						
Aug	2	Catt	5f	GF	2	**100**

ROTUMA 6						
May	20	Hayd	10½f	G	8	99
Jun	11	Leic	10f	G	6	99
Jly	19	Ayr	10f	G	3	**102**

ROUGE ET NOIR 7						
Jun	18	Rdcr	14f	G	2	**100**

ROWAN LODGE 3						
Jun	25	Ches	7f	G	3	101
Jly	27	Sand	7f	GS	5	101
Sep	2	NmkJ	8f	G	10	**103**

ROWAN PURSUIT 4						
Feb	21	Ling	8f	SD	1	**100**
Mar	21	Ling	10f	SD	4	**100**
Jun	4	Ling	10f	SD	2	**100**

ROWAN WARNING 3						
Jly	7	Donc	8f	GF	4	99
Sep	13	Yarm	11½f	G	6	**102**

ROYAL ALCHEMIST 3						
Apr	16	Newb	7f	GS	2	101
May	13	York	7f	GS	5	99
Jun	17	York	8f	G	5	107
Sep	24	NmkR	8f	G	6	**109**
Oct	2	Lonc	10f	G	7	108
Oct	13	NmkR	10f	G	2	107
Nov	5	Donc	10½f	S	3	103

ROYAL ATALZA 8						
Jan	22	Ling	16f	FT	10	100
Jun	18	NmkJ	15f	G	5	**105**
Aug	28	Yarm	14f	G	5	99

ROYAL AUDITON 4						
Jun	11	Ling	12f	SW	3	**99**

ROYAL AXMINSTER 10						
Jan	3	Sthl	12f	SD	3	**102**
Jun	29	Chep	12f	G	5	101
Jly	19	Yarm	11½f	G	6	100

ROYAL CAVALIER 8						
May	1	NmkR	12f	G	7	**107**
Jly	2	Hayd	12f	GF	13	100
Jly	16	Ripn	12f	G	5	105
Aug	3	Pont	12f	G	7	101
Sep	3	Hayd	14f	GF	10	103

ROYAL CHALLENGE 4						
May	25	NmkR	7f	G	5	101
Aug	3	Yarm	6f	G	1	**107**
Aug	27	York	6f	G	7	100
Sep	25	Muss	7f	G	9	101
Oct	16	Muss	7f	G	4	101

ROYAL DIGNITARY 5						
May	21	Catt	7f	GF	6	102
Jun	3	Epsm	8½f	G	5	**105**
Aug	6	Rdcr	7f	G	3	102
Aug	16	Haml	9f	F	3	102
Aug	22	Haml	8½f	F	1	104

ROYAL HIGHNESS 3						
Sep	11	Lonc	12f	G	2	**111**

ROYAL ISLAND 3						
Jly	30	Thsk	8f	G	4	106
Aug	6	Hayd	8f	GF	1	104
Sep	10	Donc	8f	GS	2	**108**
Oct	7	York	8f	G	4	106

ROYAL JELLY 3						
Jun	25	NmkJ	8f	G	7	**99**

ROYAL JET 3						
May	16	Bath	10f	G	1	**106**
Jly	17	Rdcr	11f	G	2	102
Aug	1	Ripn	10f	G	2	101
Aug	7	Leic	12f	GF	1	101
Aug	20	Bevl	10f	GF	10	99
Aug	31	York	12f	G	4	104
Sep	21	Gdwd	11f	G	3	104
Oct	4	Leic	12f	G	2	**106**

ROYAL MASTER 3						
Jan	19	Ling	6f	FT	3	**100**
Sep	19	Carl	8f	G	2	**100**

ROYAL MELBOURNE 5						
Jan	10	Wolv	12f	SD	3	101
Apr	20	Catt	12f	S	1	**103**
May	11	Newc	12½f	G	2	99
Jly	8	Wolv	14f	FT	2	99
Oct	9	Newc	12½f	G	3	99

ROYAL MILLENNIUM 7						
Apr	2	Donc	6f	G	4	106
May	11	York	6f	S	10	101
Jun	18	York	6f	GF	4	**110**
Jly	7	NmkJ	6f	G	15	99

ROYAL ORISSA 3
Mar 26 Kemp 6f G 1 100
Apr 27 Ling 6f GS 3 102
Jun 2 Hayd 6f G 5 100
Jly 2 Sand 7f G 11 100
Jly 23 Newb 7f GF 16 **104**

ROYAL PRINCE 4
Apr 23 Sand 8f G 2 106
May 28 Gdwd 8f G 5 102
Jun 15 York 8f G 4 110
Jly 23 Newb 10f GF 3 101
Jly 30 NmkJ 8f GF 4 **111**
Sep 10 Gdwd 7f G 5 110
Sep 17 Newb 9f GF 2 101

ROYAL REBEL 9
May 30 Sand 16½f G 8 **99**

ROYAL STORM 6
Jun 2 Hayd 7f G 7 103
Jun 12 Sals 6f G 3 105
Jun 25 NmkJ 7f G 4 104
Jly 26 Gdwd 7f G 4 **112**
Aug 7 Deau 6½f G 9 109
Aug 29 Wwck 7f GF 7 99

ROYAL WEDDING 3
Jan 5 Sthl 8f SD 1 **99**

ROYAL WINDMILL 6
May 9 Rdcr 6f GS 4 **100**

RUBIES 3
Sep 13 Yarm 6f G 1 **108**

RUBY BROWN 3
Aug 7 Ling 8f SD 2 **99**

RUBY LEGEND 7
Jly 19 Ayr 10f G 4 101
Aug 12 Newc 10f GS 2 100
Aug 26 Newc 9f GF 2 **104**
Sep 5 Newc 10f G 5 101

RUBY ROCKET 4
Apr 14 NmkR 6f G 7 101
May 7 Ling 7f G 4 106
Sep 26 Haml 6f F 1 107
Oct 13 NmkR 6f G 2 107
Nov 1 MsnL 6f GF 4 **113**

RUBY WINE 3
Jun 8 Newb 10f GF 1 100
Jly 2 Hayd 12f GF 4 101
Jly 31 Newb 12f G 5 **108**

RUBY'S DREAM 3
Jly 2 Leic 6f GF 1 **102**
Aug 10 Yarm 6f GF 4 100

RUDAKI 3
Sep 15 Pont 10f G 4 **100**

RUDI'S PET 11
May 9 Rdcr 6f GS 6 99
May 28 Muss 5f G 4 102
Jun 16 Bevl 5f G 2 100
Jly 4 Muss 5f GF 1 **106**
Jly 20 Catt 5f GF 1 103

RULE FOR EVER 3
Jly 5 Pont 12f G 6 **99**

RULING REEF 3
Jun 22 Bath 8f G 1 101
Aug 28 Bevl 10f GS 1 **104**

RUNAWAY 3
Aug 2 Deau 10f G 1 109
Sep 11 Lonc 12f G 2 **114**
Oct 1 Lonc 9½f G 3 105

RUSSIAN BLUE 3
Apr 3 Curr 7f S 4 **102**

RUSSIAN HILL 5
Aug 21 Deau 10f G 6 **110**

RUSSIAN SYMPHONY 4
Jan 7 Wolv 7f SW 2 107
Feb 8 Ling 6f SD 1 **110**
Mar 4 Wolv 6f SD 2 105
Mar 12 Wolv 6f SD 3 105
Jun 2 Hayd 6f G 3 104
Jun 25 Wind 6f G 7 105
Jly 5 Pont 6f G 4 104
Jly 29 Gdwd 6f G 6 102
Aug 8 Wind 6f GF 2 103
Oct 30 Ling 6f SD 2 109
Nov 19 Ling 7f FT 7 107

RUSSIAN TSAR 4
Apr 3 Curr 10f S 8 **104**

RUSTLER 3
Jun 17 NmkJ 8f GF 2 103
Aug 13 NmkJ 8f G 2 102
Sep 8 Epsm 8½f G 2 **104**
Sep 20 Brig 8f G 1 101
Oct 19 Bath 8f GS 1 **104**

RUWI 3
Apr 10 Lonc 10½f S 1 110
May 9 Lonc 11f G 4 103
Jun 5 Chan 10½f G 5 103
Aug 20 Deau 10f GS 2 **114**
Sep 17 Lonc 10f G 2 108
Oct 1 Lonc 9½f G 2 107
Oct 30 StCl 8f G 4 113

RYAN'S FUTURE 5
Sep 2 NmkJ 12f G 4 **105**
Sep 17 Ayr 10f G 1 103
Oct 5 Nott 10f G 5 104
Oct 25 Yarm 10f S 7 101

RYDAL 4
Jan 7 Wolv 6f SW 2 **111**
Mar 12 Wolv 6f SD 2 106
Mar 19 Ling 7f SD 3 106
Mar 31 Donc 6f G 5 101
Apr 30 NmkR 6f G 11 108
Jly 1 Sand 5f G 7 100
Jly 8 Ling 6f SW 2 106
Dec 6 Sthl 5f FT 2 105

RYEDANE 3
Jly 13 Catt 5f G 1 **102**
Sep 9 Donc 5f G 13 99

RYNINCH 4
Jun 1 Leop 7f G 5 **108**
Jun 8 Leop 8f F 2 106
Jly 2 Leop 7f F 4 103

RYONO 6
May 1 StCl 8f HD 4 **115**
Jly 24 MsnL 8f F 4 113

S

SAADIGG 3
May 14 Newb 11f G 3 **103**

SAAMEQ 4
Jan 10 Wolv 12f SD 1 **104**

SABBEEH 4
Aug 6 NmkJ 7f G 4 **112**
Aug 27 Gdwd 7f G 2 108
Sep 10 Donc 8f GS 3 108
Sep 27 Gdwd 7f G 2 106
Oct 22 Donc 7f S 2 101

SABBIOSA 3
Apr 21 Bath 8f GS 1 **101**

SABLIER NOIR 3
Jly 24 MsnL 10f F 9 **104**

SABRE D'ARGENT 5
Jun 4 Donc 10½f GF 1 **105**

SABRINA BROWN 4
Sep 15 Pont 6f G 1 **114**

SACHIN 4
Apr 8 Ling 10f SD 3 **100**
Jun 18 Ling 10f SW 6 **100**

SACRANUN 3
May 1 Sals 10f GS 3 100
May 23 Leic 10f G 2 100
Jun 6 Pont 10f GF 1 **103**

SAFARI SUNSET 3
May 20 Gdwd 5f G 5 100
Jun 30 Epsm 6f G 4 **103**
Jly 28 Gdwd 7f G 6 100
Sep 11 Gdwd 6f G 6 **103**
Sep 23 Ling 6f G 5 100

SAFE SHOT 6
Jun 27 Muss 12f G 5 **99**

SAFENDONSEABISCUIT 3
Jan 4 Ling 6f FT 2 **100**

SAFFRON FOX 4
May 26 Bath 17½f G 3 **102**
Jun 30 Hayd 14f GF 6 101

SAFIRAH 4
Jly 1 Hayd 12f G 4 **105**

SAFSOOF 3
Jun 11 Sand 7f G 6 **105**
Sep 16 Newb 7f GF 1 103
Sep 30 NmkR 7f G 9 101

SAHARA PRINCE 5
May 25 Leop 7f GF 1 **109**
Jun 8 Leop 8f F 8 102

Sep 4 Curr 8f G 12 103

SAHARA SILK 4
Apr 28 Sthl 5f G 3 100
Jun 8 Bevl 5f G 1 99
Jun 20 Muss 5f G 1 103
Jun 28 Haml 5f F 2 102
Jly 30 Haml 5f F 1 **105**

SAIDA LENASERA 4
Apr 19 Sthl 16f GF 1 **104**
May 7 Bevl 16f G 2 102
May 25 Ripn 16f G 3 102

SAIF SAREEA 5
Sep 20 Bevl 10f GF 1 107

SAINT ETIENNE 4
Mar 28 Kemp 6f G 5 **105**
May 15 Ripn 6f G 3 101
Jun 21 Newb 6f GF 1 102
Jly 8 York 6f G 8 103

SAINTE JUST 6
Jan 21 Wolv 12f SD 1 **105**

SAINTLY RACHEL 7
Apr 3 Curr 10f S 1 **111**
Apr 10 Leop 12f GS 2 110
May 12 York 10½f S 3 105
Jun 18 York 12f G 7 101

SAINTLY THOUGHTS 10
Feb 23 Ling 16f G 1 **102**
Aug 31 Ling 16f G 6 99

SAKE 3
Jun 7 Rdcr 7f G 1 **104**
Aug 31 York 8f G 8 99

SALAMANCA 3
Jun 11 Ripn 6f G 11 99
Jun 18 Wwck 7f G 11 103
Jly 5 NmkJ 7f G 2 104
Jly 28 Gdwd 7f G 2 105
Aug 7 Leic 7f G 5 101
Aug 27 York 6f G 3 107
Sep 24 NmkR 8f G 1 **112**
Oct 14 NmkR 8f G 11 103

SALINGER 3
Dec 30 Ling 10f FT 3 **99**

SALINJA 3
May 18 Gdwd 9f G 2 **109**
Jun 9 Ripn 8f G 2 104
Jly 6 NmkJ 10f G 7 101
Aug 13 Gdwd 10f G 1 107
Sep 10 Gdwd 9f G 10 104
Oct 1 NmkR 10f G 3 103

SALISHAN 3
Jly 20 Naas 6f GF 2 **104**

SALON PRIVE 5
Jan 6 Wolv 5f GF 1 99
Feb 11 Wolv 5f SD 4 102
Feb 26 Ling 5f SD 3 102
Mar 18 Ling 6f SD 3 99
Apr 6 Ling 5f FT 1 **103**

SALSELON 6
Jly 24 MsnL 8f F 3 **113**

SALTANGO 6
Sep 16 Newb 11f G 12 103

SALTBURN LAD 3
May 30 Chep 12f G 2 **103**

SALTINO 3
May 9 Lonc 11f G 5 **101**

SALUT THOMAS 3
Mar 28 StCl 8f GS 2 **111**
May 15 Lonc 8f G 4 **111**
Jly 3 Chan 8f G 8 104

SALUTE 6
Jan 13 Ling 12f SD 4 **110**
May 20 NmkR 12f G 7 99
Jun 12 Sals 12f G 2 104
Jun 25 Wind 11½f G 1 109
Jly 9 Ling 16f SD 7 **110**
Jly 23 Newb 12f GF 12 101

SALVIATI 8
Jun 6 Wind 5f G 2 **104**
Jun 18 Ling 5f G 7 102
Jun 23 Sals 5f G 3 102
Jly 2 Bevl 5f G 2 **104**
Jly 15 Pont 5f GF 2 102
Jly 22 York 5f G 5 101
Aug 23 Yarm 5f G 6 101
Oct 7 York 5f G 5 99

SAM'S SECRET 3
Sep 4 York 7f GF 2 100
Sep 12 Rdcr 7f G 2 **102**

SAMANDO 5
Apr 3 Lonc 10f S 3 **115**
Oct 2 Lonc 12f G 13 104
Oct 23 Lonc 15½f GS 4 111

SAMUEL CHARLES 7
Mar 12 Wolv 7f SD 3 99
Apr 1 Ling 7f SD 1 **102**
Apr 2 Wolv 6f FT 2 100
Aug 19 Wolv 7f FT 2 100
Nov 15 Sthl 8f FT 5 99

SAMURAI WAY 3
Oct 19 Newc 12½f GS 2 **102**

SAN ANTONIO 5
Apr 18 Pont 8f S 1 107
Apr 27 Pont 8f GS 1 102
May 2 Kemp 8f G 1 105
May 25 Ripn 8f G 4 106
Jun 11 Sand 7f G 2 **113**
Jly 24 Pont 8f G 3 105
Aug 11 Sand 7f GF 5 107
Aug 29 Ripn 8f G 3 108
Oct 30 Ling 6f SD 2 111
Nov 26 Ling 8f FT 4 106

SAN DENG 3
Jun 4 Ling 7f G 2 **103**
Sep 28 Ling 12f SD 6 102

SAN HERNANDO 5
Jan 22 Ling 16f FT 7 **104**

SANCHI 3
Sep 21 Rdcr 10f GF 1 **102**
Oct 22 Donc 12f S 4 100

SAND AND STARS 4
May 20 NmkR 12f G 3 101
Oct 7 York 12f G 3 **103**

SAND FAIRY 3
May 21 Ling 10f GS 3 102
Jly 1 Hayd 8f G 3 104
Sep 14 Sand 8f G 3 **105**
Oct 9 Gdwd 8f G 5 103

SAND REPEAL 3
May 30 Chep 12f G 3 **102**
Jly 1 Wolv 12f G 5 99

SANDY OWEN 9
May 25 Leop 14f GF 7 **102**

SANDY'S LEGEND 3
Apr 20 Ling 10f FT 7 **99**

SANFRANCULLINAN 3
Jly 6 Naas 6f GF 1 107
Aug 20 Curr 6f GF 5 102
Oct 23 Curr 6f S 2 **108**

SANGIOVESE 6
Mar 8 Sthl 8f SD 8 99
Apr 23 Hayd 10½f G 3 104
May 6 Nott 10f G 1 101
Jly 27 Leic 10f G 4 102
Sep 16 Newb 11f G 5 **106**

SANSERIF 3
May 22 Curr 8f G 6 **111**
Jun 8 Leop 7f G 5 105
Jly 17 Curr 9f F 4 107

SANTA FE 3
May 21 NmkR 7f G 4 **100**

SANTANDO 5
Feb 5 Ling 12f G 6 100
Feb 12 Ling 10f SD 5 **106**
Sep 23 Ling 12f SD 10 99

SAOIRE 3
May 1 NmkR 8f G 6 107
May 22 Curr 8f G 1 113
Jun 25 Curr 10f G 8 111
Jly 17 Curr 12f F 6 108
Sep 10 Leop 8f GF 5 **115**

SAPAS 3
Jun 12 Chan 10½f G 9 **101**

SARABA 4
Feb 4 Wolv 9½f SD 2 102
Feb 16 Ling 12f SD 2 99
Mar 30 Folk 12f HY 2 **105**
May 25 Ling 10f G 3 **105**

SARIMA 3
Aug 7 Curr 16f G 12 **100**

SAROS 4
Apr 21 Sthl 7f FT 2 99
May 21 Carl 8f G 3 **103**

SARRAAF 9
- May 16 Muss 7f G 1 103
- May 21 Catt 7f GF 2 100
- Jun 13 Thsk 7f G 5 99
- Jun 27 Muss 7f GF 4 102
- Jly 28 Muss 7f G 3 102
- Aug 25 Muss 8f G 3 **105**
- Sep 4 York 8f G 10 100
- Sep 25 Muss 8f G 4 99
- Dec 16 Wolv 9½f FT 3 99

SASSO 3
- Sep 15 Pont 10f G 2 **103**

SATCHEM 3
- Apr 30 NmkR 8f G 9 **107**

SATWA QUEEN 3
- Jun 12 Chan 10½f G 7 104
- Aug 2 Deau 10f G 1 **116**
- Oct 2 Lonc 10f G 5 108

SAUCY 4
- Mar 22 Ling 10f SD 1 99
- Mar 31 Ling 10f SD 4 **105**

SAVILE'S DELIGHT 6
- Jan 1 Sthl 6f SD 4 100
- Jan 31 Wolv 7f SD 7 99
- Feb 24 Sthl 6f FT 2 101
- Feb 28 Wolv 5f SD 1 106
- Mar 8 Sthl 5f SD 5 100
- Apr 2 Kemp 5f GS 3 **107**
- Jun 6 Wind 5f G 1 105
- Jun 19 Wwck 6f G 8 104
- Aug 10 Sand 5f GF 5 99
- Sep 10 Ches 5f GS 5 105
- Dec 2 Wolv 6f SD 3 103

SAVIOURS SPIRIT 4
- Jan 20 Sthl 5f FT 3 101
- Feb 26 Ling 5f SD 8 100
- Apr 2 Kemp 5f GS 6 **105**

SAVOIE 3
- Jly 15 Wwck 11f G 5 **101**

SAVOY CHAPEL 3
- Feb 11 Wolv 7f SD 1 **102**
- Feb 25 Wolv 7f SD 1 100

SAWWAAH 8
- Apr 12 Muss 8f G 2 105
- May 6 Ches 7½f GS 5 **106**
- May 30 Sand 8f G 9 102
- Jun 3 Epsm 8½f G 6 103
- Aug 10 Haml 8½f F 2 100
- Aug 25 Muss 9f G 2 102
- Sep 12 Muss 9f GF 3 103
- Sep 15 Ayr 9f G 1 105

SAXON LIL 3
- Mar 29 Wwck 7f GS 3 101
- Jun 4 Ling 7f G 1 **105**
- Jun 9 Brig 7f G 3 99
- Jly 18 Bevl 7½f G 1 103
- Jly 27 Sand 7f GS 3 103
- Aug 10 Sand 7f GF 3 99

SCALADO 6
- Jun 15 Leop 9f GF 4 **103**

SCAMPERDALE 3
- Dec 19 Wolv 8½f FT 2 **104**

SCARLET INVADER 3
- May 24 Ling 7f G 1 **103**

SCARLETT ROSE 4
- Oct 30 Ling 7f SD 3 **99**

SCARRABUS 4
- Apr 26 Wwck 12½f GS 10 100

SCORPION 3
- May 8 Leop 10f S 1 109
- May 22 Curr 10f GS 2 101
- Jun 26 Curr 12f F 2 110
- Jly 14 Lonc 12f F 1 **114**
- Sep 10 Donc 14½f S 1 106
- Oct 2 Lonc 12f G 10 113

SCOTLAND THE BRAVE 5
- May 9 Rdcr 7f GS 3 **105**
- May 26 Ayr 7f G 3 99
- Oct 10 Ayr 8f S 2 101
- Oct 29 Ayr 7f HY 1 102

SCOTT 4
- Jun 30 Newb 11f G 5 **104**
- Jly 30 NmkJ 12f GF 8 100
- Aug 1 Wind 11½f GS 4 101
- Sep 17 Wolv 12f FT 2 102

SCOTTISH RIVER 6
- Jan 10 Wolv 9½f SD 11 100
- Jan 29 Ling 10f SD 14 100
- Feb 4 Wolv 12f SD 1 104
- Mar 8 Sthl 8f SD 5 **105**
- Apr 16 Wolv 8½f FT 2 103
- Jly 4 Wind 10f G 5 99
- Jly 14 Epsm 10f G 5 101
- Oct 31 Wolv 8½f SD 4 103
- Dec 3 Wolv 9½f SD 4 100
- Dec 17 Ling 10f FT 5 99

SCOTTY'S FUTURE 7
- Apr 12 Muss 8f G 3 **104**
- Sep 15 Ayr 9f G 3 101

SCREEN TEST 3
- Jun 25 Ling 10f SW 4 **102**

SCREENPLAY 4
- Jan 15 Ling 10f SD 5 102
- Mar 4 Wolv 12f SD 2 103
- Mar 24 Wolv 12f SD 1 100
- Aug 20 Ches 16f G 4 108

SCREWDRIVER 3
- Aug 10 Sals 8f G 2 104
- Aug 19 Sals 7f GS 4 102
- Aug 29 Wwck 7f GF 6 101
- Sep 6 Ling 7f SD 8 99
- Nov 15 Ling 7f FT 3 **105**
- Nov 29 Ling 8f FT 10 101
- Dec 20 Ling 8f FT 6 102

SCRIPTED 3
- Oct 9 Curr 5f GS 2 **101**

SCRIPTWRITER 3
- Jly 11 Wind 11½f G 1 **105**

SCURRA 6
- Jly 9 Ches 16f GF 5 **103**

SCUTCH MILL 3
- Jan 8 Ling 6f SD 4 99
- Feb 12 Ling 8f SD 3 **100**
- Apr 20 Ling 8f FT 1 99

SEA GIFT 3
- May 31 Rdcr 10f G 1 **102**

SEA HEIR 3
- Apr 29 Muss 9f G 5 **100**

SEA HUNTER 3
- May 13 Nott 8f F 3 101
- Jun 12 Donc 7f F 3 99
- Jun 18 NmkJ 7f G 1 103
- Jun 25 Ches 7f G 1 103
- Aug 7 Leic 7f G 1 105
- Sep 24 NmkR 7f G 7 **111**

SEA MAP 3
- Jly 23 Ling 10f SW 4 100
- Nov 25 Wolv 12f FT 1 **102**

SEA STORM 7
- Apr 12 Muss 8f G 4 103
- May 21 Catt 7f GF 3 **106**
- May 28 Muss 7f G 3 102
- Jun 8 Haml 8½f G 3 **106**
- Jun 17 Ayr 8f G 1 104
- Aug 19 Ches 7f GF 11 99
- Nov 12 Ling 8f FT 6 101

SEA WALL 3
- May 30 Chep 12f G 1 **107**
- Aug 9 Bath 11½f GF 1 104
- Aug 18 York 14f G 4 106

SEAFIELD TOWERS 5
- Jly 18 Ayr 5f GF 1 **103**

SEASONS ESTATES 3
- Apr 21 Bath 8f GS 2 100
- Jun 15 Chep 8f GS 1 **105**
- Jly 18 Wind 8½f G 1 100
- Aug 15 Wind 8½f GF 5 101

SEASONS PARKS 3
- Aug 26 Sals 8f G 2 **99**

SEATTLE ROBBER 3
- Aug 25 Muss 8f G 2 **106**

SECAM 6
- Jan 12 Ling 8f SD 1 **100**
- Apr 1 Ling 8f SD 7 **100**

SECLUDED 5
- Jun 1 Leop 16f G 11 **104**

SECOND REEF 3
- Apr 28 Rdcr 7f GF 1 **99**

SECRET AFFAIR 3
- Jly 13 Ling 8f SW 3 **102**

SECRET COVE 7
- Jun 1 Leop 14f G 23 **106**

SECRET HISTORY 3
Apr 14 Ripn 8f S 1 104
Apr 21 Bevl 7½f S 1 103
Apr 30 Gdwd 8f S 2 **107**
May 11 York 10½f S 1 99
Jun 16 York 12f G 5 102

SECRET KEY 5
Jun 1 Leop 7f G 18 **108**

SECRET PLACE 4
Feb 1 Ling 8f SD 2 **110**
May 29 NmkR 7f GF 4 105

SECRETARY GENERAL 4
May 1 NmkR 12f G 11 102
Jly 23 Newb 12f GF 10 101
Aug 8 Wind 8½f GF 5 100
Aug 26 Sals 10f G 4 100
Sep 19 Leic 8½f G 3 **105**
Oct 5 Nott 8f GF 5 99

SEDGE 5
Jan 27 Sthl 6f SD 3 **103**
Feb 4 Wolv 7f SD 1 99
Sep 1 Carl 7f G 4 101

SEIFI 6
May 7 Bevl 16f G 1 **103**

SELDEMOSA 4
Jan 13 Ling 8f SD 3 100
Jan 21 Wolv 8½f SD 1 **105**
Mar 23 Ling 8f SD 2 99
Apr 4 Wolv 9½f FT 4 100
Apr 22 Wolv 8½f SD 4 100

SELEBELA 4
May 12 York 10½f S 4 **102**
Jly 16 NmkJ 12f GF 6 100

SELECTIVE 6
May 21 Catt 7f GF 5 104
Jly 5 NmkJ 8f G 3 **106**

SELF DEFENSE 8
Aug 13 Newb 13½f G 3 102
Sep 3 NmkJ 12f G 6 100
Sep 25 NmkR 12f G 2 103
Sep 30 NmkR 12f G 7 99
Oct 22 Newb 12f G 2 108

SELF RESPECT 3
Apr 25 Wind 11½f GS 2 100
May 13 York 12f GS 1 **106**
May 31 Sand 14f G 5 101
Jun 17 York 12f G 7 101
Jly 24 Newb 12f G 2 99
Jly 30 Gdwd 11f G 2 101

SELIKA 3
Mar 29 Pont 10f S 2 **103**
Dec 12 Wolv 14f FT 9 100

SELMA 3
Feb 21 Ling 8f SD 1 **99**

SEMENOVSKII 5
Jly 11 Ayr 6f GF 3 99
Aug 3 Yarm 6f G 7 **102**
Oct 14 Brig 5½f G 1 101

SENATOR'S ALIBI 7
Mar 20 Curr 8f HY 10 104
May 21 Curr 8f G 8 107
Jun 8 Leop 8f F 7 102
Aug 14 Leop 7f F 7 100
Sep 4 Curr 8f G 6 **109**
Sep 10 Leop 7f HD 9 104
Oct 23 Curr 6f S 9 103

SENDINTANK 5
Jun 25 Newc 16f G 7 109
Aug 17 York 14f G 7 106
Sep 9 Donc 14½f G 1 106
Sep 24 NmkR 16f G 3 **112**

SENESCHAL 4
May 20 Hayd 8f G 9 101
Jun 3 Gdwd 7f GS 2 **106**
Jun 22 Epsm 7f G 7 100
Jly 16 Newb 8f GF 9 99
Dec 5 Ling 7f FT 3 100
Dec 20 Ling 6f FT 3 101

SENIOR WHIM 3
Aug 11 Chep 12f G 4 **99**

SENOR BENNY 6
Mar 20 Curr 5f HY 4 99
Apr 3 Curr 7f S 6 104
Jun 26 Curr 5f GF 9 **106**
Sep 17 Curr 5f G 14 101
Oct 23 Curr 6f S 6 105

SENOR BOND 4
Apr 29 Muss 8f G 3 101
May 16 Muss 7f G 4 101
Jly 4 Muss 8f GF 1 104
Jly 15 Haml 8½f F 1 101
Jly 27 Muss 8f GF 2 102
Dec 29 Ling 10f GF 3 **107**

SENOR EDUARDO 8
Feb 8 Sthl 11f SD 9 99
Feb 21 Ling 10f FT 2 100
Feb 22 Ling 10f SD 3 **104**
Apr 13 Bevl 10f G 10 99

SENOR SET 4
Feb 19 Wolv 8½f G 6 **100**

SENTIERO ROSSO 3
Jun 24 Newc 5f G 1 **105**
Oct 1 Epsm 5f G 6 102
Nov 3 Muss 5f GS 4 103

SENTINEL 6
Jly 6 NmkJ 16f G 3 100
Jly 23 Newb 12f GF 5 **106**
Aug 6 NmkJ 16f G 8 99

SERBELLONI 5
Jan 12 Wolv 14f SD 1 107
Mar 12 Wolv 16½f SD 1 100
Jly 1 Sand 14f G 4 102

SERGEANT CECIL 6
May 14 Newb 12f G 2 109
Jun 4 Epsm 12f G 3 108
Jun 25 Newc 16f G 1 **112**
Jly 26 Gdwd 14f G 3 107
Aug 17 York 14f G 1 109
Sep 8 Donc 18f G 2 110
Oct 15 NmkR 18f G 1 107

SERGEANT SLIPPER 8
Apr 26 Yarm 6f GS 1 **101**

SERIEUX 6
Apr 16 Thsk 8f HY 6 99
May 23 Thsk 7f G 1 **106**
Jly 28 Gdwd 7f G 5 101

SERJEANT AT ARMS 6
Jan 21 Wolv 12f SD 9 99
May 21 Curr 12f G 13 **100**

SEROV 7
Mar 20 Curr 5f HY 1 101
Sep 17 Curr 5f G 5 **106**
Oct 9 Curr 5f GS 5 100

SERPENTA 6
Apr 24 Lonc 10½f GS 9 **101**

SERRAMANNA 4
Jly 29 NmkJ 12f G 3 102
Aug 4 Chep 12f G 1 **103**
Aug 5 Ling 10f GS 2 102
Sep 5 Wwck 11f G 1 100
Sep 17 Wwck 11f G 1 99
Sep 28 Ling 12f SD 5 102

SERRE CHEVALIER 4
Apr 23 Leic 6f G 3 105
May 25 NmkR 7f G 1 108
Aug 19 Ches 7f GF 1 110
Aug 27 Gdwd 7f G 1 110
Sep 10 Gdwd 7f G 1 **114**
Sep 27 Gdwd 7f G 5 105

SET ALIGHT 4
Jan 5 Sthl 7f SD 2 100
Jan 25 Sthl 7f FT 1 99
Jan 27 Sthl 7f SD 1 102
Feb 17 Sthl 7f SD 1 103
Feb 24 Sthl 7f FT 1 **107**
May 29 NmkR 6f GF 3 101

SETTLEMENT CRAIC 4
Jun 25 Wind 11½f G 4 **105**

SEULEMENT 3
Aug 2 Deau 10f G 4 **106**

SEVEN MAGICIANS 3
May 7 Ling 11½f G 2 **102**
Jun 2 Sand 10f G 1 99
Jly 2 Hayd 12f GF 6 101

SEVEN NO TRUMPS 8
Mar 28 Wwck 5f GS 1 101
Apr 4 Yarm 5f G 2 104
Jun 6 Wind 5f G 9 100
Jun 15 Haml 5f G 1 **105**
Aug 22 Leic 5f G 2 101
Aug 26 Bath 5f G 4 100
Sep 21 Rdcr 5f GF 5 101

SEVERELY 3
Aug 29 Chep 16f G 1 **101**

SEW'N'SO CHARACTER 4
Apr 1 Donc 8f G 3 104
Apr 23 Sand 8f G 5 104

May 6 Ches 7½f GS 1 **108**
May 20 Hayd 8f G 10 101
Jun 26 Wind 8½f G 3 106
Jly 13 Ling 8f SW 3 **108**
Jly 26 Gdwd 10f G 8 104
Aug 6 Hayd 8f GF 3 102
Sep 4 Curr 8f G 8 **108**
Sep 23 Hayd 8f G 3 104
Sep 30 NmkR 8f G 4 103
Oct 14 NmkR 8f G 13 100

SEWMUCH CHARACTER 6
Mar 21 Ling 6f G 10 99
May 5 Folk 6f G 5 **102**

SEYAADI 3
Apr 1 Donc 10½f GS 4 **102**

SFORZANDO 4
Jly 19 Yarm 7f G 5 **107**

SHAABAN 4
Feb 19 Wolv 8½f G 3 **103**

SHABERNAK 6
Apr 6 Nott 14f GS 4 108
May 6 Ches 13½f GS 2 107
May 28 Gdwd 12f G 6 104
Jly 2 Sand 16½f G 1 **113**

SHADE COZY 3
Nov 29 Ling 6f FT 1 **101**

SHADES OF BEIGE 3
Jun 19 Pont 12f G 3 **101**

SHADOW JUMPER 4
Dec 16 Wolv 6f FT 3 **101**

SHAHEER 3
Nov 26 Wolv 8½f FT 2 **99**

SHAHZAN HOUSE 6
Mar 29 Pont 10f S 2 108
Apr 20 Epsm 10f GS 2 **110**
Jly 26 Gdwd 10f G 4 105
Aug 6 Wind 8½f GF 10 99

SHALAPOUR 3
Jun 26 Curr 12f F 3 **108**
Aug 14 Leop 12f F 2 107
Sep 17 Curr 14f G 7 101

SHAMARDAL 3
May 15 Lonc 8f G 1 **113**
Jun 5 Chan 10½f G 1 105
Jun 14 York 8f G 1 **113**

SHAMDALA 3
Jly 14 Lonc 12f F 1 113
Aug 17 York 12f G 6 106
Oct 1 Lonc 15f G 1 **114**
Oct 23 Lonc 15½f GS 3 112

SHAME ON YOU 3
Jun 27 Lonc 10½f G 6 **106**

SHAMROCK BAY 3
Jun 7 Ches 10½f GF 1 **100**

SHAMWARI FIRE 5
Sep 3 Folk 9½f GF 4 **99**

SHANKLY BOND 3
May 21 Carl 9½f G 3 100
Jly 5 Pont 10f G 3 102
Jly 13 Catt 12f GF 3 99
Dec 12 Wolv 9½f FT 1 **103**

SHANNON SPRINGS 3
Apr 12 NmkR 12f GF 1 100
May 5 Ches 12½f GS 5 99
Sep 7 Epsm 10f G 1 107
Sep 22 Pont 10f G 4 **108**
Oct 9 Gdwd 10f G 9 102

SHAPE UP 5
Feb 4 Wolv 12f SD 2 103
Feb 19 Wolv 12f SD 3 106
Feb 26 Sthl 12f FT 1 **107**
Mar 8 Sthl 12f SD 3 100

SHAPIRA 4
May 1 NmkR 9f G 4 107
Jly 31 Deau 8f G 2 **115**
Oct 1 NmkR 8f G 4 104

SHARAAB 4
Mar 7 Wolv 12f SD 10 **100**

SHARABY 3
May 10 Yarm 7f GF 2 99
May 17 Rdcr 7f G 1 101
Jun 24 Wolv 7f SD 3 100
Jly 11 Wolv 7f SD 7 99
Jly 22 Chep 7f G 1 **102**
Aug 4 Yarm 7f GF 4 99

SHARADI 4
Jun 6 Pont 17f GF 5 **100**

SHARED DREAMS 3
Jly 4 Wind 8½f G 2 101
Aug 12 Folk 9½f G 3 104
Sep 14 Yarm 10f G 3 **105**

SHARP REPLY 3
Jun 20 Wind 11½f G 1 **103**

SHARPLAW STAR 3
Jun 18 NmkJ 5f G 2 **99**

SHASHANA 3
Jly 5 Pont 10f G 2 **99**

SHASTYE 4
Jun 19 Pont 12f G 2 **110**
Jly 2 Hayd 12f GF 5 101

SHAUNAS VISION 6
Jly 2 Leop 12f GF 2 **110**

SHAWANDA 3
Jly 17 Curr 12f F 1 115
Sep 11 Lonc 12f G 1 112
Oct 2 Lonc 12f G 6 **118**

SHAYRAZAN 4
Sep 17 Curr 8f GF 3 **109**

SHE'S MY OUTSIDER 3
Jun 18 Wwck 7f G 10 **104**
Aug 3 Brig 8f G 8 102
Aug 13 Gdwd 8f G 3 99
Oct 9 Gdwd 8f G 6 100

SHE'S SUPERSONIC 5
Jun 15 Leop 14f G 4 **105**

SHEBOYGAN 3
Apr 27 Ling 7½f S 1 100
May 22 Curr 8f G 14 **104**

SHERIFF'S DEPUTY 5
Jan 12 Wolv 8½f SD 2 **103**
Mar 4 Wolv 8½f SD 4 101
Aug 11 Chep 8f G 4 100
Sep 4 York 8f G 7 **103**
Sep 28 Ling 12f SD 10 100

SHERSHA 6
Aug 20 Curr 6f GF 7 **106**
Sep 10 Leop 7f HD 11 103

SHIELALIGH 4
Jan 31 Wolv 6f SD 3 99
May 3 Bath 5½f HY 3 101
Jun 29 Chep 6f G 3 **102**
Aug 18 Chep 8f GF 5 101

SHIFTY 6
Jan 13 Sthl 8f SD 2 100
Feb 7 Wolv 8½f FT 4 99
Feb 24 Sthl 8f FT 4 101
Mar 2 Sthl 8f SD 3 100
Mar 12 Sthl 8f SD 1 100
Apr 26 Sthl 7f FT 1 **104**
May 7 Thsk 7f GS 1 101
May 23 Carl 8f GS 1 101

SHIFTY NIGHT 4
Jan 27 Sthl 6f SD 1 **108**
Feb 17 Sthl 6f SD 2 101
Feb 24 Sthl 6f FT 1 104
Mar 28 Yarm 7f GS 1 101

SHINGLE STREET 3
May 5 Folk 9½f GS 6 **100**

SHINY THING 3
Jly 25 Yarm 10f GS 3 100

SHIRLEY OAKS 7
Jan 24 Wolv 6f SD 1 **99**
Jly 16 Ling 6f G 2 **99**

SHIROCCO 4
Sep 11 Lonc 12f G 3 118
Oct 2 Lonc 12f G 4 **119**

SHOHRAH 3
Jly 29 Gdwd 7f G 5 **108**
Aug 14 Bath 8f G 6 104
Sep 14 Yarm 10f G 7 103

SHORT CHANGE 6
Aug 4 Chep 12f G 3 **101**

SHORT PAUSE 6
Apr 3 Lonc 10f S 2 115
Apr 24 Lonc 10½f GS 5 110
Jun 5 Chan 12f G 3 **117**

SHOT TO FAME 6
May 9 Wind 8½f GF 5 106
Jun 25 Wind 8½f G 6 101
Jly 16 Newb 10f GF 8 **107**
Oct 14 NmkR 8f G 6 **107**

SHOTLEY DANCER 6						
Aug	11	Bevl	16f	GF	4	99
Aug	28	Bevl	10f	GS	3	**102**

SHOW ME THE LOLLY 5						
Jly	19	Yarm	8f	G	1	**102**
Aug	22	Wolv	8½f	G	3	99
Oct	15	Ling	10f	SD	2	99

SHOWTIME ANNIE 4						
Feb	14	Wolv	9½f	SD	4	101
Mar	21	Sthl	8f	SD	4	102
Jly	19	Ayr	8f	G	2	**107**

SHRINK 4						
May	19	Newc	5f	G	1	102
May	23	Thsk	5f	G	1	**104**
May	27	Catt	5f	GF	2	102

SHUSH 7						
Jun	1	Yarm	10f	G	2	99
Jun	9	Wolv	12f	SD	1	**104**

SIAN THOMAS 4						
May	9	Wolv	14f	FT	2	103
Jun	1	Wolv	14f	FT	2	103
Sep	10	Leop	12f	GF	10	**107**

SICHILLA 3						
Jun	27	Lonc	7f	G	1	**109**

SIERRA VISTA 5						
Apr	30	Thsk	5f	S	2	104
May	15	Ripn	6f	G	4	100
Jun	25	Newc	6f	G	1	110
Jly	6	NmkJ	5f	GF	1	105
Jly	10	Hayd	6f	GF	4	99
Jly	27	Gdwd	5f	G	1	106
Jly	29	Gdwd	6f	G	5	103
Aug	14	Pont	6f	G	13	100
Aug	20	Bevl	5f	G	8	99
Sep	3	Hayd	5f	F	1	**112**
Sep	10	Ches	6f	GS	2	107
Sep	17	Ayr	6f	G	18	101
Sep	29	NmkR	6f	GF	4	101
Oct	13	NmkR	5f	G	1	111

SIGN OF THE WOLF 5						
Aug	21	Deau	15f	G	10	**101**

SIGNATORY 3						
Sep	15	Pont	10f	G	1	**104**
Oct	9	Gdwd	11f	G	2	102

SIGNIFICANT 3						
Jly	6	Naas	10f	GF	3	**103**

SIGNORA ROSSA 5						
Jly	16	Curr	10f	GF	3	**102**

SILENT JO 3						
Jun	4	Hayd	12f	G	5	102
Jun	30	Yarm	11½f	G	4	101
Jly	20	Ling	11½f	G	2	**105**
Aug	5	Ling	14f	GS	2	101
Aug	14	Bath	11½f	G	1	100
Sep	7	Epsm	12f	G	4	103

SILENT NAME 3						
May	15	Lonc	8f	G	9	106
Oct	1	Lonc	7f	G	4	**113**
Oct	30	StCl	8f	G	6	111

SILENT STORM 5						
Jan	17	Wolv	8½f	SD	6	103
Feb	8	Ling	6f	SD	5	102
Feb	9	Ling	7f	SD	8	99
Mar	3	Ling	8f	SW	4	103
Mar	12	Wolv	7f	SD	8	100
May	25	Ling	8f	SD	1	100
Jly	11	Wolv	7f	SD	2	103
Jly	22	Wolv	8½f	FT	4	100
Sep	1	Sals	8f	G	3	99
Sep	6	Ling	7f	SD	7	100
Sep	23	Ling	12f	SD	7	100
Oct	31	Wolv	8½f	SD	8	101
Dec	3	Wolv	9½f	SD	5	99
Dec	20	Ling	6f	SD	1	**105**

SILK AND SCARLET 3						
May	15	Lonc	8f	G	4	**108**
Jun	3	Epsm	12f	G	5	103

SILK FAN 4						
Jun	11	Sand	7f	G	6	**111**

SILK ROAD 3						
Aug	7	Deau	6½f	SD	1	**102**

SILK SCREEN 5						
Nov	6	Leop	16f	S	8	105

SILSONG 3						
Aug	27	Wind	8½f	G	6	100
Nov	21	Sthl	12f	SW	2	**102**

SILVALINE 6						
May	30	Rdcr	10f	G	12	101
Aug	29	Epsm	10f	G	6	**103**
Sep	3	NmkJ	10f	G	10	101

SILVER CROSS 3						
Apr	10	Lonc	10½f	S	3	107
May	9	Lonc	11f	G	2	104
Jun	5	Chan	10½f	G	15	99
Sep	11	Lonc	12f	G	5	**108**

SILVER DANE 3						
Jly	14	Donc	5f	GF	1	101
Jly	17	Rdcr	5f	G	2	**105**

SILVER DREAMER 3						
Jly	6	Ling	12f	SW	5	**102**

SILVER PROPHET 6						
Apr	26	Wwck	12½f	GS	4	105
May	23	Wind	11½f	GF	5	100

SILVER SEEKER 5						
Jun	27	Muss	12f	G	2	102

SILVER SONG 3						
Aug	29	Chep	16f	G	3	**99**

SILVER VISAGE 3						
Jly	6	Ling	7f	G	1	**102**

SILVERHAY 4						
May	17	Bevl	8½f	GF	5	101
Jun	1	Newc	8f	G	4	**104**
Jun	8	Bevl	7½f	G	4	100
Jly	16	Ripn	10f	G	2	102
Aug	17	Nott	8f	F	3	100
Oct	9	Newc	10f	G	4	**104**

SILVERTOWN 10						
Jly	6	Carl	14f	G	1	**106**
Jly	16	Hayd	16f	GF	1	**106**

SIMON'S SEAT 6						
Feb	7	Sthl	14f	SD	2	101
Feb	10	Sthl	16f	SD	2	99
Apr	8	Sthl	14f	SD	2	101

SIMONDA 4						
Jly	28	Gdwd	14f	G	5	99
Sep	24	Hayd	14f	GF	9	101
Oct	9	Gdwd	12f	G	3	**109**

SIMPLE EXCHANGE 4						
Jun	8	Leop	7f	G	3	**108**
Jun	17	York	10½f	G	8	104
Nov	19	Ling	10f	FT	6	101

SIMPLEX 4						
Oct	16	Lonc	12f	G	4	**104**

SIMPLIFY 3						
Feb	22	Ling	7f	SD	5	100
Jly	8	Ling	8f	SW	2	100
Jly	16	Ling	8f	SW	2	**103**
Jly	30	Haml	8½f	F	2	100
Sep	13	Sals	8f	G	7	100

SIMPLY ST LUCIA 3						
May	28	Muss	8f	G	2	**103**
Jun	1	Wolv	8½f	FT	6	100
Jun	18	Rdcr	7f	GF	3	99
Jun	27	Pont	8f	G	6	101
Nov	16	Sthl	8f	FT	2	102

SIMPLY SUNSHINE 3						
Jun	18	Wwck	7f	G	4	**107**

SIMPLY THE GUEST 6						
Feb	8	Sthl	11f	SD	1	**111**
Mar	7	Wolv	12f	SD	1	110

SIMPSONS MOUNT 4						
Apr	19	Folk	5f	GS	1	105
May	6	Ling	5f	G	1	107
Jly	7	Folk	5f	G	2	**108**
Jly	20	Sand	5f	GF	3	102
Jly	27	Gdwd	5f	G	4	102
Jly	31	Newb	5f	G	4	102
Aug	10	Sand	5f	GF	4	101

SINA COVA 3						
Jun	25	Curr	10f	G	5	104
Sep	10	Leop	12f	GF	8	**108**
Sep	18	Curr	16f	G	9	101

SINGALONG 3						
Jly	4	Wind	8½f	G	3	100
Jly	24	Pont	8f	G	2	101
Aug	11	Sand	9f	GF	3	**104**

SINGHALONGTASVEER 3						
Jly	4	Muss	9f	GF	4	**105**

SINGLET 4						
Jun	1	Wolv	14f	FT	6	99
Aug	6	NmkJ	10f	G	1	99
Aug	26	Sals	10f	G	2	**103**
Sep	27	Nott	10f	GF	3	99
Oct	21	Newb	10f	GS	2	101

SION HILL 4
Apr 8 Sthl 6f GS 3 **102**

SIR BLUEBIRD 3
May 25 NmkR 6f G 3 **99**

SIR BOND 4
Feb 1 Sthl 8f FT 1 **109**
Mar 12 Sthl 8f SD 2 99
Apr 21 Bevl 7½f S 2 101
Apr 29 Muss 7f G 1 100

SIR DESMOND 7
Jly 9 York 6f G 7 101
Jly 29 NmkJ 6f G 3 **105**
Aug 27 Gdwd 6f G 8 100
Sep 29 Ayr 6f G 2 **105**
Nov 25 Wolv 6f FT 8 101
Dec 16 Wolv 6f FT 5 101

SIR DRINKSALOT 4
Jun 1 Leop 14f G 22 **106**

SIR EDWARD ELGAR 3
Jun 17 Gdwd 9f G 4 100
Jly 4 Bath 10f G 3 **102**
Jly 18 Wind 10f G 3 99

SIR EDWIN LANDSEER 5
Jly 4 Wind 6f G 1 103
Jly 27 Gdwd 5f G 6 102
Jly 29 Gdwd 6f G 2 105
Aug 13 NmkJ 6f G 2 105
Aug 27 Gdwd 6f G 6 101
Sep 3 Hayd 5f F 3 **107**

SIR ERNEST 4
Feb 11 Wolv 5f SD 1 **101**

SIR FRANCIS 7
Mar 16 Wolv 7f SD 4 **100**

SIR HAYDN 5
Jan 29 Ling 10f SD 2 **109**
Feb 5 Ling 10f SD 1 103
Feb 16 Ling 10f SD 2 105
Apr 8 Ling 10f SD 1 103
Apr 16 Wolv 8½f FT 1 106
Dec 6 Sthl 11f FT 7 103
Dec 12 Wolv 9½f FT 5 100
Dec 21 Ling 10f FT 2 101

SIR LOIN 4
Sep 28 Newc 5f GF 8 **99**

SIR MONTY 3
Aug 11 Sals 14f GF 2 **101**
Aug 28 Yarm 14f G 3 100
Sep 27 Gdwd 16f G 2 100

SIR NIGHT 5
May 23 Bevl 10f G 1 100

SIR NOD 3
Aug 3 Pont 6f G 2 101
Aug 27 York 6f G 1 **105**
Oct 29 Wolv 6f SD 2 102

SIR SANDROVITCH 9
Jan 5 Sthl 5f FT 1 99
Jan 19 Ling 5f FT 2 99
Feb 28 Wolv 5f SD 3 103
Jly 12 Bevl 5f GF 2 101
Aug 26 Newc 5f GF 1 **106**
Oct 1 Rdcr 5f GF 4 100
Dec 27 Sthl 5f SD 3 101

SIR SIDNEY 5
May 20 Hayd 10½f G 4 **103**
Jun 4 Donc 12f GF 6 101

SIRAJ 6
Jan 27 Sthl 6f SD 2 103
Feb 17 Sthl 6f SD 1 103
Mar 21 Ling 6f SD 5 104
May 5 Folk 6f G 3 **105**

SIRCE 3
Apr 7 Leic 10f S 1 99
May 16 Wind 11½f G 3 104
Jun 16 Newb 12f G 2 103
Jly 2 Leic 12f GF 2 99
Sep 23 Ling 12f GF 1 105
Oct 9 Gdwd 12f G 2 **109**
Oct 19 Bath 11½f GS 1 103

SISTER SOX 5
May 22 Curr 6f G 3 105
Jly 16 Curr 5f F 7 **107**
Sep 17 Curr 5f G 4 **107**

SIX OF ONE 7
Mar 7 Ling 16f SD 10 **99**

SKERRIES 4
Jun 15 Leop 10f G 3 102
Sep 4 Curr 10f G 6 **105**

SKI JUMP 5
May 12 York 14f S 2 **110**
May 28 Muss 14f G 5 102
Jly 8 York 12f GS 1 109
Jly 22 York 14f G 3 109
Sep 19 Carl 12f G 2 107

SKIDDAW WOLF 3
Apr 12 Muss 5f G 6 100
Jun 27 Pont 6f G 2 **107**
Jly 14 Haml 6f GF 2 102
Jly 21 Donc 6f GF 4 99

SKIDMARK 4
Jan 15 Ling 10f SD 6 **104**
Feb 12 Ling 10f SD 6 101
Feb 26 Ling 10f SD 6 **104**
Nov 19 Ling 12f FT 10 100
Nov 26 Ling 8f FT 9 103
Dec 21 Ling 10f FT 7 100

SKIDROW 3
May 18 Gdwd 9f G 9 100
Jun 16 York 8f G 5 **107**
Jly 2 Bevl 8½f G 1 100
Jly 24 NmkJ 8f G 5 99
Sep 23 Hayd 8f G 2 106

SKY CRUSADER 3
May 2 Kemp 9f G 5 99
Jun 3 Epsm 7f G 1 105
Jun 16 York 8f G 4 **110**
Jly 2 Sand 7f G 6 102
Aug 7 Leic 7f G 2 104
Aug 29 Ripn 8f G 9 103
Sep 10 Gdwd 9f G 9 105
Sep 30 NmkR 7f G 3 105
Oct 7 York 8f G 8 105
Oct 27 Ling 7f SD 5 107

SKY HIGH FLYER 3
Mar 20 Curr 7f HY 2 103
May 8 Leop 7f S 2 104
Jly 17 Curr 9f F 6 107
Sep 10 Leop 8f GF 8 **110**

SKY QUEST 7
May 30 Rdcr 10f G 10 101
Jun 11 Ripn 9f G 7 102
Sep 3 NmkJ 10f G 7 102
Sep 16 Newb 11f G 10 **104**
Oct 9 Bath 11½f G 5 99

SKY TO SEA 7
Apr 3 Curr 16f HY 8 **99**

SKYE'S FOLLY 5
Oct 21 Newb 16f GS 3 **101**

SKYLARKER 7
May 20 NmkR 12f G 2 **105**
Jun 4 Epsm 12f G 9 102
Jun 23 Sals 14f G 3 104
Jly 7 NmkJ 12f G 10 99
Jly 23 Newb 12f GF 8 104
Aug 20 Sand 10f G 3 101
Oct 9 Bath 11½f G 4 100

SLAP SHOOT 3
Jun 27 Lonc 9½f G 3 **106**

SLAVONIC 4
Jly 29 Thsk 7f G 4 **104**
Sep 3 Thsk 8f G 1 101

SLEEPING INDIAN 4
Jun 2 Hayd 7f G 1 **115**
Jly 27 Gdwd 8f GS 5 113
Aug 13 Newb 7f G 1 111
Sep 8 Donc 7f GF 2 111
Sep 24 NmkR 8f G 5 109
Oct 15 NmkR 7f G 2 **115**

SLING BACK 4
Feb 11 Wolv 7f SD 2 102
Aug 7 Curr 7f G 9 **103**
Nov 12 Wolv 8½f FT 3 102
Dec 2 Wolv 6f SD 7 100

SLIP DANCE 3
Apr 13 NmkR 7f G 4 106
May 1 NmkR 8f G 14 100
May 22 Curr 8f G 13 106
Jun 4 Hayd 6f G 2 102
Jun 15 York 7f G 9 99
Jun 26 Curr 6½f GF 6 100
Jly 8 York 6f G 7 104
Sep 10 Ches 6f GS 4 101
Sep 18 Haml 5f F 1 **107**

SMART JOHN 5
Apr 26 Wwck 12½f GS 6 **104**
Jun 12 Sals 12f G 4 **104**
Jun 19 Wwck 12½f G 1 102
Jly 10 Hayd 14f GF 3 99
Sep 23 Hayd 12f G 2 102

SMIDDY HILL 3
Apr 28 Rdcr 5f GF 5 **100**

SMIRFYS NIGHT 6
Jun 27 Wolv 6f SD 2 **102**
Jly 18 Ayr 6f GF 4 99
Jly 29 Thsk 6f G 11 99
Oct 24 Wolv 7f SD 1 99

SMIRFYS PARTY 7
Jly 29 Thsk 6f G 8 **101**
Aug 6 Rdcr 6f G 3 99

SMOKIN BEAU 8
Mar 19 Ling 5f SD 4 **103**
Apr 30 Gdwd 5f G 2 102
Jly 9 Ling 5f SD 1 **103**
Jly 30 Gdwd 6f G 19 101
Aug 6 Hayd 5f G 15 102
Sep 7 Donc 5½f GF 14 102
Sep 24 Hayd 6f GF 3 102

SMOKIN JOE 4
Jan 29 Ling 7f SD 4 **108**
Feb 12 Ling 8f SD 4 99
Mar 1 Ling 6f SD 7 103
Mar 18 Ling 7f SD 6 99

SMOOTH JAZZ 3
Apr 29 Muss 9f G 2 **102**
May 30 Rdcr 11f G 5 99
Jun 17 NmkJ 8f GF 4 100

SMOOTHIE 7
Dec 10 Wolv 12f FT 5 **99**

SMOOTHLY DOES IT 4
May 3 Bath 8f HY 3 101
May 5 Chep 8f GS 2 103

SMUGGLER'S SONG 6
Sep 17 Curr 8f GF 11 **102**

SNAP 4
Apr 19 Sthl 7f GF 4 99
Apr 30 Thsk 7f S 2 103
May 18 Gdwd 7f G 7 100
May 31 Sand 8f G 10 99
Jly 1 Bevl 8½f G 4 104
Nov 6 Leop 8f S 1 **106**

SNEEM'S ROCK 4
Jan 22 Ling 10f FT 6 99
Mar 3 Ling 10f SW 3 **101**
Mar 21 Ling 10f SW 3 **101**

SNOW BUNTING 7
Jun 18 NmkJ 6f G 4 100
Jun 24 Newc 6f G 4 **102**

SNOW WOLF 4
Jan 4 Ling 5f FT 6 101
May 27 Brig 5½f GF 3 **102**
Aug 6 Hayd 6f G 4 101
Sep 21 Rdcr 5f GF 7 100

SNOWED UNDER 4
May 31 Leic 10f G 1 103
Jun 11 Leic 10f G 1 **105**
Jun 21 Bevl 10f G 3 102
Jly 27 Leic 10f G 2 103
Aug 7 Leic 10f GF 1 99

Aug 30 Ripn 10f F 5 101
Oct 17 Wind 10f G 12 99

SO ELEGANT 3
Oct 15 Ling 13f SD 1 **101**

SOAR 3
Sep 6 Leic 5f GF 6 **100**

SOAVE 6
Nov 1 MsnL 6f GF 3 **113**

SOBA JONES 8
Jan 11 Sthl 6f SW 2 **103**
Jan 21 Wolv 6f SD 4 **103**
Mar 12 Wolv 7f SD 6 102
Mar 21 Sthl 6f SD 2 100
Jly 2 Hayd 5f GF 3 **103**
Dec 27 Sthl 5f SD 4 99

SOCIAL ORDER 7
Jun 15 Leop 14f G 8 **101**

SOCIETY HOSTESS 3
Sep 10 Leop 7f HD 2 **107**

SOCIETY MUSIC 3
Jun 17 Ayr 8f G 1 102
Jly 1 Hayd 8f G 1 **107**

SOGNO VERDE 3
Jun 15 Leop 8f GF 2 **104**

SOHGOL 3
May 12 Sals 10f G 2 **102**
May 31 Rdcr 10f G 3 100
Jun 16 Newb 12f G 5 **102**
Jun 30 Newb 10f G 5 101
Sep 2 NmkJ 8f G 11 **102**

SOL ROJO 3
Apr 23 Wolv 8½f SD 1 **99**

SOLAR POWER 4
Apr 26 Bath 5f HY 5 101
Jun 24 NmkJ 6f G 5 100
Jly 8 Ling 6f SW 7 105
Aug 17 Epsm 7f G 2 106
Sep 1 Sals 7f G 4 107
Sep 25 NmkR 7f G 10 **108**
Sep 29 NmkR 6f GF 2 101
Oct 20 Brig 6f GS 2 103

SOLARIAS QUEST 3
Jly 31 Ches 12½f G 1 **102**

SOLDIER'S TALE 4
May 13 York 6f GS 1 **110**
Jun 25 Newc 6f G 1 108
Jly 7 NmkJ 6f G 4 108

SOLENT 3
Apr 2 Donc 8f G 1 **104**
Jun 4 Epsm 10f G 5 101
Aug 6 Wind 11½f GF 1 99

SOLERINA 8
Nov 6 Leop 16f S DSQ 110

SOLIZA 4
Aug 7 Curr 10f G 2 **109**

SOLO FLIGHT 8
Apr 20 Epsm 12f GS 6 103
May 14 Newb 12f G 9 99
May 25 NmkR 10f G 1 103
Jly 9 York 10½f G 5 102
Jly 23 Newb 10f GF 6 99
Sep 17 Newb 10f GF 11 **108**
Sep 30 NmkR 12f G 4 103
Oct 22 Newb 10f G 9 105

SOLOMON'S MINE 6
Jan 7 Wolv 8½f SW 10 100
Feb 8 Sthl 11f SD 4 **105**

SOLSKJAER 5
Apr 3 Curr 7f S 7 102
May 5 Ches 10½f G 2 **112**
May 8 Leop 8f S 2 101
Jun 1 Leop 8f G 8 103
Jun 8 Leop 10f F 4 104
Aug 7 Curr 10f G 4 **112**
Sep 18 Curr 8f GF 2 109

SOMERSET WEST 5
Jan 28 Wolv 5f SD 2 **99**

SOMETHING 3
May 29 NmkR 7f GF 1 **108**

SOMETHING EXCITING 3
May 18 Gdwd 10f G 1 101
Jun 3 Epsm 12f G 2 **106**
Jun 16 York 12f G 4 102
Jly 30 Gdwd 10f G 5 105
Aug 10 Sals 10f G 3 **106**
Sep 11 Lonc 12f G 6 104

SOMNUS 5
May 11 York 6f S 4 109
Jly 7 NmkJ 6f G 13 100
Aug 7 Deau 6½f G 10 109
Sep 3 Hayd 6f F 4 105
Oct 1 Lonc 7f G 6 **111**
Oct 15 NmkR 7f G 5 109

SON OF THUNDER 4
May 21 Carl 9½f G 1 **102**
Jun 27 Pont 8f G 5 **102**
Jly 6 Carl 9½f G 1 100
Jly 28 Carl 9½f G 4 100
Aug 16 Haml 9f F 5 100
Aug 25 Muss 8f G 11 99
Sep 10 Muss 8f G 6 100

SONDERBORG 4
Sep 17 Catt 7f G 2 99
Oct 13 Sthl 8f SD 2 99
Nov 19 Sthl 8f SW 2 **101**

SONG OF SONGS 3
Jun 25 Donc 10½f GF 1 **102**
Jly 30 Donc 10½f G 6 100

SONG OF VALA 4
Jun 15 Nott 8f GF 6 101
Aug 3 Brig 8f G 1 **107**
Aug 23 Brig 8f G 2 101

SONG SPARROW 3
Jly 6 Ling 12f SW 6 **102**
Jly 19 Yarm 11½f G 4 101

SONG THRUSH 3						
Jly	23	York	10½f	GS	6	**99**

SONGERIE 3						
Jly	30	Gdwd	10f	G	4	105
Sep	7	Donc	14½f	GF	3	101
Oct	1	Lonc	12½f	G	4	**111**

SONGLARK 5						
Jun	19	Pont	12f	G	1	**111**
Aug	16	York	16f	G	3	103
Oct	22	Newb	12f	G	6	103

SONIC ANTHEM 3						
Jun	27	Muss	7f	GF	2	**100**

SONNTAG BLUE 3						
Dec	30	Ling	7f	FT	1	**102**

SONNY PARKIN 3						
Mar	28	Yarm	8f	GS	3	102
Jun	17	NmkJ	8f	GF	1	104
Jly	22	NmkJ	8f	G	4	101
Sep	2	NmkJ	8f	G	3	**107**
Nov	10	Ling	8f	SD	6	101
Nov	19	Ling	8f	FT	3	100
Dec	30	Ling	8f	FT	6	101

SORBIESHARRY 6						
Jan	11	Sthl	11f	SW	4	101
Feb	3	Sthl	8f	SD	4	100
Feb	4	Wolv	8½f	SD	1	105
Feb	25	Wolv	9½f	SD	1	102
Feb	28	Wolv	9½f	SD	5	106
Mar	4	Wolv	8½f	SD	3	101
Mar	17	Sthl	12f	SD	2	105
Mar	24	Wolv	8½f	SD	1	**107**
Apr	2	Wolv	8½f	FT	1	103
Apr	21	Sthl	8f	FT	2	106
Nov	12	Wolv	9½f	FT	5	99
Nov	15	Sthl	8f	FT	4	100
Dec	6	Sthl	11f	FT	9	101
Dec	12	Wolv	9½f	FT	7	99

SOTERIO 5						
Apr	30	Lonc	15½f	GS	7	**111**

SOUL PROVIDER 4						
Jly	11	Wind	8½f	G	7	**100**

SOULACROIX 4						
May	4	Ches	10½f	GS	7	105
Jly	7	NmkJ	12f	G	7	100
Aug	6	NmkJ	16f	G	7	100
Sep	16	Newb	11f	G	3	107
Sep	30	NmkR	12f	G	1	107
Oct	13	NmkR	12f	G	2	**108**

SOUND AND VISION 3						
Jun	15	Haml	8½f	GS	2	**101**
Jun	23	Leic	10f	GF	5	**101**

SOUND BREEZE 3						
Jly	4	Ripn	8f	G	1	102
Jly	18	Ayr	8f	GF	1	**110**
Jly	24	Pont	8f	G	1	109

SOUND OF FLEET 4						
Jly	20	Leic	12f	GF	5	**100**

SOUND THAT ALARM 3						
May	3	Bath	5½f	HY	1	**102**

SOUTH O'THE BORDER 3						
May	2	Wwck	12½f	G	6	101
Jun	22	Sals	10f	G	2	101
Jly	21	Folk	9½f	G	1	**103**
Aug	3	Brig	10f	G	3	101
Aug	25	Ling	10f	GS	1	**103**
Sep	9	Sand	10f	GS	2	**103**
Dec	21	Ling	10f	GS	9	100

SOUTH WEST NINE 6						
Jun	1	Leop	16f	G	9	**104**

SOVEREIGN DREAMER 5						
Jun	2	Brig	12f	G	2	**102**
Jun	21	Brig	12f	G	4	99

SOVEREIGN SPIRIT 3						
Apr	11	Sthl	10f	G	5	101
Dec	12	Wolv	14f	FT	1	**105**
Dec	31	Wolv	14f	SD	2	99

SOVEREIGN STATE 8						
Jun	29	Catt	12f	G	8	99

SOVEREIGNTY 3						
Jun	13	Thsk	7f	G	3	100
Jun	30	Hayd	8f	GF	4	100
Oct	14	Rdcr	7f	GF	2	**103**

SOVIET SCEPTRE 4						
Jun	29	Chep	12f	G	1	**104**

SOVIET SONG 5						
Jun	15	York	8f	G	3	111
Jly	5	NmkJ	8f	G	1	108
Jly	27	Gdwd	8f	GS	2	**118**

SOVIET THREAT 4						
Mar	16	Wolv	7f	SD	1	**104**
May	6	Ling	8f	SD	3	101

SOVIET TREAT 4						
May	25	Leop	7f	GF	3	**106**

SOVIETTA 4						
Mar	30	Folk	12f	HY	6	**100**
May	3	Bath	11½f	HY	1	99

SPANISH ACE 4						
Apr	20	Epsm	5f	GS	11	100
Jun	12	Sals	5f	G	4	**106**

SPANISH DON 7						
May	7	NmkR	9f	GF	2	104
Jun	3	Epsm	10f	G	10	108
Jly	16	Newb	8f	GF	8	101
Jly	30	NmkJ	8f	GF	7	103
Sep	17	Newb	9f	GF	4	99

SPANISH MUSIC 3						
May	28	Donc	5f	G	3	**101**

SPANISH RIDGE 3						
Jun	22	Sals	10f	G	4	99
Jly	9	Sals	12f	G	1	**103**
Oct	1	NmkR	14f	G	7	100

SPARK UP 5						
Apr	22	Wolv	8½f	SD	6	100
Jly	1	Wolv	8½f	SD	1	**101**

SPARKWELL 3						
Aug	17	Epsm	7f	G	2	99
Aug	29	Wwck	7f	GF	1	**103**

SPEAGLE 3						
Feb	26	Ling	12f	SD	1	**101**

SPEAR 3						
May	16	Wind	11½f	G	4	**103**
May	28	Donc	10½f	GF	3	99
Jun	9	Yarm	14f	G	4	101
Jun	27	Wolv	12f	SD	1	**103**
Jly	5	Wolv	12f	FT	2	100
Sep	23	Ling	12f	FT	5	101

SPEAR THISTLE 3						
Aug	13	Newb	10f	G	5	100
Sep	3	NmkJ	10f	G	4	103
Sep	16	Newb	11f	G	2	**109**
Oct	1	NmkR	14f	G	4	104
Nov	3	Muss	16f	GS	2	100

SPECIAL GOLD 3						
May	28	Donc	5f	G	4	100
Jun	1	Nott	5f	G	1	**101**
Jun	24	Newc	5f	G	2	**101**

SPECIAL KALDOUN 6						
Mar	28	StCl	8f	GS	2	113
May	1	StCl	8f	HD	6	115
Jun	12	Chan	8f	GF	2	102
Jly	24	MsnL	8f	F	2	**116**
Aug	15	Deau	10f	G	3	113
Aug	28	Deau	8f	G	1	104
Oct	1	Lonc	8f	G	1	**116**
Oct	30	StCl	8f	G	3	113

SPECIAL LAD 3						
Aug	12	Newb	6f	G	1	102
Aug	17	Carl	7f	GF	3	99
Aug	28	Gdwd	6f	G	6	102
Sep	12	Folk	6f	GF	1	102
Oct	30	Ling	6f	SD	5	**107**

SPECTAIT 3						
Jly	20	Ling	7f	SD	1	99
Jly	22	Wolv	8½f	FT	1	102
Jly	27	Sand	7f	GS	1	**107**
Aug	4	Hayd	8f	GF	4	104

SPECTESTED 4						
Feb	14	Wolv	12f	GF	7	**102**
Mar	7	Wolv	14f	SD	2	101

SPECTRAL STAR 3						
Aug	31	Ling	12f	SD	2	**101**

SPECTROFOLLE 3						
Aug	21	Deau	10f	G	2	102
Oct	2	Lonc	10f	G	4	**108**

SPEED DIAL HARRY 3						
Mar	7	Ling	5f	SD	5	102
Apr	19	Folk	5f	GS	1	101
Dec	20	Sthl	7f	SW	2	**107**

SPEIGHTSTOWN 3						
Aug	26	Bath	13f	G	5	**99**

SPENCE APPEAL 3						
Feb	9	Ling	8f	G	2	**102**
Jly	8	Wolv	8½f	FT	3	99

SPHINX 7
Dec 21 Ling 12f FT 4 **100**

SPIN KING 4
Jly 29 Thsk 7f G 10 **99**

SPINDOR 6
Aug 6 Ling 7f SD 1 **103**

SPINETAIL RUFOUS 7
Feb 23 Ling 7f SD 5 **101**

SPINNING COIN 3
Jun 27 Wind 11½f G 1 101
Jly 1 Hayd 12f G 2 105
Oct 1 NmkR 14f G 3 **106**

SPIRIT OF CHESTER 3
Jly 12 Brig 6f G 2 **108**

SPIRIT OF FRANCE 3
Apr 22 Sand 8f G 7 101
May 14 Nott 6f F 4 103
May 21 NmkR 6f G 4 102
Jun 11 Ripn 6f G 6 105
Jun 20 Ripn 6f G 4 102
Jly 8 Chep 7f GF 2 106
Jly 15 Haml 6f F 1 103
Jly 28 Gdwd 7f G 3 103
Aug 6 NmkJ 7f G 8 **109**
Aug 13 Ripn 6f G 5 100
Sep 10 Muss 8f G 1 108
Sep 17 Ayr 8f G 3 101
Oct 14 NmkR 7f G 10 105

SPITTING IMAGE 5
Jun 3 Wolv 14f FT 4 99
Jun 10 Catt 16f GF 6 99
Jun 17 Rdcr 16f G 1 103
Jly 22 Chep 16f G 2 102
Aug 6 Rdcr 14f G 6 99
Aug 14 Pont 17f G 3 **104**
Nov 5 Wolv 16½f FT 1 103
Dec 9 Wolv 14f FT 6 99

SPORTING GESTURE 8
May 28 Donc 12f GF 1 104
Jly 23 York 12f GS 1 **105**
Aug 14 Bath 11½f G 2 101
Sep 3 Thsk 12f G 1 102
Sep 19 Carl 12f G 4 101
Oct 7 York 12f G 4 102

SPREE 3
May 29 NmkR 6f GF 4 **100**

SPRING BREEZE 4
Apr 6 Catt 16f G 1 102
Jun 10 Catt 16f GF 5 103
Jly 9 Ches 16f GF 2 105
Aug 24 Catt 16f G 1 102

SPRING GODDESS 4
May 21 Ling 8f SD 1 **106**
Jun 3 Epsm 10f G 11 105
Jly 5 NmkJ 8f G 11 100
Jly 26 Gdwd 8f G 7 99
Oct 7 Newb 7f GF 2 103

SPRING JIM 4
May 2 Donc 10½f G 1 **109**
May 25 NmkR 10f G 6 100
Jly 1 Sand 10f G 3 101

SPRING PURSUIT 9
Oct 10 Ayr 15f S 1 102

SPY GUN 5
Apr 4 Sthl 6f SD 2 **102**
Jun 15 Chep 6f GS 4 100
Nov 5 Sthl 7f FT 1 100

SQUAW DANCE 3
Jly 2 Sand 8f G 3 **106**
Sep 14 Yarm 10f G 5 104

SRI DIAMOND 5
Feb 12 Ling 8f SD 1 100
Mar 1 Ling 10f SD 1 **110**
Mar 12 Wolv 8½f SD 4 108
Sep 27 Gdwd 8f G 1 103
Nov 19 Ling 12f FT 1 105
Nov 29 Ling 10f FT 5 108

SRIOLOGY 4
Feb 22 Ling 10f SD 6 **102**

ST ANDREWS 5
Mar 26 Kemp 10f GS 2 106
Apr 14 Ripn 10f S 2 103
May 5 Ches 10½f G 4 109
Jly 2 Sand 8f G 6 112
Jly 30 NmkJ 8f GF 1 **114**
Sep 10 Donc 8f GS 7 102
Sep 30 NmkR 8f G 5 103
Oct 15 NmkR 9f G 3 103
Oct 29 NmkR 8f S 1 109

ST ANDREWS STORM 3
May 1 NmkR 7f G 6 **103**

ST AUSTELL 5
Jan 4 Ling 6f FT 2 **100**

ST IVIAN 5
Feb 24 Sthl 6f FT 4 99
Oct 10 Wolv 5f FT 2 **103**

ST PETERSBURG 5
Apr 23 Leic 7f G 4 105
May 7 Hayd 7f GS 5 99
May 12 York 7f GS 9 101
Jly 7 NmkJ 7f G 18 99
Jly 28 Gdwd 7f G 1 106
Jly 29 Gdwd 8f G 6 **113**
Oct 1 NmkR 9f G 11 99
Oct 14 NmkR 8f G 5 107
Oct 29 NmkR 8f S 2 109

ST SAVARIN 4
Apr 23 Hayd 10½f G 1 **107**
May 2 Donc 10½f G 5 106

STAFF NURSE 5
Apr 4 Sthl 11f SD 1 **105**

STAGBURY HILL 3
May 2 Donc 8f G 4 **102**

STAGE SCHOOL 3
Apr 20 Catt 7f S 1 **100**
Jun 12 Donc 10½f GF 1 99

STAGE SECRET 4
Jan 5 Ling 7f SD 2 105
Mar 18 Ling 7f SD 3 105
May 18 Gdwd 7f G 1 109
May 21 Ling 7f G 3 100
Jun 11 Sand 7f G 11 108
Jly 22 Newb 6f G 2 104
Aug 5 NmkJ 6f GF 6 99
Sep 10 Gdwd 7f G 2 **111**

STAGNITE 5
Feb 14 Wolv 5f G 3 99
Jun 9 Brig 5½f G 3 100
Jun 21 Brig 5½f G 1 99
Jly 20 Sand 5f GF 2 **102**
Jly 22 Chep 5f G 5 99
Dec 21 Ling 6f G 3 100
Dec 30 Ling 7f FT 5 99

STALLONE 8
Jan 6 Wolv 12f FT 2 **107**
Jan 12 Wolv 14f SD 6 101

STAMFORD BLUE 4
May 23 Leic 6f G 1 **102**
Jun 23 Thsk 8f G 1 **102**

STAN'S GIRL 3
Apr 19 Brig 5½f G 1 **101**

STANCOMB WILLS 3
May 27 Catt 12f GF 1 **100**
Jun 25 Ches 12½f G 5 **100**
Oct 14 NmkR 12f G 6 **100**
Oct 24 Ling 12f SW 11 99

STAR APPLAUSE 5
Apr 12 Muss 5f G 8 **99**

STAR FERN 4
Oct 11 Sthl 8f G 3 99
Dec 28 Wolv 8½f G 5 **100**

STAR MAGNITUDE 4
Feb 21 Ling 7f SD 1 **103**

STAR MEMBER 6
Jun 25 Newc 16f G 14 **106**
Aug 17 York 14f G 15 100

STAR OF LIGHT 4
Apr 27 Ling 8f FT 2 104
May 31 Sand 8f G 3 109
Jun 15 Nott 8f GF 1 105
Jly 5 NmkJ 8f G 5 103
Jly 23 Newb 10f GF 1 103
Aug 17 York 10½f G 2 109
Sep 17 Newb 10f GF 1 **113**

STAR OF RUSSIA 3
Aug 7 Curr 7f G 7 **104**

STAR SIDE 3
Jun 25 Ling 10f SW 5 **101**

STAR VALLEY 5
May 22 Lonc 7f GF 3 **108**
Jly 9 Deau 6f GF 6 106

STAR WELCOME 4
Mar 3 Ling 10f SW 2 101
Jly 18 Wind 10f G 3 **102**

Jly 29 NmkJ 12f G 4 99

STARCHY 3
Apr 2 Donc 7f G 3 **102**
May 5 Ches 7½f GS 6 100

STARCRAFT 5
Jun 14 York 8f G 3 114
Jly 2 Sand 10f G 6 104
Sep 4 Lonc 8f GF 1 **120**
Sep 24 NmkR 8f G 1 115

STARDUSTER 3
Jly 9 Nott 5f F 4 101
Jly 20 Leic 5f F 1 **103**
Aug 7 Ling 5f G 4 99

STARGAZER JIM 3
Jly 5 Wolv 8½f FT 1 103
Jly 24 Pont 10f G 2 **104**
Sep 9 Sand 10f GS 3 100
Nov 4 Yarm 10f HY 4 99

STARGEM 4
Feb 19 Wolv 6f HY 1 103
Feb 26 Ling 6f SD 2 99
Mar 8 Sthl 5f SD 1 104
Jun 6 Wind 5f G 7 101
Jun 20 Muss 5f G 2 99
Jun 28 Brig 5½f F 2 105
Jly 7 Folk 5f G 3 **108**

STARPIX 3
Jun 12 Chan 8f GF 7 105
Jly 3 Chan 8f G 2 **116**

STARWOMAN 3
Aug 2 Deau 10f G 9 **110**

STATE DILEMMA 4
Feb 1 Ling 8f SD 7 **102**
Jly 29 Nott 5f G 8 99

STATE OF BALANCE 7
Feb 21 Ling 10f FT 5 99
Mar 3 Ling 10f SW 6 99
Mar 21 Ling 10f SW 5 **100**

STAY CLOSE 3
Feb 1 Ling 7f SD 1 **101**
Apr 21 Bevl 7½f S 4 99
Jly 2 Sand 7f G 8 **101**

STEDFAST MCSTAUNCH 3
Jan 28 Wolv 8½f SD 3 **105**

STEED 3
Jun 12 Chan 8f GF 6 **108**

STEEL BLUE 5
Apr 30 NmkR 6f G 23 100
Aug 1 Ripn 6f G 4 103
Aug 27 York 6f G 4 103
Oct 1 Epsm 7f GS 1 104
Oct 14 NmkR 7f G 13 104
Oct 22 Donc 5f S 3 **111**

STEELY DAN 6
Feb 22 Ling 7f SD 1 **107**
Mar 1 Ling 10f SD 7 106
Apr 11 Ling 12f SD 9 99

STEENBERG 6
Apr 3 Curr 7f S 2 110
May 11 York 6f S 2 **111**
Jun 25 Newc 6f G 3 105
Jly 9 Deau 6f GF 3 108
Jly 26 Gdwd 7f G 6 **111**
Aug 7 Deau 6½f G 11 109
Sep 3 Hayd 6f F 9 102

STELLA BLUE 3
Jun 5 Chan 8f GF 8 **103**

STELLA MARAIS 4
Feb 4 Wolv 7f SD 1 **103**

STELLAR BRILLIANT 3
Oct 19 Bath 10f GS 1 **108**

STELLITE 5
Feb 7 Wolv 8½f FT 2 102
Feb 18 Wolv 7f SD 4 99
Aug 19 Ayr 8f GF 2 99
Sep 29 Ayr 7f S 1 **106**
Nov 12 Wolv 8½f FT 2 102

STETCHWORTH PRINCE 3
Apr 13 NmkR 7f G 3 **108**
May 28 Gdwd 8f G 4 104
Jun 16 York 7f GF 3 105
Jly 5 NmkJ 6f G 4 **108**
Jly 30 Donc 6f G 1 106
Sep 8 Donc 5f F 6 103

STEVEDORE 4
Jun 29 Chep 8f G 2 99
Jly 9 Nott 8f F 1 99
Jly 14 Epsm 7f G 2 104
Aug 15 Brig 7f G 2 104
Sep 8 Epsm 7f G 10 99
Sep 25 Muss 8f G 1 102
Nov 16 Sthl 8f FT 1 104
Dec 10 Sthl 8f FT 3 100
Dec 15 Sthl 8f SD 1 **106**

STILL GOING ON 8
Jly 16 Curr 16f GF 5 **101**

STING LIKE A BEE 6
Jly 11 Ayr 11f F 5 **104**
Jly 19 Ayr 10f G 2 102

STOIC LEADER 5
Jan 5 Ling 7f SD 5 104
Jan 8 Ling 8f SD 8 101
Feb 18 Wolv 8½f SD 5 106
Apr 27 Ling 8f FT 6 101
Apr 29 Muss 8f G 1 103
May 17 Rdcr 8f G 1 103
May 21 Catt 7f GF 1 **108**
May 23 Thsk 7f G 5 100
Jun 18 Ayr 7f G 5 101
Jun 25 Newc 7f G 3 104
Jun 30 Hayd 8f GF 4 101
Jly 13 Hayd 8f G 5 103
Jly 23 Newc 7f GF 3 99
Jly 30 Thsk 8f G 7 102
Aug 29 Ripn 8f G 5 107
Nov 29 Ling 8f FT 6 105
Dec 9 Wolv 8½f FT 7 103
Dec 30 Ling 8f FT 5 102

STOKESIES WISH 5
Jly 25 Wind 6f G 3 99
Aug 1 Wind 6f G 3 **100**

STOLEN HOURS 5
May 17 Leic 12f G 2 103
Jun 7 Sals 12f G 4 99
Jun 30 Epsm 12f G 1 **104**

STOLEN SONG 5
Aug 10 Yarm 10f G 1 100
Nov 21 Sthl 14f SW 3 **105**

STOOP TO CONQUER 5
May 12 York 14f S 4 **107**

STOP MAKING SENSE 3
Aug 28 Deau 8f G 4 101
Oct 1 Lonc 9½f G 4 105
Oct 30 StCl 8f G 5 **111**

STORM CENTRE 3
Oct 17 Wind 8½f G 5 **101**

STORM CHASE 3
Mar 29 Wwck 7f GS 2 **101**
Jun 4 Ling 6f G 1 99
Aug 19 Ayr 8f GF 5 100

STORMINA 3
Jun 5 Chan 8f GF 3 **110**

STORMY NATURE 4
Feb 9 Ling 7f GF 7 99
Jly 11 Wolv 7f SD 6 100
Aug 6 Ling 7f SD 5 99
Aug 27 Wind 8½f G 4 101
Sep 13 Sals 8f G 4 **102**

STORY NINE 5
Jun 1 Leop 7f G 16 **108**

STRAFFAN 3
Jan 31 Wolv 6f SD 1 99
May 6 Haml 5f GS 1 **103**

STRATHCLYDE 6
Dec 28 Wolv 6f GS 2 **101**

STRAVMOUR 9
Feb 1 Sthl 14f FT 1 **99**

STRAWBERRY DALE 3
Sep 3 Thsk 8f G 1 107
Sep 24 NmkR 8f G 7 107
Nov 5 Donc 10½f S 1 **108**

STRAWBERRY LEAF 3
Jun 30 Hayd 8f GF 1 104
Jly 27 Gdwd 9f GS 1 **105**

STREAM OF GOLD 4
Apr 2 Donc 8f G 1 **115**
Apr 23 Sand 8f G 4 103
Jun 4 Epsm 8½f G 4 103

STREETS OF GOLD 3
Aug 7 Curr 16f G 4 **107**

STRENGTH 'N HONOUR 5
May 28 Gdwd 12f G 8 **102**
Aug 22 Wind 10f G 2 99

STRENSALL 8
Apr 30 Thsk 5f S 5 101
May 28 Muss 5f G 5 101
Jun 23 Thsk 5f GF 1 **104**
Jly 4 Muss 5f GF 7 100
Jly 20 Catt 5f GF 3 99
Jly 23 Newc 5f GF 3 103
Aug 20 Ches 5f G 6 99
Sep 21 Rdcr 5f GF 3 102

STRETTON 7
May 30 Rdcr 10f G 15 99
Jun 7 Ches 10½f GF 9 100
Sep 17 Catt 12f G 7 103
Oct 7 York 12f G 2 **105**
Nov 7 Wolv 12f FT 1 100

STRIDER 4
Jun 10 Chep 10f G 1 99
Jun 21 Newb 10f G 3 **101**

STRIDES OF FIRE 4
Sep 4 Curr 10f G 11 99

STRIKE 4
May 8 Leop 12f S 5 **106**
May 25 Leop 14f GF 10 99

STRIKING AMBITION 5
May 11 York 6f S 6 107
Jly 9 Deau 6f GF 1 113
Aug 7 Deau 6½f G 13 107
Oct 2 Lonc 5f G 2 **114**

STROLLER 4
Jan 15 Ling 10f SD 1 **105**
Feb 12 Ling 10f SD 4 103

STRONG HAND 5
May 12 Carl 9½f G 1 105
May 20 Hayd 10½f G 1 **107**
Jun 2 Hayd 10½f G 1 101
Jly 8 York 10½f GS 3 105
Jly 23 York 10½f GS 4 100

STRONGHOLD 3
May 2 Kemp 8f G 2 99
May 20 Hayd 8f G 1 105
Jun 2 Sand 10f G 3 101
Jly 24 NmkJ 8f G 1 107
Aug 4 Hayd 8f GF 1 **111**

STRUDEL 3
Jly 29 Nott 8f G 1 104
Aug 28 Gdwd 9f G 7 **106**
Sep 14 Sand 8f G 6 104
Sep 23 Hayd 10½f G 5 101
Oct 10 Ayr 10f S 1 102
Oct 24 Ling 12f SW 7 103

STUTTGART 5
Sep 10 Leop 12f GF 12 **100**

STYLING IT 4
May 22 Curr 6f G 6 **103**

STYLISH SUNRISE 4
Feb 23 Ling 16f G 4 **99**

STYLISTIC 4
Aug 14 Leop 6f G 2 **101**

SUALDA 6
Jly 8 York 12f GS 3 105
Jly 16 Ripn 12f G 3 **108**
Jly 23 York 12f GS 2 104
Aug 14 Pont 12f G 4 102

SUBLIMITY 5
Apr 3 Curr 10f S 1 **107**

SUBPOENA 3
May 20 NmkR 8f G 3 **110**
Aug 18 Ches 7½f F 3 99
Aug 29 Wwck 7f GF 3 107
Sep 9 Donc 8f G 2 105
Nov 2 Nott 8f GS 2 102

SUBTLE AFFAIR 3
May 10 Yarm 11½f GS 1 **103**
Nov 5 Donc 16½f S 4 100

SUBYAN DREAMS 3
Mar 23 Ling 7f SD 1 100
Apr 13 NmkR 7f G 10 **101**

SUCCESSION 3
Aug 14 Bath 8f G 9 **103**

SUCCESSOR 5
Jly 16 Ling 10f SW 3 99
Aug 10 Yarm 10f G 3 99
Dec 29 Ling 10f G 2 **107**

SUGARHONEYBABY 4
Sep 10 Leop 7f HD 4 106
Sep 18 Curr 8f GF 3 107
Nov 6 Leop 7f GS 1 **110**

SUGGESTIVE 7
May 7 Ling 7f G 3 112
Jun 15 York 8f G 9 108
Jly 9 Ches 7f GF 3 **113**
Jly 26 Gdwd 7f G 9 107
Aug 18 York 7f GF 6 107
Sep 8 Epsm 7f G 1 109
Oct 1 Rdcr 7f GF 2 110
Dec 9 Wolv 7f FT 1 108

SUIVEZ MOI 3
Jly 5 Pont 10f G 2 **103**
Jly 22 Newb 10f G 2 100
Aug 3 Newc 9f G 3 99

SUMMER BOUNTY 9
Apr 25 Wind 10f GS 2 100
May 15 Ripn 10f G 9 100
Jly 27 Leic 10f G 5 102
Dec 29 Ling 10f G 5 **104**

SUMMER CHARM 3
Apr 11 Sthl 10f G 1 **107**
May 2 Wwck 12½f G 3 104
May 9 Wind 11½f GF 2 99
Sep 28 Ling 12f SD 1 104
Dec 21 Ling 12f SD 8 99

SUMMER MAGIC 4
Apr 3 Curr 10f S 11 **101**

SUMMER RECLUSE 6
Mar 24 Wolv 7f SD 5 99
Jun 19 Wwck 6f G 3 **107**
Jly 12 Brig 6f G 2 102
Aug 12 Newb 6f G 3 101
Aug 14 Bath 5½f G 1 103
Sep 8 Epsm 7f G 6 102
Sep 17 Wwck 5½f G 1 101
Sep 21 Rdcr 6f GF 2 100
Sep 27 Nott 6f G 2 102
Dec 2 Wolv 6f SD 5 102

SUMMER SHADES 7
Jan 10 Wolv 7f SD 2 **102**
Feb 8 Ling 8f SD 3 101
May 9 Rdcr 7f GS 7 99
May 27 Catt 7f GF 3 99
Aug 17 Nott 8f F 4 99

SUMMERISE 4
Jun 1 Yarm 10f G 1 100
Jun 4 Ling 10f SD 1 104
Jun 11 Ling 10f SW 1 **105**
Jun 27 Wind 11½f G 3 99
Jly 16 Ling 10f SW 3 102
Jly 25 Yarm 10f GS 2 101
Aug 22 Leic 10f G 3 101
Oct 24 Ling 12f SW 9 100

SUMMITVILLE 5
May 1 NmkR 9f G 2 **111**
Jun 6 Pont 8f GF 2 104
Jun 23 Newc 10f GF 3 103
Jly 8 Chep 10f GF 3 106
Aug 14 Bath 8f G 1 110
Sep 4 Curr 9f G 4 108
Oct 1 NmkR 8f G 2 109

SUMORA 3
Mar 19 Ling 7f SD 5 102
Apr 26 Bath 5f HY 2 105
May 14 Nott 6f F 5 102
Jly 9 Ling 5f SD 6 99
Aug 6 Hayd 5f G 8 105
Aug 17 York 5f F 2 102
Sep 7 Donc 5½f GF 4 **107**
Sep 18 Haml 5f F 5 104

SUN AND SHOWERS 3
Oct 5 Nott 10f G 4 **99**

SUN HILL 5
Jan 13 Ling 12f SD 9 102
May 7 Thsk 16f GS 2 **106**
Jun 1 Wolv 14f FT 4 101
Nov 21 Sthl 14f SW 1 **106**

SUN KISSED 3
Jun 11 Ripn 9f G 9 **100**

SUNDAY CITY 4
Aug 14 Bath 11½f G 4 99

SUNDAY SYMPHONY 3
Jun 17 York 12f G 2 106
Jly 8 York 12f GS 2 **108**
Aug 18 York 14f G 3 107
Aug 31 York 12f G 3 105

SUNDRIED TOMATO 6
Jan 21 Wolv 6f SD 3 **105**

SUNDROP 4
Jun 15 York 8f G 2 **113**

SUNGIO 7
Jan 22 Ling 16f FT 4 **105**
Feb 23 Ling 16f FT 2 101

SUNISA 4
Jun 4 Donc 12f GF 7 **100**

SUNLIT SKIES 3
Jly 19 Yarm 7f G 5 **101**

SUNNY TIMES 3
May 24 Ling 7f G 1 **99**

SUNRIDGE FAIRY 6
Apr 4 Sthl 11f SD 2 101
May 18 Sthl 12f FT 2 **103**

SUNSET DREAMER 4
Jly 12 Brig 6f G 4 **102**

SUNSET STRIP 3
Feb 11 Wolv 7f SD 3 101
Apr 25 Wolv 8½f FT 1 101
May 4 Ches 12½f GS 5 99
May 18 Gdwd 9f G 6 **104**

SUNSHINE ON ME 4
Feb 25 Wolv 12f G 4 **100**
Apr 16 Wolv 9½f FT 3 99
Jly 30 Ling 10f SD 1 99

SUPER DOMINION 8
Jan 7 Wolv 8½f SW 1 **109**
Jan 22 Ling 10f FT 1 102
Feb 1 Ling 10f SD 3 100
Feb 22 Ling 10f SD 5 103
Mar 3 Ling 10f SW 5 100
Apr 4 Wolv 8½f FT 3 00

SUPERSTITIOUS 3
Jun 1 Nott 6f G 1 **103**
Jun 23 Newc 6f G 2 100

SUPREME SALUTATION 9
Aug 27 Wind 8½f G 13 **104**
Oct 25 Yarm 7f S 5 100

SURAK 5
Aug 7 Deau 10f GF 10 **105**

SURDOUE 5
Feb 1 Sthl 12f FT 1 100
Feb 8 Sthl 11f SD 3 **104**
Feb 24 Sthl 8f FT 5 101
Mar 17 Sthl 12f FT 3 103
Dec 4 Sthl 11f FT 2 99

SUTURIA 3
Mar 29 Wwck 7f GS 4 **100**

SVEDOV 4
Mar 28 StCl 8f GS 4 **110**

SWAHILI DANCER 4
Apr 9 Newc 9f S 6 **99**

SWAINS BRIDGE 3
Jly 7 Donc 8f GF 3 **99**

SWAINSON 4
Jun 22 Epsm 12f G 3 **99**

SWEET EMILY 3
Sep 20 Brig 8f G 4 99
Oct 4 Leic 7f G 1 **102**

SWEET INDULGENCE 4
May 2 Kemp 8f G 6 99
Jun 24 NmkJ 10f G 4 103
Jly 7 NmkJ 12f G 4 101
Jly 30 NmkJ 12f GF 3 104
Aug 13 NmkJ 12f G 1 **109**
Sep 24 Hayd 14f GF 3 104

SWEET PICKLE 4
May 27 Wolv 7f SD 1 99
Jun 21 Brig 7f G 3 **101**
Aug 2 Brig 7f G 4 99
Sep 3 Wolv 7f FT 3 99
Nov 16 Sthl 7f FT 1 99

SWEET STREAM 5
Aug 15 Deau 10f G 1 **115**
Sep 7 Donc 14½f GF 1 103

SWEET TREAT 3
Apr 10 Leop 7f GS 2 100
Jun 1 Leop 6f G 6 **108**
Nov 6 Leop 7f GS 5 105

SWEETEST REVENGE 4
Jan 5 Ling 6f SD 5 101
Apr 8 Ling 6f SD 9 99
Jun 27 Wolv 6f SD 3 101
Jly 4 Bath 5f G 1 100
Jly 20 Ling 5f SD 1 101
Aug 1 Wind 5f G 1 99
Aug 9 Bath 5f GF 3 **102**
Aug 21 Folk 5f G 6 101

SWEETWATER 5
Jan 14 Wolv 14f SW 3 **102**
Jan 21 Wolv 12f SD 6 101
Feb 18 Wolv 12f SD 2 101

SWIFT OSCAR 3
Jan 5 Ling 8f SD 1 **108**
Jly 9 Ling 8f SD 2 101
Jly 20 Sand 7f G 5 106
Aug 11 Sand 7f GF 2 **108**
Sep 17 Newb 7f GF 5 103

SWIFT SAILOR 4
May 4 Ches 18½f GS 2 103
May 28 Muss 14f G 3 103
Jun 25 Newc 16f G 11 108
Jly 9 Ling 16f SD 3 **114**
Jly 26 Gdwd 14f G 7 103
Sep 15 Pont 18f G 1 103

SWINBROOK 4
Sep 6 Ling 7f SD 6 100
Sep 21 Gdwd 6f GF 2 **107**
Oct 8 Sals 7f GF 3 101
Oct 19 Nott 6f GS 1 99

SWINDON 3
Jun 10 Chep 12f G 3 **99**

SWISS COTTAGE 3
Jun 25 Curr 10f G 4 **105**
Aug 20 Curr 10f GF 6 102

SYDNEY SYMPHONY 3
Feb 19 Wolv 8½f GF 1 **106**
Jun 27 Wolv 12f SD 5 99

SYDNEYROUGHDIAMOND 3
Mar 2 Sthl 6f SD 2 **99**

SYUKHTUN 3
May 22 Curr 8f G 7 **102**

T

TAAKEED 3
Jun 4 Hayd 8f G 3 **100**

TABADUL 4
Jun 8 Bevl 10f G 1 101
Jly 26 Gdwd 8f G 6 102
Sep 23 Hayd 8f G 4 104
Oct 8 Sals 8f GF 2 103
Oct 29 NmkR 8f S 5 **105**

TABOOR 7
Aug 2 Catt 5f GF 1 101
Aug 13 NmkJ 5f GS 1 **103**
Aug 22 Leic 5f G 3 100
Dec 21 Ling 6f G 4 99

TAG TEAM 4
Feb 5 Ling 5f G 6 103
May 9 Rdcr 6f GS 3 100
May 25 Ling 6f SD 2 101
Nov 5 Wolv 5f FT 2 99
Dec 6 Sthl 5f FT 6 100
Dec 17 Ling 5f FT 4 100
Dec 27 Sthl 5f SD 1 **105**

TAGULA BAY 3
May 23 Thsk 5f G 3 100
Aug 13 Ripn 5f G 2 **105**
Aug 20 Bevl 5f G 2 100

TAGULA BLUE 5
Jun 23 Thsk 8f G 5 **99**

TAGULA SUNRISE 3
May 21 Hayd 8f GF 12 101
Jun 3 Epsm 7f G 4 100
Jly 28 Gdwd 7f G 1 **106**
Sep 10 Muss 8f G 5 102
Sep 24 Hayd 6f GF 7 99

TAHIRAH 5
Jan 7 Wolv 8½f SW 3 **112**

TAHRIR 3
Apr 13 NmkR 7f G 1 103
Jun 15 York 8f G 6 101
Jly 5 NmkJ 7f G 3 104
Sep 1 Sals 7f G 1 **110**
Oct 13 NmkR 6f G 7 100
Nov 5 Donc 6f HY 2 105

TAHTHEEB 4
Feb 26 Ling 10f SD 3 **107**
Sep 1 Sals 14f G 3 106
Sep 21 Gdwd 10f G 3 106
Oct 9 Gdwd 12f G 6 103

TAKAFU 3
Jly 15 Pont 10f GF 1 **101**

TAKE A BOW 4
May 9 Wind 8½f GF 2 110
Jun 1 Nott 8f G 1 **112**

TAKE A MILE 3
Sep 8 Bath 10f GF 2 101

TAKE IT THERE 3
Sep 26 Bath 8f G 5 **99**

TAKES TUTU 6
Jan 29 Ling 7f SD 2 **109**
Feb 22 Ling 7f SD 10 101
Mar 18 Ling 8f SD 5 102
Mar 19 Ling 8f SD 2 105
May 17 Rdcr 8f G 3 101
May 23 Thsk 7f G 2 102
Jun 7 Rdcr 8f G 1 105
Jun 11 Ripn 8f G 5 100
Aug 3 Brig 8f G 11 99
Nov 15 Ling 7f FT 4 105
Dec 5 Ling 8f FT 5 103
Dec 19 Wolv 8½f FT 4 103

TAKHLEED 3
Apr 12 NmkR 7f GF 4 99
Apr 30 Gdwd 7f S 4 **106**
May 17 Leic 6f G 1 104

TAKHMIN 3
Mar 29 Pont 10f S 1 **110**
Apr 20 Catt 12f S 2 103
May 14 Newb 11f G 7 100

TALBOT AVENUE 7
May 6 Ches 5f GS 3 107
May 12 York 5f GS 3 107
May 28 Gdwd 5f G 8 99
May 31 Sand 5f G 10 103
Jun 18 York 6f GF 4 **109**
Jly 2 Hayd 6f GF 3 **109**
Jly 31 Ches 6f G 5 104
Aug 6 Hayd 5f G 2 108
Aug 18 York 5f GF 11 **109**
Sep 6 Leic 5f GF 4 103
Sep 17 Ayr 6f G 9 **109**

TALCEN GWYN 3
May 22 Brig 5½f G 1 101
Jun 28 Brig 5½f F 4 103
Jly 29 Gdwd 5f G 4 102
Sep 10 Ches 5f GS 6 **104**
Dec 17 Ling 5f FT 3 100

TALLY 5
Feb 11 Wolv 5f SD 2 100
Mar 21 Ling 6f SD 5 **102**

TAMALAIN 3
Aug 20 Sand 8f G 2 **102**

TAMINOULA 4
Jan 5 Ling 13f SD 4 99
Jan 14 Wolv 12f SW 4 102
Aug 2 Brig 7f G 3 100
Aug 18 Chep 8f GF 2 **103**
Sep 11 Gdwd 8f G 8 **103**

TANDORI 3
Aug 2 Deau 10f G 6 **105**

TANFORAN 3
Apr 6 Nott 8f GS 5 100
May 23 Thsk 8f G 1 100
Jun 23 Thsk 7f G 3 103
Jly 6 Catt 7f GS 1 **104**
Jly 31 Ches 7½f G 1 103

TANGIBLE 3
Aug 15 Nott 14f GF 2 **102**

TANGO STEP 5
Oct 23 Curr 6f S 12 **100**

TANNENBERG 4
Jun 17 Rdcr 11f G 2 101
Jly 5 Pont 12f G 3 **104**

TANWIR 4
Apr 26 Wwck 12½f GS 12 **99**

TANZANITE 3
Jly 27 Sand 8f GS 1 105
Aug 4 Chep 8f G 4 100
Aug 15 Wind 8½f GF 4 103
Sep 2 Hayd 8f G 1 **110**
Sep 14 Sand 8f G 2 105
Oct 1 NmkR 10f G 5 102
Oct 22 Newb 10f G 12 103

TAPA 3
Mar 30 Folk 6f S 1 **101**

TARABUT 3
Jun 10 Gdwd 14f G 2 99
Jly 23 Sals 14f G 3 **102**

TARAGAN 3
Jly 19 Yarm 11½f G 1 **104**

TARANAKI 7
Feb 12 Ling 6f SD 6 **106**
May 28 Ling 7f GF 2 101
Jun 13 Wwck 7f GF 3 105

TARANDOT 4
Jly 2 Leic 12f GF 3 99
Oct 25 Yarm 14f S 1 **101**

TARFAH 4
Mar 26 Kemp 8f GS 1 108
May 1 NmkR 9f G 1 **112**
Jun 15 York 8f G 5 105

TARKESAR 3
May 25 Leop 8f GF 3 **106**

TARRAMAN 3
Mar 31 Donc 8f G 1 99
Jun 9 Ripn 8f G 5 101
Aug 20 Bevl 10f GF 2 **106**

TARTATARTUFATA 3
Apr 16 Nott 5f G 2 **99**
Jun 10 Wolv 5f SD 1 **99**
Jly 29 Gdwd 5f G 8 **99**

TARTOUCHE 4
Jly 28 Gdwd 14f G 1 **103**

TARUSKIN 4
May 21 Curr 8f G 11 **107**

TASDEED 3
May 13 York 7f GS 2 **106**

TASS HEEL 6
Jan 22 Ling 16f FT 8 **101**

TATA NAKA 5
Sep 14 Yarm 10f G 10 99
Sep 20 Bevl 10f GF 8 **100**

TAU CETI 6
Oct 28 NmkR 10f GS 1 **110**

TAURANGA 3
Aug 20 Curr 10f GF 2 **107**

TAVALU 3
Oct 1 Rdcr 14f GF 4 **100**

TAWQEET 3
Jun 16 Newb 12f G 1 107
Jly 7 NmkJ 12f G 5 101
Jly 27 Gdwd 12f GS 3 103
Aug 18 York 14f G 1 **111**
Sep 10 Donc 14½f S 3 102
Sep 29 NmkR 14f GF 3 105

TAX FREE 3
Apr 30 Thsk 7f S 1 103
May 14 Thsk 8f G 3 103
Jun 12 Donc 7f F 1 100
Jly 5 NmkJ 6f G 1 **111**
Aug 27 York 6f G 1 **111**

TAXMAN 3
Sep 6 Catt 14f GF 2 **102**
Sep 28 Newc 16f GF 1 100

TAYIF 9
Jan 5 Ling 6f SD 4 **101**
Jan 13 Ling 6f SD 6 **101**

TCHERINA 3
May 13 York 12f GS 2 105
Aug 18 York 14f G 5 105
Oct 7 York 12f G 1 **106**
Oct 28 NmkR 12f GS 3 104

TE QUIERO 7
Jan 1 Sthl 8f SD 3 **112**
Jan 20 Sthl 7f SD 1 **112**
Dec 9 Wolv 8½f FT 9 102

TEDSDALE MAC 6
May 12 Carl 6f G 1 101
Jly 1 Bevl 8½f G 5 **103**
Aug 12 Newc 6f GS 4 **103**

TEDSTALE 7
Jan 28 Wolv 9½f SD 2 **105**
Feb 18 Wolv 8½f SD 9 **105**
Mar 19 Ling 8f SD 5 103
Apr 12 Muss 8f G 8 100
May 15 Ripn 10f G 7 102
May 26 Ayr 10f G 4 103
Jly 7 NmkJ 12f G 2 102
Sep 7 Donc 10½f GF 9 103

TEE JAY KASSIDY 5
Apr 21 Sthl 8f FT 5 **101**

TEEBA 3
Jun 12 Sals 8f G 1 101
Jly 22 Newb 8f G 2 **102**
Aug 20 Sand 8f G 3 100

TEES COMPONENTS 10
Jun 25 Newc 16f G 16 103
Sep 24 Hayd 14f GF 8 101
Oct 8 York 20f HY 3 103

TEMPER TANTRUM 7
Feb 5 Ling 7f HY 7 99
Mar 3 Ling 10f SW 7 99
Mar 21 Ling 10f SW 2 **101**
Mar 23 Ling 8f SD 1 100
Jly 12 Brig 10f G 6 100
Oct 30 Ling 7f SD 4 99

TEMPLE PLACE 4
Apr 20 Epsm 10f GS 10 99
May 20 Hayd 8f G 1 **109**
May 30 Sand 8f G 11 99
Jun 23 Newc 8f G 3 99

TEMPLET 5
Jan 17 Wolv 8½f SD 3 **108**
Feb 18 Wolv 8½f SD 4 106
Mar 12 Wolv 7f SD 4 103
May 21 Carl 8f G 7 100
Jun 8 Haml 8½f G 8 99

TEMPSFORD 5
Sep 19 Carl 12f G 1 **108**
Sep 26 Haml 13f G 2 99

TENDER FALCON 5
Apr 20 Epsm 12f GS 1 **111**
Jun 4 Epsm 12f G 10 101

TENDER TRAP 7
May 21 Ling 16f SD 7 **102**

TERENZIUM 3
Jun 15 Nott 8f GF 7 **100**

TERMINATE 3
Jan 26 Ling 10f FT 1 99
Feb 5 Ling 10f FT 2 **101**
Jun 25 Ches 10½f G 2 100

TERRA VERDE 3
Oct 1 Lonc 9½f G 8 **101**

TESARY 3
Apr 14 Ripn 6f S 1 100
May 19 Donc 6f GF 2 102
Jun 12 Donc 7f F 2 99
Jly 9 Sals 7f G 1 101
Jly 29 Gdwd 7f G 6 **108**
Aug 14 Pont 6f G 6 107

TETRAGON 5
Jun 2 Haml 9f GS 3 **102**
Jun 8 Haml 11f G 1 **102**

TEXAS GOLD 7
Apr 30 NmkR 5f G 8 99
May 20 Gdwd 5f G 6 99
Jun 4 Epsm 5f G 6 103
Jun 25 Wind 6f G 3 109
Jly 1 Sand 5f G 2 107
Jly 9 Ling 5f SD 2 101
Aug 6 Hayd 5f G 1 109
Aug 29 Epsm 5f G 1 109
Sep 8 Donc 5f F 2 **110**
Sep 17 Newb 5f GF 7 105
Sep 25 NmkR 6f G 8 109
Oct 2 Lonc 5f G 11 106

THAI HILL 3
Jun 27 Lonc 9½f G 9 **99**

THAKAFAAT 3
May 18 Gdwd 10f G 2 99
Jun 16 York 12f G 1 104
Jly 17 Curr 12f F 7 **106**

THE ABBESS 3
May 31 Leic 7f GF 5 **101**

THE BARONESS 5
Mar 22 Ling 5f SD 4 **102**

THE BONUS KING 5
Aug 17 Carl 7f GF 1 100
Sep 1 Carl 8f G 3 **102**
Sep 19 Carl 8f G 6 99

THE CARBON UNIT 3
Aug 14 Leop 9f F 1 101
Aug 20 Curr 10f GF 1 **108**
Sep 10 Leop 9f GF 15 102

THE CAT'S WHISKERS 5
Sep 25 NmkR 7f G 11 **105**

THE COIRES 3
Jly 21 Folk 9½f G 2 102
Aug 10 Sals 8f G 1 106
Aug 28 Gdwd 9f G 2 **108**
Sep 7 Donc 10½f GF 2 106

THE COMPOSER 3
Apr 22 Sand 8f G 6 **102**
Sep 23 Hayd 10½f G 7 100

THE CROOKED RING 3
Apr 6 Nott 5f S 2 104
Jly 16 Newb 6f GF 7 **107**
Jly 31 Ches 6f G 4 105
Aug 6 Wind 6f GF 5 102
Aug 13 Newb 7f G 6 101

THE FISIO 5
Jun 6 Wind 5f G 6 **101**
Aug 20 Bevl 5f G 1 99
Sep 14 Bevl 5f G 7 99
Dec 17 Ling 5f FT 3 **101**

THE FUN MERCHANT 4
Feb 9 Ling 8f FT 5 99
May 5 Chep 8f GS 1 104
Jun 1 Newc 8f G 7 99
Jun 27 Wind 8½f G 1 **107**

THE GAIKWAR 6
Mar 16 Wolv 9½f SD 5 99
May 4 Chep 8f S 7 99
May 26 Bath 8f G 1 99
Jun 10 Chep 7f G 2 99
Jun 29 Chep 8f G 2 100
Jly 8 Chep 8f GF 2 **104**
Jly 17 Rdcr 9f G 2 103
Aug 1 Wind 8½f GS 4 101
Aug 29 Chep 8f G 2 100
Oct 19 Bath 8f GS 2 102
Oct 31 Wolv 8½f SD 9 101

THE GEEZER 3
May 12 York 10½f S 2 109
Jun 4 Epsm 12f G 8 103
Jun 17 York 12f G 3 106
Jly 2 Hayd 12f GF 1 102
Jly 26 Gdwd 12f G 1 107
Aug 16 York 12f G 2 104
Sep 10 Donc 14½f S 2 105
Oct 1 Lonc 15f G 4 **112**

THE IRON GIANT 3
Jun 1 Leop 7f G 7 **100**

THE JOBBER 4
Jly 1 Sand 5f G 1 **108**
Jly 31 Newb 5f G 1 105
Oct 30 Ling 6f SD 4 **108**

THE KIDDYKID 5
Apr 2 Donc 6f G 2 108
Apr 14 NmkR 6f G 3 105
May 11 York 6f S 1 **112**
Sep 16 Newb 7f GF 5 103
Sep 27 Gdwd 7f G 7 99

THE LAST HURRAH 5
Apr 3 Curr 10f S 2 **109**
May 22 Curr 12f GS 10 103

THE LEATHER WEDGE 6
Mar 2 Sthl 5f SD 1 101
May 13 Haml 5f F 1 103
May 27 Catt 5f GF 1 103
Jun 18 Ayr 5f G 2 **105**
Jly 4 Muss 5f GF 3 103
Aug 17 Nott 5f GF 3 103
Aug 25 Muss 5f G 7 100
Sep 21 Rdcr 5f GF 2 103
Oct 18 Sthl 5f SW 2 101

THE LORD 5
Jan 1 Sthl 5f FT 5 104
Jan 7 Wolv 6f SW 5 102
Feb 5 Ling 5f SW 8 103
Mar 27 Muss 5f G 1 109
Apr 2 Kemp 5f GS 1 **110**
Apr 13 Bevl 5f G 3 103
May 6 Ches 5f GS 5 105
May 20 Gdwd 5f G 2 102
May 28 Muss 5f G 13 100
Jly 9 Ches 5f GF 7 104
Nov 16 Sthl 5f FT 10 101
Dec 3 Wolv 5f FT 5 101
Dec 6 Sthl 5f FT 3 104
Dec 17 Ling 6f FT 9 101

THE NAWAB 3
Jun 17 NmkJ 12f GF 4 **108**
Aug 20 Ches 16f G 2 **108**
Sep 10 Gdwd 16f G 1 103
Oct 8 York 20f HY 1 107

THE NUMBER 4
Apr 6 Catt 7f G 1 **103**

THE PEN 3
Aug 26 Newc 9f GF 10 101
Sep 5 Newc 10f G 6 100

THE PLAINSMAN 3
Jly 23 Ling 10f SW 5 **99**

THE PRINCE 11
Jun 27 Wind 8½f G 1 **102**

THE TATLING 8
May 15 Lonc 5f G 7 103
May 31 Sand 5f G 5 113
Jun 14 York 5f G 7 102
Jun 18 York 6f GF 8 106
Jly 2 Sand 5f G 3 105
Jly 28 Gdwd 5f G 2 112
Aug 18 York 5f GF 2 113
Sep 4 Curr 5f G 2 **115**
Sep 17 Newb 5f GF 1 111
Oct 2 Lonc 5f G 6 111
Oct 14 NmkR 6f G 5 111

THE TRADER 7
Jun 5 Chan 5f G 1 **113**
Aug 7 Deau 6½f G 7 111
Aug 18 York 5f GF 14 106
Sep 4 Curr 5f G 3 **113**
Sep 17 Newb 5f GF 6 106
Oct 2 Lonc 5f G 8 107

THE VIOLIN PLAYER 4
Feb 19 Wolv 12f G 2 **106**
Mar 3 Ling 12f SW 1 99
Apr 20 Epsm 12f GS 10 99
Aug 11 Bevl 10f GF 4 103
Sep 7 Donc 10½f GF 5 105
Oct 24 Ling 12f SW 4 **106**
Nov 19 Ling 12f FT 7 101
Dec 16 Wolv 12f FT 5 101

THE WAY WE WERE 4
Jun 23 Sals 10f G 4 **99**

THE WHISTLING TEAL 9
Jly 29 Gdwd 12f G 4 100
Sep 3 NmkJ 12f G 3 103
Sep 17 Curr 14f G 2 **104**

THE WIZARD MUL 5
May 11 Newc 9f G 3 **99**

THEATRE 6
May 1 Sals 14f GS 8 100
Sep 10 Gdwd 16f G 2 101

THEATRE LADY 7
Jan 21 Wolv 12f SD 4 **102**

THEATRE OF DREAMS 3
May 31 Rdcr 5f G 6 **99**
Jly 13 Catt 5f G 3 **99**

THEATRE TINKA 6
Jan 21 Wolv 12f SD 5 102
Apr 2 Wolv 12f FT 2 **103**

THEBESTISYETTOCOME 3
Aug 20 Ling 10f SD 1 **103**

THIRD EMPIRE 4
Apr 9 Newc 9f S 1 **108**

THIS IS MY SONG 3
May 5 Folk 9½f GS 3 **106**

THISTLE 4
Jun 17 Rdcr 8f G 4 99
Jly 11 Ayr 11f F 4 **104**

THORNABY GREEN 4
Apr 25 Haml 6f G 4 102
Jly 20 Catt 6f G 6 99
Aug 25 Muss 8f G 6 **104**
Sep 10 Muss 8f G 4 101
Nov 22 Sthl 8f SW 1 103

THORNTOUN PICCOLO 3
Jun 18 Ayr 6f G 2 **101**

THORNY MANDATE 3
Jly 23 Ling 10f SW 1 **104**
Jly 31 Ches 10½f G 2 100

THREE GRACES 5
Jun 2 Hayd 7f G 4 111
Jly 9 Ches 7f GF 1 **115**
Aug 18 York 7f GF 8 105

THREE MIRRORS 5
May 22 Curr 12f GS 12 **100**

THREE WRENS 3
Apr 21 Bath 8f GS 3 99
May 14 Nott 8f F 1 **107**
Oct 5 Nott 8f GF 2 102
Nov 19 Ling 8f FT 1 105
Dec 17 Ling 8f FT 4 103

THREEZEDZZ 7
Aug 29 Chep 8f G 3 **100**

THROUGH THE RYE 9
May 25 Ripn 16f G 2 103

THROW THE DICE 3
May 14 Nott 6f F 2 **105**

THUNDER CALLING 3
Oct 22 Newb 10f GS 6 **99**

THUNDER ROCK 3
Jun 30 Yarm 11½f G 1 103
Aug 27 York 10½f G 3 **104**

THUNDERWING 3
Oct 3 Pont 8f G 7 100
Oct 29 Ayr 9f HY 4 **101**

THURLESTONE ROCK 5
Jan 5 Ling 7f SD 8 **100**
Feb 8 Ling 6f SD 11 99
Mar 4 Wolv 6f SD 9 99

THYOLO 4
Apr 30 NmkR 10f G 5 103
May 30 Rdcr 10f G 6 103
Jun 17 York 10½f G 3 **109**
Jly 9 York 10½f G 10 99
Aug 6 Hayd 10½f GF 11 102
Sep 17 Newb 10f GF 14 107
Oct 7 York 10½f G 6 102

TI ADORA 3
Sep 17 Wolv 12f FT 1 **104**
Oct 3 Wind 11½f GF 6 99
Nov 16 Sthl 12f FT 6 99

TIAMO 3
May 31 Sand 14f G 4 101
Jun 10 Gdwd 14f G 1 100
Jly 6 Catt 16f GS 1 99
Jly 24 NmkJ 15f GS 3 102
Aug 26 Thsk 16f GF 7 99
Oct 1 NmkR 14f G 6 **103**

TIBER TIGER 5
May 7 Ling 7f G 1 99
May 31 Rdcr 7f G 1 **105**
Jun 15 Nott 8f GF 5 102
Jun 30 Yarm 7f G 4 99
Oct 3 Wind 8½f GF 5 103

TICERO 4
Jan 29 Ling 10f SD 1 **110**
Feb 12 Ling 10f SD 6 101
Apr 20 Catt 12f S 3 102

TICKI TORI 3
Apr 5 Folk 9½f S 2 **102**

TIDY 5
Mar 24 Wolv 7f SD 4 100
Apr 9 Newc 8f S 3 **102**

TIFFANY GARDENS 3
Oct 9 Curr 5f GS 6 **99**

TIGANELLO 4
Mar 28 StCl 8f GS 3 **112**
May 1 StCl 8f HD 9 111
Jun 12 Chan 8f GF 3 102
Oct 1 Lonc 8f G 6 110
Oct 30 StCl 8f G 8 110

TIGER DANCE 3
Oct 15 NmkR 7f G 6 **108**

TIGER ROYAL 9
Sep 17 Curr 5f G 9 **104**
Oct 23 Curr 6f S 7 **104**

TIGER TIGER 4
Apr 20 Epsm 10f GS 7 107
May 4 Ches 10½f GS 1 **110**
May 11 York 10½f S 3 105
Jly 26 Gdwd 10f G 5 104
Aug 27 Wind 11½f G 4 104
Dec 16 Wolv 12f FT 4 101

TIGHT SQUEEZE 8
Jan 10 Wolv 9½f SD 10 **102**
Jan 19 Ling 10f FT 7 101
Jun 17 Gdwd 12f G 4 **102**
Jly 8 Ling 10f G 7 101
Jly 30 NmkJ 12f GF 7 100
Aug 21 Folk 12f G 3 99
Aug 28 Bevl 12f GS 2 100
Sep 12 Rdcr 14f G 2 **102**

TIGIM 6
Jly 16 Curr 5f F 3 **110**
Sep 17 Curr 5f G 12 103

TILT 3
Jly 5 Wolv 12f FT 4 100
Aug 15 Nott 14f GF 3 101
Sep 27 Nott 16f GF 4 **103**

TIMBERLAKE 3
Jun 25 Ling 10f SW 7 **100**

TIME DISCLOSES ALL 5
May 8 Leop 8f S 2 **111**
May 21 Curr 8f G 4 **111**
Sep 10 Leop 9f GF 7 106

TIME MARCHES ON 7
Jun 27 Muss 16f G 2 100

TIME N TIME AGAIN 7
Jan 11 Sthl 6f SW 5 100
Feb 18 Wolv 6f SD 10 99
Mar 4 Wolv 6f SD 3 104
Mar 12 Wolv 6f SD 6 **105**
Aug 2 Catt 6f G 3 103
Aug 6 Hayd 6f G 7 99
Sep 12 Rdcr 6f G 3 **105**

TIME TO REGRET 5
Aug 2 Catt 7f G 4 **99**

TIMES REVIEW 4
Feb 11 Wolv 5f SD 5 102
Mar 4 Wolv 6f SD 8 99
Sep 22 Pont 5f G 2 **103**
Oct 1 Rdcr 5f GF 5 99

TINCTURE 3
May 4 Ches 11½f GS 3 **101**

TINY TIM 7
Feb 14 Ling 6f SD 2 99
Jun 15 Chep 6f GS 2 **105**

TIPPERARY ALL STAR 5
Mar 20 Curr 8f HY 7 **106**
May 21 Curr 8f G 15 103
Oct 9 Curr 12f GS 4 103

TIPSY LAD 3
Nov 26 Ling 7f FT 2 **99**
Nov 29 Sthl 7f SD 2 **99**

TIRWANAKO 3
Apr 3 Lonc 10f S 4 **103**

TITIAN TIME 3
May 22 Curr 8f G 12 **107**
Jly 2 Sand 8f G 4 104

TITINIUS 5
Jun 29 Catt 7f G 3 **100**

TITUS SALT 4
Jly 15 Haml 8½f F 2 **99**
Jly 27 Muss 8f GF 4 **99**

TIVISKI 3
Apr 26 Wwck 7f GS 8 100
Dec 16 Wolv 6f FT 1 **102**

TIYOUN 7
May 1 NmkR 16f G 4 **103**

TOBEROGAN 4
May 5 Chep 6f GS 7 100
May 22 Curr 6f G 2 **107**
Jly 6 Naas 6f GF 2 105
Aug 20 Curr 6f GF 4 102

TODMAN AVENUE 3
Aug 20 Bevl 10f GF 9 99
Sep 19 Carl 12f G 5 **101**

TOFANA 3
Jly 20 Naas 6f GF 5 **99**

TOFFEE VODKA 3
May 14 Newb 7f F 3 99
Aug 7 Ling 8f SD 1 **100**

TOGETHER 5
Mar 28 StCl 8f GS 6 **109**
May 22 Lonc 7f GF 8 106

TOKEWANNA 5
Feb 28 Wolv 9½f SD 1 **110**
Jly 2 Hayd 8f GF 3 101
Aug 17 Carl 8f GF 4 103
Aug 25 Muss 8f G 9 102
Sep 10 Muss 8f G 1 103

TOLDO 3
May 4 Ches 12½f GS 4 99
May 15 Ripn 12f G 1 **104**
May 30 Rdcr 11f G 4 101
Jun 9 Ripn 12f GF 2 99
Oct 21 Donc 14½f S 1 100
Nov 5 Donc 16½f S 2 103

TOLPUDDLE 5
Mar 20 Curr 8f HY 9 105
Apr 3 Curr 10f S 4 104
Apr 23 Sand 10f G 3 **106**
May 8 Leop 8f S 1 102
May 22 Lonc 9f GF 6 104

TOM FOREST 3
Apr 26 Wwck 7f GS 1 **109**
May 11 Newc 7f G 1 101
Jly 2 Sand 7f G 10 100

TOM FROM BOUNTY 5
Jan 7 Wolv 8½f SW 6 **103**

TOM TUN 10
Mar 31 Donc 6f G 2 103
Apr 6 Nott 5f S 3 99
Apr 16 Thsk 6f S 1 102
Jun 25 Newc 6f G 6 102
Oct 22 Donc 5f S 4 **110**

TOMASINO 7
May 1 Haml 13f S 4 **102**
May 23 Carl 12f GS 1 99
Jly 15 Carl 12f G 2 **102**
Aug 12 Catt 12f G 3 101
Aug 29 Newc 14½f GF 2 100
Sep 3 Thsk 12f G 3 100

TOMMY SMITH 7
Jun 23 Thsk 5f GF 2 **102**

TOMMYTYLER 6
Mar 17 Sthl 8f GF 2 **99**

TOMTHEVIC 7
Jly 21 Bath 5f G 2 **99**

TONI ALCALA 6
Mar 7 Wolv 14f SD 4 99
Apr 19 Sthl 16f GF 4 102
Apr 29 Muss 14f G 3 102
May 7 Bevl 16f G 5 100
May 21 Catt 14f GF 5 103
Jun 10 Catt 16f GF 3 107
Jun 23 Newc 16f GF 3 99
Jly 30 Thsk 16f G 3 104

TONY JAMES 3
Apr 13 NmkR 7f G 4 **107**
Apr 30 NmkR 8f G 8 **107**
May 15 Lonc 8f G 11 105

TONY THE TAP 4
Apr 30 NmkR 6f G 6 **109**
May 7 NmkR 6f GF 2 104
May 21 Catt 7f GF 4 104
Jun 4 Epsm 6f G 5 104
Jun 12 Sals 5f G 5 105
Jly 6 NmkJ 5f GF 2 102
Sep 24 Hayd 5f GF 7 104
Oct 21 Newb 6f G 2 104
Oct 30 Ling 6f SD 6 103

TONY TIE 9
Apr 12 Muss 8f G 9 100
May 26 Ayr 10f G 3 103
Jun 17 Ayr 8f G 4 100
Jly 11 Ayr 8f F 3 103
Jly 19 Ayr 8f G 4 **106**
Sep 17 Ayr 10f G 3 100
Sep 28 Newc 8f GF 1 99
Oct 9 Newc 10f G 8 103

TOP DIRHAM 7
Apr 9 Newc 8f S 4 101
Jun 4 Donc 7f G 1 106
Jun 22 Carl 8f GF 6 102
Jly 30 Thsk 8f G 2 **107**

TOP MAN TEE 3
Sep 27 Nott 8f GF 3 102
Oct 5 Nott 10f G 2 102
Oct 22 Newb 10f GS 1 **106**
Nov 29 Ling 8f FT 8 103

TOP MARK 3
Sep 13 Sals 7f G 2 **103**
Sep 30 Ling 7f FT 1 **103**

TOP SEED 4
Mar 26 Kemp 10f GS 9 100
Apr 2 Donc 12f G 5 **107**
Apr 30 NmkR 10f G 6 103
May 11 York 10½f S 6 99
May 25 NmkR 10f G 7 99
Jun 4 Epsm 12f G 12 101

TOP SPEC 4
May 2 Donc 10½f G 10 102
May 30 Sand 10f G 2 100
Jun 10 Sand 10f GF 3 102
Jly 7 NmkJ 12f G 6 100
Jly 21 Sand 10f GF 5 101
Sep 3 NmkJ 10f G 3 **105**
Sep 19 Leic 10f G 1 99

TOP STRATEGY 5
May 25 Leop 14f GF 8 102

TOP THE CHARTS 3
May 30 Chep 8f G 2 101
Jly 5 NmkJ 10f G 4 100

Jly 18 Wind 10f G 2 99
Aug 4 Hayd 10½f GF 3 104
Aug 13 Newb 10f G 4 101
Sep 8 Bath 11½f GF 1 104
Sep 21 Gdwd 12f G 1 **110**
Oct 1 NmkR 14f G 8 99
Oct 14 NmkR 12f G 2 104

TOP TREES 7
Dec 28 Wolv 14f G 4 **102**

TOPARUDI 4
Sep 23 Hayd 10½f G 2 **105**
Oct 25 Yarm 10f S 2 104
Nov 2 Nott 10f S 3 102

TOPATOO 3
Apr 29 Nott 8f G 3 99
May 11 York 7f GS 2 99
Aug 27 York 8f G 1 106
Aug 31 York 8f G 3 **108**
Sep 14 Sand 8f G 8 102
Oct 8 York 9f GS 5 102

TOPKAT 4
Jun 12 Sals 12f G 1 105
Jly 1 Sand 14f G 7 101
Jly 16 NmkJ 15f GF 4 101
Aug 2 Brig 12f G 2 106
Oct 14 NmkR 12f G 5 103

TOPTON 11
Jun 17 NmkJ 8f GF 3 99
Jun 24 NmkJ 8f G 3 99
Aug 7 Rdcr 8f G 2 99
Aug 12 NmkJ 8f G 3 99
Aug 18 Chep 8f GF 8 100
Sep 2 NmkJ 8f G 7 **104**
Nov 5 Wolv 8½f FT 1 101

TORINMOOR 4
May 2 Donc 10½f G 3 107
May 25 NmkR 10f G 2 102
Sep 17 Newb 10f GF 9 **110**
Oct 9 Gdwd 10f G 2 106

TORQUEMADA 4
Jun 1 Yarm 7f G 2 99
Jun 13 Wwck 7f GF 5 101
Sep 20 Bevl 7½f GF 2 **104**

TORRENS 3
Jun 23 Leic 10f GF 4 101
Jly 4 Ripn 12f G 1 102
Jly 8 Ches 10½f F 1 104
Jly 14 Haml 11f GF 3 100
Aug 19 Ches 10½f GF 1 102
Aug 27 York 10½f G 7 99
Sep 22 Pont 10f G 5 **108**
Oct 1 NmkR 10f G 8 100

TORRENT 10
Apr 5 Sthl 5f FT 1 101
Jun 9 Ripn 5f G 6 100
Jun 29 Catt 5f GF 3 99
Jly 18 Ayr 5f GF 3 **102**
Sep 28 Newc 5f GF 6 100
Nov 30 Wolv 5f SD 2 99

TORRID KENTAVR 8
Apr 9 Newc 8f S 1 103
Jly 8 York 10½f GS 2 105

Sep 3 Thsk 12f G 4 99
Sep 14 Sand 10f G 2 100

TOSCO 5
Feb 23 Ling 7f G 9 **100**

TOSHI 3
Apr 1 Donc 10½f GS 2 **104**
May 31 Rdcr 10f G 2 101
Aug 10 Haml 9f F 2 **104**
Oct 3 Pont 8f G 3 99
Dec 10 Wolv 9½f FT 6 100

TOSS THE CABER 3
Jly 4 Muss 9f GF 1 **107**

TOTAL TURTLE 6
Jun 25 Newc 16f G 17 103
Oct 15 NmkR 18f G 9 102
Oct 30 Ling 16f SD 4 **105**

TOTALLY SCOTTISH 9
Apr 18 Pont 21½f S 2 104

TOTALLY YOURS 4
May 23 Wind 6f F 7 **100**

TOUCH OF EBONY 6
Jan 2 Sthl 11f SD 2 **108**

TOUCH OF LAND 5
May 22 Lonc 9f GF 4 106
Jun 15 York 10½f G 4 105
Oct 1 Lonc 9½f G 1 **108**
Oct 15 NmkR 10f G 13 99

TOUGH LOVE 6
Apr 12 Muss 8f G 6 102
May 17 Rdcr 8f G 4 101
May 21 Catt 7f GF 2 **107**
Jun 4 Donc 7f G 2 103
Jly 17 Rdcr 8f G 2 102
Aug 6 Rdcr 8f G 4 **107**
Aug 29 Ripn 8f G 8 103

TOUPIE 3
May 15 Lonc 8f G 2 112
Jun 5 Chan 8f GF 2 112
Jly 31 Deau 8f G 4 **113**
Oct 1 Lonc 7f G 8 108

TOURNEDOS 3
Jun 25 Newc 6f G 7 100
Jly 9 Ches 5f GF 1 **111**
Jly 28 Gdwd 5f G 7 106
Aug 20 Bevl 5f G 5 105
Aug 29 Epsm 5f G 4 107
Sep 4 Lonc 5f GF 4 109
Sep 17 Newb 5f GF 12 99

TOYLSOME 6
May 22 Lonc 7f GF 7 **106**

TRAFALGAR SQUARE 3
Jun 10 Sand 8f GF 6 100
Aug 10 Sand 7f GF 4 99
Sep 1 Rdcr 7f G 1 101
Sep 10 Muss 8f G 3 **106**

TRAGIC LOVER 9
Jun 1 Leop 16f G 10 **104**

TRANCE 5
May 21 NmkR 14f GS 1 **107**
May 28 Muss 14f G 4 103
Sep 17 Ayr 13f G 6 100
Dec 6 Sthl 14f FT 2 104
Dec 10 Sthl 14f FT 1 104
Dec 15 Sthl 12f SD 4 105

TRANSACTION 3
May 1 NmkR 7f G 8 **102**

TRANSVESTITE 3
May 7 NmkR 8f GF 2 101
Jun 20 Nott 8f F 4 **102**
Jly 14 Epsm 10f G 4 101
Aug 13 Gdwd 8f G 1 101
Oct 17 Wind 10f G 10 99

TRAPRAIN 3
May 7 Ling 10f G 3 102
May 28 Muss 8f G 3 105
Oct 5 Nott 10f G 1 **109**

TRAYTONIC 4
Jly 2 Hayd 6f GF 1 **112**
Jly 23 Newb 7f GF 5 **112**
Aug 27 NmkJ 6f G 3 103
Sep 17 Ayr 6f G 19 99
Sep 25 NmkR 6f G 12 105

TREASON TRIAL 4
Jun 23 Leic 12f GF 5 99
Oct 8 York 14f S 1 **102**

TREASURE CAY 4
Jan 1 Sthl 5f FT 2 106
Jan 27 Sthl 5f FT 4 101
Feb 5 Ling 5f FT 1 **107**
Feb 19 Wolv 5f FT 4 105
Mar 19 Ling 5f SD 5 101
Mar 27 Muss 5f G 3 100
May 14 Thsk 5f G 6 103
May 27 Brig 5½f GF 2 102
Jun 4 Epsm 5f G 8 101
Jun 7 Ches 5f GF 3 104
Jun 25 Ches 5f G 2 101
Jly 15 Wwck 5½f G 6 101
Aug 5 NmkJ 6f GF 2 103
Aug 23 Yarm 5f G 2 **107**
Sep 19 Leic 5f F 1 104

TREBLE SEVEN 3
Sep 26 Bath 8f G 3 **99**

TREETOPS HOTEL 6
Feb 5 Ling 7f G 5 **100**
Sep 20 Brig 8f G 3 **100**

TREMAR 3
Mar 19 Ling 7f SD 3 103
Oct 14 NmkR 6f G 6 **107**

TRESOR SECRET 5
Jun 24 Wolv 12f SD 2 99
Jly 5 Wolv 12f FT 1 **101**
Aug 8 Wolv 12f SD 1 **101**

TREVIAN 4
Jly 19 Ayr 8f G 9 100
Aug 23 Brig 7f G 2 **101**
Aug 29 Chep 8f G 1 **101**

TREW CLASS 4
Jun 10 Sand 10f GF 1 103
Jun 23 Newc 10f GF 5 99
Jly 23 York 10½f GS 1 **106**
Aug 10 Sals 10f G 5 **106**
Aug 23 Yarm 10f G 3 103
Sep 17 Newb 10f GF 16 105

TRIALS 'N TRIBS 3
Nov 10 Ling 12f SD 3 **100**

TRIBUTE 4
Jly 14 Leic 6f GF 10 99
Jly 20 Catt 6f G 1 **107**
Aug 2 Catt 6f G 4 101
Aug 14 Bath 5½f G 3 102

TRICK CYCLIST 4
Jly 15 Carl 5f GF 1 99
Jly 20 Catt 5f GF 2 102
Jly 23 Newc 5f GF 2 **104**
Sep 16 Ayr 5f GF 5 100
Oct 1 Rdcr 5f GF 3 101

TRICK OF LIGHT 3
Aug 17 Nott 10f G 1 **105**

TRICKSTEP 4
Jan 3 Sthl 12f SD 5 **100**

TRICKY VENTURE 5
Apr 26 Sthl 11f FT 2 99
Dec 20 Ling 10f FT 5 **103**

TRIFTI 4
Jan 29 Ling 10f SD 8 105
Feb 8 Ling 7f SD 1 103
Mar 16 Wolv 7f SD 1 103
Jly 22 Wolv 8½f FT 6 100
Sep 13 Yarm 11½f G 7 101
Oct 1 Wolv 8½f FT 1 103
Oct 29 Wolv 9½f SD 3 **106**
Nov 12 Ling 8f FT 8 100
Nov 26 Wolv 9½f FT 1 105

TRINCULO 8
Jan 7 Wolv 6f SW 4 102
Jun 1 Newc 5f G 1 102
Jun 10 Sand 5f GF 1 105
Jly 2 Bevl 5f G 1 105
Jly 15 Pont 5f GF 4 101
Sep 10 Ches 5f GS 1 **110**

TRIPLE JUMP 4
Jly 8 York 10½f GS 6 **102**

TRIPLE TWO 3
Jly 5 NmkJ 7f G 6 **102**
Jly 23 Sals 7f G 3 99

TRIPLE ZERO 3
Aug 31 Ling 6f GF 1 **99**

TRITONVILLE LODGE 3
Jly 1 Wolv 12f GF 3 103
Jly 25 Wind 10f GS 2 102
Oct 19 Bath 11½f GS 5 100

TRIVANDRUN 3
Apr 12 Muss 9f G 4 100
May 28 Muss 8f G 1 **109**

TROJAN FLIGHT 4
Apr 23 Ripn 6f S 2 106
Apr 30 Thsk 5f S 1 105
May 7 Bevl 5f GF 3 104
May 14 Thsk 6f G 3 100
May 27 Catt 6f GF 1 104
Jun 17 Rdcr 6f G 6 104
Jun 25 Donc 6f GF 3 106
Jly 2 Bevl 5f G 6 100
Jly 15 Pont 5f GF 6 99
Jly 24 Pont 6f G 2 105
Jly 29 Thsk 6f G 9 101
Aug 1 Ripn 6f G 6 102
Sep 9 Donc 5f G 4 **109**
Nov 1 Catt 7f GS 2 102

TROMP 4
Apr 1 Ling 12f SD 1 103
Jun 17 Gdwd 12f G 6 99
Oct 24 Ling 12f SW 5 **105**

TROPICAL LADY 5
Mar 20 Curr 8f HY 2 99
Jun 26 Curr 8f F 6 102
Jly 2 Leop 7f F 5 107
Jly 17 Curr 7f F 3 106
Aug 7 Curr 10f G 1 **117**

TROPICAL SON 6
Jan 10 Wolv 12f SD 5 **99**

TROTTERS BOTTOM 4
Jun 2 Sand 5f G 6 **100**

TROUBLE MAKER 4
Oct 24 Ling 6f SW 3 **99**

TROUBLE MOUNTAIN 8
Apr 23 Hayd 10½f G 6 101
Jly 8 York 10½f GS 4 **105**
Oct 9 Newc 10f G 7 103
Nov 2 Nott 10f S 5 99

TRUCKLE 3
Feb 10 Sthl 11f SD 5 **99**

TRUE 4
Jun 29 Catt 12f G 4 **102**

TRUE COMPANION 6
Feb 19 Wolv 12f G 4 **106**
Apr 6 Nott 10f GS 1 103
Apr 16 Newb 10f GS 2 99
May 4 Ches 10½f GS 10 103
May 23 Thsk 12f G 5 100
Oct 17 Wind 10f G 4 101
Oct 25 Yarm 10f S 4 102
Nov 26 Wolv 9½f FT 6 99
Dec 21 Ling 12f FT 2 101

TRUE LOVER 8
Oct 15 NmkR 18f G 13 **100**

TRUE MAGIC 4
May 21 Carl 5f GF 2 **106**
Aug 17 Carl 5f GF 3 100

TRUE NIGHT 8
May 28 Muss 7f G 2 **102**
Jun 24 Newc 8f G 1 99
Jun 30 Epsm 7f G 7 99
Jly 23 Newb 7f GF 19 **102**

TRUE TO YOURSELF 4
Jan 20 Sthl 12f SD 2 **101**

TRUMAN 4
Sep 14 Yarm 10f G 2 **99**

TRUST RULE 5
Jun 18 York 12f G 8 99
Jly 12 Bevl 16f GF 4 **100**
Jly 31 Ches 12½f G 4 **100**

TRYMORE 3
Jan 15 Ling 8f SD 3 **99**

TSAROXY 3
May 14 Thsk 8f G 1 106
Jun 16 York 8f G 15 100
Jly 9 York 8f G 5 **107**
Sep 4 York 6f G 8 99

TUCKER 3
Apr 12 NmkR 7f GF 1 101
Apr 30 NmkR 8f G 10 107
May 20 NmkR 8f G 1 **113**
May 28 Gdwd 8f G 2 107
Jun 14 York 8f G 6 104
Jly 27 Gdwd 8f GS 10 110

TUNGSTEN STRIKE 4
Jun 4 Epsm 12f G 7 103
Jun 25 Newc 16f G 2 **111**
Jly 28 Gdwd 16f G 7 108
Sep 1 Sals 14f G 1 110
Oct 15 NmkR 16f G 2 **111**

TUNING FORK 5
Sep 11 Gdwd 8f G 11 **102**

TURBO 6
Mar 26 Kemp 10f GS 7 102
Apr 20 Epsm 12f GS 7 103

TURIBIUS 6
Feb 8 Ling 6f SD 7 **102**
Aug 23 Brig 5½f G 1 100
Sep 9 Sand 5f G 7 100
Dec 17 Ling 5f FT 5 100

TURKS WOOD 3
May 14 Nott 8f F 2 **106**
May 21 Carl 7f G 2 102
Jun 1 Yarm 7f G 1 101
Jun 18 NmkJ 7f G 4 99
Jun 23 Thsk 7f G 4 102

TURN 'N BURN 4
Feb 8 Ling 12f SD 6 99
Apr 20 Ling 12f FT 4 99
May 21 Ling 16f SD 6 103
Jun 23 Sals 14f G 4 103
Sep 15 Yarm 16f GS 3 **105**

TURN AROUND 5
Apr 28 Sthl 6f FT 1 99
May 27 Wolv 6f SD 2 **101**

TURN OF PHRASE 6
Jly 26 Bevl 12f G 3 **101**

TURN ON THE STYLE 3
Jly 18 Wind 6f G 2 **99**

TURNER 4
Jun 19 Wwck 12½f G 4 100
Jun 27 Pont 10f G 5 99
Jly 9 Ches 16f GF 1 **106**

TURNER'S TOUCH 3
Dec 29 Ling 10f GF 1 **108**

TURNKEY 3
Apr 7 Leic 6f S 1 **113**
Aug 28 Deau 6f G 5 108
Nov 1 MsnL 6f GF 9 109
Nov 6 Leop 7f GS 3 109

TURNSTILE 4
Aug 12 Newb 13½f G 10 103

TURNSTONE 3
Jan 20 Sthl 8f SD 1 **99**

TURTLE BOWL 3
May 15 Lonc 8f G 8 106
Jun 12 Chan 8f GF 1 115
Jly 3 Chan 8f G 1 **117**

TURTLE PATRIARCH 4
Apr 26 Wwck 12½f GS 5 **105**

TUSCAN FLYER 7
Aug 15 Brig 6f G 2 **101**
Sep 24 Brig 5½f GF 1 100

TUSCAN TREATY 5
Sep 20 Brig 8f G 2 **100**

TUSCARORA 6
Jan 31 Wolv 7f SD 4 **102**
May 23 Leic 7f G 3 101
Jun 13 Brig 8f G 3 101
Jly 23 Sals 7f G 2 100
Aug 2 Brig 7f G 2 101

TUVALU 3
Feb 10 Sthl 11f SD 3 **100**
Apr 25 Wind 11½f GS 3 **100**

TWENTYTWOANDCHANGE 6
Mar 20 Curr 8f HY 11 104
May 21 Curr 8f G 14 105
Jun 1 Leop 7f G 17 **108**

TWILIGHT BREEZE 6
Jun 1 Leop 16f G 5 104
Jun 26 Curr 12f F 11 **107**

TWIN PEAKS 3
Jan 10 Wolv 7f SD 1 **99**

TWYLA THARP 3
May 20 Gdwd 9f GS 1 102
Jun 16 York 12f G 2 103
Jly 2 Hayd 12f GF 8 100
Oct 1 Lonc 12½f G 6 **106**

TYBALT 3
Jly 25 Wind 10f GS 1 **104**
Oct 10 Wind 11½f G 4 99

TYBERIOR 6
Jun 27 Lonc 7f G 6 **109**

TYCHEROS 3
Oct 22 Wolv 12f SD 1 99
Dec 12 Wolv 14f FT 7 **102**

TYCHY 6
Aug 29 Epsm 5f G 7 **105**

TYCOON'S HILL 6
May 15 Lonc 5f G 3 108
Jun 5 Chan 5f G 4 110
Jly 9 Deau 6f GF 5 108
Aug 7 Deau 6½f G 6 **111**
Aug 28 Deau 6f G 4 109

TYPHOON GINGER 10
Sep 4 York 8f G 1 **111**

TYPHOON TILLY 8
Jan 6 Wolv 12f G 1 **108**
Mar 7 Wolv 12f SD 7 107
Jly 16 NmkJ 15f GF 5 100
Sep 12 Rdcr 14f G 1 103

TYRONE SAM 3
Aug 7 Rdcr 6f G 2 **104**

U

UHOOMAGOO 7
Mar 12 Wolv 7f SD 1 109
Apr 12 NmkR 7f GF 7 99
May 7 Ling 7f G 5 **111**
Jun 3 Epsm 8½f G 4 105
Jun 11 Sand 7f G 10 109
Jun 16 York 7f GF 10 101
Jly 23 Newc 7f GF 1 101
Sep 30 NmkR 7f G 11 100
Oct 14 NmkR 7f G 4 107
Oct 27 Ling 7f SD 11 102

UIG 4
May 25 Ling 10f G 5 102
Jun 7 Sals 10f G 4 100
Jun 15 Chep 10f GS 1 105
Jly 4 Wind 10f G 3 100
Jly 8 Ling 10f G 1 **107**
Jly 27 Gdwd 9f GS 4 102
Aug 12 Folk 9½f G 2 105
Aug 22 Leic 10f G 4 101

ULSHAW 8
Jun 29 Chep 12f G 7 **100**

ULYSEES 6
Apr 25 Haml 6f G 1 **104**
May 26 Ayr 7f G 4 99
Jun 17 Ayr 8f G 5 99
Jly 19 Ayr 8f G 5 102
Sep 16 Ayr 8f G 6 100

UMNIYA 3
Apr 13 NmkR 7f G 13 100
Sep 24 NmkR 8f G 10 **105**
Oct 11 Leic 8½f G 4 100

UMOJA 5
Jun 15 Leop 14f G 9 **99**

UNAVAILABLE 4
Mar 1 Ling 10f SD 6 **106**
May 14 Newb 12f G 10 99

Sep 17 Ayr 13f G 4 101

UNBRIDLED'S DREAM 4
Jun 23 Sals 10f G 5 **99**

UNCLE BULGARIA 3
May 11 Newc 8f G 1 **100**

UNCLE JOHN 4
Jan 21 Wolv 12f SD 7 101

UNDER MY SPELL 4
Jun 19 Wwck 6f G 4 **107**
Aug 4 Chep 8f G 3 100

UNDERSCORE 3
Aug 26 Sals 8f G 1 **105**

UNDETERRED 9
May 27 Catt 6f GF 6 100
Jly 5 Pont 6f G 7 101
Jly 20 Catt 6f G 4 101
Jly 24 Pont 6f G 3 **105**
Aug 10 Haml 6f GF 1 103
Aug 22 Haml 6f F 1 100
Aug 24 Catt 6f G 1 100

UNFURLED 3
Apr 30 Gdwd 10f S 1 102
May 18 Gdwd 11f G 1 106
Jun 4 Epsm 12f G 7 104
Jly 26 Gdwd 12f G 2 103
Aug 27 Gdwd 14f G 2 **109**

UNITED IN SPIRIT 4
Jun 1 Leop 14f G 11 **106**

UNITED SPIRIT 4
Jan 12 Wolv 8½f SD 8 100
Feb 12 Wolv 8½f FT 3 **104**
Aug 6 Ayr 10f F 2 101
Sep 5 Newc 10f G 7 99

UNLIMITED 3
May 13 Haml 5f F 2 102
Jly 6 Carl 5f G 1 **104**
Sep 22 Pont 5f G 4 100

UNSHAKABLE 6
May 30 Sand 8f G 10 100
Jly 5 NmkJ 8f G 2 106
Jly 29 Gdwd 8f G 1 **115**
Oct 14 NmkR 8f G 4 108

UNTIMELY 3
Sep 19 Carl 8f G 1 **101**

UP TEMPO 7
Jan 7 Wolv 7f SW 7 102
Feb 10 Sthl 6f SD 3 99
Mar 8 Sthl 8f SD 6 **104**
Apr 23 Hayd 6f G 2 99
May 9 Rdcr 6f GS 1 103
May 16 Wind 6f G 3 99

USHINDI 3
Aug 24 Catt 12f G 1 **99**

UTTERLY HEAVEN 3
May 22 Curr 8f G 4 111
Sep 10 Leop 8f GF 7 **112**

V

VADAWINA 3
May 1 StCl 10½f F 1 106
May 22 Lonc 10f GF 1 **108**
Jun 12 Chan 10½f G 4 107

VADEMECUM 4
Apr 4 Sthl 6f SD 1 **103**

VAGUE STAR 3
Jly 7 Folk 5f G 6 104
Jly 30 Donc 5f G 1 **107**

VAL DE MAAL 5
Jun 27 Wolv 6f SD 4 100
Jly 5 Wolv 6f FT 2 99
Aug 12 Newc 6f GS 1 103
Aug 19 Wolv 6f FT 4 101
Sep 12 Rdcr 6f G 2 **107**

VALANCE 5
Aug 12 Newb 13½f G 6 104

VALE DE LOBO 3
Jly 30 Gdwd 11f G 5 99
Aug 13 Ripn 12f GS 4 101

VALENTIN 3
May 31 Leic 7f GF 7 **100**

VALENTINA GUEST 4
Nov 6 Leop 8f S 7 **101**

VALENTINO 6
Mar 28 StCl 8f GS 1 **115**
May 1 StCl 8f HD 7 114
Jun 12 Chan 8f GF 6 101
Aug 28 Deau 8f G 3 102

VALEUREUX 7
Dec 9 Wolv 14f FT 5 **100**

VALIANT ROMEO 5
Jun 19 Wwck 5f GF 4 100
Jly 18 Ayr 5f GF 2 **102**
Jly 28 Muss 5f F 2 100
Aug 12 Folk 5f GF 1 **102**

VALIXIR 4
Apr 13 NmkR 9f G 3 108
May 22 Lonc 9f GF 1 109
Jun 14 York 8f G 1 116
Jly 24 MsnL 8f F 1 **117**
Aug 14 Deau 8f GF 3 114
Sep 4 Lonc 8f GF 5 113

VALJARV 4
Apr 30 NmkR 6f G 7 **109**
May 15 Ripn 6f G 2 101
May 28 Donc 7f G 8 100
Jun 24 NmkJ 6f G 6 99

VALLEY GER 6
Jun 1 Leop 14f G 13 **106**
Jun 15 Leop 14f G 7 102

VAMOSE 4
Jan 6 Wolv 8½f G 7 99
Aug 2 Brig 12f G 4 **105**

VAMP 4
May 31 Sand 9f G 2 99
Jun 18 NmkJ 10f G 3 99
Aug 30 Ripn 10f F 8 99
Oct 21 Newb 10f GS 1 **104**

VANADIUM 3
May 19 Donc 7f GF 3 **102**
May 30 Sand 7f G 1 **102**
Jun 20 Nott 8f F 5 100
Sep 2 Hayd 6f GF 2 100

VANBRUGH 5
Jan 5 Sthl 16f SD 1 101
Feb 3 Sthl 16f SD 1 **103**
Apr 26 Sthl 11f FT 1 102

VANDERLIN 6
May 20 Gdwd 7f GS 1 109
Jun 2 Hayd 7f G 2 **113**
Jly 9 Ches 7f GF 2 **113**
Jly 26 Gdwd 7f G 8 108

VAR 6
May 31 Sand 5f G 8 106
Jun 14 York 5f G 6 105
Jun 18 York 6f GF 5 **109**

VATORI 3
Mar 28 StCl 8f GS 4 **108**
Jun 5 Chan 10½f G 12 100
Jly 24 MsnL 10f F 8 107

VAUGHAN 4
May 20 NmkR 12f G 1 106
Jun 18 York 12f G 5 104
Jly 2 Hayd 12f GF 9 104
Jly 26 Gdwd 14f G 10 99
Aug 17 York 14f G 16 99
Sep 25 NmkR 12f G 3 **107**
Oct 14 NmkR 12f G 1 106

VELVET HEIGHTS 3
Aug 15 Nott 14f GF 6 100
Sep 27 Nott 16f GF 3 **106**

VELVET WATERS 4
Jun 1 Yarm 11½f G 2 103
Aug 11 Sals 14f GF 5 99
Sep 13 Yarm 11½f G 2 **105**
Oct 27 Ling 12f SD 8 100

VENABLES 4
Apr 14 NmkR 6f G 9 **99**

VENETIAN KING 3
May 23 Thsk 7f G 4 101
Jly 5 Pont 10f G 1 **104**

VENETIAN PRINCESS 3
Oct 11 Sthl 8f G 2 **99**
Nov 5 Sthl 8f FT 1 **99**

VERY WISE 3
Sep 9 Sand 8f GS 4 **102**

VIABLE 3
Jun 23 Leic 10f GF 2 **102**

VIANE ROSE 3
Aug 2 Deau 10f G 2 **115**
Aug 21 Deau 10f G 1 103

VIBE 4
May 16 Bath 8f G 2 **101**

VICARS DESTINY 7
Apr 18 Pont 21½f S 1 **108**
Jly 30 Thsk 16f G 5 101

VICIOUS KNIGHT 7
Jun 27 Muss 7f GF 1 **109**
Aug 26 Thsk 8f GF 3 99

VICIOUS PRINCE 6
May 25 Ripn 16f G DSQ **107**
Jun 8 Haml 12f G 5 101
Aug 10 Bevl 16f GF 3 105

VICIOUS WARRIOR 6
May 20 Hayd 8f G 11 101
May 30 Rdcr 10f G 7 102
Jun 7 Rdcr 8f G 4 101
Jly 9 York 8f G 3 **107**
Jly 18 Ayr 8f GF 2 105
Aug 6 Rdcr 8f G 6 102
Aug 18 York 8f G 11 106
Sep 16 Ayr 8f G 4 101
Nov 12 Ling 8f FT 3 102
Nov 26 Ling 8f FT 6 105

VICKY LANE 4
Jun 1 Leop 7f G 13 **108**

VICTORIA PEEK 3
Jly 6 Catt 6f GS 1 **103**

VICTORY DESIGN 3
Jun 10 Sand 8f GF 2 101
Jun 24 NmkJ 10f G 6 **102**

VICTRAM 5
Mar 20 Curr 8f HY 1 **115**

VIENNA'S BOY 4
May 25 NmkR 7f G 6 101
Jly 8 Chep 8f GF 9 99
Aug 6 Ling 7f SD 4 100
Sep 8 Epsm 7f G 8 101
Oct 27 Ling 7f SD 1 **102**

VIEWFORTH 7
Apr 11 Sthl 5f FT 2 103
Jun 8 Haml 5f G 1 **107**
Jly 2 Carl 6f GF 4 101
Sep 29 Ayr 6f G 4 102

VIGATA 4
Aug 21 Deau 10f G 7 **109**

VIKING SPIRIT 3
May 28 Gdwd 6f G 2 103
Jun 11 Ripn 6f G 3 106
Jly 5 NmkJ 6f G 3 **109**
Aug 7 Leic 7f G 7 101
Aug 27 York 6f G 10 100

VILLAGO 5
Jly 30 Thsk 16f G 1 **105**
Aug 14 Pont 17f G 4 103
Aug 26 Thsk 16f GF 3 **105**

VINANDO 4
Sep 10 Donc 12f S 2 108
Sep 24 NmkR 16f G 4 **112**

Oct 15 NmkR 18f G 4 104

VINDICATION 5
Jun 21 Brig 7f G 2 **103**

VINNIE ROE 7
May 25 Leop 14f GF 1 **107**
Aug 14 Leop 12f F 3 106
Sep 17 Curr 14f G 3 104

VIOLET PARK 4
May 9 Rdcr 7f GS 6 102
Aug 25 Ling 7f FT 4 100
Sep 27 Gdwd 7f G 2 106
Oct 29 NmkR 8f S 2 **107**

VIOLETS EMPIRE 3
Apr 3 Curr 7f S 3 **106**

VIRGINIA WATERS 3
Apr 10 Leop 7f GS 1 104
May 1 NmkR 8f G 1 112
May 22 Curr 8f G 8 110
Jun 3 Epsm 12f G 4 103
Jun 17 York 8f G 6 106
Jly 30 Gdwd 10f G 6 105
Sep 10 Leop 8f GF 3 **115**

VIRGINIA WOOLF 3
Jun 8 Leop 12f F 1 99
Oct 9 Curr 16f GS 8 106
Nov 6 Leop 16f S 2 **110**

VISIONIST 3
Jun 30 Newb 6f G 2 100
Aug 6 Wind 6f GF 9 99
Sep 24 NmkR 7f G 5 **112**
Oct 14 NmkR 7f G 17 102

VISIT WEXFORD 4
Aug 7 Curr 10f G 7 106
Sep 10 Leop 9f GF 5 **107**

VISTA BELLA 3
Feb 16 Ling 7f SD 1 104
Mar 26 Kemp 8f GS 1 108
May 1 NmkR 8f G 3 **109**

VIZ 3
Aug 20 Ling 12f SD 1 **102**
Aug 31 York 14f G 2 99

VLASTA WEINER 5
Feb 6 Wolv 7f SD 1 99
Nov 26 Ling 7f FT 1 **100**

VOCATINE 4
Jun 27 Lonc 7f G 1 **100**

VOICE MAIL 6
May 20 Hayd 10½f G 3 105
Jun 11 Leic 10f G 7 99
Jun 22 Bath 8f G 1 102
Jly 12 Brig 8f G 3 103
Aug 3 Brig 8f G 2 **106**
Aug 11 Bevl 10f GF 7 100
Aug 23 Brig 8f G 3 100
Aug 30 Ripn 10f F 6 100
Sep 13 Sals 8f G 6 100

VOILE 4
May 7 Ling 7f G 3 **108**

VOIX DU NORD 4
Apr 24 Lonc 10½f GS 4 111
Jun 5 Chan 12f G 4 **117**
Jun 26 StCl 12f GF 6 112

VOL DE NUIT 4
Sep 11 Lonc 12f G 4 **114**

VOLCAN MAGIQUE 5
May 8 Leop 8f S 7 **108**
Sep 4 Curr 10f G 7 104
Oct 9 Curr 8f GS 4 99

VOLTMETER 3
Oct 2 Lonc 12f G 15 **101**

VORTEX 6
Mar 12 Wolv 8½f SD 2 **111**
Apr 2 Donc 8f G 5 109
Apr 9 Ling 7f FT 1 **111**
May 29 NmkR 7f GF 1 107
Jun 25 NmkJ 7f G 1 109
Jly 9 Ling 8f SD 3 **111**
Sep 16 Newb 7f GF 2 107

VRACCA 3
Jun 27 Lonc 9½f G 1 **108**
Aug 3 Epsm 10f G 3 105

W

WAHCHI 6
Jun 1 Newc 8f G 8 99
Jun 27 Pont 10f G 1 101
Jly 11 Ayr 11f F 7 **102**

WAHOO SAM 5
May 13 Nott 8f F 5 100
Jun 28 Haml 8½f F 1 102
Jly 9 Haml 9f F 4 100
Aug 30 Ripn 10f F 1 **106**

WAINWRIGHT 5
Feb 18 Wolv 6f SD 3 **105**
Feb 24 Sthl 6f FT 3 101
Apr 26 Sthl 6f FT 1 101
Jun 28 Haml 6f F 1 100
Aug 25 Muss 8f G 8 102
Dec 2 Wolv 6f SD 2 104
Dec 20 Sthl 7f SW 3 103

WAIT FOR THE WILL 9
Jun 17 Gdwd 12f G 2 103
Jun 25 Wind 11½f G 6 103
Aug 12 Newb 13½f G 7 104
Sep 23 Ling 12f G 9 100
Oct 24 Ling 12f SW 6 **105**

WALK IN THE PARK 3
Jun 4 Epsm 12f G 2 **110**

WALKONTHEWILDSIDE 3
May 2 Wwck 7f G 1 103
Jly 2 Sand 7f G 1 **108**

WALTZING WIZARD 6
Apr 4 Sthl 8f SD 2 **99**

WANCHAI LAD 4
May 14 Thsk 5f G 1 108
Jly 4 Muss 5f GF 6 100
Jly 9 York 6f G 9 100
Jly 24 Newb 5f G 3 **112**
Jly 29 Gdwd 6f G 7 101
Sep 24 Hayd 5f GF 8 104
Oct 22 Donc 5f S 14 100

WANNA SHOUT 7
Apr 18 Wolv 8½f FT 1 **101**

WANSDYKE LASS 3
Apr 9 Newc 9f S 3 **106**

WAR AT SEA 3
Jun 26 Wind 10f G 4 103
Sep 16 Newb 11f G 7 **105**

WAR OWL 8
Oct 27 Ling 12f SD 3 **101**
Oct 31 Wolv 14f SD 1 100
Nov 7 Wolv 12f FT 2 99

WARDEN WARREN 7
Sep 6 Leic 7f GF 1 **99**

WARLINGHAM 7
Feb 7 Wolv 8½f FT 3 102
May 11 Brig 7f G 1 **105**

WARRSAN 7
May 1 NmkR 12f G 4 99
Jun 3 Epsm 12f G 4 108
Jun 15 York 10½f G 5 101
Jly 23 Newb 12f GF 4 110
Oct 2 Lonc 12f G 8 **116**

WASALAT 3
Jun 13 Brig 7f G 2 **99**

WATCHMYEYES 3
Oct 12 Ling 10f G 7 **100**

WATCHTOWER 3
Oct 17 Wind 8½f G 4 **102**

WATERSIDE 6
Jan 5 Ling 7f SD 1 106
Jan 29 Ling 7f SD 9 104
Feb 9 Ling 7f SD 4 101
Mar 18 Ling 7f SD 3 105
Apr 2 Kemp 7f GS 5 103
Apr 19 Sthl 7f GF 5 99
Jun 3 Gdwd 7f GS 3 105
Jun 30 Epsm 8½f G 1 102
Jly 14 Epsm 7f G 3 103
Jly 26 Gdwd 8f G 4 106
Aug 3 Brig 8f G 4 104
Aug 8 Wind 8½f GF 3 107
Nov 12 Ling 8f FT 5 102
Nov 29 Ling 8f FT 1 **109**
Dec 20 Ling 8f FT 4 103

WAVERLEY 6
Jly 16 Newb 10f GF 6 **108**
Aug 17 York 14f G 9 104

WAVERTREE ONE OFF 3
Aug 5 Ling 10f GS 5 99
Dec 30 Ling 10f FT 5 **100**

WAVERTREE WARRIOR 3
Jly 9 Ling 8f SD 1 102
Oct 1 Epsm 8½f GS 2 101

Nov 29 Ling 8f FT 9 **103**
Dec 20 Ling 8f FT 5 **103**

WAYWARD SHOT 3
May 7 Bevl 8½f GS 1 **100**
Sep 12 Muss 8f GF 1 99

WAZIR 3
Jun 11 Sand 7f G 2 **109**
Jly 2 Sand 7f G 9 101

WE'LL MEET AGAIN 5
Jun 9 Wolv 8½f SD 3 100
Jly 11 Wolv 8½f SD 2 100
Dec 3 Wolv 8½f SD 5 100

WE'RE STONYBROKE 6
Jan 5 Ling 6f SD 1 **105**
Jan 21 Wolv 6f SD 5 103

WEAKEST LINK 4
Jun 2 Haml 5f G 2 **100**
Jun 17 Rdcr 5f G 2 **100**

WEBBSWOOD LAD 4
Nov 10 Ling 12f SD 4 **99**

WEDDING PARTY 3
Aug 15 Wind 8½f GF 3 **103**
Sep 14 Sand 8f G 12 99

WEECANDOO 7
Jan 10 Wolv 9½f SD 8 **102**
Jan 19 Ling 10f FT 6 101

WEET A HEAD 4
Oct 5 Nott 10f G 7 **102**
Nov 12 Wolv 9½f FT 6 99

WEIGHTLESS 5
Apr 23 Sand 10f G 1 **109**
Jly 1 Sand 10f G 6 100
Aug 27 Wind 10f G 5 **109**
Sep 21 Gdwd 10f G 5 105

WELCOME STRANGER 5
Apr 23 Sand 8f G 10 100
May 12 York 7f GS 4 109
Jun 15 York 8f G 10 107
Jun 25 Wind 8½f G 2 106
Jly 16 Newb 10f GF 1 **112**
Aug 27 Wind 10f G 6 107
Sep 16 Newb 11f G 5 100

WELL ESTABLISHED 3
Sep 9 Sand 10f GS 1 **101**

WELLING 3
May 28 Ling 10f SW 5 **104**

WELLINGTON HALL 7
Apr 4 Yarm 10f GS 2 101
Jun 17 NmkJ 12f GF 2 **108**
Jly 7 NmkJ 12f G 3 102
Oct 17 Wind 10f G 6 101
Nov 19 Ling 12f FT 5 102
Dec 16 Wolv 12f FT 6 99

WELSH EMPEROR 6
May 7 Hayd 7f GS 1 111
May 11 York 6f S 3 109
Jun 2 Hayd 7f G 6 106

Oct 14 NmkR 6f G 1 **114**
Nov 1 MsnL 6f GF 2 **114**

WELSH WIND 9
Mar 4 Wolv 8½f SD 4 **102**
Nov 12 Wolv 8½f FT 4 99

WENDY'S GIRL 4
Jan 31 Wolv 6f SD 1 **100**

WESSEX 5
Feb 3 Sthl 8f SD 1 105
Feb 19 Wolv 7f SD 1 107
Feb 26 Sthl 8f FT 2 **112**
Mar 8 Sthl 8f SD 3 111
Mar 12 Wolv 7f SD 2 105
Jly 8 Chep 7f GF 8 100
Oct 20 Brig 6f GS 7 99
Nov 29 Sthl 6f SD 1 101
Dec 31 Wolv 7f SD 1 107

WEST END WONDER 6
Jan 24 Wolv 14f SD 3 99
Feb 21 Wolv 14f FT 4 99

WESTBROOK BLUE 3
Apr 4 Yarm 5f G 3 102
Apr 16 Thsk 5f S 1 103
May 5 Ches 5f GS 1 **105**
Aug 17 York 5f F 5 99

WESTCOTE 4
Feb 4 Wolv 9½f SD 1 **104**

WESTCOURT DREAM 5
May 10 Muss 9f G 2 100
Jly 13 Hayd 10½f G 1 **102**
Jly 28 Carl 9½f G 3 **102**
Sep 20 Bevl 10f GF 3 **102**

WESTER LODGE 3
May 15 Ripn 12f G 3 **101**
Aug 9 Bath 11½f GF 4 100

WESTERN FLYER 6
Jun 15 Leop 14f G 6 **102**

WESTERN HOUSE 3
Sep 17 Ayr 13f G 7 **100**

WESTERN ROOTS 4
Jan 12 Wolv 8½f SD 2 **105**
Jan 31 Wolv 7f SD 2 103
Feb 5 Ling 10f SD 2 102
Feb 16 Ling 10f SD 6 103
Jun 8 Bevl 7½f G 3 101
Sep 12 Muss 9f GF 5 99
Nov 7 Wolv 9½f FT 1 100
Dec 12 Wolv 9½f FT 1 101

WESTERNER 6
Apr 30 Lonc 15½f GS 1 115
May 22 Lonc 15½f GF 1 115
Oct 2 Lonc 12f G 2 **120**

WESTLAND 3
Jun 2 Sand 8f G 2 **101**

WHAT'S UP DOC 4
Jun 8 Leop 8f F 1 **107**

WHAT-A-DANCER 8
Jan 7 Wolv 6f SW 6 100
Jan 15 Ling 10f SD 5 **104**
Feb 22 Ling 7f SD 7 **104**
Mar 19 Ling 7f SD 6 103
May 27 Brig 7f GF 1 100
Jly 14 Epsm 7f G 4 102
Jly 22 York 7f G 4 100
Jly 28 Muss 8f G 1 103
Aug 15 Brig 7f G 3 103

WHATATODO 3
Aug 26 Bath 8f G 1 **105**

WHAZZAT 3
Oct 15 NmkR 10f G 12 101
Nov 5 Donc 10½f S 2 **107**

WHINHILL HOUSE 5
Jan 4 Ling 6f FT 1 102
Jan 10 Wolv 6f SD 1 99
Feb 12 Ling 6f SD 9 100
Feb 17 Sthl 5f SD 1 105
Mar 1 Ling 6f SD 5 103
Apr 26 Wwck 5f G 2 101
May 12 Carl 5f GF 1 104
May 21 Carl 5f GF 1 **107**
Jun 2 Sand 5f G 2 105
Jun 7 Ches 5f GF 7 99
Jun 24 Newc 5f G 14 99
Jly 11 Ayr 5f GF 1 105
Aug 6 Hayd 5f G 7 106

WHIPPASNAPPER 5
Oct 24 Ling 6f SW 2 100
Oct 30 Ling 7f SD 2 **101**

WHIPPER 4
May 1 StCl 8f HD 3 **117**
Jun 12 Chan 8f GF 4 102
Aug 7 Deau 6½f G 1 **117**
Aug 14 Deau 8f GF 2 115
Sep 4 Lonc 8f GF 4 116

WHIRLING 3
Jly 26 Bevl 12f G 1 99

WHIRLY BIRD 4
May 6 Ling 10f G 1 100
May 25 Ling 10f G 1 109
Sep 16 Newb 11f G 1 **110**
Oct 10 Wind 11½f G 3 101

WHISPERING DEATH 3
Sep 1 Rdcr 14f G 2 99
Oct 1 Rdcr 14f GF 1 **103**

WHISTLER 8
Apr 1 Donc 5f G 9 99
May 12 York 5f GS 7 104
May 20 Gdwd 5f G 1 103
May 28 Muss 5f G 9 102
Jun 18 York 6f GF 9 102
Jun 24 Newc 5f G 13 100
Jly 1 Sand 5f G 8 99
Jly 8 York 5f G 2 102
Aug 6 Hayd 5f G 16 101
Sep 3 Hayd 5f F 7 **106**
Oct 16 Muss 5f GF 6 102
Oct 22 Donc 5f S 13 102

WHITBARROW 6						
Apr	1	Donc	5f	G	8	100
Jun	4	Epsm	6f	G	8	102
Oct	22	Donc	5f	S	6	**109**
Nov	12	Ling	5f	FT	3	101
Dec	3	Wolv	5f	FT	4	102

WHITBY ECHO 3						
Sep	13	Thsk	12f	G	2	**101**

WHITE BEAR 3						
Jan	29	Ling	8f	SD	3	**104**
Jly	27	Leic	6f	G	3	99
Dec	15	Sthl	7f	SD	2	101

WHITE MOUNTAIN 3						
Jun	1	Leop	7f	G	6	**100**

WHITETHORNE 3						
Jly	28	Carl	7f	GS	1	100
Aug	19	Ayr	7f	GF	2	**103**

WHITGIFT ROCK 4						
Mar	3	Ling	8f	SW	5	102
Apr	1	Ling	8f	SD	2	102
Jun	3	Gdwd	9f	GS	2	99
Jun	17	Gdwd	12f	G	3	**103**

WHITSBURY CROSS 4						
May	29	NmkR	8f	GF	1	**99**
Jun	22	Sals	10f	G	1	**99**

WHO'D OF GUEST 4						
Jly	16	Curr	10f	GF	1	**107**

WHO'S WINNING 4						
Feb	26	Ling	5f	SD	9	99
Mar	1	Ling	6f	SD	2	**106**
Mar	18	Ling	6f	SD	2	101
Apr	20	Epsm	5f	GS	8	105
May	7	NmkR	6f	GF	1	**106**
Jly	1	Sand	5f	G	4	104
Aug	5	NmkJ	6f	GF	4	102
Sep	3	NmkJ	6f	G	12	100
Sep	13	Yarm	6f	G	4	101
Sep	21	Gdwd	6f	GF	12	101

WHONEEDSWINGS 3						
Nov	6	Leop	12f	S	4	**100**

WHOOPSIE 3						
Jly	29	Nott	16f	G	1	**102**
Aug	14	Pont	17f	G	5	**102**

WHORTLEBERRY 5						
Apr	10	Lonc	10f	S	8	105
Aug	21	Deau	10f	G	3	**112**

WHY NOW 3						
Jun	22	Carl	5f	GF	1	**105**
Nov	15	Ling	7f	FT	7	104

WICKED UNCLE 6						
Nov	5	Wolv	5f	FT	1	**100**

WIDELY ACCEPTED 3						
Apr	10	Leop	7f	GS	3	**99**

WIGGY SMITH 6						
May	2	Donc	10½f	G	11	101
Aug	20	Sand	10f	G	4	101
Aug	29	Epsm	10f	G	4	**107**
Sep	23	Ling	10f	G	4	105

WIGWAM WILLIE 3						
Aug	27	NmkJ	7f	G	10	99
Sep	16	Ayr	8f	G	2	**104**

WILD PITCH 4						
Jan	5	Ling	10f	SD	2	99
Jan	15	Ling	10f	SD	4	**102**
Jun	4	Ling	12f	SD	1	101

WILD SAVANNAH 3						
May	13	Newb	10f	GF	1	99
Jun	4	Hayd	12f	G	2	106
Sep	17	Newb	10f	GF	6	**111**
Nov	19	Ling	12f	FT	2	104
Nov	29	Ling	10f	FT	3	108

WILL HE ROCK 4						
May	21	Curr	12f	G	1	**109**
Jun	26	Curr	12f	F	2	**109**
Sep	4	Curr	10f	G	8	104

WILL HE WISH 9						
Jun	4	Donc	7f	G	3	102
Jly	8	Chep	7f	GF	5	103
Jly	19	Yarm	7f	G	3	**110**
Aug	11	Sand	7f	GF	1	**110**
Nov	25	Wolv	6f	FT	4	104
Dec	16	Wolv	6f	FT	1	107

WILL THE TILL 3						
Aug	26	Bath	8f	G	3	**101**

WILLHECONQUERTOO 5						
Jan	4	Ling	5f	FT	3	104
Feb	26	Ling	5f	SD	4	102
Mar	18	Ling	6f	SD	3	104
Mar	21	Ling	6f	SD	3	**105**
Jun	6	Wind	5f	G	3	103
Jun	28	Brig	5½f	F	5	103
Jly	4	Wind	6f	G	3	102
Dec	2	Wolv	6f	SD	1	102

WILLHEGO 4						
Jly	15	NmkJ	10f	G	2	100
Aug	12	NmkJ	8f	G	2	**104**
Oct	3	Wind	8½f	GF	7	102
Dec	17	Ling	10f	FT	1	99

WILLHEWIZ 5						
May	20	Bath	5½f	G	2	100
Jun	7	Sals	6f	G	1	**103**
Jun	12	Sals	5f	G	6	102
Jly	15	Wwck	5½f	G	5	101
Aug	5	NmkJ	6f	GF	5	100
Aug	17	Epsm	6f	G	5	101

WILLIAM TELL 3						
Mar	29	Pont	10f	S	4	**102**
Apr	19	Sthl	10f	GF	1	100

WILTSHIRE 3						
Feb	9	Ling	8f	GF	1	**103**
Jun	22	Bath	8f	G	4	99

WIND CHIME 8						
Jun	5	Bath	8f	G	1	**103**

WINDERMERE ISLAND 3						
Jun	13	Brig	7f	G	1	100
Aug	4	Yarm	7f	GF	1	**103**

WINDHOVER 3						
May	21	Carl	7f	G	1	**106**
Jly	30	Haml	9f	F	4	103

WINDS OF TIME 3						
May	31	Leic	7f	GF	4	102
Jun	18	Wwck	7f	G	6	**106**
Aug	14	Bath	8f	G	5	104
Sep	14	Yarm	10f	G	8	103
Sep	24	NmkR	8f	G	11	105

WINDSOR KNOT 3						
Sep	17	Ayr	10f	G	3	**106**

WINDY PROSPECT 3						
Dec	27	Sthl	8f	SD	3	**100**

WINDYA 3						
Oct	2	Lonc	12f	G	14	**102**

WING COLLAR 4						
May	12	York	14f	S	7	101
Jly	6	Carl	14f	G	2	104
Jly	22	York	14f	G	1	**112**
Aug	20	Ches	16f	G	6	107
Aug	31	York	14f	G	1	100

WING COMMANDER 6						
May	17	Bevl	8½f	GF	1	**105**
Jly	24	Pont	8f	G	6	99
Aug	6	Rdcr	8f	G	7	100
Aug	18	York	8f	G	17	99
Sep	4	York	9f	G	1	100

WINGED D'ARGENT 4						
Mar	26	Kemp	16f	S	3	105
Apr	6	Nott	14f	GS	1	**112**
Apr	27	Ling	16f	S	4	107
May	22	Lonc	15½f	GF	3	**112**
Jly	28	Gdwd	16f	G	9	105

WINGMAN 3						
Apr	30	NmkR	8f	G	4	102
May	18	Gdwd	9f	G	5	105
Jun	4	Epsm	10f	G	7	99
Jun	22	Sals	12f	G	5	100
Sep	23	Ling	12f	G	8	100
Oct	9	Gdwd	11f	G	5	101
Oct	22	Donc	12f	S	2	**106**
Nov	5	Donc	12f	S	4	105
Nov	19	Ling	12f	FT	8	100

WINGSPEED 3						
Jun	6	Folk	9½f	G	2	**107**

WINNERS DELIGHT 4						
Jan	13	Ling	12f	SD	5	**110**
Feb	8	Ling	12f	SD	3	100
Feb	19	Wolv	12f	SD	9	102

WINTHORPE 5						
Jan	1	Sthl	6f	SD	3	100
Feb	12	Wolv	7f	FT	2	99
Jun	19	Wwck	6f	G	10	102
Jun	24	Newc	6f	G	3	103
Jly	26	Bevl	5f	G	2	100
Aug	2	Catt	6f	G	2	**104**
Aug	10	Bevl	5f	GF	8	99
Sep	28	Newc	5f	GF	2	**104**
Nov	4	Yarm	6f	S	4	103

WISE DENNIS 3
May 11 York 7f GS 1 **106**
Jly 30 Gdwd 8f G 6 101
Sep 16 Newb 7f GF 8 100

WISE OWL 3
Aug 28 Yarm 14f G 4 100
Sep 21 Gdwd 11f G 6 101
Oct 3 Wind 11½f GF 5 99
Nov 26 Ling 12f FT 1 **102**

WISE WAGER 3
May 31 Rdcr 5f G 4 100
Jun 22 Carl 5f GF 4 100
Jly 6 Carl 5f G 3 100
Jly 13 Catt 5f G 2 101
Jly 17 Rdcr 5f G 4 **102**

WITCHCRAFT 4
Oct 29 Sthl 8f SD 2 **100**
Nov 12 Sthl 8f FT 1 99
Dec 22 Sthl 8f SD 6 99

WITCHELLE 4
Feb 26 Sthl 8f FT 1 99
Mar 21 Sthl 8f SD 3 **103**
May 27 Catt 7f GF 2 100

WITCHRY 3
May 31 Rdcr 5f G 5 **100**

WITH REASON 7
Sep 3 Hayd 8f GF 2 **105**
Sep 8 Donc 7f GF 6 **105**

WITHERING LADY 3
Aug 9 Bath 5f GF 6 **99**

WITHOUT A TRACE 3
Jly 4 Wind 11½f G 1 101
Jly 28 Gdwd 14f G 2 102
Oct 1 Lonc 15f G 3 **112**

WITWATERSRAND 3
Aug 18 Wolv 8½f SD 6 **100**

WIZARD LOOKING 4
Jly 1 Bevl 12f G 2 **102**

WOLDS DANCER 3
Jly 15 Carl 9½f G 3 **100**

WOLFE TONE 4
May 14 Newb 13½f G 1 **101**
May 30 Sand 16½f G 4 100

WONDERFUL MIND 3
May 31 Rdcr 5f G 3 101
Jun 22 Carl 5f GF 3 **102**

WOODCOTE 3
Jun 11 Ripn 6f G 9 99
Jly 5 NmkJ 6f G 2 **109**

WOODCRACKER 4
Apr 30 NmkR 10f G 2 **106**

WOODLAND DREAM 3
Jun 8 Leop 7f G 1 99
Aug 14 Leop 7f F 4 **102**

WOOLACOMBE DREAM 3
Jly 19 Yarm 7f G 4 **101**

WOOLSTONE BOY 4
Oct 1 Sthl 12f SD 1 **99**

WORD PERFECT 3
Apr 7 Leic 6f S 6 **103**

WORLD SERIES 3
Aug 31 Ling 7f S 5 **101**

WORTH ABBEY 3
Mar 21 Ling 6f S 9 **102**
Jun 1 Wolv 8½f FT 5 100
Jun 16 Wolv 8½f FT 4 101
Jly 5 Wolv 8½f FT 1 99
Jly 8 Wolv 8½f FT 4 99

WOTCHALIKE 3
Jan 13 Ling 10f SD 3 100
Feb 19 Wolv 8½f SD 3 **102**
May 13 York 12f GS 3 100
Dec 19 Wolv 8½f FT 7 99
Dec 26 Wolv 12f SD 6 101

WRENLANE 4
Jun 8 Bevl 7½f G 6 **99**

WRIGHTY ALMIGHTY 3
Jun 25 NmkJ 6f G 1 **105**
Jly 2 Hayd 6f GF 4 101
Aug 28 Gdwd 6f G 10 99

WROOT DANIELLE 5
Apr 25 Haml 9f G 1 **102**

WUJOOD 3
Jly 27 Leic 8½f G 1 **100**

WUNDERBRA 4
Apr 28 Rdcr 5f GF 1 **104**

WUNDERWOOD 6
Apr 20 Epsm 10f GS 4 **108**
May 13 Haml 12f F 1 104

WYATT EARP 4
May 7 Bevl 5f GF 10 99
May 27 Catt 6f GF 3 103
Jun 17 Rdcr 6f G 1 **109**
Jly 9 York 6f G 4 103
Jly 16 Curr 5f F 12 104
Aug 16 York 6f GF 10 101
Sep 17 Ayr 7f G 6 99
Sep 29 Ayr 6f G 6 101
Nov 1 Catt 7f GS 1 103
Nov 15 Ling 7f FT 2 107
Nov 26 Ling 8f FT 5 106

WYCHBURY 4
Jan 17 Wolv 8½f SD 9 99
Jly 8 Chep 8f GF 4 **104**
Aug 12 Newb 9f G 1 102
Aug 18 Chep 8f GF 3 103
Oct 1 Rdcr 10f GF 7 99

X

XPRES DIGITAL 4
Feb 10 Sthl 6f SD 1 102
Feb 24 Sthl 6f FT 3 101
Mar 12 Wolv 7f SD 5 102
Mar 21 Sthl 6f SD 1 **105**

XTRA TORRENTIAL 3
Mar 26 Kemp 8f GS 3 **104**

Y

YAJBILL 3
Apr 27 Ling 6f GS 2 **105**

YAKIMOV 6
Jun 30 Hayd 8f GF 2 101
Jly 22 York 7f G 2 102
Aug 1 Wind 8½f GS 2 **104**

YAMATO PINK 4
Feb 8 Ling 7f SD 4 100
May 11 Brig 7f G 3 **104**

YANKEEDOODLEDANDY 4
Jly 16 Hayd 16f GF 4 101
Sep 23 Ling 12f GF 6 101

YARIA 3
Mar 20 Curr 7f HY 1 **104**
May 22 Curr 8f G 16 101
Jly 16 Curr 8f GF 4 **104**

YASHIN 4
Jan 29 Ling 10f SD 12 **102**
Oct 11 Leic 10f G 4 99

YAWMI 5
Feb 5 Ling 12f G 8 100
Jly 16 Ling 8f SW 3 102
Jly 23 York 10½f GS 4 **103**
Oct 27 Ling 12f SD 6 100
Nov 10 Ling 8f SD 7 101
Dec 21 Ling 10f SD 3 99

YAZAAR 3
Jun 17 Rdcr 11f G 3 **99**

YEATS 4
Jun 3 Epsm 12f G 1 **113**
Jun 26 StCl 12f GF 9 104
Sep 17 Curr 14f G 4 104

YENALED 8
Jan 1 Sthl 8f SD 5 **107**
Dec 22 Sthl 12f SD 2 105

YNYSLAS 3
Jun 25 Curr 10f G 9 **100**

YO PEDRO 3
Jan 29 Ling 8f SD 1 **111**
Jly 7 NmkJ 8f G 4 104

YOMALO 5
May 6 Ling 5f G 2 106
May 15 Ripn 6f G 5 99
May 29 NmkR 6f GF 1 102
Jun 12 Sals 6f G 2 107
Aug 8 Wind 6f GF 3 102
Sep 4 York 6f G 5 101
Sep 17 Ayr 6f G 4 **112**
Sep 29 NmkR 6f GF 6 100
Nov 16 Sthl 5f FT 2 107
Dec 2 Wolv 6f SD 9 102

YORK CLIFF 7
Jan 6 Wolv 8½f SD 2 102
Jan 12 Wolv 8½f SD 4 **104**
Jan 21 Wolv 12f SD 3 **104**
Jun 2 Haml 9f GS 4 99
Jun 27 Wind 10f G 2 103
Nov 25 Wolv 12f FT 3 99
Dec 9 Wolv 14f FT 2 102
Dec 10 Wolv 12f FT 2 102

YORKE'S FOLLY 4
Aug 26 Newc 5f GF 2 **105**

YORKIE 6
Nov 4 Yarm 6f S 5 **103**

YORKIES BOY 10
Aug 4 Brig 6f G 3 **101**

YORKSHIRE BLUE 6
Jly 7 Donc 7f GF 1 100
Jly 18 Ayr 6f GF 2 101
Jly 29 Thsk 6f G 6 102
Aug 6 Hayd 6f G 1 **103**
Aug 11 Hayd 6f GF 4 99
Aug 19 Ayr 6f GF 3 99
Sep 29 Ayr 6f G 5 102

YORKSHIRE LAD 3
Feb 12 Wolv 6f FT 1 99
May 13 Nott 6f F 1 **101**

YOUNG ELODIE 4
Jun 1 Leop 14f G 18 **106**

YOUNG KATE 4
Nov 5 Sthl 8f FT 2 **100**

YOUNG MICK 3
Dec 3 Wolv 8½f FT 4 **100**

YOUNG MR GRACE 5
Apr 9 Newc 7f S 2 **109**
May 25 Ripn 8f G 5 104
Jun 18 Ayr 7f G 6 100
Jly 9 York 8f G 8 99

YOUNG ROONEY 5
Sep 15 Pont 8f G 4 **99**
Oct 4 Catt 12f GF 4 **99**

YOUNG SCOTTON 5
May 28 Muss 8f G 4 **99**

YSOLDINA 3
Mar 28 StCl 8f GS 3 107
May 15 Lonc 8f G 3 **110**

Z

ZABEEL PALACE 3
Jly 24 Pont 10f G 1 **105**

ZAFARSHAH 6
Mar 4 Wolv 8½f SD 3 100
May 16 Muss 7f G 5 100
Sep 11 Gdwd 8f G 7 **104**

ZAFFEU 4
Jan 21 Wolv 12f SD 1 **106**
Feb 4 Wolv 12f SD 4 100
May 9 Wolv 14f FT 4 101
Jun 1 Yarm 11½f G 4 102
Jly 11 Wolv 14f SD 3 101
Dec 12 Wolv 14f FT 3 103

ZAKFREE 4
May 8 Leop 8f S 4 **110**
Aug 7 Curr 10f G 6 107
Sep 17 Curr 8f GF 4 108

ZALIMAR 3
Jun 27 Wind 11½f G 2 100
Jly 17 Rdcr 11f G 5 101
Sep 10 Muss 14f G 1 102
Sep 17 Catt 12f G 2 **106**

ZALKANI 5
Feb 8 Ling 12f SD 2 101
Feb 21 Ling 10f FT 3 **102**
Mar 29 Wwck 11f S 5 **102**
Aug 4 Folk 9½f GF 2 100
Aug 18 Chep 8f GF 4 **102**
Sep 3 Folk 9½f GF 2 99
Oct 24 Ling 8f SW 3 101
Nov 10 Ling 8f SD 2 **102**
Dec 5 Ling 8f FT 6 101
Dec 10 Wolv 9½f FT 5 101
Dec 21 Ling 12f FT 6 99
Dec 30 Ling 8f FT 8 100

ZALONGO 3
Apr 14 NmkR 10f G 2 99
May 6 Ches 10½f GS 3 106
Aug 17 York 10½f G 12 100
Sep 25 NmkR 12f G 5 105
Oct 13 NmkR 12f G 5 **107**

ZAMBOOZLE 3
Jun 30 Newb 11f G 1 **108**

ZANDEED 7
Oct 19 Newc 8f GS 3 **99**

ZANJEER 5
Jly 26 Bevl 8½f G 2 102
Aug 1 Carl 7f G 1 100
Aug 17 Carl 7f GF 4 99
Sep 15 Ayr 7f G 1 **103**
Sep 20 Bevl 7½f GF 3 **103**

ZARABAD 3
Oct 3 Pont 8f G 6 **102**

ZARAD 4
Apr 3 Curr 7f S 3 **109**
Jun 8 Leop 7f G 2 108
Jun 26 Curr 8f F 3 102

ZARANDJA 3
May 8 Leop 8f S 11 103
Jun 1 Leop 7f G 1 **108**
Jun 15 Leop 7f G 2 106

ZARIANO 5
Jan 5 Ling 8f SD 1 100
Jan 14 Wolv 9½f SW 2 **105**
Feb 24 Sthl 7f FT 3 102
Feb 26 Sthl 7f FT 2 99

ZARZU 6
Jan 27 Sthl 5f FT 6 99
Feb 5 Ling 5f FT 4 **105**
Feb 19 Wolv 5f FT 9 100
Mar 19 Ling 5f SD 3 103
Mar 27 Muss 5f G 2 104
Apr 20 Epsm 5f GS 9 103
May 28 Muss 5f G 3 103
Jly 15 Wwck 5½f G 8 100

ZAVILLE 3
Jly 13 Ling 16f G 4 **99**

ZAYN ZEN 3
Apr 29 Nott 8f G 1 103
May 13 Nott 8f F 6 100
Aug 6 NmkJ 8f G 2 103
Aug 22 Leic 10f G 1 103
Sep 21 Gdwd 11f G 2 104
Oct 13 NmkR 10f G 5 **105**
Oct 30 Ling 8f SD 1 104
Nov 19 Ling 10f FT 4 101

ZAZOUS 4
Sep 11 Gdwd 8f G 5 **105**

ZEALAND 5
Jan 1 Sthl 11f SD 3 **99**

ZEEBA 3
Aug 31 Ling 12f SD 2 102
Oct 14 Brig 12f G 1 **105**

ZEITGEIST 4
Jly 2 Hayd 12f GF 1 **109**
Aug 17 York 14f G 5 106

ZELKOVA 3
Aug 20 Curr 10f GF 7 99
Sep 10 Leop 9f GF 12 **104**

ZELOSO 7
Jan 14 Wolv 14f SW 4 **100**
Mar 8 Sthl 14f SD 1 99
Apr 5 Sthl 14f SD 2 **100**

ZENNO ROB ROY 5
Aug 16 York 10½f G 2 **115**

ZERLINA 4
May 21 Ling 8f SD 2 **105**
Aug 25 Ling 7f FT 3 101
Oct 10 Wolv 7f FT 4 100
Nov 19 Ling 8f FT 5 101

ZERO TOLERANCE 5
May 11 York 10½f S 1 108
Aug 27 York 9f G 5 103
Oct 14 NmkR 8f G 3 109
Oct 29 NmkR 8f S 1 **111**

ZEROBERTO 5
May 21 Curr 12f G 4 107
Jun 26 Curr 16f F 2 103
Jly 2 Leop 12f GF 1 **111**

ZEYDNAA 5
Aug 7 Rdcr 11f G 3 **101**
Sep 13 Thsk 12f G 3 100
Oct 1 Rdcr 14f GF 6 99

ZHITOMIR 7
Apr 15 Thsk 7f S 2 103
Apr 22 Wolv 7f SD 2 101
May 3 Catt 7f GS 1 **108**

Jun 13 Thsk 7f G 2 102
Jly 29 Thsk 7f G 2 106
Oct 15 Catt 7f GS 2 100
Nov 1 Catt 7f GS 4 100

ZIDANE 3
Oct 14 Rdcr 6f GF 1 **104**

ZIET D'ALSACE 5
Jan 7 Wolv 8½f SW 4 **106**
Feb 23 Ling 7f SW 2 103

ZILCH 7
Apr 9 Newc 7f S 1 **110**
May 6 Ches 7½f GS 7 101
Jun 16 York 7f GF 13 99

ZIMBALI 3
Aug 21 Folk 5f G 7 **101**

ZOHAR 3
Jly 2 Sand 7f G 3 **105**

ZOMERLUST 3
Jun 11 Ripn 6f G 4 106
Jun 20 Ripn 6f G 1 **109**
Jly 5 NmkJ 6f G 15 100
Aug 19 Ches 7f GF 8 103
Sep 16 Ayr 6f GF 4 100
Oct 14 NmkR 7f G 6 107

ZONERGEM 7
May 4 Ches 10½f GS 8 104
Nov 29 Ling 10f FT 6 **107**

ZONIC BOOM 5
May 14 Nott 8f F 1 99
Jun 3 Gdwd 9f GS 1 **102**

ZOOM ZOOM 5
Jan 6 Wolv 6f GS 1 103
Feb 18 Wolv 6f SD 5 104
Mar 4 Wolv 6f SD 2 **108**
Apr 23 Hayd 6f G 1 105

ZORN 6
Jan 14 Wolv 7f SW 3 99
Feb 24 Sthl 6f FT 1 **102**
May 30 Leic 6f G 6 100

ZOWINGTON 3
May 17 Leic 6f G 4 100
Jly 8 Wolv 6f FT 1 102
Aug 20 Sand 5f GS 2 101
Oct 21 Newb 6f G 1 **106**
Oct 30 Ling 6f SD 10 100

ZUHAIR 12
May 27 Catt 5f GF 5 **100**

ZWEIBRUCKEN 4
May 8 Leop 8f S 9 106
Jun 1 Leop 7f G 12 **108**

TWO-YEAR-OLDS of 2005

A

ABIGAIL PETT 2
Oct 15 NmkR 7f G 3 **106**

ACHILL BAY 2
Oct 14 NmkR 8f G 1 **100**

ADVANCED 2
Jly 29 NmkJ 7f G 2 99
Sep 28 Sals 6f G 1 **102**

AEROPLANE 2
Jly 27 Leic 6f G 2 **99**

AJIGOLO 2
Sep 17 Newb 6f GF 6 100
Oct 8 Sals 5f GF 2 **102**

ALESSANDRIA 2
Sep 27 Nott 8f GF 1 **100**

ALEXANDER ALLIANCE 2
Oct 9 Curr 6f GS 1 **100**

ALEXANDROVA 2
Jly 28 Gdwd 7f G 3 100
Sep 24 NmkR 8f G 2 **111**

ALHAITHAM 2
Sep 30 NmkR 7f G 2 **99**

ALL THE GOOD 2
Nov 26 Ling 10f FT 1 **100**

ALMOST SPINNING 2
Sep 10 Gdwd 8f G 5 **99**

ALOCIN 2
Nov 6 Leop 7f GS 3 **100**

ALTIUS 2
Oct 9 Curr 8f GS 3 **108**

ALWAYS HOPEFUL 2
Jly 29 Gdwd 6f G 1 106
Aug 21 Deau 6f G 3 **108**
Sep 30 NmkR 6f G 3 104

ALYZEA 2
Nov 1 MsnL 6f GF 5 **107**

AMADEUS MOZART 2
Aug 7 Curr 6f G 2 **105**

AMADEUS WOLF 2
Jun 14 York 6f G 3 104
Aug 17 York 6f F 1 104
Sep 30 NmkR 6f G 1 **109**

AMAETHON 2
Oct 16 Lonc 9f GF 4 **105**

AMBER GLORY 2
May 11 York 5f S 1 **103**

AMBIKA 2
Sep 4 Curr 7f G 8 **100**

AMIGONI 2
Jun 14 York 6f G 8 99
Jly 17 Curr 6½f F 1 99
Jly 29 Gdwd 6f G 4 102
Sep 9 Donc 7f G 5 99
Sep 18 Curr 7f GF 6 **105**

ANDRAMAD 2
Jun 1 Leop 6f G 2 **100**

ANGEL VOICES 2
Aug 6 NmkJ 7f G 3 **100**

ANGUS NEWZ 2
Oct 14 NmkR 6f G 4 **101**

ANN SUMMERS GOLD 2
Sep 3 NmkJ 6f G 2 **100**

ANNABELLE JA 2
Nov 29 Ling 8f FT 3 100
Dec 21 Ling 7f FT 1 **101**

ARAAFA 2
Sep 29 NmkR 7f GF 6 101
Oct 22 Newb 7f G 3 **103**

ARABIAN PRINCE 2
Oct 8 Sals 8f GF 3 100
Oct 22 Donc 8f S 5 **106**

ARDBRAE LADY 2
Sep 4 Curr 7f G 3 **106**

AREYOUTALKINGTOME 2
Sep 25 NmkR 8f G 6 **105**

ARISTOFILIA 2
Sep 1 Sals 7f G 4 **99**

ARM CANDY 2
Sep 30 NmkR 7f G 1 **103**
Oct 15 NmkR 7f G 10 99

ARMINIUS 2
Jun 25 NmkJ 7f G 1 **102**

ART MARKET 2
Sep 3 NmkJ 6f G 3 **99**

ART MUSEUM 2
Sep 4 Curr 6f G 1 99
Sep 18 Curr 6f G 1 **100**

ASAAWIR 2
Jly 22 Chep 6f G 1 99
Aug 11 Chep 6f G 1 **103**
Oct 22 Newb 7f G 3 102

ASSERTIVE 2
Jun 30 Newb 6f G 1 **106**
Jly 24 MsnL 5½f G 6 100
Aug 17 York 6f F 3 100

ASSET 2
Aug 20 Sand 7f G 3 **106**

ATLANTIC HIGH 2
Jly 31 Deau 6f G 2 **104**

ATLANTIC WAVES 2
Aug 7 Leic 7f G 1 **101**
Oct 8 Sals 8f GF 5 99

ATTIMA 2
Oct 2 Lonc 8f G 11 **103**

AUSSIE RULES 2
Jly 27 Gdwd 7f G 4 103
Sep 29 NmkR 7f GF 1 **104**

AUSTRALIA DAY 2
Oct 9 Curr 7f GS 5 **100**

AZYGOUS 2
Apr 27 Ling 5f FT 1 **100**

B

BA FOXTROT 2
Jun 4 Epsm 6f G 1 101
Sep 17 Newb 6f GF 4 **102**

BAAN 2
Jly 18 Bevl 7½f G 1 103
Aug 15 Nott 8f GF 2 101
Oct 1 Epsm 8½f GS 1 **104**

BAILEYS POLKA 2
Nov 3 Muss 7f GS 2 **99**

BAJAN PARKES 2
Sep 26 Bath 5½f G 1 **99**

BALIK PEARLS 2
Oct 14 NmkR 6f G 7 **99**

BALTHAZAAR'S GIFT 2
Oct 8 York 6f G 1 103
Nov 1 MsnL 6f GF 1 **114**

BASRA 2
Oct 9 Curr 8f GS 5 **101**

BATHWICK ALICE 2
Aug 22 Wind 5f G 2 100
Oct 22 Newb 6f G 4 **101**

BATHWICK EMMA 2
Aug 4 Chep 6f G 3 **101**

BEAUCHAMP UNIQUE 2
Dec 19 Ling 7f SD 1 **100**

BEAUTY BRIGHT 2
Aug 18 York 6f GF 3 **107**
Oct 15 NmkR 7f G 8 102

BEFORE YOU GO 2
Dec 17 Ling 8f FT 1 **101**

BEST ALIBI 2
Oct 22 Donc 8f S 4 **108**

BEST DOUBLE 2
Nov 10 Ling 5f SD 2 **101**

BEST NAME 2
Oct 16 Lonc 9f GF 2 **106**

BINIOU 2
Aug 15 Deau 5f G 3 **101**

BLACK CHARMER 2
Jun 4 Donc 6f G 3 99
Jly 27 Gdwd 7f G 3 **105**

BLADES GIRL 2
Sep 29 NmkR 6f GF 2 **100**

BLING 2
Aug 26 Sals 6f G 1 **101**

BLITZKRIEG 2
Sep 14 Sand 7f G 2 **104**
Oct 8 Sals 8f GF 1 102

BLOODSTOCKTV 2
Jly 2 Leic 5f GF 1 **99**

BLU MANRUNA 2
Dec 5 Ling 7f FT 4 **99**

BLUE BLUE SKY 2
Oct 2 Lonc 8f G 12 **101**

BLUE JEANS 2
Aug 3 Epsm 6f G 2 **100**

BLUE MIRAGE 2
Oct 21 Donc 7f GS 1 **105**

BLUSHING HILARY 2
Sep 10 Muss 8f G 2 **99**

BOLD AND FREE 2
Sep 6 Leic 7f GF 1 **100**

BOMBER COMMAND 2
Oct 24 Ling 8f SW 2 **100**

BONNIE PRINCE BLUE 2
Aug 27 Wind 6f GF 1 99
Oct 1 Rdcr 6f GF 4 **101**

BOQUILOBO 2
Oct 16 Muss 9f G 3 **102**

BOW BRIDGE 2
May 13 York 5f GS 1 **99**

BRANDYWELL BOY 2
Nov 12 Ling 6f FT 2 **99**

BRENDA MEOVA 2
Jly 23 Newb 6f GF 6 **101**
Aug 13 Newb 5f G 3 100

BRIBON 2
Oct 30 StCl 8f G 5 **100**

BRIDAL PATH 2
Aug 25 Muss 5f G 1 **99**
Sep 20 Brig 6f G 5 **99**

BRILAND 2
Jly 26 Gdwd 5f G 5 **100**

BULL MARKET 2
Dec 10 Sthl 8f FT 1 **99**

BUNOOD 2
Oct 29 NmkR 8f S 2 **103**

C

CACTUS KING 2
Nov 12 Ling 8f FT 1 **100**

CALL MY NUMBER 2
Jun 16 Bevl 7½f G 1 **101**

CAMPBELTOWN 2
Sep 16 Ayr 5f GF 2 **99**

CANTABRIA 2
Aug 1 Wind 6f G 2 **104**
Sep 1 Sals 6f G 7 99
Oct 1 NmkR 7f G 2 99
Oct 22 Newb 7f G 2 102

CARLOTAMIX 2
Sep 17 Lonc 8f G 1 108
Oct 30 StCl 8f G 1 **111**

CARMENERO 2
Sep 20 Brig 6f G 4 **101**

CASSANDRA JADE 2
Oct 9 Curr 7f GS 7 **99**

CATBANG 2
Dec 16 Wolv 6f FT 3 **101**

CAVEWARRIOR 2
Aug 8 Wolv 6f SD 1 **102**

CELEBRATION SONG 2
Sep 10 Ches 7f GS 1 **103**

CELTIC WARRIOR 2
Nov 6 Leop 7f GS 1 **104**

CHALENTINA 2
Oct 20 Brig 7f GS 3 **99**

CHAMPARA 2
Jun 21 Brig 6f G 1 **100**

CHAMPIONSHIP POINT 2
Jun 14 York 7f GF 1 **101**

CHARLIE COOL 2
Sep 25 NmkR 8f G 7 **103**

CHARLIE TOKYO 2
Oct 17 Wind 8½f G 2 **103**

CHARLTON 2
Aug 4 Chep 6f G 1 **102**
Oct 14 NmkR 6f G 5 100

CHASE THE ACE 2
Sep 24 Ripn 5f GF 2 **101**
Oct 3 Pont 6f G 2 99

CHATILA 2
Sep 2 NmkJ 7f G 3 99
Oct 2 Lonc 8f G 8 **104**

CHEAP N CHIC 2
Aug 15 Brig 6f G 1 99

Oct 1 Rdcr 6f GF 7 **100**

CHEVIOT HEIGHTS 2
Oct 20 Brig 7f GS 2 **101**

CHEYENNE STAR 2
Oct 23 Curr 8f S 6 **103**

CHOOSY 2
Oct 22 Newb 7f G 4 **100**

CHRIS CORSA 2
Jly 1 Hayd 6f G 4 99
Aug 12 Newc 7f GS 1 **100**

CITY FOR CONQUEST 2
Jly 14 Donc 5f GF 1 **101**

CITY OF TROY 2
Jly 16 Newb 7f GF 1 100
Sep 25 NmkR 8f G 4 **106**

CLARE HILLS 2
Jun 1 Bevl 5f G 1 **101**

CLASSIC ENCOUNTER 2
May 29 NmkR 5f GF 1 **106**

CLOSE TO YOU 2
Jly 24 Newb 7f G 1 102
Aug 20 Sand 7f G 6 **105**
Sep 9 Donc 7f G 1 103

CLOUD ATLAS 2
Aug 8 Wolv 6f SD 2 **99**

COBURN 2
Sep 7 Donc 6f GF 4 **99**

COLLATERAL DAMAGE 2
Sep 10 Ches 7f GS 2 **100**

COLMAR SUPREME 2
Oct 20 Brig 7f GS 1 **103**

COME OUT FIGHTING 2
Sep 12 Muss 5f GF 1 **100**

COMMENTARY 2
Oct 15 Catt 7f GS 2 **102**

CONFIDENTIAL LADY 2
Jun 29 Catt 7f G 1 99
Jly 2 Bevl 7½f G 1 105
Jly 21 Sand 7f GF 1 **108**
Aug 6 NmkJ 7f G 2 106
Aug 20 Deau 7f GS 1 100
Oct 2 Lonc 8f G 10 103

CONFUCIUS MIRACLE 2
Sep 15 Yarm 6f G 1 **100**

COOL CREEK 2
Jly 27 Gdwd 7f G 2 105
Aug 20 Curr 6f GF 2 **107**
Sep 9 Donc 7f G 4 100
Sep 17 Newb 6f GF 1 105

CORRIB 2
Jun 10 Chep 6f G 1 **103**

COTE D'ARGENT 2
Nov 3 Muss 7f GS 1 **105**

COUNTRYWIDE BELLE 2
May 2 Donc 5f G 2 **104**

CRIMSON FLAME 2
Oct 16 Muss 9f G 4 **101**

CRITIC 2
Jun 4 Donc 6f G 2 99
Jly 2 Bevl 7½f G 3 **102**

CROCODILE BAY 2
May 2 Donc 5f G 1 **105**
May 18 Gdwd 5f G 2 101
Jun 14 York 7f GF 3 99

CROONER 2
Oct 14 NmkR 6f G 9 **99**

CROSBY HALL 2
Oct 1 Rdcr 6f GF 5 **101**

CROSS CHANNEL 2
Jly 15 NmkJ 7f G 3 **107**
Jly 30 NmkJ 7f GF 1 100
Sep 24 NmkR 8f G 5 104

CULTURE EXCHANGE 2
Nov 1 MsnL 7f GF 5 **99**

CULTURE QUEEN 2
Sep 16 Nott 6f GF 1 **100**

CURTAIL 2
Sep 16 Ayr 5f GF 1 102
Oct 8 Sals 5f GF 4 101
Nov 1 MsnL 6f GF 3 **110**

D

DAGGERNOUGHT 2
Jun 21 Brig 6f G 2 99
Oct 22 Newb 7f G 5 **102**

DAME HESTER 2
Aug 7 Curr 6f G 3 **100**

DANEHILL MUSIC 2
Nov 6 Leop 9f S 2 **102**

DANJET 2
Apr 27 Ling 5f FT 2 99
Aug 20 Curr 6f GF 6 **100**

DARK ISLANDER 2
Sep 14 Sand 7f G 3 **104**

DAWN QUEST 2
Oct 4 Leic 10f G 3 **100**

DAYLAMI STAR 2
Oct 3 Pont 10f G 1 **100**

DE ROBERTO 2
Aug 20 Curr 6f GF 5 **101**

DEE DAY 2
Sep 12 Rdcr 9f G 1 **99**

DEGAS ART 2
Oct 29 NmkR 7f S 2 **107**

DEVERON 2
Jly 15 NmkJ 7f G 2 107
Jly 28 Gdwd 7f G 1 103
Aug 6 NmkJ 7f G 3 105
Aug 28 Gdwd 7f G 6 100
Oct 2 Lonc 8f G 3 **108**

DICKENSIAN 2
Jly 18 Bevl 7½f G 2 **100**
Oct 22 Newb 7f G 8 99

DISSITATION 2
Oct 9 Curr 7f GS 3 **101**

DIXIE BELLE 2
May 17 Rdcr 6f G 1 **103**
Jun 25 NmkJ 6f G 1 **103**
Aug 18 York 6f GF 5 **103**

DOCTOR DASH 2
Aug 26 Sals 8f G 1 **102**
Sep 25 NmkR 8f G 8 **102**

DOCTOR OF LAWS 2
Aug 6 Ling 8f SD 1 **105**

DONNA BLINI 2
Jun 1 Bevl 5f G 2 99
Jly 5 NmkJ 6f G 1 **103**
Sep 29 NmkR 6f GF 1 101

DONNELLY'S HOLLOW 2
Oct 9 Curr 7f GS 4 **100**

DONT DILI DALI 2
Sep 4 Curr 7f G 7 **102**

DREAM FANTASY 2
Jun 4 Chep 6f G 1 99
Oct 1 Epsm 8½f GS 2 **103**
Oct 17 Pont 8f G 2 **103**

DREAM IN BLUE 2
Oct 16 Lonc 9f GF 5 **102**

DREAM ROSE 2
Jly 27 Sand 7f GS 2 **102**

DUBAI ON 2
Oct 4 Leic 10f G 1 **106**

DUBAI TYPHOON 2
Aug 23 Yarm 8f G 1 **100**

DUELLING 2
May 28 Ling 6f GF 1 **99**

DUFF 2
Sep 18 Curr 7f GF 4 **108**
Oct 9 Curr 8f GS 4 102

DUNE MELODY 2
Aug 20 Curr 6f GF 4 **101**

DUNELIGHT 2
Aug 10 Sand 7f GF 3 **103**

DUSTY CITY 2
Apr 2 Donc 5f G 1 **100**

Apr 27 Ling 5f FT 3 99

DYLAN THOMAS 2
Sep 10 Leop 7f HD 1 100
Oct 8 Sals 8f GF 2 101
Oct 22 Donc 8f S 6 **105**

DYNACAM 2
Nov 4 Yarm 10f HY 1 **99**

E

EDAARA 2
Sep 1 Sals 7f G 3 **101**
Oct 14 NmkR 8f G 2 99

EGYPTIAN LORD 2
Dec 26 Wolv 5f SD 2 **100**

EILEAN BAN 2
Aug 6 NmkJ 7f G 2 101
Sep 2 NmkJ 7f G 1 104
Oct 2 Lonc 8f G 6 **105**

ELISE 2
Oct 20 Brig 8f GS 1 **100**

EMIRATES GOLD 2
Aug 5 NmkJ 7f GF 2 100
Aug 26 Sals 8f G 2 **101**

EMIRATES SKYLINE 2
Jly 30 Donc 7f G 1 101
Sep 14 Sand 7f G 1 **105**

EMPRESS JAIN 2
May 6 Nott 5f G 1 **101**

ERYTHEIS 2
Oct 14 NmkR 6f G 1 **103**

ESCAPE PLAN 2
Aug 1 Ripn 6f G 1 **99**

EXPENSIVE 2
Jly 1 Hayd 6f G 2 102
Aug 26 Thsk 6f GF 1 **104**
Sep 17 Newb 6½f GF 1 100

F

FAMCRED 2
Sep 13 Yarm 7f G 1 **99**

FAMILIAR TERRITORY 2
Oct 1 Epsm 8½f GS 3 **100**

FAST BOWLER 2
Aug 28 Yarm 6f G 1 **100**

FAUVELIA 2
Oct 16 Lonc 9f GF 3 **105**

FELICITOUS 2
Sep 2 NmkJ 6f G 2 **100**

FENICE 2
Oct 2 Lonc 7f G 4 **109**

FIGARO FLYER 2
Jly 23 York 5f G 1 **100**

FIGJAM 2
Jly 6 Ling 5f G 1 **99**

FINAL VERSE 2
Jly 7 Donc 6f GF 1 100
Aug 16 York 6f GF 2 101
Oct 22 Newb 7f G 2 **104**

FIRE AND RAIN 2
Sep 29 NmkR 8f GF 1 **99**

FISOLA 2
Jly 14 Donc 5f GF 2 **100**

FLASHY WINGS 2
Jun 15 York 5f G 1 105
Aug 18 York 6f GF 1 **110**
Sep 17 Newb 6½f GF 2 99
Sep 29 NmkR 6f GF 3 100

FLIGHT CAPTAIN 2
Aug 5 NmkJ 7f GF 1 **101**

FLOR Y NATA 2
Jly 25 Sthl 7f GF 1 **103**

FORCES SWEETHEART 2
May 6 Nott 5f G 2 **100**

FOXYSOX 2
Sep 29 NmkR 6f GF 3 **99**

FREE ROSES 2
Jly 20 Naas 6f GF 2 **104**

FREGATE ISLAND 2
Nov 15 Ling 8f FT 3 101
Nov 29 Ling 8f FT 1 **103**

FUSILI 2
Aug 26 NmkJ 8f G 2 **99**

G

GALANTAS 2
Aug 20 Curr 7f GF 2 **110**

GALILEO'S STAR 2
Jly 15 NmkJ 7f G 5 102
Jly 27 Sand 7f GS 1 **104**
Aug 12 Newb 7f G 2 100

GALLERY GIRL 2
Sep 17 Ayr 6f G 2 101
Oct 1 Rdcr 6f GF 3 **102**

GAMBLE IN GOLD 2
Apr 25 Wind 5f GS 1 **100**

GEE DEE NEN 2
Oct 8 York 8f S 1 **101**

GEMINI GOLD 2
Oct 23 Curr 8f S 3 **106**

GENARI 2
Sep 3 Hayd 8f GF 1 **99**

GENRE 2
Jly 9 Sals 7f G 3 101
Aug 10 Sand 7f GF 5 102
Aug 27 Gdwd 8f G 2 102
Oct 21 Donc 8f GS 1 **103**

GEORGE WASHINGTON 2
Aug 7 Curr 6f G 1 **116**
Sep 18 Curr 7f GF 1 113

GEORGE'S FLYER 2
Dec 19 Wolv 8½f FT 1 **99**

GILT LINKED 2
Sep 30 Ling 5f G 1 **105**

GIPSY TOUCH 2
Oct 9 Curr 7f GS 2 **103**

GIVE ME THE NIGHT 2
Oct 15 Catt 5f G 1 **102**

GLAZIER MIST 2
Oct 9 Curr 7f GS 6 **99**

GLOBAL GENIUS 2
Jun 14 York 7f GF 2 **100**
Aug 20 Ches 7f G 1 **100**

GO FIGURE 2
Oct 9 Gdwd 7f G 5 **99**

GODFREY STREET 2
May 24 Ling 5f G 1 102
Jun 25 Ches 5f G 2 101
Jly 26 Gdwd 5f G 6 99
Sep 10 Donc 5f GS 1 **107**

GOLDEN ACER 2
Jun 11 Bath 5f G 1 **105**
Jly 8 Chep 5f GF 1 103
Aug 15 Deau 5f G 2 102

GOLDEN ARROW 2
Sep 18 Curr 7f GF 2 **110**

GRACECHURCH 2
Jly 20 Sand 7f G 2 99
Aug 10 Sand 7f GF 6 **101**
Aug 31 York 8f G 2 99

GRAMM 2
Oct 4 Leic 10f G 2 **104**
Oct 13 NmkR 8f G 1 102

GRAND REPORTER 2
Jly 24 MsnL 5½f G 4 **102**

GRANTLEY ADAMS 2
Jly 14 Haml 6f GF 1 99
Jly 30 Gdwd 6f G 2 100
Sep 18 Haml 6f F 1 **102**
Sep 28 Sals 6f G 2 100

GRAZEON GOLD BLEND 2
Aug 28 Bevl 5f GS 1 **99**

GREEN PRIDE 2
May 18 Gdwd 5f G 5 **100**

GRENANE 2
Aug 11 Chep 6f G 2 **100**

GREY OUTLOOK 2
Nov 3 Muss 8f GS 2 **101**

GUEST CONNECTIONS 2
Aug 7 Curr 6f G 5 **100**

GUILIA 2
Sep 13 Thsk 7f G 1 **102**

GUTO 2
Sep 24 Ripn 5f GF 1 **102**

GWENSEB 2
Jly 24 MsnL 5½f G 3 103
Nov 1 MsnL 6f GF 2 **113**

H

HAITI DANCER 2
Jly 25 Yarm 7f G 1 **99**

HANOONA 2
Jly 21 Sand 7f GF 5 **102**

HARD TO EXPLAIN 2
Oct 16 Muss 9f G 2 **102**

HAZEYMM 2
Sep 18 Curr 7f GF 5 **108**

HEADACHE 2
Aug 15 Deau 5f G 4 100
Nov 1 MsnL 6f GF 8 **103**

HEATSEEKER 2
Jly 20 Naas 6f GF 1 105
Sep 18 Curr 7f GF 3 **110**

HEAVEN CAN WAIT 2
Oct 9 Gdwd 7f G 2 **102**

HEAVEN SENT 2
Jly 15 NmkJ 7f G 7 **100**

HIDDEN CHARM 2
Jly 17 Curr 5f F 1 **102**

HIGH CURRAGH 2
Oct 14 NmkR 6f G 6 **99**

HIGH HEEL SNEAKERS 2
Sep 8 Donc 8f GF 2 **109**
Sep 24 NmkR 8f G 4 107

HIGH SEASONS 2
Jun 19 Wwck 7f G 2 **99**

HILL OF ALMHUIM 2
Jly 1 Hayd 6f G 1 **103**

HITS ONLY JUDE 2
Nov 1 Catt 6f GS 2 **99**

HOPEFUL PURCHASE 2
Oct 29 NmkR 7f S 3 **106**

HORATIO NELSON 2
Jly 7 NmkJ 7f G 1 107
Aug 20 Curr 7f GF 1 113
Oct 2 Lonc 7f G 1 **114**
Oct 15 NmkR 7f G 2 110

HOT 2
May 30 Leic 5f G 1 **102**
Sep 17 Newb 6f GF 7 99

HOTHAM 2
Oct 22 Newb 6f G 3 **101**

HUMUNGOUS 2
Jly 9 Sals 7f G 1 **102**
Oct 15 NmkR 7f G 6 100

HUNTER STREET 2
Jly 26 Gdwd 5f G 4 101
Aug 15 Deau 5f G 5 100
Sep 10 Donc 5f GS 2 **105**
Oct 8 Sals 5f GF 1 103

HURRICANE CAT 2
Oct 22 Newb 7f G 1 **105**

I

IDARAH 2
Nov 3 Muss 8f GS 1 **102**

IL CASTAGNO 2
Oct 15 Catt 7f GS 1 **104**

IN DUBAI 2
Jly 28 Gdwd 7f G 4 **99**
Oct 21 Donc 8f S 1 **99**

IN THE FASHION 2
Jly 20 Sand 7f G 1 **100**

INDECENT PROPOSAL 2
Sep 20 Brig 6f G 2 **102**

INDIGO NIGHTS 2
Jun 25 Ches 5f G 1 **102**

INGLEBY ARCH 2
Oct 1 Rdcr 6f GF 9 **99**

INNOCENT AIR 2
Jly 28 Gdwd 7f G 2 102
Aug 12 Newb 7f G 1 **103**

IT'S A DREAM 2
Dec 20 Ling 8f G 1 **99**

IVAN DENISOVICH 2
Jun 1 Leop 6f G 1 106
Jly 6 NmkJ 6f GF 1 99
Aug 21 Deau 6f G 2 **108**
Sep 30 NmkR 6f G 4 103

J

JADALEE 2
Aug 10 Sand 7f GF 7 100
Sep 26 Bath 10f G 1 **104**

JAISH 2
Oct 29 NmkR 8f S 3 **101**

JAMIESON GOLD 2
Jly 6 NmkJ 6f GF 2 **99**

JEANMAIRE 2
Aug 1 Wind 6f G 1 **105**
Sep 1 Sals 6f G 3 102

JEREMY 2
Oct 10 Wind 6f G 1 100
Oct 22 Donc 6f S 2 **108**

JEU DE MOT 2
Jly 2 Bevl 7½f G 2 **102**
Aug 13 Newb 7f G 1 100
Aug 26 Sals 8f G 3 100

JIMMY THE GUESSER 2
Oct 22 Newb 6f G 2 102
Nov 7 Wolv 6f FT 1 99
Dec 16 Wolv 6f FT 1 **103**

JIOCONDA 2
Oct 23 Curr 8f S 1 **110**

JOHANNES 2
Aug 29 Ripn 6f G 2 **101**

JOHN KEATS 2
Oct 3 Pont 6f G 1 **100**

JOHNNY THE FISH 2
Sep 7 Donc 6f GF 1 **101**

JUMBAJUKIBA 2
Sep 13 Sals 6f G 1 **99**

JUROR 2
Aug 10 Sand 7f GF 2 **103**

JUST OBSERVING 2
Aug 28 Bevl 8½f GS 3 **99**

K

KAKOFONIC 2
Oct 30 StCl 8f G 6 **100**

KALANKARI 2
Sep 27 Gdwd 8f G 2 **99**

KEPT FAITH 2
Aug 28 Yarm 6f G 2 **99**

KILLYBEGS 2
Sep 9 Donc 7f G 3 101
Sep 29 NmkR 7f GF 2 **103**

KILWORTH 2
Aug 20 Sand 7f G 5 105
Aug 29 Chep 8f G 1 100
Sep 25 NmkR 8f G 2 **108**

KING ORCHISIOS 2
Jun 4 Hayd 5f G 1 **100**

KINGSDALE OCEAN 2
Sep 17 Curr 5f GF 1 **103**

KINSYA 2
Aug 26 NmkJ 8f G 1 **100**

L

LA CHUNGA 2
Jun 17 York 6f GF 1 103
Jly 23 Newb 6f GF 4 105
Aug 18 York 6f GF 2 **108**

LADY ANGELE 2
Aug 15 Deau 5f G 1 **106**

LADY LIVIUS 2
Jly 16 Newb 5f GF 1 **100**

LADY ROMANOV 2
Oct 18 Sthl 7f SD 1 **99**

LAKE HERO 2
Oct 9 Bath 5f G 3 **99**

LE COLOMBIER 2
Aug 10 Sand 7f GF 4 **103**

LEAGUE CHAMPION 2
Jun 14 York 6f G 7 101
Jly 16 Newb 7f GF 3 99
Jly 27 Gdwd 7f G 5 **103**
Sep 10 Gdwd 8f G 4 102

LENOIR 2
Dec 5 Ling 7f FT 3 **100**

LEO 2
Jly 7 NmkJ 7f G 2 104
Sep 10 Gdwd 8f G 2 103
Sep 25 NmkR 8f G 1 **110**

LEVERA 2
Jly 27 Leic 6f G 1 **104**

LINDA'S LAD 2
Sep 17 Lonc 8f G 2 **107**
Oct 16 Lonc 9f GF 1 **107**

LIVE FAST 2
Aug 10 Sals 6f G 2 **101**

LONDON EXPRESS 2
Oct 13 NmkR 8f G 2 **101**

LONELY AHEAD 2
Aug 18 York 6f GF 4 **105**
Sep 4 Curr 7f G 5 **105**

LOOKER 2
Oct 13 NmkR 8f G 4 **99**

LOUA 2
Jly 1 Hayd 6f G 3 **102**

LOYAL ROYAL 2
Oct 21 Newb 6f G 2 **102**

LUBERON 2
Jun 16 Bevl 7½f G 2 100
Jun 27 Muss 7f GF 1 99
Jly 7 Wwck 7f G 2 100
Sep 15 Ayr 8f G 1 **102**

LUCAYOS 2
Oct 9 Bath 5f G 1 **101**

M

MACADEMY ROYAL 2
Nov 10 Ling 5f SD 3 **100**

MACORVILLE 2
Aug 15 Nott 8f GF 3 **99**

MACVEL 2
Jly 23 Ling 5f GF 1 **100**

MAGADAR 2
Sep 5 Wwck 6f G 2 100
Oct 7 Newb 6f GF 1 **101**

MAGICAL MUSIC 2
Dec 10 Sthl 8f FT 1 **101**

MAMBO SUN 2
Nov 29 Sthl 8f SD 2 **100**

MANSTON 2
Oct 7 York 6f GF 1 101
Oct 22 Donc 6f S 1 **112**
Nov 1 MsnL 6f GF 6 105

MARC OF BRILLIANCE 2
Sep 26 Bath 10f G 2 **101**

MARCUS ANDRONICUS 2
Jun 14 York 6f G 5 103
Oct 22 Donc 6f S 4 **106**

MARIOL 2
Jly 31 Deau 6f G 3 104
Nov 1 MsnL 6f GF 4 **109**

MAROUSSIES WINGS 2
Oct 10 Ayr 8f S 1 **103**
Oct 29 NmkR 8f S 5 99

MASTA PLASTA 2
Jun 1 Newc 5f G 1 101
Jun 16 York 5f GF 1 **103**
Oct 8 York 6f G 2 99

MATTEROFACT 2
Oct 9 Bath 5f G 2 **100**

MAURALAKANA 2
Jly 31 Deau 6f G 1 108
Aug 21 Deau 6f G 4 104
Oct 2 Lonc 7f G 3 **110**

MAYONGA 2
Jly 6 Naas 6f GF 2 **101**

MEDNAYA 2
Nov 1 MsnL 7f GF 2 **109**

MEMPHIS MAN 2
May 18 Gdwd 5f G 6 **99**

METROPOLITAN MAN 2
Sep 4 York 6f G 1 100
Sep 29 NmkR 7f GF 5 **102**

MILITARY CROSS 2
Sep 17 Wwck 7f G 1 **105**
Sep 28 Sals 7f G 1 100

MILLION WAVES 2
Oct 23 Curr 8f S 2 **107**

MISPHIRE 2
Sep 29 NmkR 6f GF 4 99
Oct 17 Pont 6f G 1 **100**

MISSOULA 2
Aug 31 York 8f G 1 **101**

MISTER CHOCOLATE 2
Aug 15 Deau 5f G 6 **99**

MISTRESS BAILEY 2
Oct 23 Curr 8f S 7 **101**

MISU BOND 2
Oct 1 Rdcr 6f GF 1 **108**

MIXED BLESSING 2
Jun 30 Newb 6f G 3 103
Jly 23 Newb 6f GF 1 **110**
Aug 28 Gdwd 7f G 3 103

MOI AUSSI 2
Nov 29 Sthl 8f SD 1 **102**
Dec 27 Sthl 8f SD 1 99

MONT ETOILE 2
Jly 15 NmkJ 7f G 4 **102**

MONTHLY MEDAL 2
Nov 6 Leop 7f GS 2 **101**

MONTREUX 2
Nov 15 Ling 8f FT 4 **99**

MOONLIGHT MUSIC 2
Aug 26 NmkJ 7f G 2 **99**

MORE TIME 2
Oct 22 Newb 6f G 5 **99**

MORGHIM 2
Aug 26 NmkJ 7f G 1 **100**

MORTARBOARD 2
Oct 8 York 8f S 2 **100**

MOSTAQELEH 2
Aug 12 Newb 6f G 1 **99**

MOUNTAIN 2
Nov 6 Leop 9f S 4 **99**

MR FLOODLIGHT 2
Aug 10 Sand 7f GF 8 **100**

MR SANDICLIFFE 2
May 30 Leic 5f G 2 99
Sep 7 Donc 6f GF 2 **100**

MRS SNAFFLES 2
Aug 7 Curr 6f G 1 **104**
Sep 1 Sals 6f G 4 100

MULAQAT 2
Jly 9 Sals 7f G 4 99
Aug 6 Ling 8f SD 2 **102**
Sep 27 Gdwd 8f G 1 100
Oct 11 Leic 7f G 1 101

MULL OF DUBAI 2
Oct 9 Gdwd 7f G 6 **99**

MULLAAD 2
May 19 Newc 5f G 1 99
Jly 29 Gdwd 6f G 3 **102**

MULTAKKA 2
Sep 30 NmkR 7f G 3 **99**

MUNNINGS 2
Oct 13 NmkR 8f G 2 **101**

MURFREESBORO 2
Jun 7 Rdcr 6f G 1 99
Jly 16 Newb 7f GF 2 99
Sep 29 NmkR 6f GF 1 **101**

MUSIC NOTE 2
Aug 23 Yarm 8f G 2 **99**

MUSICAL GUEST 2
Aug 4 Chep 6f G 4 99
Aug 19 Sals 6f G 1 100
Oct 14 NmkR 6f G 3 **101**

MUTAMARRES 2
Sep 10 Ches 7f GS 1 **101**
Oct 15 Catt 7f GS 3 **101**

MUTAWAJID 2
Jly 6 NmkJ 6f GF 1 **102**
Aug 17 York 6f F 4 99

MY AMALIE 2
Sep 8 Donc 8f GF 7 **103**

N

NAKHEEL 2
Oct 17 Pont 8f G 1 **107**

NAMAYA 2
Jly 6 Naas 6f GF 1 **104**

NAMID REPROBATE 2
Nov 1 Catt 6f GS 1 **100**

NANNINA 2
Jly 5 NmkJ 6f G 5 100
Jly 23 Newb 6f GF 3 106
Aug 28 Gdwd 7f G 1 106
Sep 24 NmkR 8f G 1 **112**

NANTYGLO 2
Aug 4 Chep 6f G 2 101
Sep 17 Newb 6f GF 3 **102**

NARVIK 2
Sep 20 NmkR 7f G 1 **99**

NASHEEJ 2
Jly 21 Sand 7f GF 3 105
Aug 6 NmkJ 7f G 1 107
Sep 8 Donc 8f GF 1 **110**
Sep 24 NmkR 8f G 3 108

NATURAL FORCE 2
Sep 13 Thsk 7f G 3 99
Nov 15 Ling 8f FT 1 **103**

NEILA 2
Nov 1 MsnL 7f GF 4 **102**

NELSONS COLUMN 2
Aug 28 Bevl 8½f GS 2 **100**

NESNO 2
Sep 13 Thsk 7f G 3 **99**

NEW ART 2
Aug 16 York 6f GF 3 **100**

NEW GIRLFRIEND 2
Jly 24 MsnL 5½f G 1 **108**
Aug 21 Deau 6f G 5 100

NIDHAAL 2
Jly 7 NmkJ 6f G 1 105
Jly 23 Newb 6f GF 2 **107**
Sep 1 Sals 6f G 1 **107**

NIGELLA 2
Jun 16 Wolv 5f G 1 101
Jly 16 Newb 5f GF 2 99
Sep 8 Donc 5f F 4 **108**

NIGHT CRESCENDO 2
Oct 24 Ling 8f SW 1 **101**

NORTHERN BOY 2
Sep 13 Thsk 7f G 2 **100**

NORTHERN EMPIRE 2
Jun 13 Wind 5f GF 1 **99**

O

OCEAN PRIDE 2
Oct 11 Leic 7f G 3 **99**

OCEANS APART 2
Sep 1 Sals 6f G 5 **100**

OCHRE BAY 2
Dec 16 Wolv 6f FT 4 **99**

OH HOW LOVELY 2
Oct 15 NmkR 7f G 5 **104**

OLYMPIAN ODYSSEY 2
Oct 29 NmkR 7f S 1 **109**

ON A CLOUD 2
Oct 2 Lonc 8f G 7 **105**

ONE NIGHT IN PARIS 2
Oct 9 Gdwd 7f G 3 **101**

OOH AAH CAMARA 2
May 4 Ches 5f GS 1 **107**
Jly 26 Gdwd 5f G 7 99

OPERA CAPE 2
Jly 9 Sals 7f G 2 101
Jly 30 Gdwd 7f G 1 99
Aug 20 Sand 7f G 1 **112**
Oct 2 Lonc 7f G 2 **112**
Oct 15 NmkR 7f G 3 108

ORCHARD SUPREME 2
Dec 5 Ling 7f FT 2 100
Dec 16 Wolv 6f FT 2 **102**
Dec 30 Ling 6f FT 1 99

ORPSIE BOY 2
Sep 28 Ling 6f SD 1 **100**
Nov 12 Ling 6f FT 3 99

OSCILLATOR 2
Nov 3 Muss 8f GS 4 **101**

OUR SHEILA 2
Oct 1 Rdcr 6f GF 8 **99**

OVERSTAYED 2
Apr 14 Ripn 5f S 1 **101**
Jun 30 Newb 6f G 5 99

OVERWING 2
Oct 9 Bath 5f G 4 **99**

P

PACIFIC PRIDE 2
Jun 14 York 6f G 2 **105**

PACKING HERO 2
Sep 7 Epsm 6f G 1 **101**

PALACE EPISODE 2
Aug 16 York 7f GF 1 99
Sep 25 NmkR 8f G 3 108
Oct 15 NmkR 7f G 5 102
Oct 22 Donc 8f S 1 **112**

PATRONISE 2
Sep 17 Curr 5f GF 3 **99**

PELHAM CRESCENT 2
Nov 29 Ling 8f FT 2 **101**

PHANTOM WHISPER 2
Mar 31 Donc 5f G 1 **100**

PICCELINA 2
Aug 12 Folk 5f GF 1 **104**

PICKETT 2
Jly 26 Gdwd 5f G 2 **103**
Oct 8 Sals 5f GF 6 99

PIGEON ISLAND 2
Nov 26 Ling 10f FT 2 **99**

PLAYFUL 2
Jun 1 Nott 5f G 1 **100**
Aug 13 Newb 5f G 4 99

POMMES FRITES 2
Dec 5 Ling 7f FT 5 **99**

PORTO SANTO 2
Oct 30 StCl 8f G 3 **107**

POSEIDON ADVENTURE 2
Oct 30 StCl 8f G 4 **105**

POSSESSED 2
Nov 29 Ling 8f FT 5 **99**

POUND SIGN 2
Jly 26 Bevl 7½f G 2 **100**

POWER POLITICS 2
Jun 25 Ling 5f G 2 **101**

PRETTILINI 2
Oct 9 Bath 5f G 5 **99**

PRICE TAG 2
Aug 7 Deau 7f G 1 **100**

PRIMARY 2
Aug 22 Leic 7f G 1 **99**

PRINCE OF LIGHT 2
Aug 16 York 6f GF 1 **104**
Sep 3 NmkJ 6f G 1 101

PRINCE TAMINO 2
Oct 24 Ling 6f SW 2 **99**

PRINCE WOODMAN 2
Oct 21 Newb 6f G 1 **104**

PRINCESS NADA 2
Oct 10 Ayr 8f S 2 **100**

PRIORS HILL 2
Sep 16 Newb 8f GF 3 **99**

PRIVATE BUSINESS 2
Jly 7 NmkJ 7f G 5 100
Sep 10 Gdwd 8f G 3 **102**
Oct 22 Newb 7f G 4 **102**

PSYCHIC STAR 2
Aug 28 Gdwd 7f G 5 **101**

PURE ILLUSION 2
Aug 6 NmkJ 7f G 1 **105**
Sep 8 Donc 8f GF 5 104

PUSKAS 2
May 18 Gdwd 5f G 3 **100**
Aug 21 Deau 6f G 6 99

Q

QUALIFY 2
Oct 25 Yarm 8f S 1 **99**

QUEEN CLEOPATRA 2
Oct 15 NmkR 7f G 9 **101**

QUEEN OF FIRE 2
Jly 5 NmkJ 6f G 4 **101**

QUEEN'S BEST 2
Oct 28 NmkR 6f G 1 **99**

QUEENSALSA 2
Jly 24 MsnL 5½f G 2 **104**

QUIET ROYAL 2
Oct 2 Lonc 8f G 2 110
Nov 1 MsnL 7f GF 1 **112**

QUINCE 2
Sep 17 Catt 7f G 1 **99**

QUSOOR 2
Aug 3 Epsm 6f G 1 **101**

R

RACE FOR THE STARS 2
Aug 7 Curr 6f G 2 101
Sep 4 Curr 7f G 9 99
Oct 1 NmkR 7f G 1 **103**

RACE TO THE MUSIC 2
Jun 25 Ling 5f G 1 **104**

RACER FOREVER 2
Aug 10 Sals 6f G 1 **104**
Sep 17 Newb 6f GF 5 100
Oct 8 Sals 5f GF 5 99

RAISE AGAIN 2
Sep 18 Curr 6f G 3 **99**

RAJEEM 2
Sep 27 Nott 8f GF 1 101
Oct 29 NmkR 8f S 1 **104**

RAMPALLION 2
Oct 14 NmkR 8f G 1 **99**

RAPSGATE 2
Dec 26 Wolv 5f SD 1 **101**

RED CAPE 2
Dec 17 Ling 8f FT 2 **99**

RED CLUBS 2
May 25 NmkR 6f G 1 99
Jun 14 York 6f G 1 **108**
Aug 7 Curr 6f G 3 102
Aug 17 York 6f F 2 102
Sep 30 NmkR 6f G 2 107
Oct 15 NmkR 7f G 4 104

RED ROCKS 2
Oct 14 NmkR 8f G 2 **99**

REFORM ACT 2
Oct 23 Curr 8f S 4 **105**

REGAL CONNECTION 2
Aug 31 York 8f G 3 **99**

REKAAB 2
Aug 20 Curr 7f GF 4 108
Oct 9 Curr 8f GS 2 **110**

RIBH 2
Jly 7 NmkJ 6f G 2 **99**

RICHTERHOFFEN 2
Jly 14 Epsm 7f G 1 **99**

RIGHT AGAIN 2
Jly 7 NmkJ 7f G 4 **101**
Sep 10 Gdwd 8f G 6 99

RISING CROSS 2
Jly 21 Sand 7f GF 4 104
Jly 29 NmkJ 7f G 1 100
Aug 6 NmkJ 7f G 4 104
Aug 20 Sand 7f G 4 **106**
Aug 28 Gdwd 7f G 2 104
Sep 8 Donc 8f GF 6 103

RISK RUNNER 2
Nov 4 Yarm 8f S 1 **100**

RIVER BRAVO 2
Oct 17 Wind 6f G 1 **99**

RIVER CROSSING 2
Jun 17 Rdcr 5f G 1 **99**

RIVER KINTYRE 2
May 4 Ches 5f GS 1 **99**

RIVER LENA 2
Jly 26 Bevl 7½f G 1 **103**

RIVER THAMES 2
Sep 10 Donc 5f GS 3 **100**
Sep 17 Newb 6f GF 8 99

ROAD TO LOVE 2
Aug 28 Bevl 8½f GS 1 **104**

ROL'OVER BEETHOVEN 2
Oct 21 Newb 6f G 3 **100**

ROMANTIC EVENING 2
Aug 12 Newb 7f G 3 **100**

ROSINKA 2
Jly 27 Gdwd 6f G 1 **101**

ROYAL INTRIGUE 2
Nov 6 Leop 9f S 3 **100**

ROYAL POWER 2
Jun 3 Thsk 5f G 2 **102**
Jun 13 Thsk 7f G 1 99
Sep 10 Leop 7f HD 2 99

ROYAL PROPOSAL 2
Sep 2 NmkJ 7f G 2 **103**

RUBENSTAR 2
Oct 9 Gdwd 7f G 1 **104**

RUMPLESTILTSKIN 2
Aug 7 Curr 7f G 1 101
Sep 4 Curr 7f G 1 110
Oct 2 Lonc 8f G 1 **111**

RYEDALE OVATION 2
Apr 28 Rdcr 5f GF 1 **101**

S

SAABIQ 2
Sep 1 Sals 6f G 2 **105**

SABANA PERDIDA 2
Oct 2 Lonc 8f G 14 **99**

SAKKARA STAR 2
Sep 4 Curr 7f G 6 **103**

SALSALAVA 2
Sep 17 Lonc 8f G 4 **103**

SALT MAN 2
Oct 30 Ling 8f SD 1 **99**

SALUT D'AMOUR 2
May 30 Sand 5f G 1 100
Jun 15 York 5f G 2 100
Jly 5 NmkJ 6f G 2 **102**

Sep 24 NmkR 8f G 6 99

SALUTE THE GENERAL 2
Nov 15 Ling 8f FT 2 **102**

SAMSA 2
Oct 2 Lonc 8f G 5 **106**

SANDIE 2
Sep 4 Curr 7f G 4 **105**

SANDS CROONER 2
Dec 26 Wolv 5f SD 3 **99**

SANDS OF BARRA 2
Dec 5 Ling 7f FT 1 **101**

SANTIAGO STAR 2
Aug 5 NmkJ 7f GF 1 **101**

SAVILLE ROAD 2
Jun 4 Donc 6f G 1 **101**
Jly 22 NmkJ 7f G 2 **101**

SAXON SAINT 2
Aug 22 Wind 5f G 1 **101**

SCARLET FLYER 2
Sep 20 Brig 6f G 1 **103**

SCARLET KNIGHT 2
Oct 24 Ling 6f SW 1 **100**
Nov 15 Ling 8f FT 5 99

SCARLETT'S PRIDE 2
Jly 24 MsnL 5½f G 5 **101**

SCOTTISH STAGE 2
Oct 1 NmkR 7f G 2 **102**

SECRET NIGHT 2
Sep 24 Ripn 5f GF 3 **101**
Nov 12 Ling 6f FT 1 100

SENSUOUS 2
Sep 1 Sals 7f G 2 **101**

SEPTIMUS 2
Oct 9 Curr 8f GS 1 **111**
Oct 22 Donc 8f S 3 109

SEVEN SAMURAI 2
Oct 17 Wind 8½f G 3 **102**
Nov 10 Ling 7f SD 1 99

SHAHIN 2
Sep 16 Newb 8f GF 2 100
Oct 21 Newb 8f G 1 **107**

SHAPERELLI 2
Sep 18 Curr 6f G 1 **103**

SHAYDREAMBELIEVER 2
Sep 10 Ches 7f GS 4 **99**
Sep 17 Ayr 8f G 1 **99**

SHERMEEN 2
Oct 8 Sals 5f GF 3 **101**

SHES MINNIE 2
Jun 11 Bath 5f G 2 **99**

SHINKO DANCER 2
Sep 17 Curr 5f GF 2 **101**

SHORT DANCE 2
Sep 2 NmkJ 6f G 1 101
Oct 1 NmkR 7f G 4 100
Oct 22 Newb 7f G 1 **103**

SHORT SKIRT 2
Aug 26 NmkJ 7f G 1 **106**
Oct 15 NmkR 7f G 7 102

SHORTEST DAY 2
Jly 15 NmkJ 7f G 8 100
Oct 17 Wind 8½f G 1 **104**

SILCA'S SISTER 2
Jly 22 Newb 6f G 1 99
Aug 21 Deau 6f G 1 **111**

SILENT TIMES 2
Jly 8 York 7f G 1 100
Aug 20 Curr 7f GF 3 **108**
Sep 9 Donc 7f G 1 103

SILIDAN 2
Sep 4 York 7f GF 1 99
Oct 11 Leic 7f G 2 **100**

SILVA 2
Nov 1 MsnL 6f GF 7 **103**

SILVER BLUE 2
Jly 20 Ling 7f SD 1 **99**

SILVER DIP 2
Sep 1 Sals 7f G 1 **102**

SIN CITY 2
Sep 15 Yarm 8f G 1 **101**

SINDIRANA 2
Oct 29 NmkR 8f S 4 **99**

SIR PERCY 2
Jun 23 Sals 6f G 1 100
Jly 27 Gdwd 7f G 1 106
Oct 15 NmkR 7f G 1 **111**

SIR XAAR 2
May 27 Pont 6f GF 1 101
Jun 14 York 6f G 4 103
Aug 29 Ripn 6f G 1 102
Sep 17 Newb 6f GF 2 **104**

SIRENE DOLOISE 2
Oct 2 Lonc 8f G 13 **101**

SKHILLING SPIRIT 2
Sep 18 Haml 6f F 2 **101**
Oct 21 Donc 6f S 1 **101**

SKYELADY 2
Jun 25 NmkJ 6f G 2 **101**

SLEEPING STORM 2
Jly 15 NmkJ 7f G 6 **102**
Aug 6 Hayd 6f G 1 100

SMITTEN KITTEN 2
Aug 6 NmkJ 7f G 4 **99**

SOHO SQUARE 2
Nov 3 Muss 8f GS 3 **101**

SOLVA 2
Sep 27 Nott 8f GF 2 **99**

SONG OF SILENCE 2
Dec 10 Sthl 8f FT 2 **100**

SONNY SANTINO 2
Jun 19 Wwck 7f G 1 **100**

SOTO 2
May 11 York 5f S 2 **102**

SOUNDS SIMLA 2
Jun 10 Chep 6f G 3 **101**

SOUTH CAPE 2
Oct 22 Donc 6f S 5 **105**

SPEARIT 2
Nov 10 Ling 5f SD 1 **103**

SPECIOSA 2
Sep 8 Donc 8f GF 3 108
Oct 15 NmkR 7f G 1 **109**

SPEEDY SAM 2
Sep 15 Ayr 8f G 2 **99**

SPIDER POWER 2
Sep 20 Brig 6f G 3 **101**

SPINNING QUEEN 2
Jly 5 NmkJ 6f G 3 102
Aug 6 NmkJ 7f G 5 **103**
Aug 28 Gdwd 7f G 4 102
Sep 8 Donc 8f GF 8 102
Oct 15 NmkR 7f G 6 **103**

SPIRITO DEL VENTO 2
Oct 2 Lonc 7f G 5 **108**

SPUNGER 2
Sep 10 Muss 8f G 1 **100**

STAGE FLIGHT 2
Sep 14 Bevl 7½f G 1 102
Oct 15 NmkR 7f G 4 **104**

STAINLEY 2
Sep 10 Ches 7f GS 2 **102**

STAR CLUSTER 2
Jly 15 NmkJ 7f G 1 **108**

STARSHIP 2
Dec 21 Ling 7f G 2 **99**

STARTORI 2
Oct 1 NmkR 7f G 1 **100**
Oct 17 Pont 8f G 3 99

STEPPING UP 2
Sep 5 Newc 6f F 1 101
Sep 29 NmkR 7f GF 3 **102**
Oct 22 Newb 7f G 7 99

STONEACRE LAD 2
Dec 6 Sthl 5f FT 1 **99**

STORMY RIVER 2
Oct 30 StCl 8f G 2 **108**

STRATHAM 2
Jly 23 Sals 6f G 1 **99**

STRIKE UP THE BAND 2
Apr 27 Pont 5f GS 1 100
May 4 Ches 5f GS 2 **106**
May 18 Gdwd 5f G 1 103
Jun 16 York 5f GF 2 99
Jun 18 York 5f GF 2 104
Jly 26 Gdwd 5f G 1 105

STRUT 2
Aug 6 Wind 5f GF 1 99
Aug 13 Newb 5f G 1 **103**

SUNRISE SAFARI 2
Oct 1 Rdcr 6f GF 6 **101**

SUPASEUS 2
Oct 21 Newb 8f G 2 **104**

SUPERCAST 2
Jly 8 Chep 5f GF 2 **101**

SURELY TRULY 2
Jun 16 Wolv 5f GF 2 **99**
Oct 14 NmkR 6f G 8 **99**
Oct 24 Ling 6f SW 3 **99**

SUZY BLISS 2
Aug 10 Sand 7f GF 1 104
Sep 8 Donc 8f GF 4 **107**
Oct 1 NmkR 7f G 5 99

SWEET AFTON 2
Jly 23 Newb 6f GF 5 **104**
Aug 13 Newb 5f G 2 102

SWEET PETITE 2
Oct 23 Curr 8f S 5 **104**

SWING THE RING 2
Sep 7 Donc 6f GF 3 **99**

T

TABARET 2
Jun 18 York 5f GF 3 102
Jly 1 Bevl 5f G 1 **105**

TAKODA 2
May 11 York 5f S 3 **99**

TARA TOO 2
Sep 1 Sals 6f G 6 100
Sep 14 Sand 7f G 4 **101**

TEN DOWNING STREET 2
Oct 19 Bath 5f G 1 **99**

THAMARAT 2
Jly 31 Deau 6f G 4 **103**
Oct 2 Lonc 8f G 9 **103**

THE SNATCHER 2
Jun 10 Chep 6f G 2 102
Sep 20 NmkR 6f G 1 99
Oct 28 NmkR 6f GS 2 **105**

THE VISUALISER 2
Aug 10 Bevl 7½f GF 1 **99**

THE WILD SWAN 2
Oct 22 Donc 6f S 3 **107**

THREE THIEVES 2
Oct 3 Pont 10f G 2 99
Oct 16 Muss 9f G 1 **103**

TIANA 2
Oct 1 NmkR 7f G 3 **101**

TIBER TILLY 2
Jly 30 Gdwd 6f G 1 **101**

TIME FOR LIFE 2
Nov 29 Ling 8f FT 4 **99**
Dec 17 Ling 8f FT 3 **99**

TITUS ALONE 2
Jun 18 York 5f GF 1 **106**

TO SENDER 2
May 14 Newb 6f F 1 **101**

TOUR D'AMOUR 2
Oct 9 Gdwd 7f G 4 **100**

TRAFALGAR BAY 2
Oct 22 Newb 6f G 1 **104**

TRISKAIDEKAPHOBIA 2
Jun 3 Thsk 5f G 1 **103**

TROPHY PRIDE 2
Oct 27 Ling 5f SD 1 **102**

TRUE CAUSE 2
Aug 15 Nott 8f GF 1 103
Sep 10 Gdwd 8f G 1 104
Sep 25 NmkR 8f G 5 **105**

TUFTON 2
Sep 28 Sals 7f G 2 **99**

TURN ME ON 2
Jun 3 Thsk 5f G 3 **101**

TWILL 2
Nov 21 Sthl 8f SW 1 **106**

TWINSPOT 2
Oct 2 Lonc 8f G 4 **106**

U

UGO FIRE 2
May 8 Leop 6f GS 1 99
Aug 7 Curr 6f G 4 101
Aug 20 Curr 6f GF 3 104
Sep 4 Curr 7f G 2 **109**

UNDER MY THUMB 2
Jly 22 NmkJ 7f G 1 **102**
Oct 4 Leic 10f G 4 99

UPPER HAND 2
Jly 29 Gdwd 6f G 2 **102**

V

VAGUE 2
Jly 21 Sand 7f GF 2 **106**

VEGAS BOYS 2
Sep 5 Wwck 6f G 1 **101**

VIOLANI 2
Aug 20 Curr 7f GF 5 **104**

VIOLETTE 2
Aug 6 Hayd 6f G 2 99
Sep 17 Ayr 6f G 1 105
Oct 1 Rdcr 6f GF 2 107
Oct 15 NmkR 7f G 2 **108**
Nov 1 MsnL 7f GF 3 104

W

WAITINGFORANALIBI 2
Oct 9 Curr 7f GS 1 **104**

WAKE UP MAGGIE 2
Aug 20 Curr 6f GF 1 **109**
Sep 29 NmkR 6f GF 2 100

WASSEEMA 2
Sep 2 NmkJ 6f G 3 **99**

WATERWAYS 2
Apr 3 Curr 5f S 1 99
May 21 Curr 5f GF 1 101
Jly 26 Gdwd 5f G 3 **103**

WELL ARMED 2
Oct 8 Sals 8f GF 4 **100**

WEST OF AMARILLO 2
Sep 29 NmkR 7f GF 7 **99**

WHERE'S THAT TIGER 2
May 18 Gdwd 5f G 4 **100**

WILD SUNDAY 2
Oct 2 Lonc 7f G 6 **99**

WILSON STAR 2
Jun 30 Newb 6f G 4 **99**

WINGED CUPID 2
Sep 16 Newb 8f GF 1 102
Oct 22 Donc 8f S 2 **110**

WITH INTEREST 2
Oct 7 Newb 7f GF 1 **99**

WITHOUT A PADDLE 2
Sep 18 Curr 6f G 2 **101**

WOVOKA 2
Aug 19 Sals 6f G 2 99
Sep 10 Ches 7f GS 3 101
Nov 6 Leop 9f S 1 **104**

Y

YANKEE GEORGE 2
Jly 7 Donc 7f GF 1 99

Oct	14	NmkR	6f	G	2	**102**

YARQUS 2

Sep	15	Yarm	8f	G	2	**100**
Oct	14	Brig	8f	G	1	99

YASOODD 2

Jun	18	Ayr	7f	G	1	100
Jly	7	NmkJ	7f	G	3	103
Jly	27	Gdwd	7f	G	6	101
Aug	20	Sand	7f	G	2	**110**
Sep	29	NmkR	7f	GF	4	102
Oct	22	Newb	7f	G	6	99

YELLOW CARD 2

Nov	10	Ling	5f	SD	4	**99**

YOUMZAIN 2

Aug	27	Gdwd	8f	G	1	**103**

YOUR AMOUNT 2

Aug	6	Ling	8f	SD	3	**101**

Z

ZAAL 2

Jly	28	Carl	6f	G	1	**99**
Aug	18	Wolv	7f	SD	1	**99**

ZABEEL TOWER 2

Oct	17	Wind	8½f	G	4	**101**

ZAMALA 2

Jly	27	Sand	7f	GS	3	**100**

ZATO 2

Jun	14	York	6f	G	6	101
Jun	30	Newb	6f	G	2	**104**
Sep	17	Lonc	8f	G	3	**104**

ZAVONE 2

Jly	1	Sand	5f	G	1	**101**

ZENNERMAN 2

Jly	7	Wwck	7f	G	1	**101**

FASTEST PERFORMERS 2005

THREE-YEAR-OLDS AND UPWARDS

5f-6f

Reverence 119
Benbaun 118
Baron's Pit 117
Cape Of Good Hope ... 117
Whipper 117
Beckermet 116
Iffraaj 116
Indian Trail 116
Ace 115
Ashdown Express 115
Avonbridge 115
Bali Royal 115
Baltic King 115
Celtic Mill 115
Majestic Missile 115
Miss Emma 115
Noelani 115
Osterhase 115
The Tatling 115

7f-9f

Martillo 119
Proclamation 119
Le Vie Dei Colori 118
Rakti 118
Soviet Song 118
Attraction 117
Autumn Glory 117
Court Masterpiece 117
Divine Proportions 117
Dubawi 117
Gorella 117
Majors Cast 117
Turtle Bowl 117
Valixir 117
Whipper 117
Ace Of Hearts 116
Ad Valorem 116
Chic 116
Creskeld 116
Eccentric 116
Fayr Jag 116
Galeota 116
Goodricke 116
Iffraaj 116
Jack Sullivan 116
Layman 116
Moayed 116
Special Kaldoun 116
Starpix 116

10f-12f

Hurricane Run 122
Pride 121
Westerner 120
Alkaased 119
Bago 119
Geordieland 119
Motivator 119
Pinson 119
Shirocco 119
Artiste Royal 118
Fracassant 118
Shawanda 118
Autumn Glory 117
Diamond Green 117
Echo Of Light 117
Policy Maker 117
Short Pause 117
Tropical Lady 117
Voix Du Nord 117
Alost 116
Blu Canari 116
Cairdeas 116
Charmo 116
Delfos 116
Eccentric 116
Electrocutionist 116
Levitski 116
Mohandas 116
Oratorio 116
Satwa Queen 116
Warrsan 116

13f+

Distinction 117
Golden Quest 116
High Action 115
Westerner 115

TWO-YEAR-OLDS

5f-6f

George Washington.. 116
Balthazaar's Gift 115
Gwenseb 113
Manston 112
Silca's Sister 111
Curtail 110
Flashy Wings 110
Mixed Blessing 110

7f+

Horatio Nelson 114
George Washington 113
Nannina 112
Opera Cape 112
Palace Episode 112
Quiet Royal 112
Alexandrova 111
Carlotamix 111
Rumplestiltskin 111
Septimus 111
Sir Percy 111
Galantas 110
Golden Arrow 110
Heatseeker 110
Jioconda 110
Leo 110
Mauralakana 110
Nasheej 110
Rekaab 110
Winged Cupid 110
Yasoodd 110

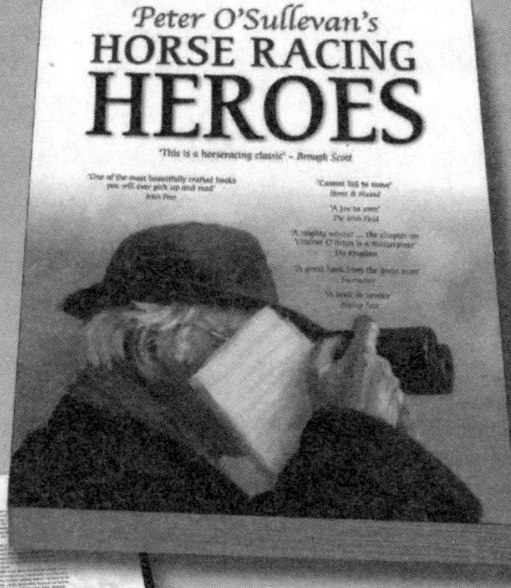

GROUP ONE SURVEY

The tables represent those races which held Group One status in 2005, together with the winners and their Speed Figure for the race. Speed figures for 2001 and after are on a different scale to previous seasons.

ULTIMATEPOKER.COM 1000 GUINEAS

2005	Virginia Waters (USA)	112
2004	Attraction	112
2003	Russian Rhythm (USA)	112
2002	Kazzia (GER)	104
2001	Ameerat	111
2000	Lahan	68
1999	Wince	60
1998	Cape Verdi (IRE)	93
1997	Sleepytime (IRE)	73
1996	Bosra Sham (USA)	66

ULTIMATEPOKER.COM 2000 GUINEAS

2005	Footstepsinthesand	112
2004	Haafhd	116
2003	Refuse To Bend (IRE)	114
2002	Rock Of Gibraltar (IRE)	112
2001	Golan (IRE)	113
2000	King's Best (USA)	83
1999	Island Sands (IRE)	62
1998	KIng Of Kings (IRE)	89
1997	Entrepreneur	92
1996	Mark of Esteem	77

JUDDMONTE LOCKINGE STAKES

2005	Rakti	118
2004	Russian Rhythm (USA)	115
2003	Hawk Wing (USA)	120
2002	Keltos (FR)	112
2001	Medicean	89
2000	Aljabr (USA)	72
1999	Fly To The Stars	77
1998	Cape Cross (IRE)	94
1997	First Island (IRE)	77
1996	Soviet Line (IRE)	51

VODAFONE DERBY

2005	Motivator	114
2004	North Light (IRE)	113
2003	Kris Kin (USA)	111
2002	High Chapparal (IRE)	112
2001	Galileo (IRE)	111
2000	Sinndar (IRE)	97
1999	Oath (IRE)	83
1998	High-Rise (IRE)	89
1997	Benny The Dip (USA)	91
1996	Shaamit (IRE)	82

VODAFONE OAKS

2005	Eswarah	107
2004	Ouija Board	114
2003	Casual Look (USA)	103
2002	Kazzia (GER)	110
2001	Imagine (IRE)	110
2000	Love Divine	76
1999	Ramruma (USA)	86
1998	Shahtoush (IRE)	85
1997	Reams of Verse	79
1996	Lady Carla	84

VODAFONE CORONATION CUP

2005	Yeats (IRE)	113
2004	Warrsan (IRE)	112
2003	Warrsan (IRE)	111
2002	Boreal (GER)	109
2001	Mutafaweq	113
2000	Daliapour (IRE)	86
1999	Daylami (IRE)	76
1998	Silver Patriarch (IRE)	90
1997	Singspiel (IRE)	65
1996	Swain (IRE)	48

QUEEN ANNE STAKES

2005	Valixir (IRE)	116
2004	Refuse To Bend (IRE)	112
2003	Dubai Destination (USA)	111
2002	No Excuse Needed	109
2001	Medicean	111
2000	Kalanisi (IRE)	117
1999	Cape Cross (IRE)	79
1998	Intikhab (USA)	108
1997	Allied Forces (USA)	87
1996	Charnwood Forest (IRE)	95

ST JAMES'S PALACE STAKES

2005	Shamardal (USA)	113
2004	Azamour (IRE)	119
2003	Zafeen	114

2002	Rock Of Gibraltar (IRE)	114
2001	Black Minnaloushe (USA)	110
2000	Giant's Causeway (USA)	77
1999	Sendawar (IRE)	80
1998	Dr Fong (USA)	99
1997	Starborough	96
1996	Bijou d'Inde	78

PRINCE OF WALES'S STAKES

2005	Azamour (IRE)	114
2004	Rakti	117
2003	Nayef (USA)	119
2002	Grandera (IRE)	123
2001	Fantastic Light (USA)	110
2000	Dubai Millennium	112
1999	Lear Spear (USA)	91
1998	Faithful Son (USA)	82
1997	Bosra Sham (USA)	95
1996	First Island (IRE)	103

CORONATION STAKES

2005	Maids Causeway (IRE)	116
2004	Attraction	118
2003	Russian Rhythm (USA)	112
2002	Sophisticat (USA)	107
2001	Banks Hill	113
2000	Crimplene (IRE)	91
1999	Balisada	57
1998	Exclusive	88
1997	Rebecca Sharp	71
1996	Shake the Yoke	76

ASCOT GOLD CUP

2005	Westerner	---
2004	Papineau	109
2003	Mr Dinos (IRE)	109
2002	Royal Rebel	97
2001	Royal Rebel	107
2000	Kayf Tara	59
1999	Enzeli (IRE)	66
1998	Kayf Tara	68
1997	Celeric	79
1996	Classic Cliche	66

GOLDEN JUBILEE STAKES

2005	Cape Of Good Hope	117
2004	Fayr Jag (IRE)	114
2003	Choisir (AUS)	113
2002	Malhub (USA)	114
2001	Harmonic Way	116
2000	Superior Dream	113
1999	Bold Edge	75
1998	Tomba	89
1997	Royal Applause	86
1996	Atraf	69

CORAL-ECLIPSE STAKES

2005	Oratorio (IRE)	113
2004	Refuse To Bend (IRE)	116
2003	Russian Rhythm (USA)	112
2002	Hawk Wing (USA)	112
2001	Medicean	115
2000	Giant's Causeway (USA)	71
1999	Compton Admiral	64
1998	Daylami (IRE)	94
1997	Pllsudski (IRE)	63
1996	Halling (USA)	78

UAE EQUESTRIAN AND RACING FEDERATION FALMOUTH STAKES

2005	Soviet Song (IRE)	108
2004	Soviet Song (IRE)	115

DARLEY JULY CUP

2005	Pastoral Pursuits	114
2004	Frizzante	116
2003	Oasis Dream	117
2002	Continent	113
2001	Mozart (IRE)	118
2000	Agnes World (USA)	72
1999	Stravinsky (USA)	93
1998	Elnadim (USA)	85
1997	Compton Place	64
1996	Anabaa (USA)	80

KING GEORGE VI AND QUEEN ELIZABETH DIAMOND STAKES

2005	Azamour (IRE)	115
2004	Doyen (IRE)	107
2003	Alamshar (IRE)	114
2002	Golan (IRE)	118
2001	Galileo (IRE)	120
2000	Montjeu	100
1999	Daylami (IRE)	99
1998	Swain (IRE)	93
1997	Swain (IRE)	83
1996	Pentire	92

CANTOR SPREADFAIR SUSSEX STAKES

2005	Proclamation (IRE)	119
2004	Soviet Song (IRE)	118
2003	Reel Buddy (USA)	109
2002	Rock Of Gibraltar (IRE)	116
2001	Noverre	112
2000	Giant's Causeway (USA)	76
1999	Aljabr (USA)	81
1998	Among Men (USA)	76
1997	Ali-Royal (IRE)	81
1996	First Island (IRE)	87

VODAFONE NASSAU STAKES

2005	Alexander Goldrun (IRE)	108
2004	Favourable Terms	106
2003	Russian Rhythm (USA)	111
2002	Islington (IRE)	112
2001	Lailani	109
2000	Crimplene (IRE)	73
1999	Zahrat Dubai	71
1998	Alborada	--
1997	Ryafan (USA)	84
1996	Last Second (IRE)	59

JUDDMONTE INTERNATIONAL STAKES

2005	Electrocutionist (USA)	116
2004	Sulamani (IRE)	114
2003	Falbrav (IRE)	118
2002	Nayef (USA)	117
2001	Sakhee (USA)	119
2000	Giant's Causeway (IRE)	80
1999	Royal Anthem (USA)	104
1998	One So Wonderful	93
1997	Singspiel (IRE)	90
1996	Halling (USA)	94

ASTON UPTHORPE YORKSHIRE OAKS

2005	Punctilious	110
2004	Quiff	106
2003	Islington (IRE)	113
2002	Islington (IRE)	115
2001	Super Tassa (IRE)	106
2000	Petrushka (IRE)	45
1999	Ramruma (USA)	76
1998	Catchascatchcan	75
1997	My Emma	83
1996	Key Change (IRE)	67

VC BET NUNTHORPE STAKES

2005	La Cucaracha	114
2004	Bahamian Pirate (USA)	117
2003	Oasis Dream	117
2002	Kyllachy	110
2001	Mozart (IRE)	116
2000	Nuclear Debate (USA)	104
1999	Stravinsky (USA)	83
1998	Lochangel	81
1997	Ya Malak	79
	Coastal Bluff	79
1996	Pivotal	80

WILLIAM HILL SPRINT CUP

2005	Goodricke	108
2004	Tante Rose (IRE)	113
2003	Somnus	115
2002	Invincible Spirit (IRE)	111
2001	Nuclear Debate (USA)	111
2000	Pipalong (IRE)	83
1999	Diktat	64
1998	Tamarisk (IRE)	73
1997	Royal Applause	59
1996	Iktamal (USA)	86

LADBROKES ST LEGER

2005	Scorpion (IRE)	106
2004	Rule Of Law (USA)	103
2003	Brian Boru	114
2002	Bollin Eric	115
2001	Milan	115
2000	Millenary	76
1999	Mutafaweq	83
1998	Nedawi	56
1997	Silver Patriarch (USA)	54
1996	Shantou (USA)	84

MEON VALLEY STUD FILLIES' MILE

2005	Nannina	112
2004	Playful Act (IRE)	108
2003	Red Bloom	109
2002	Soviet Song (IRE)	110
2001	Gossamer	109
2000	Crystal Music (USA)	61
1999	Teggiano (IRE)	56
1998	Sunspangled (IRE)	57
1997	Glorosia (FR)	64

1996	Reams of Verse (USA)	53
1996	Bosra Sham (USA)	85

QUEEN ELIZABETH II STAKES

2005	Starcraft (NZ)	115
2004	Rakti	120
2003	Falbrav (IRE)	118
2002	Where Or When (IRE)	114
2001	Summoner	119
2000	Observatory (USA)	94
1999	Dubai Millennium	93
1998	Desert Prince (IRE)	99
1997	Air Express (IRE)	92
1996	Mark of Esteem (IRE)	85

SKYBET CHEVELEY PARK STAKES

2005	Donna Blini	101
2004	Magical Romance (IRE)	105
2003	Carry On Katie (USA)	101
2002	Airwave	107
2001	Queen's Logic (IRE)	114
2000	Regal Rose	54
1999	Seazun (IRE)	68
1998	Wannabe Grand (IRE)	45
1997	Embassy	65
1996	Pas De Reponse (USA)	63

SHADWELL STUD MIDDLE PARK STAKES

2005	Amadeus Wolf	109
2004	Ad Valorem (USA)	106
2003	Three Valleys (USA)	109
2002	Oasis Dream	107
2001	Johannesburg (USA)	111
2000	Minardi (USA)	57
1999	Primo Valentino (IRE)	79
1998	Lujain (USA)	57
1997	Hayil (USA)	61
1996	Bahamian Bounty	66

KINGDOM OF BAHRAIN SUN CHARIOT STAKES

2005	Peeress	111
2004	Attraction	113

DARLEY DEWHURST STAKES

2005	Sir Percy	111
2004	Shamardal (USA)	117
2003	Milk It Mick	114
2002	Tout Seul (IRE)	114
2001	Rock Of Gibraltar (IRE)	109
2000	Tobougg (IRE)	63
1999	Distant Music (USA)	67
1998	Mujahid (USA)	79
1997	Xaar	84
1996	In Command (IRE)	76

EMIRATES AIRLINE CHAMPION STAKES

2005	David Junior (USA)	113
2004	Haafhd	116
2003	Rakti	116
2002	Storming Home	117
2001	Nayef (USA)	114
2000	Kalanisi (IRE)	94
1999	Alborada	69
1998	Alborada	92
1997	Pilsudski (IRE)	84
1996	Bosra Sham (USA)	74

RACING POST TROPHY

2005	Palace Episode (USA)	112
2004	Motivator	113
2003	American Post	103
2002	Brian Boru	113
2001	High Chaparral (IRE)	109
2000	Dilshaan	68
1999	Aristotle (IRE)	72
1998	Commander Collins (IRE)	64
1997	Saratoga Springs (CAN)	73
1996	Medaaly	64

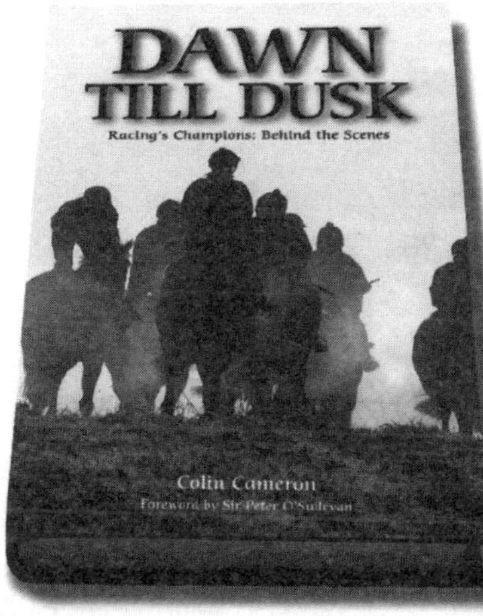

RACEFORM RECORD TIMES (FLAT)

ASCOT

Dist	Time	Age& wt		Going	Horse	Date
5f	59.7 secs	2	8-8	Gd to Firm	Lyric Fantasy	Jun 17 1992
5f	59.1 secs	3	8-8	Firm	Orient	Jun 12 1986
6f	1m 13.6	2	8-12	Gd to Firm	Three Valleys	Jun 17 2003
6f	1m 12.1	5	9-3	Firm	Ratio	Jun 21 2003
6f	1m 12.1	4	9-6	Firm	Fayr Jag (IRE)	Jun 21 2003
7f	1m 27.2	2	8-11	Gd to Firm	Celtic Swing	Oct 8 1994
7f	1m 25.8	4	8-2	Gd to Firm	Master Robbie	Sep 27 2003
1m	1m 40.8	2	8-10	Gd to Firm	Red Bloom	Sep 27 2003
1m	1m 38.0	4	7-8	Gd to Firm	Colour Sergeant	Jun 17 1992
1m	1m 38.5	3	9-0	Gd to Firm	Russian Rhythm	Jun 20 2003
1m 2f	2m 2.7	4	9-3	Gd to Firm	First Island (IRE)	Jun 18 1996
1m 4f	2m 26.5	4	8-9	Firm	Doyen (IRE)	Jun 19 2004
2m 45y	3m 25.2	3	8-11	Gd to Firm	Landowner	Jun 17 1992
2m 4f	4m 15.3	5	9-0	Gd to Firm	Royal Gait (disq)	Jun 16 1988
2m 6f 34y	4m 47.8	6	9-3	Firm	Cover Up (IRE)	Jun 21 2003

AYR

Dist	Time	Age& wt		Going	Horse	Date
5f	56.9 secs	2	8-11	Good	Boogie Street	Sep 18 2003
5f	57.2 secs	4	9-5	Gd to Firm	Sir Joey	Sep 16 1993
6f	69.7 secs	2	7-10	Good	Sir Bert	Sep 17 1969
6f	68.9 secs	7	8-8	Gd to Firm	Sobering Thoughts	Sep 18 1993
7f	1m 25.7	2	9-0	Gd to Firm	Jazeel	Sep 16 1993
7f	1m 24.9	5	7-11	Firm	Sir Arthur Hobbs	Jun 19 1992
7f 50y	1m 28.9	2	9-0	Good	Tafaahum (USA)	Sep 19 2003
7f 50y	1m 28.2	4	9-2	Gd to Firm	Flur Na H Alba	Jun 21 2003
1m	1m 39.2	2	9-0	Gd to Firm	Kribensis	Sep 17 1986
1m	1m 36.0	4	7-13	Firm	Sufi	Sep 16 1959
1m 1f 20y	1m 50.3	4	9-3	Good	Retirement	Sep 19 2003
1m 2f	2m 4.0	4	9-9	Gd to Firm	Endless Hall	Jly 17 2000
1m 2f192y	2m 13.3	4	9-0	Gd to Firm	Azzaam	Sep 18 1991
1m 5f 13y	2m 45.8	4	9-7	Gd to Firm	Eden's Close	Sep 18 1993
1m 7f	3m 13.1	3	9-4	Good	Romany Rye	Sep 19 1991
2m 1f105y	3m 45.0	4	6-13	Good	Curry	Sep 16 1955

BATH

Dist	Time	Age& wt		Going	Horse	Date
5f 11y	60.1 secs	2	8-11	Firm	Double Fantasy	Aug 25 2000
5f 11y	59.9 secs	6	9-2	Firm	Cauda Equina	Aug 25 2000
5f 161y	69.1 secs	2	8-7	Firm	Sibla	Aug 25 2000
5f 161y	68.1 secs	6	9-0	Firm	Madraco	May 22 1989
1m 5y	1m 39.7	2	8-9	Firm	Casual Look	Sep 16 2002

1m 5y	1m 37.2	5	8-12	Gd to Firm	Adobe	Jun 17 2000
1m 5y	1m 37.2	3	8-7	Firm	Alasha (IRE)	Aug 18 2002
1m 2f 46y	2m 5.8	3	9-0	Gd to Firm	ConnoisseurBay	May 29 1998
1m 3f144y	2m 25.74	3	9-0	Hard	Top Of The Charts	Sep 8 2005
1m 5f 22y	2m 47.2	4	10-0	Firm	Flown	Aug 13 1991
2m 1f 34y	3m 43.4	6	7-9	Firm	Yaheska (IRE)	Jun 14 2003

BEVERLEY

Dist	Time	Age&	wt	Going	Horse	Date
5f	61.0 secs	2	8-2	Gd to Firm	Addo (IRE)	Jly 17 2001
5f	60.1 secs	4	9-5	Firm	Pic Up Sticks	Apr 16 2003
7f 100y	1m 31.1	2	9-7	Gd to Firm	Champagne Prince	Aug 10 1995
7f 100y	1m 31.1	2	9-0	Firm	Majal (IRE)	Jly 30 1991
7f 100y	1m 29.5	3	7-8	Firm	Who's Tef	Jly 30 1991
1m 100y	1m 43.3	2	9-0	Firm	Arden	Sep 24 1986
1m 100y	1m 42.2	3	8-4	Firm	Legal Case	Jun 14 1989
1m 1f 207y	2m 1.8	3	9-7	Firm	Rose Alto	Jly 5 1991
1m 3f 216y	2m 30.8	3	8-1	Hard	Coinage	Jun 18 1986
1m 4f 16y	2m 35.8	4	9-3	Gd to Firm	Red River Rebel	Aug 25 2002
2m 35y	3m 29.5	4	9-2	Gd to Firm	Rushen Raider	Aug 14 1996

BRIGHTON

Dist	Time	Age&	wt	Going	Horse	Date
5f 59y	60.1 secs	2	9-0	Firm	Bid for Blue	May 6 1993
5f 59y	59.3 secs	3	8-9	Firm	Play Hever Golf	May 26 1993
5f 213y	68.1 secs	2	8-9	Firm	Song Mist (IRE)	Jly 16 1996
5f 213y	67.3 secs	3	8-9	Firm	Third Party	Jun 3 1997
5f 213y	67.3 secs	5	9-1	Gd to Firm	Blundell Lane	May 4 2000
6f 209y	1m 19.9	2	8-11	Hard	Rain Burst	Sep 15 1988
6f 209y	1m 19.4	4	9-3	Gd to Firm	Sawaki	Sep 3 1991
7f 214y	1m 32.8	2	9-7	Firm	Asian Pete	Oct 3 1989
7f 214y	1m 30.5	5	8-11	Firm	Mystic Ridge	May 27 1999
1m 1f 209y	2m 4.7	2	9-0	Gd to Soft	Esteemed Master	Nov 2 2001
1m 1f 209y	1m 57.2	3	9-0	Firm	Get The Message	Apr 30 1984
1m 3f 196y	2m 25.8	4	8-2	Firm	New Zealand	Jly 4 1985

CARLISLE

Dist	Time	Age&	wt	Going	Horse	Date
5f	60.1 secs	2	8-5	Firm	La Tortuga	Aug 2 1999
5f	58.8 secs	3	9-8	Gd to Firm	Esatto	Aug 21 2002
5f 193y	1m 12.45	2	9-6	Gd to Firm	Musical Guest (IRE)	Sep 11 2005
5f 193y	1m 10.83	4	9-0	Gd to Firm	Bo McGinty (IRE)	Sep 11 2005
6f 192y	1m 24.3	3	8-9	Gd to Firm	Marjurita (IRE)	Aug 21 2002
6f 206y	1m 26.5	2	9-4	Hard	Sense of Priority	Sep 10 1991
6f 206y	1m 25.3	4	9-1	Firm	Move With Edes	Jly 6 1996
7f 200y	1m 37.34	5	9-7	Gd to Firm	Hula Ballew	Aug 17 2005
7f 214y	1m 44.6	2	8-8	Firm	Blue Garter	Sep 9 1980
7f 214y	1m 37.3	5	7-12	Hard	Thatched (IRE)	Aug 21 1995

1m 1f 61y	1m 53.8	3	9-0	Firm	Little Jimbob	Jun 14 2004
1m 3f 206y	2m 29.13	5	9-8	Gd to Firm	Tempsford (USA)	Sep 19 2005
1m 4f	2m 28.8	3	8-5	Firm	Desert Frolic (IRE)	Jun 27 1996
1m 6f 32y	3m 2.2	6	8-10	Firm	Explosive Speed	May 26 1994
2m 1f 52y	3m 46.2	3	7-10	Gd to Firm	Warring Kingdom	Aug 25 1999

CATTERICK

Dist	Time	Age& wt		Going	Horse	Date
5f	57.6 secs	2	9-0	Firm	H Harrison	Oct 8 2002
5f	57.1 secs	4	8-7	Fast	Kabcast	Jly 7 1989
5f 212y	1m 11.4	2	9-4	Firm	Captain Nick	Jly 11 1978
5f 212y	69.8 secs	9	8-13	Gd to Firm	Sharp Hat	May 30 2003
7f	1m 24.1	2	8-11	Firm	Lindas Fantasy	Sep 18 1982
7f	1m 22.5	6	8-7	Firm	Differential (USA)	May 31 2003
1m 3f 214y	2m 30.5	3	8-8	Gd to Firm	Rahaf	May 30 2003
1m 5f 175y	2m 54.8	3	8-5	Firm	Geryon	May 31 1984
1m 7f 177y	3m 20.8	4	7-11	Firm	Bean Boy	Jly 8 1982

CHEPSTOW

Dist	Time	Age& wt		Going	Horse	Date
5f 16y	57.6 secs	2	8-11	Firm	Micro Love	Jly 8 1986
5f 16y	56.8 secs	3	8-4	Firm	Torbay Express	Sep 15 1979
6f 16y	69.4 secs	2	9-0	Fast	Royal Fifi	Sep 9 1989
6f 16y	68.1 secs	3	9-7	Firm	America Calling(USA)	Sep 18 2001
7f 16y	1m 20.8	2	9-0	Gd to Firm	Royal Amaretto(IRE)	Sep 12 1996
7f 16y	1m 19.3	3	9-0	Firm	Taranaki	Sep 18 2001
1m 14y	1m 33.1	2	8-11	Gd to Firm	Ski Academy (IRE)	Aug 28 1995
1m 14y	1m 31.6	3	8-13	Firm	Stoli (IRE)	Sep 18 2001
1m 2f 36y	2m 4.1	5	8-9	Hard	Leonidas	Jly 5 1983
1m 2f 36y	2m 4.1	5	7-8	Gd to Firm	It's Varadan	Sep 9 1989
1m 2f 36y	2m 4.1	3	8-5	Gd to Firm	Ela Athena	Jly 23 1999
1m 4f 23y	2m 31.0	3	8-9	Gd to Firm	Spritsail	Jly 13 1989
1m 4f 23y	2m 31.0	7	9-6	Hard	Maintop	Aug 27 1984
2m 49y	3m 27.7	4	9-0	Gd to Firm	Wizzard Artist	Jly 1 1989
2m 2f	3m 56.4	5	8-7	Gd to Firm	Laffah	Jly 8 2000

CHESTER

Dist	Time	Age& wt		Going	Horse	Date
5f 16y	60.2 secs	2	9-0	Gd to Firm	Majestic Missile(IRE)	Jly 11 2003
5f 16y	59.2 secs	3	10-0	Firm	Althrey Don	Jly 10 1964
6f 18y	1m 12.8	2	8-10	Gd to Firm	Flying Express	Aug 31 2002
6f 18y	1m 12.7	3	8-3	Gd to Firm	Play Hever Golf	May 4 1993
6f 18y	1m 12.7	6	9-2	Good	Stack Rock	Jun 23 1993
7f 2y	1m 25.2	2	9-0	Gd to Firm	Due Respect (IRE)	Sep 25 2002
7f 2y	1m 23.75	5	8-13	Gd to Firm	Three Graces (GER)	Jly 9 2005
7f 122y	1m 32.2	2	9-0	Gd to Firm	Big Bad Bob (IRE)	Sep 25 2002
7f 122y	1m 30.91	3	8-12	Gd to Firm	Cupid's Glory	Aug 18 2005
1m 2f 75y	2m 7.7	3	8-9	Gd to Firm	Fragrant View	May 7 2002

1m 3f 79y	2m 22.5	3	8-9	Gd to Firm	Rockerlong	May 9 2001
1m 4f 66y	2m 33.7	3	8-10	Gd to Firm	Fight Your Corner	May 7 2002
1m 5f 89y	2m 45.4	5	8-11	Firm	Rakaposhi King	May 7 1987
1m 7f 195y	3m 20.3	4	9-0	Gd to Firm	Grand Fromage (IRE)	Jly 13 2002
2m 2f 147y	4m 0.2	6	8-9	Gd to Firm	Fantasy Hill (IRE)	May 8 2002

DONCASTER

Dist	Time	Age&	wt	Going	Horse	Date
5f	58.4 secs	2	9-5	Firm	Sing Sing	Sep 11 1959
5f	58.4 secs	2	9-0	Good	D'Urberville	Sep 13 1967
5f	57.2 secs	6	9-12	Gd to Firm	Celtic Mill	Sep 9 2004
5f 140y	67.2 secs	2	9-0	Gd to Firm	Cartography (IRE)	Jun 29 2003
5f 140y	65.6 secs	9	9-10	Good	Halmahera (IRE)	Sep 8 2004
6f	69.6 secs	2	8-11	Good	Caesar Beware (IRE)	Sep 8 2004
6f	69.6 secs	2	8-11	Good	Caesar Beware (IRE)	Sep 8 2004
6f 110y	1m 17.9	2	8-13	Good	Swan Nebula (USA)	Sep 8 2004
7f	1m 22.6	2	9-1	Good	Librettist (USA)	Sep 8 2004
7f	1m 21.6	3	8-10	Gd to Firm	Pastoral Pursuits	Sep 9 2004
1m	1m 36.5	2	8-6	Gd to Firm	Singhalese	Sep 9 2004
1m (R)	1m 35.4	2	8-10	Good	Playful Act (IRE)	Sep 9 2004
1m	1m 35.3	3	9-0	Gd to Firm	Gneiss	May 2 1994
1m (R)	1m 36.6	7	9-9	Gd to Firm	Invader	Jun 29 2003
1m 2f 60y	2m 13.4	2	8-8	Good	Yard Bird	Nov 6 1981
1m 2f 60y	2m 5.4	3	8-8	Gd to Firm	Carlito Brigante	Jly 26 1995
1m 4f	2m 27.7	3	8-12	Gd to Firm	Takwin (IRE)	Sep 9 2000
1m 6f 132y	3m 2.2	3	8-3	Gd to Firm	Brier Creek	Sep 10 1992
2m 110y	3m 34.4	4	9-12	Gd to Firm	Farsl	Jun 12 1992
2m 2f	3m 50.2	7	9-1	Gd to Firm	Boreas	Sep 12 2002

EPSOM

Dist	Time	Age&	wt	Going	Horse	Date
5f	55.0 secs	2	8-9	Gd to Firm	Prince Aslia	Jun 9 1995
5f	53.6 secs	4	9-5	Firm	Indigenous	Jun 2 1960
6f	67.8 secs	2	8-11	Gd to Firm	Showbrook	Jun 5 1991
6f	67.3 secs	5	8-12	Good	Loyal Tycoon (IRE)	Jun 7 2003
7f	1m 21.3	2	8-9	Gd to Firm	Red Peony	Jul 29 2004
7f	1m 20.1	4	8-7	Firm	Capistrano	Jun 7 1972
1m 114y	1m 42.8	2	8-5	Gd to Firm	Nightstalker	Aug 30 1988
1m 114y	1m 40.7	3	8-6	Gd to Firm	Sylva Honda	Jun 5 1991
1m 2f 18y	2m 3.5	5	7-13	Good	Crossbow	Jun 7 1967
1m 4f 10y	2m 32.3	3	9-0	Gd to Firm	Lammtarra	Jun 10 1995

FOLKESTONE

Dist	Time	Age&	wt	Going	Horse	Date
5f	58.4 secs	2	9-2	Gd to Firm	Pivotal	Nov 6 1995
5f	58.6 secs	3	9-0	Gd to Firm	Zarzu	Jun 28 2002
6f	1m 10.8	2	8-9	Good	Boomerang Blade	Jly 16 1998
6f	69.5 secs	4	8-12	Gd to Firm	Double Oscar (IRE)	Jly 14 1997

6f 189y	1m 23.7	2	8-11	Good	Hen Harrier	Jly 3 1996
6f 189y	1m 21.4	3	8-9	Firm	Cielamour (USA)	Aug 9 1988
7f	1m 25.2	2	8-11	Gd to Firm	Persian Jasmine	Aug 12 2002
7f	1m 24.5	4	9-2	Good	Roffey Spinney(IRE)	Jly 15 1998
1m 1f 149y	1m 59.7	3	8-6	Gd to Firm	Dizzy	Jly 23 1991
1m 4f	2m 33.2	4	8-8	Hard	Snow Blizzard	Jun 30 1992
1m 7f 92y	3m 23.1	3	9-11	Firm	Mata Askari	Sep 12 1991
2m 93y	3m 34.9	3	8-12	Gd to Firm	Candle Smoke(USA)	Aug 20 1996

GOODWOOD

Dist	Time	Age& wt		Going	Horse	Date
5f	57.5 secs	2	8-12	Gd to Firm	Poets Cove	Aug 3 1990
5f	56.0 secs	5	9-0	Gd to Firm	Rudi's Pet	Jly 27 1999
6f	69.8 secs	2	8-11	Gd to Firm	Bachir (IRE)	Jly 28 1999
6f	69.5 secs	4	8-3	Firm	For The Present	Jly 30 1994
7f	1m 24.9	2	8-11	Gd to Firm	Ekraar	Jly 29 1999
7f	1m 23.8	3	8-7	Firm	Brief Glimpse (IRE)	Jly 25 1995
1m	1m 38.1	2	8-11	Good	Rimrod (USA)	Sep 13 2002
1m	1m 35.6	3	8-13	Gd to Firm	Aljabr (USA)	Jly 28 1999
1m 1f	1m 52.8	3	9-6	Good	Vena (IRE)	Jly 27 1995
1m 1f 192y	2m 3.4	3	8-12	Good	Moon Ballad (IRE)	Sep 14 2002
1m 3f	2m 23.0	3	8-8	Gd to Firm	Asian Heights	May 22 2001
1m 4f	2m 31.5	3	8-10	Firm	Presenting	Jly 25 1995
1m 6f	2m 58.5	4	9-2	Gd to Firm	Mowbray	Jly 27 1999
2m	3m 21.6	5	9-2	Gd to Firm	Jardine's Lookout	Aug 1 2002
2m 4f	4m 11.7	3	7-10	Firm	Lucky Moon	Aug 2 1990

HAMILTON

Dist	Time	Age& wt		Going	Horse	Date
5f 4y	58.0 secs	3	7-8	Firm	Fair Dandy	Sep 25 1972
5f 4y	58.0 secs	5	8-6	Firm	Golden Sleigh	Sep 6 1972
6f 5y	1m 10.0	2	8-12	Gd to Firm	Break The Code	Aug 24 1999
6f 5y	69.3 secs	4	8-7	Firm	Marcus Game	Jly 11 1974
1m 65y	1m 45.8	2	8-11	Firm	Hopeful Subject	Sep 24 1973
1m 65y	1m 42.7	6	7-7	Firm	Cranley	Sep 25 1972
1m 1f 36y	1m 53.6	5	9-6	Gd to Firm	Regent's Secret	Aug 10 2005
1m 3f 16y	2m 19.8	3	8-1	Gd to Firm	McEldowney	Aug 22 2005
1m 4f 17y	2m 32.0	4	10-0	Firm	Hold Tight	Aug 22 1983
1m 4f 17y	2m 32.0	4	7-4	Firm	Fine Point	Aug 24 1981
1m 5f 9y	2m 45.1	6	9-6	Firm	Mentalasanythin	Jun 14 1995

HAYDOCK

Dist	Time	Age& wt		Going	Horse	Date
5f	59.2 secs	2	9-4	Firm	Money For Nothing	Aug 21 1964
5f	58.2 secs	5	8-9	Good	Sierra Vista	Sep 3 2005
6f	1m 10.9	4	9-9	Gd to Firm	Wolfhound (USA)	Sep 4 1993
6f	69.9 secs	4	9-0	Gd to Firm	Iktamal (USA)	Sep 7 1996
7f 30y	1m 29.4	2	9-0	Gd to Firm	Apprehension	Sep 7 1996

7f 30y	1m 26.8	3	8-7	Gd to Firm	Lady Zonda	Sep 28 2002
1m 30y	1m 40.6	2	8-12	Gd to Firm	Besiege	Sep 7 1996
1m 30y	1m 40.1	3	9-2	Firm	Untold Riches(USA)	Jly 11 1999
1m 2f 120y	2m 22.2	2	8-11	Soft	Persian Haze	Oct 9 1994
1m 2f 120y	2m 8.5	3	8-7	Gd to Firm	Fahal (USA)	Aug 5 1995
1m 3f 200y	2m 26.4	5	8-2	Firm	New Member	Jly 4 1970
1m 6f	2m 59.5	3	8-3	Gd to Firm	Castle Secret	Sep 30 1989
2m 45y	3m 27.0	4	8-13	Firm	Prince of Peace	May 26 1984
2m 1f 130y	3m 55.0	3	8-12	Good	Crystal Spirit	Sep 8 1990

KEMPTON

Dist	Time	Age& wt		Going	Horse	Date
5f	58.3 secs	2	9-0	Firm	Schweppeshire Lad	Jun 3 1978
5f	57.4 secs	4	9-3	Gd to Firm	Almaty (IRE)	May 31 1997
6f	1m 10.6	2	8-10	Gd to Firm	Don Puccini	May 29 1999
6f	69.7 secs	4	9-1	Gd to Firm	Magic Rainbow	May 29 1999
7f	1m 26.7	2	8-8	Good	Exclusive	Sep 10 1997
7f	1m 24.7	2	9-0	Gd to Firm	Canons Park	Jun 28 1995
7f	1m 23.5	3	9-2	Gd to Firm	Wild Rice	Aug 2 1995
7f	1m 23.6	3	9-0	Gd to Firm	Shaheen (USA)	May 31 1997
1m	1m 43.4	2	7-0	Good	Fascinating	Nov 3 1956
1m	1m 38.7	2	9-0	Gd to Firm	Taverner Society(IRE)	Sep 22 1997
1m	1m 35.8	4	9-1	Firm	County Broker	May 23 1984
1m	1m 35.3	3	8-12	Gd to Firm	Private Line	Jun 28 1995
1m 1f	1m 50.0	4	9-11	Gd to Firm	Bahrqueen (USA)	Jun 25 2003
1m 2f	1m 59.5	4	9-6	Firm	Batshoof	Apr 6 1990
1m 3f 30y	2m 16.2	4	9-2	Firm	Shernazar	Sep 6 1985
1m 4f	2m 30.1	6	8-5	Firm	Going Going	Sep 7 1985
1m 6f 92y	3m 6.5	4	9-8	Gd to Firm	Renzo (IRE)	Sep 21 1997
2m	3m 24.3	4	8-9	Gd to Firm	Eminence Grise(IRE)	May 29 1999

LEICESTER

Dist	Time	Age& wt		Going	Horse	Date
5f 2y	58.4 secs	2	9-0	Firm	Cutting Blade	Jun 9 1986
5f 2y	58.0 secs	3	7-13	Gd to Firm	Emerald Peace (IRE)	Sep 5 2000
5f 218y	1m 10.1	2	9-0	Firm	Thordis (IRE)	Oct 24 1995
5f 218y	69.4 secs	3	8-12	Gd to Firm	Lakeland Beauty	May 29 1990
7f 9y	1m 22.8	2	8-6	Good	Miss Dragonfly (IRE)	Sep 22 1997
7f 9y	1m 20.8	3	8-7	Firm	Flower Bowl	Jun 9 1986
1m 8y	1m 34.5	2	8-9	Firm	Lady Carla	Oct 24 1995
1m 8y	1m 33.6	5	7-13	Gd to Firm	Derryquinn	Aug 13 2000
1m 9y	1m 39.2	4	8-11	Firm	Nashaab (USA)	May 28 2001
1m 1f 218y	2m 5.3	2	9-1	Gd to Firm	Windsor Castle	Oct 14 1996
1m 1f 218y	2m 2.4	3	8-11	Firm	Effigy	Nov 4 1985
1m 1f 218y	2m 2.4	4	9-6	Gd to Firm	Lady Angharad(IRE)	Jun 18 2000
1m 3f 183y	2m 27.1	5	8-12	Gd to Firm	Murghem (IRE)	Jun 18 2000

LINGFIELD (TURF)

Dist	Time	Age& wt		Going	Horse	Date
5f	57.1 secs	2	8-9	Good	Emerald Peace	Aug 6 1999
5f	56.2 secs	3	9-1	Gd to Firm	Eveningperformance	Jly 25 1994
6f	68.6 secs	2	9-3	Firm	The Ritz	Jun 11 1965
6f	68.2 secs	6	9-10	Firm	Al Amead	Jly 2 1986
7f	1m 21.3	2	7-6	Firm	Mandav	Oct 3 1980
7f	1m 20.1	3	8-7	Gd to Firm	Zelah (IRE)	May 13 1998
7f 140y	1m 29.9	2	8-12	Firm	Rather Warm	Nov 7 1978
7f 140y	1m 26.7	3	8-6	Fast	Hiaam	Nov 7 1978
1m 1f	1m 52.4	4	9-2	Gd to Firm	Quandary (USA)	Jly 15 1995
1m 2f	2m 4.6	3	9-3	Firm	Usran	Jly 15 1989
1m 3f 106y	2m 23.9	3	8-5	Firm	Night-Shirt	Jly 14 1990
1m 6f	2m 59.1	5	9-5	Firm	Ibn Bey	Jly 1 1989
2m	3m 23.7	3	9-5	Gd to Firm	Lauries Crusader	Aug 13 1988

LINGFIELD (A.W)

Dist	Time	Age& wt		Going	Horse	Date
5f	58.6 secs	2	9-7	Standard	Classy Cleo (IRE)	Nov 28 1997
5f	57.3 secs	4	9-5	Standard	No Time (IRE)	Mar 20 2004
6f	1m 11.5	2	8-8	Standard	Two Step Kid (USA)	Oct 27 2003
6f	1m 10.48	4	8-4	Standard	Desert Lord	Dec 18 2004
7f	1m 24.0	2	8-12	Standard	Scottish Castle	Nov 2 1990
7f	1m 22.7	6	9-12	Standard	Vortex	Apr 9 2005
1m	1m 36.5	2	9-5	Standard	San Pier Niceto	Nov 30 1989
1m	1m 35.86	4	9-0	Standard	Eccentric	Feb 1 2005
1m 2f	2m 2.6	3	8-10	Standard	Compton Bolter	Nov 18 2000
1m 4f	2m 29.2	6	8-13	Standard	Ursa Major	Dec 28 2000
1m 5f	2m 42.9	3	9-7	Standard	Global Dancer	Dec 7 1994
2m	3m 20.0	3	9-0	Standard	Yenoora	Aug 8 1992

MUSSELBURGH

Dist	Time	Age& wt		Going	Horse	Date
5f	57.7 secs	2	8-2	Firm	Arasong	May 16 1994
5f	57.3 secs	3	8-12	Firm	Corunna	Jun 3 2000
7f 30y	1m 28.4	2	8-8	Firm	Sand Bankes	Jun 26 2000
7f 30y	1m 26.3	3	9-5	Firm	Waltzing Wizard	Aug 22 2002
1m	1m 40.3	2	8-12	Gd to Firm	Succession	Sep 26 2004
1m	1m 38.8	6	9-4	Gd to Firm	Sea Storm (IRE)	May 29 2004
1m 1f	1m 50.8	3	9-2	Firm	Short Respite	Aug 22 2002
1m 4f	2m 33.7	3	9-11	Firm	Alexandrine	Jun 26 2000
1m 5f	2m 48.9	6	8-10	Gd to Firm	Tojoneski	July 27 2005
1m 6f	2m 59.2	3	9-7	Firm	Forum Chris	Jly 3 2000
2m	3m 26.6	5	9-6	Gd to Firm	Jack Dawson (IRE)	Jun 1 2002

NEWBURY

Dist	Time	Age& wt		Going	Horse	Date
5f 34y	59.1 secs	2	8-6	Gd to Firm	Superstar Leo	Jly 22 2000

5f 34y	59.2 secs	3	9-5	Gd to Firm	The Trader (IRE)	Aug 18 2001
6f 8y	1m 11.19	2	8-9	Gd to Firm	Mixed Blessing	Jly 23 2005
6f 8y	69.42secs	3	8-11	Gd to Firm	Nota Bene	May 13 2005
7f	1m 23.0	2	8-11	Gd to Firm	Haafhd	Aug 15 2003
7f	1m 21.5	3	8-4	Gd to Firm	Three Points	Jly 21 2000
1m	1m 37.5	2	9-1	Gd to firm	Winged Cupid (IRE)	Sep 16 2005
1m	1m 33.59	6	9-0	Firm	Rakti	May 14 2005
1m 1f	1m 49.6	3	8-0	Gd to Firm	Holtye	May 21 1995
1m 2f 6y	2m 1.2	3	8-7	Gd to Firm	Wall Street (USA)	Jly 20 1996
1m 3f 5y	2m 16.5	3	8-9	Gd to Firm	Grandera (IRE)	Sep 22 2001
1m 4f 5y	2m 28.26	4	9-7	Gd to Firm	Azamour (IRE)	Jul 23 2005
1m 5f 61y	2m 44.9	5	10-0	Gd to Firm	Mystic Hill	Jly 20 1996
2m	3m 25.4	8	9-12	Gd to Firm	Moonlight Quest	Jly 19 1996

NEWCASTLE

Dist	Time	Age& wt		Going	Horse	Date
5f	58.8 secs	2	9-0	Firm	Atlantic Viking (IRE)	Jun 4 1997
5f	58.0 secs	4	9-2	Firm	Princess Oberon	Jly 23 1994
6f	1m 12.18	2	9-0	Gd to Firm	Stepping Up (IRE)	Sep 5 2005
6f	1m 10.6	8	9-5	Firm	Tedburrow	Jly 1 2000
7f	1m 24.2	2	9-0	Gd to Firm	Iscan (IRE)	Aug 31 1998
7f	1m 23.3	4	9-2	Gd to Firm	Quiet Venture	Aug 31 1998
1m	1m 38.9	2	9-0	Gd to Firm	Stowaway	Oct 2 1996
1m	1m 38.9	3	8-12	Firm	Jacamar	Jly 22 1989
1m 3y	1m 37.1	2	8-3	Gd to Firm	Hoh Steamer (IRE)	Aug 31 1998
1m 3y	1m 37.3	3	8-8	Gd to Firm	Its Magic	May 27 1999
1m 1f 9y	2m 3.2	2	8-13	Soft	Response	Oct 30 1993
1m 1f 9y	1m 52.3	3	6-3	Good	Ferniehurst	Jun 23 1936
1m 2f 32y	2m 6.5	4	8-9	Fast	Missionary Ridge	Jly 29 1990
1m 4f 93y	2m 37.3	5	8-12	Firm	Retender	Jun 25 1994
1m 6f 97y	3m 6.4	3	9-6	Gd to Firm	One Off	Aug 6 2003
2m 19y	3m 24.3	4	8-10	Good	Far Cry (IRE)	Jun 26 1999

NEWMARKET (ROWLEY)

Dist	Time	Age& wt		Going	Horse	Date
5f	58.7 secs	2	8-5	Gd to Firm	Valiant Romeo	Oct 3 2002
5f	56.8 secs	6	9-2	Gd to Firm	Lochsong	Apr 30 1994
6f	69.6 secs	2	8-11	Gd to Firm	Oasis Dream	Oct 3 2002
6f	69.9 secs	5	8-6	Gd to Firm	Indian Trail	Apr 30 2005
7f	1m 22.9	2	8-11	Gd to Firm	Grosvenor Square	Sep 21 2004
7f	1m 22.2	4	9-5	Gd to Firm	Perfolia	Oct 17 1991
1m	1m 35.7	2	9-0	Gd to Firm	Forward Move (IRE)	Sep 21 2004
1m	1m 34.5	4	9-0	Gd to Firm	Desert Deer	Oct 3 2002
1m 1f	1m 47.2	4	9-5	Firm	Beauchamp Pilot	Oct 5 2002
1m 2f	2m 4.6	2	9-4	Good	Highland Chieftain	Nov 2 1985
1m 2f	2m 1.0	3	8-10	Good	Palace Music	Oct 20 1984
1m 4f	2m 27.1	5	8-12	Gd to Firm	Eastern Breeze	Oct 3 2003
1m 6f	2m 51.59	3	8-7	Good	Art Eyes (USA)	Sep 29 2005

2m	3m 19.5	5	9-5	Gd to Firm	Grey Shot	Oct 4 1997
2m 2f	3m 47.5	3	7-12	Hard	Whiteway	Oct 15 1947

NEWMARKET (JULY)

Dist	Time	Age&	wt	Going	Horse	Date
5f	58.5 secs	2	8-10	Good	Seductress	Jly 10 1990
5f	57.3 secs	6	8-12	Gd to Firm	Rambling Bear	Jan 1 1999
6f	1m 10.6	2	8-10	Gd to Firm	Mujtahid	Jly 11 1990
6f	69.5 secs	3	8-13	Gd to Firm	Stravinsky (USA)	Jly 8 1999
7f	1m 24.1	2	8-11	Good	My Hansel	Aug 27 1999
7f	1m 22.5	3	9-7	Firm	Ho Leng (IRE)	Jly 9 1998
1m	1m 39.0	2	8-11	Good	Traceability	Aug 25 1995
1m	1m 35.5	3	8-6	Gd to Firm	Lovers Knot	Jly 8 1998
1m 110y	1m 44.1	3	8-11	Good	Golden Snake	Apr 15 1999
1m 2f	2m 0.9	4	9-3	Gd to Firm	Elhayq (IRE)	May 1 1999
1m 4f	2m 25.2	4	9-2	Good	Craigsteel	Jly 6 1999
1m 6f 175y	3m 4.2	3	8-5	Good	Arrive	Jly 11 2001
2m 24y	3m 20.2	7	9-10	Good	Yorkshire	Jly 11 2001

NOTTINGHAM

Dist	Time	Age&	wt	Going	Horse	Date
5f 13y	57.9 secs	2	8-9	Firm	Hoh Magic	May 13 1994
5f 13y	57.6 secs	6	9-2	Gd to firm	Catch The Cat (IRE)	May 14 2005
6f 15y	1m 11.4	2	8-11	Firm	Jameelapi	Aug 8 1983
6f 15y	1m 10.0	4	9-2	Firm	Ajanac	Aug 8 1988
1m 54y	1m 40.8	2	9-0	Gd to Firm	King's Loch	Sep 2 1991
1m 54y	1m 39.6	4	8-2	Gd to Firm	Blake's Treasure	Sep 2 1991
1m 1f 213y	2m 5.6	2	9-0	Firm	Al Salite	Oct 28 1985
1m 1f 213y	2m 2.3	2	9-0	Firm	Ayaabi	Jly 21 1984
1m 6f 15y	2m 57.8	3	8-10	Firm	Buster Jo	Oct 1 1985
2m 9y	3m 24.0	5	7-7	Firm	Fet	Oct 5 2036
2m 2f 18y	3m 55.1	9	9-10	Gd to Firm	Pearl Run	May 1 1990

PONTEFRACT

Dist	Time	Age&	wt	Going	Horse	Date
5f	61.1 secs	2	9-0	Firm	Golden Bounty	Sep 20 2001
5f	60.8 secs	4	8-9	Firm	Blue Maeve	Sep 29 2004
6f	1m 14.0	2	9-3	Firm	Fawzi	Sep 6 1983
6f	1m 12.6	3	7-13	Firm	Merry One	Aug 29 1970
1m 4y	1m 42.8	2	9-13		Star Spray	Sep 6 1970
1m 4y	1m 42.8	2	9-0	Firm	Alasil (USA)	Sep 26 2002
1m 4y	1m 40.6	4	9-10	Gd to Firm	Island Light	Apr 13 2002
1m 2f 6y	2m 10.1	2	9-0	Firm	Shanty Star	Oct 7 2002
1m 2f 6y	2m 8.2	4	7-8	Hard	Happy Hector	Jly 9 1979
1m 2f 6y	2m 8.2	3	7-13	Hard	Tom Noddy	Aug 21 1972
1m 4f 8y	2m 34.1	3	9-5	Gd to Firm	High Action	Aug 6 2003
2m 1f 22y	3m 40.67	4	8-7	Gd to Firm	Paradise Flight	June 6 2005
2m 1f 216y	3m 51.1	3	8-8	Firm	Kudz	Sep 9 1986
2m 5f 122y	4m 47.8	4	8-4	Firm	Physical	May 14 1984

REDCAR

Dist	Time	Age& wt		Going	Horse	Date
5f	56.9 secs	2	9-0	Firm	Mister Joel	Oct 24 1995
5f	56.1 secs	5	9-10	Firm	Salviati (USA)	Jun 4 2002
6f	68.8 secs	2	8-3	Gd to Firm	Obe Gold	Oct 2 2004
6f	68.6 secs	3	9-2	Gd to Firm	Sizzling Saga	Jun 21 1991
7f	1m 21.9	2	8-11	Firm	Nagwa	Sep 27 1975
7f	1m 21.0	3	9-1	Firm	Empty Quarter	Oct 3 1995
1m	1m 36.1	2	7-11	Gd to Soft	Master Soden	Nov 1 1999
1m	1m 33.1	3	9-5	Firm	Night Wink (USA)	Oct 24 1995
1m 1f	1m 52.4	2	9-0	Firm	Spear (IRE)	Sep 13 2004
1m 1f	1m 48.5	5	8-12	Firm	Mellottie	Jly 25 1990
1m 2f	2m 10.1	2	8-11	Good	Adding	Nov 10 1989
1m 2f	2m 1.4	5	9-2	Firm	Eradicate	May 28 1990
1m 3f	2m 17.2	3	8-9	Firm	Photo Call	Aug 7 1990
1m 5f 135y	2m 54.7	6	9-10	Firm	Brodessa	Jun 20 1992
1m 6f 19y	2m 59.9	3	8-7	Firm	Trainglot	Jly 25 1990
2m 4y	3m 24.9	3	9-3	Gd to Firm	Subsonic	Oct 8 1991

RIPON

Dist	Time	Age& wt		Going	Horse	Date
5f	57.8 secs	2	8-8	Firm	Super Rocky	Jly 5 1991
5f	57.6 secs	5	8-5	Good	Broadstairs Beauty	May 21 1995
6f	1m 10.4	2	9-2	Good	Cumbrian Venture	Aug 17 2002
6f	69.8 secs	4	9-8	Gd to Firm	Tadeo	Aug 16 1997
6f	69.8 secs	5	7-10	Firm	Quoit	Jly 23 1966
1m	1m 39.79	2	8-6	Good	Top Jaro (FR)	Sep 24 2005
1m	1m 36.62	4	8-11	Gd to Firm	Granston (IRE)	Aug 29 2005
1m 1f	1m 50.4	3	9-2	Gd to Firm	Bold Words (CAN)	Apr 9 1997
1m 2f	2m 2.6	3	9-4	Firm	Swift Sword	Jly 20 1990
1m 4f 60y	2m 32.2	7	8-3	Hard	Crusaders Horn	Aug 8 1950
1m 4f 60y	2m 32.2	6	8-7	Firm	Cholo	Sep 27 1941
2m	3m 27.07	5	9-12	Gd to Firm	Greenwich Meantime	Aug 30 2005

SALISBURY

Dist	Time	Age& wt		Going	Horse	Date
5f	59.3 secs	2	9-0	Gd to Firm	Ajigolo	May 12 2005
5f	59.3 secs	2	9-0	Gd to Firm	Ajigolo	May 12 2005
6f	1m 12.1	2	8-0	Gd to Firm	Parisian Lady (IRE)	Jun 10 1997
6f	1m 11.5	4	8-7	Gd to Firm	Prince Sky	Jun 25 1986
6f 212y	1m 25.9	2	9-0	Firm	More Royal (USA)	Jun 29 1995
6f 212y	1m 24.9	3	9-7	Firm	High Summer (USA)	Sep 5 1996
1m	1m 40.4	2	8-13	Firm	Choir Master (USA)	Sep 17 2002
1m	1m 38.29	3	8-7	Gd to Firm	Layman (USA)	Aug 11 2005
1m 1f 198y	2m 4.9	3	8-6	Gd to Firm	Zante	Aug 12 1998
1m 4f	2m 31.6	3	9-5	Gd to Firm	Arrive	Jun 27 2001
1m 6f 15y	2m 59.4	3	8-6	Gd to Firm	Tabareeh	Sep 2 1999

SANDOWN

Dist	Time	Age& wt		Going	Horse	Date
5f 6y	59.4 secs	2	9-3	Firm	Times Time	Jly 22 1982
5f 6y	58.8 secs	6	8-9	Gd to Firm	Palacegate Touch	Sep 17 1996
7f 16y	1m 27.8	2	8-12	Gd to Firm	Red Camellia	Jly 25 1996
7f 16y	1m 26.3	3	9-0	Firm	Mawsuff	Jun 14 1983
1m 14y	1m 41.1	2	8-11	Fast	Reference Point	Sep 23 1986
1m 14y	1m 39.0	3	8-8	Firm	Linda's Fantasy	Aug 19 1983
1m 1f	1m 54.6	2	8-8	Gd to Firm	French Pretender	Sep 20 1988
1m 1f	1m 52.4	7	9-3	Gd to Firm	Bourgainville	Aug 11 2005
1m 2f 7y	2m 2.1	4	8-11	Firm	Kalaglow	May 31 1982
1m 3f 91y	2m 21.6	4	8-3	Fast	Aylesfield	Jly 7 1984
1m 6f	2m 56.9	4	8-7	Gd to Firm	Lady Rosanna	Jly 19 1989
2m 78y	3m 29.9	6	9-2	Firm	Sadeem	May 29 1989

SOUTHWELL (TURF)

Dist	Time	Age& wt		Going	Horse	Date
6f	1m 15.6	2	8-11	Gd to Firm	Yaselda	Jly 4 2001
6f	1m 14.1	4	9-12	Gd to Firm	Miss Haggis	Jly 26 1993
7f	1m 29.1	2	9-0	Gd to Firm	Dulcet Spear	Jly 4 2001
7f	1m 26.5	3	9-5	Gd to Firm	Sea Storm (IRE)	Jly 5 2001
1m 2f	2m 10.0	3	9-4	Good	Bronze Maquette(IRE)	Jly 26 1993
1m 3f	2m 21.9	3	8-5	Gd to Firm	Pims Gunner (IRE)	Aug 15 1991
1m 4f	2m 34.4	5	9-3	Gd to Firm	Corn Lily	Aug 10 1991
2m	3m 34.1	5	9-1	Gd to Firm	Triplicate	Sep 20 1991

SOUTHWELL (A.W.)

Dist	Time	Age& wt		Going	Horse	Date
5f	58.50secs	2	8-1	Standard	Primrose and Rose	Apr 4 2001
5f	57.70secs	3	9-6	Standard	Case Law	Aug 15 1990
5f	57.70secs	5	9-12	Standard	Goretski (IRE)	Jul 17 1998
6f	1m 14.00	2	8-5	Standard	Panalo	Nov 8 1989
6f	1m 13.50	4	10-02	Standard	Saladan Knight	Dec 30 1989
7f	1m 27.10	2	8-2	Standard	Mystic Crystal	Nov 20 1990
7f	1m 26.80	5	8-4	Standard	Amenable	Dec 13 1990
1m	1m 38.00	2	8-9	Standard	Alpha Rascal	Nov 13 1990
1m	1m 38.00	2	8-10	Standard	Andrew's First	Dec 30 1989
1m	1m 37.25	3	8-6	Standard	Valira	Nov 3 1990
1m 3f	2m 21.50	4	9-7	Standard	Tempering	Dec 5 1990
1m 4f	2m 33.90	4	9-12	Standard	Fast Chick	Nov 8 1989
1m 6f	3m 1.60	3	7-8	Standard	Erevnon	Dec 29 1990
2m	3m 37.60	9	8-12	Standard	Old Hubert	Dec 5 1990

THIRSK

Dist	Time	Age& wt		Going	Horse	Date
5f	57.2 secs	2	9-7	Gd to Firm	Proud Boast	Aug 5 2000
5f	56.9 secs	5	9-6	Firm	Charlie Parkes	April 11 2003
6f	69.2 secs	2	9-6	Gd to Firm	Westcourt Magic	Aug 25 1995

6f	68.8 secs	6	9-4	Firm	Johayro	Jly 23 1999
7f	1m 23.7	2	8-9	Firm	Courting	Jly 23 1999
7f	1m 22.8	4	8-5	Firm	Silver Haze	May 21 1988
1m	1m 37.9	2	9-0	Firm	Sunday Symphony	Sep 4 2004
1m	1m 34.8	4	8-13	Firm	Yearsley	May 5 1990
1m 4f	2m 29.9	5	9-12	Firm	Gallery God	Jun 4 2001
2m	3m 22.3	3	8-11	Firm	Tomaschek	Jul 17 1981

WARWICK

Dist	Time	Age& wt		Going	Horse	Date
5f	58.4 secs	2	9-7	Gd to Firm	Prenonamoss	Oct 9 1990
5f	57.7 secs	4	9-6	Gd to Firm	Little Edward	Jly 7 2002
5f 110y	63.6 secs	5	8-6	Gd to Firm	Dizzy In The Head	Jun 27 2004
6f 21y	1m 10.6	2	9-0	Gd to Firm	Viking Spirit	Sep 6 2004
6f 21y	69.6 secs	6	9-2	Firm	Parkside Pursuit	Jun 20 2004
7f 26y	1m 22.9	2	9-0	Firm	Country Rambler(USA)	Jun 20 2004
7f 26y	1m 21.2	3	8-11	Gd to Firm	Lucky Spin	Jun 19 2004
1m 22y	1m 37.1	3	8-11	Firm	Orinocovsky (IRE)	Jun 26 2002
1m 2f 188y	2m 16.2	6	7-12	Gd to Firm	Scented Air	Apr 21 2003
1m 4f 134y	2m 39.5	3	8-13	Gd to Firm	Maimana (IRE)	Jun 22 2002
1m 6f 135y	3m 7.5	3	9-7	Gd to Firm	Burma Baby (USA)	Jly 2 1999
2m 39y	3m 27.9	3	8-1	Firm	Decoy	Jun 26 2002

WINDSOR

Dist	Time	Age& wt		Going	Horse	Date
5f 10y	58.9 secs	2	9-0	Firm	Strictly Private	Jly 22 1974
5f 10y	58.9 secs	2	9-0	Gd to Firm	Bad As I Wannabe	Jly 31 2000
5f 10y	58.3 secs	5	7-10	Gd to Firm	Beyond The Clouds	Jun 2 2001
5f 217y	69.0 secs	2	8-7	Gd to Firm	Options Open	Jly 25 1994
5f 217y	1m 10.1	3	8-4	Firm	Sweet Relief	Sep 11 1978
6f	1m 10.5	2	9-5	Gd to Firm	Cubism (USA)	Aug 17 1998
6f	1m 10.26	5	9-1	Gd to Firm	Baltic King	May 23 2005
1m 67y	1m 44.38	2	9-0	Good	Genre	Oct 3 2005
1m 67y	1m 40.6	7	9-8	Gd to Firm	Gateman	Jun 26 2004
1m 2f 7y	2m 3.0	2	9-1	Firm	Moomba Masquerade	May 19 1990
1m 3f 135y	2m 21.5	3	9-2	Firm	Double Florin	May 19 1980

WOLVERHAMPTON (A.W.)

Dist	Time	Age& wt		Going	Horse	Date
5f 20y	61.87 sec	2	9-2	Standard	Thoughtsofstardom	Oct 1 2005
5f 20y	60.86 sec	4	8-7	Fast	Misaro (GER)	Oct 10 2005
5f 216y	1m 14.59	2	9-0	Standard	Outlook	Jly 22 2005
5f 216y	1m 13.32	5	8-12	Standard	Desert Opal	Sep 17 2005
7f 32y	1m 29.24	2	8-12	Standard	Bomber Command	Nov 7 2005
7f 32y	1m 27.71	8	8-3	Standard	Hand Chime	Sep 3 2005
1m 141y	1m 48.74	2	9-7	Standard	Dream Fantasy	Sep 3 2005
1m 141y	1m 48.20	4	9-1	Standard	Trifti	Oct 1 2005
1m 1f 103y	2m 0.120	5	8-6	Standard	Nevada Desert (IRE)	Oct 30 2005

1m 4f 50y	2m 37.00	4	8-13	Standard	Bethanys Boy (IRE)	Oct 1 2005
1m 5f 194y	3m 2.140	8	8-0	Standard	Bid For Fame (USA)	Jun 3 2005
2m 119y	3m 39.57	5	8-8	Standard	Spitting Image (IRE)	Nov 5 2005

YARMOUTH

Dist	Time	Age&	wt	Going	Horse	Date
5f 43y	60.4 secs	2	8-6	Gd to Firm	Ebba	Jly 26 1999
5f 43y	59.8 secs	4	8-13	Gd to Firm	Roxanne Mill	Aug 25 2002
6f 3y	1m 10.4	2	9-0	Fast	Lanchester	Aug 15 1988
6f 3y	69.9 secs	4	8-9	Firm	Malhub (USA)	Jun 13 2002
7f 3y	1m 22.2	2	9-0	Gd to Firm	Warrshan	Sep 14 1988
7f 3y	1m 22.2	3	8-7	Firm	Cielamour	Sep 15 1988
1m 3y	1m 36.3	2	8-2	Gd to Firm	Outrun	Sep 15 1988
1m 3y	1m 33.9	3	8-8	Firm	Bonne Etoile	Jun 27 1995
1m 2f 21y	2m 3.1	4	8-9	Gd to Firm	Supreme Sound	Aug 9 1998
1m 3f 101y	2m 23.1	3	8-9	Firm	Rahil	Jly 1 1993
1m 6f 17y	2m 57.8	3	8-2	Gd to Firm	Barakat	Jly 24 1990
2m	3m 26.7	4	8-2	Gd to Firm	Alhesn (USA)	Jly 26 1999
2m 2f 51y	3m 56.8	4	9-10	Firm	Provence	Sep 19 1991

YORK

Dist	Time	Age&	wt	Going	Horse	Date
5f	57.3 secs	2	7-8	Gd to Firm	Lyric Fantasy	Aug 20 1992
5f	56.1 secs	3	9-3	Gd to Firm	Dayjur	Aug 23 1990
5f 3y	58.4 secs	2	8-11	Gd to Firm	Howick Falls (USA)	Aug 20 2003
5f 3y	56.2 secs	3	9-9	Gd to Firm	Oasis Dream	Aug 21 2003
6f	69.5 secs	2	9-0	Gd to Firm	Indiscreet (CAN)	Aug 22 1996
6f	68.58secs	7	9-4	Firm	Cape Of Good Hope	Jun 16 2005
6f 3y	1m 10.6	2	8-11	Gd to Firm	Carry on Katie (USA)	Aug 21 2003
6f 3y	69.4 secs	3	8-2	Gd to Firm	Dazzling Bay	Jun 14 2003
6f 214y	1m 22.9	2	8-10	Gd to Firm	Options Open	Aug 16 1994
6f 214y	1m 21.3	3	9-0	Firm	Bold Fact (USA)	Aug 20 1998
6f 217y	1m 22.6	2	9-0	Gd to Firm	Moonlight Man	Oct 9 2003
6f 217y	1m 22.0	4	9-0	Gd to Firm	Vanderlin	Aug 21 2003
7f 202y	1m 37.2	2	9-4	Gd to Firm	The Wife	Sep 2 1999
7f 202y	1m 34.8	4	8-10	Gd to Firm	Concer Un	Aug 22 1996
7f 205y	1m 36.0	5	8-7	Gd to Firm	Faithful Warrior(USA)	Jly 11 2003
1m 205y	1m 52.4	2	8-1	Gd to Firm	Oral Evidence	Oct 6 1988
1m 205y	1m 47.0	3	8-10	Gd to Firm	Gold Academy	Sep 2 1999
1m 208y	1m 48.9	4	8-5	Gd to Firm	Krugerrand (USA)	Jun 14 2003
1m 2f 88y	2m 6.09	4	8-11	Gd to Firm	Imperial Stride	Jun 17 2005
1m 3f 195y	2m 25.1	3	8-9	Gd to Firm	Sea Wave (IRE)	Aug 18 1998
1m 3f 198y	2m 27.4	4	9-4	Gd to Firm	Islington (IRE)	Aug 20 2003
1m 5f 194y	2m 51.8	3	8-7	Gd to Firm	Tuning	Aug 19 1998
1m 5f 197y	2m 52.5	4	8-9	Gd to Firm	Mamool (IRE)	May 15 2003
1m 7f 195y	3m 18.4	3	8-0	Gd to Firm	Dam Busters	Aug 16 1988

"THE 120 CLUB"

(those horses, not necessarily race winners, who have recorded a Speed Figure of 120 or more since January 2001)

Pearly Shells.................125
Ana Marie.....................125
Century City..................124
Fantastic Light...............124
Lady Zonda....................124
Refuse To Bend................124
Creekview.....................123
Crystal Castle................123
Grandera......................123
High Chaparral................123
Marienbard....................123
Nicobar.......................123
Bago..........................122
Bright Sky....................122
Ghannam.......................122
High Pitched..................122
Hurricane Run.................122
Kalanisi......................122
King Harson...................122
Nayyir........................122
Sulamani......................122
Swallow Flight................122
Alamshar......................121
Albanova......................121
Aquarelliste..................121
Castle Gandolfo...............121
Cherry Mix....................121
Dalakhani.....................121
Fair Mix......................121
Head In The Clouds............121
Hightori......................121
Island Sands..................121
Islington.....................121
Latino Magic..................121
Masani........................121
Ouija Board...................121
Pride.........................121
Royal Millennium..............121
Soviet Song...................121
Anabaa Blue...................120
Attraction....................120
Best Of The Bests.............120
Doyen.........................120
Galileo.......................120
Hawk Wing.....................120
Kyllachy......................120
Mister Cosmi..................120
Mubtaker......................120
Observatory...................120
Passing Glance................120
Rakti.........................120
Sholokhov.....................120
Vinnie Roe....................120
Westerner.....................120

NOTES